Google Certified Associate Cloud Engineer

Technology Workbook

---

www.ipspecialist.net

Document Control

Proposal Name	:	Google Certified Associate Cloud Engineer
Document Version	:	Version 1
Document Release Date	:	24th June 2019

Registered in England and Wales
Company Registration No: 10883539
Registration Office at: Office 32, 19-21 Crawford Street, London W1H 1PJ, United Kingdom
www.ipspecialist.net

Feedback:
If you have any comments regarding the quality of this book, or otherwise alter it to better suit your needs, you can contact us through email at info@ipspecialist.net
Please make sure to include the book's title and ISBN in your message.

About IPSpecialist

IPSPECIALIST LTD. IS COMMITTED TO EXCELLENCE AND DEDICATED TO YOUR SUCCESS.

Our philosophy is to treat our customers like family. We want you to succeed, and we are willing to do everything possible to help you make it happen. We have the proof to back up our claims. We strive to accelerate billions of careers with great courses, accessibility, and affordability. We believe that continuous learning and knowledge evolution are the most important things to keep re-skilling and up-skilling the world.

Planning and creating a specific goal is where IPSpecialist helps. We can create a career track that suits your visions as well as develop the competencies you need to become a professional Network Engineer. We can also assist you with the execution and evaluation of your proficiency level, based on the career track you choose, as they are customized to fit your specific goals.

We help you STAND OUT from the crowd through our detailed IP training content packages.

Course Features:

- Self-Paced learning
    - Learn at your own pace and in your own time
- Covers Complete Exam Blueprint
    - Prep-up for the exam with confidence
- Case Study Based Learning
    - Relate the content with real life scenarios
- Subscriptions that suits you
    - Get more and pay less with IPS subscriptions
- Career Advisory Services
    - Let the industry experts plan your career journey
- Virtual Labs to test your skills
    - With IPS vRacks, you can evaluate your exam preparations
- Practice Questions
    - Practice questions to measure your preparation standards
- On Request Digital Certification
    - On request digital certification from IPSpecialist LTD

About the Authors:

This book has been compiled with the help of multiple professional engineers. These engineers specialize in different fields e.g. Networking, Security, Cloud, Big Data, IoT etc. Each engineer develops content in his/her own specialized field that is compiled to form a comprehensive certification guide.

About the Technical Reviewers:

Nouman Ahmed Khan

AWS-Architect, CCDE, CCIEX5 (R&S, SP, Security, DC, Wireless), CISSP, CISA, CISM, Nouman Ahmed Khan is a Solution Architect working with a major telecommunication provider in Qatar. He works with enterprises, mega-projects, and service providers to help them select the best-fit technology solutions. He also works as a consultant to understand customer business processes and helps select an appropriate technology strategy to support business goals. He has more than 14 years of experience working in Pakistan/Middle-East & UK. He holds a Bachelor of Engineering Degree from NED University, Pakistan, and M.Sc. in Computer Networks from the UK.

Abubakar Saeed

Abubakar Saeed has more than twenty-five years of experience, managing, consulting, designing, and implementing large-scale technology projects, extensive experience heading ISP operations, solutions integration, heading Product Development, Pre-sales, and Solution Design. Emphasizing on adhering to Project timelines and delivering as per customer expectations, he always leads the project in the right direction with his innovative ideas and excellent management skills.

Areeba Tanveer

Areeba Tanveer is an AWS Certified Solution Architect – Associate working professionally as a Technical Content Developer. She holds a Bachelor's of Engineering degree in Telecommunication Engineering from NED University of Engineering and Technology. She also worked as a project Engineer in Pakistan Telecommunication Company Limited (PTCL). She has both the technical knowledge and industry sounding information, which she utilizes effectively when needed.

Syed Hanif Wasti

Syed Hanif Wasti is a Computer Science graduate working professionally as a Technical Content Developer. He is a part of a team of professionals operating in the E-learning and digital education sector. He holds a Bachelor's Degree in Computer Sciences from PAF-KIET, Pakistan. He has completed his training of MCP and CCNA. He has both the technical knowledge and industry sounding information, which he uses efficiently in his career. He previously worked as a Database and Network administrator and obtained a good experience in software development.

Afia Afaq

Afia Afaq works as a Technical Content Developer. She holds a Bachelor of Engineering Degree in Telecommunications Engineering from NED University of Engineering and Technology. She also has worked as an intern in Pakistan Telecommunication Company Limited (PTCL) as well as in Pakistan Meteorological Department (PMD). Afia Afaq uses her technical knowledge and industry sounding information efficiently in her career.

Hira Arif

Hira Arif is an Electrical Engineer Graduate from NED University of Engineering and Technology, working professionally as a Technical Content Writer. Prior to that, she worked as a Trainee Engineer at Sunshine Corporation. She utilizes her knowledge and technical skills profoundly when required.

Free Resources:

With each workbook bought from Amazon, IPSpecialist offers free resources to our valuable customers.

Once you buy this book, you will have to contact us at support@ipspecialist.net or tweet @ipspecialistnet to get this limited time offer without any extra charges.

Free Resources Include:

Exam Practice Questions in Quiz Simulation: IP Specialists' Practice Questions have been developed keeping in mind the certification exam perspective. The collection of these questions from our technology workbooks is prepared keeping the exam blueprint in mind, covering not only important but necessary topics as well. It is an ideal document to practice and revise your certification.

Career Report: This report is a step-by-step guide for a novice who wants to develop his/her career in the field of computer networks. It answers the following queries:

- Current scenarios and future prospects.
- Is this industry moving towards saturation or are new opportunities knocking at the door?
- What will the monetary benefits be?
- Why to get certified?
- How to plan and when will I complete the certifications if I start today?
- Is there any career track that I can follow to accomplish specialization level?

Furthermore, this guide provides a comprehensive career path towards being a specialist in the field of networking and highlights the tracks needed to obtain certification.

IPS Personalized Technical Support for Customers: Good customer service means helping customers efficiently, in a friendly manner. It is essential to be able to handle issues for customers and do your best to ensure they are satisfied. Providing good service is one of the most important things that can set our business apart from the others of its kind.

Great customer service will result in attracting more customers and attain maximum customer retention.

IPS is offering personalized TECH support to its customers to provide better value for money. If you have any queries related to technology and labs, you can simply ask our technical team for assistance via Live Chat or E-mail.

Become an Author & Earn with Us

If you are interested in becoming an author and start earning passive income, IPSpecialist offers "Earn with us" program. We all consume, develop and create content during our learning process, certification exam preparations, and while searching, developing and refining our professional careers. That content, notes, guides, worksheets and flip cards among other material is normally for our own reference without any defined structure or special considerations required for formal publishing.

IPSpecialist can help you craft this 'draft' content into a fine product with the help of our global team of experts. We sell your content via different channels as:

1. Amazon – Kindle
2. eBay
3. LuLu
4. Kobo
5. Google Books
6. Udemy and many 3rd party publishers and resellers

Our Products

Technology Workbooks

IPSpecialist Technology workbooks are the ideal guides to developing the hands-on skills necessary to pass the exam. Our workbook covers official exam blueprint and explains the technology with real life case study based labs. The content covered in each workbook consists of individually focused technology topics presented in an easy-to-follow, goal-oriented, step-by-step approach. Every scenario features detailed breakdowns and thorough verifications to help you completely understand the task and associated technology.

We extensively used mind maps in our workbooks to visually explain the technology. Our workbooks have become a widely used tool to learn and remember the information effectively.

vRacks

Our highly scalable and innovative virtualized lab platforms let you practice the IP Specialist Technology Workbook at your own time and your own place as per your convenience.

Quick Reference Sheets

Our quick reference sheets are a concise bundling of condensed notes of the complete exam blueprint. It is an ideal and handy document to help you remember the most important technology concepts related to the certification exam.

Practice Questions

IP Specialists' Practice Questions are dedicatedly designed from a certification exam perspective. The collection of these questions from our technology workbooks is prepared keeping the exam blueprint in mind covering not only important but necessary topics as well. It is an ideal document to practice and revise your certification.

Content at a glance

Chapter 01: Cloud Concepts 19

Chapter 02: Getting Started 43

Chapter 03: Basic Services 130

Chapter 04: Scaling and Security 237

Chapter 05: Networking 279

Chapter 06: Google Engines 356

Answers: 385

Acronyms: 408

References: 411

About Our Products 415

Table of Contents

Chapter 01: Cloud Concepts 19

What is Cloud Computing? 19

Advantages of Cloud Computing 19
Types of Cloud Computing 20
Cloud Computing Deployments Models 21

Google Cloud Platform 21

GCP Resources 22
Global, Regional, and Zonal Resources 22
Ways to Interact with the Services 23
GCP's Design and Structure 25
What are Google Cloud Platform (GCP) Services? 27

Practice Questions: 38

Chapter 02: Getting Started 43

Introduction 43

GCP Cheat Sheet Introduction 43

Products/ Services as Building Block 44

Key Building Blocks 47

GCP- Getting Started 55

GCP Resources 55
Accessing resources through services 56
Global, regional, and zonal resources 56
Projects 56
Ways to interact with the services 57
Pricing 58

Free- Tier GCP Accounts 58

Always Free 59

Create Free-Tier GCP Account (LAB) 60

Incognito Mood 60

Lab 2.1: Create a GCP Account 60

Explore GCP Console 73

Set up Billing Export 77

Lab 2.2: Billing Export 78

Set Up Billing Alerts 88

Budget Alert Threshold Rules 89

Lab 2.3: Set up Billing Alerts 89

Set Up Non- Admin User Access 93

Lab 2.4: Set up Non-Admin User 94

Cloud Shell and Editor 104

Lab 2.5: Cloud Shell 105

Data Flows 119

Mental Models 119

Cloud Shell Data Flow 119

Lab 2.6: Update Course Lab Files 121

Milestone: Open World 123

Practice Questions: 125

Chapter 03: Basic Services 130

Introduction 130

Google Cloud Storage 130

Key Terms 130

Projects 132

Storage Classes 133

Lab 3.1- Creating a Bucket via GCP Console and Cloud SDK 136

Features 176

Access Control 179

Encryption 179

Consistency 180

Cache Control and Consistency 181

Gcloud 181

Overview 181

Syntax 181

Configuration Properties 182
Configurations 182
Lab 3-2: Creating VM 183
Google Compute Engine 192
Virtual Machine Instances 193
Instance Templates 197
Instance Group 197
Sole-Tenant Nodes 197
Storage Options 198
Access Control 199
Lab 3-3 – Configuration on GCE 199
GCE in Console 216
Lab 3.4- Creating a Virtual Machine and Attaching GCS to it 218
Practice Questions: 233
Chapter 04: Scaling and Security 237
Introduction 237
Scaling 237
Lab 4.1: Managed Instance Groups 237
Security 265
Proper Data flow 265
Controlling Data flow 265
AAA Data flow 266
What enables security in GCP? 266
IAM Resources Hierarchy 268
IAM Permissions & Roles 268
IAM Members & Groups 270
IAM Policies 271
Billing Access Control 272
Practice Questions 275
Chapter 05: Networking 279
Introduction 279
OSI Model 279

OSI Layers ... 279

Routing ... 280

Routing to Google's Network ... 280
Routing to the Right Resources ... 280
Routing Among Resources ... 281

Lab 5.1: Creating Auto-Mode VPCs ... 282

Lab 5.2: Custom-Mode VPCs ... 291

Lab 5.3: Two-Tier Custom Mode VPC ... 335

Challenge ... 351

Practice Questions ... 353

Chapter 06: Google Engines ... 356

Introduction ... 356

Google Kubernetes Engine (GKE) ... 356

Cluster Orchestration with GKE ... 356
GKE on GCP ... 356
GKE Workloads ... 357
Cluster Architecture ... 357
What is POD? ... 358
What is Deployment? ... 359
What are Stateful Sets? ... 359
What is a Daemon Set? ... 360
What is a Service? ... 361
HTTP(S) Load Balancing with Ingress ... 362
Storage Overview ... 362

Google App Engine (GAE) ... 363

Codelabs ... 363
Lab 6.1 – For Analyzing Data ... 364
Qwiklabs ... 370
Lab 6.2- Qwiklabs ... 371

Practice Questions ... 380

Answers: ... 385

Acronyms: ... 408

References:..**411**
About Our Products **415**

Google Cloud Certifications

We will be discussing the general structure, basic stuff, advanced stuff and much more during the entire course. These things all-together make the foundation of Google Cloud, for your concepts building and your continuous learning. You are going to be challenged by Google in its exam to demonstrate what you have learned.

Logistics

In the exam, you have to answer 50 questions in 120 minutes, and its fee is USD 125 for each time you attempt it. Now, this is not something you can do online. You either have to appear in this exam at an authorized testing center, or you can give it on-site at Google Cloud Next. All of the questions in the exam will be in the form of Multiple Choice Questions (MCQs) with at least four options in each question. Also, some of the questions require multiple responses, for example, you may select 2 out of 5 options given in the questions.

If you fail the exam in the first attempt, you have to wait for 14 days and re-pay the full exam fee then retake the exam. If you are unable to pass the exam in the second attempt as well, then you have to wait for another 60 days for the third attempt. If you fail the exam even for the third time, then you have to wait for a whole year for another attempt.

One of the things you can do to check how much prepared you are for the exam is to take the official practice exam that Google offers. In this exam, you have got around 20 questions. This official practice exam is free to take because it is available online using a Google Forum based UI. This official practice exam is repeatable, and you can do it as many times as you want.

For the registration of your exam, you need to create a Web Assessor account with your email address. You can cancel or reschedule your exam without having to pay any extra fee before 72 hours of the exam. If you make changes within the 72 hours, it will cost some or maybe all of your exam fees. Remember to bring your IDs and your exam code which you get at the time of registration of the exam. During the exam, you can see there is an exam count down timer visible on every page, and you can flag any of the questions for later review. The overview page shows flags and lets you jump to any question. The responses can be changed until the exam ends. Double check your answers before moving on.

All GCP Certifications expire after two years. Re-certification expires two years after the renewal exam date, not the original date.

Quick Summary of the Exam

- Wide variety of Google Cloud services and their working. It focuses on IAM, Compute, Storage and also, a bit of network and data service is included.
- Covers Cloud SDK commands and Console operations which are required for day-to-day work. If you have not used GCP before, ensure that you do a lot of labs or else, you will be clueless about some of the questions and commands
- Tests are updated for the latest enhancements. There is no reference of Google Container Engine, and Google Kubernetes Engine, also covers Cloud Functions, and Cloud Spanner
- The list of topics is quite long, but some topics that you need to cover are General Services, Billing, Cloud SDK, Network Services, VPC, Load Balancer, Identity Service, Cloud IAM, Compute Services, GCE, Google AE, GKE, Storage Services, Cloud Storage, Cloud SQL, Cloud Spanner, BigQuery, Data Services, Google Stackdriver, DevOps Services, Deployment Manager and Cloud Launcher

Final Preparation

Let's discuss some exam tips. You will get several questions in exams on Kubernetes, and what happens when you deploy something on Kubernetes. You should be aware of the best practices for working with Google Cloud. Google has published valuable documents for the knowledge of Best Practices for Enterprise Organizations. This work book form IPSpecialist covers the whole exam blueprint and it will help you in getting familiar with IAM roles which describes the Cloud IAM roles that you grant to identities to access Cloud Platform resources. You should spend some time playing with the GCP Pricing Calculator. Several questions appear on how GCP Calculator works and understand the pricing structure of the different services. Several questions appear on how it works. Review gcloud structure before your exam. Another thing that comes up several times in the exam is Cloud Audit Logging.

Before the exam, re-read this exam guide and make sure you can do every task. Revise the key tips or exam tips provided in the course outline. Revise the key official documentation pages. Another important thing is to repeat the course practice exams because they are designed to identify your gaps and areas of weaknesses and research targets that matters. This is how you will understand the scenarios of the questions and suggest the best response. Go through the practice questions multiple times to make yourself ready for the exam.

You must identify the gaps and overcome those gaps by going through this exam guide, attempting the practice exams and reading of the student reports about their exams. Fill those gaps by going through our course, going through the official documentation, watching videos that Google has provided.

Soaring

Throughout the course, you will learn a lot of stuff which will prepare you for the exam. But, this is not the end; this is the beginning of your learning journey. You are going to take what you will learn into its practical use where you build a real system and teach your peers about it. The entire technology landscape has massively developed and expanded in the last 20 years; the technology will be better as the development occurs.

About Google Cloud Certifications

Google Cloud Platform (GCP) Certifications are industry-recognized credentials that validate your technical cloud skills and expertise while assisting you in your career growth. These are one of the most valuable IT certifications right now since GCP has established an overwhelming lead in the public cloud market. Even with the presence of several tough competitors such as Microsoft Azure, AWS, and Rackspace, GCP is gaining ground in the public cloud platform today, with an astounding collection of proprietary services that continues to grow.

The two key reasons as to why GCP certifications are prevailing in the current cloud-oriented job market:

- There is a dire need for skilled cloud engineers, developers, and architects – and the current shortage of experts is expected to continue into the foreseeable future.
- The Google Cloud Certified assignment means you've exhibited the important aptitudes to use Google Cloud innovation in a manner that can change organizations and definitively sway the general population and clients they serve.

Types of Certification

Role-based Certification

- *Associate*- Technical role-based certifications. No pre-requisite.
- *Professional*- Highest level technical role-based certification. Relevant Associate certification required.

About GCP - Associate Cloud Engineer Exam

Exam Questions	Multiple choice and multiple answer
Number of Questions	50
Time to Complete	120 minutes
Available Languages	English, Japanese, Spanish, French, German, and Portuguese
Exam Fee	125 USD

The Google Certified Associate Cloud Engineer exam validates and individual's ability to deploy applications, monitor operations, and manage enterprise solutions. This individual is able to use GCP Console and the CLI to perform common platform-based tasks to maintain one or more deployed solutions that leverage Google-managed or self-managed services on Google Cloud. Example concepts you should understand for this exam include:

- Creation of projects and billing accounts
- Planning and configuring compute resources, data storage options, and network resources
- Deployment and implementation of a cloud solution
- Managing App Engine, Compute Engine, and Kubernetes Engine
- Management of IAM and Service accounts

Recommended Google Cloud Knowledge

- 6-month hands-on experience on Google Cloud Console and CLI
- Understanding of core GCP services and their uses
- This exam has no prerequisites

	Domain
Domain 1	Set up a cloud solution environment
Domain 2	Plan and configure a cloud solution
Domain 3	Deploy and implement a cloud solution
Domain 4	Ensure successful operation of a cloud solution

Domain 5	Configure access and security

Chapter 01: Cloud Concepts

What is Cloud Computing?

Cloud Computing is the practice of using a network of remote servers hosted on the internet to store, manage, and process data rather than using a local server or personal computer. It is the on-demand delivery of computing resources through a Cloud service platform with pay-as-you-go pricing.

Advantages of Cloud Computing

- **Cost Savings**
  The most important advantage of Cloud computing is IT cost savings. Businesses exist to earn money whilst keeping capital and operating expenses to a minimum, regardless of their type or size. You can save significant capital costs with zero in-house server storage and application requirements with Cloud Computing

- **Reliability**
  Cloud Computing is far more reliable and consistent than in-house IT infrastructure with a managed service platform. Most suppliers offer a Service Level Agreement that guarantees availability 24/7/365 and 99.99 percent

- **Manageability**
  Cloud Computing delivers enhanced and simplified IT management and maintenance capabilities by centralized resource management, vendor - managed infrastructure and SLA - backed agreements

- **Scalability**
  With the use of Cloud Computing, you do not need to worry about scaling as it depends on your requirements. It has multiple services that perform scaling up and down

- **Improved Collaboration**
  Cloud applications enhance collaboration by enabling dispersed groups of people to meet in real time and through shared storage, to share information virtually and easily. This capability can reduce time - to - market and improve customer service and product development.

1. **<u>Stop Spending Money on Running and Maintaining Data Centers</u>**
   It saves you from the traditional need for spending money on running and maintaining data centers, which are now managed by the Cloud Provider.

2. **<u>Go Global in Minutes</u>**
   It provides lower latency at minimal cost by easily deploying your application in multiple regions around the world.

Types of Cloud Computing

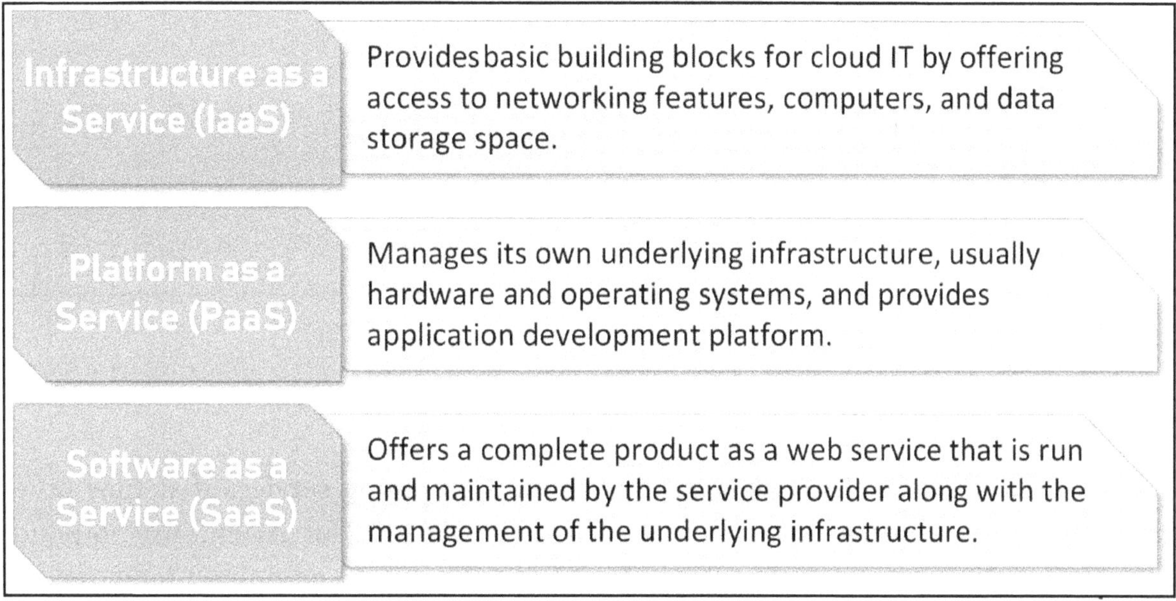

Infrastructure as a Service (IaaS)
Providesbasic building blocks for cloud IT by offering access to networking features, computers, and data storage space.
Platform as a Service (PaaS)
Manages its own underlying infrastructure, usually hardware and operating systems, and provides application development platform.
Software as a Service (SaaS)
Offers a complete product as a web service that is run and maintained by the service provider along with the management of the underlying infrastructure.

Figure 1-01: Types of Cloud Computing

Cloud Computing Deployments Models

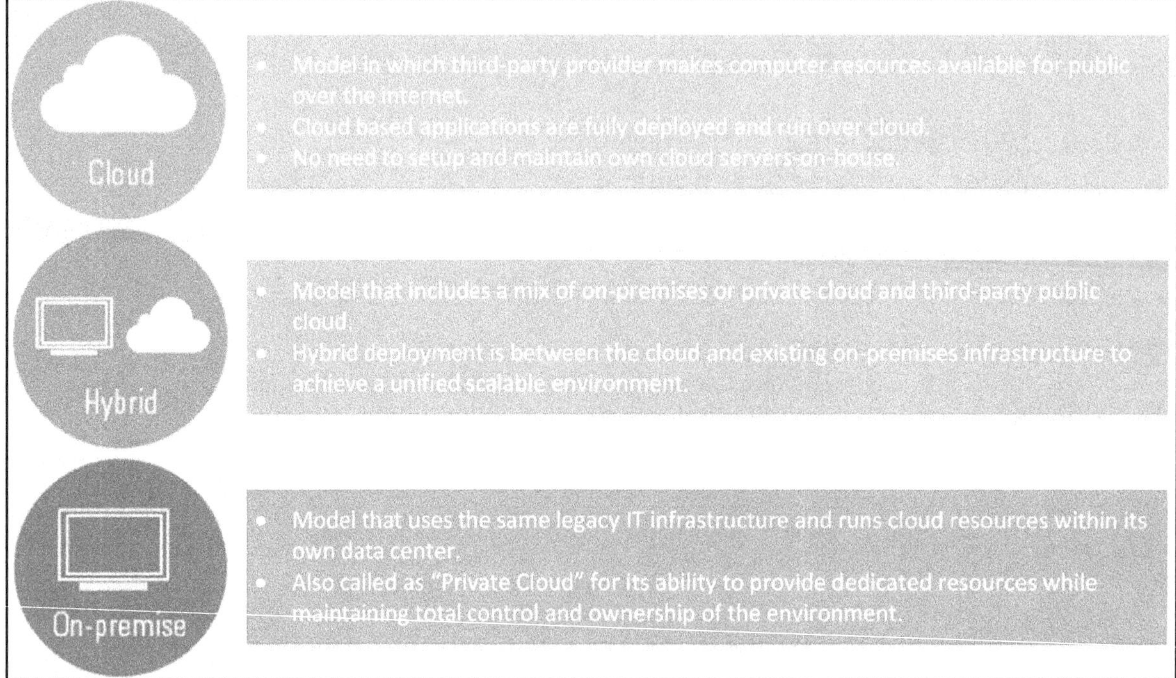

Figure 1-02: Cloud Computing Deployment Model

Google Cloud Platform

Google Cloud Platform (GCP), is a suite of Cloud Computing services that runs on the same internally operating infrastructure, which Google uses for its end-user products, such as Google Search and YouTube. It offers a range of modular Cloud services, including computing, data storage, data analysis and automated learning, along with a number of management tools. In April 2008, Google announced App Engine, which was Google's first Cloud Computing service, as the platform for developing and hosting web applications. In November 2011, the service was generally offered to everyone. Google has added several Cloud services to the platform since the announcement of App Engine. Google Cloud Platform is an integral part of Google Cloud, which includes the Public Cloud Infrastructure for Google Cloud Platform as well as the G Suite, Android, and Chrome OS business versions, and APIs for machine and business mapping.

Figure 1-03: Google Cloud Platform

GCP Resources

GCP consists of a number of physical assets. These include computers, hard drives and virtual resources such as, VMs contained in data centers around the globe. Each location of the data center is expanded to a worldwide area, which includes Central America, Western Europe, and East Asia. Each region is a group of areas that is isolated within the region from one another. Every zone has a name that combines a letter identification with the region's name for example, Asia-East1-a, is called zone one in Eastern Asia.

This allocation of resources provides a number of advantages, including redundancy and reduced latency by close customer contacts. This distribution also sets out some rules for the joint use of resources.

Global, Regional, and Zonal Resources

Some resources are accessible throughout regions and areas through any other resource. These global resources include disk images, disk snapshots, and networks that are pre-configured. Only resources located in the same region can access certain resources. These regional resources include external IP addresses that are static. Only resources located in the same area can access other resources. These areas include VM instances, types, and disks.

The following diagram illustrates the relationship between the global scope, regions and areas, and certain of their resources:

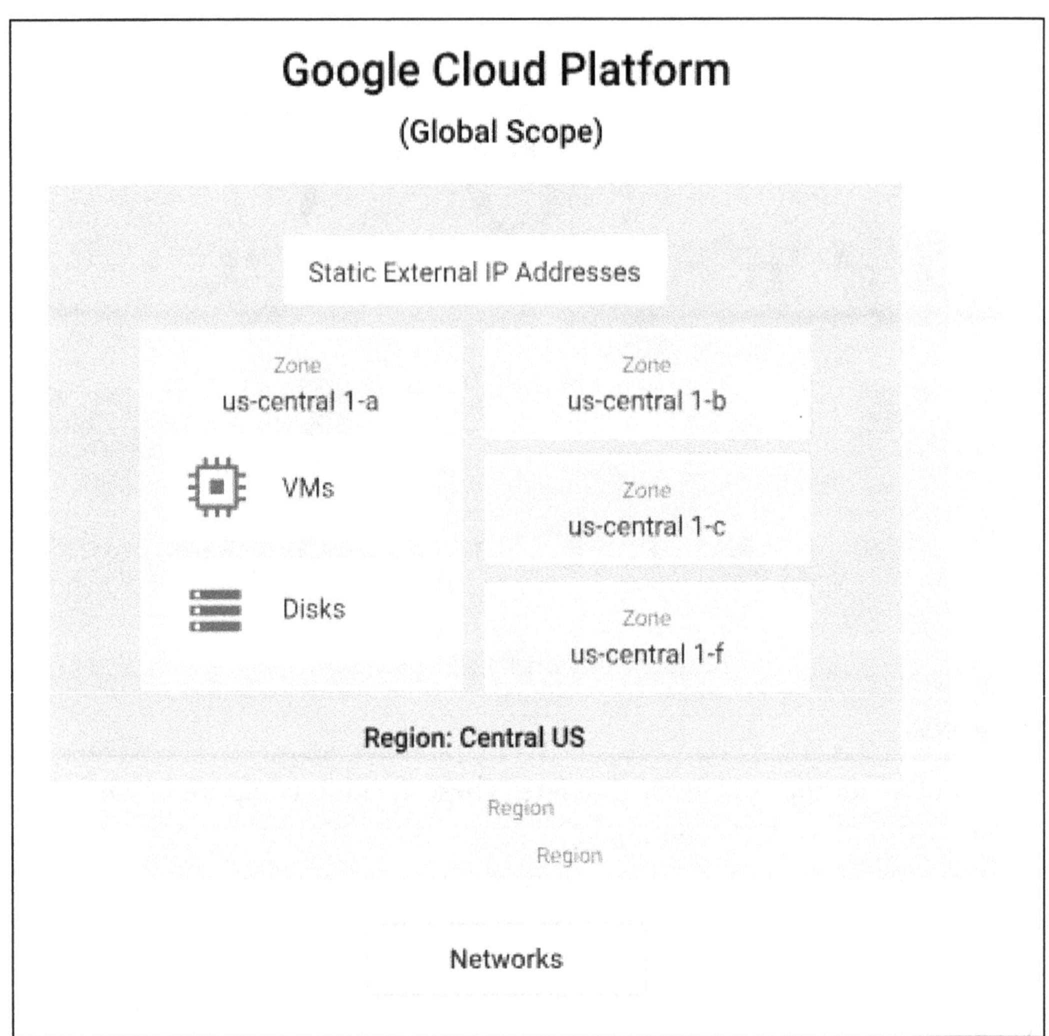

Figure 1-04: GCP Global Scope

For instance, building a network is a global operation as networking is a global resource, while booking an IP address, is a regional operation because the address is a regional resource. The scope of operation varies according to the type of resources you are working with. You may or may not have to think about how and where the resources are allocated depending on the level of self-management required by the computing and hosting service you choose.

Ways to Interact with the Services

There are three different ways to interact with GCP, which are CLI, SDK, and Console.

Google Cloud Platform Console

You can use the Google Cloud Platform Console to manage your GCP projects and resources with a web-based graphical user interface. You can create a new project or work on an existing project by using the GCP Console and use the resources you create in that project. You can create multiple projects so that you can use projects in any way that makes sense to separate your work. For example, if you want to make sure that only certain team members have access to the resources of a project and all team members have access to resources in another project, you could launch a new project.

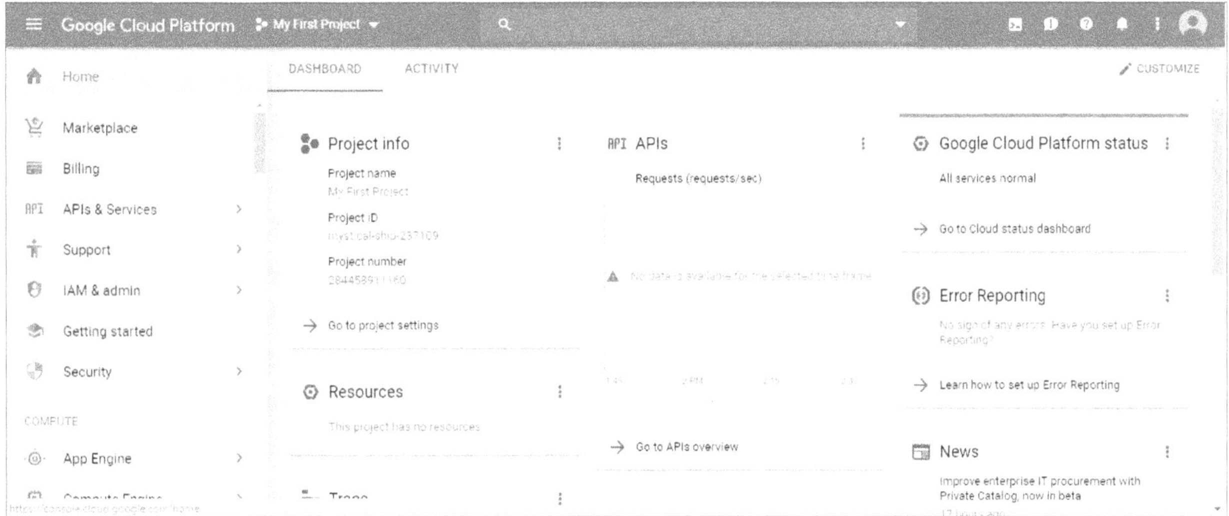

Figure 1-05: GCP Console

Command Line Interface

If you prefer to work in a terminal window, Google Cloud SDK provides the gcloud command-line tool, which gives you access to the commands you need. The gcloud tool can be used to manage both your development workflow and your GCP resources.

GCP also provides the GCP interactive browser shell environment, Cloud Shell. The GCP console allows you to access the Cloud Shell. A temporary instance for a virtual machine, Compute Engine Cloud Shell provides instance control from a web browser access to the instance. It also provide a built-in code editor and 5GB persistence disk storage. Google Cloud SDK and other tools have been pre-installed. Java, Go, Python, Node.js, PHP, Ruby and.NET linguistic are also supported. The functionality of web preview is also provided by Cloud Shell. Built-in authorization for accessing the GCP Project and Resources is also provided by Cloud Shell.

```
test-project-165220 ×   +
Welcome to Cloud Shell! Type "help" to get started.
ipspecialist @test-project-165220:~$ gcloud version
Google Cloud SDK 158.0.0
alpha 2017.03.24
app-engine-go
app-engine-java 1.9.53
app-engine-python 1.9.54
beta 2017.03.24
bq 2.0.24
cloud-datastore-emulator 1.2.1
core 2017.06.02
datalab 20170525
docker-credential-gcr
gcd-emulator v1beta3-1.0.0
gcloud
gsutil 4.26
kubectl
pubsub-emulator 2017.03.24
ipspecialist @test-project-165220:~$
```

Figure 1-06: GCP Cloud Shell

Client Libraries

The Cloud SDK consists of client libraries, which allow you to build and manage resources easily. GCP client libraries expose APIs for two principal purposes:

- App APIs allow service access. For supported languages like Node.js and Python, the App APIs are optimized. The libraries are designed for service metaphors to work more naturally with the services and to write fewer boilerplates. The libraries also offer authentication and permission helpers
- Admin APIs provide resource management functionality; For instance, if you want to build your own automated tools, you can use admin APIs

GCP's Design and Structure

GCP is designed to be offered globally, and it is scalable, unlimited with security built in it. GCP is used to serve worldwide customers; that is why it is intrinsically global. With the global model as compared to the regional model, it is easier to handle the latency and failures in a global but more sensitive way in terms of multiple region failures.

Physical Infrastructure

From the bottom level, there are some programs that run on CPU, which exist in a physical server that are on Racks in the Google data center. In Google, they have entirely separated duties, which means that a person who has access to the data center, has no access to the services; while those who have access to the services have no access to the data center.

The zone is a concept where two or more data centers are logically grouped together. There are multiple zones around the globe, but each zone is independent of another zone. They are grouped together in a region. Zones within the region can communicate with each other very quickly but not as quick as compared to the communication between the data centers in the zone.

When multiple regions are grouped together, they are called multi-region, and they are 100 miles apart from each other. All region and zones are connected to each other with a private global network. In this private network, there is Google Fiber, which is spread all over the world and it is connected to its Datacenter. Hence, the traffic from one server to another does not go through the internet as it goes through the fiber. But if still the things that need to connect to the internet so for that Point of Presence (POP) came, which are at the edges of google private network. They are connected to the internet and CDN locations.

Network Ingress/Egress

In normal network, the data goes to the edge location, which is closest to the destination via the internet, but in Google network, the traffic enters from the internet to the edge location closest to the source. This is some unique way as if we use a single global IP which has the capability to balance the load across the servers all over the world. If the request is first generated, it goes to the closest edge location, but if that edge location is overloaded, then the load is balanced by distributing some of the traffic to another region with latency. With the use of single global IP, DNS issues are resolved.

Pricing

In GCP, there is customer friendly pricing. There is no upfront cost; you only have to pay as you go depending on its provisioning and usage. There is no termination fee, which means that you stop paying for the service from the very next second you terminated it. In GCP, you pay per second, and there are some discount schemes that are also available.

Network traffic is also charged, but only for traffic going out of the network, not for incoming traffic. Egress traffic pricing depends on the traffic amount in GBs. Some GCP

services are free when they are communicating with other GCP services, depending on their location and the type of service you are using.

Security

As we discussed above, in GCP, there is a separation of duties and physical securities. In GCP, everything is encrypted at rest, so there is no need to enable encryption manually. In that, there is a strong key and identity management. Network encryption is also done in GCP, which means that all control information is encrypted and all WAN traffic is to be encrypted automatically soon between regions. Within the data center, all local traffic is encrypted.

Quotas

Some resources have set project-wide quota limits and per-region quota limits such as static IPs, images, firewall rules or VPC networks. The total quota for your project or per-region quota is counted when you create these resources if applicable. You will not be able to add further resources of the same kind in this project or region if any of the quota limits are exceeded.

What are Google Cloud Platform (GCP) Services?

Google offers a wide range of Services, i.e. approximately 90 products. Followings are the major Google Cloud Services:

- Compute
- Networking
- Storage and Databases
- Big Data
- Machine Learning
- Identity and Security

Computing and Hosting

Google Cloud Platform offers various options for Computing and Hosting:

- Using a managed application platform
- Working in a server-less environment
- Building your own cloud-based infrastructure to have the most control and flexibility
- Leveraging container technologies in order to gain high flexibility

Application Platform

Google App Engine is Platform as a Service (PaaS). Many of the resources are managed by Google for the user by using App Engine.

You can obtain the following by using the Google App Engine:

- Management of app hosting, scaling, monitoring, and infrastructure made for the user by Google
- Build the app on top of the App Engine standard environment runtime in the supported languages (Python 2.7, Java 8, Java 7, PHP 5.5, and Go 1.8,1.6)
- Build the app on top of App Engine flexible environment runtimes in the flexible supported languages (Python 2.7/3.6, Java 8, Go 1.8, Node.js, PHP 5.6, 7, .NET and Ruby). User can also use custom runtimes
- To develop or test on your local machine in an environment, use App Engine SDK
- Use the supported storage technologies
- Use Cloud Endpoints in the standard environment for generating APIs and Client libraries
- For activities like E-mail and user management, built-in and managed services are provided
- For the identification of security vulnerabilities, Cloud Security Scanner is provided
- Deploy applications by using App Engine Launcher GUI application on Microsoft Windows or MacOS or by CLI

Note: Run the app from Central US or Western Europe region for the standard environment.

Server-less Computing

GCP is Function as a Service (FaaS), i.e., Google Cloud Function provides a server-less environment for building and connecting cloud services. There is no need to provision any infrastructure or manage any server.

Cloud Function format is JavaScript, and it executes in a Node.js v6.11.5 environment in GCP. User can execute the Cloud Function in any standard Node.js Runtime.

Use Cases of Cloud Function

- Lightweight APIs consisting of loosely linked logic in applications
- Mobile backend functions
- For scenarios such as video transcoding and IoT streaming data, data processing and ETL operations

- Webhooks to respond to HTTP triggers

Containers

Google Kubernetes Engine is a GCP's Container as a Service (CaaS). In Container-based service, users do not have to consume time on deployment and integration into the hosting environment. Only the application code is the responsibility of the user. Google Kubernetes Engine is built on the Kubernetes open source system, which provides you with on-site or hybrid cloud flexibility in addition to the Public Cloud Infrastructure of GCP.

User can perform the following tasks by using Kubernetes Engine:

- State your Docker container requirements by creating a simple JSON configuration file
- Create an external network load balancer
- Create and Manage services; Services create an abstraction layer that separates customers from pods with backend functions. This allows customers to work at any given time without any concern about the pods created or deleted
- Create and manage Compute Engine groups of instances running Kubernetes, called clusters. Kubernetes Engine uses Compute Engine instances as cluster nodes. Each node runs the Docker runtime; a Kubernetes node agent monitors the node's health, and a simple network proxy
- Use the Google Container Registry to store Docker images securely and privately. You can push images to your registry and then use an HTTP endpoint to pull images to any instance of the Compute Engine or your own hardware
- Create single-container and multi-container pods. Each pod is a logical host capable of containing one or more containers. By sharing resources, such as networking resources, containers in a pod work together
- Create and manage replication controllers that manage on the basis of a template to create and delete pod replicas. Replication controllers help ensure that the resources your application needs to run are reliable and scale appropriately.

Virtual Machines

Google Compute Engine is an unmanaged service of GCP that works as Infrastructure as a Service (IaaS). User should select and configure the platform components. When using Google Compute Engine, system configuration, administration and monitoring are on the user's end. Complete control of system and flexibility is available for the user. Google will make sure of the availability and reliability of the resources.

Following are the tasks a user can perform:

- Select global regions and zones for the deployment of resources
- Use VM instances for building an application
- Select the required operating system, development stacks, languages, frameworks, services, and other software technologies
- Create instances from public or private images
- Avail any third-party technology or GCP storage technology
- For deploying quickly, Google Cloud Launcher provides pre-configured software packages
- Attach or Detach disk as required
- Create instance groups for multiple instances management
- Auto-scaling of instances
- SSH connection to instances

Option for Combined Computing and Hosting

User can combine multiple services for more facilities; for example, combining Compute Engine and App Engine.

Storage Services

GCP offers various storage services for its users, which include:

- Cloud Datastore and Cloud Bigtable for NoSQL data storage
- Cloud Storage is the consistent, large-capacity and scalable data storage service. It has further options:
    - ✓ Multi-Regional (Highly available and geo-redundant)
    - ✓ Regional (High availability and localized storage location)
    - ✓ Nearline (Cheap archival storage suitable for the data accessed less than once in a month)
    - ✓ Coldline (Cheap archival storage ideal for backup and disaster recovery)
- Cloud SQL database provides either MySQL or PostgreSQL databases
- A fully managed, mission-critical, relational database service in Cloud Spanner, which provides transactional consistency at a global scale, schemas, SQL querying, and automatic, synchronous replication for high availability
- Persistent disks on Compute Engine (Standard persistent disk, which is a hard disk based persistent disk and Solid state persistent disk)

Note: User can set the required storage technology on Compute Engine by using the persistent disk.

Big Data Services

Big data is the service, which helps the user in querying, analyzing and processing large data stored in Cloud in a faster way. Cloud provides various Big Data services regarding Data Analysis, Asynchronous Messaging, and Batch and Streaming Data Processing.

Data Analysis

GCP offers BigQuery for data analysis services. User can avail the following features by using BigQuery:

- Data management and protection by using permissions
- User can load, export, query and copy data by using jobs
- Using the web UI, CLI or API
- Quickly querying massive datasets by using SQL-like commands
- Loading data from various sources including streaming data
- Organizing data into datasets and tables creating custom schemas

Batch and Streaming Data Processing

GCP provides managed services and sets of SDKs used for Batch and Streaming data processing tasks. This service is named as Cloud Dataflow. Dataflow is ideal for the processing task, which can be easily divided into parallel workloads. Dataflow is designed for High-Volume computations. Extract-Transform-Load (ETL) tasks are for the transferring of data between different storage media, transforming data into any other format, or data loading in a new storage system. Dataflow is a great service for ETL.

Asynchronous Messaging

GCP provides Cloud Pub/Sub (Asynchronous Messaging Service). This application is able to send messages in JSON format to a publishing unit called topic. Other applications of the project can receive the messages in HTTP requests or in response bodies by subscribing to the topic because Cloud Pub/Subtopics are global resources. Cloud Pub/Sub is not only for Big Data, but it can be also used with any message service.

Networking

Compute Engine offers a number of network services. These services help you load resource traffic, create DNS records, and link your existing network to the Google network.

The services that are included in networking are:

- **VPC** - the Private Virtual Cloud to manage the Cloud software network. In this, sets of networking services are included, which are used by VM instances. At a time, an instance can connect to only one network
- **Balancing of Cloud Load** – A software-defined and managed Load Balancing service for traffic across multiple instances. There are two types of server-side Load Balancing; Network Load Balancing and HTTP/ HTTPS Load Balancing. In Network Load Balancing, you can distribute traffic among server instances in the same region based on incoming IP protocol data, such as an address, port, and protocol. In HTTP/HTTPS Load Balancing, the traffic is distributed across the regions, to ensure that requests are routed into the nearest region, or to a healthy instance in the next nearest region, if there are any failures or overcapacity constraints
- **CDN** - Content Delivery Network based on the global edge points of presence of Google
- **Cloud Interconnect** -You can use a highly available, low-latency, corporate-grade connection to connect your existing network to your VPC network
- **Cloud VPN** - It allows you to connect an IPsec connection to your existing VPC network. It is also possible to use a VPN to connect two Cloud VPN gates together
- **Cloud DNS** - Domain Name System (DNS) records can be published and maintained using the same infrastructure as Google. You can work with managed zones and DNS records using the Google Cloud Platform Console, command line and a REST API

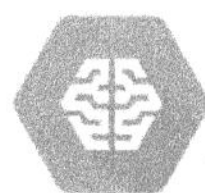

Machine Learning Services

A variety of powerful Machine Learning (ML) services are provided by GCP Cloud AI. You can either use APIs that provide pre-trained models that are optimized for particular application or build and train your own sophisticated, large-scale models through the TensorFlow frame.

ML APIs

GCP offers a variety of APIs that allow you to make use of Google ML without your own models.

- **Google Cloud Video Intelligence API** lets you use video analysis technology that provides label detection, explicit content detection, shot-change detection, and regionalization features
- You can easily integrate the vision detection function with the **Google Cloud Vision API** that includes image labeling, visual or landmark detection, OCRs and explicit contents tagging
- You can quickly translate source text in over 100 languages via **Google Cloud Translation API**. In cases where the source language is not known, language detection assists
- The **Google Cloud Speech API** allows you to convert speech to text to support your global user base and to recognize more than 110 languages and variants
- You can quickly convert your source text into more than a hundred supported languages by **Google Cloud Translation API**. In cases where the source language is not known, language detection helps
- You can add sentimental assessment, entity analysis, entity - sense analysis, the content classification and syntax analysis to the **Google Natural Language API**

Cloud ML Engine

Cloud Machine Learning Engine combines GCP's managed infrastructure with TensorFlow's power and flexibility. It can be used to train models learning on a scale and to host trained models to predict new cloud data. With Cloud ML Engine, you can train machine learning patterns using TensorFlow GCP-based training applications and host these trained patterns to help you gather new data forecasting. Cloud ML Engine manages the computing resources your training needs to perform so that you can focus more on your model than on configuring hardware or managing resources.

Identity and Security

Security is really important in every cloud system. The security model of Google Cloud, is a worldwide infrastructure. Its unique, innovative capability will help to make your business safe and compliant. In GCP, there are multiple identities and security services such as:

Roles

These are the collection of permissions that are used to manage the GCP resources. Roles are global. In permission, you define the action, which you want to perform by allowing it. It will be written as "Service.Resource.Verb".

In Roles, there is a type called primitive roles in which Owner, Editor and Viewer role are defined. The Owner has the right to control who can access and change billings; the Editor can modify the resource like create, delete any resource for most services.while the Viewer has read-only rights. Another type of role is known as Pre-defined roles that give granular access to specific GCP resources (IAM). It is more specific to a particular task.

Custom role is also a type of role in which you define granular permission to project or organize level collections.

Cloud IAM

Cloud IAM controls access to GCP resources, which allows you to manage access control by defining who (identity) has which access (role) for which resource.. In Cloud IAM, the member is the user, group, domain, service account or the public. As cloud IAM does not manage identity, so it uses individual Google accounts, Google groups, G Suite/Cloud Identity domains. In Cloud IAM, it is better to use google group and service account rather than an individual account. Service account belongs to application or instance. In Cloud IAM, the E-mail address,which is tied to each identity, has a unique E-mail address.

Cloud IAM policies are something that attaches the members to roles at a hierarchy level: Org, Folder, Project, Resource. Policies control who can do what to which resource IAM is free in GCP.

Service Accounts

A Service Account (SAC), instead of an individual end user, is a particular kind of Google Account that belongs to your application or VM. Your application assumes the identity of the Google API service account so that users do not participate directly. The important thing to remember is almost in every case, whether you are producing application or developing it outside the cloud environemet, you should use service account rather than user account or API keys.

When you create a service account, you must ensure that what resources and what permissions your application requires and then give the least privilege.

Cloud Identity

Identity Cloud is a Service Identity (IDaaS). The Cloud Identity can be used to manage your users, applications, and devices centrally through the Google Admin Console. If you are using GCP without the Cloud Identity service, then most probably you can use GSuite or Gmail/Google Account. So for Non-G Suite users via this, you can create free Google account and tie it with the verified domain.

With central management, you can use 2 step verification and enforcement including security keys. Via Google Cloud Directory Sync, you can sync from AD and LDAP directories. You can also use Cloud Identity with other apps by using SSO. It is also free to use.

Security Key Enforcement

This is USB or Bluetooth 2 step verification device that prevents unauthorized access. 2SV poses an additional barrier among businesses and cybercriminals who try to steal passwords and usernames from business information. The only thing you can do to protect your business is turning to 2SV. It ensures that your users log into the services with the security key that was originally registered and verifies that it is also the right security key.

Cloud Resource Manager

Centrally manage and secure an organization's projects with custom folder hierarchy. It is the root node in hierarchy, after which you create a folder as per requirement. To use Cloud Resource Manager, you need an account in G Suite. By using this hierarchical organization, you can easily manage common aspects of your resources, for example, access control and configuration settings. Hence, if you do not use this, each identity will have its own GCP project.

In Cloud Resource Manager, there is a recycle bin option, which allows undeleting of project. With the Resource Manager, you can create and manage Cloud IAM policies for your organization and project. This service is not charged like other services.

Cloud Audit Logging

For each project, folder, and organization, Cloud Audit Logging maintains three audit logs: admin activity, data access, and system event. The services of the Google Cloud Platform write log entries to these logs to help reply to "who did what, where, and when?".

Admin activity has a retention period of 7 days for free, while data access has 7 days retention period free and after that, you will have to pay. Data access is for GCP visible services.

Cloud Key Management Service

Cloud KMS is a key management service hosted in the cloud that allows you to use the same methods to manage cryptographic keys on your cloud. AES256, RSA 2048, RSA 3072, RSA 4096, EC P256, and EC P384 encrypted keys can be generated, used, rotated, and destroyed. By including Cloud KMS, you can manage permissions on individual keys and monitor how these are used in Cloud IAM and Cloud Audit Logging. Use Cloud KMS to guard secrets and other sensitive data to the Google Cloud Platform. As we know that in Cloud KMS, rotation of key is used to create new encryption on demand or automatically but old keys versions are stored, so you must not lose it. In this, you will have to pay for the active key version you stored over the time and the key used for operation.

Cloud Identity Aware Proxy

The Cloud Identity-Aware Proxy (Cloud IAP) controls access to your Google Cloud-based applications and VMs. Cloud IAP functions to detect if a user should be permitted to access an application or VM by verifying user identity and context of the application. Cloud IAP is a building block for the company's Security Model BeyondCorp, which allows all employees to work from unauthorized networks without a VPN.

With this, you can grant access to group and service accounts. During its set up, you only need to pay for Load Balancing / Protocol Forwarding rules and traffic.

Cloud Security Scanner

Cloud security scanner is an App Engine, Compute Engine, and Google Kubernetes Engine. Web security scanner is used for common vulnerabilities. Four common vulnerabilities, including cross-site scripting (XSS), injection flash injecting, HTTP mixed-content and outdated / unsecure libraries may be automatically scanned and detected. It makes it possible to identify early and delivers very low false positives. The security scans are easy to install, run, plan, and manage and are free for users on Google Cloud Platform.

After the scan is set up, your Cloud Security Scanner automatically scans your application and attempts to train as many user inputs and event managers as possible, following all links on your startup URLs.

Cloud Data Loss Prevention API

Cloud DLP helps you understand and manage sensitive information more effectively. It allows quick, scalable classification and writing of sensitive data elements. You can also

edit your data optionally with methods such as masking, safe hacking, tokenization, bucketing and format preservation. Cloud DLP classifies sensitive information using more than 90 pre-defined detectors, which detect patterns, formats, and checksums.

With this, you can scan text and images, and pay for the volume of data processed.

Operations and Management

Google offers various services for Operation and management purpose:

Google Stackdriver

It is used for monitoring, logging and diagnosing the application in GCP and AWS. This is a Global Service.

Google provides free tier Stackdriver only for GCP services. The free tier is with short retention and storage. Whereas, Premium Tier is for both GCP and AWS with charges per resource and provides user-defined metrics and VM monitoring agents.

Stackdriver Monitoring is for checking the performance, uptime, and health of the applications on Cloud. This service consists of built-in and custom metrics, dashboards, monitoring, and alerts. It allows the user to follow the Trail.

Stackdriver Logging allows the user to store, search, monitor, and alert on log data and events. It also allows collecting logs from AWS with agent or custom API. User can send real-time log data to BigQuery for advanced analytics. It also includes a powerful interface to browse, search, and slice log data. When logs are close to expiring, then this service allows you to transfer them in GCS.

Stackdriver Error Reporting counts, analyzes, aggregates, and tracks crash.

Stackdriver Debugger grabs program state in live deploys. User can share debugging sessions with others by using URLs. This service is free to use.

Cloud Deployment Manager

By using declarative templates "Infrastructure as Code", this service is used to Create/Manage resources.

Cloud Billing API

User can manage their project bill or get GCP pricing.

Mind Map

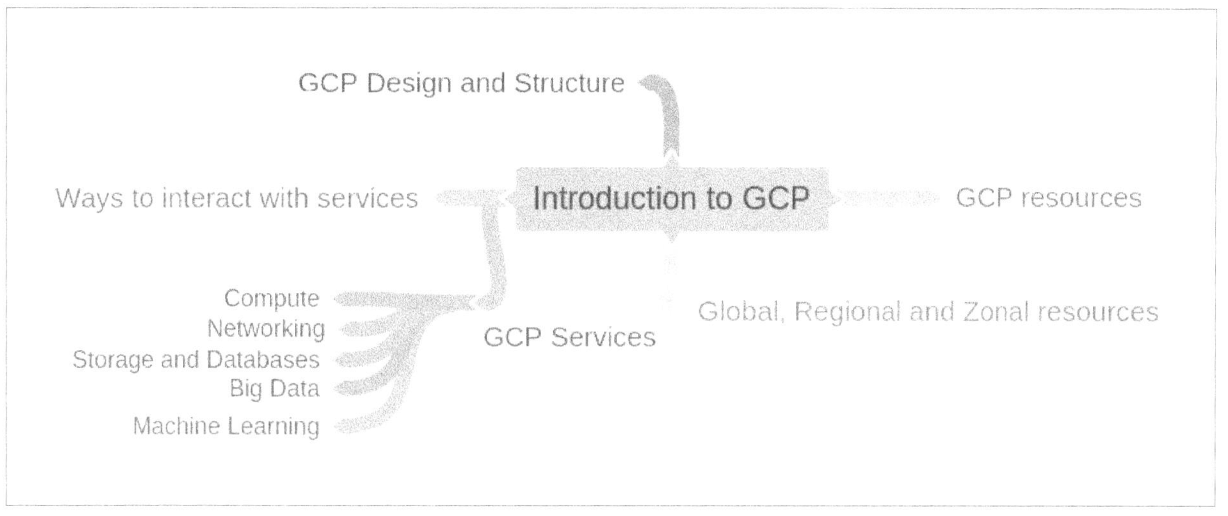

Figure 1-07: Mind Map of GCP

Practice Questions:

1. Which Cloud Computing type is used to provide Basic Building Block for Cloud?
   A. IaaS
   B. SaaS
   C. PaaS
   D. FaaS

2. Which type of Deployment model includes a mixture of on-premises Public third part Cloud and Private Cloud?
   A. Cloud
   B. Hybrid
   C. On-Premises
   D. Cloud and Hybrid Both

3. From the following options, which is the logical grouping of the data center?
   A. Zone
   B. Region
   C. Edge Location
   D. None of the above

4. _______________ is the name given to the grouping of zones.
   A. Zone
   B. Region
   C. Edge Location
   D. None of the above

5. In Google network, the traffic enters from the internet to the edge location closest to ___________.
   A. Source
   B. Destination
   C. Both

6. In GCP, for network you are charged for _____________.
   A. Ingress
   B. Egress

7. Google App Engine is ____________________.

A. IaaS
B. FaaS
C. PaaS
D. None of the above

8. Management of app hosting, scaling, monitoring and infrastructure are done for user by Google via the service ____________________.
A. Google App Engine
B. Storage
C. Big Data
D. ML

9. Google Kubernetes Engine is GCP's ___________.
A. PaaS
B. CaaS
C. IaaS
D. FaaS

10. Creating and managing Compute Engine groups of instances running Kubernetes is called __________.
A. App Engine
B. Cluster
C. Nodes
D. None of the above

11. Google Compute Engine is an unmanaged service of GCP that works as ______________.
A. PaaS
B. CaaS
C. IaaS
D. FaaS

12. Cloud Datastore and Cloud Bigtable is for ______________.
A. SQL
B. NoSQL

C. MySQL
D. Redshift

13. In GCP, for data analysis, which service is used?
A. BigQuery
B. Cloud IAM
C. Cloud Audit Logging
D. Cloud Resource Manager

14. GCP provides managed services and sets of SDKs used for Batch and Streaming data processing tasks. It is known as __________.
A. Cloud KMS
B. Cloud DataFlow
C. Cloud Pub/Sub
D. Cloud Security Scanner

15. ________________ is a particular kind of Google Account that belongs to your application or VM.
A. Cloud Identity
B. Cloud IAM
C. Service Accounts
D. None of the above

16. When you create a free trial account, you receive some credit which is available for:
A. Six months.
B. 12 months.
C. One month.
D. Three months.

17. When you are on the free trial, you are not allowed to have:
A. More than 3 Virtual CPUs together at once.
B. More than 6 Virtual CPUs together at once.
C. More than 8 Virtual CPUs together at once.
D. More than 12 Virtual CPUs together at once.

18. In Always Free Tier, from the Compute Side of things, each day you can run

______________ worth of f1-micro instance in most of the US regions, and you would not get charged for it.

A. 24 hours.
B. 12 hours.
C. 6 hours.
D. 3 hours.

19. In the Always Free Compute Category, we have App Engine, where an application can run ____________ each day in North America without getting charged.
    A. 7 hours.
    B. 14 hours.
    C. 21 hours.
    D. 28 hours.

20. Cloud Pub/Sub has:
    A. 10 GB/ month of data.
    B. 5 GB/ month of data.
    C. 20 GB/ month of data.
    D. 1 GB/ month of data.

21. Every day you can perform __________ of build, in Google Cloud Container Builders and can perform _____________ of Voice recognition each month in Google Cloud Speech API.
    A. 120 minutes of build and 60 minutes of Voice Recognition.
    B. 60 minutes of build and 120 minutes of Voice Recognition.
    C. 60 minutes of build and 60 minutes of Voice Recognition.
    D. 120 minutes of build and 120 minutes of Voice Recognition.

22. Always Free Tier account contains:
    A. 1000 unit/ month of Cloud Vision API calls.
    B. 5000 unit/ month Google Cloud Natural Language API.
    C. Both A and B.
    D. None of the Above.

23. Google also has a Cloud Shell existing in the console with ______________ of persistent disk storage quota.
    A. 5 GB.
    B. 10 GB.

C. 1 GB.
D. None of the Above.

24. In Google assigned project:
    A. The name of the project can be changed, but the project number and ID cannot be changed.
    B. The name of the project cannot be changed, but the project number and ID can be changed.
    C. The name, number, and ID of the project remains the same.
    D. The name, number, and ID of the project can be changed.

25. According to GCP Documentation, tools for ________________ now become an important part of the managing development.
    A. Monitoring.
    B. Analyzing.
    C. Optimizing Cost.
    D. All of the Above.

Chapter 02: Getting Started

Introduction

Google Cloud Platform (GCP) is a platform of cloud computing services that grew with the Google App Engine framework which is used for hosting web applications from Google's data centers. Since the launch of Google App Engine in 2008, GCP has grown into one of the highest quality cloud computing platforms in the marketplace, though it still trails Amazon Web Services (AWS) and Microsoft Azure in terms of marketplace percentage. That said, Google continues to preserve it's very own inside the cloud wars and keeps to invest in GCP to make it competitive with different public cloud vendors, and extra attractive to big clients. This chapter includes the basics of Google Cloud Platform and all the details which are required for setting up a new account using GCP service. In this chapter, you will get to know about creating a GCP Free-Tier Account and the methods to export billing and generating alarms for billing alerts.

What is Google Cloud Platform? Google Cloud Platform, is a platform used for cloud computing which provides infrastructure tools and services for users which helps in building applications and services.

Why does Google Cloud Platform matter? Google Cloud Platform is considered as the third biggest cloud provider in terms of revenue.

Who does Google Cloud Platform affect? An organization willing to perform cloud computing must consider Google Cloud platform for their needs.

When was Google Cloud Platform announced? Google announced its first cloud platform, Google App Engine, in 2008, and they continuously added more tools and services until it became known as the Google Cloud Platform later on.

How can I use Google Cloud Platform? This book that you are reading, developed and published by IPSpecialist is enough to enable you to start using Google Cloud Platform. Also, Google provides Documentations for getting started and a frequently asked questions page for IT leaders and developers and to investigate the platform.

GCP Cheat Sheet Introduction

In the GCP Cheat Sheet Introduction, the topic starts with the first and foremost question, what is the meaning of cheating and why it is used here? Well, Google's dictionary defines that cheating is to act dishonestly and unfairly to gain some advantage, especially in the examination or somewhere in the game.

It all comes back to a document made by Greg Wilson, who is the director of Developer relations at Google. He used to call his document GCP Products described in four words or less but then renamed the document as Google Cloud Developer's Cheat Sheet, but it has nothing to do with actual cheating off course. The Cheat Sheet is just something which you can refer to either remind yourself to get a very basic idea about something, and you do not have time to research it fully. The cheat sheet is updated very regularly. The Google Cloud Cheat Sheet is provided below (Figure 2-01). You might find it unreadable, so, pieces of this cheat sheet are discussed later in this chapter.

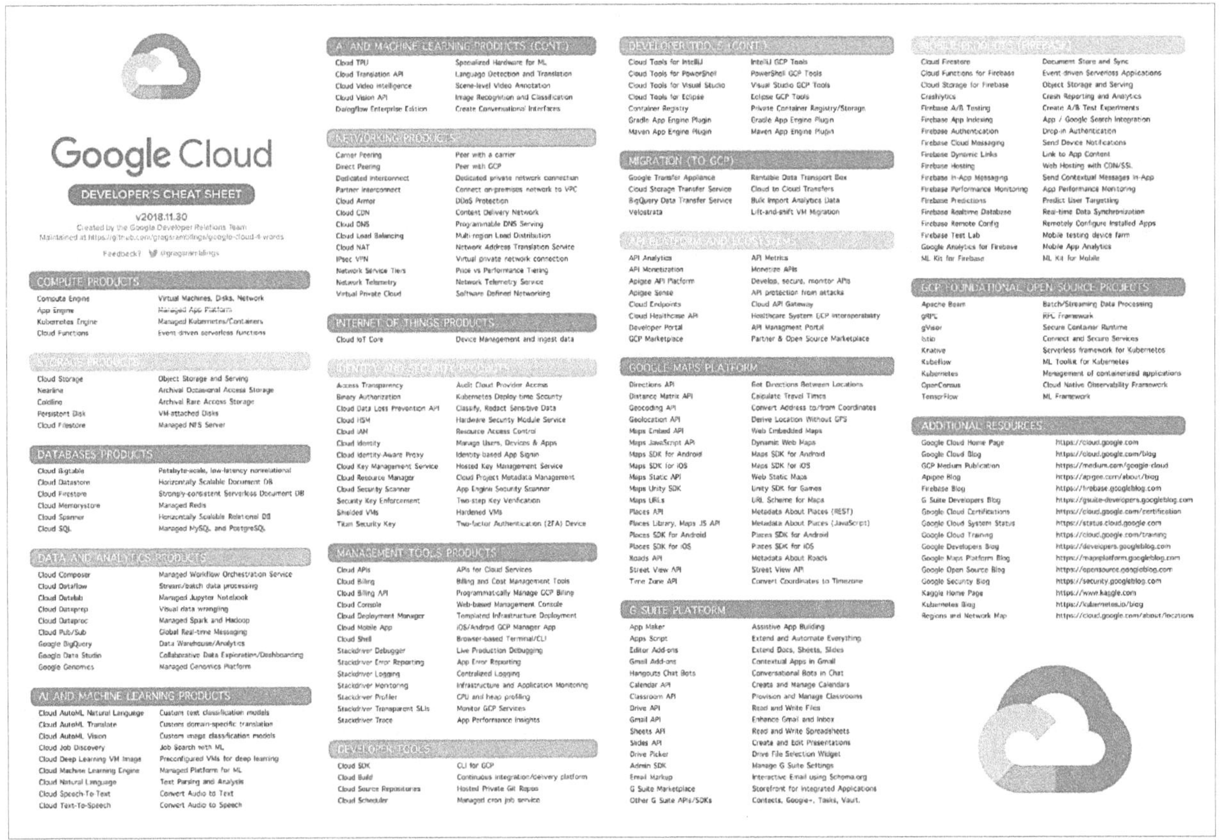

Figure 2-01: The Google Cloud Developer's Cheat Sheet.

Products/ Services as Building Block

When you look closely at this cheat sheet, you will come to know that the cheat sheet is divided into multiple categories. We have Compute Products, Storage Products, Networking Products, Management Tools, Developer Tools, and many more. And in each section, we have several Google Cloud Products. Does the question arise why these products and services are grouped in this way? The fundamental reason for this question is because Greg Wilson who puts together the original version of the whole document decided to use the document in this way, as it will be useful. Each product enlisted here is

like a piece of a puzzle; they fit together with each other and with other parts of the system. These pieces are more like LEGO bricks, building blocks. Now every building block has a different shape and served different functions. You can co-relate each of the section of developer's cheat sheet with the bucket of LEGO bricks.

Imagine one of the buckets has a whole bunch of huge flat sheet pieces, and these pieces are used as the foundation of the building. The other bucket has a whole bunch of tiny and flexible pieces; they are very useful for certain circumstances when you are building something with the block, you need to select the block with the right shape to form a product.

Most of the systems will require some amount of support for Compute, Storage, Networking, or Messaging products. An easy example is a database, it combines both services, i.e., Compute and Storage, and in this way, it will create a particular category by their own. It will remember all the data and perform computation when required. Similarly, filtering all the data and transforming into the format which you can use and, if you have replication for your database, then we can also move data from one place to another. The section named as Data and Analytic Products list the whole bunch of services that are likely to be used together.

DATA AND ANALYTICS PRODUCTS	
Cloud Composer	Managed Workflow Orchestration Service
Cloud Dataflow	Stream/batch data processing
Cloud Datalab	Managed Jupyter Notebook
Cloud Dataprep	Visual data wrangling
Cloud Dataproc	Managed Spark and Hadoop
Cloud Pub/Sub	Global Real-time Messaging
Google BigQuery	Data Warehouse/Analytics
Google Data Studio	Collaborative Data Exploration/Dashboarding
Google Genomics	Managed Genomics Platform

Figure 2-02: Data and Analytics Product is GCP Cheat Sheet.

Continuing with this LEGO analogy, two specific items should be called out. The first one is in Management Tool Products section called the Cloud Deployment Manager. The cheat sheet calls this Template Infrastructure Deployment. This product is like buying a box of LEGO pieces with instructions to build some particular things, you get all the pieces you need to be listed in the template, but this is your template, and you can

change it however you want; just like with the LEGO set which might combine several things.

MANAGEMENT TOOLS PRODUCTS	
Cloud APIs	APIs for Cloud Services
Cloud Billing	Billing and Cost Management Tools
Cloud Billing API	Programmatically Manage GCP Billing
Cloud Console	Web-based Management Console
Cloud Deployment Manager	Templated Infrastructure Deployment
Cloud Mobile App	iOS/Android GCP Manager App
Cloud Shell	Browser-based Terminal/CLI
Stackdriver Debugger	Live Production Debugging
Stackdriver Error Reporting	App Error Reporting
Stackdriver Logging	Centralized Logging
Stackdriver Monitoring	Infrastructure and Application Monitoring
Stackdriver Profiler	CPU and heap profiling
Stackdriver Transparent SLIs	Monitor GCP Services
Stackdriver Trace	App Performance Insights

Figure 2-03: Cloud Deployment Manager under the Management Tools.

The next thing is the API Platform and Ecosystem section, in particular, the GCP Market Place is a partner and open source market place. This place has all the packages together, but instead of you controlling all of the details and building it yourself, the GCP Market Place is more about buying completed things.

API PLATFORM AND ECOSYSTEMS

API Analytics	API Metrics
API Monetization	Monetize APIs
Apigee API Platform	Develop, secure, monitor APIs
Apigee Sense	API protection from attacks
Cloud Endpoints	Cloud API Gateway
Cloud Healthcase API	Healthcare System GCP Interoperability
Developer Portal	API Managment Portal
GCP Marketplace	Partner & Open Source Marketplace

Figure 2-04: GCP Marketplace in API Platforms and Ecosystems Section.

Key Building Blocks

Before jumping into the document of the GCP Cheat sheet described in Figure 2-01, let me reassure you that we will not discuss every product. The purpose is to make you familiar with the different products that Google Cloud offers and describe some of the services that you are going to come across. There are some items on the list that you never have to deal with in your entire life. But we discuss some of the ones that you are likely to deal with, but the text documentation of GCP Developers Cloud Cheat Sheet is available and contains all the details of the services and products for their users. Most of them have two links; one link goes for the marketing tape, which is the friendly version of the documentation. This version describes the product, describing why you might want to use it, what it does and other information like that. While the other link goes to the developer documentation, where you can learn all the information that you need to know for the particular product effectively.

Let's start at the top of the list. The first one is Compute Engine in Compute products which are described as Virtual Machines, disks, and networks. This is the most relatable Google Cloud Product, just like computers you might buy from stores, and you can run whatever you want to run, and perform virtually anything you want to perform. Cloud Function which is a little way down in the list describes as Event-driven server-less function. Cloud Function even perform faster than the Compute Engine within the 10th of the second and manages all the scaling for you automatically. This is Google Cloud Function as a service product or (FaaS). Just like Amazon Lambda, this is a key building block of server-less systems. In terms of running server programs that set around and wait for clients to connect to them. In Cloud functions you set up an event and Google

will run the code that you give whenever that event happens again. And if a bunch of the whole events is happening at the same time, then Google runs your code in parallel slots of time, and Google does it automatically. There are all sorts of events that you can hooked-up, it could be requested through HTTP like connections had been made from your web page, other micro-services or something like that or it can be a new object being uploaded to Cloud or a message being sent to Cloud Pub-Sub.

Now speaking of Cloud Storage, just like Cloud Functions, Cloud Storage is also a server-less product, and they work very nicely together. Cloud Storage is like the purest service at its core. It says give me some data, and I can give it back to you. That's why it is described as object storage and serving. Nearline and Coldline are just versions of the Cloud Storage that are priced and optimized for less frequent data access, so they are perfect for backups. That's why their descriptions are "Archival Occasional Access Storage" and "Archival Rare Access Storage." Persistent Disk is a special kind of storage which is described as VM attached disks. Now the Cloud Storage Product is object storage, but the persistent disk is block storage, so it works much like a hard drive works, and it only connects to Compute Engine instances. Persistent Disk is like LEGO pieces that have a different kind of connectors on the side, but it only goes together with Compute Engines. Cloud File Store sits between Cloud Storage and Persistent Disk and it is neither object based nor block based. Cloud File Store is file-based, and it manages an NFS server. It is a bit more flexible to connect to persistent disk and may work better with certain kind of applications than the object based cloud storage.

The Kubernetes Engine in Compute Products are installed, run and managed by GKE on clusters of Compute Engine instances but it also reaches out to the Networking world, and it creates things like Cloud Load Balancer which will help in reducing the data.

COMPUTE PRODUCTS	
Compute Engine	Virtual Machines, Disks, Network
App Engine	Managed App Platform
Kubernetes Engine	Managed Kubernetes/Containers
Cloud Functions	Event-driven serverless functions

STORAGE PRODUCTS	
Cloud Storage	Object Storage and Serving
Nearline	Archival Occasional Access Storage
Coldline	Archival Rare Access Storage
Persistent Disk	VM-attached Disks
Cloud Filestore	Managed NFS Server

Figure 2-05: Compute and Storage Products in GCP Cheat Sheet.

The Cloud TPU is enlisted in AI and Machine Learning sections, but it is specialized hardware for Machine Learning (ML), so it's kind of like a Compute Engine Instances, but this one is built for Transfer Flow Processing instead of General Purpose Processing. TPU stands for Tensor Flow Processing Unit. Transfer Flow is an open source platform used for performing machine learning activities. Some of the products in AI and Machine Learning sections are pretty straight forward. The Cloud Speech-to-Text will convert Audio to Text and Cloud Text-to-Speech will convert Text to Audio. Cloud Natural Language is used for text phrasing and analysis, so you can give it some text and then it will tell you about the parts of speech and the emotions that are represented in it. The Cloud Machine Learning Engine is a managed platform used for Machine Learning where it will transfer flow for you. Or if you want to get more manual transfer flow, Cloud Deep Learning VM Image is a preconfigured VMs used for deep learning so; you would run that image as the Compute Engine instance. In the middle of the spectrum, we have the Cloud AutoML Products where the basic ML models are set up, but you can train them with your own organization's set of data whether those be a text document, images, translations or visions.

AI AND MACHINE LEARNING PRODUCTS	
Cloud AutoML Natural Language	Custom text classification models
Cloud AutoML Translate	Custom domain-specific translation
Cloud AutoML Vision	Custom image classification models
Cloud Job Discovery	Job Search with ML
Cloud Deep Learning VM Image	Preconfigured VMs for deep learning
Cloud Machine Learning Engine	Managed Platform for ML
Cloud Natural Language	Text Parsing and Analysis
Cloud Speech-To-Text	Convert Audio to Text
Cloud Text-To-Speech	Convert Audio to Speech

AI AND MACHINE LEARNING PRODUCTS (CONT.)	
Cloud TPU	Specialized Hardware for ML
Cloud Translation API	Language Detection and Translation
Cloud Video Intelligence	Scene-level Video Annotation
Cloud Vision API	Image Recognition and Classification
Dialogflow Enterprise Edition	Create Conversational Interfaces

Figure 2-06: AI and ML products in GCP Cheat Sheet.

The Databases section have quite a variety of products. The one that is most likely to be familiar with is Cloud SQL which is used to manage My SQL and Postgre SQL. Instead of managing Compute Engine instances and Persistent Disk yourself and installing MySQL, upgrading it, applying patches, here Google can perform all of the processes easily and can even manage things like Read Replica, but not everything might fit in a single instance, so Cloud Spanner is a horizontally scalable relational database. This thing is seriously massive scale. There are several non-relational options too. Cloud Fire Store, which incidentally shows up a couple of sections. It is strongly consistent server-less document DB, and it has some cool built-in things. The Cloud Data Store is a horizontally scalable document database, and you need only to pay for the services that you use. You don't have to provision or manage the certain capacity but if you have a predictable and high volume. And Cloud Bigtable might be a better choice since it is a Petabyte scale, low latency, and non-relational database.

DATABASES PRODUCTS	
Cloud Bigtable	Petabyte-scale, low-latency nonrelational
Cloud Datastore	Horizontally Scalable Document DB
Cloud Firestore	Strongly-consistent Serverless Document DB
Cloud Memorystore	Managed Redis
Cloud Spanner	Horizontally Scalable Relational DB
Cloud SQL	Managed MySQL and PostgreSQL

Figure 2-07: Databases Products in GCP Cheat Sheet.

In the Data and Analytics section, two of the core services that stand out are Cloud Dataflow and Cloud Dataproc. Spark and Hadoop manage cloud Dataproc. So, if you are already running Hadoop somewhere else, Cloud Dataproc is an efficient way to move that data to Google Cloud. This is for processing a large amount of data. The Cloud Dataflow also process a large amount of data but it is newer and better than Cloud Dataproc, and it handles both stream and batch data processing. The key technology behind Cloud Dataflow is something that Google released the open source Apache beam. Google Genomics is very specialized; it is only useful if you are working with that kind of medical data. The Cloud Pub/Sub is the most flexible product in all of Google Cloud. This is described as Global Real-Time messaging, and it can be used to connect to almost anything with anything else. In Cloud Pub/Sub you create topics and then you have one part of your system publish messages to that topic and another part of your system subscribe messages from that topic. Now speaking of Google BigQuery which is used as the Data Warehouse and Analytics. BigQuery is server-less; when you are not using it means you are not paying for it. It scales up automatically and handles it without a problem. You can store tons of data in BigQuery and still get incredibly fast responses for your queries.

DATA AND ANALYTICS PRODUCTS

Cloud Composer	Managed Workflow Orchestration Service
Cloud Dataflow	Stream/batch data processing
Cloud Datalab	Managed Jupyter Notebook
Cloud Dataprep	Visual data wrangling
Cloud Dataproc	Managed Spark and Hadoop
Cloud Pub/Sub	Global Real-time Messaging
Google BigQuery	Data Warehouse/Analytics
Google Data Studio	Collaborative Data Exploration/Dashboarding
Google Genomics	Managed Genomics Platform

Figure 2-08: Data and Analytics Products in GCP Cheat Sheet.

In the Networking section, there are a bunch of different features listed. Virtual Private Cloud or VPC is the core. You can also use Dedicated Interconnect used to have a dedicated private network connection between your VPC and external data center. You can also use Cloud NAT (Network Address Translation) to connect out to VPC, and you can have Cloud Load Balancing which deals with Multi-region load distribution into the Global VPC. Cloud Load Balancing is quite special when you combine it with the premium network service tier. Similarly, you have your clients who are connecting from all over the world, connect to one single IP address and still have all of those connections be made to the server present inside your VPC is physically closest to them. Which means your clients have much faster connections. There are more products available too. Cloud Armor is DDoS Protection and WAF service. Cloud CDN is the Content Network Delivery service which is capable of caching data where the users are physically located, and Cloud DNS allows you to take advantage of Google's Programmable DNS Serving Network.

NETWORKING PRODUCTS	
Carrier Peering	Peer with a carrier
Direct Peering	Peer with GCP
Dedicated Interconnect	Dedicated private network connection
Partner Interconnect	Connect on-premises network to VPC
Cloud Armor	DDoS Protection
Cloud CDN	Content Delivery Network
Cloud DNS	Programmable DNS Serving
Cloud Load Balancing	Multi-region Load Distribution
Cloud NAT	Network Address Translation Service
IPsec VPN	Virtual private network connection
Network Service Tiers	Price vs Performance Tiering
Network Telemetry	Network Telemetry Service
Virtual Private Cloud	Software Defined Networking

Figure 2-09: Networking Products in GCP Cheat Sheets.

Down in the Management Tools Section, Stack Driver is an important family of services. Stack Driver Monitoring is infrastructure and Application Monitoring Service, used to observe the system activities. Stack Driver Logging is Centralized Logging, so that all the different parts of your system whether they be micro-services or just multiple instances or completely different parts of your system, they can all log to one central place. Centralized Logging is really important to run a system.

MANAGEMENT TOOLS PRODUCTS	
Cloud APIs	APIs for Cloud Services
Cloud Billing	Billing and Cost Management Tools
Cloud Billing API	Programmatically Manage GCP Billing
Cloud Console	Web-based Management Console
Cloud Deployment Manager	Templated Infrastructure Deployment
Cloud Mobile App	iOS/Android GCP Manager App
Cloud Shell	Browser-based Terminal/CLI
Stackdriver Debugger	Live Production Debugging
Stackdriver Error Reporting	App Error Reporting
Stackdriver Logging	Centralized Logging
Stackdriver Monitoring	Infrastructure and Application Monitoring
Stackdriver Profiler	CPU and heap profiling
Stackdriver Transparent SLIs	Monitor GCP Services
Stackdriver Trace	App Performance Insights

Figure 2-10: Management Tool Products in GCP Cheat Sheet.

The Identity and Security Section has several interesting products too. The core ones are Cloud Identity, and Cloud IAM is the resource access control. Cloud IAM ties everything together with a security perspective where you can define the operations performed as per desire. There is more security-related stuff too. Cloud HSM is the Hardware Security Module Service used to manage encryption key certificates, and the Cloud Data Load Prevention API is an ML service that can classify, and redact sensitive data.

IDENTITY AND SECURITY PRODUCTS

Access Transparency	Audit Cloud Provider Access
Binary Authorization	Kubernetes Deploy-time Security
Cloud Data Loss Prevention API	Classify, Redact Sensitive Data
Cloud HSM	Hardware Security Module Service
Cloud IAM	Resource Access Control
Cloud Identity	Manage Users, Devices & Apps
Cloud Identity-Aware Proxy	Identity-based App Signin
Cloud Key Management Service	Hosted Key Management Service
Cloud Resource Manager	Cloud Project Metadata Management
Cloud Security Scanner	App Engine Security Scanner
Security Key Enforcement	Two-step Key Verification
Shielded VMs	Hardened VMs
Titan Security Key	Two-factor Authentication (2FA) Device

Figure 2-11: Identity and Security Products in GCP Cheat Sheet.

GCP- Getting Started

This overview is designed to make you understand the overall scenario of Google Cloud Platform (GCP). Here, you will take a detailed look at some of the get pointers to documentation and commonly used features, and that can help you to understand deeper. Knowing what is available and how the parts are working together can help you in making the decisions about how to proceed.

GCP Resources

GCP consists of a set of physical components, such as computers and hard disk drives, and virtual resources, such as VMs, that resides in Google's data centers around the globe. Each data center is located in the global region. Regions include Western Europe, Central US, and East Asia. Each region is the collection of zones, which are isolated from each other within the same region. Each zone is classified by a name that combines a letter identifier with the name of the region, for example, Asia-east1-a.

The distribution of this resource provides multiple benefits, including redundancy in case of failure and reduced latency by locating the resources closer to clients. This distribution introduces some rules related to how resources can be used together.

Accessing resources through services

When talking about cloud computing, sometimes what you might be used to thinking of as hardware and software products, become services. These services are used to provide access to the underlying resources. The GCP service list is long, and it is increasing continuously. When you develop your application or website on GCP, you mix and match these services to provide the infrastructure which you need, and then create your code to enable the scenarios you want to build.

Global, regional, and zonal resources

Some resources can be accessed by another resource, across the regions and zones. These global resources contain preconfigured images of disk, snapshots of the disk, and networks. Some resources can be accessed by the resources that are located in the same region. These regional resources consist of static external IP addresses. Other resources can be accessed only by the resources that are located in the same zone. These zonal resources include instances, their types, and disks of Virtual Machines.

The scope of operation varies depending on which type of resources you are working with. For example, network creation is a global operation because a network is a global resource, while the IP address reservation is a regional operation because the address is a regional resource.

As you begin to optimize your GCP applications, it is important to understand the interaction between regions and zones. For example, you would not want to attach a disk in one region to a computer in a different region because the latency you would introduce results in poor performance. In GCP, disks can only be attached to computers in the same zone.

Projects

GCP resources which you allocate and use must belong to a project. A project is an organizing entity. A project is made up of the permissions, settings, and other metadata which describes your applications. Resources inside a single project can work together easily, for example, internal network communication, subject to the regions-and-zones rules. The resources remain separate across project boundaries that each project contains; you can only interconnect them via an external network connection.

Each GCP project contains:

- A project name
- A project ID
- A project number

Across GCP, each project ID must be unique. You have created a project, and you can delete the project, but its ID can never be used again.

Each project is associated particularly with one billing account when billing is enabled. Multiple projects have their resource usage billed to the same account.

A project serves as a namespace. This means every resource in each project must contain a unique name, but you can reuse the resource names if they are present in separate projects. Some resource names must be globally unique.

Ways to interact with the services

To interact with the services and resources, GCP gives you three basic ways.

Google Cloud Platform Console

The GCP Console provides a web-based GUI which is used to manage your GCP projects and resources. When using the GCP Console, you can create a new project, or choose an existing project, and you can use the resources that you create for the project. Multiple Projects can be created, so you can use projects to separate your work in whatever way makes sense for you.

Command-line interface

If you want to work in a terminal window, the Google Cloud SDK provides the "gcloud" CLI tool which gives you access to the commands. The gcloud tool is used to manage your development workflow and GCP resources.

Cloud Shell provided by GCP, is an interactive shell environment used for GCP. Cloud Shell can be accessed via GCP Console. Cloud Shell provides:

- A temporary Compute Engine VM instance.
- Access to the instances through Command Line from a web browser.
- Code Editor.
- Persistent disk storage of 5GB.
- Google Cloud SDK and other tools are pre-installed.
- Supported languages are Java, Go, Python, Node.js, PHP, Ruby, and .NET.
- The functionality of web preview.
- Built-in authorization is present to access the GCP Console resources and projects.

Client libraries

The Cloud SDK contains Client Libraries that enable you to create and manage resources. For two main purposes, GCP client libraries expose APIs:

- App APIs provide access to the services. Application APIs are optimized for supported languages, like Node.js and Python. These libraries provide help for authentication and authorization.
- Admin APIs offer services for resource management. For example, admin APIs can be used for building automated tools.

You can also use the Google API client libraries to access APIs for services and products such as Google Drive, Google Maps, and YouTube.

Pricing

You can also take benefits of some tools which help you to evaluate the costs of using GCP.

- The pricing calculator is used to provides a quick and easy way to estimate what your GCP usage will look like. You can also provide the details about the services you want to use and then check the pricing estimate.
- TCO tool is used to evaluate the estimated cost for running your compute load in the cloud to provide financial estimate. The tool provides multiple inputs for cost modelling, which you can adjust and then compare the estimated costs on GCP and AWS. This tool is not capable of modelling all components of a typical application, such as networking, and storage.

Free- Tier GCP Accounts

The Free-Tier Account in GCP is the billing account that does not get charged. The key factor is that you need to upgrade in order to become a paying account, manually. Setting up an account for GCP requires a credit card for verification, but it does not get charged. When you create a free tier account for GCP, you also get 300 USD credit, which you can use for up to 12 months, and this feature defines your free-tier account. If you either use your $300 or let the 12 months go by, then your free trial will be over. When your free trial comes to an end, then you will have the option to upgrade to a paid account. You need to upgrade the account when the free trial finishes whether it happens in 12 months or you run out of credit you. Business Accounts are not eligible for the free trial account. Free – tier account has some restrictions. When you are on the free trial, you are not allowed to have more than 8 Virtual CPUs together at once.

Similarly, you cannot attach any GPUs (Video Card Chips) to your machine nor any TPUs for boosting tensor flow. You are not allowed any Quota increases while you run on the free trial account. You are not allowed to do any Crypto mining. They are providing you $300 credit so that you can learn the platform, not for exchanging some other currency

also, you can run anything you want on it, they do not recommend running of the production environment, and they do not give you any Service Level Agreements (SLAs). During the free trial, you also cannot use any premium OS licenses or Cloud Launcher Product with extra usage fee.

Always Free

"Always Free" contains certain amount of different services which you can use without having to pay for it and "Always Free" usage does not count against your free trial credit, which means that your $300 will last even longer. From the Compute side of things, each day you can run 24 hours' worth of f1-micro instance in most of the US regions, and you would not get charged for it. If you are running all of this all day, you will be charged for the additional services that you might use. In the Always Free Compute Category, we have App Engine, where an application can run for 24 hours of App Engine runtime in North America without getting charged. You can also run two million Cloud Functions within certain size and time limits.

In the Storage category, the storage is averaged entirely over the month, storing Terabyte of data and then deleting it within a minute does not cost a lot. In the Always Free Tier, you can store 5GB of Regional Cloud Storage, 1GB of data in Cloud Data Store and 10GB of data in BigQuery and for BigQuery every month you can do 1TB of query processing in the free tier. More free storage includes 30GB of HDD storage on GCE (Google Compute Engine) and AE (App Engine), 5GB of snapshot storage on GCE and AE and 5GB of Stack Driver logs with the retention period of 7 days.

Moving on to Networking aspect of Always Free account, if your data is headed to China and Australia, it does not qualify for the Always Free tier but could be applied for the free trial you have got. You can have 1GB/ month of data that leads for App Engine project for free. Similarly, for compute engine, 1GB per month is allowed. Google Cloud Functions are even more generous, Google Cloud functions provide you with 5GB of data that can be transferred each month and 5GB for Cloud Storage based in North America. Cloud Pub/Sub have 10GB/ month of data because Cloud Pub/Sub is the global messaging service in which you can write data from one region in the world and read from the other region.

Every day you can perform 120 minutes of build in Google Cloud Container Builders and can perform 60 minutes of Voice recognition each month in Google Cloud Speech API. You can do 1000 unit/ month of Cloud Vision API calls and 5000 unit/ month of Google Cloud Natural Language API. Google also has a Cloud Shell existing in the console with 5GB of persistent disk storage quota. You can also do 1GB of Google Cloud Source Repository Private Hosting.

Create Free-Tier GCP Account (LAB)

Does a question arise that why do we create a separate Gmail account? The mean reason is Least Privilege. This is the principle where every privileged user and every program of the system must operate by using the least amount of privilege, which is necessary to complete the job. It is an awful habit to use administrative privileges for performing normal activities.

Incognito Mood

To perform this lab, we are going to open Incognito Window in Chrome. In Firefox, it is called "Private Browsing". Sign in to the Console of GCP and select "Open link in Incognito Window."

Lab 2.1: Create a GCP Account

Scenario: Create a GCP free tier account and activate two-factor authentication. Also, provide a way to get the snapshot of the emails to another account for backup purposes.

Solution: Create Free-Tier GCP Account but do not link it with your existing email address. Create a new Gmail Account for billing and secure it with 2FA (Two-Factor Authentication) and you can also forward mail to your normal account so that you can get any notifications.Open an Incognito Window.

1. Go to the resource link. "https://console.cloud.google.com/freetrial"
2. Click on Create account.

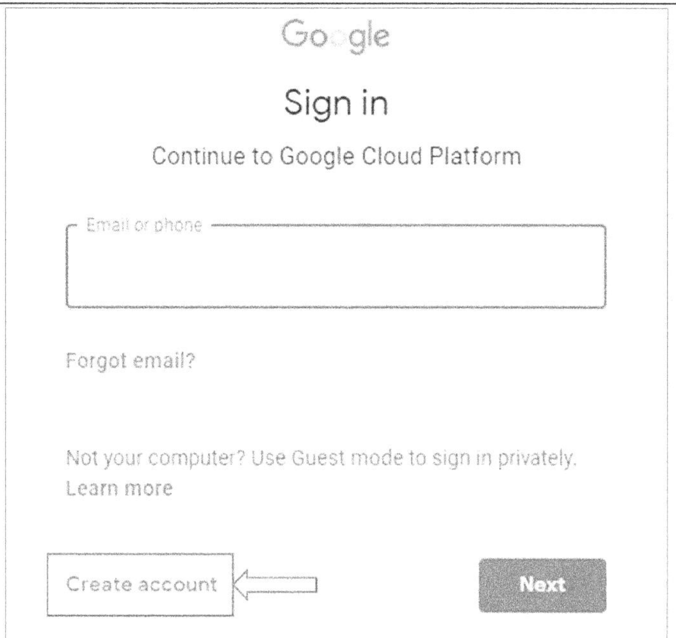

3. In the next step, click on "Create Account"
4. Create an individual account.

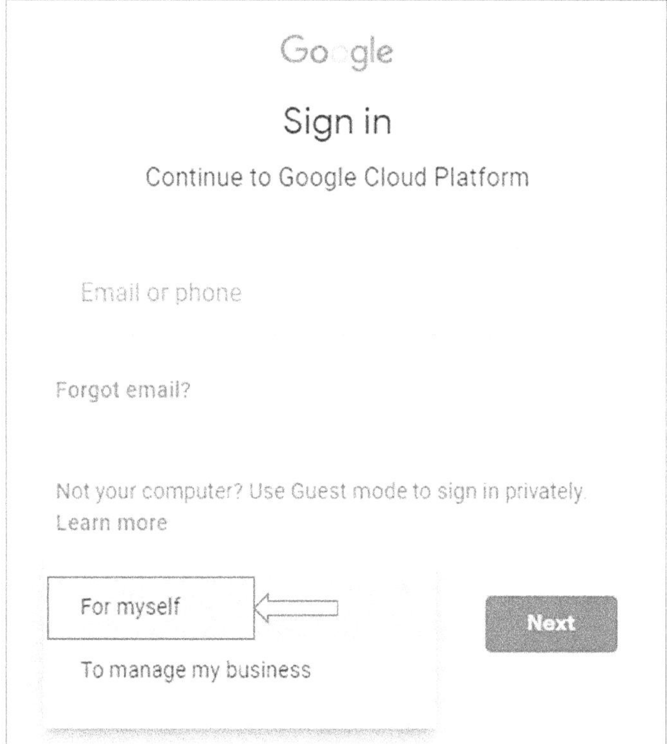

5. Provide your name, address, and password, click on Next.

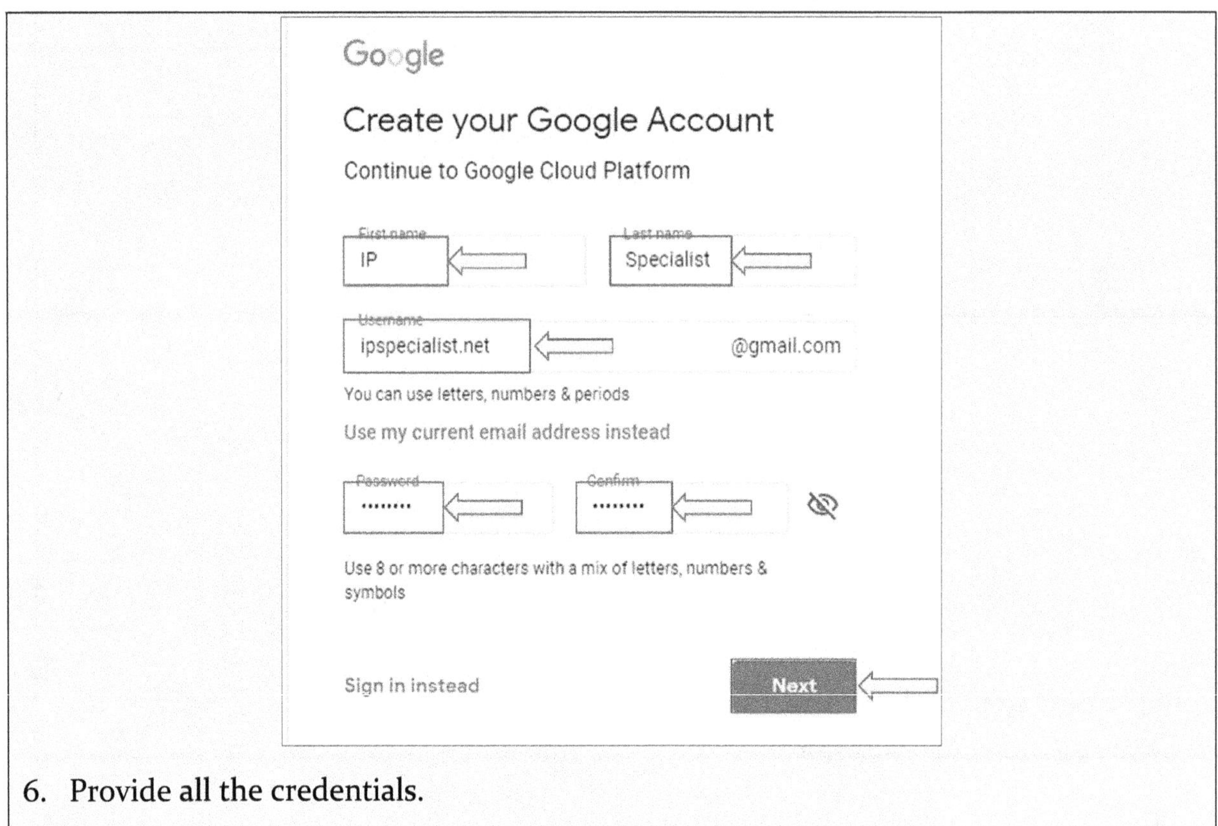

6. Provide all the credentials.

Welcome to Google

Ipspecialist.net@gmail.com

Phone number (optional)

We'll use your number for account security. It won't be visible to others.

Recovery email address (optional)
info@ipspecialist.com

We'll use it to keep your account secure

Day Month Year

Your date of birth

Gender

Your personal info is private and safe

Why we ask for this information

Back Next

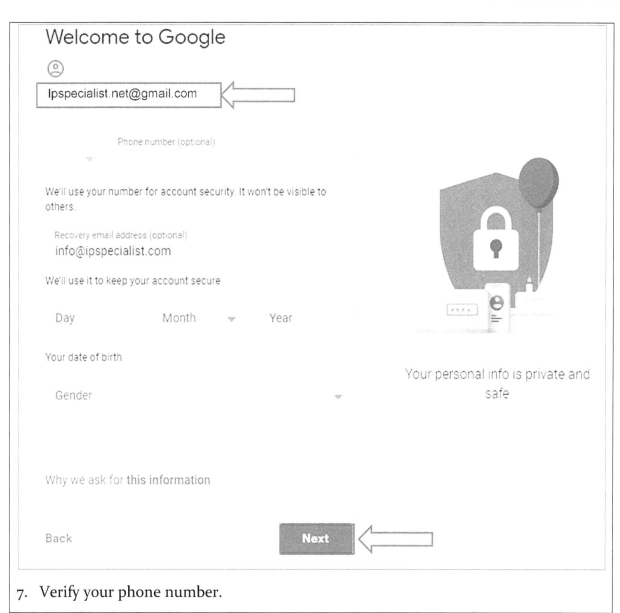

7. Verify your phone number.

Google

Verifying your phone number

To make sure that this number is yours, Google will send you a text message with a 6-digit verification code. *Standard rates apply*

Enter verification code

G- 537062

Back Call instead **Verify**

Your personal info is private and safe

Google

Get more from your number

If you like, you can add your phone number to your account for use across Google services. Learn more

For example, your number will be used to

Receive video calls & messages

Make Google services, including ads, more relevant to you

More options

Your personal info is private and safe

Back Skip **Yes, I'm in**

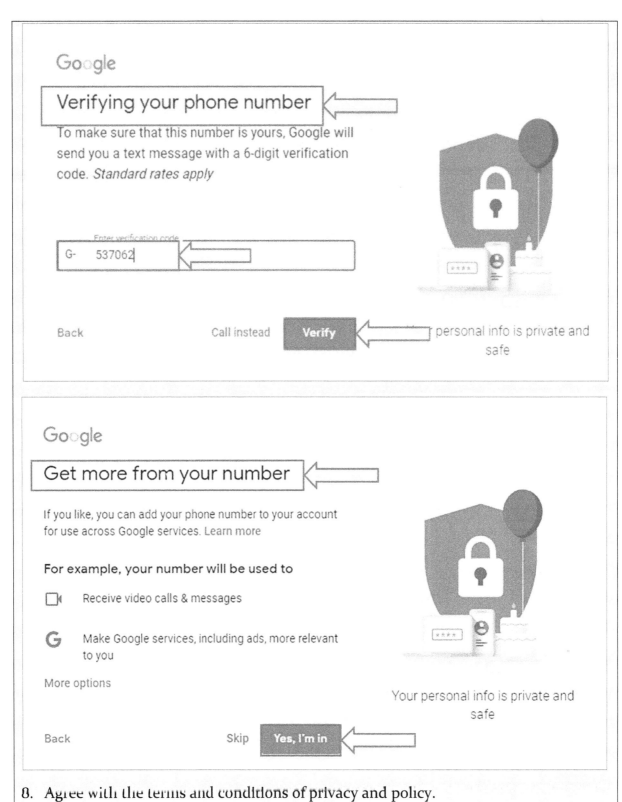

8. Agree with the terms and conditions of privacy and policy.

Google

Privacy and Terms

Combining data

We also combine this data among our services and across your devices for these purposes. For example, depending on your account settings, we show you ads based on information about your interests, which we can derive from your use of Search and YouTube, and we use data from trillions of search queries to build spell-correction models that we use across all of our services.

You're in control

Depending on your account settings, some of this data may be associated with your Google Account and we treat this data as personal information. You can control how we collect and use this data now by clicking 'More Options' below. You can always adjust your controls later or withdraw your consent for the future by visiting My Account (myaccount.google.com).

You're in control of the data we collect and how it's used

MORE OPTIONS

Cancel

I agree

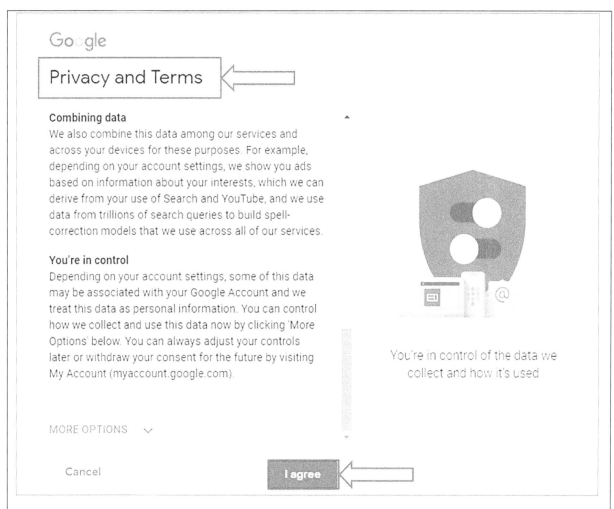

9. Make sure that this is an individual payment account.
10. Enter your required credentials including your credit card details.
11. Click on"Start my Free Trial".

Try Google Cloud Platform for free

Step 1 of 2

Country

Terms of Service

I agree to the Google Cloud Platform Terms of Service, and the terms of service of any applicable services and APIs.I have also read and agree to the Google Cloud Platform Free Trial Terms of Service.

Required to continue

Email updates

I would like to receive periodic emails on news, product updates and special offers from Google Cloud and Google Cloud Partners.

AGREE AND CONTINUE

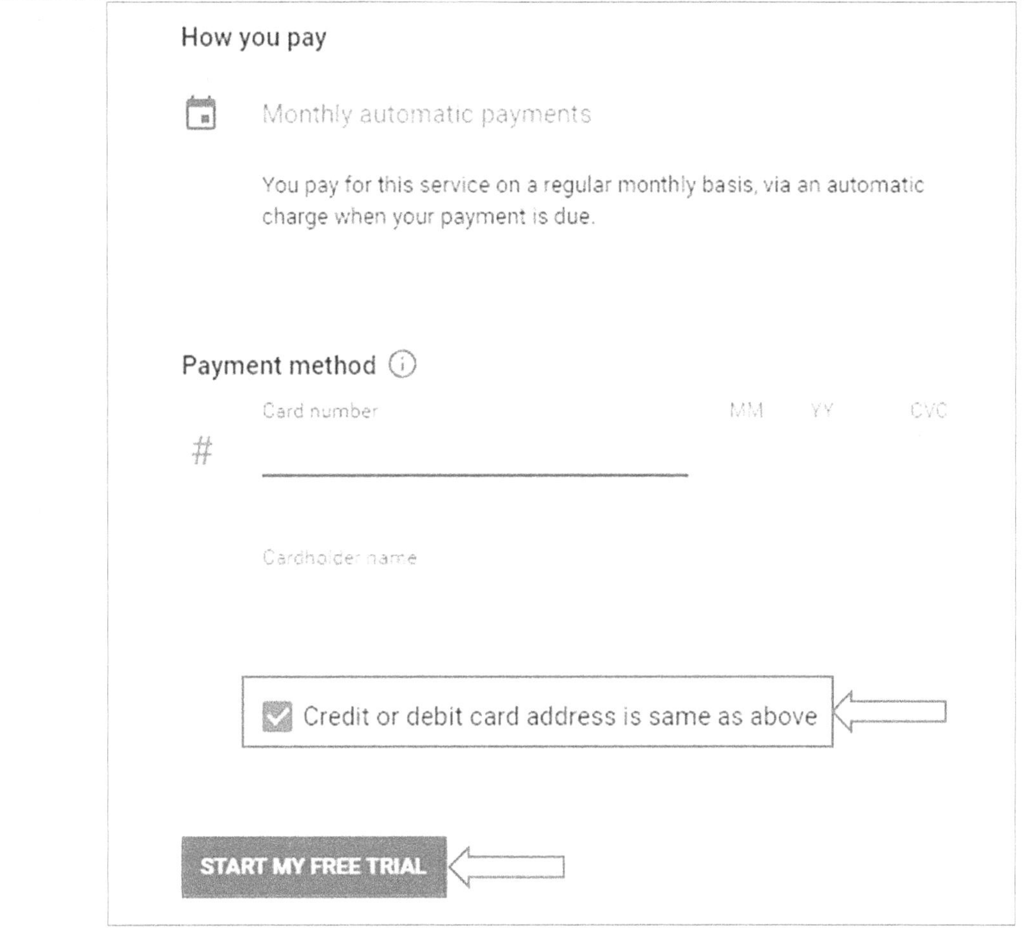

12. Your account is live now.

Welcome!

Thanks for signing up for the 12-month free trial.

We've given you $300 in free trial credit to spend. If you run out of credit, don't worry, you won't be billed until you give your permission.

GOT IT

13. Enable the 2FA (two-factor authentication).
14. Click on the little icon located at the top right corner on the screen.

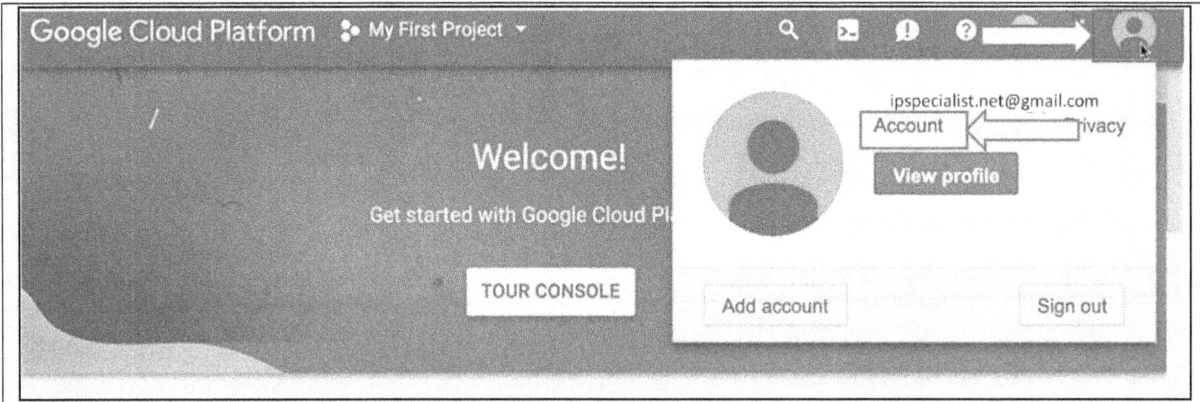

15. Click on Account> Signing into Google> 2-Step Verification.

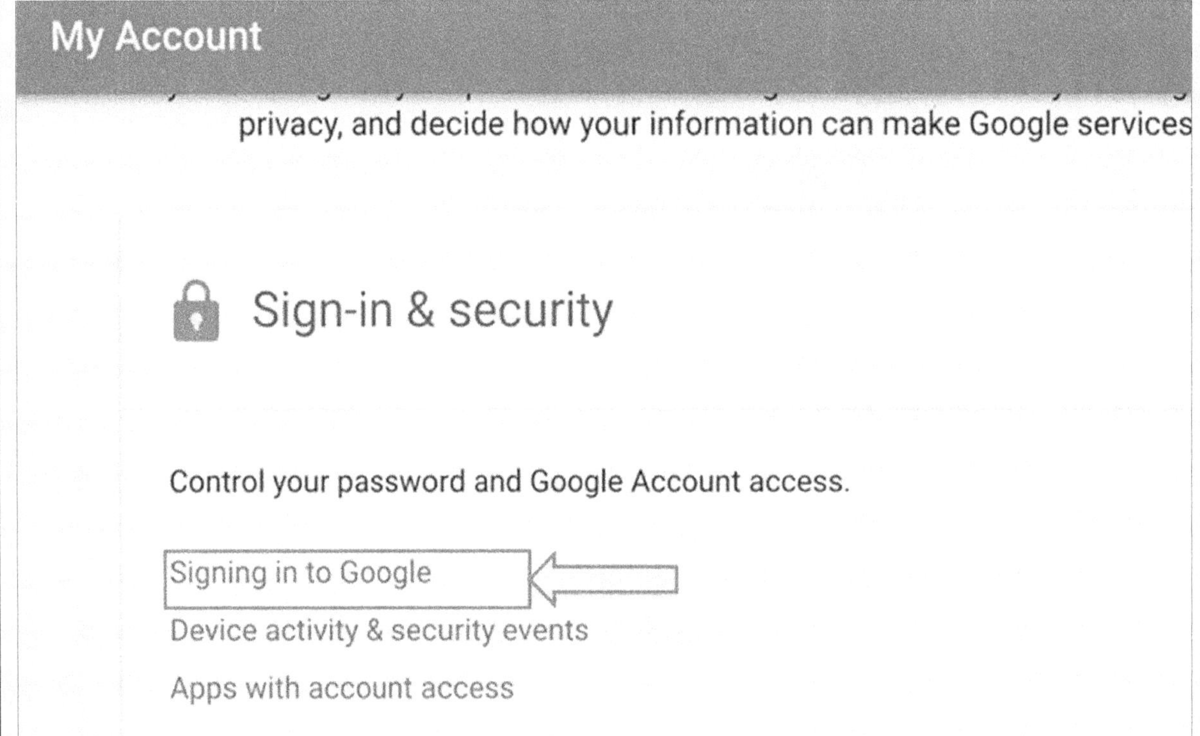

My Account

Sign-in & security

Welcome

Sign-in & security

Signing in to Google

Device activity & security events

Apps with account access

Personal info & privacy

Your personal info

Contacts

Manage your Google activity

protection with 2-Step Verification, which sends a single-use code to your phone for you to enter when you sign in. So even if somebody manages to steal your password, it is not enough to get into your account.

Note: To change these settings, you will need to confirm your password.

Password — Last changed: 11 minutes ago

2-Step Verification — Off

Account recovery options

16. Get Started.

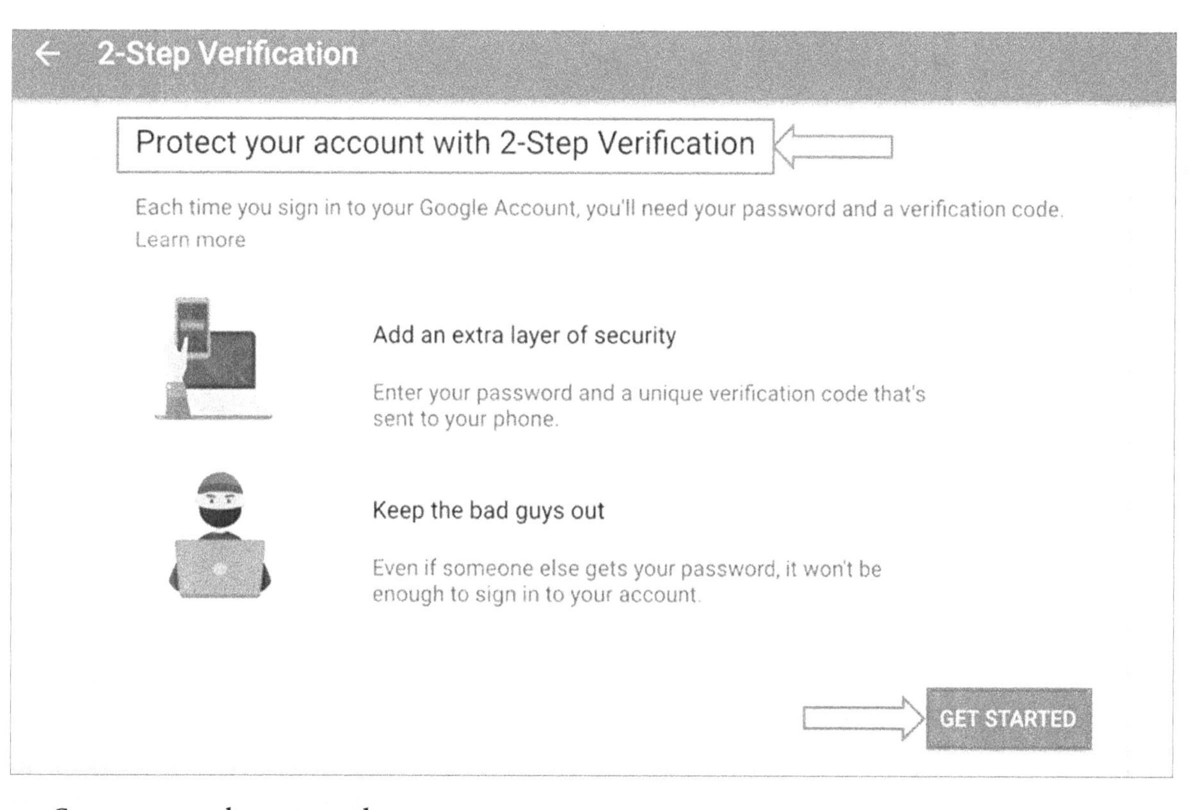

17. Setup your phone number.

What phone number do you want to use?

Google will only use this number for account security.
Don't use a Google Voice number.
Message and data rates may apply.

How do you want to get codes?

Text message call

Step 1 of 3 NEXT

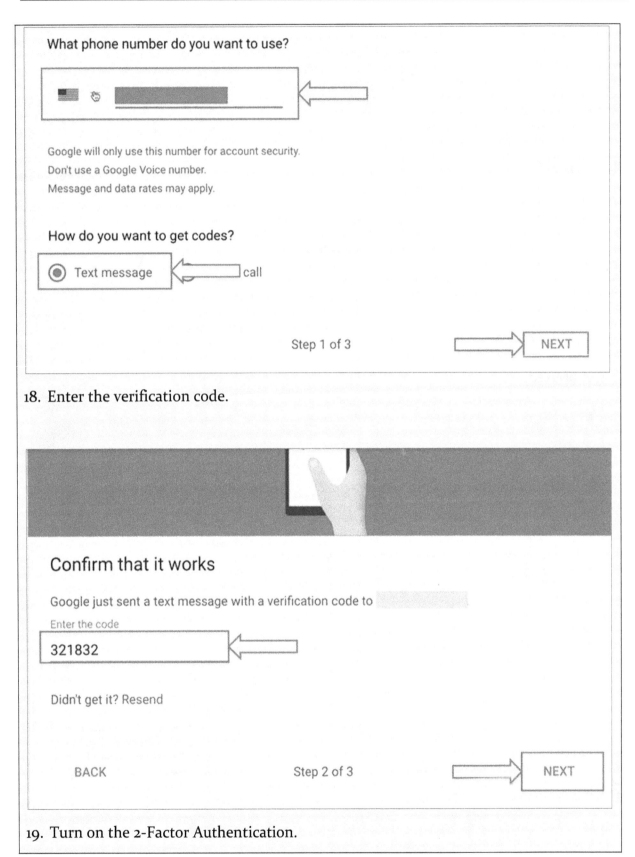

18. Enter the verification code.

Confirm that it works

Google just sent a text message with a verification code to

Enter the code

321832

Didn't get it? Resend

BACK Step 2 of 3 NEXT

19. Turn on the 2-Factor Authentication.

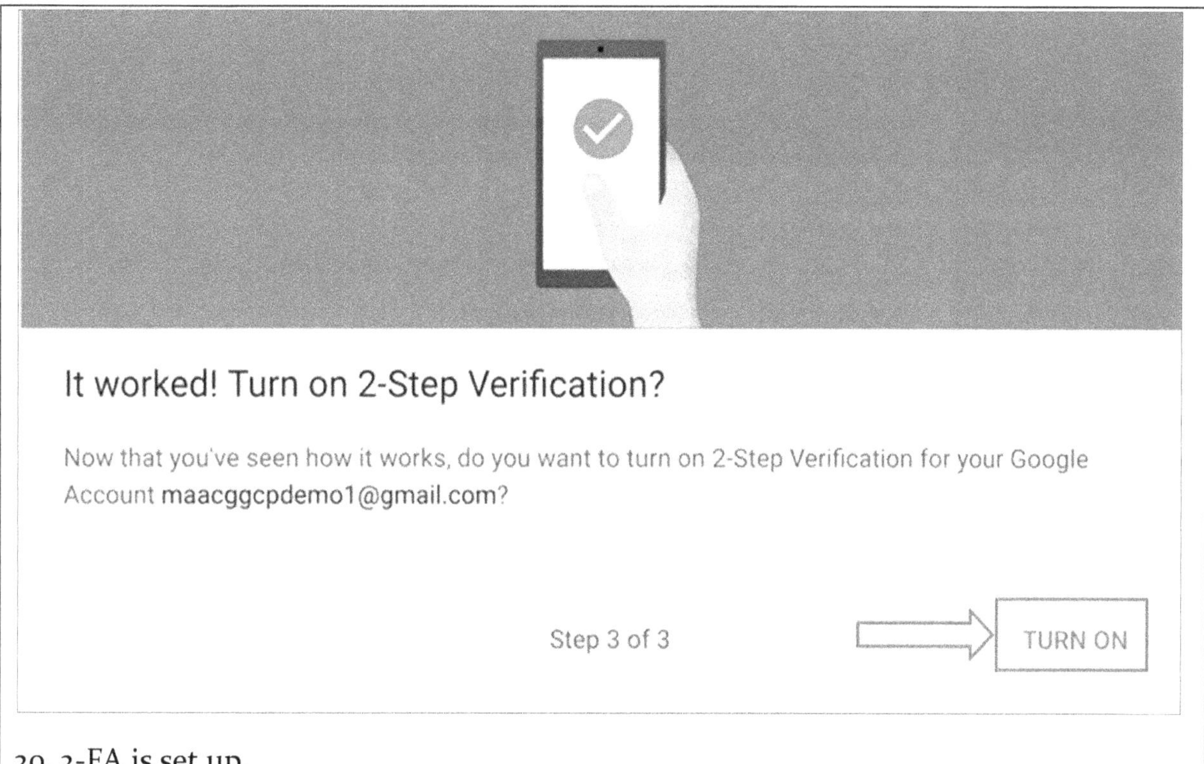

20. 2-FA is set up.
21. Log out and log in back again to make sure that 2-FA works or not properly.
22. To setup, the forwarding with Gmail, go to Gmail and click on the little gear icon, click on settings> Forwarding and POP/IMAP and then add the forwarding address.

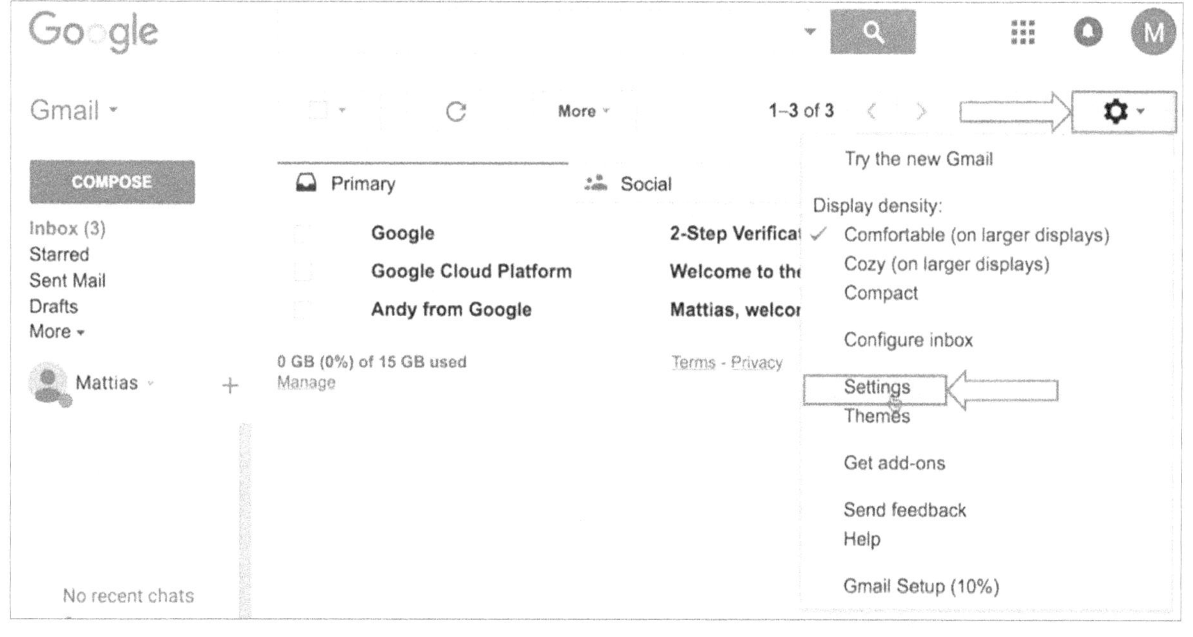

Gmail ▾ Settings

COMPOSE

Inbox (3)
Starred
Sent Mail
Drafts
More ▾
Mattias

General Labels Inbox Accounts and Import Filters and Blocked Addresses
Forwarding and POP/IMAP Chat Labs Offline Themes

Forwarding: Learn more — Add a forwarding address

Tip: You can also forward only some of your mail by creating a filter!

POP Download: Learn more
1. Status: POP is disabled
Enable POP for all mail
Enable POP for mail that arrives from now on

2. When messages are accessed with POP
keep Gmail's copy in the Inbox

3. Configure your email client (e.g. Outlook, Eudora, Netscape Mail)
Configuration instructions

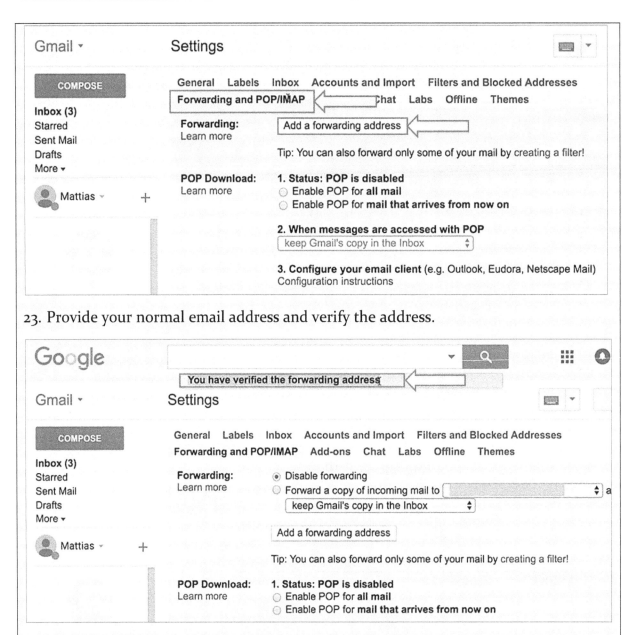

23. Provide your normal email address and verify the address.

Google

You have verified the forwarding address

Gmail ▾ Settings

COMPOSE

Inbox (3)
Starred
Sent Mail
Drafts
More ▾
Mattias

General Labels Inbox Accounts and Import Filters and Blocked Addresses
Forwarding and POP/IMAP Add-ons Chat Labs Offline Themes

Forwarding: Learn more
Disable forwarding
Forward a copy of incoming mail to
keep Gmail's copy in the Inbox
Add a forwarding address

Tip: You can also forward only some of your mail by creating a filter!

POP Download: Learn more
1. Status: POP is disabled
Enable POP for all mail
Enable POP for mail that arrives from now on

24. Do not forget to save changes at the bottom of the screen.

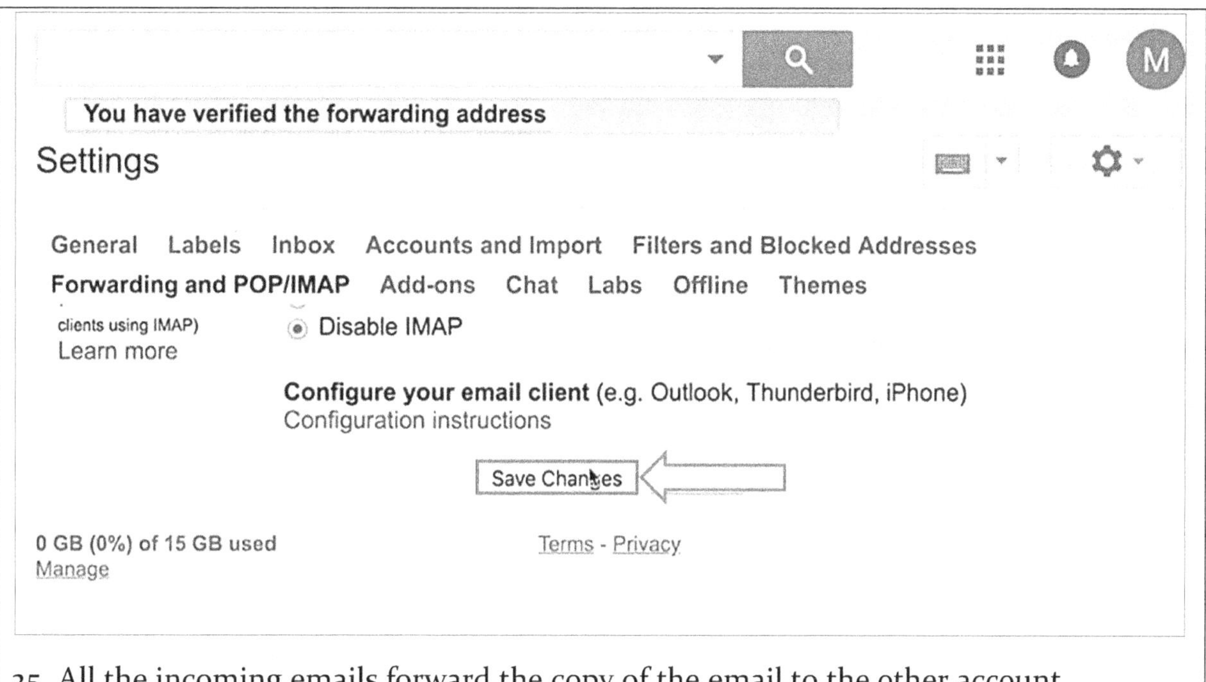

25. All the incoming emails forward the copy of the email to the other account.

Explore GCP Console

To explore different services and activities in the GCP Console, first, you need to log in to GCP Console from the account which you created earlier. Log in with the email address and password. In the Console, you have credit of $300, which is available for 365 days. You can also rename your billing account.

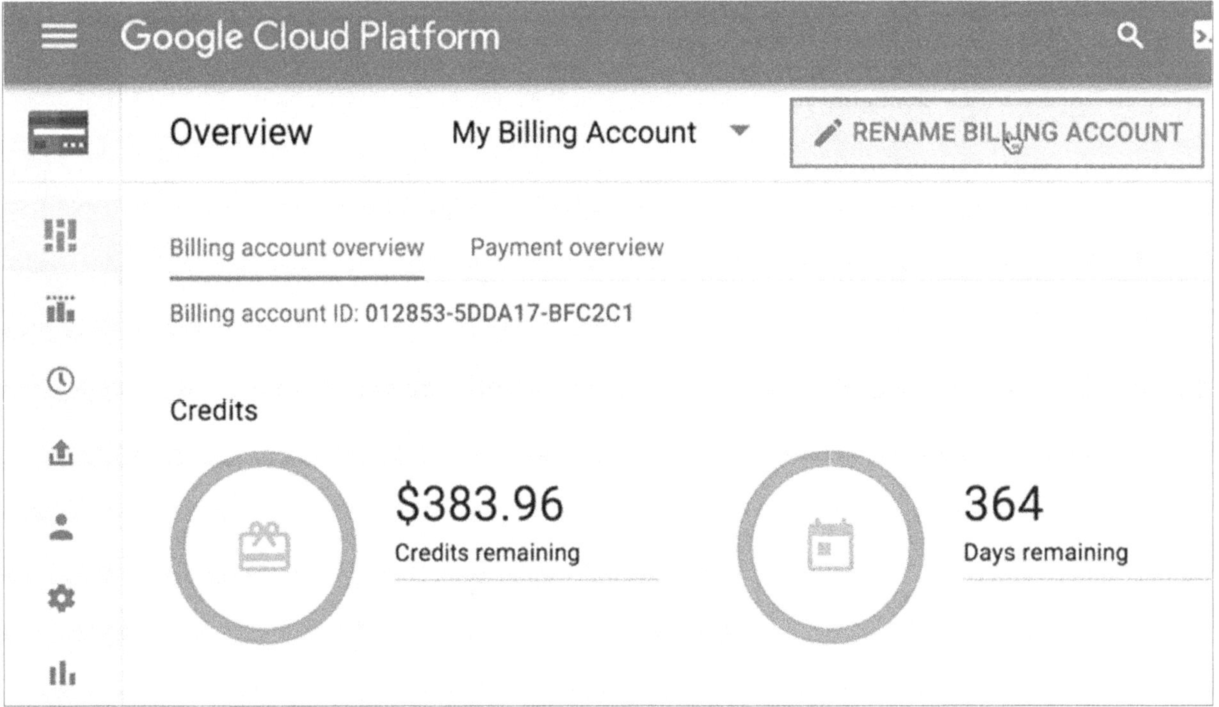

Figure 2-12: GCP Billing Console.

If you want to check the list of billing accounts you have, you can click on "All Billing Accounts" drop-down and select "Manage billing account".

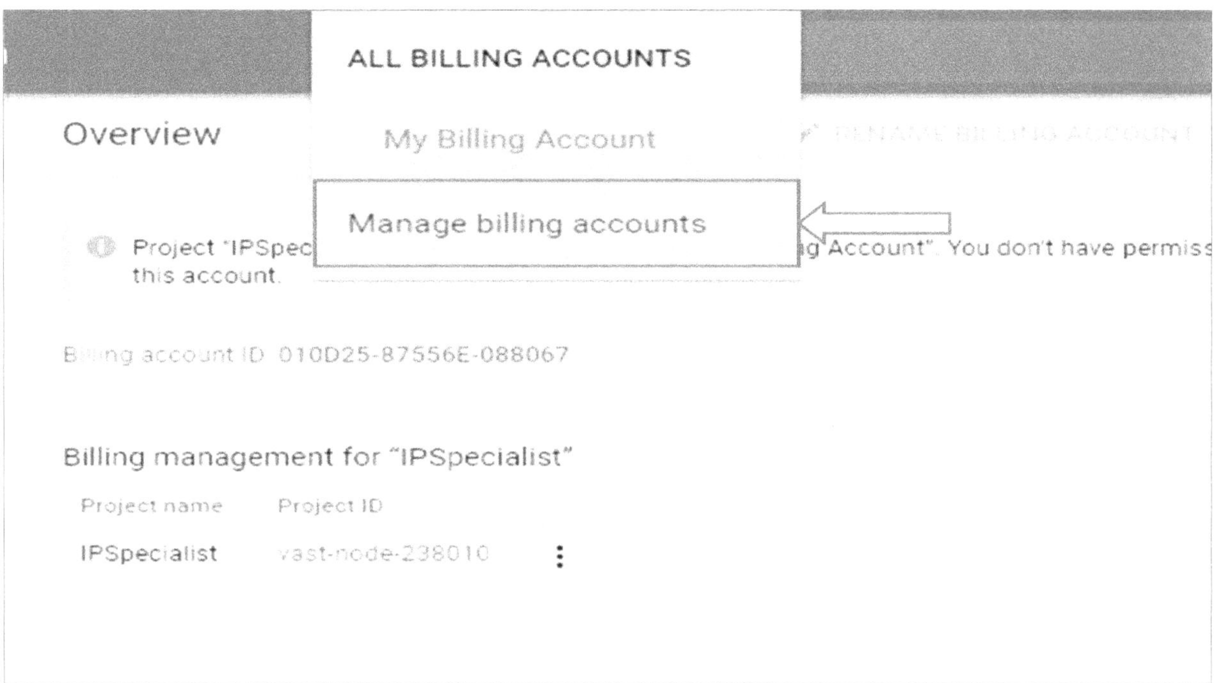

Figure 2-13: Manage Billing Account in GCP.

From the menu button located at the top left corner, you click on the Navigation Panel and go to Home. You can Customize your Dashboard as per your desire by clicking on the "Customize" button, which is located on the top right. And move thing just by drag and drop them. When you are done with the panel, press done. Now, you can see the customized view.

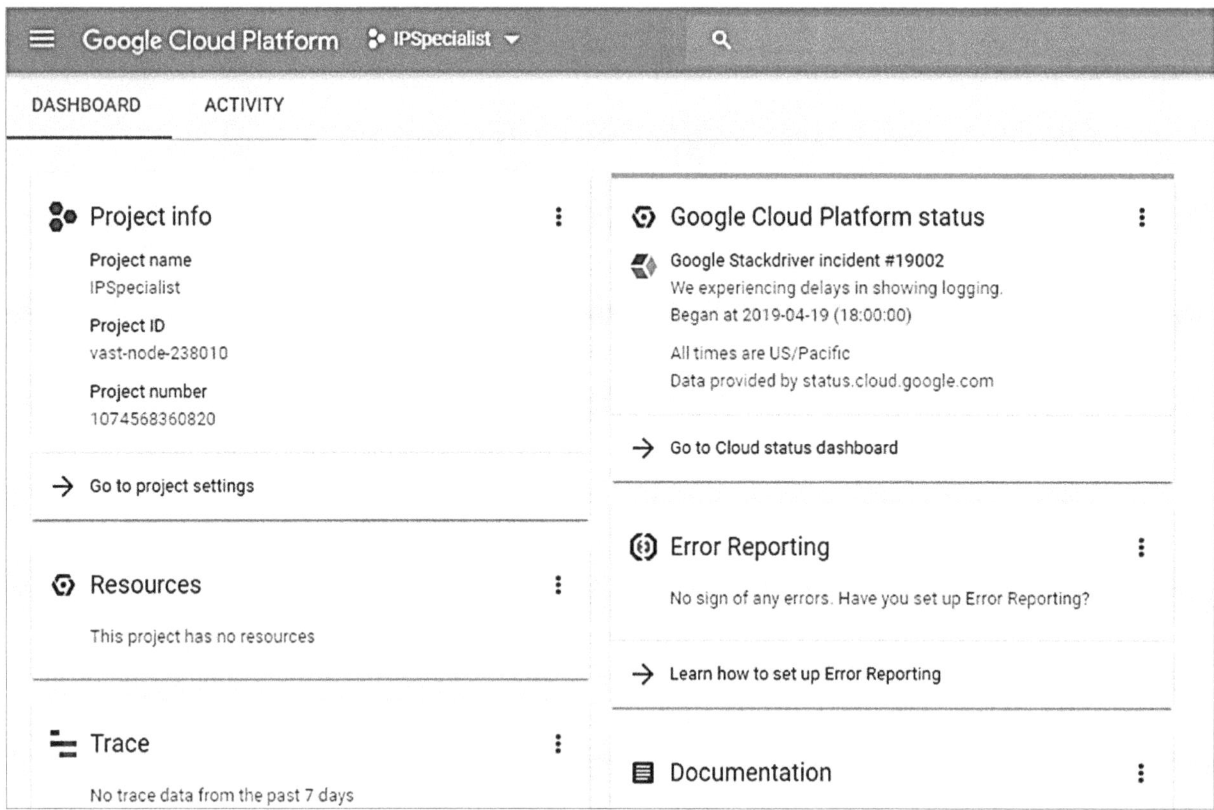

Figure 2-14: Home Page in GCP Console.

The API card represents the progress of the running project, and the news chart represents the latest update and news related to GCP. Turn this API card on, to keep yourself updated. You can also hide the card by using this drop down, named as "Hide card."

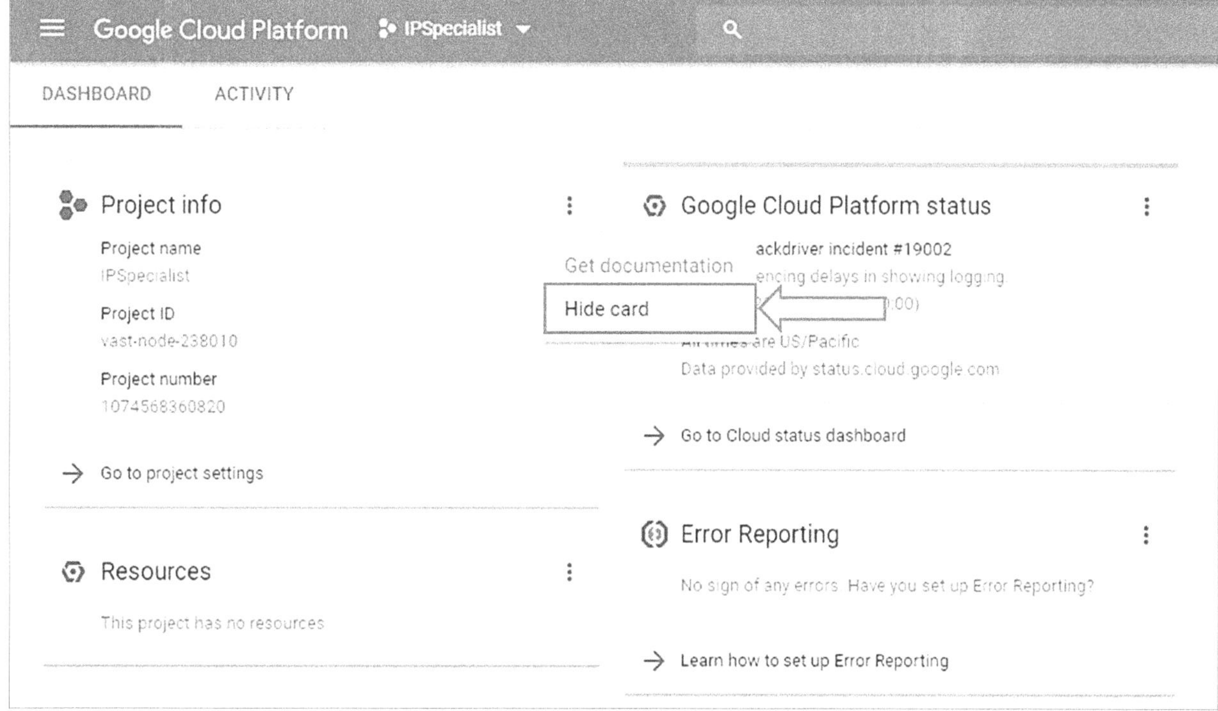

Figure 2-15: Exploring Hide Card feature in GCP Console.

You can also see the list of Activities happening in the project. When you create the account, the first project is already created. You can set up the remaining projects and can find more details by just clicking on the activity of projects.

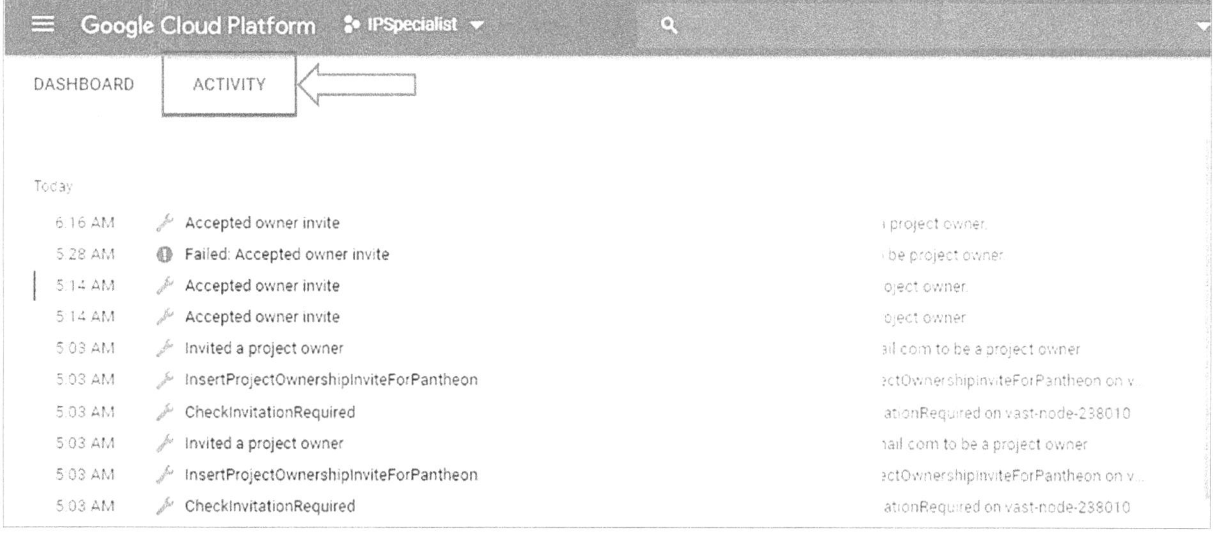

Figure 2-16: Activity List in GCP.

Google assigns a Project number and auto-generated ID to your project. The name of the project can be changed, but the project number and ID cannot be changed. Go to Project

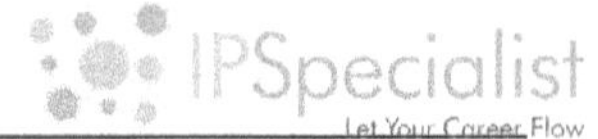

setting, where you can check this. Moreover, you can check your free trial status, notifications, and activities.

Google Cloud Platform IPSpecialist

DASHBOARD ACTIVITY

Update project

n@gmail.com updated vast-node-238010
April 18, 2019 at 3:40:19 AM GMT-7

User	
Resource name	projects/vast-node-238010
Request	
Project > name	IPSpecialist
Project id	vast-node-238010
Response	
Create time	2019-04-18T10:23:19.481Z
Lifecycle state	ACTIVE
Name	IPSpecialist
Project id	vast-node-238010
Project number	1074568360820

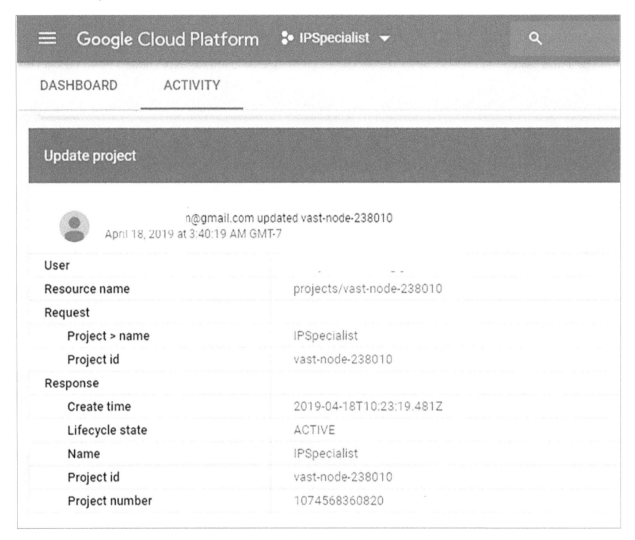

Figure 2-17: Project Name, Number and ID in Activity List.

Set up Billing Export

According to GCP Documentation, tools for monitoring, analyzing and optimizing cost have now become an important part of the managing development. Billing export to BigQuery allows you to export your daily usage and estimate the cost automatically to a BigQuery dataset that you specify throughout the day. Your billing data can be accessed through BigQuery.

Lab 2.2: Billing Export

Scenario:

An organization demands to set up the services which can export their daily usage and cost estimates for monitoring, analyzing, and optimizing the cost of the services used.

Solution:

Firstly, you need to set up the billing accounts and then export the billing details using BigQuery service. For this purpose, you need to create a project and a dataset. Then allow the dataset to export all the billing details through BigQuery service.

1. Log in to the console with the administrator account.
2. Set up and export billing information in this lab.
3. Open the Navigation Pane and click on "Billing".

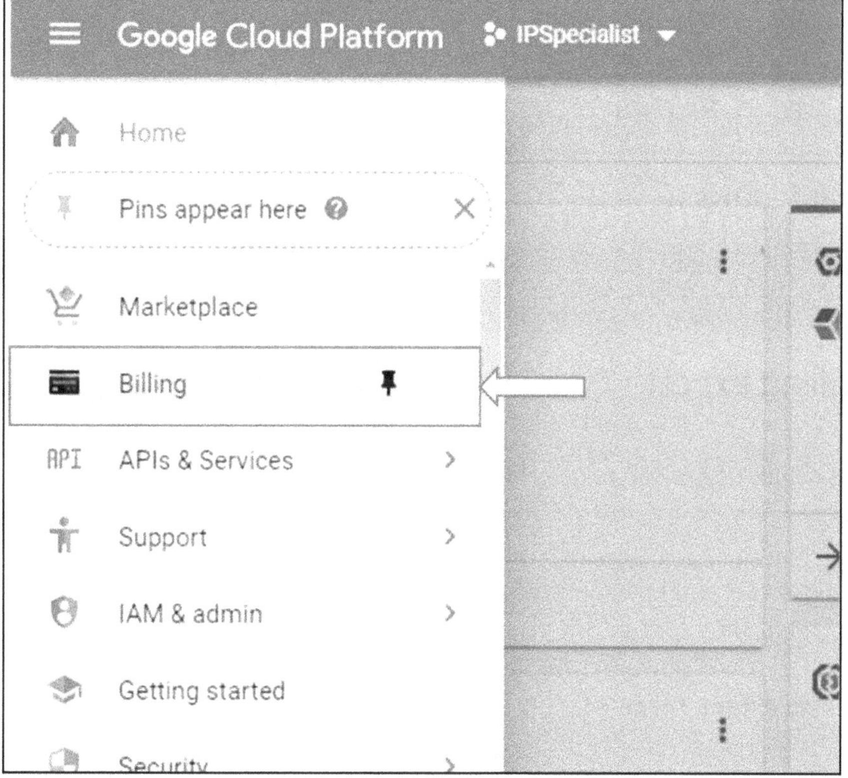

4. Click on Billing export.

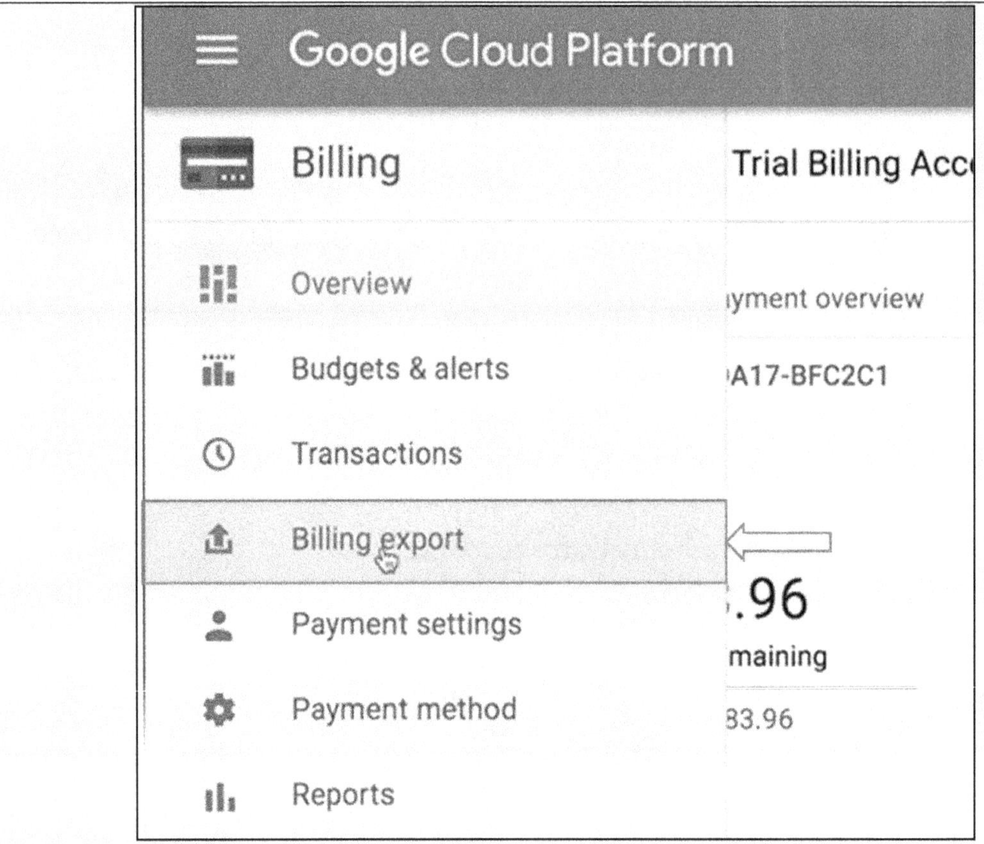

5. Click on "Edit Settings".

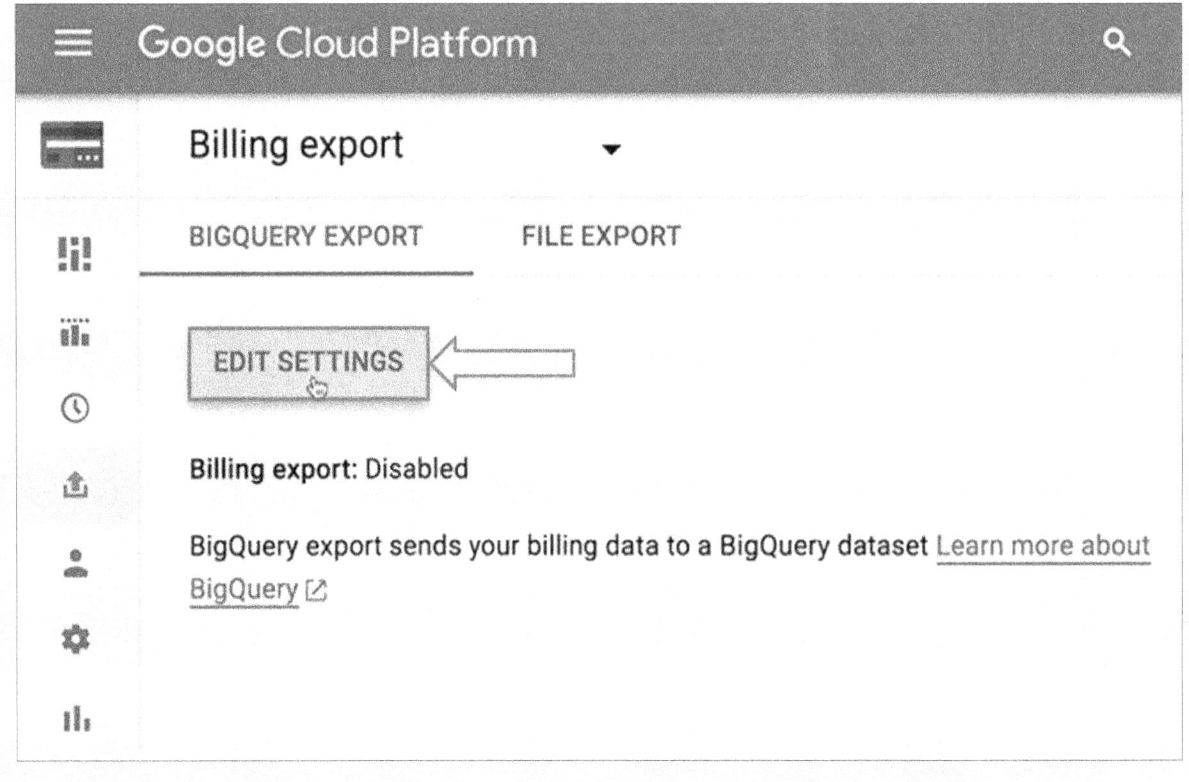

6. To create a data set in the BigQuery we could follow the link named as "Go to BigQuery".

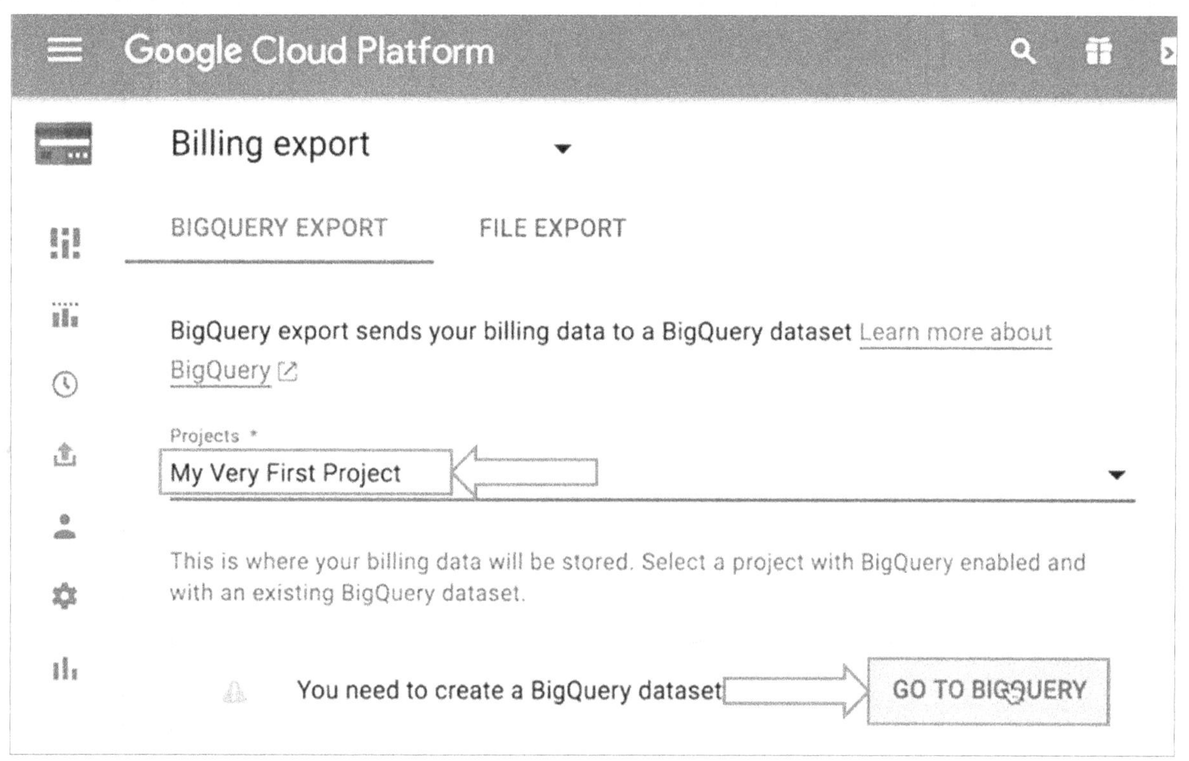

7. The dataset resides inside the project. In GCP, to avoid mixing all of the stuff, we use Projects to manage GCP resources.
8. Let's create our first new project.
9. Open up the navigation menu and click on Home.

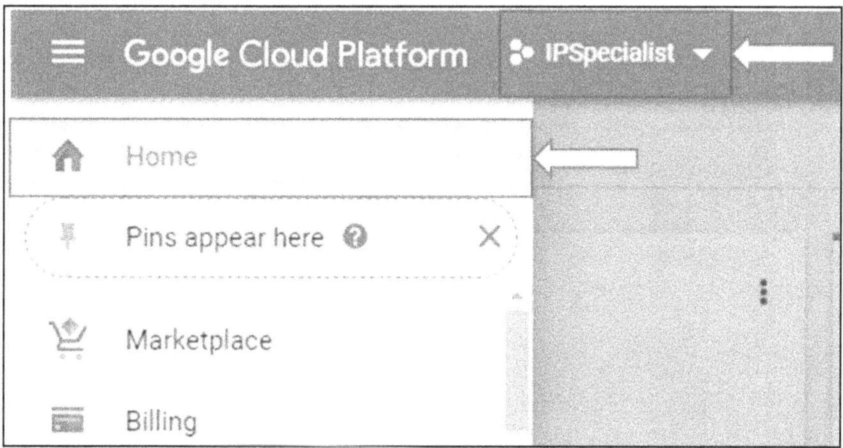

10. Create a New Project.

Select a project

NEW PROJECT

Search projects and folders

RECENT ALL

Name	ID
✓ IPSpecialist	vast-node-238010
My First Project	orbital-stage-238011

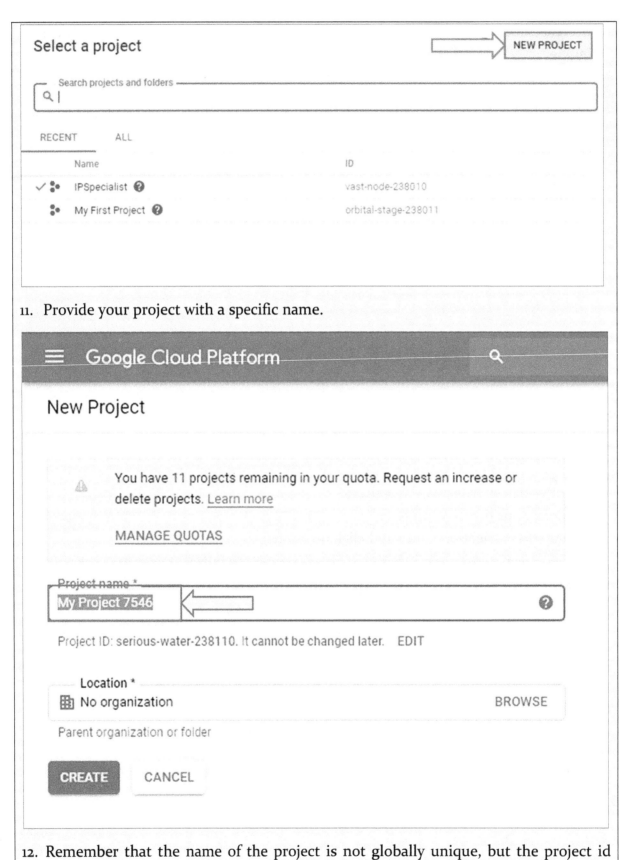

11. Provide your project with a specific name.

Google Cloud Platform

New Project

You have 11 projects remaining in your quota. Request an increase or delete projects. Learn more

MANAGE QUOTAS

Project name *

My Project 7546

Project ID: serious-water-238110. It cannot be changed later. EDIT

Location *

No organization BROWSE

Parent organization or folder

CREATE CANCEL

12. Remember that the name of the project is not globally unique, but the project id

and project number is globally unique.

13. Provide a specific name and click on "Create".

Google Cloud Platform

New Project

You have 11 projects remaining in your quota. Request an increase or delete projects. Learn more

MANAGE QUOTAS

Project name *

Admin Project

Project ID: admin-project-238110. It cannot be changed later. EDIT

Location *

No organization BROWSE

Parent organization or folder

CREATE

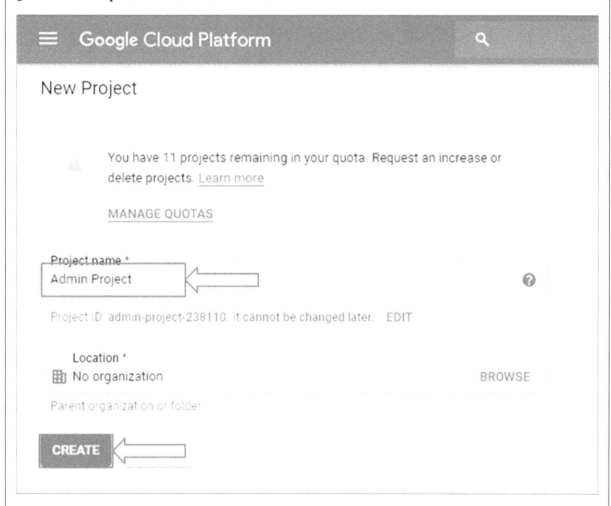

14. We can create a project, and a new notification will appear on your screen.

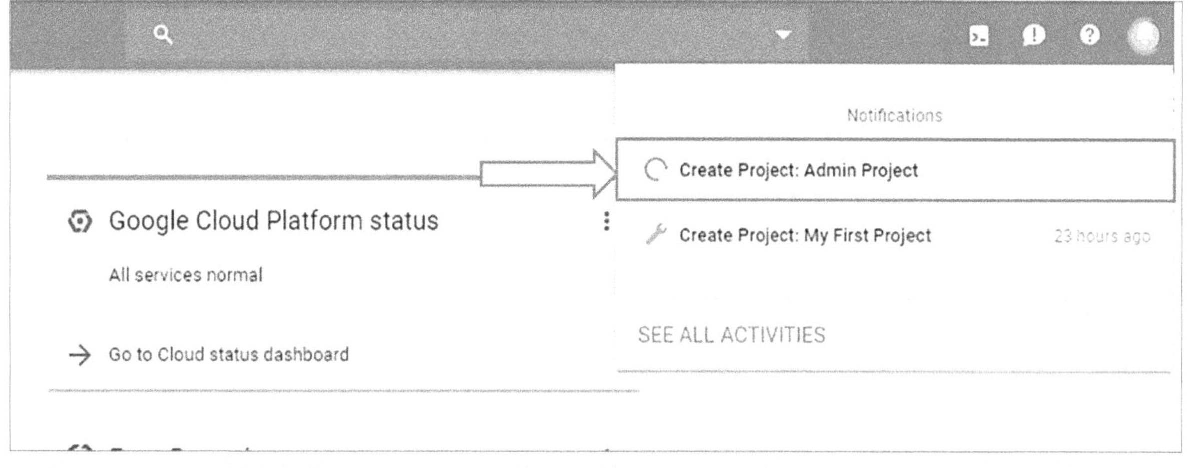

15. Inside the Admin Project, let's select the BigQuery service to export the billing dataset.

16. Select the BigQuery service. Select your project.

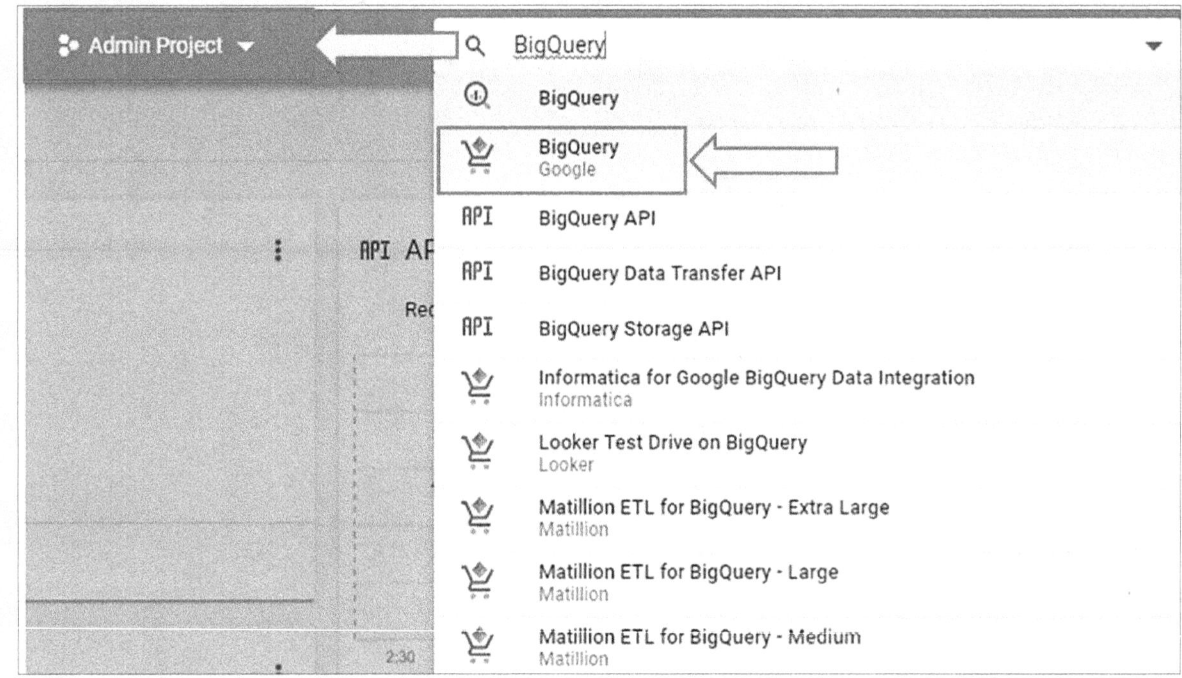

17. Click on Hide Editor.

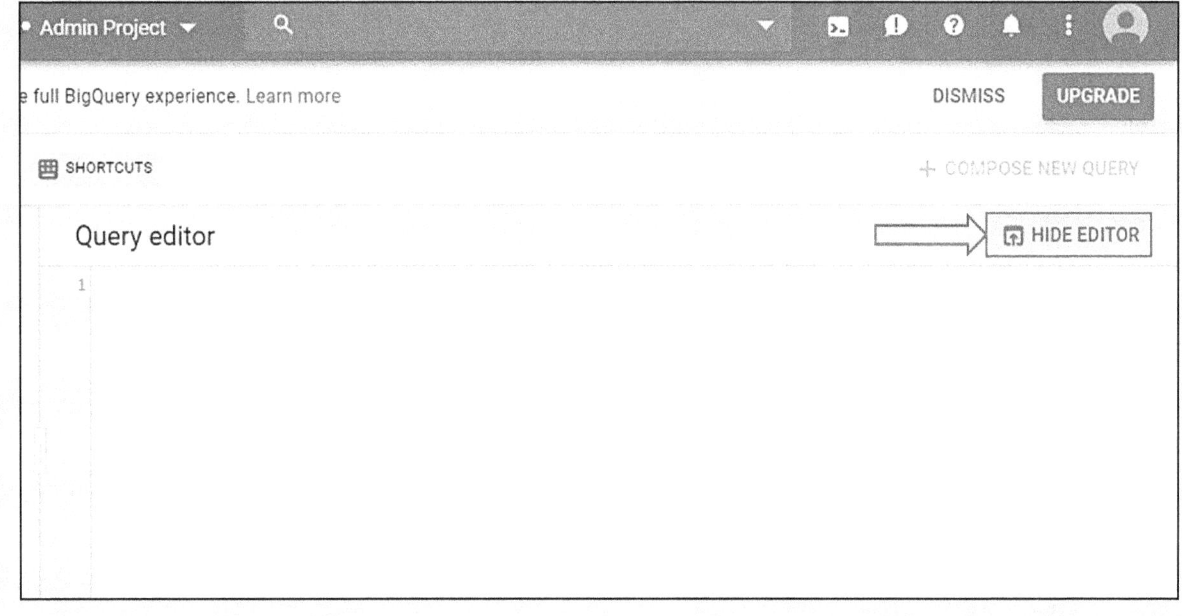

18. Click on Create Dataset.

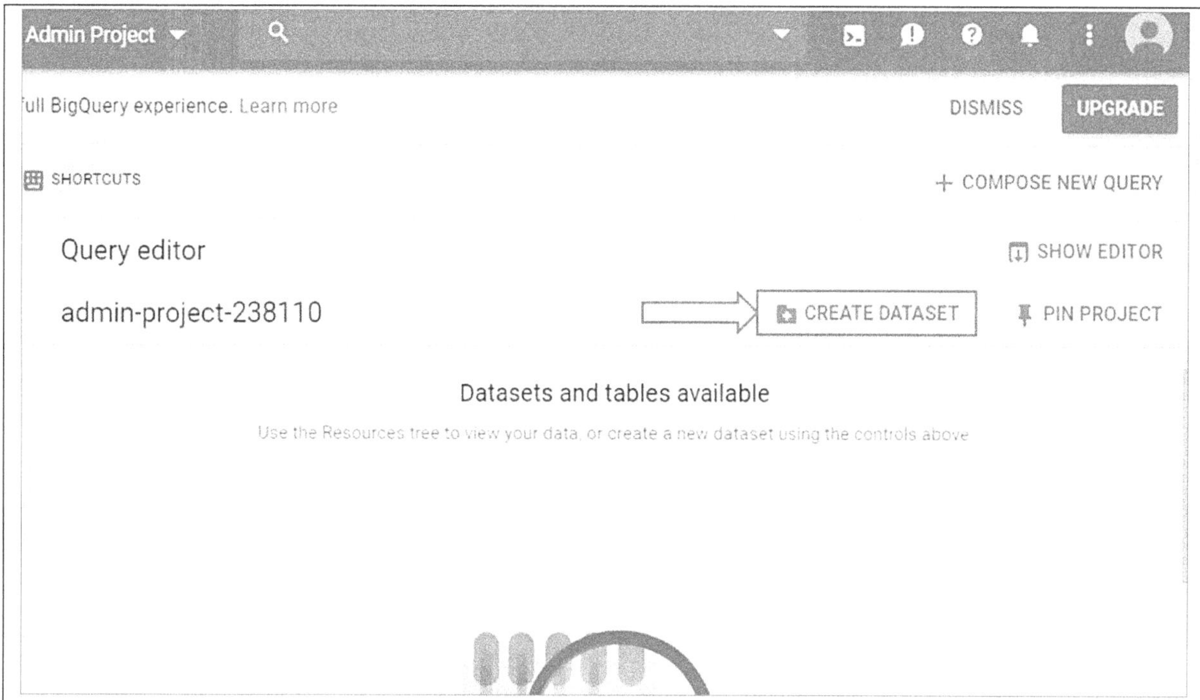

19. Provide a name for your dataset, a location and a specific date of expiration as well.
20. Create a dataset.

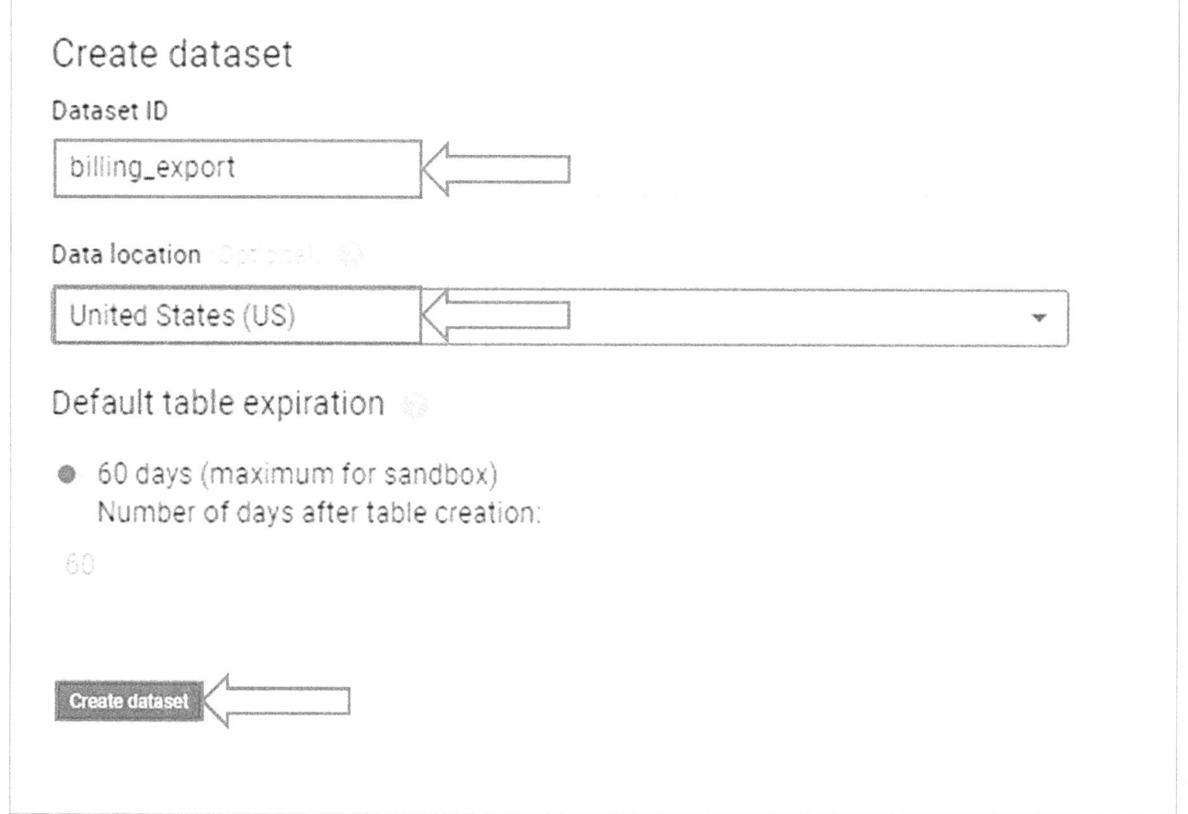

21. The data set is created. Inside the dataset, you can add the description and add the expiration date too.
22. We can add labels on the dataset.

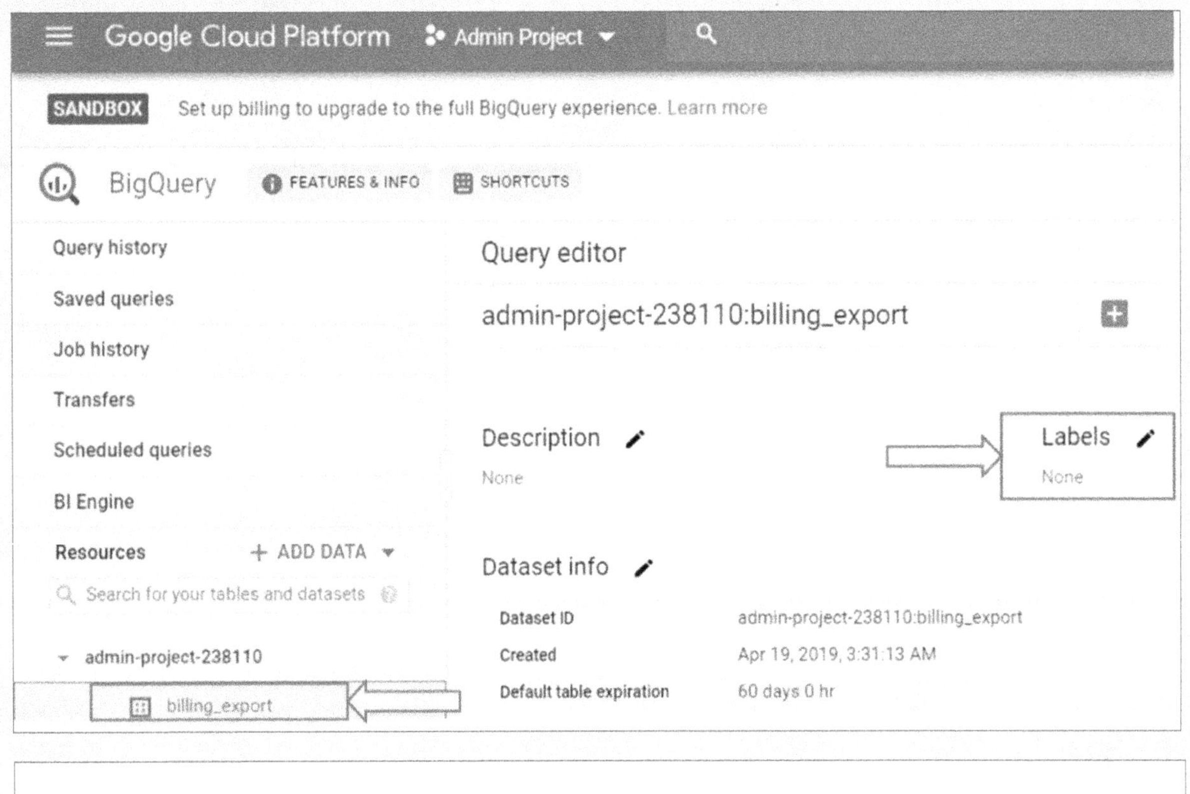

Edit labels

Labels help organize your datasets and tables (e.g., cost_center:sales or env:prod). Learn more

+ Add label

Edit labels

Labels help organize your datasets and tables (e.g., cost_center:sales or env:prod). Learn more

Key	Value
department	finance
function	billing

+ Add label

UPDATE

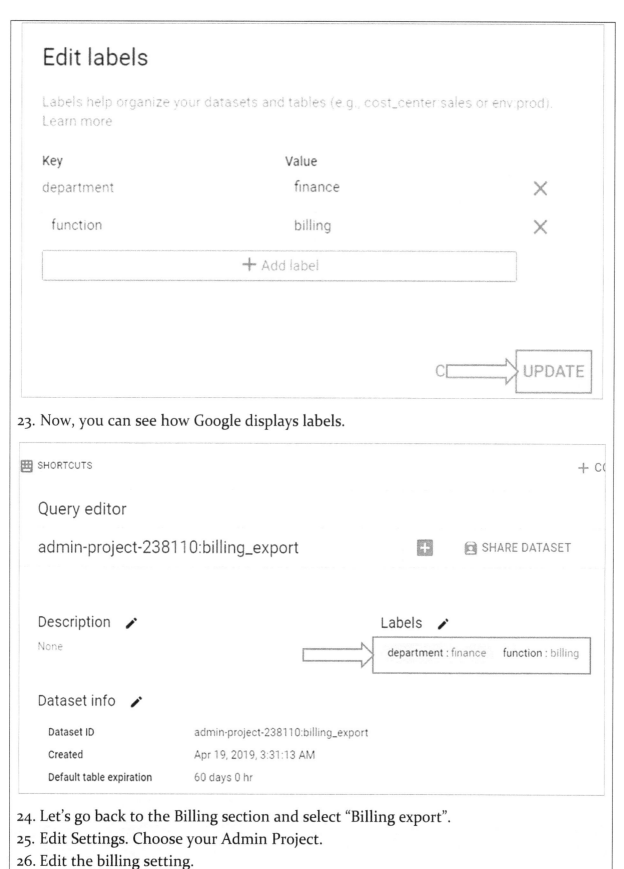

23. Now, you can see how Google displays labels.

SHORTCUTS

Query editor

admin-project-238110:billing_export

SHARE DATASET

Description

None

Labels

department : finance function : billing

Dataset info

Dataset ID	admin-project-238110:billing_export
Created	Apr 19, 2019, 3:31:13 AM
Default table expiration	60 days 0 hr

24. Let's go back to the Billing section and select "Billing export".
25. Edit Settings. Choose your Admin Project.
26. Edit the billing setting.

Google Cloud Platform

Billing export My Trial Billing Account

BIGQUERY EXPORT FILE EXPORT

BigQuery export sends your billing data to a BigQuery dataset Learn more about BigQuery

Projects *

Admin Project

This is where your billing data will be stored. Select a project with BigQuery enabled and with an existing BigQuery dataset.

Billing export dataset *

billing_export

BigQuery export will create a table with your billing data in the selected dataset

SAVE

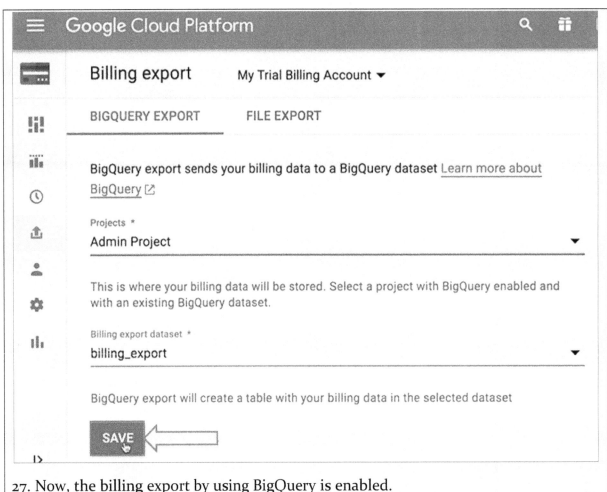

27. Now, the billing export by using BigQuery is enabled.

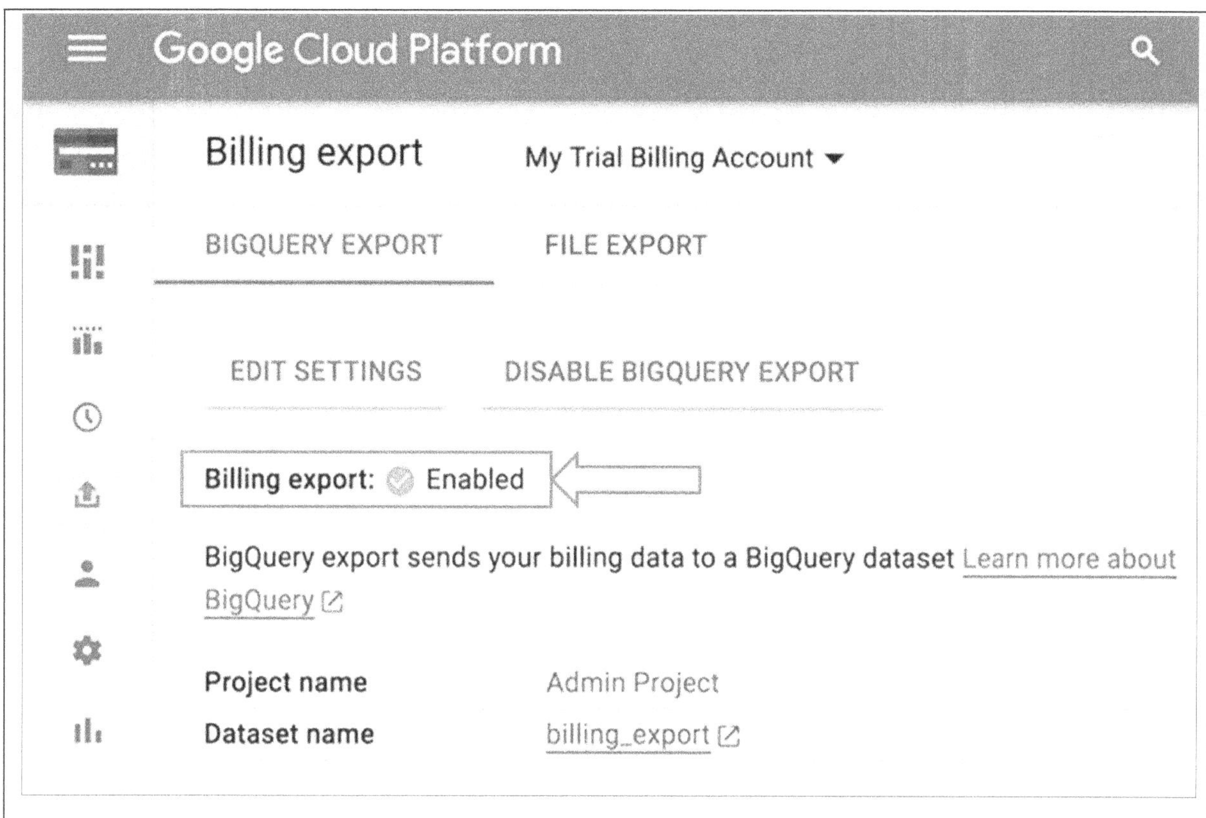

EXAM TIP: We need to set up billing export for each billing account. Resources should be placed into appropriate projects and they should be tagged with a label. Billing export is not real-time. In general, we would measure the delay in hours, not in seconds or days.

Set Up Billing Alerts

The budget amount that has been set is used to calculate the thresholds, which are used to trigger the alert notifications.

GCP documentation states that, in order to help you with project planning and controlling costs, you can set a budget. Setting a budget lets you track your expense growth towards that specific amount. You can apply a budget to either a billing account or a project, and you can set the budget at a specific amount or match it to the previous months' expense. You can also create alerts to notify billing administrators when spending exceeds a percentage of your budget.

Budget Alert Threshold Rules

The purpose behind creating a budget is that you can trigger alert notifications which are sent to the billing administrators and the billing account users when the costs exceed a percentage of the budget or the amount which is specified. After creating a budget, set the threshold rules of budget alert.

Lab 2.3: Set up Billing Alerts

Scenario:

A company's desire is to set up the alert notifications, which are to be sent to the billing administrator and billing account users after the cost gets increased to some percent of the budget or a specified amount.

Solution:

Billing Alert is set up by using the GCP Console to trigger the billing alert notifications to the administrator or billing accounts when the cost exceeds the specified amount.

1. Log in to GCP Console with the Administrative Account.
2. Go to the Navigation Menu and select Billing.

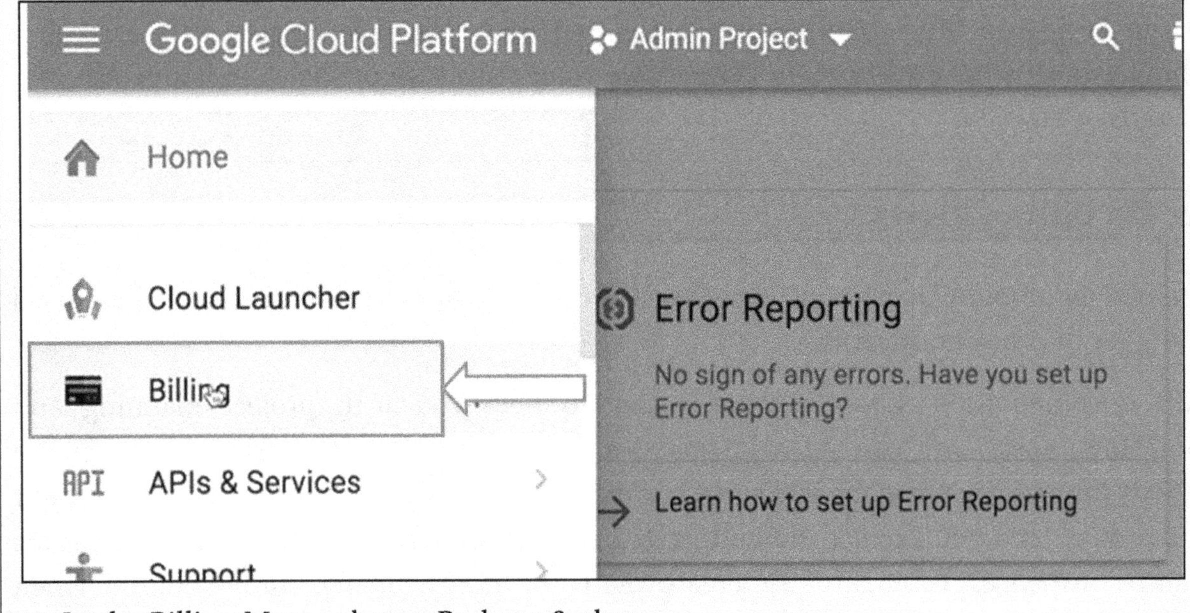

3. In the Billing Menu, choose Budgets & alerts.

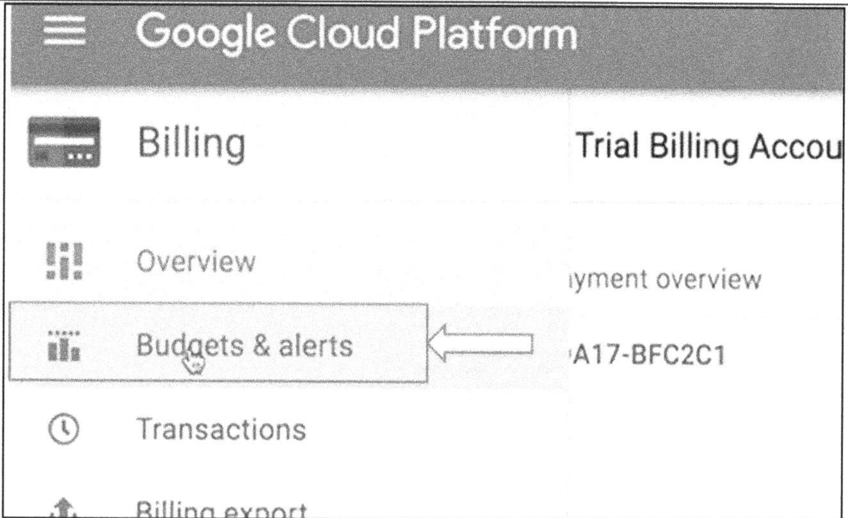

4. Select "Create Budget".

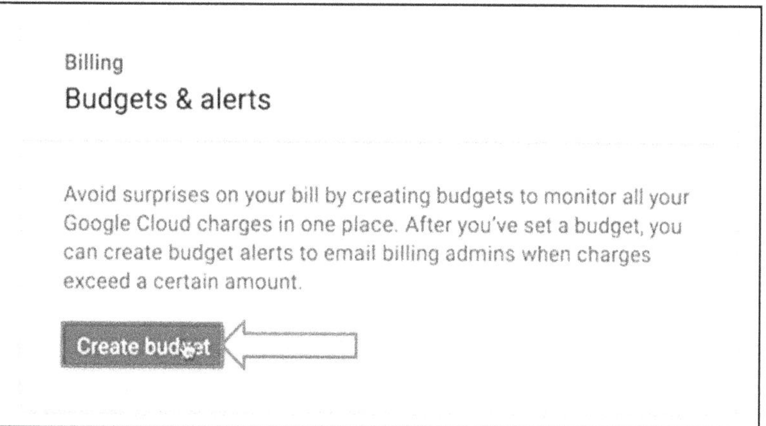

5. Provide a specific name to your budget.
6. Make sure to select your billing account.
7. Set the Budget amount.

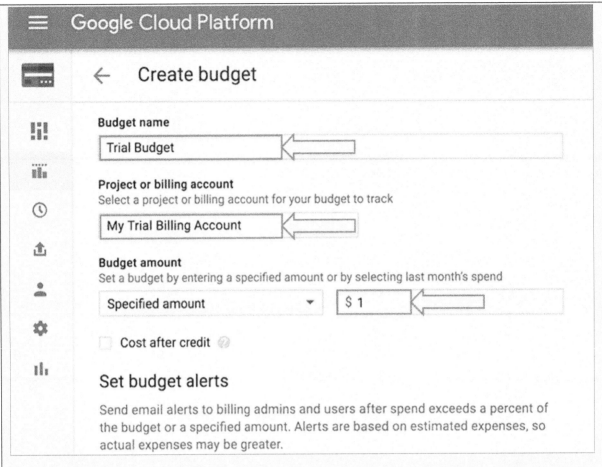

8. Optionally, you can choose Cost after credit. Cost after credit is the total cost minus any applicable credit(s). Credits may include usage discounts, promotions, and grants to use the Google Cloud Platform.
9. Save the settings.

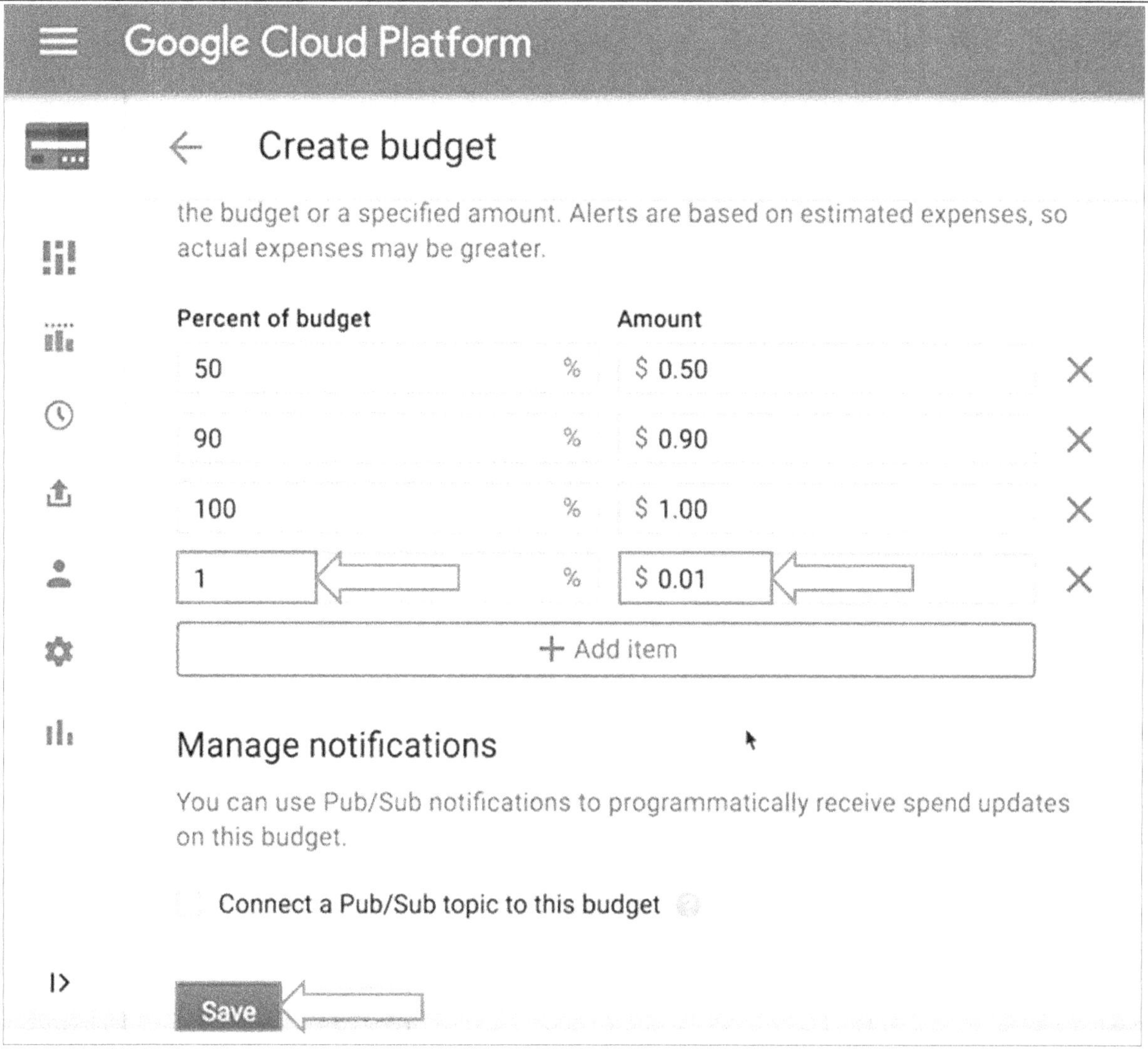

Google Cloud Platform

Create budget

the budget or a specified amount. Alerts are based on estimated expenses, so actual expenses may be greater.

Percent of budget		Amount
50	%	$ 0.50
90	%	$ 0.90
100	%	$ 1.00
1	%	$ 0.01

+ Add item

Manage notifications

You can use Pub/Sub notifications to programmatically receive spend updates on this budget.

Connect a Pub/Sub topic to this budget

Save

10. Budget is created.

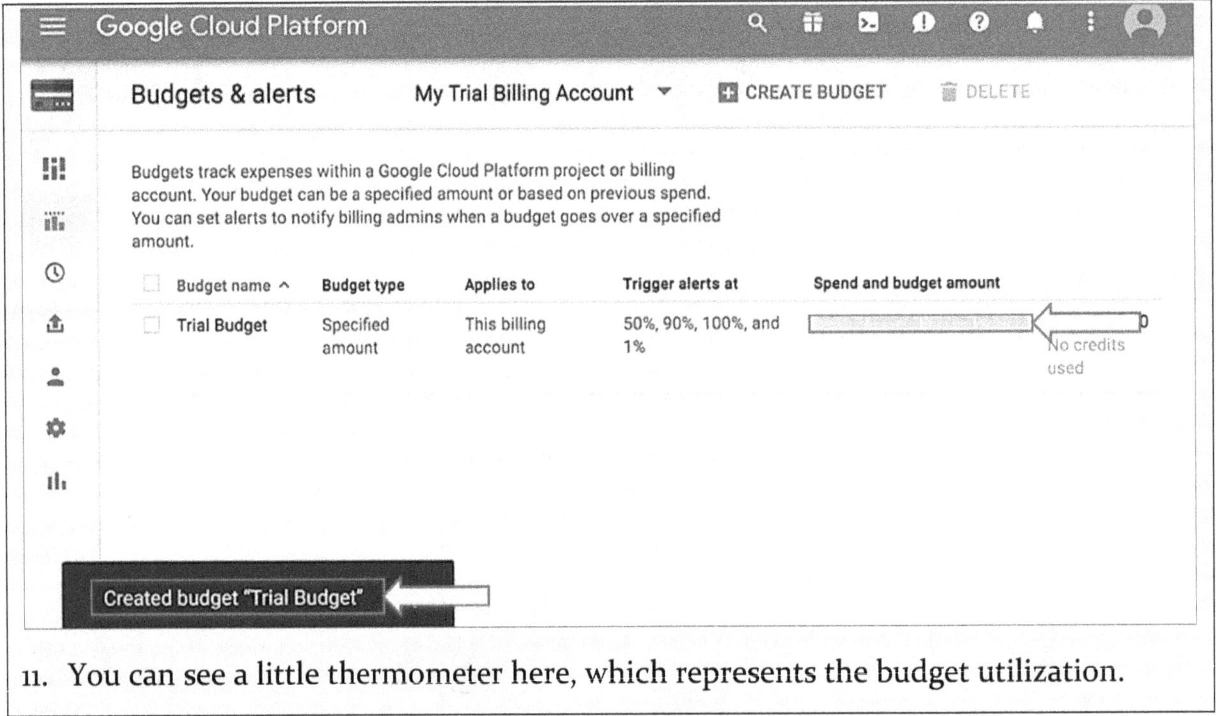

11. You can see a little thermometer here, which represents the budget utilization.

Set Up Non- Admin User Access

In this topic, there is one key role that we have to look at, which is called Billing Account User. Roles are a collection of permissions which are used to manage GCP resources. In this case, the purpose of Billing Account User is to link projects to billing accounts. You can grant this role to either an organization or to a billing account. But since we have only one billing account which is an individual account and not associated with any organization account. This role has very restricted permission so that you can grant it broadly, typically in combination with project creators and you can control the viewing permissions at different levels for different users or roles by setting access permissions at the billing account or project level. These two roles, which grant restricted permissions to the project creator and control the viewing permission at different levels to different users, allow a user to create new projects linked to the billing account on which the role is granted.

Before starting the lab, you need to get the email address of the Google Account that you control, not the admin account which you used to sign up to GCP. This account will be called the User Account. You can use a pre-existing Google Account, you can make Google Account for any existing email address, or you can make a completely separate new Gmail Account. Any of these options would be fine. Make sure that you have 2FA setup for this particular account.

Lab 2.4: Set up Non-Admin User

Scenario:

A company wants to create a non-admin user who holds the billing account same as the administrator account, but they are not able to check each other's data resources. The activities performed on a user account or the activities performed on the administrator account must be separate from each other.

Solution:

A non-admin user can be set up from the administrator account using GCP Console. The users can create their projects and perform multiple activities on it but cannot check the billing status as the permission is not granted by the admin account. Similarly, the admin account is no longer able to check the activities and projects of the user account.

1. Log in to GCP Console with the administrator access, not the user account.
2. Go to the "Navigation Menu" and select "Billing".

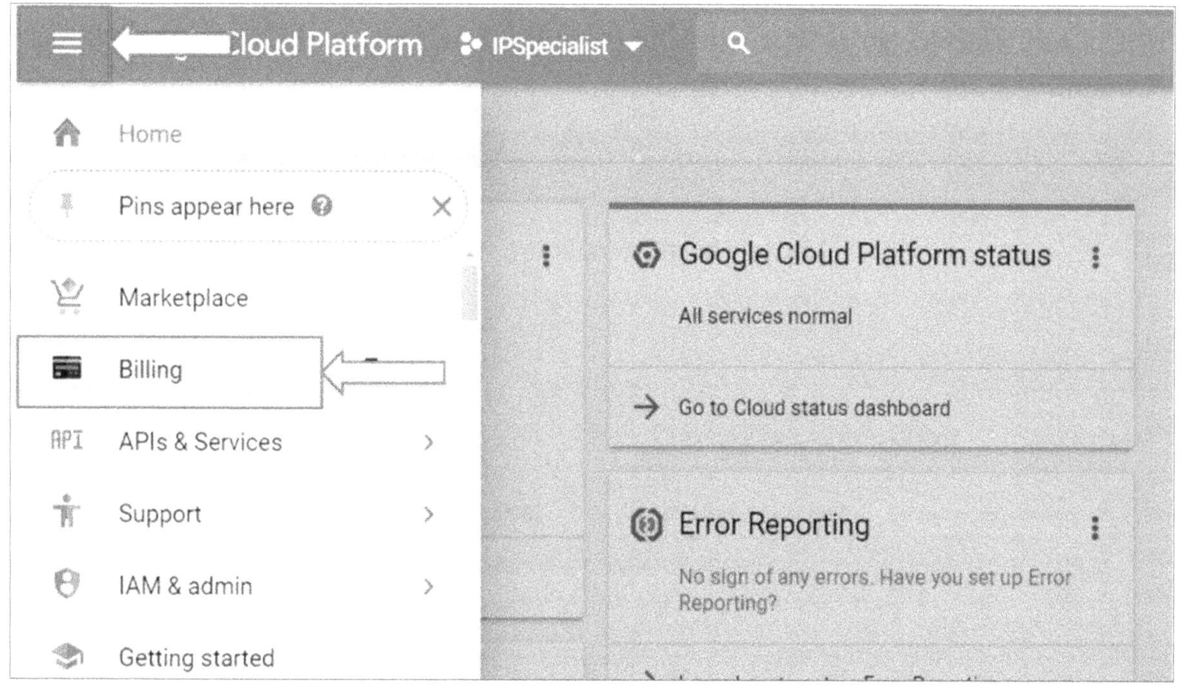

3. Select your Billing Account.

Google Cloud Platform

Overview

ALL BILLING ACCOUNTS

My Trial Billing Account

Manage billing accounts

Billing account overvi

Billing account ID: 01

Credits

$383.96

Credits remaining

348

Days remaining

Projects linked to this billing account

Project name

Project ID

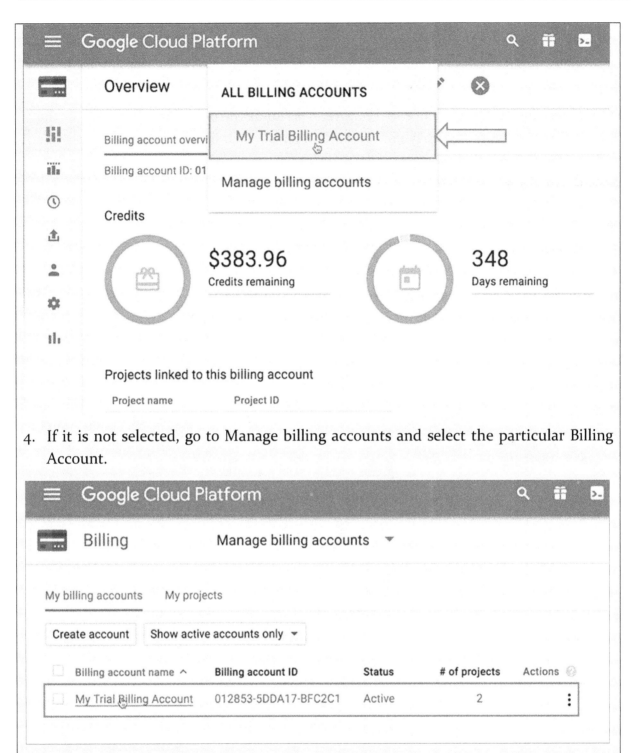

4. If it is not selected, go to Manage billing accounts and select the particular Billing Account.

Google Cloud Platform

Billing

Manage billing accounts

My billing accounts

My projects

Create account

Show active accounts only

Billing account name	Billing account ID	Status	# of projects	Actions
My Trial Billing Account	012853-5DDA17-BFC2C1	Active	2	

5. Click on Show Info Panel.

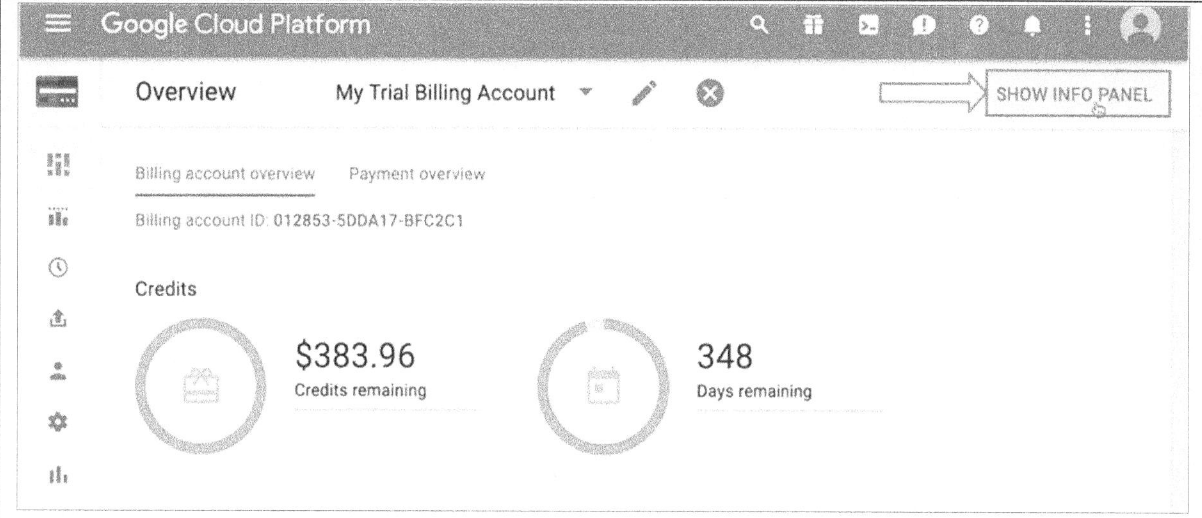

6. You can see that there is only one billing account attached, which is the administrator account.

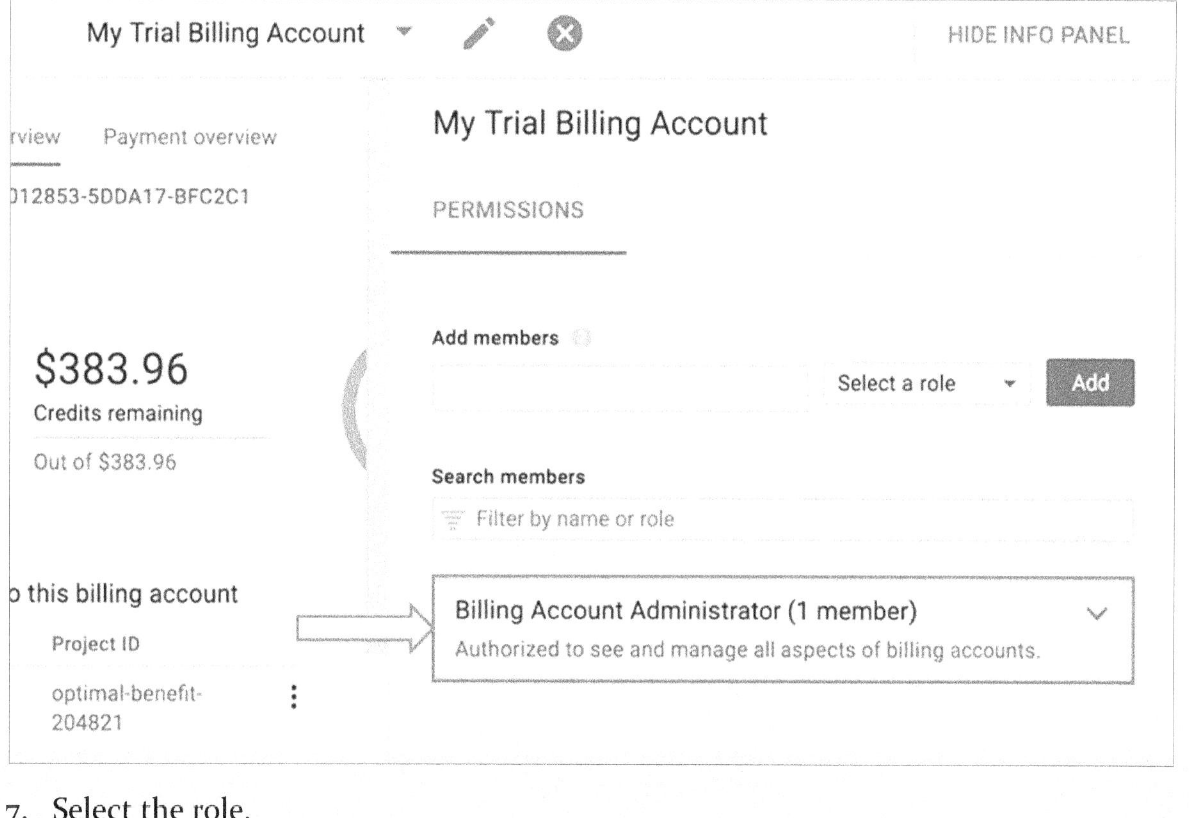

7. Select the role.

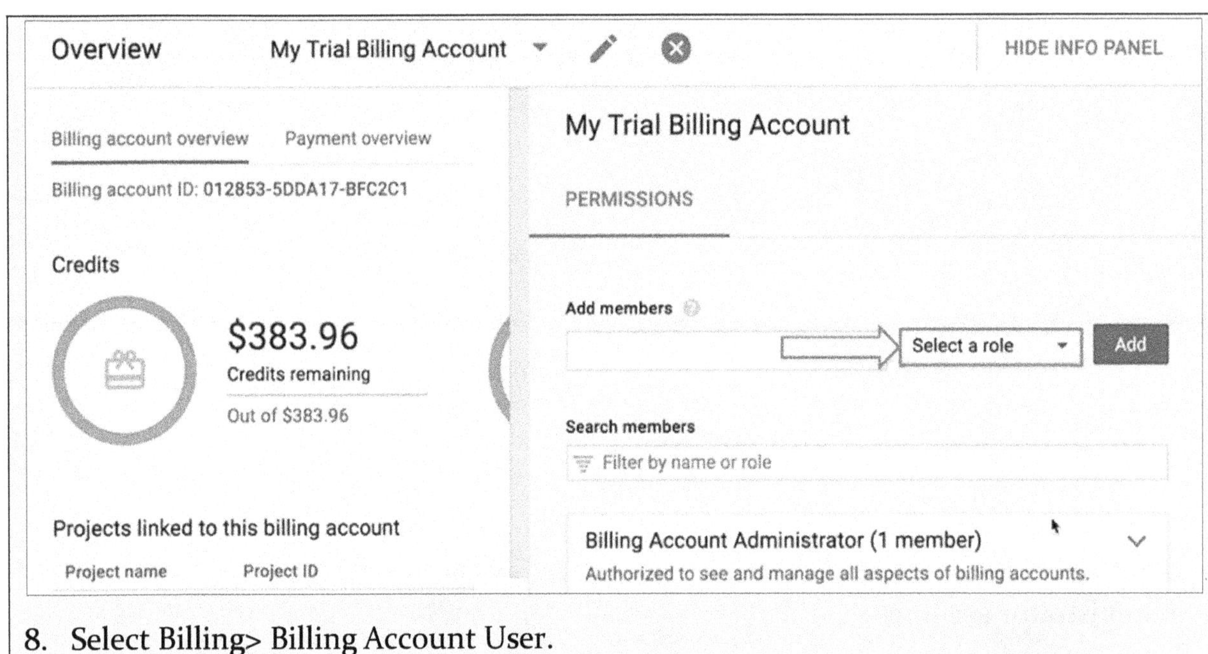

8. Select Billing> Billing Account User.

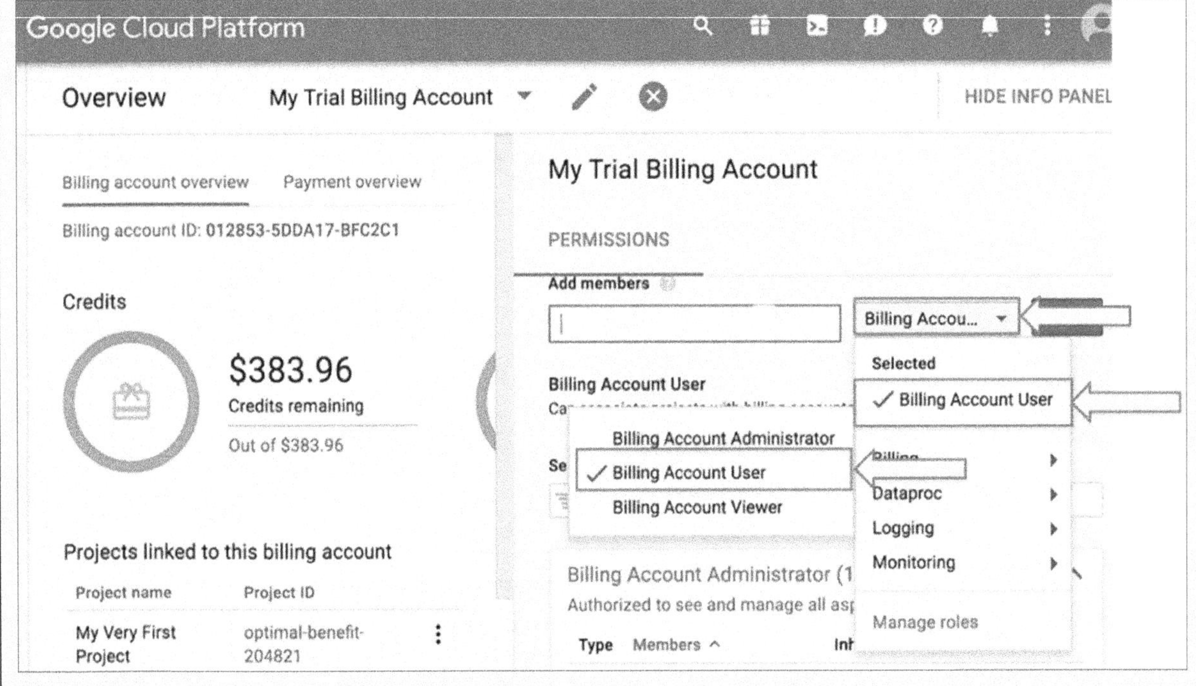

9. Now, enter the email address that we are using as the GCP User.

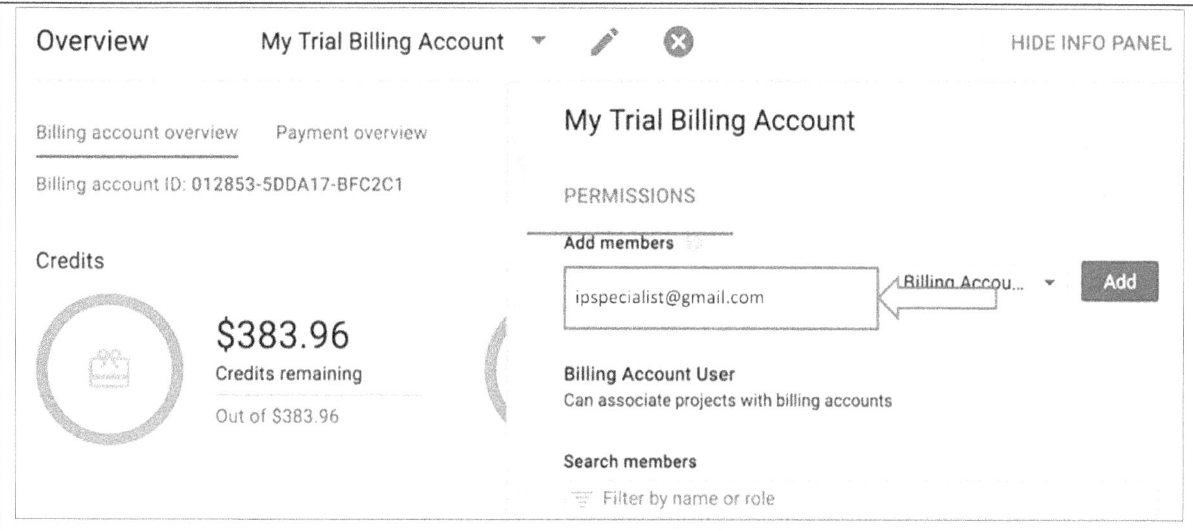

10. Sign out from the admin account and sign in from the user account.

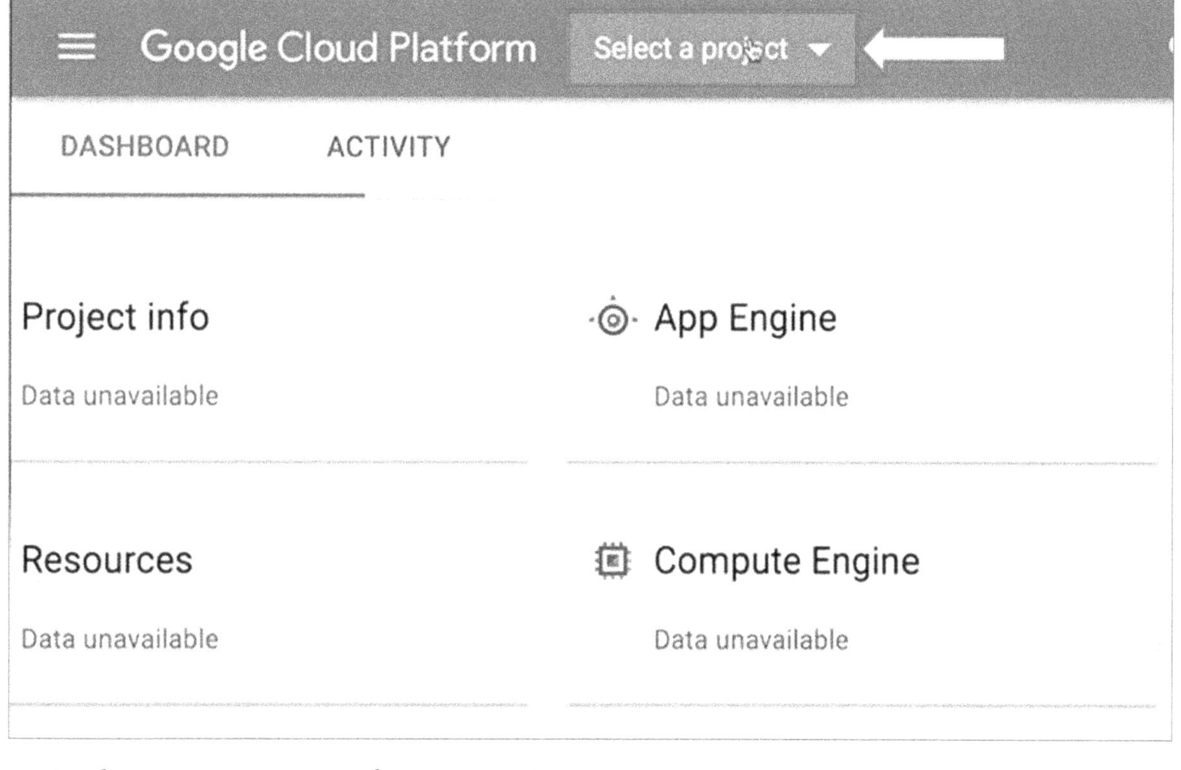

11. In the user account, we have no projects yet.
12. We create a project.

Select a project

NEW PROJECT

Search projects and folders

RECENT ALL

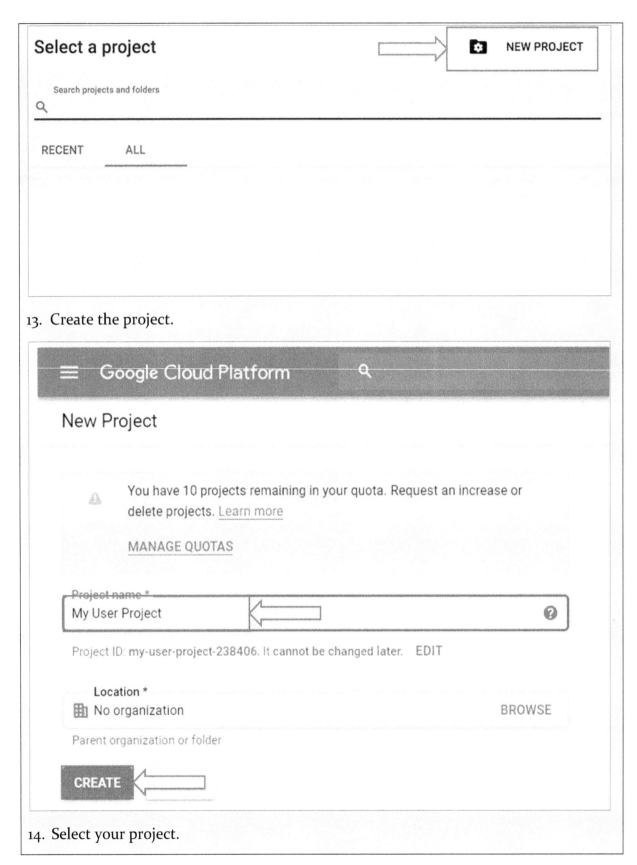

13. Create the project.

Google Cloud Platform

New Project

You have 10 projects remaining in your quota. Request an increase or delete projects. Learn more

MANAGE QUOTAS

Project name *

My User Project

Project ID: my-user-project-238406. It cannot be changed later. EDIT

Location *

No organization BROWSE

Parent organization or folder

CREATE

14. Select your project.

Select a project

NEW PROJECT

Search projects and folders

RECENT ALL

Name	ID
My User Project	my-user-project-206422

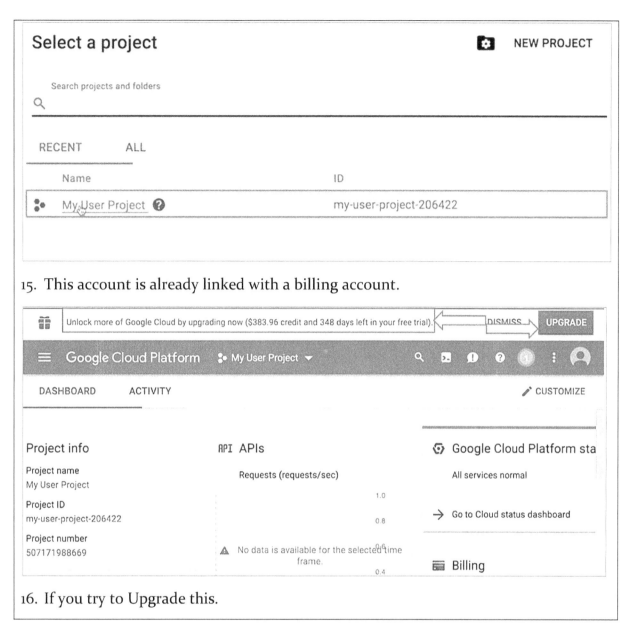

15. This account is already linked with a billing account.

Unlock more of Google Cloud by upgrading now ($383.96 credit and 348 days left in your free trial). DISMISS UPGRADE

Google Cloud Platform My User Project

DASHBOARD ACTIVITY CUSTOMIZE

Project info

Project name
My User Project

Project ID
my-user-project-206422

Project number
507171988669

API APIs

Requests (requests/sec)

1.0
0.8
0.6
0.4

No data is available for the selected time frame.

Google Cloud Platform sta

All services normal

Go to Cloud status dashboard

Billing

16. If you try to Upgrade this.

Upgrade your account

You're one step away from unlocking all of Google Cloud Platform.

You won't be charged until after your free credits run out or expire (whichever comes first). Learn more

You only pay for what you use. View pricing details

17. You will get an error because we are not able to upgrade this particular account.

Error

You do not have sufficient permissions to view this page.

Tracking Number: 8143241587812606(

Send feedback

OK

18. Go back to Billing Menu and check, if you are not allowed to view the billing status.

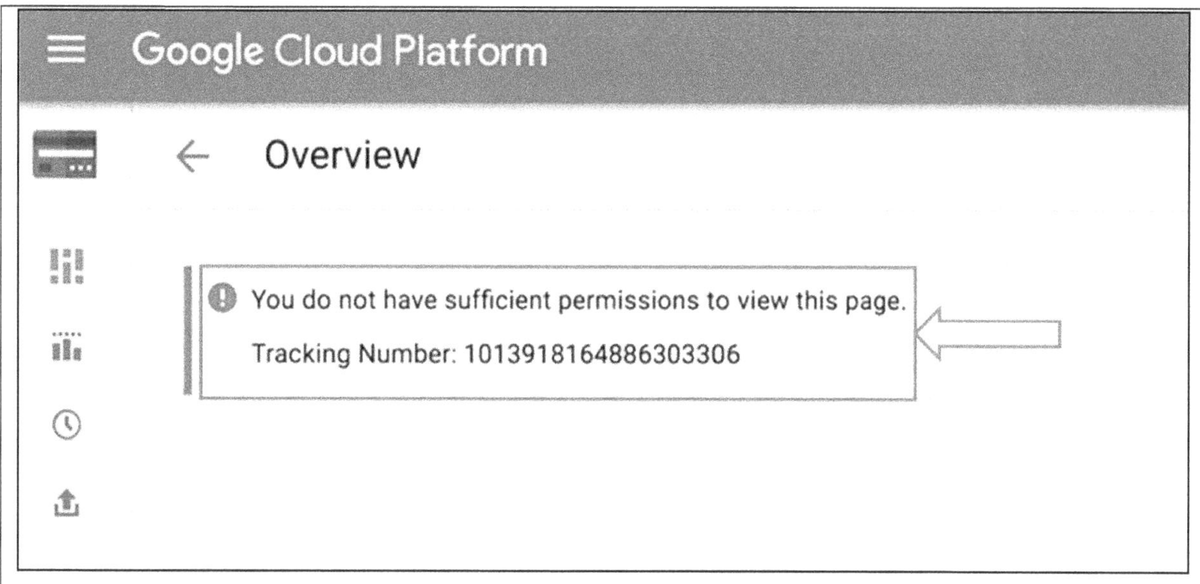

19. You can only check the number of active projects under the billing account inside My billing accounts.

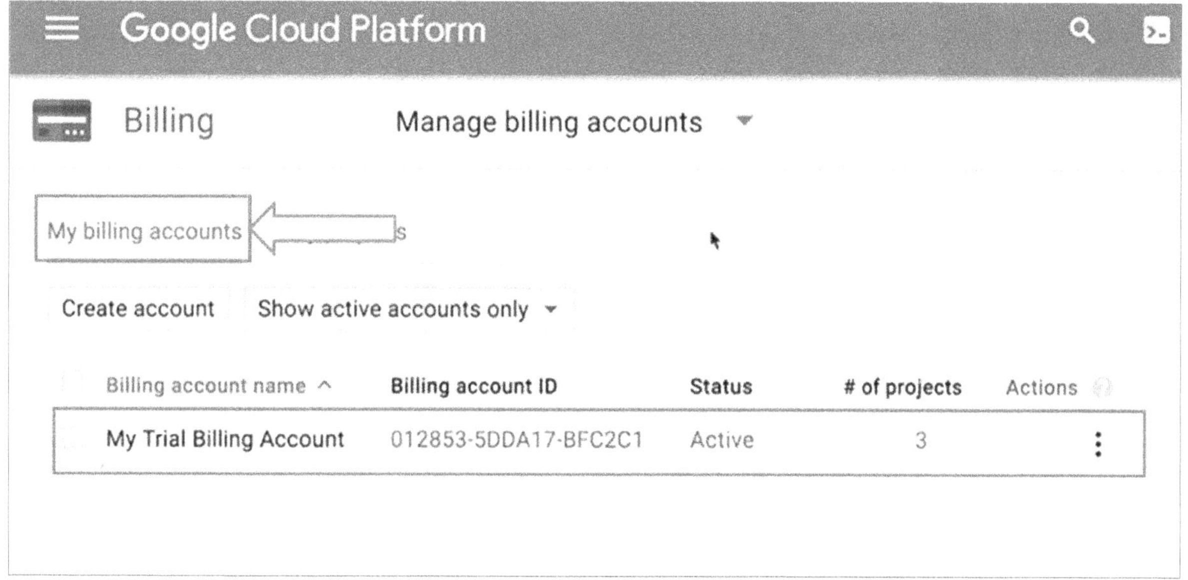

20. Inside the User Projects, you can only view the user created projects.

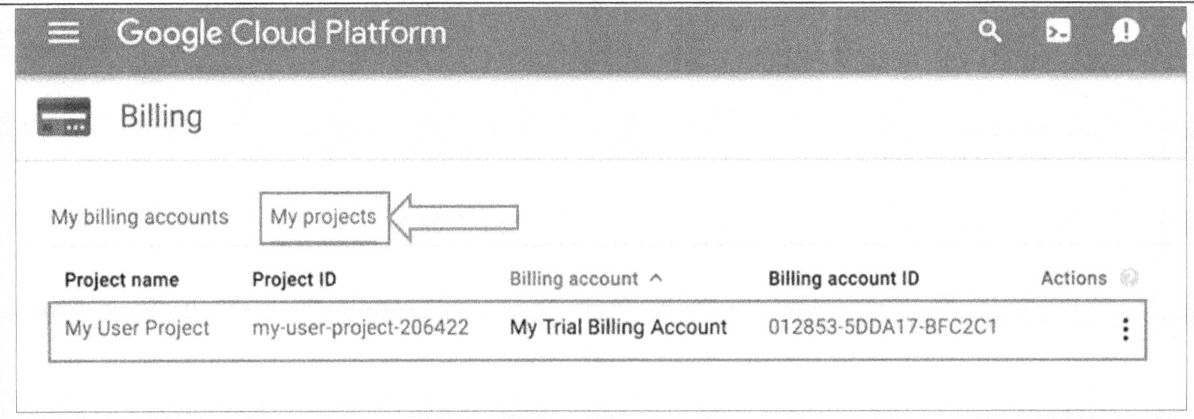

21. Go back to the dashboard. Grab the URL of this particular project. Now, sign out from user account and sign in back with the administrator account. Paste the URL. You are not allowed to view that data.

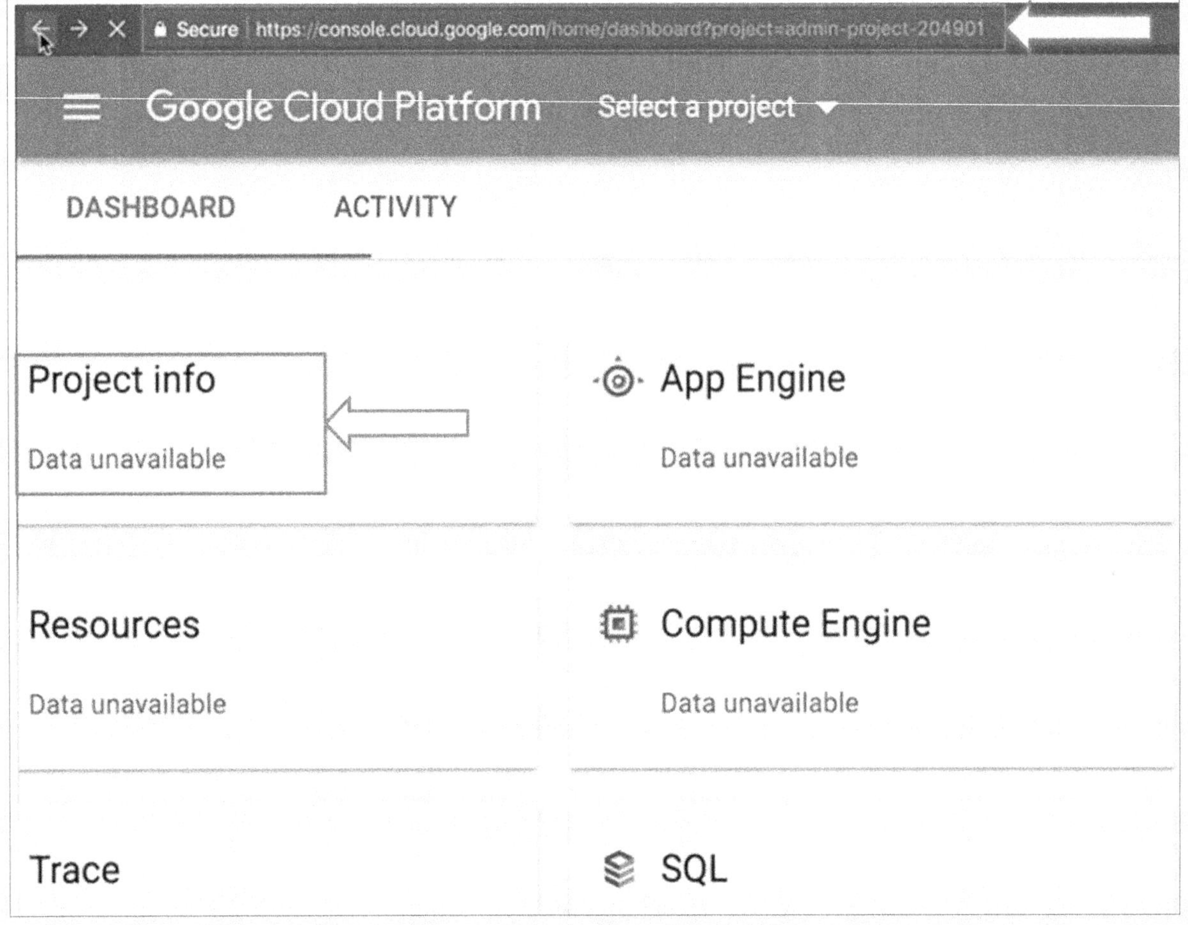

22. Similarly, the project created from the user account is not present in the list of projects of the administrator account.

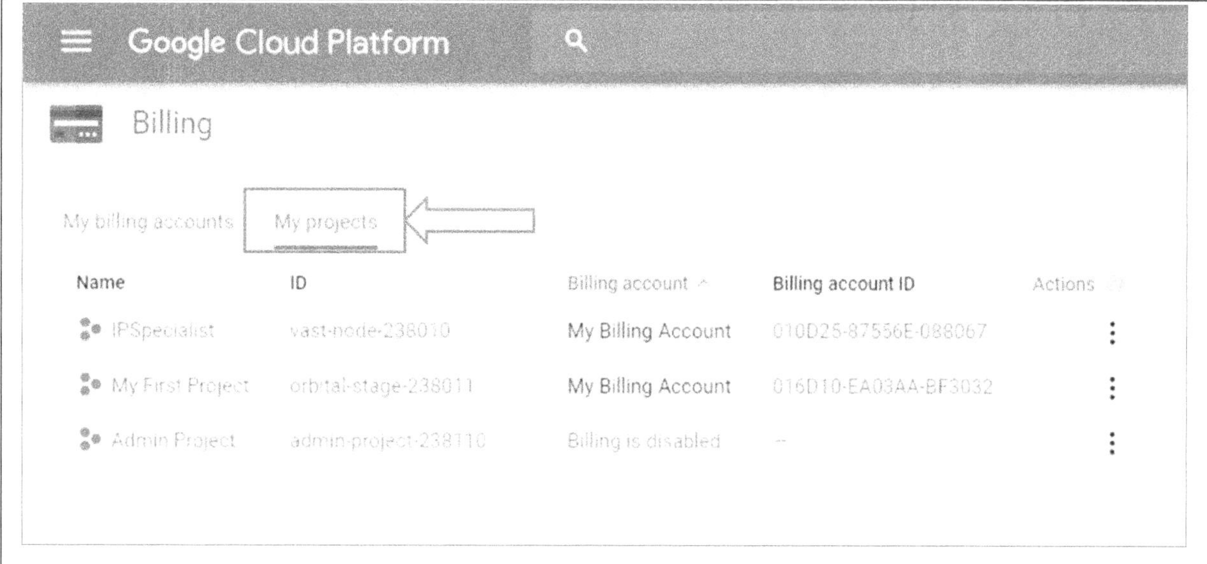

23. Owning a project and being able to hold its resources is completely separate from holding the billing accounts attached to that project.

Cloud Shell and Editor

Google Cloud Shell presents you command line access in your cloud resources directly from your browser. You can manage your tasks and sources without installing the Google Cloud SDK or different tools on your system. With Cloud Shell, the Cloud SDK gcloud command line tool and other utilities you want, are constantly available, up to date, and fully authenticated.

You can access this command line tool from any web browser, anywhere through an internet connection, which means that you do not need a local terminal program running on the computer you are using. You also escape from having to manage the keys manually. There is an automatic SSH key management in Cloud Shell. Cloud Shell provides you 5GB of persistent storage, which means if you save something in one-way session and come back to use the data later, it will reside in the data. You can easily pick up where you left off. There is an easy access to all the pre-installed tools like gcloud, bq, kubectl, docker, npm/ node, pip/ python, ruby, vim, emacs, bash, etc. when you are using these tools to interact with your GCP, they are pre-authorized and you do not need to update them, because they are always up to date when they are connecting to Cloud Shell. If you run something in this Cloud Shell, like a node app or something, you will get a URL so that you can preview the web app running on your local machine to that Cloud Shell.

Lab 2.5: Cloud Shell

Scenario:

A user wants to learn about Cloud Shell, including multiple tasks that can be performed on Cloud Shell. He wants to know how Cloud Shell is used to print working directory, go back to the previous directory and navigate the directory. Similarly, how different files are uploaded on Cloud Shell and how the changes can be made using Cloud Shell Code Editor.

Solution:

Explore the different commands used in Cloud Shell and use it. Check the active directories, print working directory, navigate to different files and Use the commands of node and nodemon to execute the changes that are performed in the Cloud Shell Code Editor.

1. Log in to the GCP Console with your non-administrative account and pay attention when you are logging in. If you do not get prompted for 2FA, then set it up now.
2. Find and click on the button named as "Activate Cloud Shell".

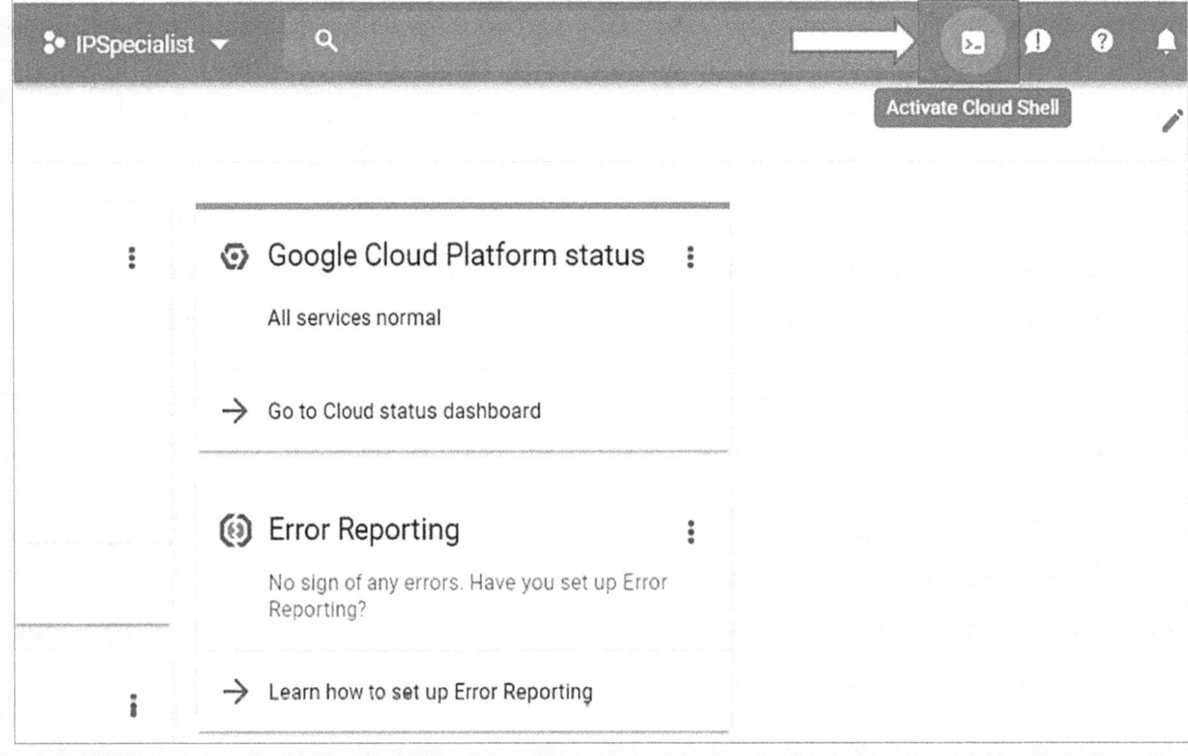

3. This little screen shows some running update on the screen.
4. Click on Start Cloud Shell.

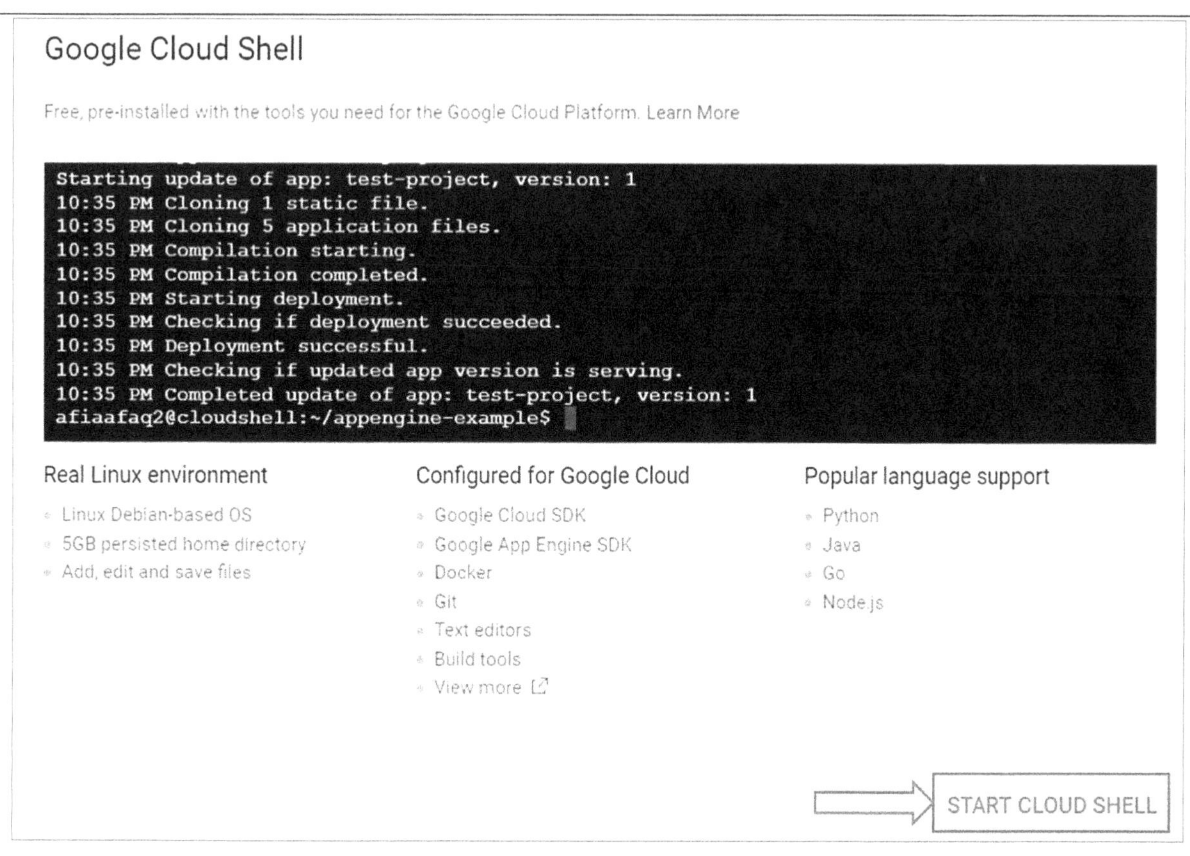

5. By default, Cloud Shell window is located at the bottom of the screen.

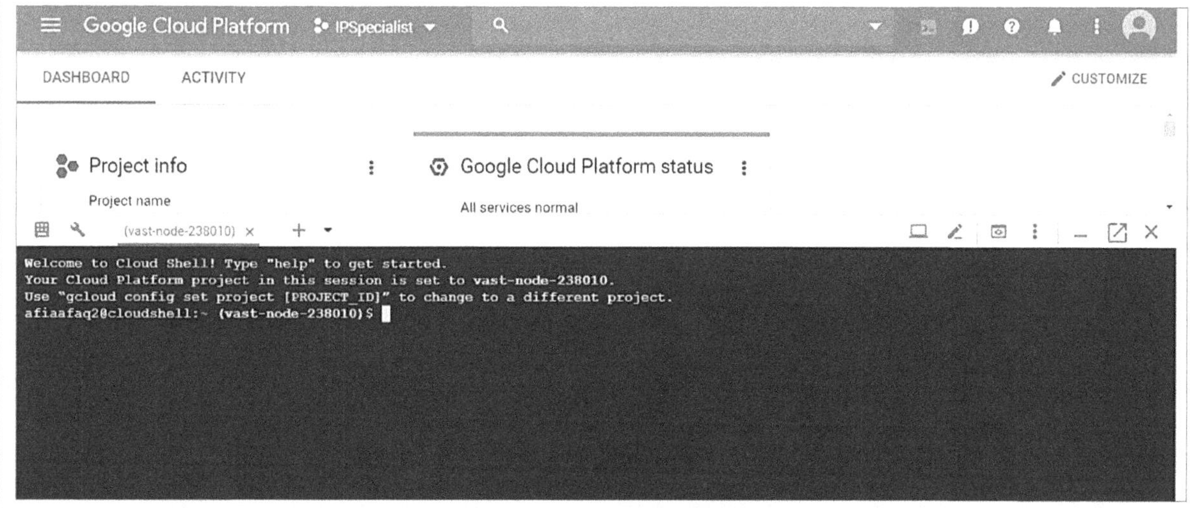

6. Press this button, and open this up in the new window.

7. This Cloud Shell is automatically connected to this project.

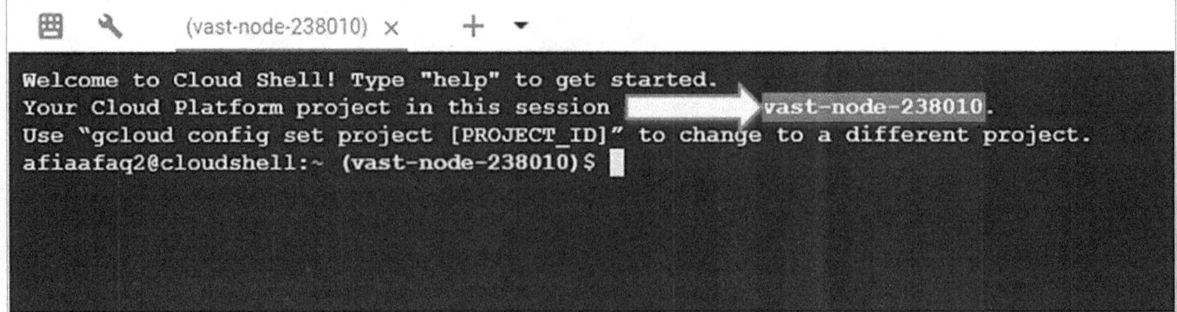

8. If you want to change the project, use this command.

```
Welcome to Cloud Shell! Type "help" to get started.
Your Cloud Platform project in this session is set to vast-node-238010.
Use "gcloud config set project [PROJECT_ID]                e to a different project.
afiaafaq2@cloudshell:~ (vast-node-238010)$
```

9. You can upload and download the files in this Cloud Shell and restart the machine.

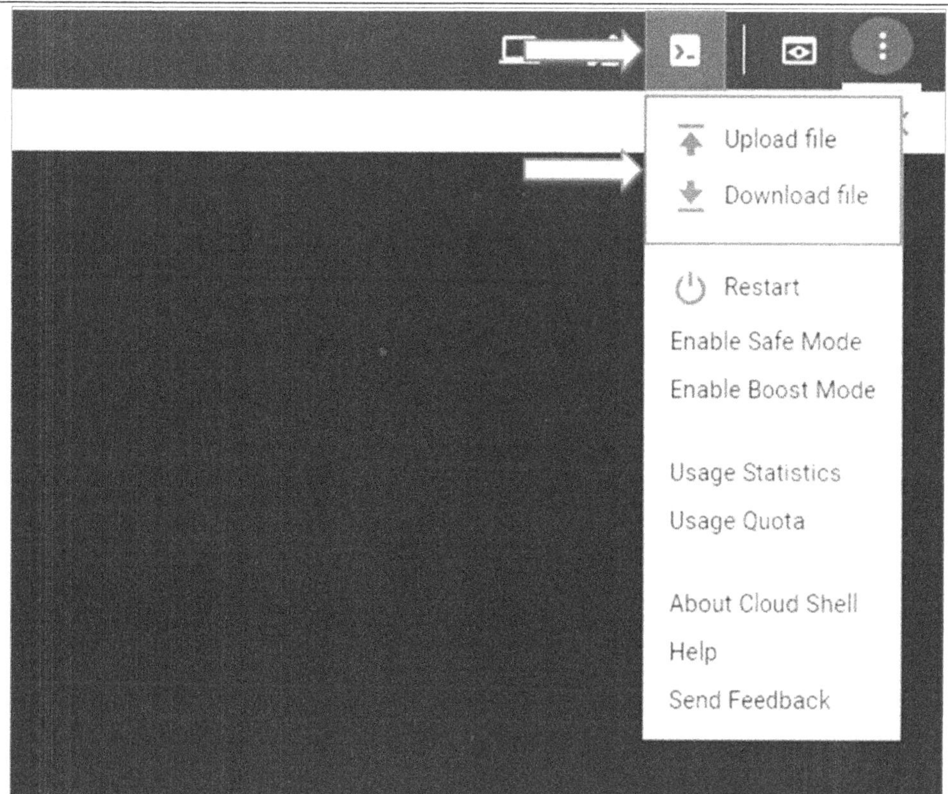

10. You might also be able to enable the "Boost Mode".

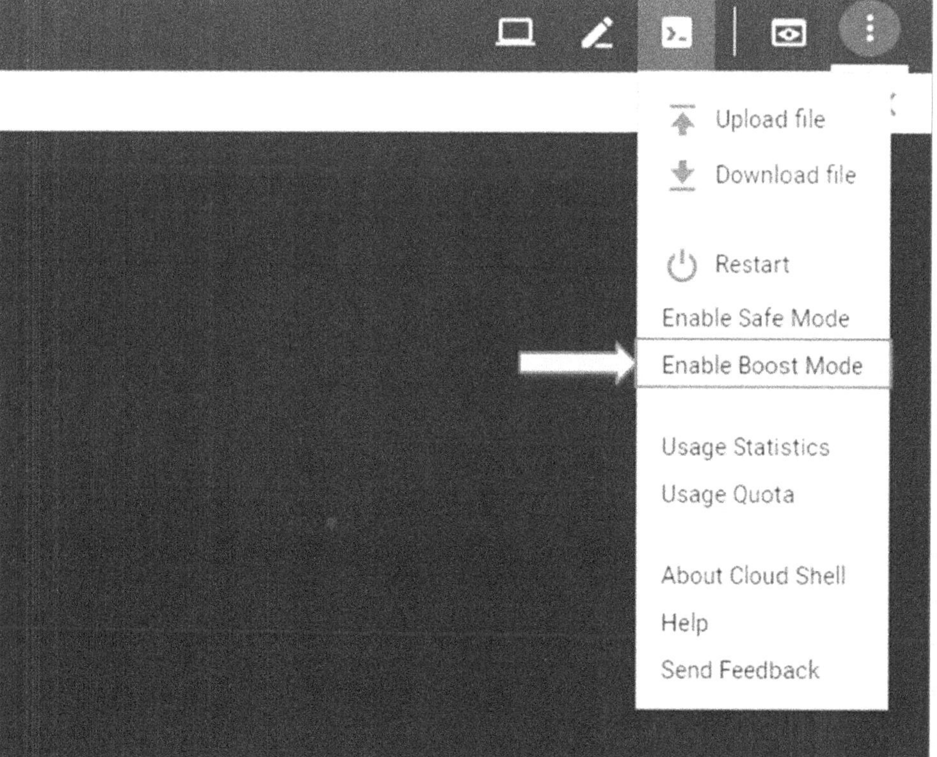

11. Enable "Boost Mode". This can take a bit of time.
12. Boost Mode is Activated. It might not look any different, but it is faster than the previous mode.

Enable Boost Mode

Boost mode temporarily increases the power of your Cloud Shell VM. Once activated, all sessions will be boosted for the next 24 hours. The usage of Cloud Shell in Boost mode is subject to regular usage limits. The feature is currently **experimental** and there may be additional limits in the future.

Enabling Boost mode may take a couple of minutes and will immediately terminate your session. A new VM will then be provisioned for you, which can take a couple of minutes. The data in your home directory will persist, but all running processes will be lost.

13. Clear the screen.

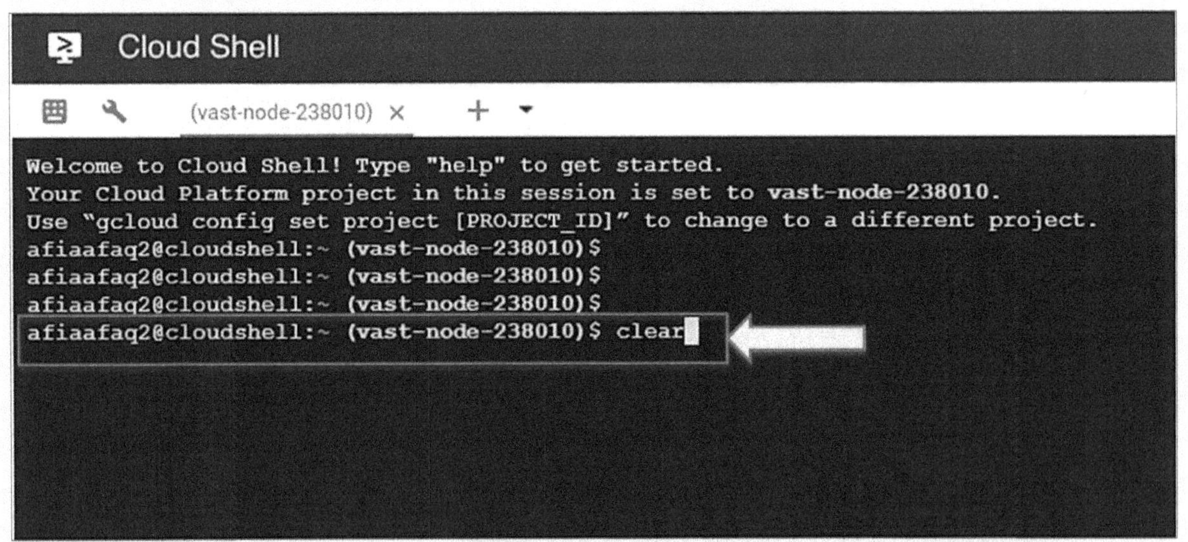

14. Print the working directory to check from where you started it.

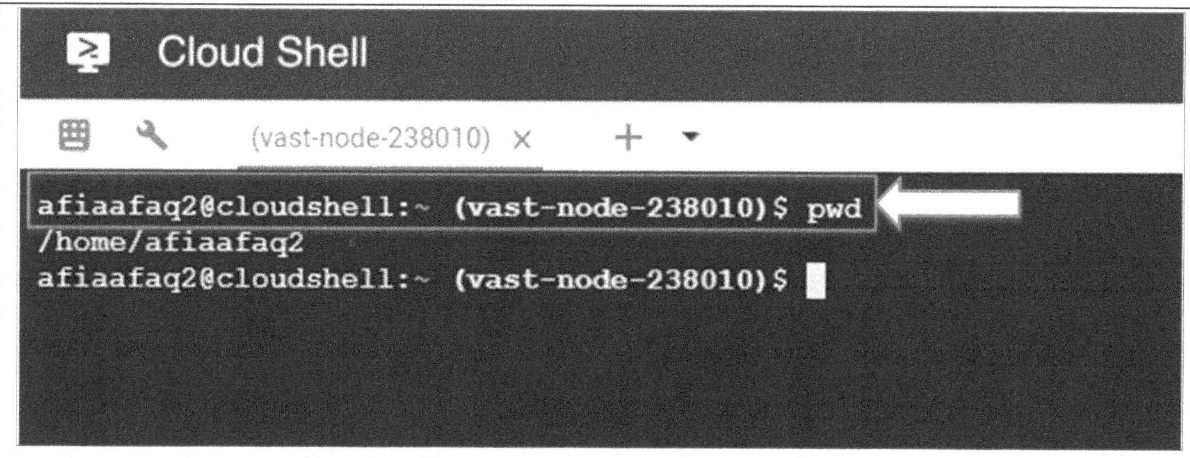

15. You can move to previous directories and come back to the new one.

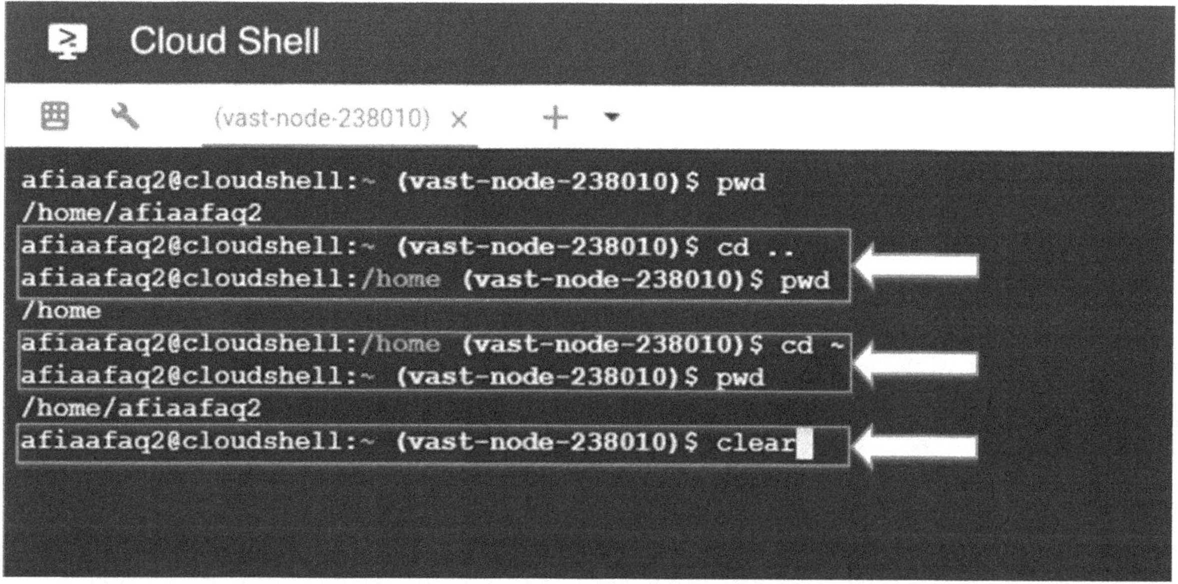

16. To start the Cloud Shell, use this command.

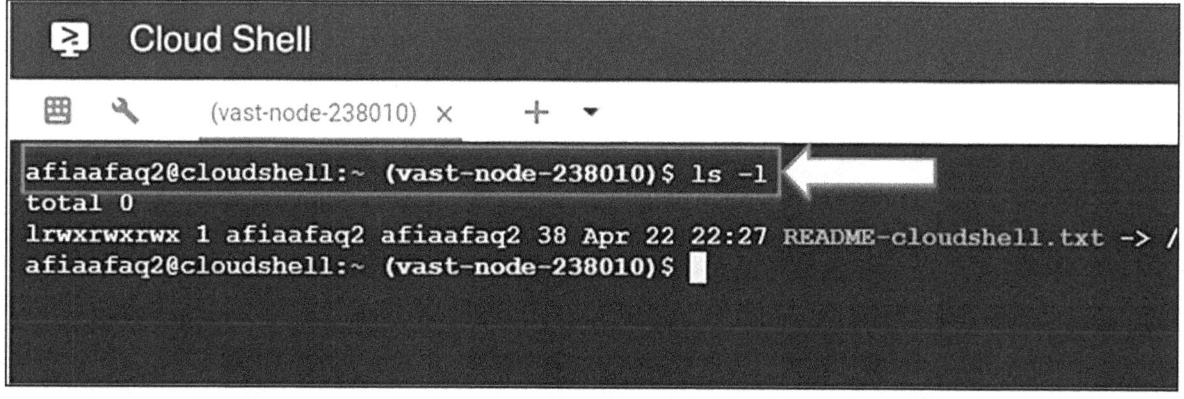

17. Use the cat command to check the information about the Read File.
18. Write cat with capital R and press tab to complete the whole command.

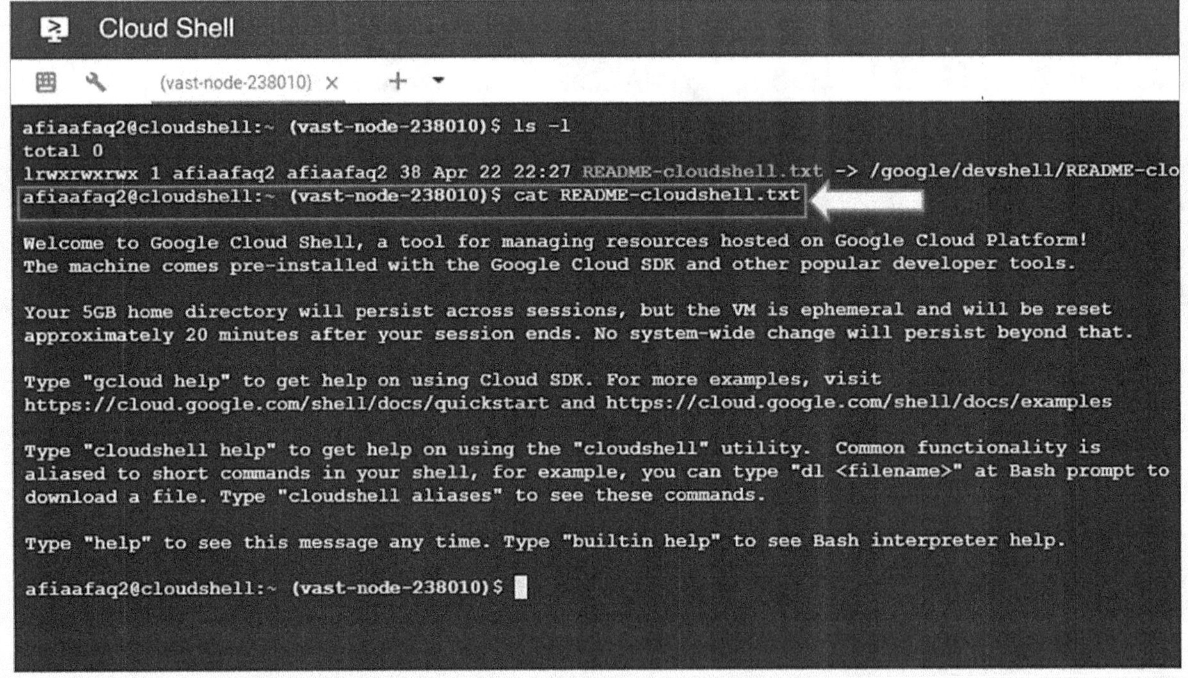

19. The VM we are using is ephemeral.

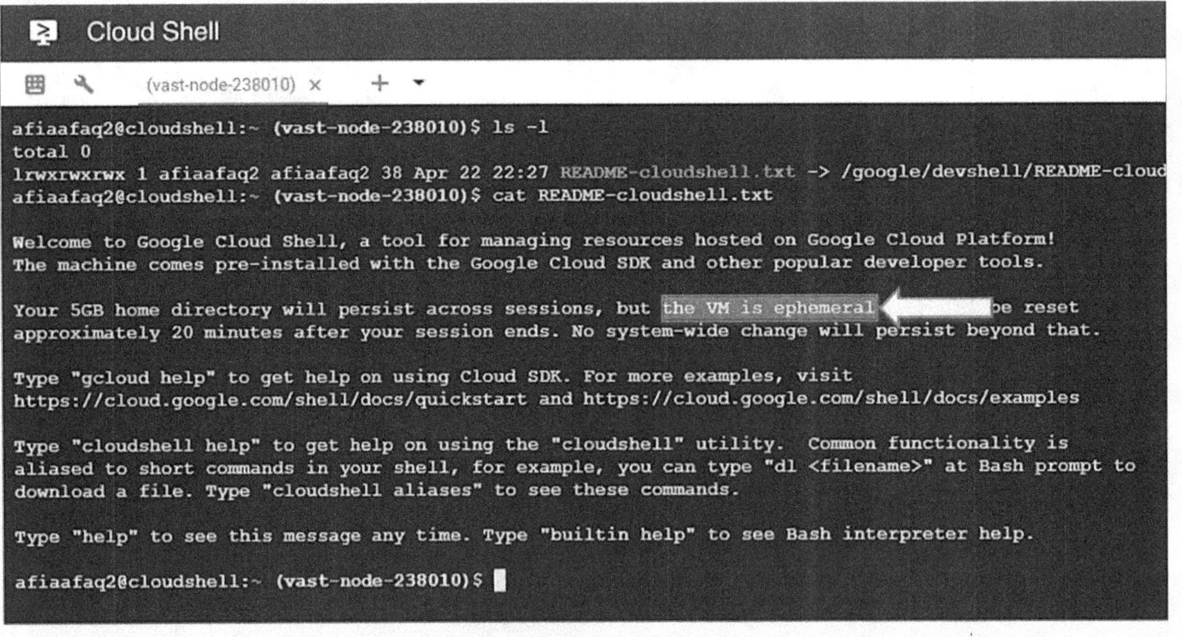

20. Dl <filename> allows us to download that particular file.

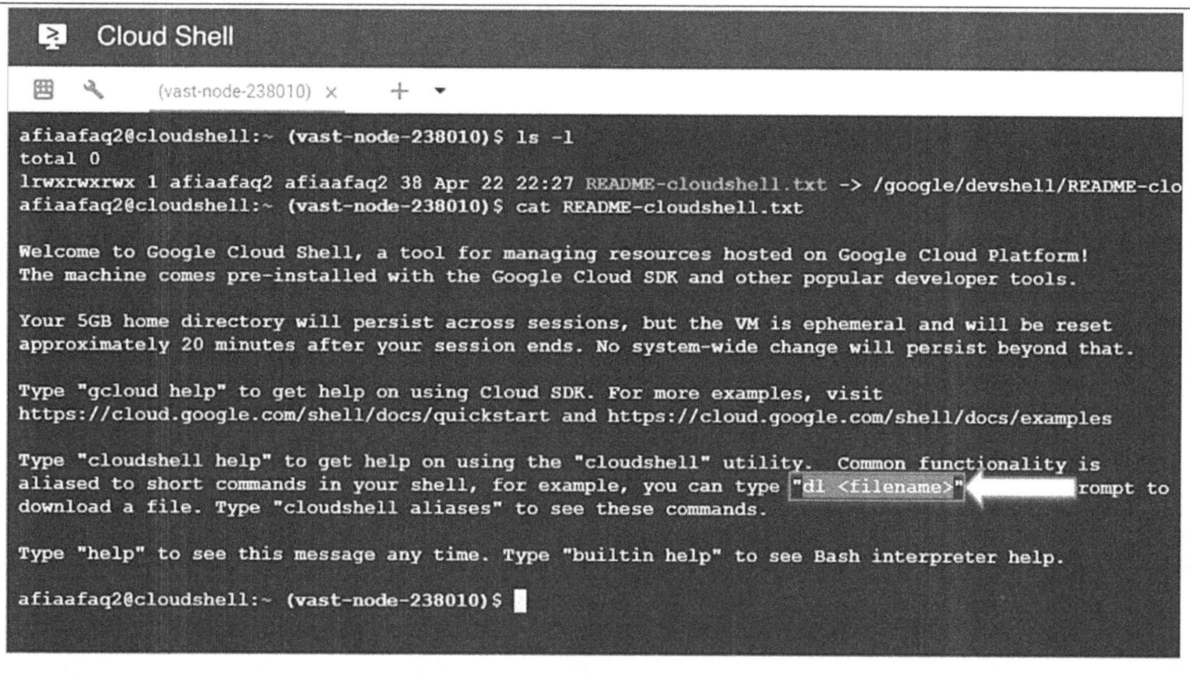

21. Let's test this command.

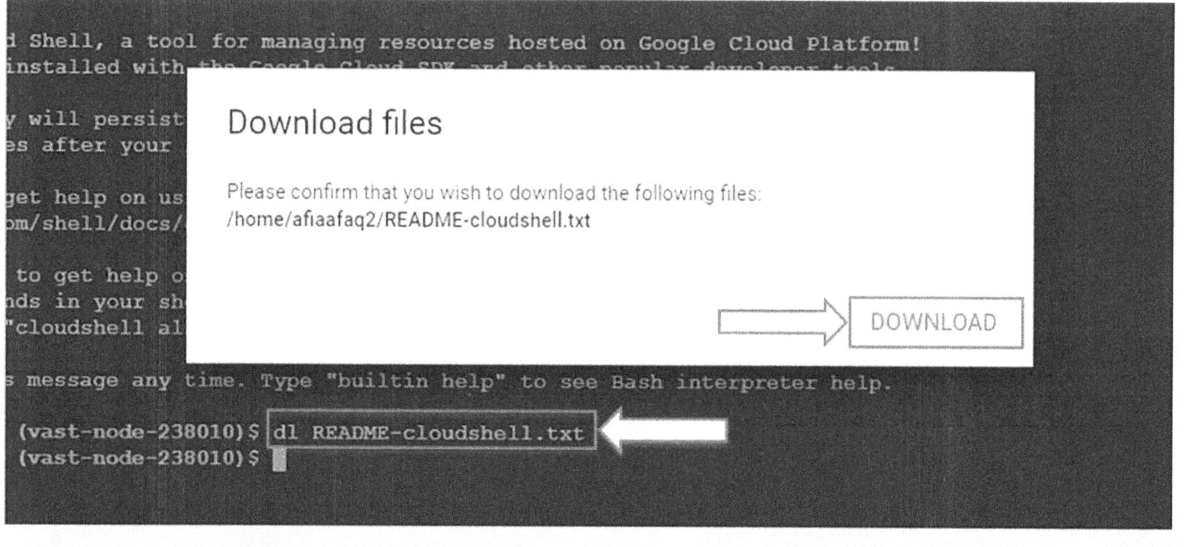

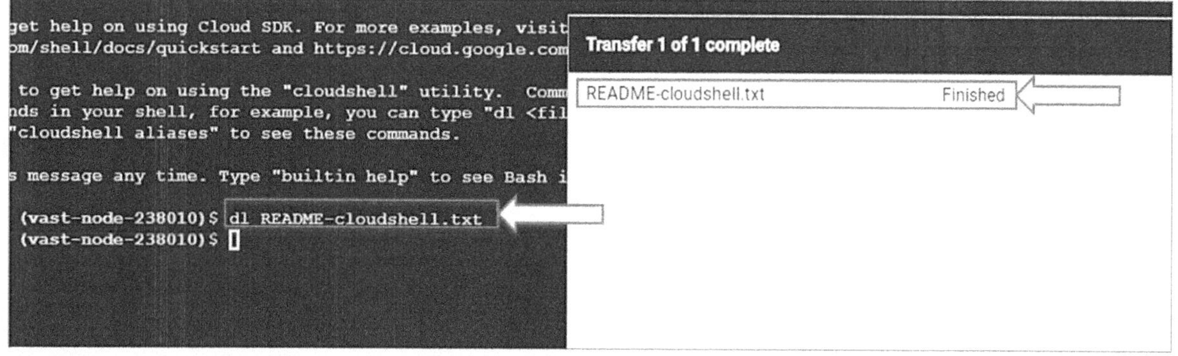

22. Now, let's take the lab files for this course.

23. Now, write this command on your editor window. The link of the repository is given below.

"https://github.com/IPSpecialist/ipspecialist-gcp-cloud-engineer.git"

```
$ git clone https://github.com/IPSpecialist/ipspecialist-gcp-cloud-engineer.git
```

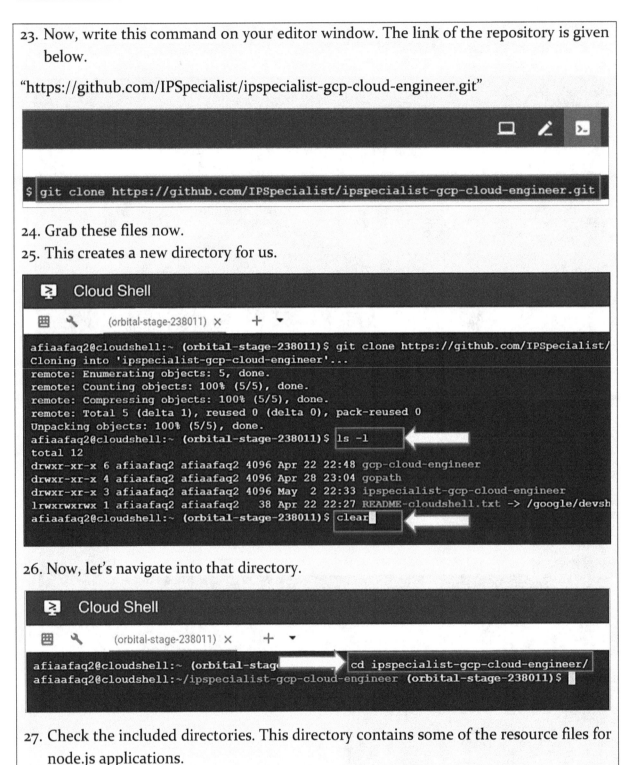

24. Grab these files now.
25. This creates a new directory for us.

```
Cloud Shell
(orbital-stage-238011) ×

afiaafaq2@cloudshell:~ (orbital-stage-238011)$ git clone https://github.com/IPSpecialist/
Cloning into 'ipspecialist-gcp-cloud-engineer'...
remote: Enumerating objects: 5, done.
remote: Counting objects: 100% (5/5), done.
remote: Compressing objects: 100% (5/5), done.
remote: Total 5 (delta 1), reused 0 (delta 0), pack-reused 0
Unpacking objects: 100% (5/5), done.
afiaafaq2@cloudshell:~ (orbital-stage-238011)$ ls -l
total 12
drwxr-xr-x 6 afiaafaq2 afiaafaq2 4096 Apr 22 22:48 gcp-cloud-engineer
drwxr-xr-x 4 afiaafaq2 afiaafaq2 4096 Apr 28 23:04 gopath
drwxr-xr-x 3 afiaafaq2 afiaafaq2 4096 May  2 22:33 ipspecialist-gcp-cloud-engineer
lrwxrwxrwx 1 afiaafaq2 afiaafaq2   38 Apr 22 22:27 README-cloudshell.txt -> /google/devsh
afiaafaq2@cloudshell:~ (orbital-stage-238011)$ clear
```

26. Now, let's navigate into that directory.

```
Cloud Shell
(orbital-stage-238011) ×

afiaafaq2@cloudshell:~ (orbital-stag      cd ipspecialist-gcp-cloud-engineer/
afiaafaq2@cloudshell:~/ipspecialist-gcp-cloud-engineer (orbital-stage-238011)$
```

27. Check the included directories. This directory contains some of the resource files for node.js applications.

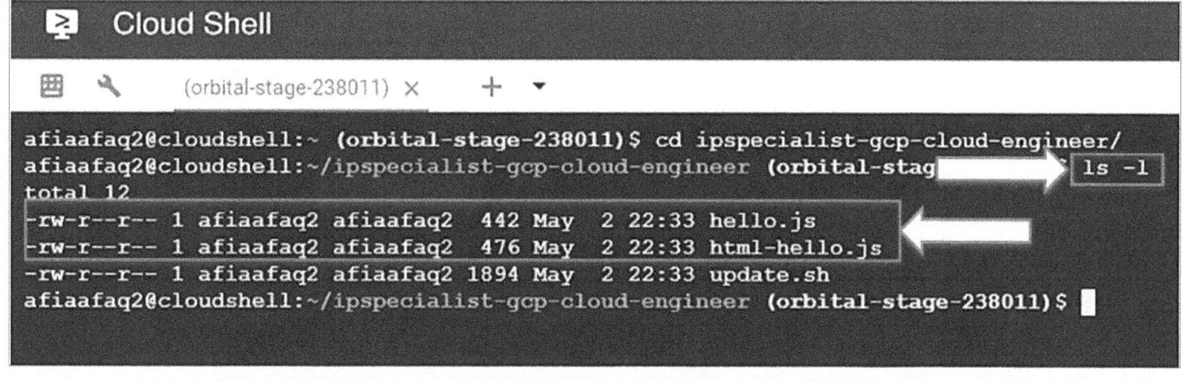

28. Run node hello.js command.
29. This application is running on this localhost address of port 8080.

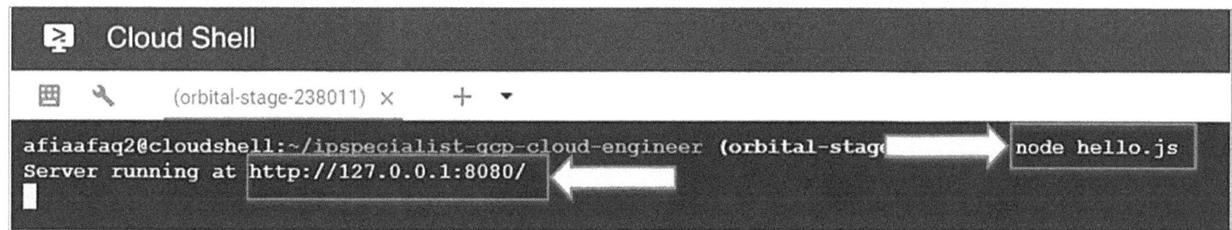

30. But if you try to navigate to the address, you can see it does not work because the local host on the browser is different from the local host of the Cloud Shell.

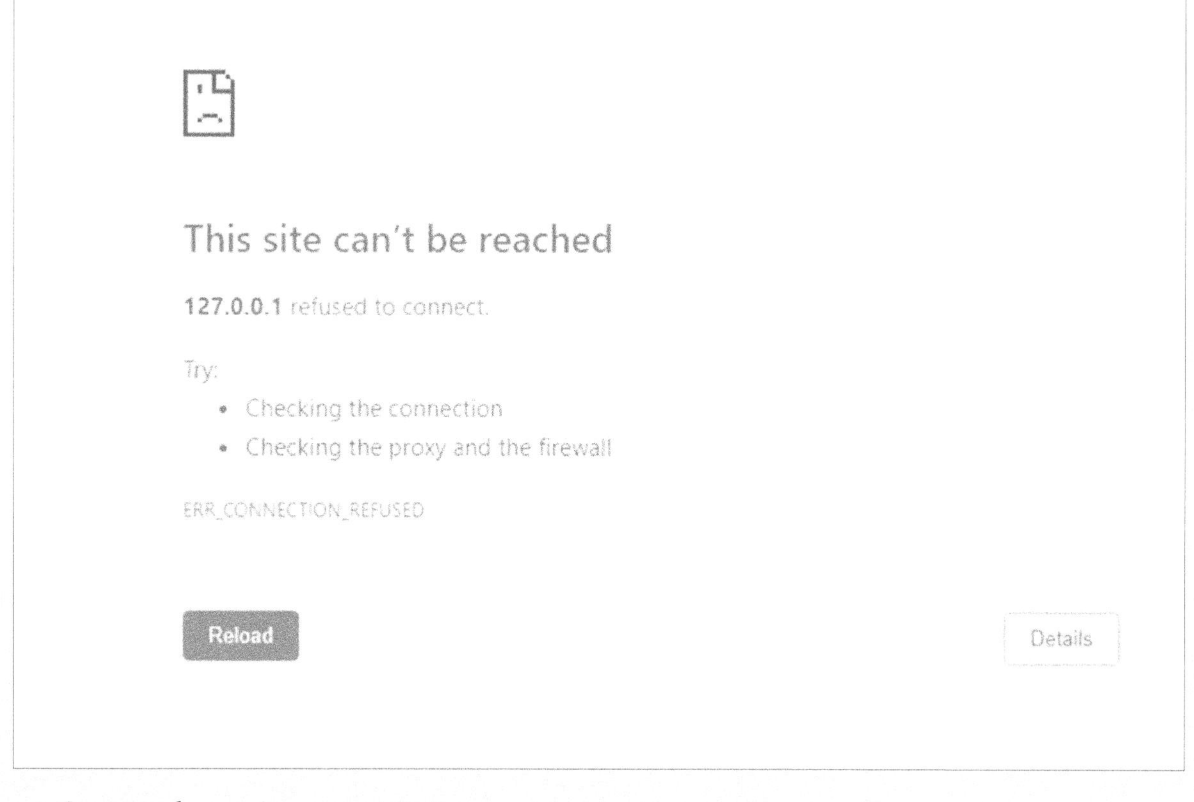

31. Go to web preview> port 8080.

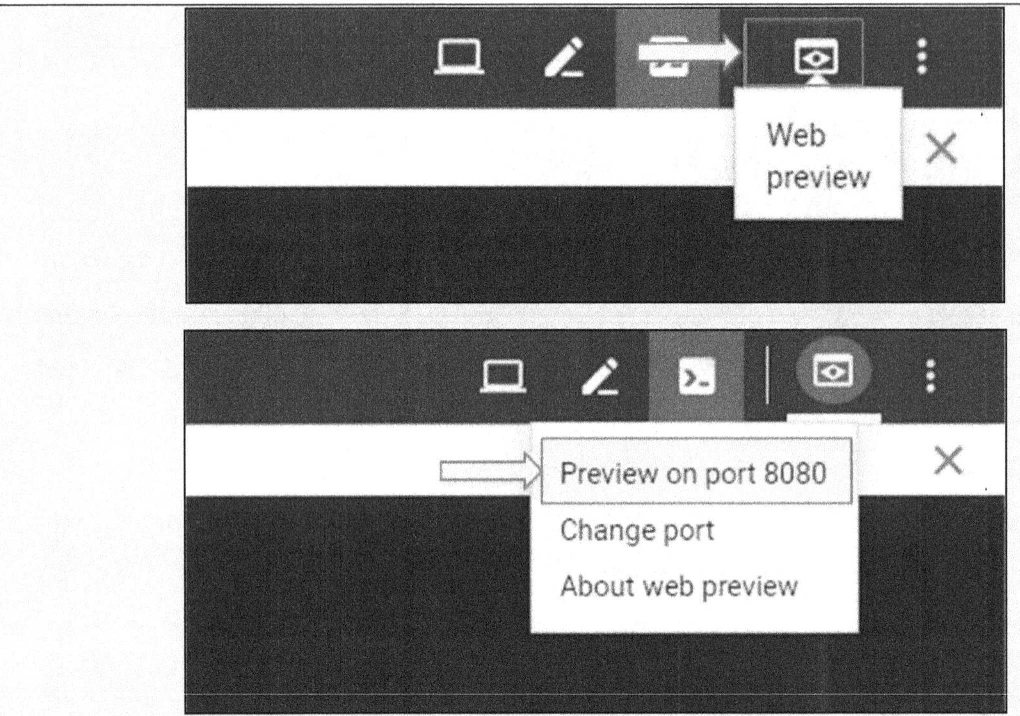

32. This app spot URL connects to the application running in the Cloud Shell.

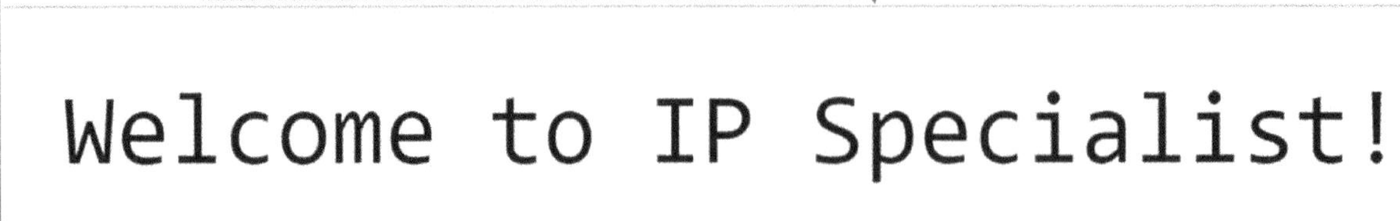

33. Go to the Editor Window, to preview the Code.
34. Click on this button to open up the Code Editor.

Cloud Shell

File Edit Selection View Go Help

afiaafaq2
gcp-cloud-engineer
gopath
ipspecialist-gcp-cloud-engineer
hello.js
html-hello.js
update.sh

hello.js html-hello.js hello.js

```
const http = require('http');

const hostname = '127.0.0.1';
const port = 8080;

const message = 'Welcome to IP Specialist!';
const fullMessage = `${message}\n`;

const server = http.createServer((request, response) => {
  response.statusCode = 200;
  response.setHeader('Content-Type', 'text/plain');
  response.end(fullMessage);
});
```

35. We can make changes in the code editor, and save it with Ctrl + S.

hello.js html-hello.js hello.js ×

```
const http = require('http');

const hostname = '127.0.0.1';
const port = 8080;

const message = 'Welcome to IP Specialist!!!!!!';
const fullMessage = `${message}\n`;

const server = http.createServer((request, response) => {
  response.statusCode = 200;
  response.setHeader('Content-Type', 'text/plain');
  response.end(fullMessage);
});
```

36. But this will not make any changes, because the node command does not execute the changes in the files.

Welcome to IP Specialist!

37. Press Ctrl + C to exit the program.
38. Run nodemon hello.js command.

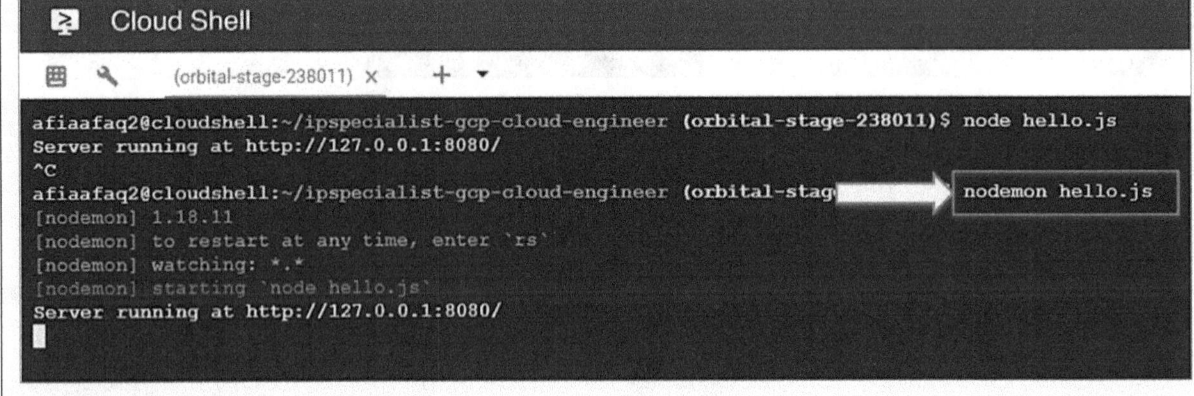

39. The changes will be executed.

Welcome to IP Specialist!!!!!!

40. Press Ctrl + C to stop the nodemon command and clear the screen.
41. Let's check the difference between a hello.js file and html-hello.js file.

Cloud Shell

(orbital-stage-238011)

```
afiaafaq2@cloudshell:~/ipspecialist-gcp-cloud-engineer (orbital-stag  diff hello.js html-hello.js
4c4
< const port = 8080;
---
> const port = 8081;
6,7c6,7
< const message = 'Welcome to IP Specialist!!!!!!';
< const fullMessage = `${message}\n`;
---
> const message = 'Welcome to IP Specialist!';
> const fullMessage = `<html><body><h1>${message}</h1></body></html>\n`;
11c11
<   response.setHeader('Content-Type', 'text/plain');
---
>   response.setHeader('Content-Type', 'text/html');
afiaafaq2@cloudshell:~/ipspecialist-gcp-cloud-engineer (orbital-stage-238011)$ clear
```

42. If we run nodemon command for html-hello.js file, it will run on a different port.

Cloud Shell

(orbital-stage-238011)

```
afiaafaq2@cloudshell:~/ipspecialist-gcp-cloud-engineer (orbital-stag nodemon html-hello.js
[nodemon] 1.18.11
[nodemon] to restart at any time, enter `rs`
[nodemon] watching: *.*
[nodemon] starting `node html-hello.js`
Server running at http://127.0.0.1:8081/
```

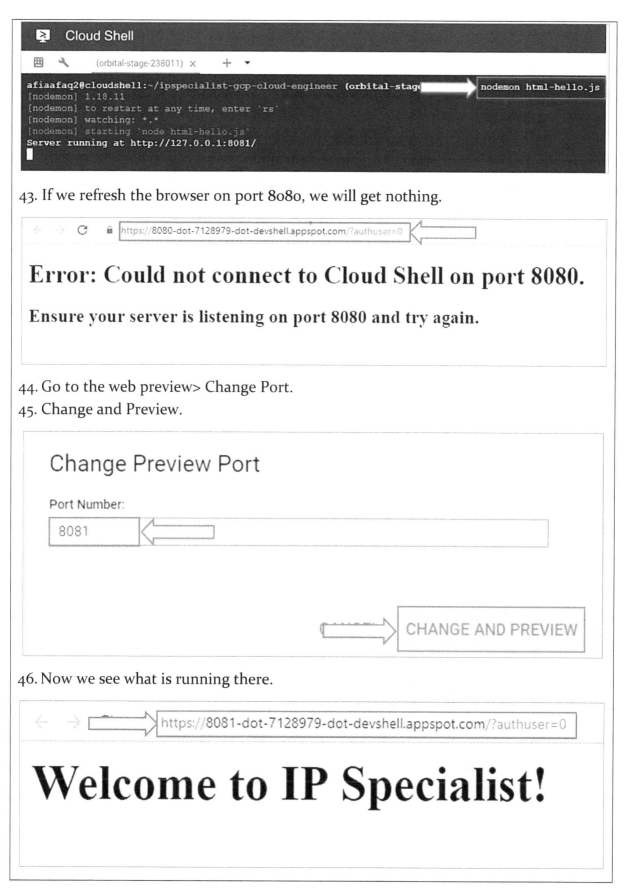

43. If we refresh the browser on port 8080, we will get nothing.

https://8080-dot-7128979-dot-devshell.appspot.com/?authuser=0

Error: Could not connect to Cloud Shell on port 8080.

Ensure your server is listening on port 8080 and try again.

44. Go to the web preview> Change Port.
45. Change and Preview.

Change Preview Port

Port Number:

8081

CHANGE AND PREVIEW

46. Now we see what is running there.

https://8081-dot-7128979-dot-devshell.appspot.com/?authuser=0

Welcome to IP Specialist!

Data Flows

The topic starts with the main concept describing, "In IT, Data Flow is everything." IT is all about applying technology in useful ways to handle information. If you try to learn and identify data flow and control data flow, you will succeed, but if you try to memorize situations and responses, then you will fail. Fundamentally, the data flow is described as taking some data or information and moving it around, processing it in interesting ways and remembering it. We associate these things with three classes of services including the network service, compute service and storage services. Moving data could also mean loading some data from disk into memory. To linking up the services through some integration that are basically in networking, this processing includes how a database might respond to a query or set a message service to filter what passes through it. Remembering also includes things like caching data in RAM or a content distribution network.

Mental Models

A Mental Model is the simplified version of reality, which is used by your mind to anticipate events or conclude what happened in the event. Beyond just one mental model, it is also important to recognize that systems do combine to build larger systems out of a smaller one, and to do that effectively, we need to use abstraction. A lot of the time it is not important what the details are, or what is happening inside the subsystem. But it is usually very helpful to understand at least the basics of what is going on and being able to zoom into subsystems and back out into the bigger system.

Cloud Shell Data Flow

Cloud Data Flow is a managed service which is used for executing a huge variety of data processing patterns. Let's start with your machine, on your machine you run a web browser; meanwhile running other things too. But those things do not affect the data flow. Inside the web browser, you open up the GCP Console and that reaches out to the Google Cloud Control Plane (a mathematical model where you can control the GCP services activities) Google Cloud makes sure that you have some persistent storage available for Cloud Shell data flow and finds a machine to host Cloud Shell instances.

On this machine, it starts a Container, and in the container, it starts a Secure Shell Server. There might be some other things running on that machine as well, but they do not disrupt the process. The Cloud Shell can now be connected from our browser to Secure Shell Server. Git command is used to get the files by connecting to Git hub and store those files to Cloud Shell Persistent Storage.

Run a Node against those files. The node will load them up and then wait for request to arrive on port 8080. In your web browser, you try to connect to port 8080, but localhost is just pointing back to your machine, means that it is not working. Instead, use the web preview where the Google Cloud sets up the proxy. Connect the URL of port 8080 through a particular proxy; it connects to port 8080 nodes running on the container of Cloud Shell Host Machine.

Open up the Cloud Shell Editor which connects to the lab files, and then make changes. Save those changes back to the persistent storage and then reload the browser, which connects back to the proxy on port 8080 on the Cloud Shell Container. There has been no data flow between the lab files and node process, so when you talk to the Node process, you will get all the versions of the page for 8080. If you want to check the effect of nodes, you have to get the data into the node process, that is why the node process should be stopped and then restarted using nodemon, again when the node process starts it reaches out and takes the files; the updated ones in this case. The nodemon process check those files. This is how the data flows through the system. We need to reload the browser, this time we will get the updated response.

If you want to check what is running on port 8081, we change the port, Google Cloud changes the proxy, opens up the web page and connects to the node. Since that proxy is configured for 8081, it does find the new node process and get the response.

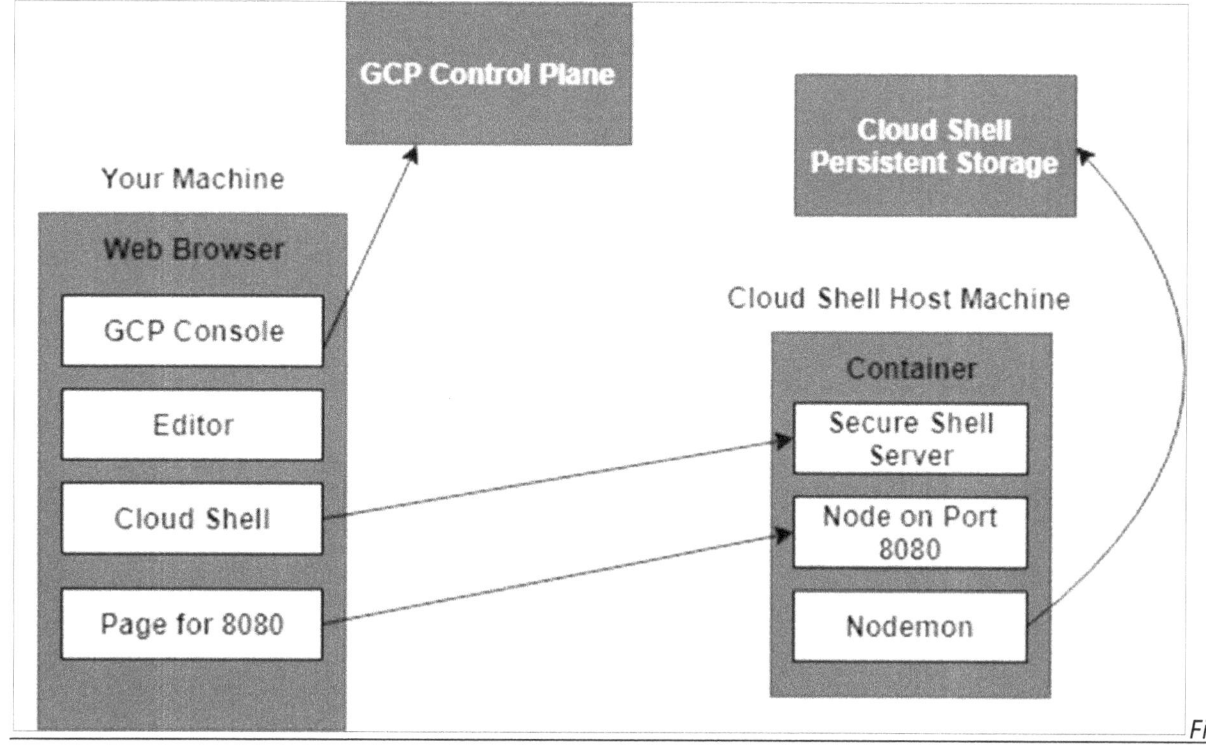

Figure 2-18: Data Flow Mental Model.

What happens if you update the files stored in Git Hub and you change the lab files? What happens if the Cloud Shell Persistent Storage becomes temporarily unavailable? When and how might you notice that? Understanding of this Mental Model and data flow must be very strong to understand this process. Data Flows are the foundation of every system, and they are made up of moving, processing and remembering information, not just network, compute and storage component. When you think about data flow, make sure you have built mental models. These models help you make predictions about what will happen and identify and think through the data flow; doing this can highlight potential issues.

Lab 2.6: Update Course Lab Files

Scenario: A user needs the update course lab file. How can the user find out that the course files are being updated and how can he/she use those updated files?

Solution: Updating the files manually is not a good approach to be taken for finding out whether the files are updated or not. First, you need to navigate to the course file and then search out the update.sh file. This file does not appear as the executable one. To make this file executable, you need to run the commands. Then the updated files will be available to use.

1. Log in to GCP Console with the user account.
2. Start Cloud Shell. In this lab, it does not matter which project you are using.

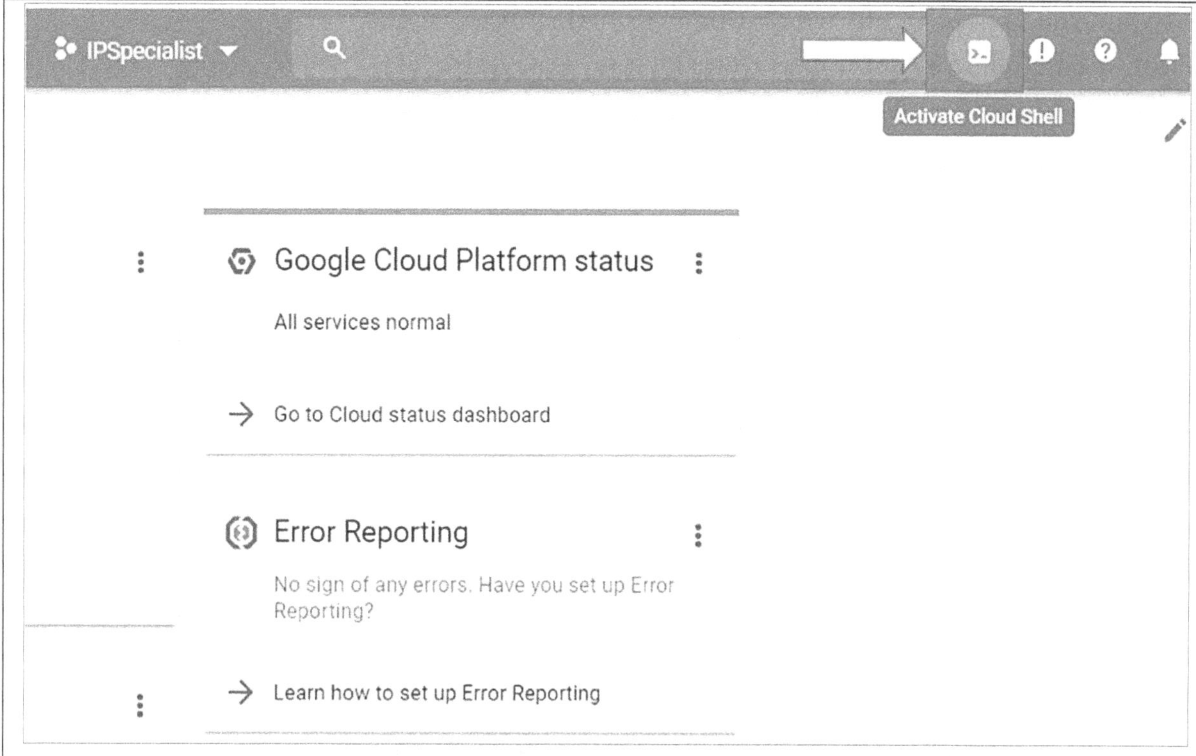

3. Let's check the present directory.

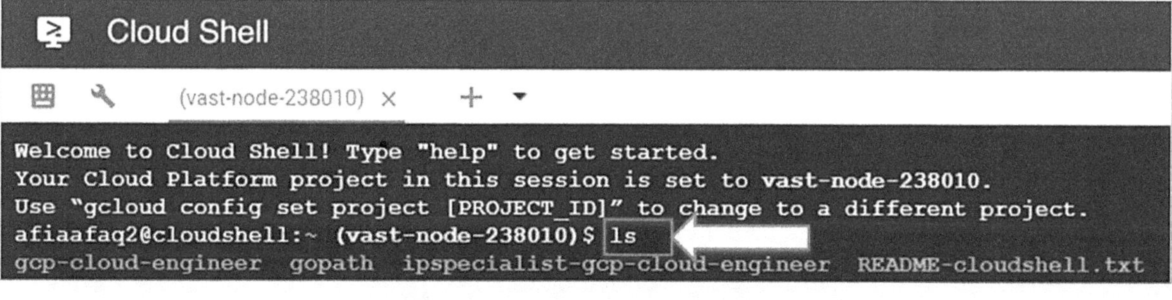

4. We have a README file and a cloned repository in the data.
5. Navigate into the ipspecialist-gcp-cloud-engineer repository.

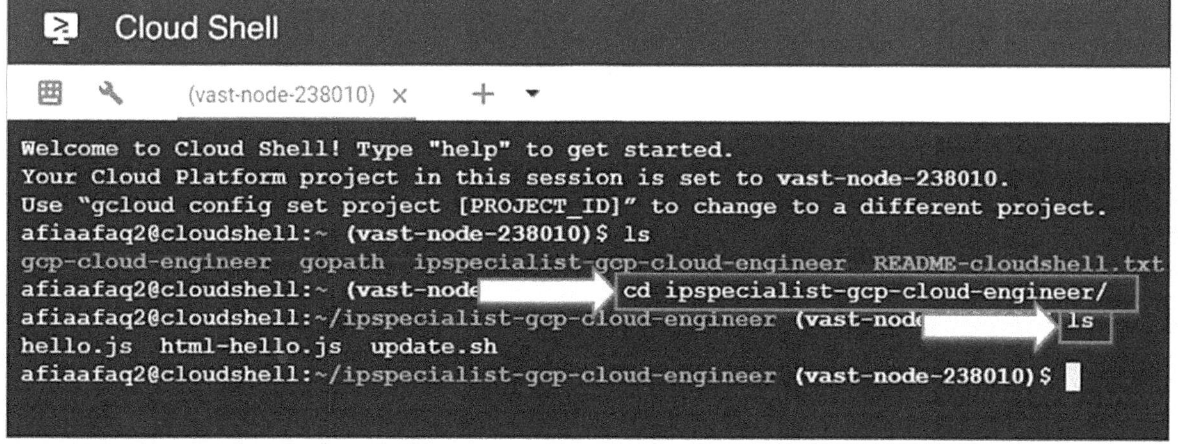

6. To run the update.sh file, we first need to make it executable.
7. Run the highlighted command to make it an executable file.

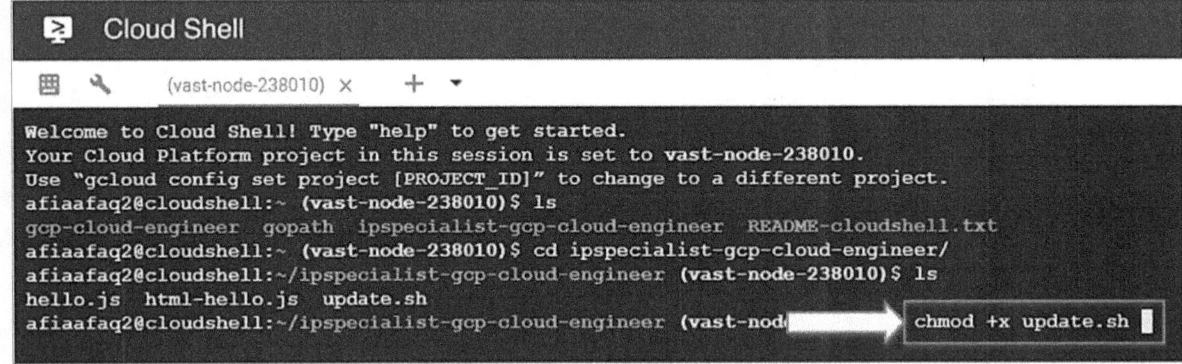

8. Run the script using "./update.sh."

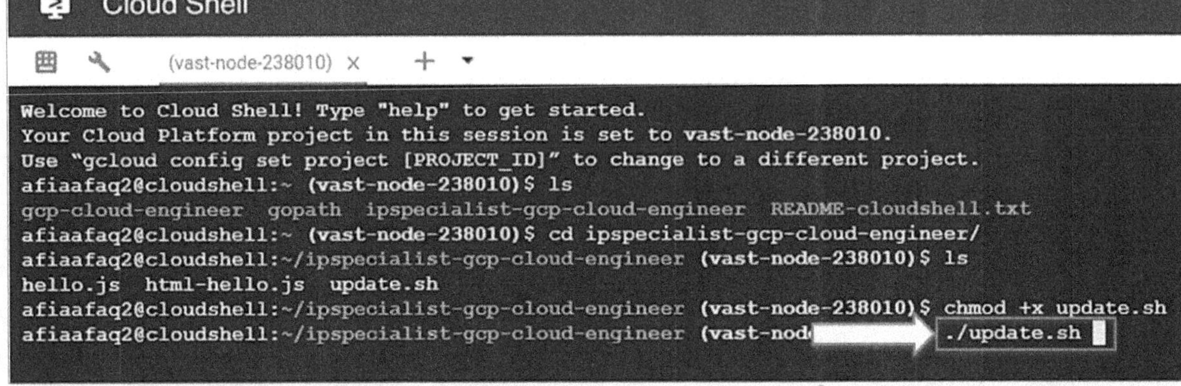

9. Here we can see all the files are updated now.

```
--------------------------------------------------------------------------------
Pulling latest changes...
--------------------------------------------------------------------------------
Already up-to-date.

--------------------------------------------------------------------------------
Finished.
--------------------------------------------------------------------------------
To get back any stashed changes, run:
  git stash apply
from inside the repo directory.

afiaafaq2@cloudshell:~/ipspecialist-gcp-cloud-engineer (vast-nod    ls
hello.js  html-hello.js  update.sh
afiaafaq2@cloudshell:~/ipspecialist-gcp-cloud-engineer (vast-node-238010)$
```

Milestone: Open World

Some people think that we have covered things a bit slowly, but that is the riskier part of what we do in this course. Looking back at the setup, we have gone through a number of real-world scenarios including how to set up billing, how to grant access to other users, etc. We have also been exposed to some services of Google Cloud, and we have taken a look at how data flows across the system, and that is something that you need to keep in mind. One of the important things is a project; you can make a project, do some activities and then delete the project. You have excellent isolation in the project. Each user has a quota of how many projects he can afford and your billing account has a separate quota of how many projects are linked to the billing account. Google automatically creates a project for your administrator account.

A Look-Back	The Road Ahead
Account properly Set up.	Explore.
Liability now limited.	The goal is to learn.
Real-world scenarios.	Do a Project.
Exposure to services.	Delete the Projects.
Data Flows.	Think About Data Flows.

Table 2-01: Milestone: Open World.

Mind Map

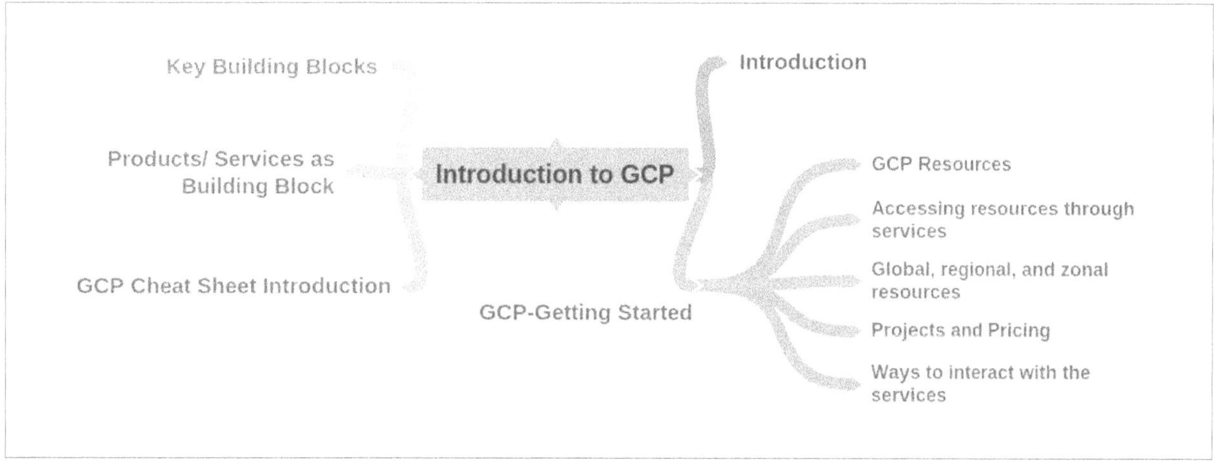

Figure 2-19: GCP Mind Map.

2-20: Chapter's Mind Map.

Practice Questions:

1. GCP Cheat Sheet was developed by Greg Wilson?
   A. True
   B. False

2. The GCP Cheat Sheet consists of:
   A. Compute Products.
   B. Storage Products.
   C. Networking Products.
   D. Management and Developer Tools.
   E. All of the Above.

3. Which search service is used by online retailers who are used for marketing their products for their site searches with several navigations?
   A. Google Site Search.
   B. Google Commerce Search.
   C. Google Search Appliance.
   D. Google Mini.

4. Which service is used as the Web traffic analysis tool for the internet?
   A. Big Analytics.
   B. Analytics.

C. BigQuery.
D. All of the Above.

5. Which of the following service provide offline access to online data?
   A. Gears.
   B. Bloggers.
   C. Offline.
   D. All of the Above.

6. _______________ is a platform used for cloud computing which provides infrastructure tools and services for users which helps in building applications and services.
   A. GCP.
   B. AWS.
   C. Azure.
   D. None of the Above.

7. ____________ is considered as the third biggest cloud provider in terms of revenue.
   A. Amazon Web Services.
   B. Google Cloud Platform.
   C. Microsoft Azure.
   D. None of the Above.

8. In which year Google announced its first cloud platform, Google App Engine?
   A. 2005.
   B. 2006.
   C. 2007.
   D. 2008.

9. Compute Engine in Compute Products can be described as:
   A. Virtual Machines.
   B. Disks.
   C. Networks.
   D. All of the Above.

10. Cloud Function is described as Event-driven server less function. Cloud Function even perform faster than the Compute Engine within the 10th of the second and

manages all the scaling for you automatically.

A. Event-driven server less function.
B. Event-driven function.
C. Serverless function.
D. None of the Above.

11. Which service is described as object storage and serving?

A. Cloud Compute.
B. Cloud Storage.
C. Data and Analytics Service.
D. Networking Products.

12. Nearline and Coldline lie under the services of:

A. Cloud Compute.
B. Cloud Storage.
C. Data and Analytics Product.
D. Networking Products.

13. The Cloud Storage Product is:

A. Object-Based Storage.
B. Block Based Storage.
C. Both A and B.
D. None of the Above.

14. The persistent disk is:

A. Object-Based Storage.
B. Block Based Storage.
C. Both A and B.
D. None of the Above.

15. Cloud File Store sits between these two applications:

A. Cloud Storage and Persistent Disk.
B. Coldline and Nearline.
C. Cloud Storage and Coldline.
D. Cloud Storage and Nearline.

16. Cloud File Store is:

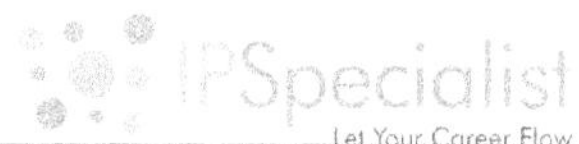

A. Object-Based Storage.
B. Block Based Storage.
C. Both A and B.
D. Neither Object-Based nor Block Based.

17. Cloud TPU stands for:
    A. Transfer Flow Processing Unit.
    B. Transfer Processing Unit.
    C. Transferring Flow Process Unit.
    D. Transferring Process Unit.

18. The Cloud TPU is enlisted in:
    A. Compute Products Section.
    B. Storage Product Section.
    C. AI and Machine Learning Section.
    D. Data and Analytics Section.

19. The Cloud Speech-to-Text will convert:
    A. Audio to Text.
    B. Text to Audio.
    C. Audio to Audio.
    D. Text to Text.

20. The Cloud Text-to-Speech will convert:
    A. Audio to Text.
    B. Text to Audio.
    C. Audio to Audio.
    D. Text to Text.

21. Spark and Hadoop manage _______________.
    A. Cloud Dataflow.
    B. Cloud Dataproc.
    C. Bigtable.
    D. BigQuery.

22. It handles both stream and batch data processing:
    A. Cloud Dataflow.

B. Cloud Dataproc.
C. Bigtable.
D. BigQuery.

23. Which service is used as a Data Warehouse and Analytics service?
A. Cloud Dataflow.
B. Cloud Dataproc.
C. Bigtable.
D. BigQuery.

24. Each GCP project contains:
A. A project name.
B. A project ID.
C. A project number.
D. All of the Above.

25. When you create a free tier account for GCP, you also get ___________ credit that you can use for up to 12 months, and this feature defines your free-tier account.
A. USD 300.
B. USD 200.
C. USD 100.
D. USD 350.

Chapter 03: Basic Services

Introduction

In this chapter, we will discuss the two main basic services of Google Cloud Platform, which are Google Cloud Storage and Google Compute Engine. We will discuss the storage classes, features and access controls of GCS. We will learn how to create a bucket in GCP. In this, we will also learn about command line tool GCloud.

We will also be discussing different machine types, instance lifecycle and many more features of GCE.

Google Cloud Storage

Cloud Storage is a service in the Google Cloud, which allows you to store or retrieve any amount of data worldwide at any time. Cloud Storage can be used for a variety of scenarios including serving website contents, storing archival and disaster recovery data or directly downloading large data objects to users.

Key Terms

To make effective use of Cloud Storage, you should understand some of the concepts that it is based on. Let us discuss an overview of key Cloud Storage terms and concepts.

Projects

Within a project, all data is in Cloud Storage. A project consists of a set of users, a set of APIs, and settings for those APIs needs to be billed, authenticated and monitored. You can have one or more projects.

Buckets

All the data you store in Cloud Storage must be stored in a bucket. Buckets are your data's basic containers. Buckets can be used to organize your data and control access to your data, but you cannot nest buckets, unlike directories and folders. Because bucket creation and deletion are limited, your storage applications should be designed to support intensive object operations and relatively few bucket operations. On creation of a bucket, you need to define its a name, location, and default Cloud Storage. Once the bucket is created, you can change the default storage type to any storage class.

The bucket must be globally unique as it exists in a single Cloud Storage namespace.

Bucket Labels

Bucket labels are key: value metadata pairs through which you can group your bucket to other GCP resources such as virtual machine instances and persistent disks. You have a limit of 64 labels per bucket. Some key points you need to remember for bucket labels are:

- Keys and values must not be longer than 63 characters each. It can only contain lowercase letters, numeric characters, underscores, and dashes. international characters are allowed
- Label keys cannot be empty. Label keys must start with a lowercase letter, and international characters are allowed

Objects

Objects are data item in Cloud Storage that you store. The number of objects you can create in a bucket is unlimited. Objects are composed of two components: data and metadata of objects. Object data is a file that you typically want to save in Cloud Storage, while metadata is the collection of name-value pairs, which defines the numerous qualities of objects. An object is considered as a chunk of object metadata, which is in 1024 bytes in length (maximum) and contains a combination of UTF-8 encoded.

Object Versions and Generation Numbers

Each object has its multiple versions; by default, whenever an object is overwritten, its older version is deleted and replaced by the new version. If versioning of object is enabled on the bucket, then all older versions are kept stored with generation number to identify it. In this way, you can restore the older version or either delete it depending on your requirement.

Resources

A resource is a Google Cloud Platform entity. In Google Cloud Platform, every project, bucket, and object is a resource, like Compute Engine instance. There is a unique name of each resource, and for indicating a specific generation of resource, you can append a number at the end of the resource name.

Geo-Redundancy

Geo-redundancy in data means that data is to be kept in redundancy in at least two separate geographical sites, separated by at least 100 miles, regardless of their storage class. With Geo-Redundancy you have maximum availability of data in case if a natural disaster occurs.

Data Opacity

The data component of an object is entirely opaque to Cloud Storage. It is a piece of data.

Object Immutability

Objects are immutable and cannot be modified throughout their storage life after uploading. The time between successfully creating (uploading) and successful object deletion is the storage duration of an object. When you overwrite an object, then until the new object successfully uploaded, the older version of the object is available to the reader. Once the object overwrites, the previous immutable object's lifetime ends and new immutable object's lifetime begins. How fast you can build or update various objects in a bucket can never be limited. However, only one object per second may be updated or overwritten.

Hierarchy

To store the objects in Google Cloud Storage, a flat namespace is used while there are still some tools that can be used to work with the objects that have a virtual hierarchy to store.

Namespace

There is only one namespace for cloud storage, so every bucket has a unique name throughout the entire Cloud Storage. Object names with in a bucket must be unique.

Projects

Let us now discuss the relationship between GCP Console and Google Cloud Storage. As we learned above, project is a place where all GCP resources are organized. A project includes a set of users; a set of APIs; and the API settings for billing, authenticating, and monitoring. You can create one or more projects to organize GCP resources.

Project Members and Permissions

Via IAM, you can add members in a project who manages it or work on it. With IAM, you can specify the roles in which you define different permissions for each member to perform various things on the project. As we discussed earlier in the section "Roles" of chapter 1, about the primitive roles that applied only to the project.

Role	**Permission**
Roles/Viewer	Members with this role can list buckets in the project
Roles/Editor	Members with this role can list, create and delete buckets in the project

Roles/Owner	Members with this role can list, build and delete project buckets. Within Google Cloud Platform, roles/owners can perform management tasks like change project members' roles or change billing.

Table 3-01: Permissions on Basis Project Member

Service Accounts

We have discussed "Service Accounts" in Chapter 1 under the services of GCP. It is also used for application authentication and GCP resources and services accessed. For instance, you can create a service account for accessing objects stored in cloud storage buckets. It can be identified via the unique E-mail address within a project. For example: service-[PROJECT_NUMBER]@gs-project-accounts.iam.gserviceaccount.com

Storage Classes

At first, when a bucket is created, you need to specify three main things; bucket name, location, and storage class. Cloud Storage has four different types of storage classes:

- Multi-Regional Storage
- Regional Storage
- Nearline Storage
- Coldline Storage

There is a default Storage Class in each bucket, which you define at creation time, but you can change it later. This will not be changed for the objects that are already present in the bucket. Default Storage Class is only changed for those who are added after the changing. To change the storage class of individual objects, you can use API.

Standard Storage

As we know, there is a default storage class, which is also known as Standard Storage in API. When your bucket is associated with a regional location, then Standard Storage is equivalent to Regional Storage class. When the bucket is at multi-regional level, then it is equivalent to Multi-Regional Storage class.

Multi-Regional Storage

Multi-regional Google Cloud storage stores data in data centers worldwide with 99.95% availability. It is suitable for businesses requiring frequent access to data, such as website content, mobile application data, and interactive workloads. In at least two separate locations, multi-regional data are stored, which improves availability; that is why it is geo-redundant. Depending on where you are, it will cost you $0.026 per gigabyte per month.

Regional Storage

Instead of spreading over a large geographic location, Regional storage stores data in one geographic location at a low cost. It is best suited for computing, analytical and machine learning work. It offers 99.9% availability. Google Cloud Regional Storage ensures high performance and availability when storing and computing resources are in the same region. Data storage can reduce network charges at a regional level. Google Cloud Regional Storage costs a monthly $0.02 per GB.

Nearline Storage

Nearline storage is for storing data that are infrequently accessed. It is a low-cost storage with low availability and a minimum of 30 days storage duration. Google Cloud Storage Nearline is intended for clients who need long-term storage of data accessibility in less than once a month. It is suitable for data archiving, data backup and disaster recovery. Google Cloud Storage Nearline provides 99% availability and has at least a 30-day storage time. Customers pay a monthly fee of $0.01 per GB, and the mandatory data collection fee is $0.01 per GB.

There is geo-redundancy of Nearline storage data in which it stored data on multi-regional location, so it provides high availability as compared to Nearline Storage data in a regional location.

Coldline Storage

Coldline Storage is a durable storage with low cost for DR, backup, and data archiving. In this, your data will be available within milliseconds. Google Cloud Storage Coldline is designed for clients who need data availability in less than once a year to save information. It requires a minimum storage period of 90 days, and while the lowest of three storage levels is $0.007/GB per month, there is a fee for $0.05 per GB of data recovery.

Comparision of Storage Classes

Storage Class	Characteristics	Price	Use Cases
Multi-Regional Storage	• >99.99% typical monthly availability • 99.95% availability SLA* • Geo-redundant	$0.026	Storing data that is frequently accessed ("hot" objects) Used around the world for serving website content, streaming videos, or gaming and mobile applications
Regional	• 99.99% typical	$0.020	Storing frequently accessed data

Storage	monthly availability • 99.9% availability SLA* • Redundant across availability zones		within the same region as your Google Cloud DataProc or GCE instances that use it for data analytics
Nearline Storage	• 99.95% typical monthly availability (multi-regional locations); 99.9% typical monthly availability (regional locations) • 99.9% availability SLA* (multi-regional locations); 99.0% availability SLA* (regional locations) • 30-day minimum storage duration	$0.010	Data, which is not expected to be accessed frequently (i.e., no more than once per month). Ideal for back-up and serving long-tail multimedia content
Coldline Storage	• 99.95% monthly availability in multi-regional locations; 99.9% monthly availability in regional locations • 99.9% availability SLA in multi-regional locations; 99.0% availability SLA in regional locations • 90-day minimum storage duration	$0.007	Data, which is accessed infrequently (i.e., no more than once per year). Typically, this is for disaster recovery or for the data that is archived and may or may not be needed at some future time

Table 3-02: Comparison between Storage Classes

Per Object Storage Class

Storage classes per object allow you to assign specific storage classes in a bucket to individual objects. You can choose to specify a storage class for an object when you upload them. The storage class of an object already present on your bucket can also be changed without moving the object to another bucket or changing the object URL. As we know that if the object storage class is not specified at uploading time, then it is stored in default storage class of bucket. You can change the storage class of bucket without affecting the existing object storage class.

When you specify the storage class of an object, then it depends on the location of the bucket that holds the object. In Google Cloud Storage, you have object life cycle management, which allows you to manage the classes of the object in a bucket.

Lab 3.1- Creating a Bucket via GCP Console and Cloud SDK

Scenario:

An organization needs to use Google Cloud as a Cloud Platform to store its files in the Cloud for security reasons. The storage must have the capability to change in any type as per the requirement with the previously uploaded objects in their storage type. To achieve this, the solution has been done in two different ways.

Solution:

By using GCS service in GCP via Console and Google Cloud SDK, they can meet their requirement.

1. Login to your GCP Console and select a project on which you want to create storage.

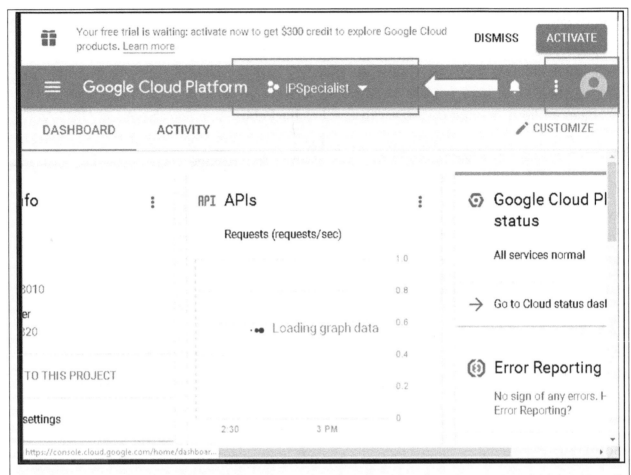

2. Go to the left side of the window on top click on the icon mention below and select "Storage".

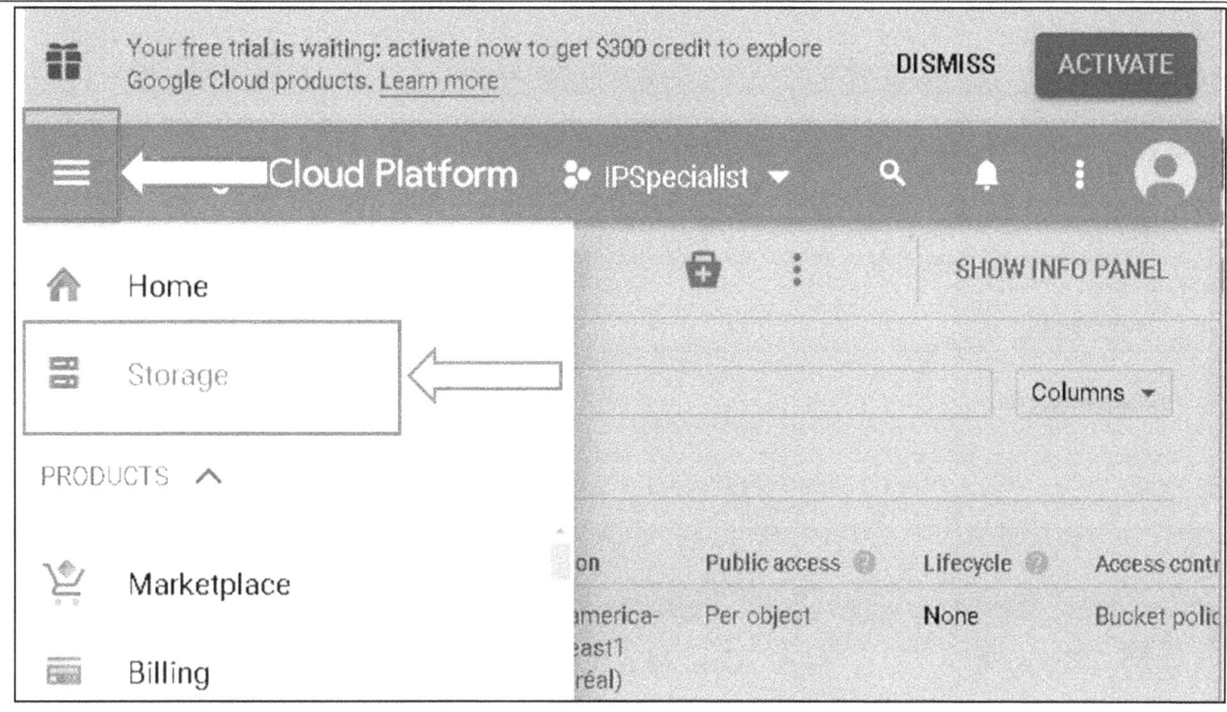

3. Click on “Create Bucket”.

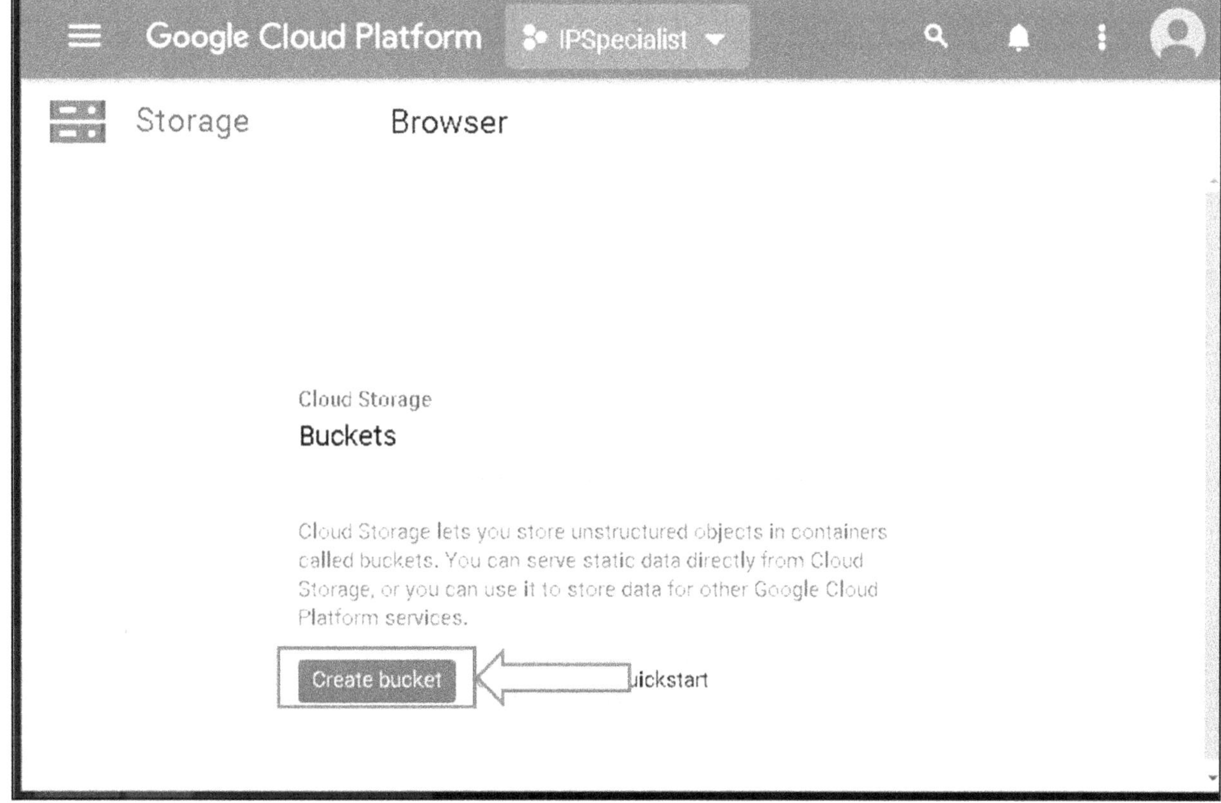

4. Now enter the name of the bucket, which must be globally unique. Also, select the storage class of your choice as per requirement.

Google Cloud Platform IPSpecialist

Storage ← Create a bucket

Name
Must be unique across Cloud Storage. If you're serving website content, enter the website domain as the name.

ips-storagelab1

Default storage class
Objects added to this bucket are assigned the selected storage class by default. An object's storage class and bucket location affect its geo-redundancy, availability, and costs. You can set storage classes for individual objects in gsutil. Learn more

Google Cloud Platform IPSpecialist

Storage ← Create a bucket

costs. You can set storage classes for individual objects in gsutil. Learn more

Nearline and Coldline data in multi-regional locations is now stored geo-redundantly. New locations nam4 and eur4 (available in beta) enable co-location of compute and storage for high performance with geo-redundancy. Learn more Dismiss

- Multi-Regional
- Regional
- Nearline
- Coldline

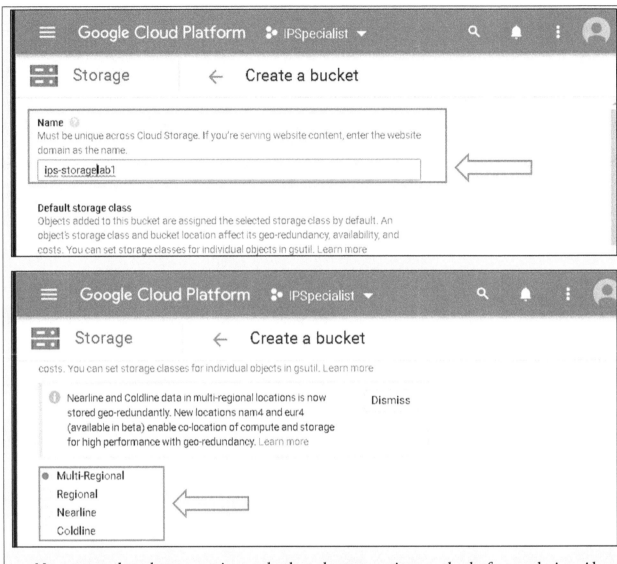

5. Now, go to the advance setting and select the encryption method of your choice. Also, add labels by clicking on "Add Labels".

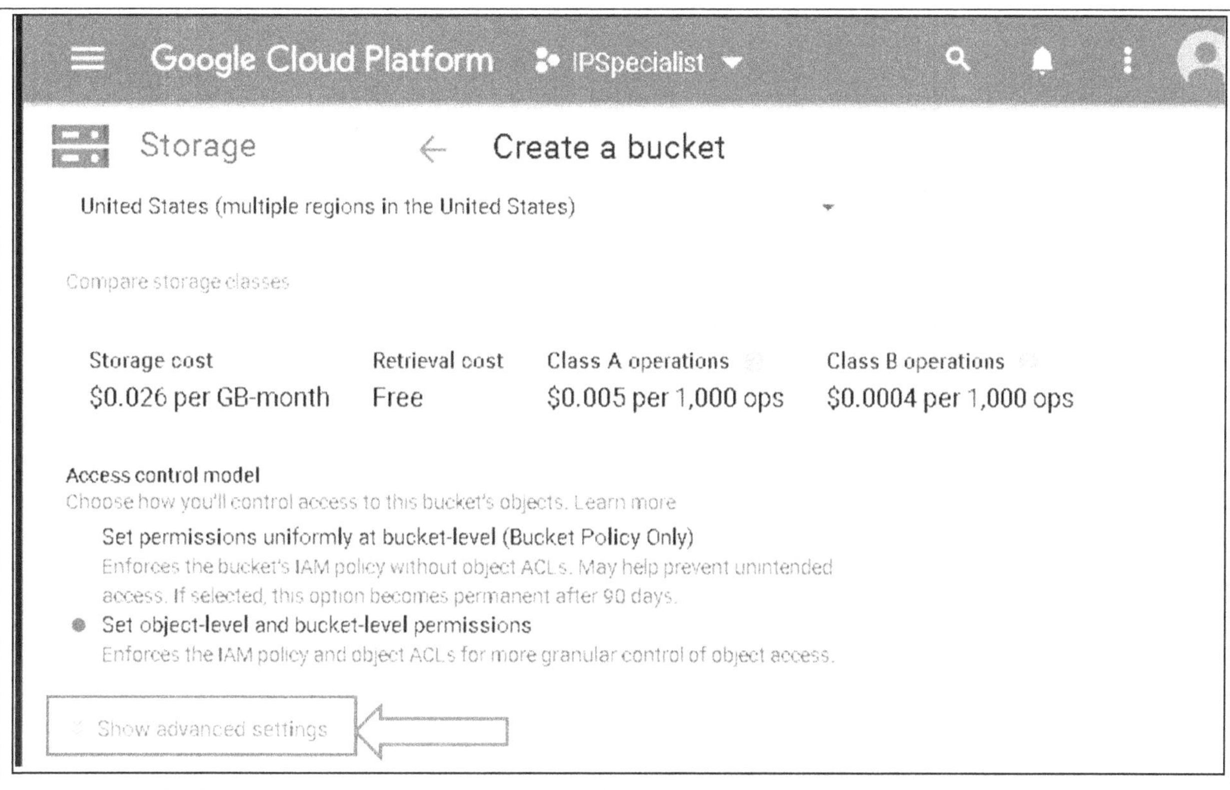
Google Cloud Platform
IPSpecialist
Storage
Create a bucket
United States (multiple regions in the United States)
Compare storage classes
Storage cost
$0.026 per GB-month
Retrieval cost
Free
Class A operations
$0.005 per 1,000 ops
Class B operations
$0.0004 per 1,000 ops
Access control model
Choose how you'll control access to this bucket's objects. Learn more
Set permissions uniformly at bucket-level (Bucket Policy Only)
Enforces the bucket's IAM policy without object ACLs. May help prevent unintended access. If selected, this option becomes permanent after 90 days.
Set object-level and bucket-level permissions
Enforces the IAM policy and object ACLs for more granular control of object access.
Show advanced settings

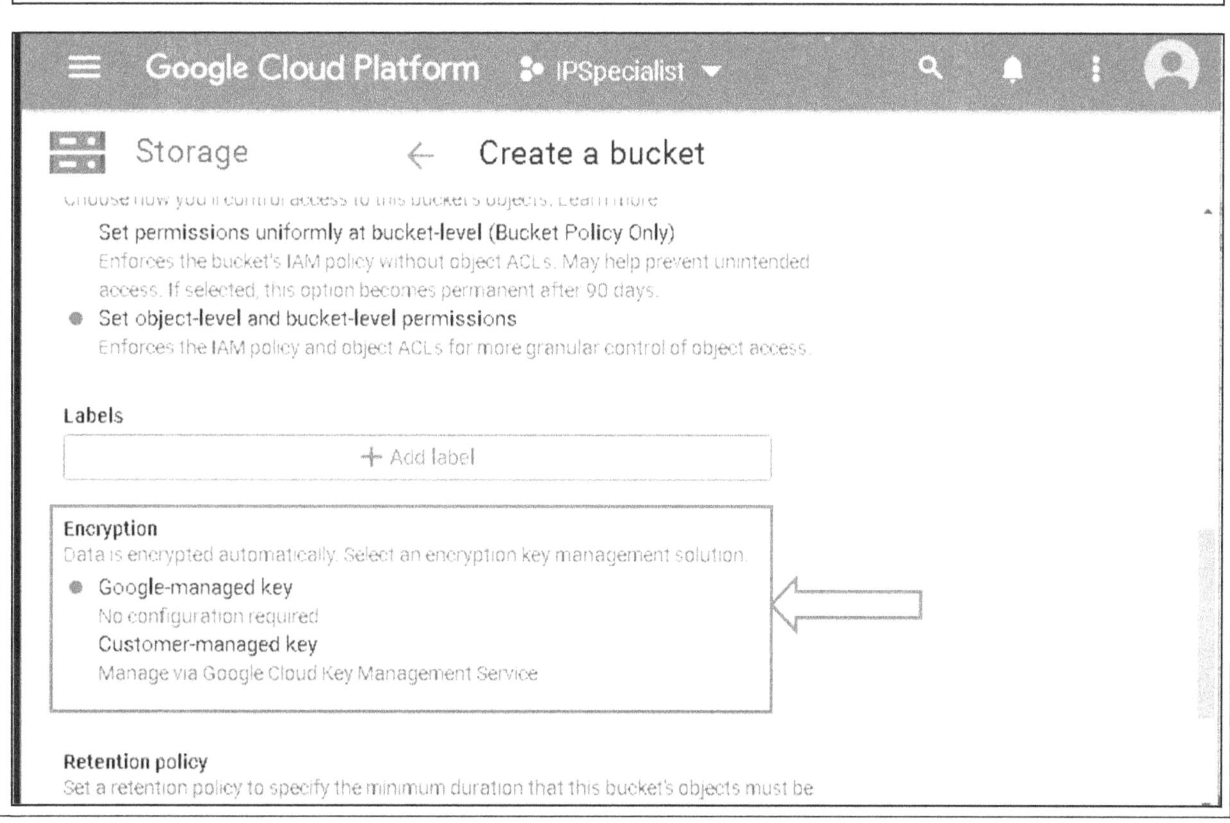
Google Cloud Platform
IPSpecialist
Storage
Create a bucket
Set permissions uniformly at bucket-level (Bucket Policy Only)
Enforces the bucket's IAM policy without object ACLs. May help prevent unintended access. If selected, this option becomes permanent after 90 days.
Set object-level and bucket-level permissions
Enforces the IAM policy and object ACLs for more granular control of object access.
Labels
+ Add label
Encryption
Data is encrypted automatically. Select an encryption key management solution.
Google-managed key
No configuration required
Customer-managed key
Manage via Google Cloud Key Management Service
Retention policy
Set a retention policy to specify the minimum duration that this bucket's objects must be

Google Cloud Platform IPSpecialist

Storage ← Create a bucket

Set permissions uniformly at bucket-level (Bucket Policy Only)
Enforces the bucket's IAM policy without object ACLs. May help prevent unintended access. If selected, this option becomes permanent after 90 days.
Set object-level and bucket-level permissions
Enforces the IAM policy and object ACLs for more granular control of object access.

Labels
+ Add label

Encryption
Data is encrypted automatically. Select an encryption key management solution.
Google-managed key
No configuration required
Customer-managed key
Manage via Google Cloud Key Management Service

Google Cloud Platform IPSpecialist

Storage ← Create a bucket

Set permissions uniformly at bucket-level (Bucket Policy Only)
Enforces the bucket's IAM policy without object ACLs. May help prevent unintended access. If selected, this option becomes permanent after 90 days.
Set object-level and bucket-level permissions
Enforces the IAM policy and object ACLs for more granular control of object access.

Labels
Key Value
task lab
+ Add label

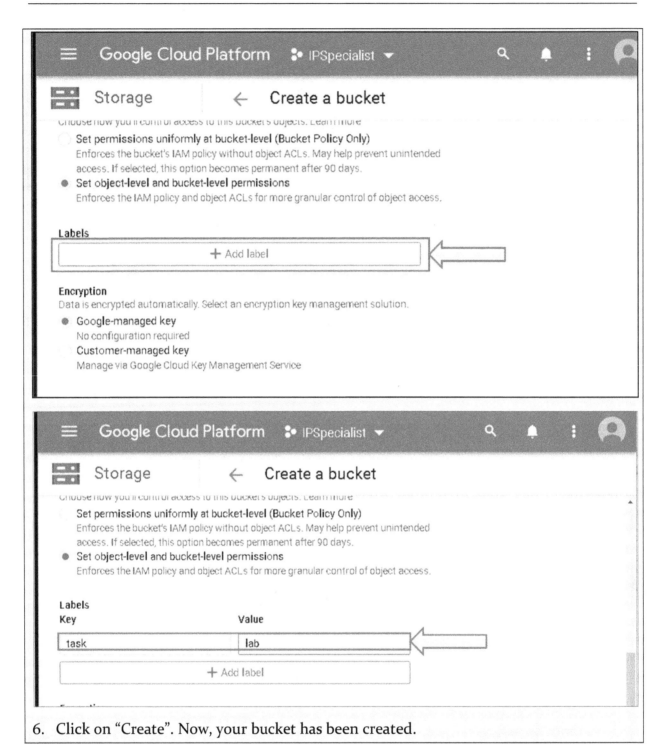

6. Click on "Create". Now, your bucket has been created.

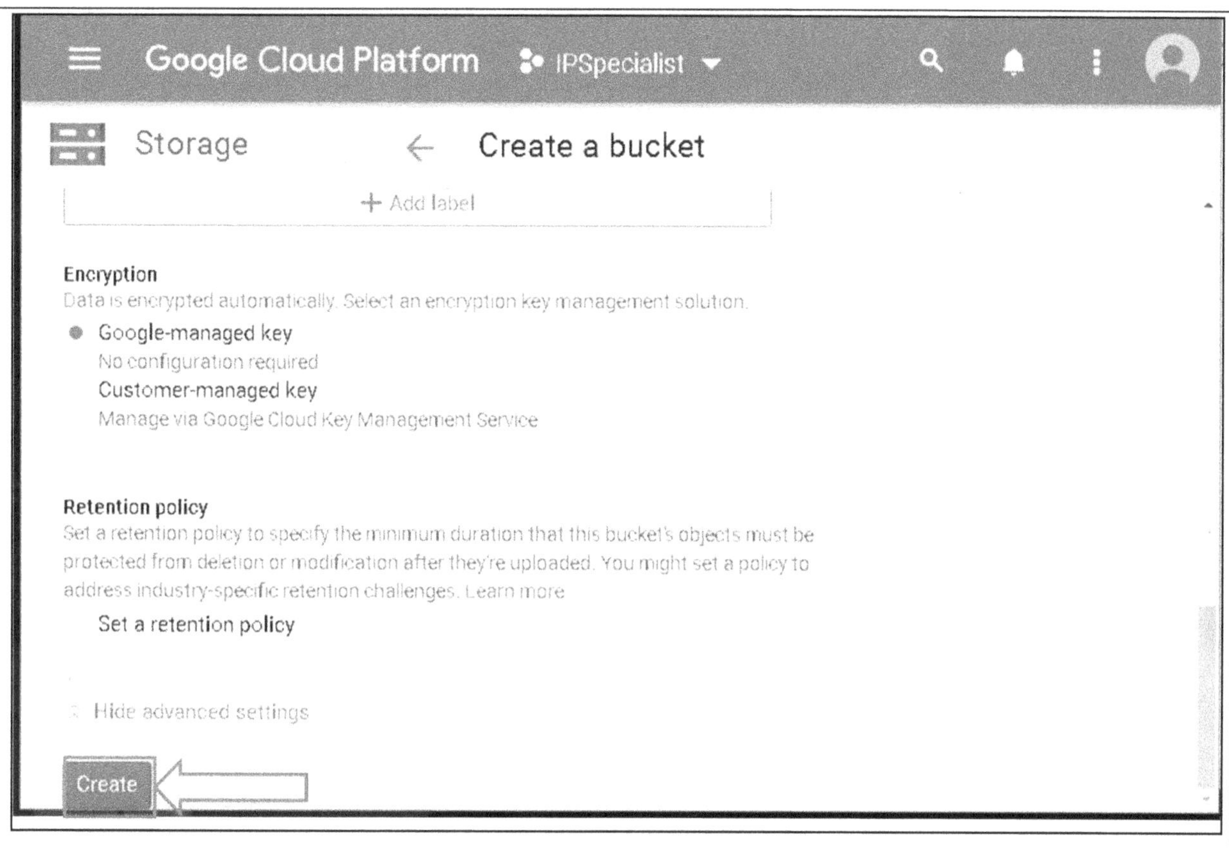

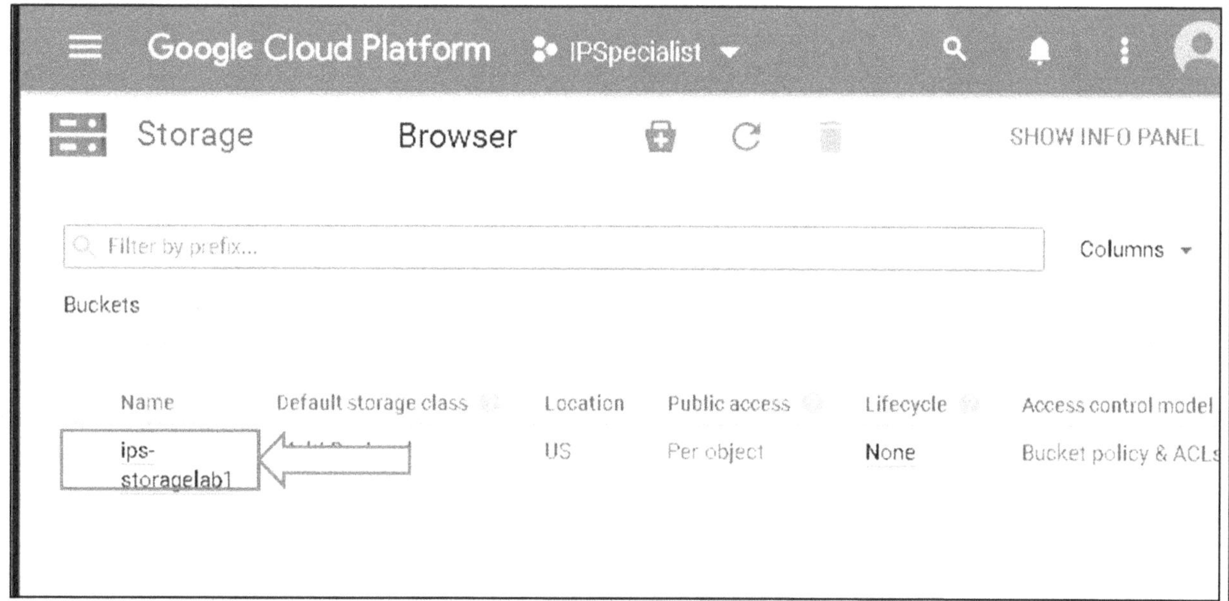

7. To upload files in the bucket, click on "Upload Files". Now, add the files you want to store in GCS.

Google Cloud Platform
IPSpecialist
Storage
Bucket details
EDIT BUCKET
ips-storagelab1
Objects
Overview
Permissions
Bucket Lock
Upload files
Create folder
Manage holds
Delete
Filter by prefix...
Buckets / ips-storagelab1
Open
This PC › Pictures › Screenshots
Search Screenshots
Organize
New folder
This PC
3D Objects
Desktop
Documents
Downloads
Galaxy S7
Music
Pictures
Videos
Local Disk (C:)
Local Disk (D:)
Network
Screenshot (33)
Screenshot (35)
Screenshot (36)
Screenshot (37)
Screenshot (38)
Screenshot (39)
Screenshot (40)
Screenshot (41)
Screenshot (42)
Screenshot (43)
Screenshot (44)
Screenshot (45)
File name: Screenshot (35)
All Files
Open

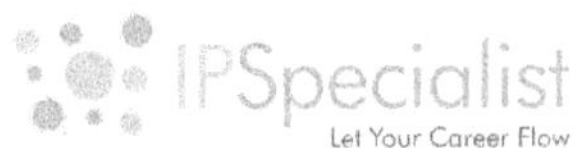

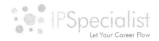

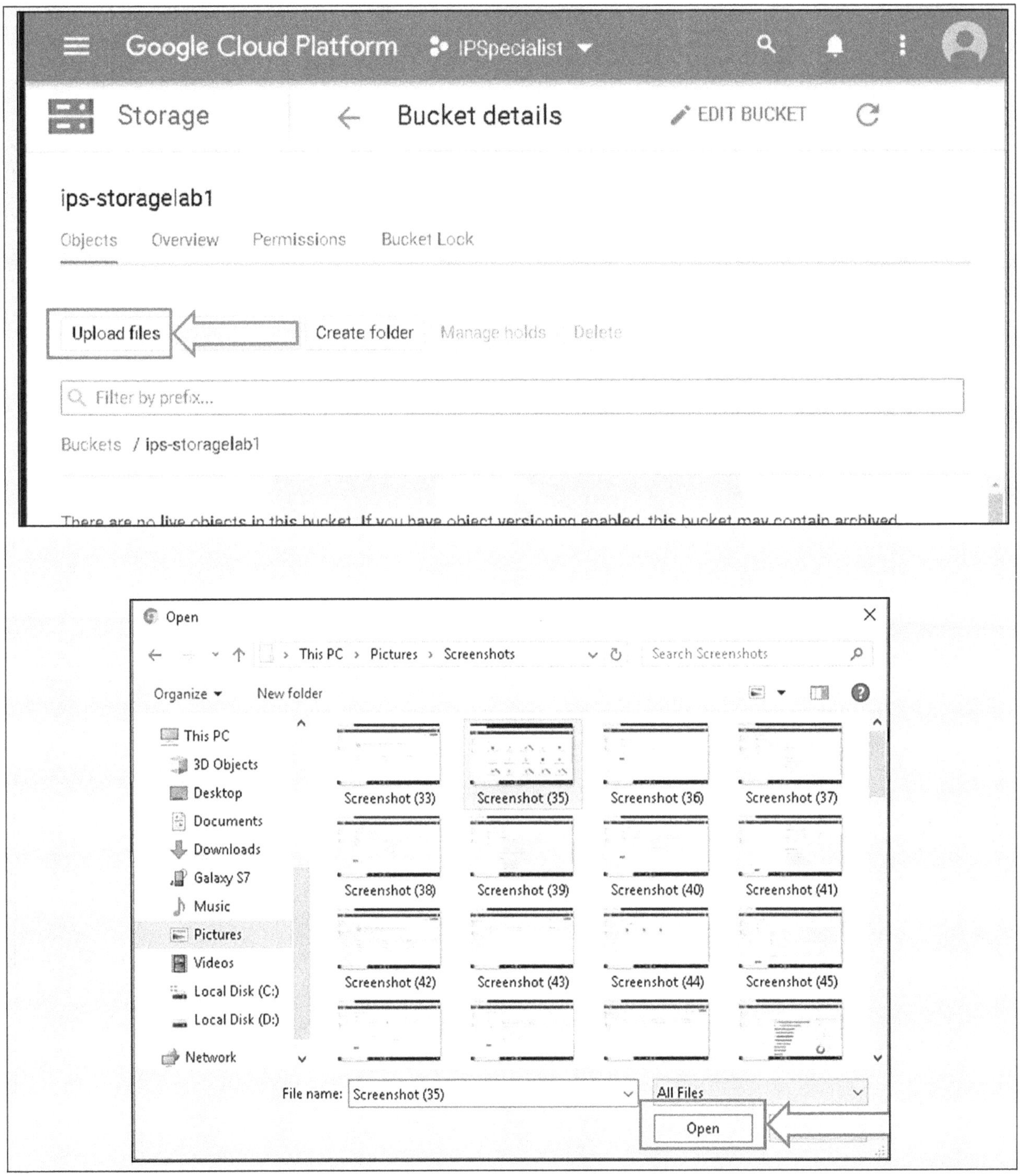

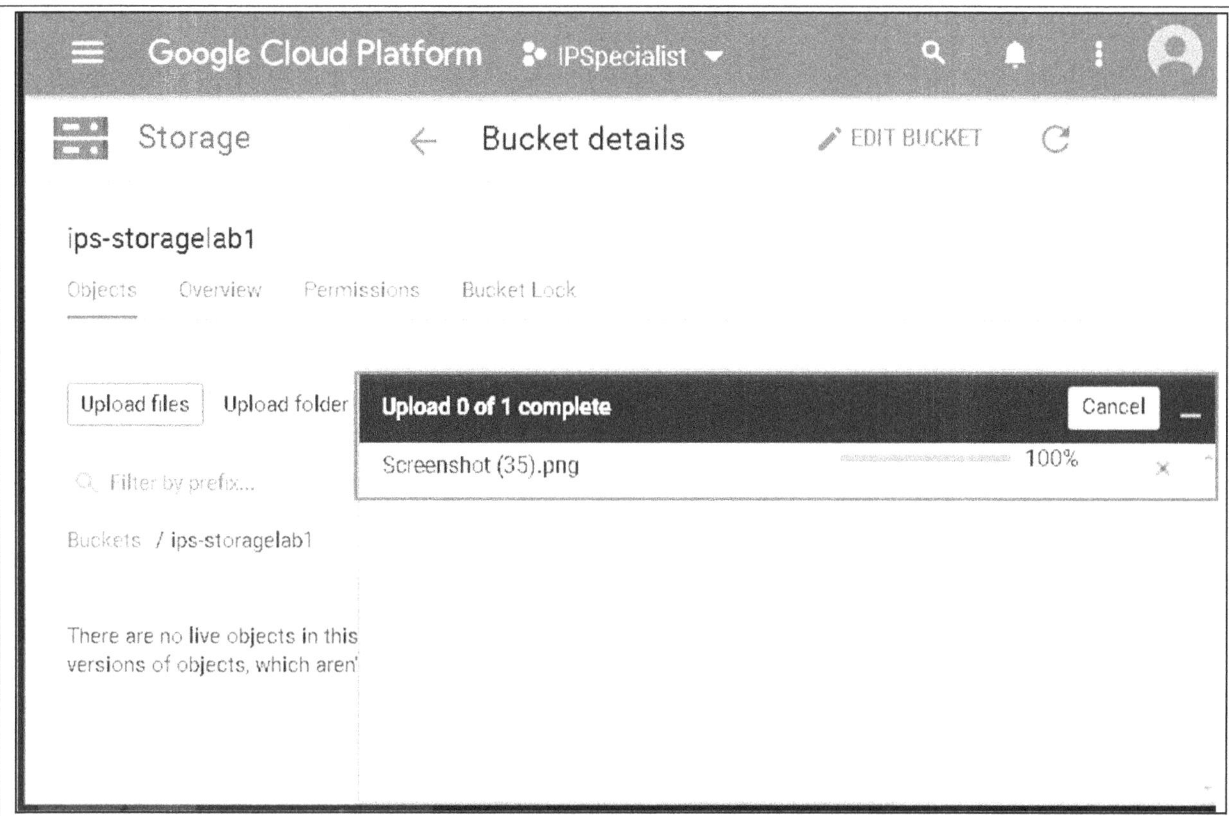

8. After successfully uploading the file, when you click on the file, it will open up in the browser as you have the right to open the file otherwise the object uploaded in the bucket are private. When you click on an object it will open in new window whose link is too large as it is the authenticated access of the file.

e.g.:

"https://00e9e64bac4b02150b679f535ee7cc8b473aa8327a39c64e11-apidata.googleusercontent.com/download/storage/v1/b/ips-storagelab1/o/Screenshot%20(35).png?qk=AD5uMEs9Yr_8L2GWHj9u0RPPgArs9VnTpVilV71tAWqnmYy4LvscorwI2pwVBpm1RfDXzke6qjZjZV8JBBYJJxK0GDElsn4OViKW4WBh5vpGcybHZN6OYu07Poe5tRobRvlQpwz7zPH9Uxov78FSRDiZ-BxINIGSJZ3PjzCGdRFIU0-NCPZtVxQ8-EaAotpM-N54nEzVg5Ks1NDeR43k3jMYPsWcZ4zjIsKHMzvSZAIj7lnTohejPFP2RHciwuJvpcfRow50W45qpUKF069hqKKnpwrQEq43DG2eKv4yQyROpE_lyvRBk3HBUUXpjIBxJuexyHGKXEpRt-au-OgHURkTC51eF1bvH-r11OYdQKsxt58PpqMKlbAWZi-3EfkHOdwCj20-ih-iVl5gB1sNC3aP52Pi6C5Tjvz5i7_3xt99kbfGn2XPlW61j-8wNAJP6QONF0Be9TprvbHb6q0b8C6Bn09ybNYaDFedLR__iaY7VcIzS1Vu2M0KLYya3l2uXAqWn41jrZDMCvz8PSqza8u350HMj4fVyoD3SfkYBa9e88QwQCOAFLJ8CsTMTCbLlyraeCrjvWFyhR2-dWG5PbpjncSVYSM3TtHiyEB-e6vnB4Pn05nq-L8uc2SRh8GXrgu7x05semLRuwOQRquplknaNMxN3uUkYntpDfO9WEJH34yocSDjebHW

80P31a01CdxSXK9K5fg4pPK2VWtcpxmkVeTPz740GcXcEky5Nr0DSdrbIrh1HWmB4l2OCB
x10RnEQGU4JZeEhw_Zn2QsBbScORthZRODgg”

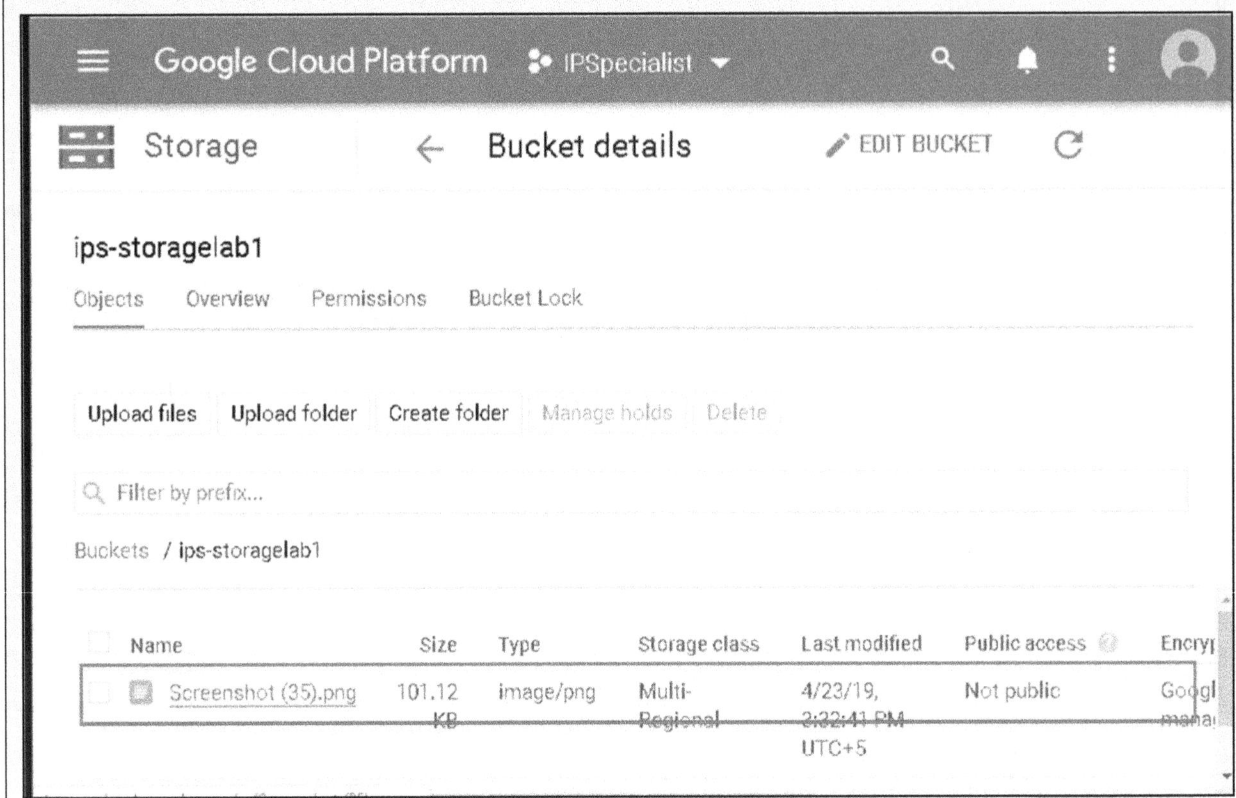

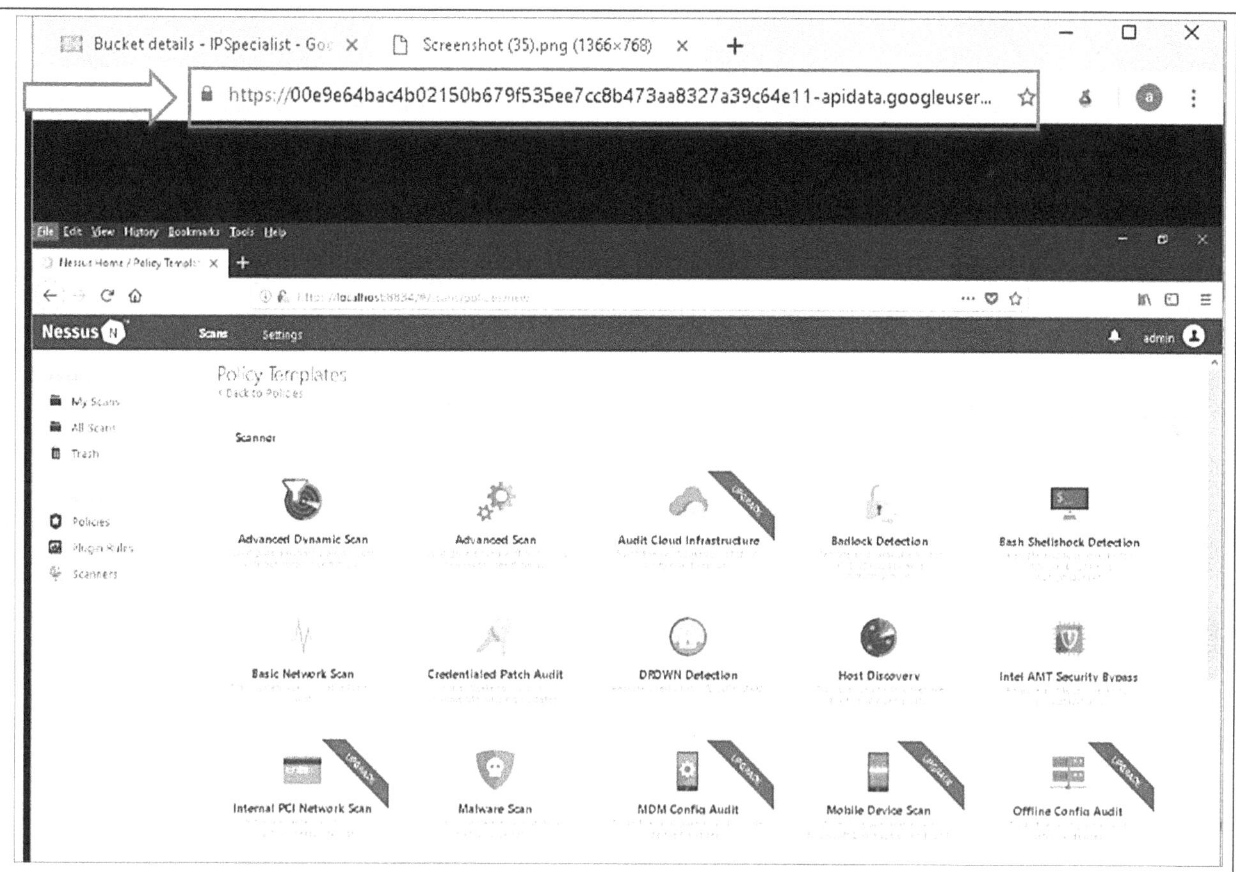

9. On the right side of the object listing, you will see a dotted icon. By clicking on this icon, you can see various options that perform on the object. Select "Edit permissions" as we want to make the object publically readable.

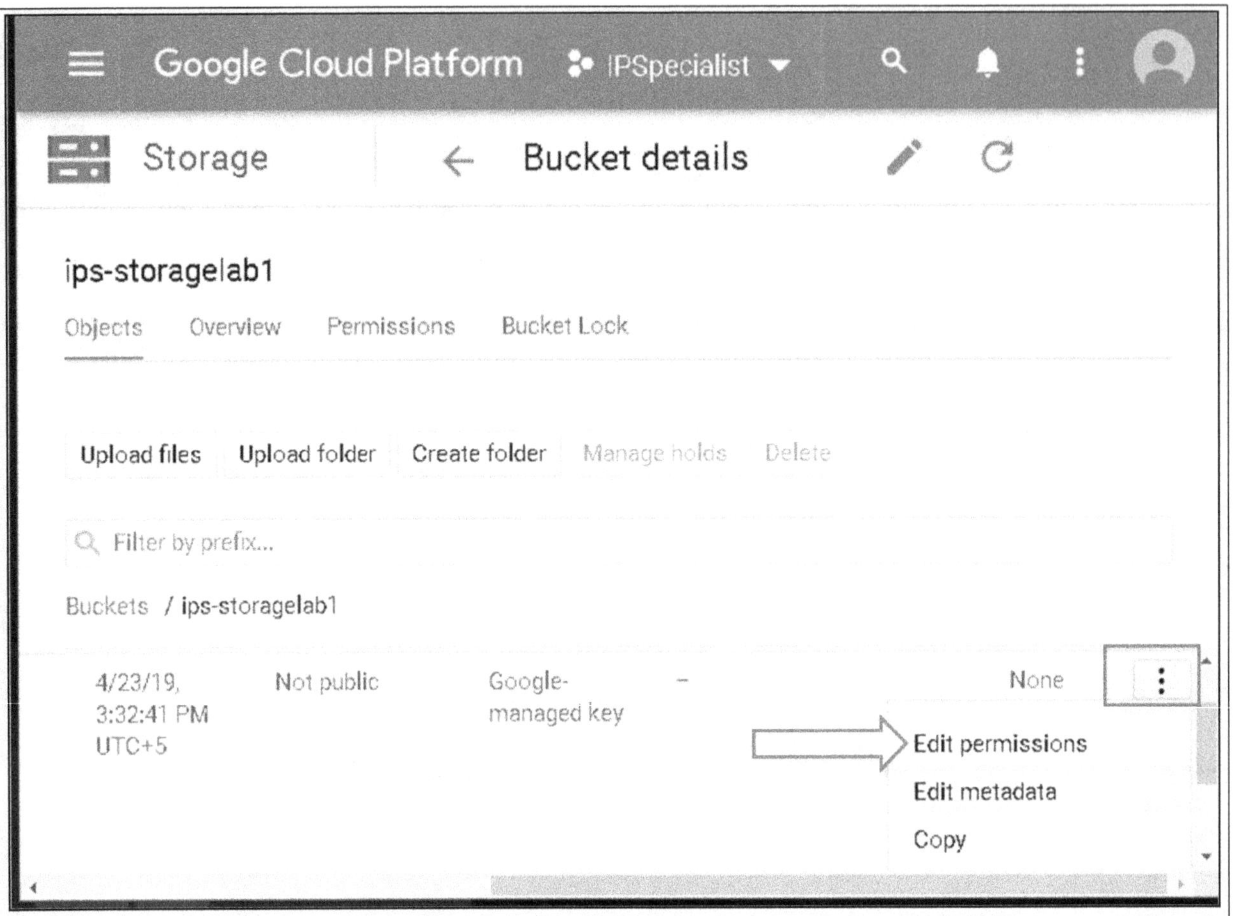

10. A pop-up window will appear in which you will need to add an item.

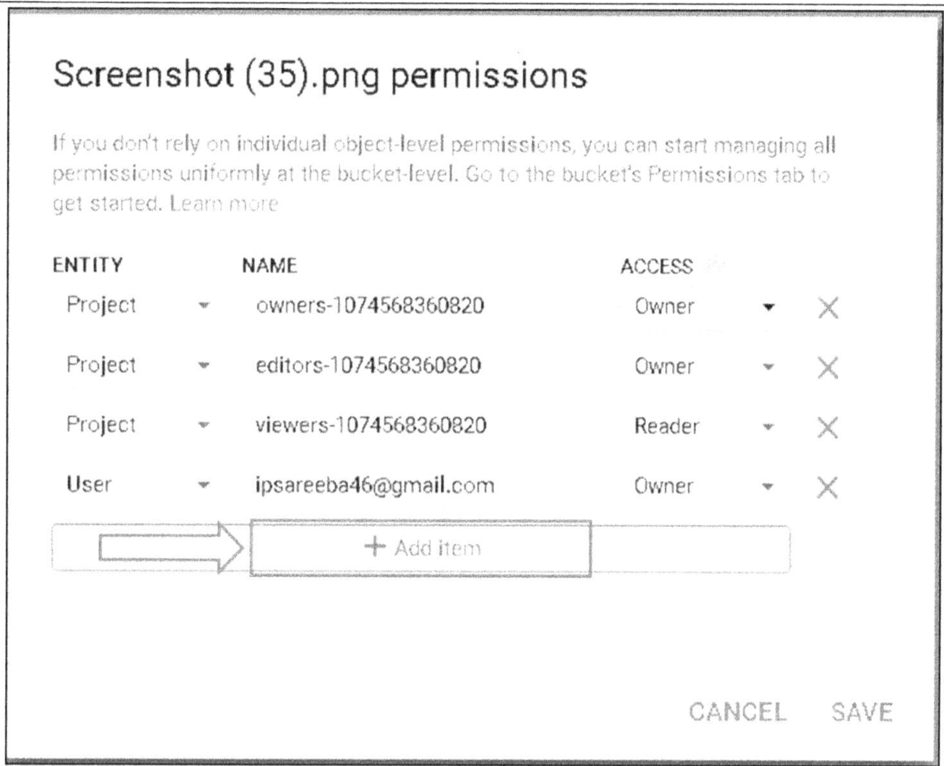

11. In **ENTITY** enter "Group" and in **NAME** enter "allusers". As you want to make it publically readable, in **ACCESS** select "Reader". Now, click "SAVE".

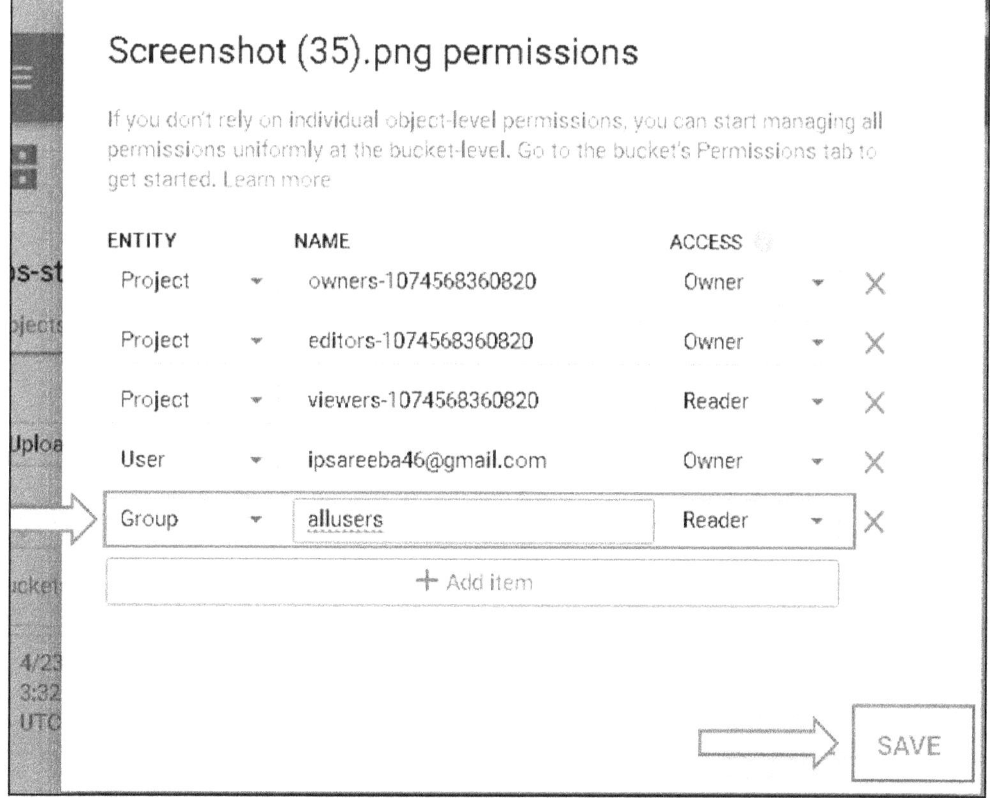

12. Now, you will see that the access list is updated, and your object becomes public with a link icon. Click on that link icon and you will that your object is publically available.

The URL of the object has now been changed to a simple url: **https://storage.googleapis.com/<bucketname>/<filename>.<format>**

"https://storage.googleapis.com/ips-storagelab1/Screenshot%20(35).png"

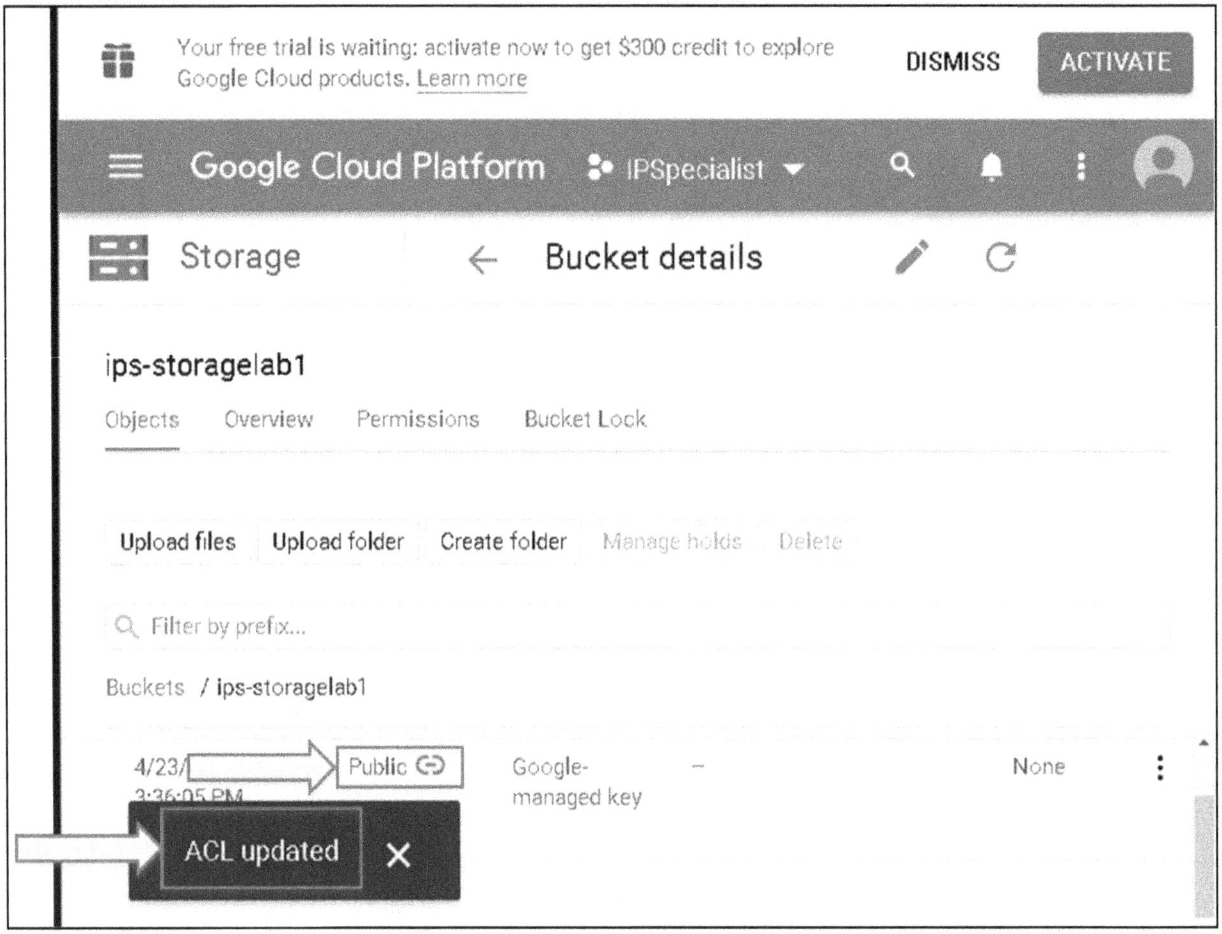

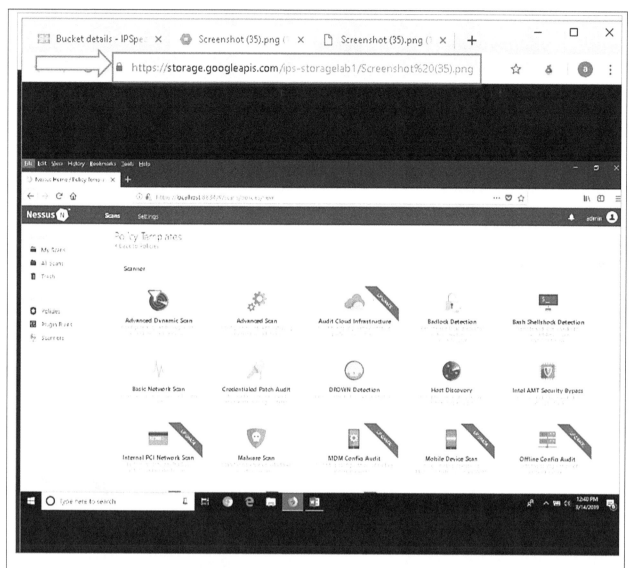

13. Now, remove public access of the object. Similarly, go to "Edit permissions" and remove the item that you created and click "SAVE". Now, your object has become private.

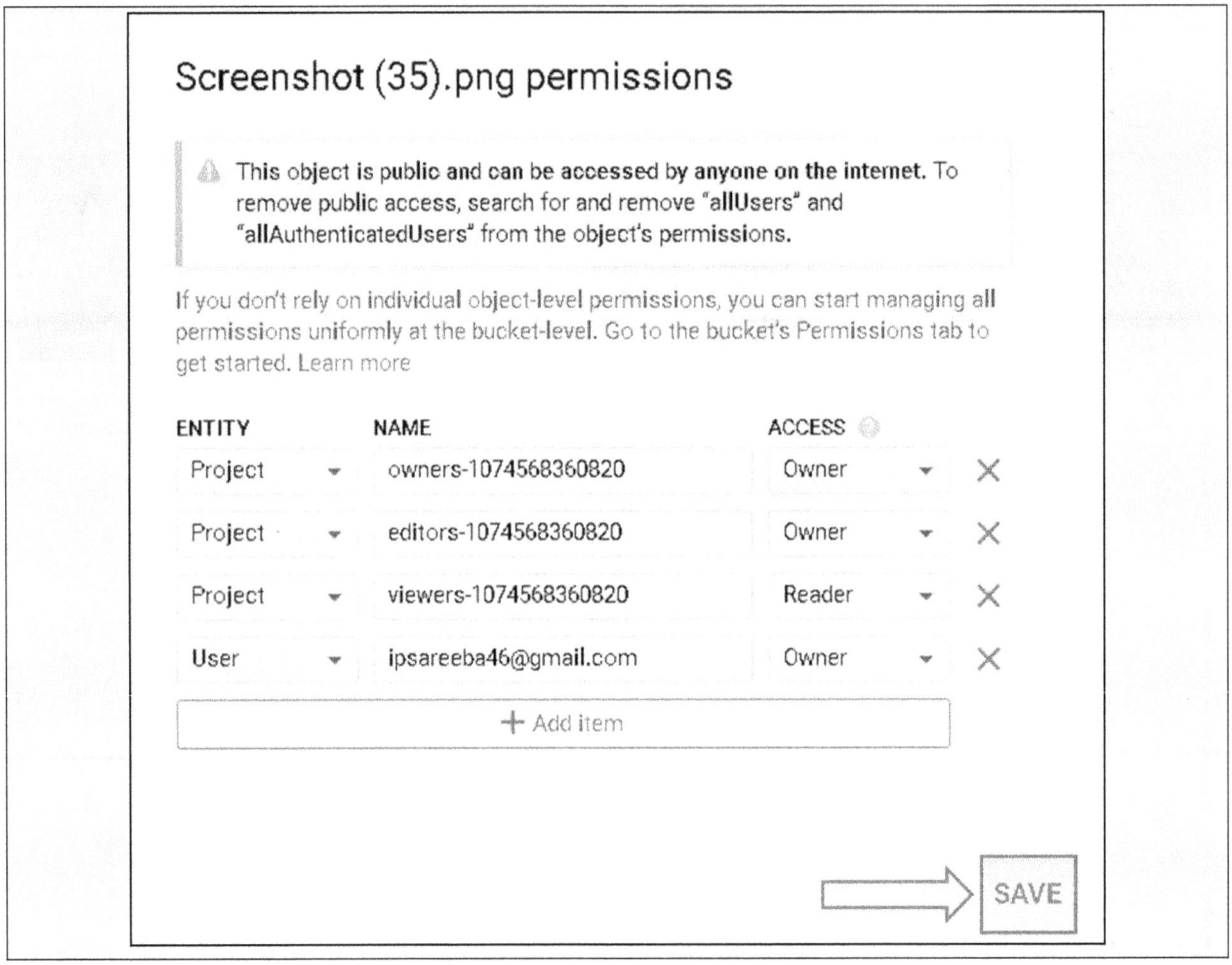

Screenshot (35).png permissions

This object is public and can be accessed by anyone on the internet. To remove public access, search for and remove "allUsers" and "allAuthenticatedUsers" from the object's permissions.

If you don't rely on individual object-level permissions, you can start managing all permissions uniformly at the bucket-level. Go to the bucket's Permissions tab to get started. Learn more

ENTITY	NAME	ACCESS
Project	owners-1074568360820	Owner
Project	editors-1074568360820	Owner
Project	viewers-1074568360820	Reader
User	ipsareeba46@gmail.com	Owner

+ Add item

SAVE

Your free trial is waiting: activate now to get $300 credit to explore Google Cloud products. Learn more
DISMISS
ACTIVATE
Google Cloud Platform
IPSpecialist
Storage
Bucket details
ips-storagelab1
Objects
Overview
Permissions
Bucket Lock
Upload files
Upload folder
Create folder
Filter by prefix...
Buckets / ips-storagelab1
Not public
Google-managed key
None
ACL updated

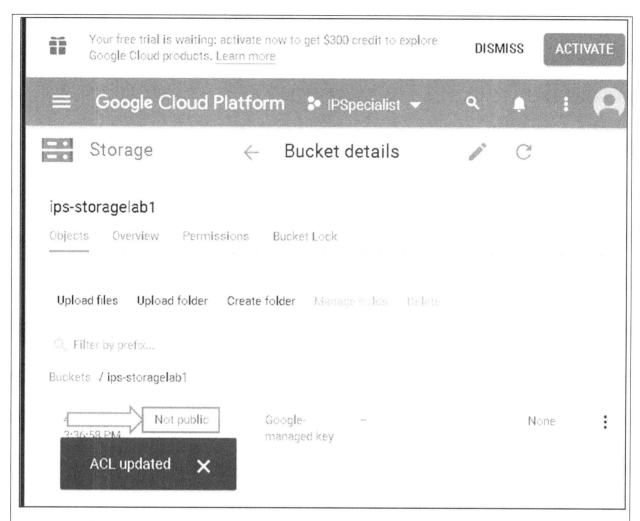

14. Now, if you try to access the object with its public url, you will get an access denied error.

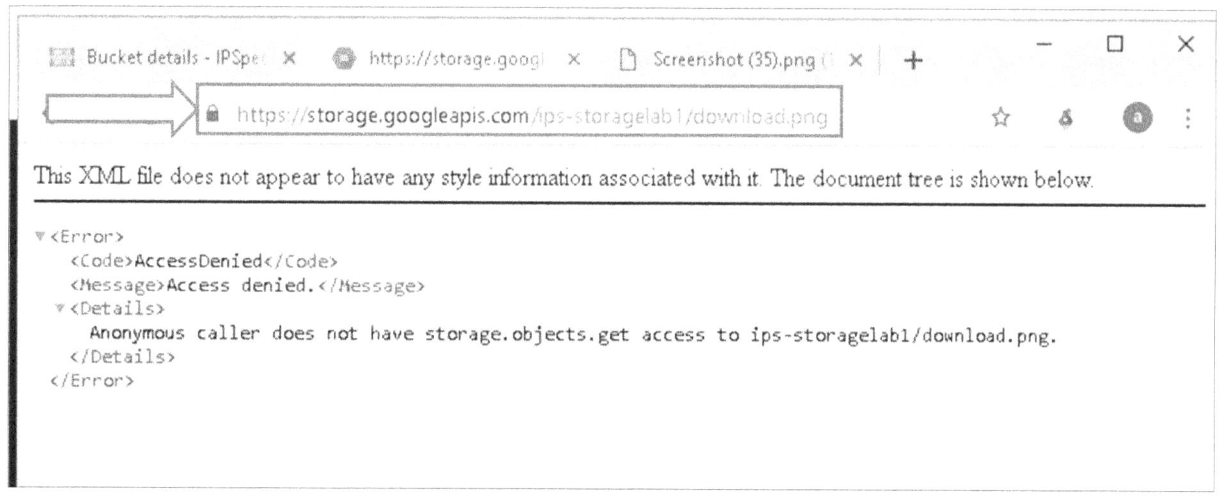

15. In the bucket, you can also create a folder by clicking on "Create folder".

Google Cloud Platform IPSpecialist

Storage ← Bucket details

ips-storagelab1

Objects Overview Permissions Bucket Lock

Upload files Create folder Manage holds Delete

Filter by prefix...

Buckets / ips-storagelab1

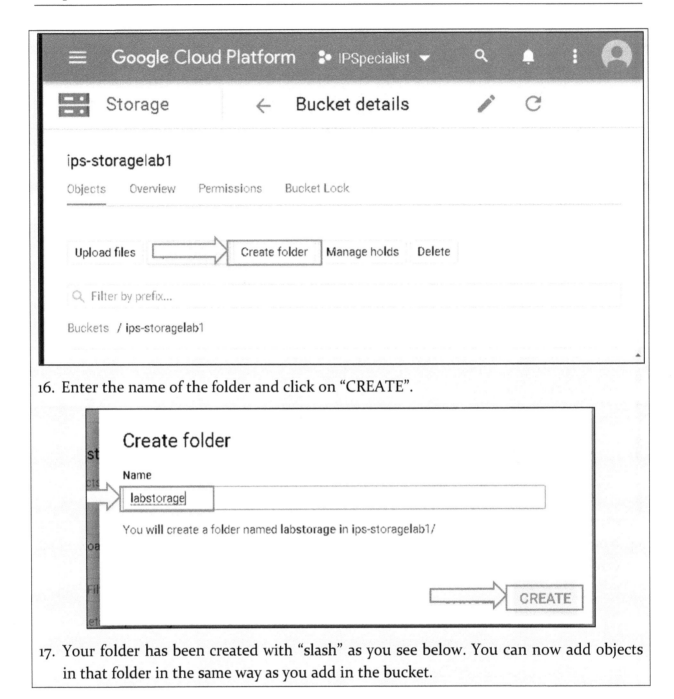

16. Enter the name of the folder and click on "CREATE".

Create folder

Name

labstorage

You will create a folder named **labstorage** in ips-storagelab1/

CREATE

17. Your folder has been created with "slash" as you see below. You can now add objects in that folder in the same way as you add in the bucket.

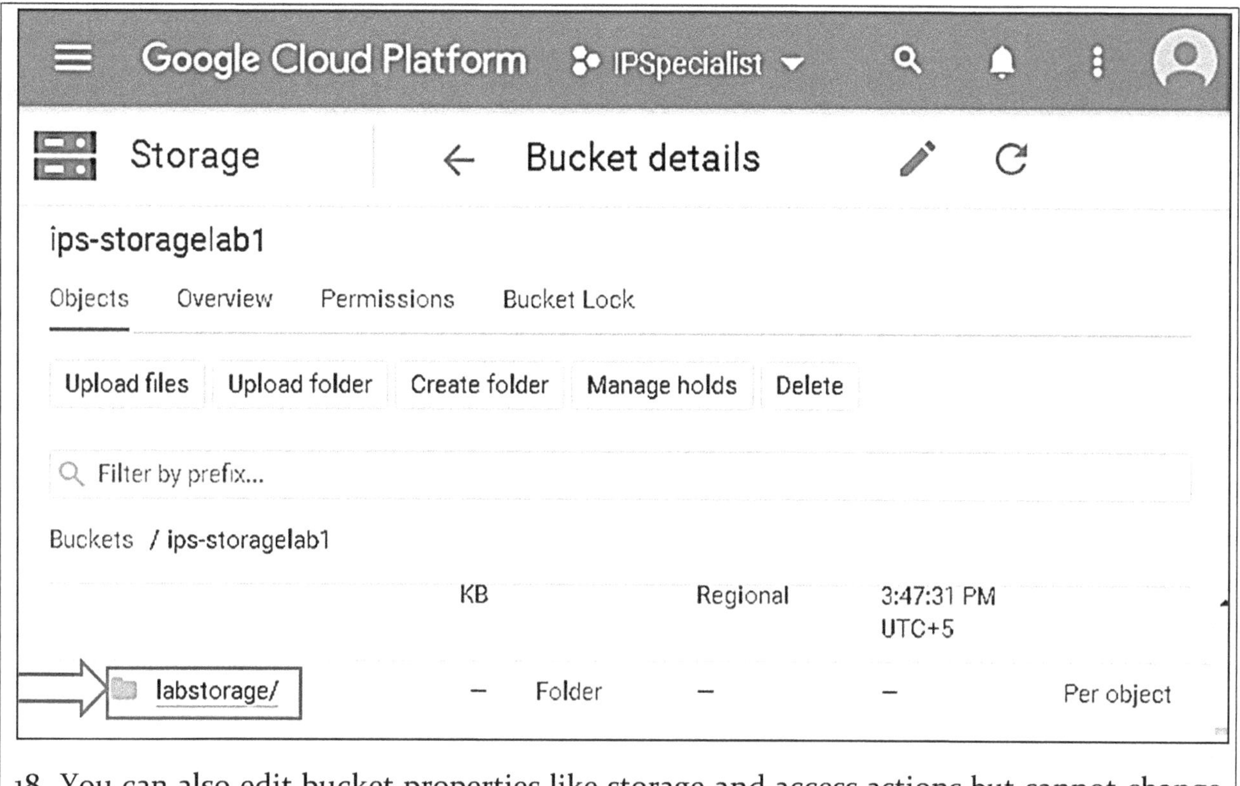

18. You can also edit bucket properties like storage and access actions but cannot change its location and name. Click on top of the console window of GCS then on "Edit bucket".

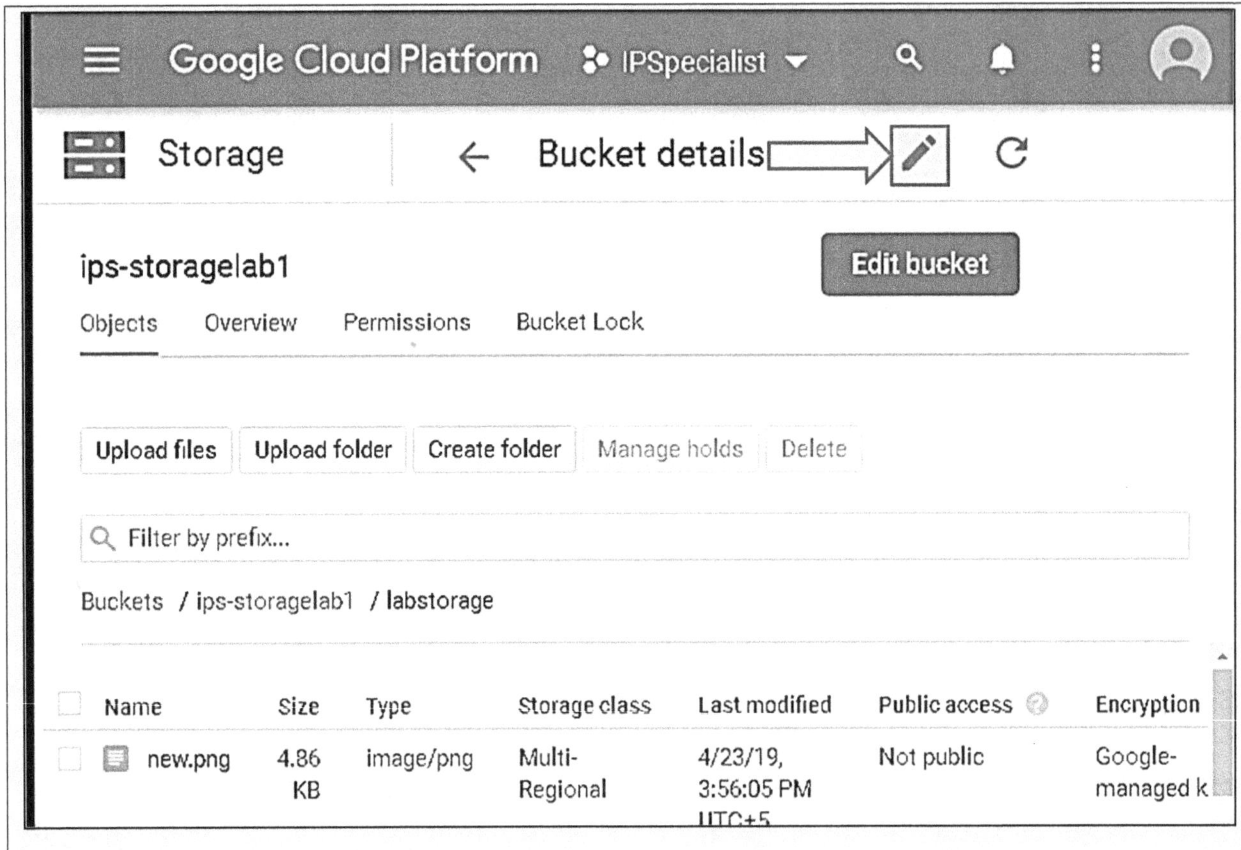

19. A new window will appear where you can change the storage class and access control model.

Your free trial is waiting: activate now to get $300 credit to explore Google Cloud products. Learn more

DISMISS ACTIVATE

Google Cloud Platform IPSpecialist

Storage ← Edit bucket

Name

ips-storagelab1

Default storage class

Multi-Regional

Regional

Nearline

Coldline

Location

United States (multiple regions in the United States)

Access control model

Choose how you'll control access to this bucket's objects. Learn more

Set permissions uniformly at bucket-level (Bucket Policy Only)

Enforces the bucket's IAM policy without object ACLs. May help prevent unintended access. If selected, this option becomes permanent after 90 days.

Set object-level and bucket-level permissions

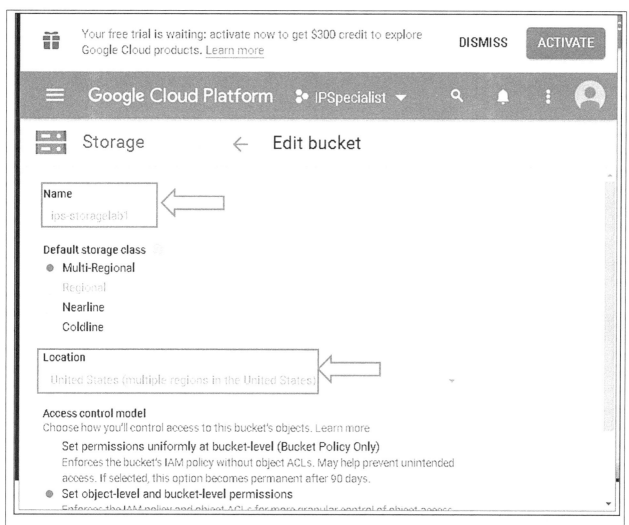

20. To delete an object from the bucket, select the bucket and click on "delete". A pop-up window will appear, click again on "DELETE". Now, your object is deleted.

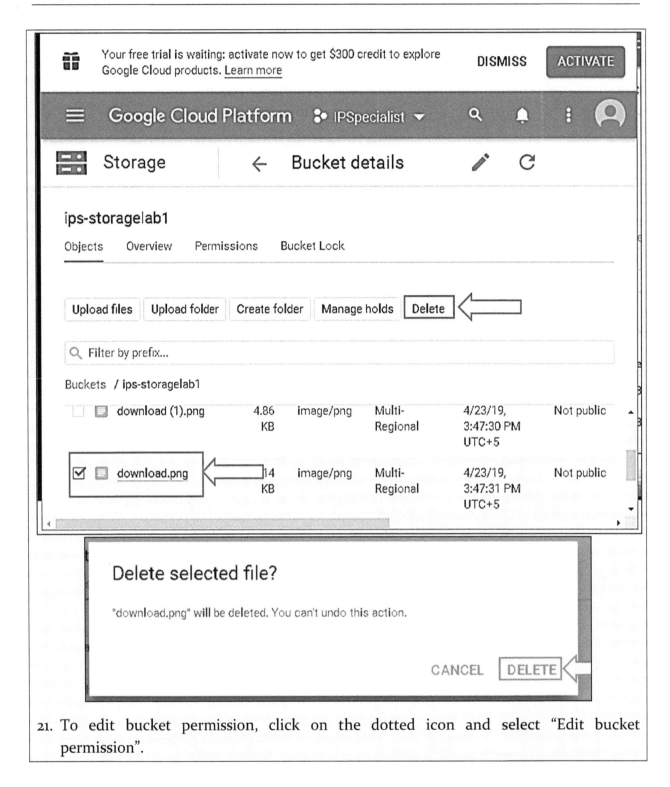

21. To edit bucket permission, click on the dotted icon and select "Edit bucket permission".

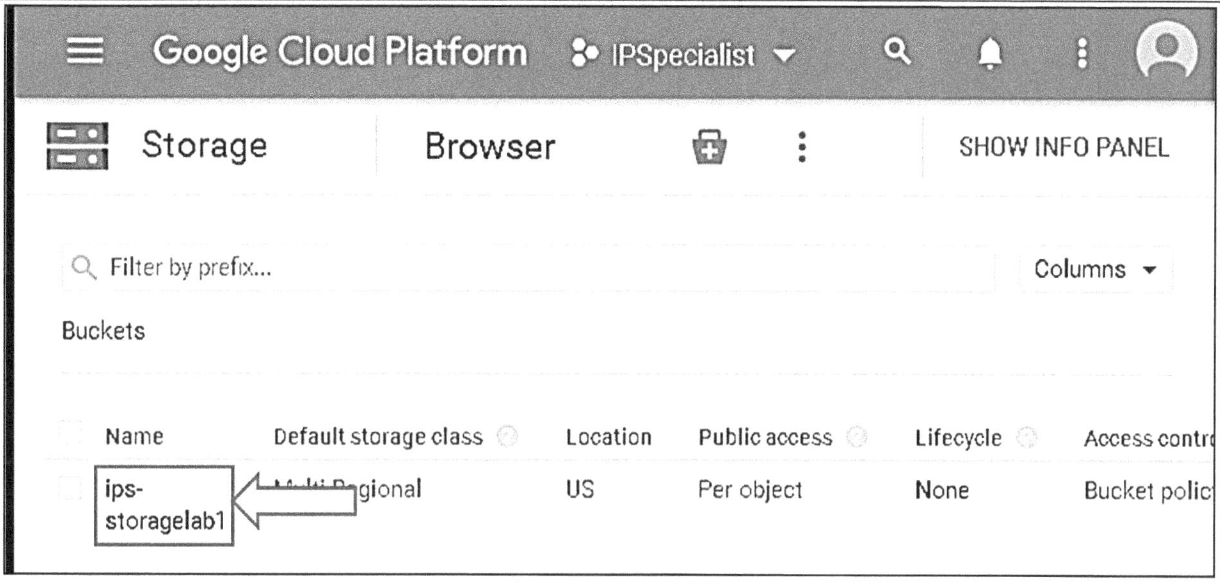

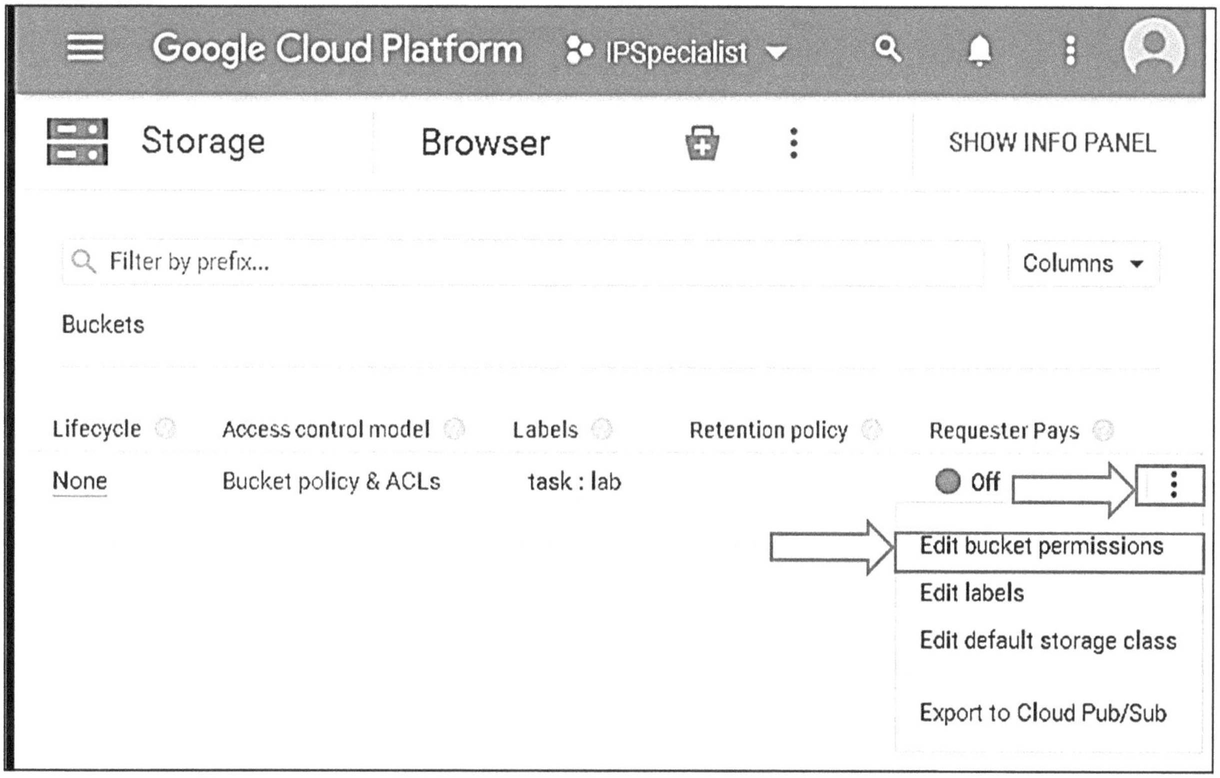

22. From the bucket permission, you can manage access control at the bucket level. You can also add members with its appropriate role to allow access to the bucket.

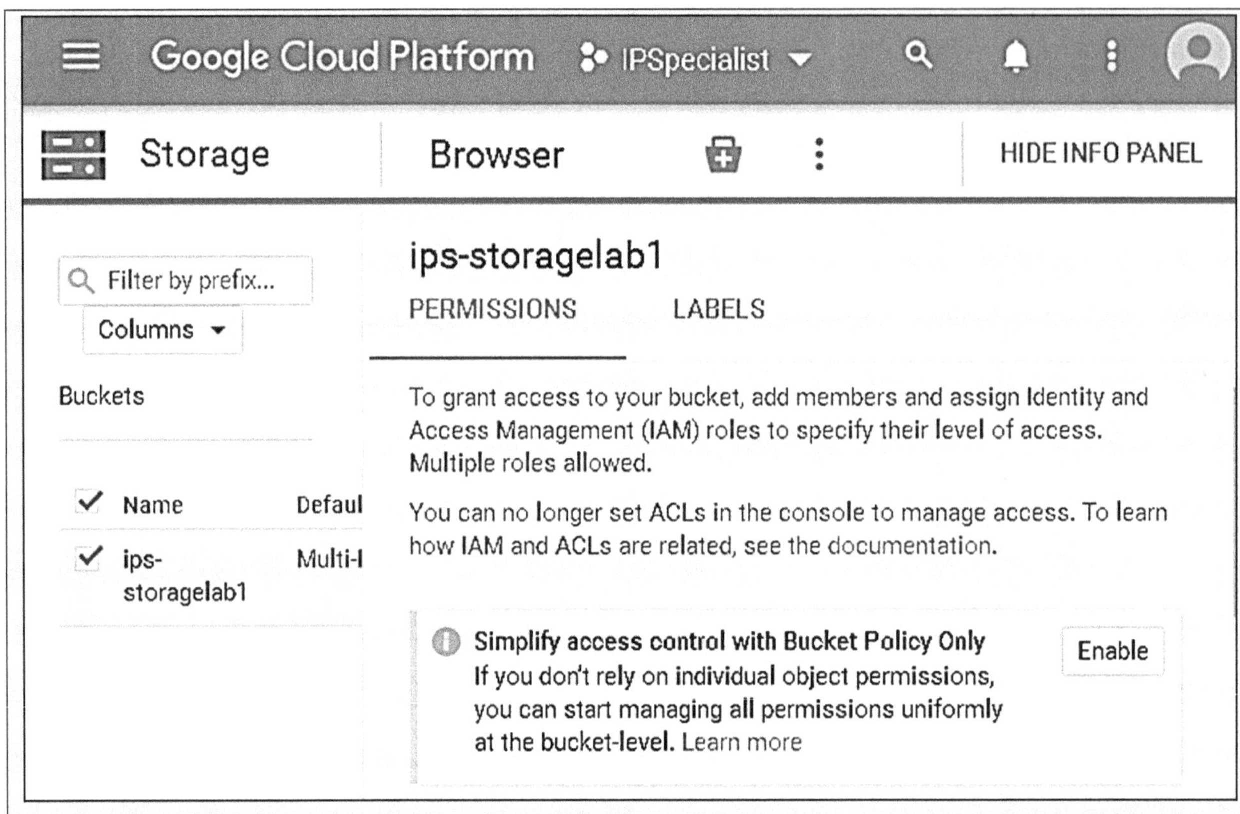

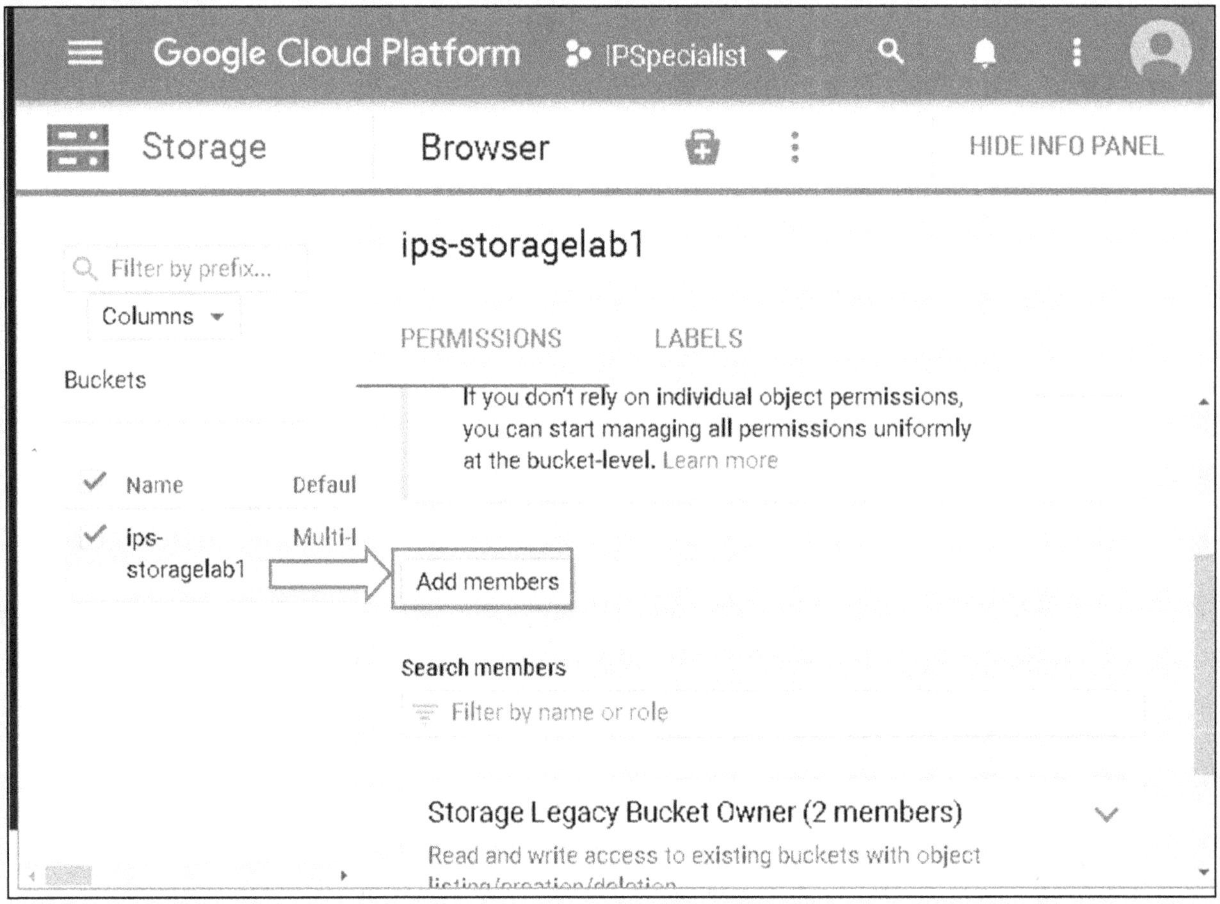

Google Cloud Platform
IPSpecialist
Storage
Browser
HIDE INFO PANEL
Filter by prefix...
Columns
Buckets
Name
Defaul
ips-storagelab1
Multi-I
ips-storagelab1
PERMISSIONS
LABELS
If you don't rely on individual object permissions, you can start managing all permissions uniformly at the bucket-level. Learn more
Add members
Search members
Filter by name or role
Storage Legacy Bucket Owner (2 members)
Read and write access to existing buckets with object listing/creation/deletion

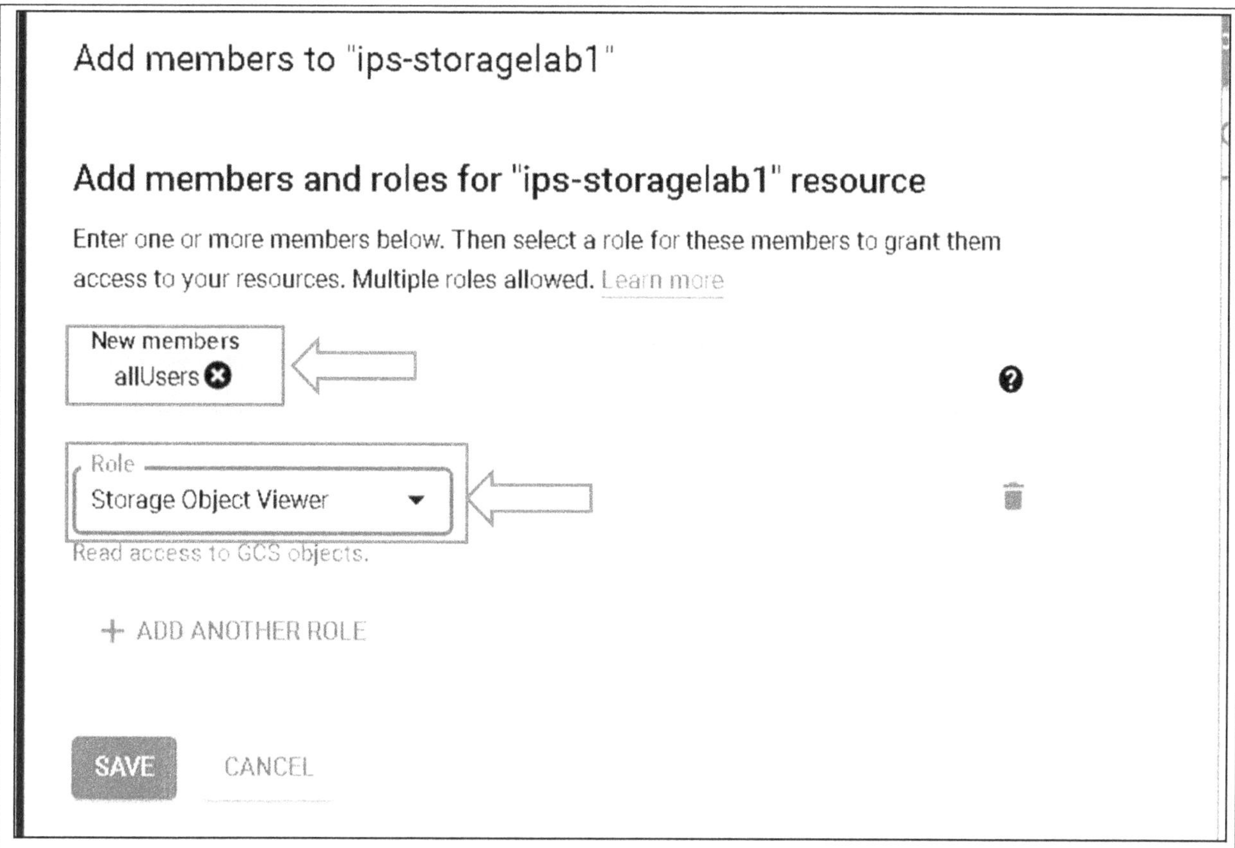

23. To use Google cloud SDK Shell, you first need to download the Google Cloud installer from this link: https://cloud.google.com/sdk/docs/quickstart-windows.
24. After downloading the installer, run it. Then, follow the steps shown below.

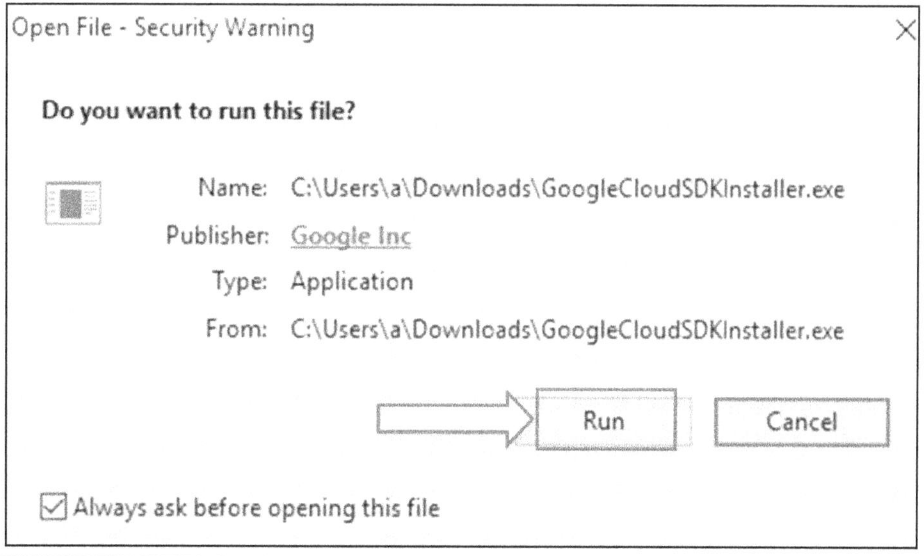

Google Cloud SDK Setup

Welcome to Google Cloud SDK Setup

This wizard will guide you through the installation of the Google Cloud SDK.

Google Cloud SDK contains tools and libraries that will enable you to easily create and manage resources on Google Cloud Platform.

Google Cloud Platform

Help make Google Cloud SDK better by automatically sending anonymous usage statistics to Google

Your privacy is important to us. Click here to learn more.

Next >

Cancel

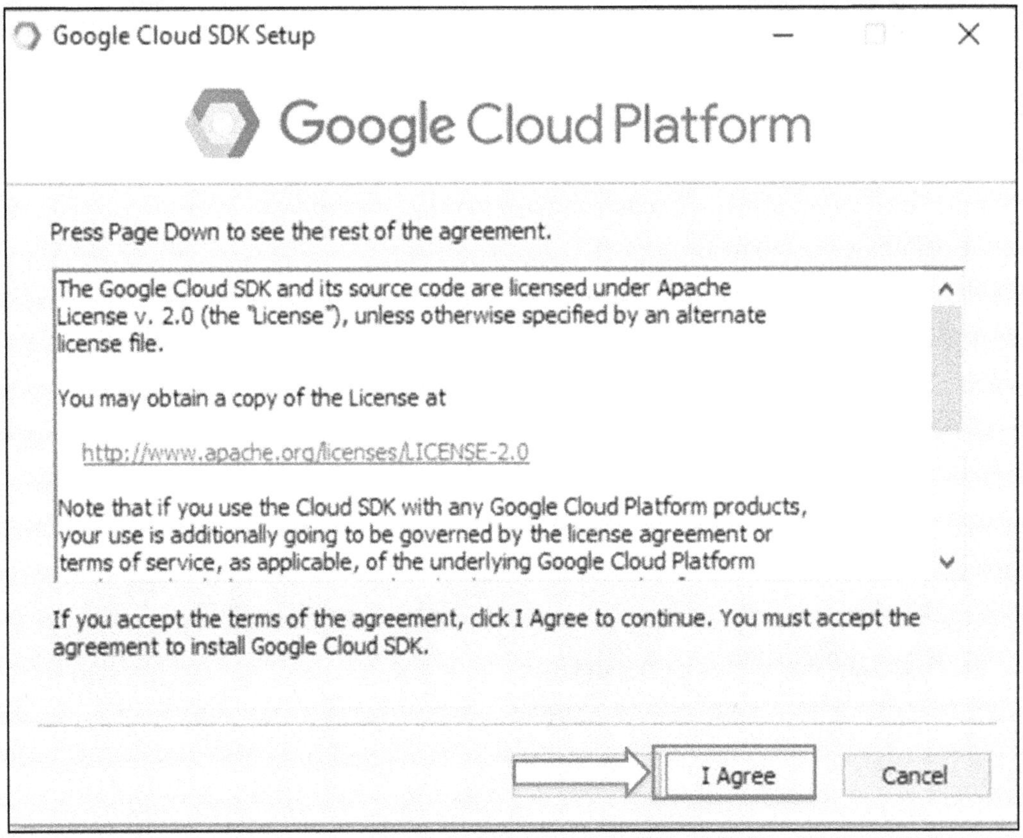

Google Cloud SDK Setup

Google Cloud Platform

Press Page Down to see the rest of the agreement.

The Google Cloud SDK and its source code are licensed under Apache License v. 2.0 (the "License"), unless otherwise specified by an alternate license file.

You may obtain a copy of the License at

http://www.apache.org/licenses/LICENSE-2.0

Note that if you use the Cloud SDK with any Google Cloud Platform products, your use is additionally going to be governed by the license agreement or terms of service, as applicable, of the underlying Google Cloud Platform

If you accept the terms of the agreement, click I Agree to continue. You must accept the agreement to install Google Cloud SDK.

I Agree

Cancel

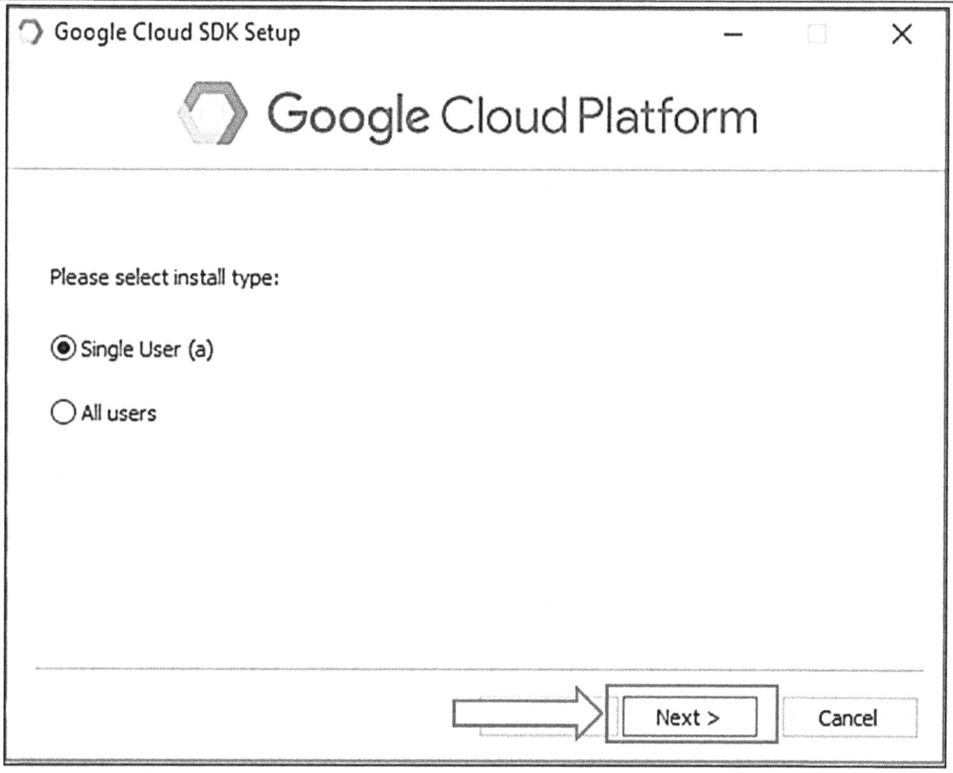

Google Cloud SDK Setup

Google Cloud Platform

Please select install type:

Single User (a)

All users

Next >

Cancel

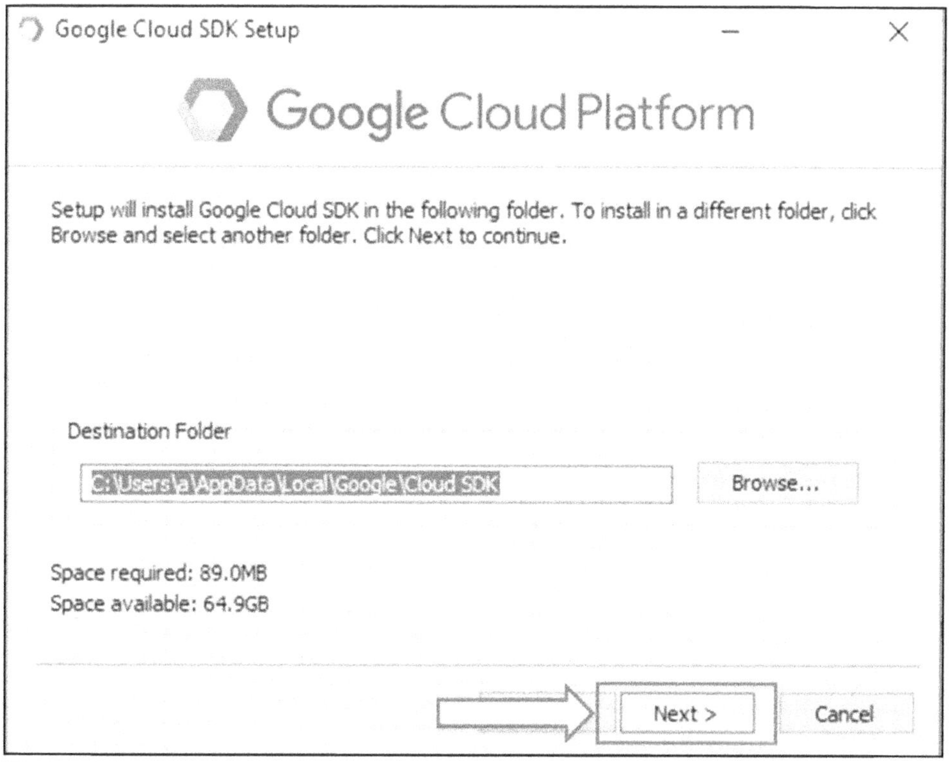

Google Cloud SDK Setup

Google Cloud Platform

Setup will install Google Cloud SDK in the following folder. To install in a different folder, click Browse and select another folder. Click Next to continue.

Destination Folder

C:\Users\a\AppData\Local\Google\Cloud SDK

Browse...

Space required: 89.0MB
Space available: 64.9GB

Next >

Cancel

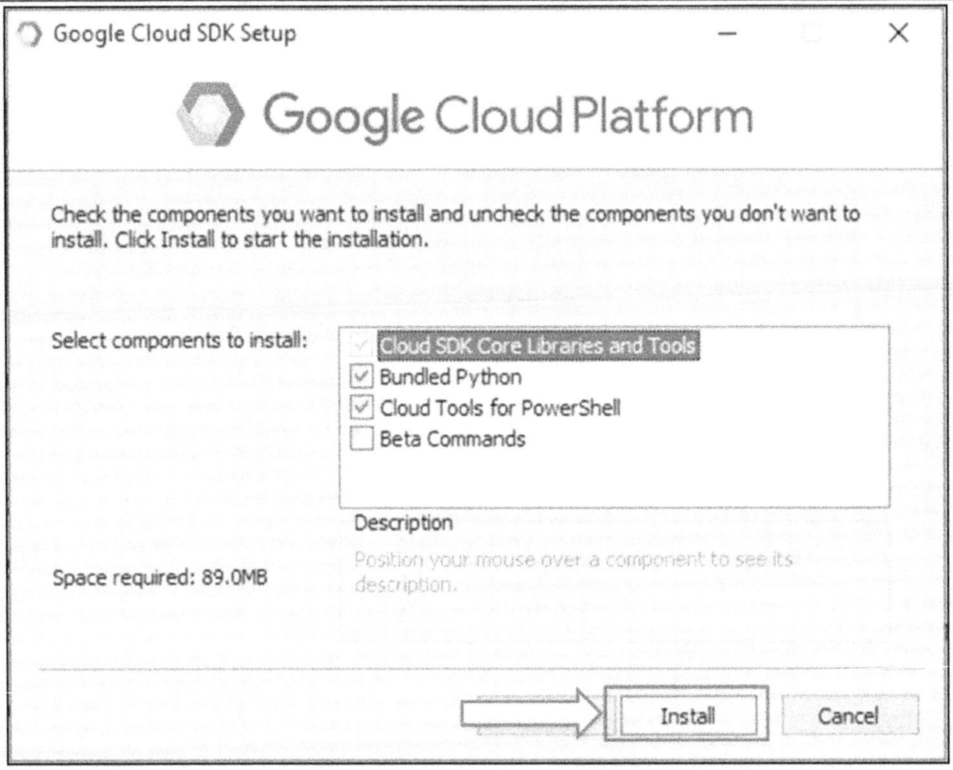

Google Cloud SDK Setup

Google Cloud Platform

Check the components you want to install and uncheck the components you don't want to install. Click Install to start the installation.

Select components to install:

- [x] Cloud SDK Core Libraries and Tools
- [x] Bundled Python
- [x] Cloud Tools for PowerShell
- [ ] Beta Commands

Description

Position your mouse over a component to see its description.

Space required: 89.0MB

Install | Cancel

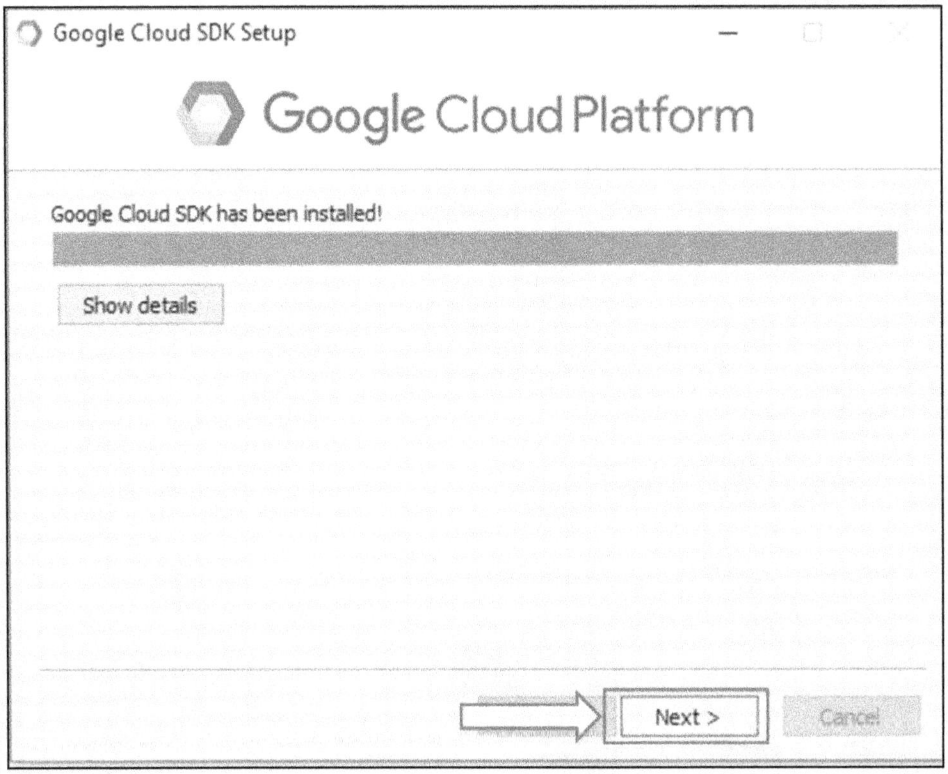

Google Cloud SDK Setup

Google Cloud Platform

Google Cloud SDK has been installed!

Show details

Next > | Cancel

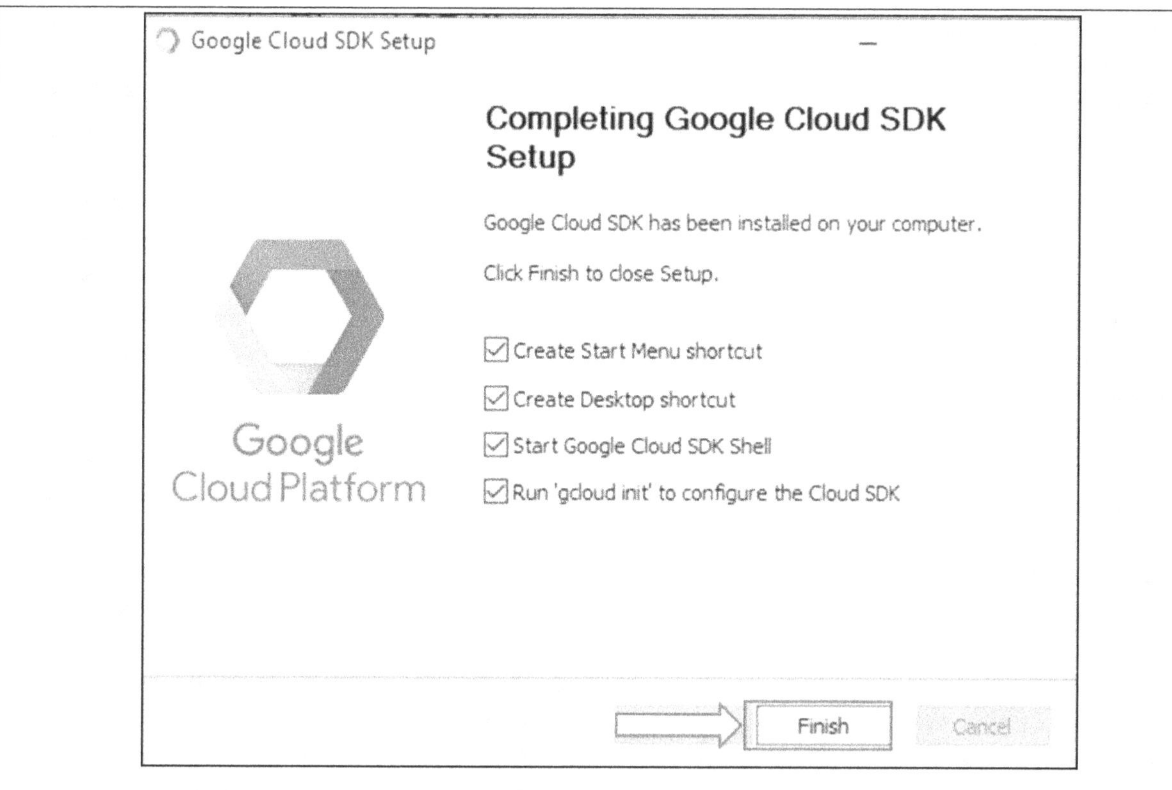

25. Click on "Google Cloud SDK", and a command line tool will open. First, enter "gcloud init" as so it launches a web browser for authorization. This is done to access the GCP using your user credentials.

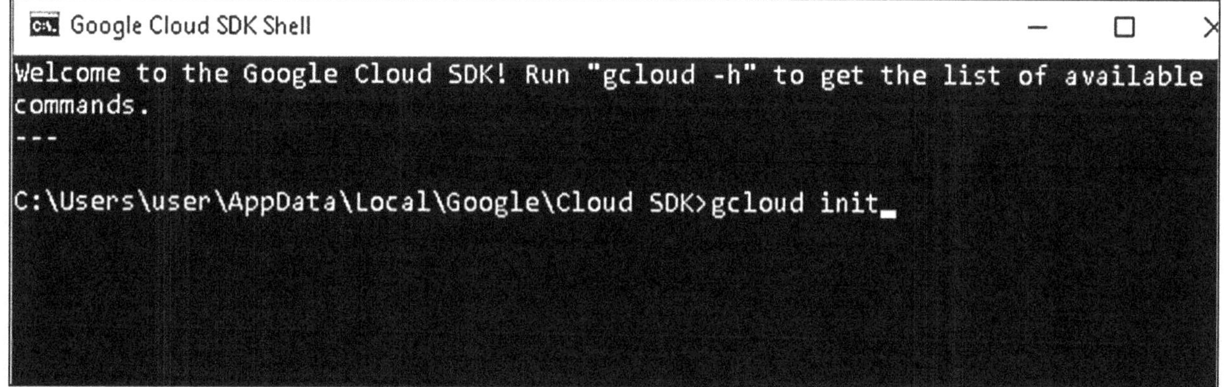

Google Cloud SDK Shell - gcloud init

```
C:\Users\user\AppData\Local\Google\Cloud SDK>gcloud init
Welcome! This command will take you through the configuration of gcloud.

Your current configuration has been set to: [default]

You can skip diagnostics next time by using the following flag:
  gcloud init --skip-diagnostics

Network diagnostic detects and fixes local network connection issues.
Checking network connection...done.
Reachability Check passed.
Network diagnostic passed (1/1 checks passed).

You must log in to continue. Would you like to log in (Y/n)?  y

Your browser has been opened to visit:

    https://accounts.google.com/o/oauth2/auth?redirect_uri=http%3A%2F%2Floc
alhost%3A8085%2F&prompt=select_account&response_type=code&client_id=3255594
0559.apps.googleusercontent.com&scope=https%3A%2F%2Fwww.googleapis.com%2Fau
th%2Fuserinfo.email+https%3A%2F%2Fwww.googleapis.com%2Fauth%2Fcloud-platfor
m+https%3A%2F%2Fwww.googleapis.com%2Fauth%2Fappengine.admin+https%3A%2F%2Fw
ww.googleapis.com%2Fauth%2Fcompute+https%3A%2F%2Fwww.googleapis.com%2Fauth%
2Faccounts.reauth&access_type=offline
```

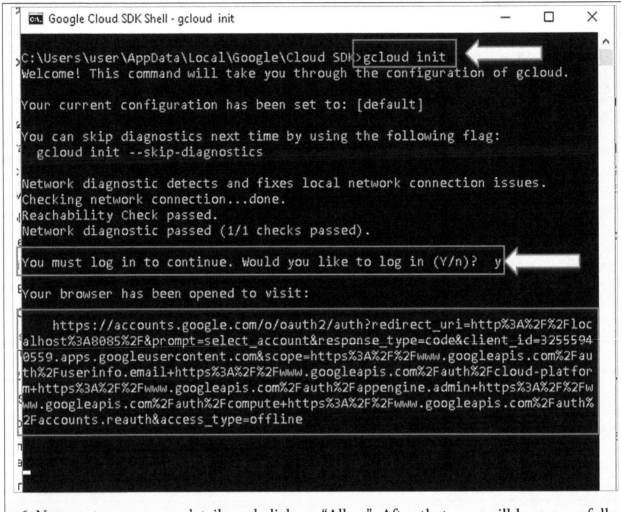

26. Now, enter your user details and click on “Allow”. After that, you will be successfully authenticated with Google Cloud SDK.

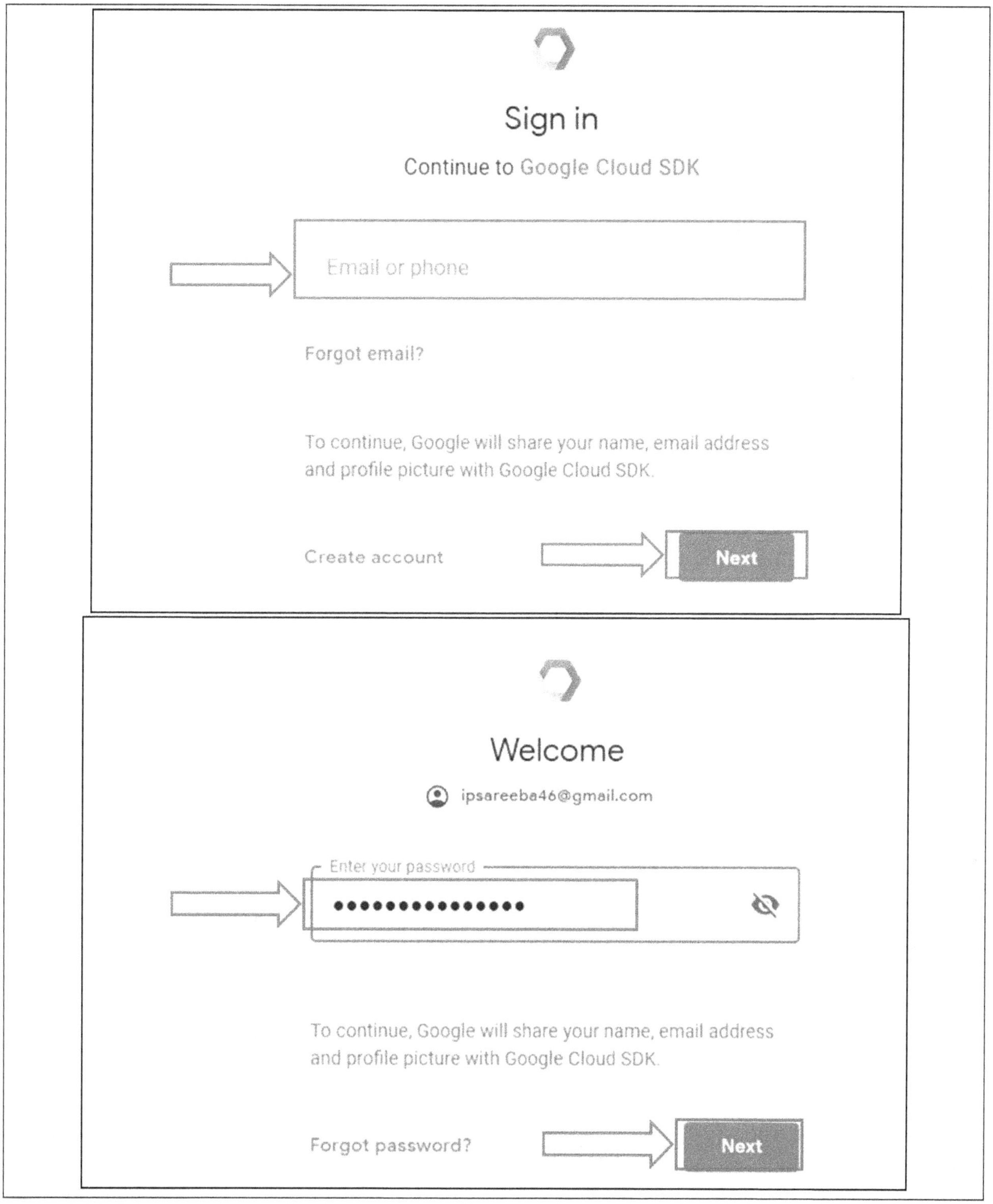

Sign in

Continue to Google Cloud SDK

Email or phone

Forgot email?

To continue, Google will share your name, email address and profile picture with Google Cloud SDK.

Create account

Next

Welcome

ipsareeba46@gmail.com

Enter your password

•••••••••••••••

To continue, Google will share your name, email address and profile picture with Google Cloud SDK.

Forgot password?

Next

View and manage your applications deployed on Google App Engine

Make sure you trust Google Cloud SDK

You may be sharing sensitive info with this site or app. Learn about how Google Cloud SDK will handle your data by reviewing its terms of service and privacy policies. You can always see or remove access in your Google Account.

Learn about the risks

Cancel

Allow

https://cloud.google.com/sdk/auth_success

Google Cloud Why Google Solutions Products Pricing Getting sta Docs Support

Developer Tools Contact sales Try free

Cloud SDK > Documentation > Google Cloud

You are now authenticated with the Google Cloud SDK!

SEND FEEDBACK

Contents

Information about command-line tools and client libraries

Tutorials

Feedback

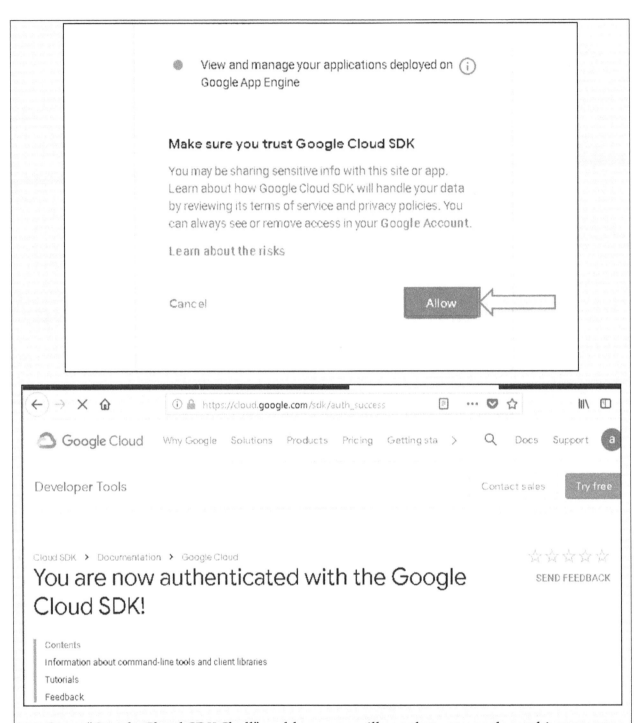

27. Go to "Google Cloud SDK Shell" and here you will see that you are logged in as a user. Now, select the project where you want to create a bucket.

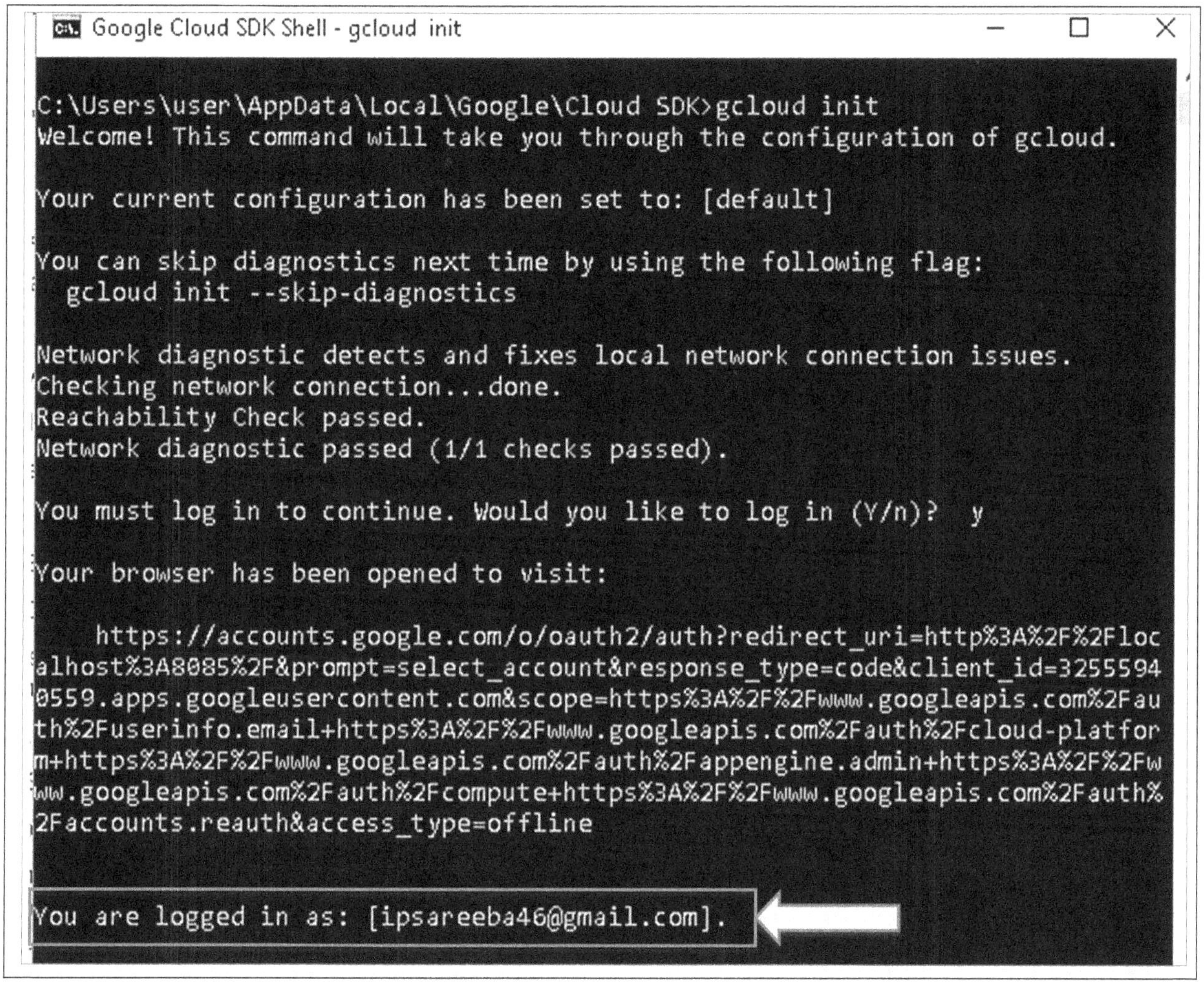

```
Google Cloud SDK Shell - gcloud init

C:\Users\user\AppData\Local\Google\Cloud SDK>gcloud init
Welcome! This command will take you through the configuration of gcloud.

Your current configuration has been set to: [default]

You can skip diagnostics next time by using the following flag:
  gcloud init --skip-diagnostics

Network diagnostic detects and fixes local network connection issues.
Checking network connection...done.
Reachability Check passed.
Network diagnostic passed (1/1 checks passed).

You must log in to continue. Would you like to log in (Y/n)?  y

Your browser has been opened to visit:

    https://accounts.google.com/o/oauth2/auth?redirect_uri=http%3A%2F%2Floc
alhost%3A8085%2F&prompt=select_account&response_type=code&client_id=3255594
0559.apps.googleusercontent.com&scope=https%3A%2F%2Fwww.googleapis.com%2Fau
th%2Fuserinfo.email+https%3A%2F%2Fwww.googleapis.com%2Fauth%2Fcloud-platfor
m+https%3A%2F%2Fwww.googleapis.com%2Fauth%2Fappengine.admin+https%3A%2F%2Fw
ww.googleapis.com%2Fauth%2Fcompute+https%3A%2F%2Fwww.googleapis.com%2Fauth%
2Faccounts.reauth&access_type=offline


You are logged in as: [ipsareeba46@gmail.com].
```

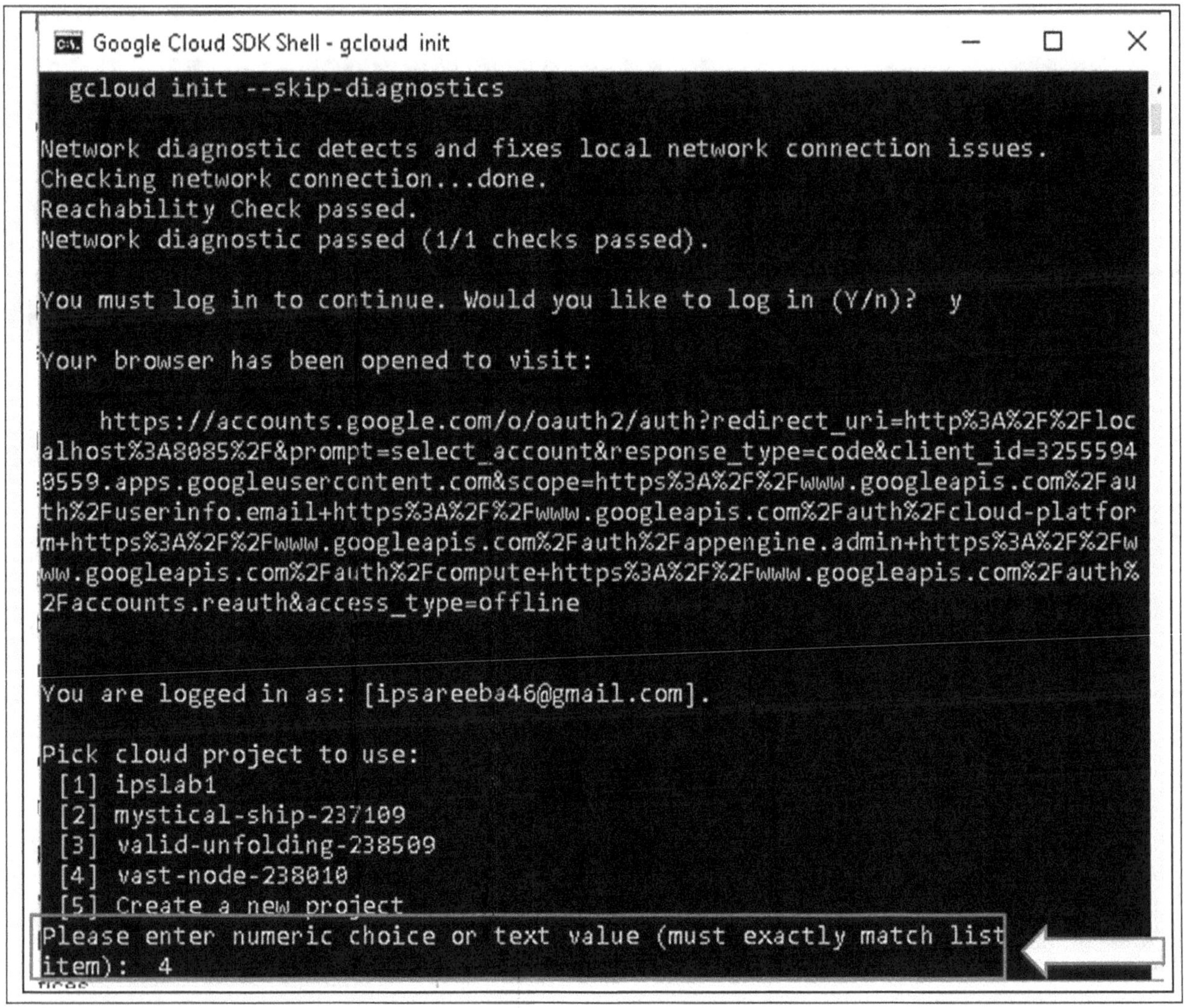

```
Google Cloud SDK Shell - gcloud init

 gcloud init --skip-diagnostics

Network diagnostic detects and fixes local network connection issues.
Checking network connection...done.
Reachability Check passed.
Network diagnostic passed (1/1 checks passed).

You must log in to continue. Would you like to log in (Y/n)?  y

Your browser has been opened to visit:

    https://accounts.google.com/o/oauth2/auth?redirect_uri=http%3A%2F%2Floc
alhost%3A8085%2F&prompt=select_account&response_type=code&client_id=3255594
0559.apps.googleusercontent.com&scope=https%3A%2F%2Fwww.googleapis.com%2Fau
th%2Fuserinfo.email+https%3A%2F%2Fwww.googleapis.com%2Fauth%2Fcloud-platfor
m+https%3A%2F%2Fwww.googleapis.com%2Fauth%2Fappengine.admin+https%3A%2F%2Fw
ww.googleapis.com%2Fauth%2Fcompute+https%3A%2F%2Fwww.googleapis.com%2Fauth%
2Faccounts.reauth&access_type=offline


You are logged in as: [ipsareeba46@gmail.com].

Pick cloud project to use:
 [1] ipslab1
 [2] mystical-ship-237109
 [3] valid-unfolding-238509
 [4] vast-node-238010
 [5] Create a new project
Please enter numeric choice or text value (must exactly match list
item):  4
```

```
Google Cloud SDK Shell - gcloud init

You can skip diagnostics next time by using the following flag:
  gcloud init --skip-diagnostics

Network diagnostic detects and fixes local network connection issues.
Checking network connection...done.
Reachability Check passed.
Network diagnostic passed (1/1 checks passed).

Choose the account you would like to use to perform operations for
this configuration:
 [1] ipsareeba46@gmail.com
 [2] Log in with a new account
Please enter your numeric choice:  1

You are logged in as: [ipsareeba46@gmail.com].

Pick cloud project to use:
 [1] ipslab1
 [2] mystical-ship-237109
 [3] valid-unfolding-238509
 [4] vast-node-238010
 [5] Create a new project
Please enter numeric choice or text value (must exactly match list
item):  4

Your current project has been set to: [vast-node-238010].
```

28. To view the detail of the project, enter the command “gcloud config list”.

```
C:\Users\user\AppData\Local\Google\Cloud SDK>gcloud config list
[compute]
region = us-east1
zone = us-east1-b
[core]
account = ipsareeba46@gmail.com
disable_usage_reporting = False
project = vast-node-238010

Your active configuration is: [default]
```

29. To view the bucket in the GCS, enter the command “gsutil ls” and for view content inside the bucket, type “gsutil ls gs://<bucketname>”.

```
C:\Users\user\AppData\Local\Google\Cloud SDK>gsutil ls
gs://ips-storagelab1/
```

```
C:\Users\user\AppData\Local\Google\Cloud SDK>gsutil ls gs://ips-storagelab1
/
gs://ips-storagelab1/Screenshot (35).png
gs://ips-storagelab1/download (1).png
gs://ips-storagelab1/labstorage/

C:\Users\user\AppData\Local\Google\Cloud SDK>
```

30. To view the folder object that you created inside the bucket, type "gsutil ls gs:<bucketname>/**".

```
C:\Users\user\AppData\Local\Google\Cloud SDK>gsutil ls gs://ips-storagelab1
/**
gs://ips-storagelab1/Screenshot (35).png
gs://ips-storagelab1/download (1).png
gs://ips-storagelab1/labstorage/
gs://ips-storagelab1/labstorage/new.png

C:\Users\user\AppData\Local\Google\Cloud SDK>
```

31. To create a bucket inside the project via command line tool, type "gsutil mb –l <zone-region> gs://<bucketname>".

```
Google Cloud SDK Shell
›perable program or batch file.

:\Users\user\AppData\Local\Google\Cloud SDK>gsutil ls gs://ips-storagelab1
/**
;s://ips-storagelab1/Screenshot (35).png
;s://ips-storagelab1/download (1).png
;s://ips-storagelab1/labstorage/
;s://ips-storagelab1/labstorage/new.png

:\Users\user\AppData\Local\Google\Cloud SDK>gsutil mb -l northamerica-nort
ieast1 gs://ips-cli-lab
```

32. Now, your bucket is being created. After creating the bucket, when you type "gsutil ls", it will show you two buckets; one created from the console and the other created from SDK Shell. To view the label of bucket, type "gsutil label get gs://<bucketname>/".

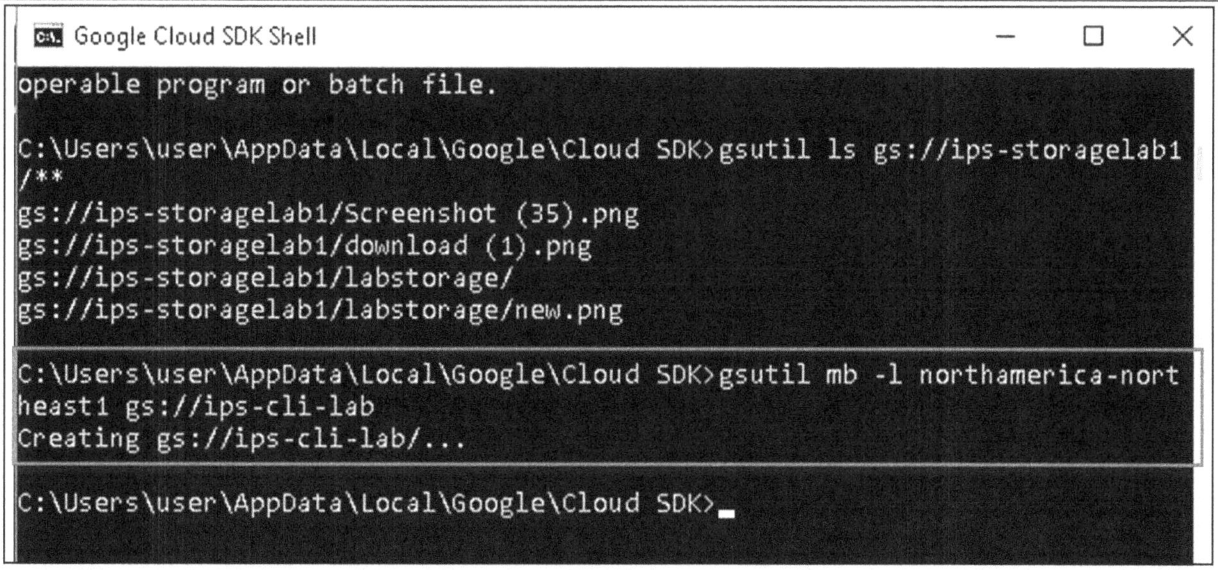

```
Google Cloud SDK Shell
operable program or batch file.

C:\Users\user\AppData\Local\Google\Cloud SDK>gsutil ls gs://ips-storagelab1
/**
gs://ips-storagelab1/Screenshot (35).png
gs://ips-storagelab1/download (1).png
gs://ips-storagelab1/labstorage/
gs://ips-storagelab1/labstorage/new.png

C:\Users\user\AppData\Local\Google\Cloud SDK>gsutil mb -l northamerica-nort
heast1 gs://ips-cli-lab
Creating gs://ips-cli-lab/...

C:\Users\user\AppData\Local\Google\Cloud SDK>
```

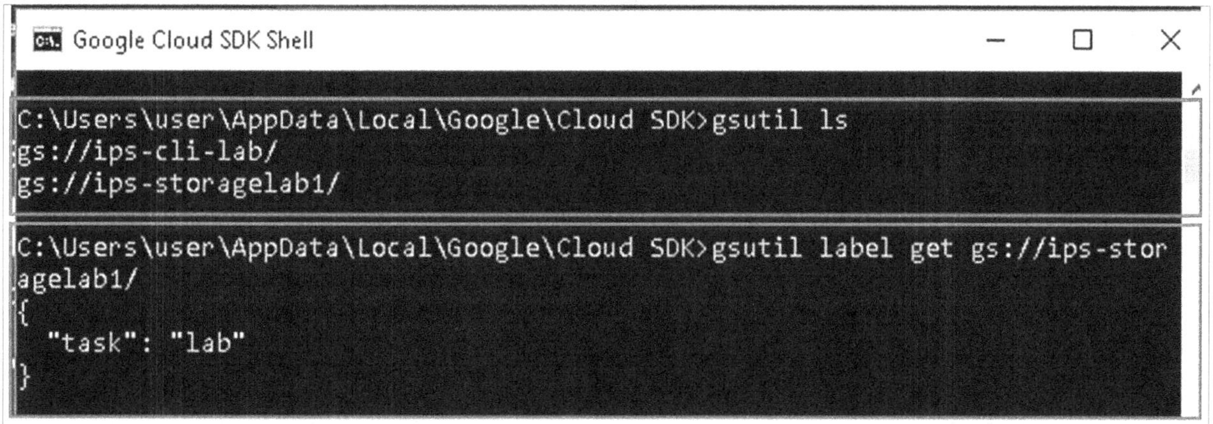

```
Google Cloud SDK Shell
C:\Users\user\AppData\Local\Google\Cloud SDK>gsutil ls
gs://ips-cli-lab/
gs://ips-storagelab1/

C:\Users\user\AppData\Local\Google\Cloud SDK>gsutil label get gs://ips-stor
agelab1/
{
  "task": "lab"
}
```

33. Now, put this label into json file via command "gsutil label get gs://<bucketname>/><filename>.json".

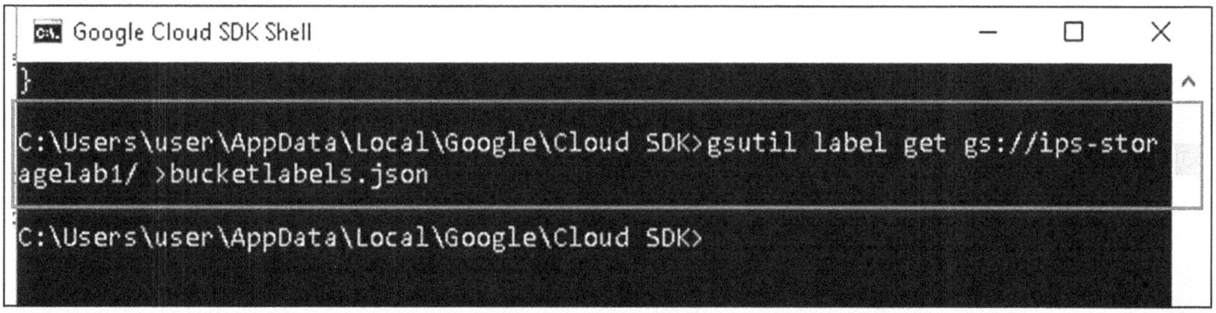

```
Google Cloud SDK Shell
}

C:\Users\user\AppData\Local\Google\Cloud SDK>gsutil label get gs://ips-stor
agelab1/ >bucketlabels.json

C:\Users\user\AppData\Local\Google\Cloud SDK>
```

34. If you view a label in the bucket that you created via Command line, then there is no label configuration. To set the label configuration in it, type "gsutil label set <filename>.json gs://<bucketname>/". Here, json file is as same as where we saved the label of the previously created bucket.

```
Google Cloud SDK Shell

C:\Users\user\AppData\Local\Google\Cloud SDK>gsutil label get gs://ips-cli-
lab/
gs://ips-cli-lab/ has no label configuration.

C:\Users\user\AppData\Local\Google\Cloud SDK>_
```

```
Google Cloud SDK Shell - gsutil label set bucketlabels.json gs://ips-cli-lab/

C:\Users\user\AppData\Local\Google\Cloud SDK>gsutil label set bucketlabels.
json gs://ips-cli-lab/
Setting label configuration on gs://ips-cli-lab/...
```

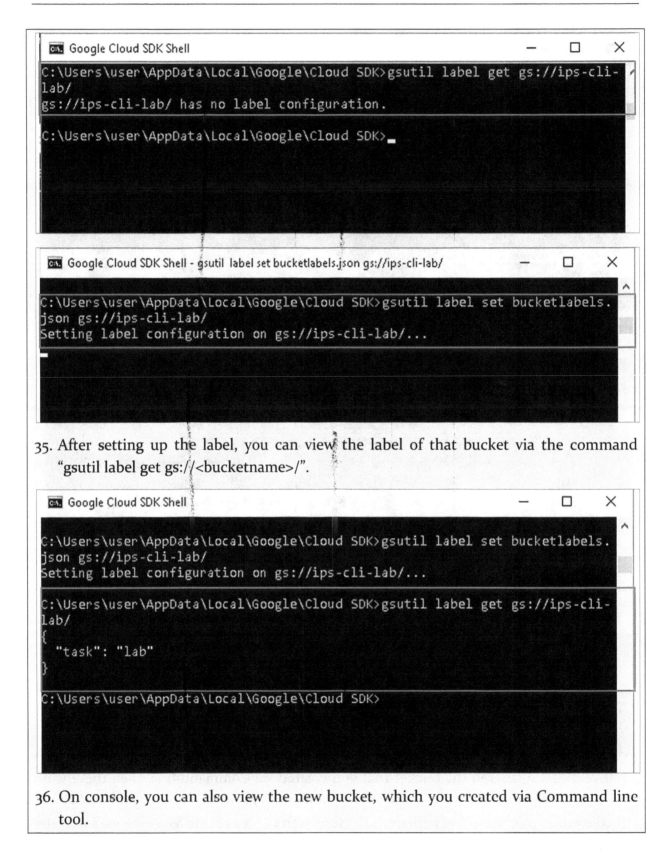

35. After setting up the label, you can view the label of that bucket via the command "gsutil label get gs://<bucketname>/".

```
Google Cloud SDK Shell

C:\Users\user\AppData\Local\Google\Cloud SDK>gsutil label set bucketlabels.
json gs://ips-cli-lab/
Setting label configuration on gs://ips-cli-lab/...

C:\Users\user\AppData\Local\Google\Cloud SDK>gsutil label get gs://ips-cli-
lab/
{
  "task": "lab"
}

C:\Users\user\AppData\Local\Google\Cloud SDK>
```

36. On console, you can also view the new bucket, which you created via Command line tool.

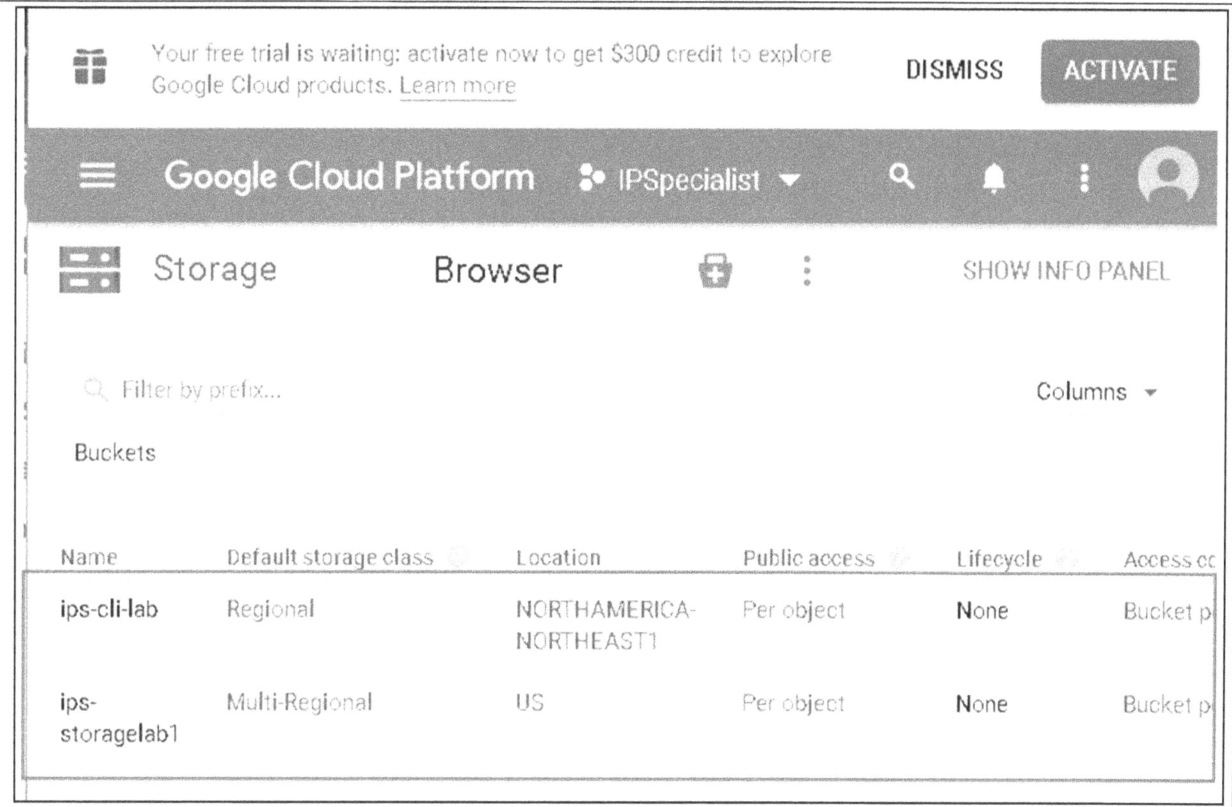

37. You can also set the new label on bucket via the command "gsutil label ch –l "<key: value>" gs://<bucketname>".

Google Cloud SDK Shell

```
C:\Users\user\AppData\Local\Google\Cloud SDK>gsutil label set bucketlabels.
json gs://ips-cli-lab/
Setting label configuration on gs://ips-cli-lab/...

C:\Users\user\AppData\Local\Google\Cloud SDK>gsutil label get gs://ips-cli-
lab/
{
  "task": "lab"
}

C:\Users\user\AppData\Local\Google\Cloud SDK>gsutil label ch -l "label:valu
e" gs://ips-cli-lab
Setting label configuration on gs://ips-cli-lab/...

C:\Users\user\AppData\Local\Google\Cloud SDK>_
```

38. On console, you can view the labels, which you have set on the newly created bucket.

Your free trial is waiting: activate now to get $300 credit to explore Google Cloud products. Learn more
DISMISS ACTIVATE
Google Cloud Platform IPSpecialist
Storage Browser SHOW INFO PANEL
Filter by prefix... Columns
Buckets

Public access	Lifecycle	Access control model	Labels	Retention p
Per object	None	Bucket policy	label : value task : lab	
Per object	None	Bucket policy & ACLs	task : lab	

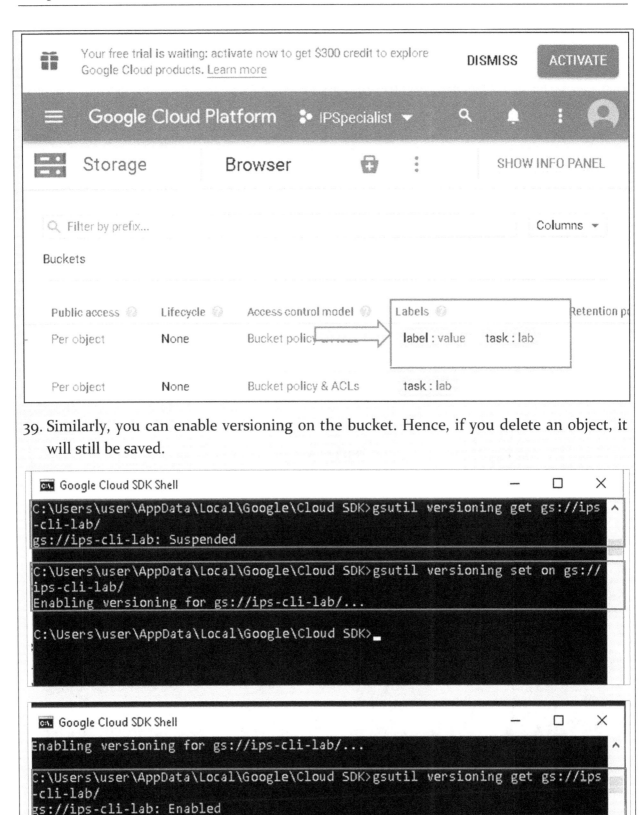

39. Similarly, you can enable versioning on the bucket. Hence, if you delete an object, it will still be saved.

Google Cloud SDK Shell

```
C:\Users\user\AppData\Local\Google\Cloud SDK>gsutil versioning get gs://ips
-cli-lab/
gs://ips-cli-lab: Suspended

C:\Users\user\AppData\Local\Google\Cloud SDK>gsutil versioning set on gs://
ips-cli-lab/
Enabling versioning for gs://ips-cli-lab/...

C:\Users\user\AppData\Local\Google\Cloud SDK>_
```

Google Cloud SDK Shell

```
Enabling versioning for gs://ips-cli-lab/...

C:\Users\user\AppData\Local\Google\Cloud SDK>gsutil versioning get gs://ips
-cli-lab/
gs://ips-cli-lab: Enabled

C:\Users\user\AppData\Local\Google\Cloud SDK>_
```

40. You can also copy a file from the SDK shell storage to the bucket via command "gsutil cp <filename>.<format> gs://<bucketname>/".

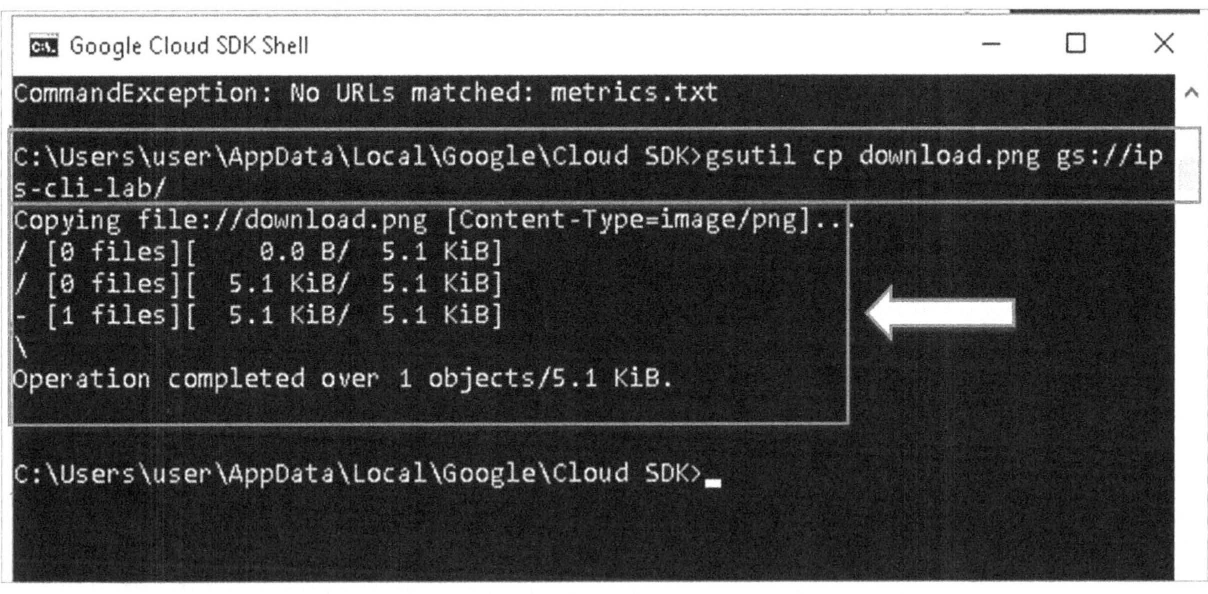

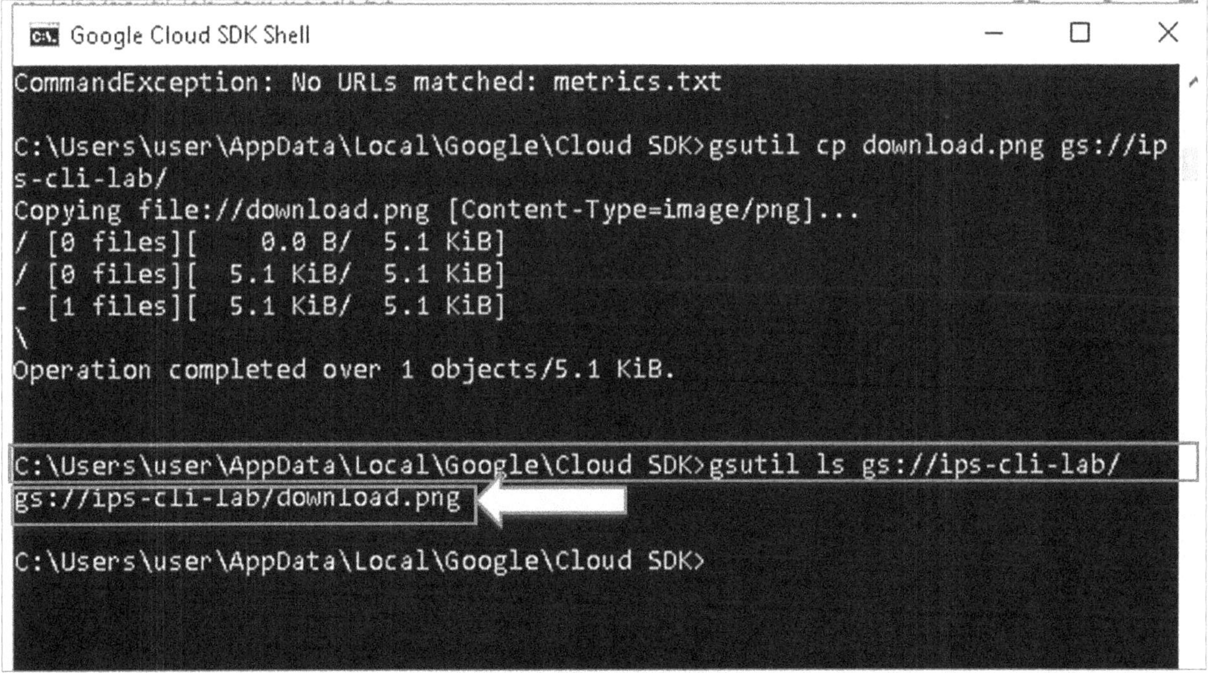

41. To get the object versioning number, type the command "gsutil ls –a gs://<bucketname>/". In this way, even if you remove the object, you still have an object in the bucket as archived.

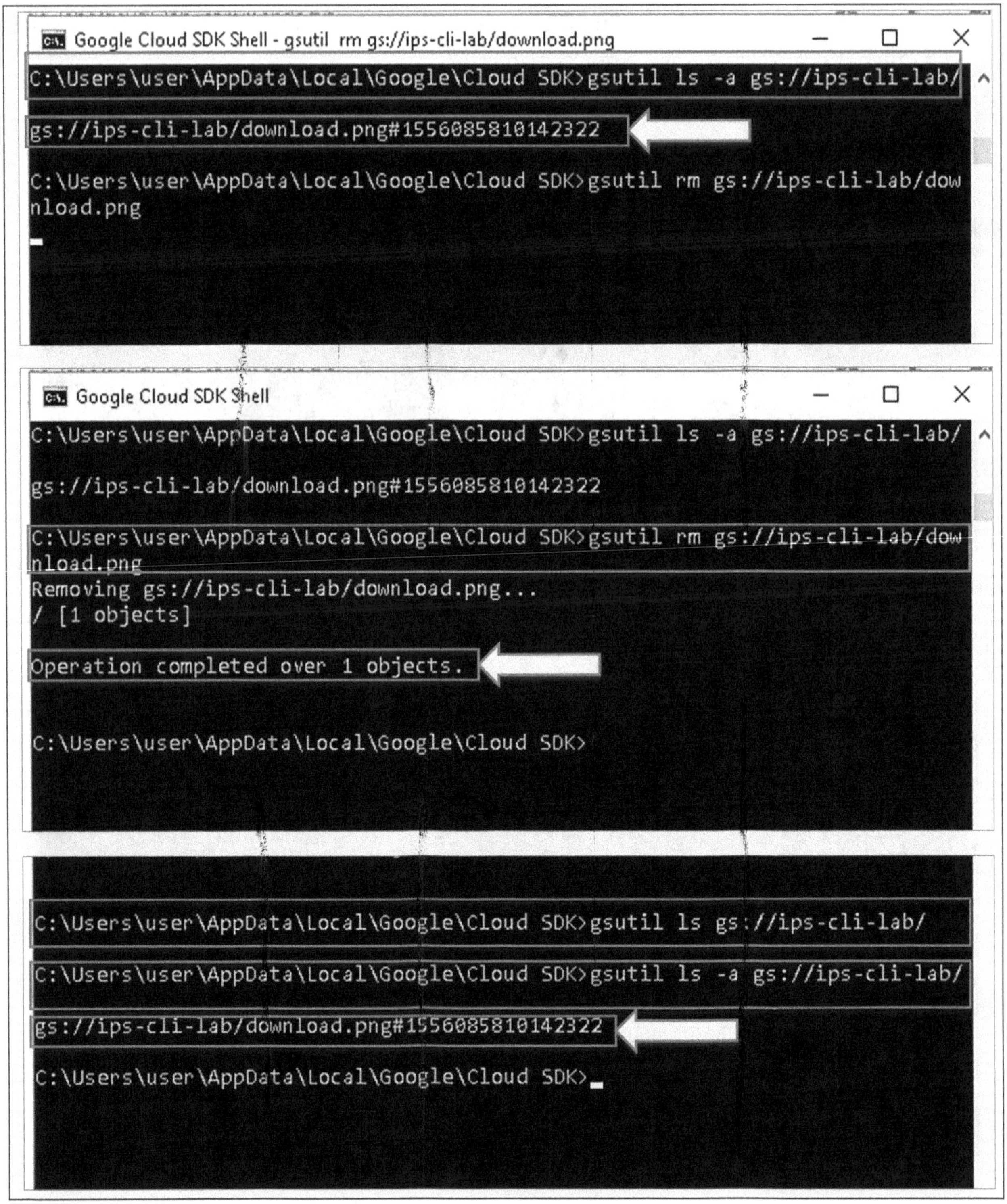

Google Cloud SDK Shell - gsutil rm gs://ips-cli-lab/download.png

```
C:\Users\user\AppData\Local\Google\Cloud SDK>gsutil ls -a gs://ips-cli-lab/

gs://ips-cli-lab/download.png#1556085810142322

C:\Users\user\AppData\Local\Google\Cloud SDK>gsutil rm gs://ips-cli-lab/dow
nload.png
```

Google Cloud SDK Shell

```
C:\Users\user\AppData\Local\Google\Cloud SDK>gsutil ls -a gs://ips-cli-lab/

gs://ips-cli-lab/download.png#1556085810142322

C:\Users\user\AppData\Local\Google\Cloud SDK>gsutil rm gs://ips-cli-lab/dow
nload.png
Removing gs://ips-cli-lab/download.png...
/ [1 objects]

Operation completed over 1 objects.


C:\Users\user\AppData\Local\Google\Cloud SDK>
```

```
C:\Users\user\AppData\Local\Google\Cloud SDK>gsutil ls gs://ips-cli-lab/

C:\Users\user\AppData\Local\Google\Cloud SDK>gsutil ls -a gs://ips-cli-lab/

gs://ips-cli-lab/download.png#1556085810142322

C:\Users\user\AppData\Local\Google\Cloud SDK>
```

Features

Object Metadata

Object metadata is the data linked with the object stored in Cloud Storage. Metadata identifies object properties and specifies how to handle the object when it is accessed. As key: value pairs, metadata is available. Metadata mutability varies; you can edit some metadata at any time, you can set some metadata only when the object has been created, and you can only view some metadata.

Editable Metadata

There are two types of metadata that users can change; Fixed Key Metadata and Custom Metadata.

Fixed Key Metadata

Fixed Key Metadata is the Metadata for which you can define value. The key is set like;

- Access Control Metadata
- Cache-Control
- Content-Disposition
- Content-Encoding
- Content-Language
- Content-Type

Custom Metadata

Metadata in which you specify both a key and a key value. You can add or remove that metadata.

Non-editable Metadata

Some of the metadata are not edited directly. This metadata is set when creating or rewriting an object. To create or rewrite objects, you can set certain metadata, like the object's storage class or the encryption keys provided by the customer. Additional metadata is added automatically and can be viewed only, such as the object generation number or the creation time.

Cloud Pub/Sub Notifications for Cloud Storage

If there are any changes in an object stored in the bucket the Cloud, Pub / Sub Notifications will send that information to Cloud Pub/Sub, then this information will be added to the Cloud Pub / Subtopic. Like for instance, in your bucket, you can track items created and deleted. Each notification contains information that describes the event that triggered it and the change in object. In every project, you have enough permission for

you can send notifications to any Cloud Pub/Sub topic. The resulting message may be sent to any number of subscribers on the subject once the Cloud Pub/Sub topic received it.

Object Change Notification

Pub/Sub notifications in your Cloud Storage buckets are the recommended way of tracking object changes since they are faster, more flexible, more configurable and more cost-effective. The object change notification is used to inform an application about any update or addition to the bucket.

A customer request may be sent to watch object changes in a particular bucket. A new notification channel is created when a watch request is completed. A notification channel is a way to send a message to an application of watching buckets. Cloud Storage notifies the application every time an object is added, updated or deleted from the bucket after a notifications channel has started.

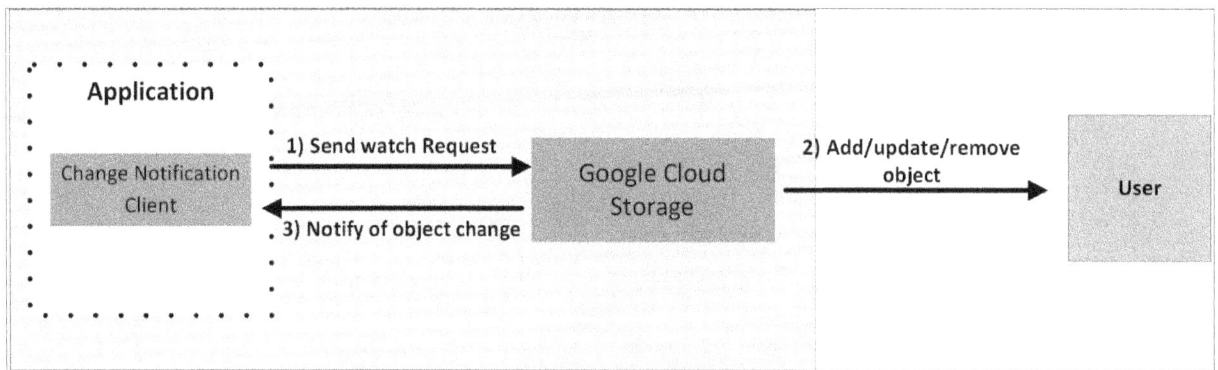

Figure 3-01: Object Change Notification

Object Versioning

Cloud Storage offers the Object Versioning feature to support the recovery of deleted or overwritten objects. With Object Versioning, you can prevent overwriting or accidentally deleting your Cloud Storage data. However, with Object Versioning, there is an increase in storage costs, which can be partially reduced with the deletion of old object versions by configuring Object Lifecycle Management. With versioning, you can archive version of an object each time the live version of the object is overwritten or deleted. These archived versions can be identified by the generation number. Versioning can be turned on and off in a bucket at any given time.

Object Lifecycle Management

There is a lifecycle management configuration, which can be assigned to manage the bucket. The setup includes a set of rules for current and future objects. When an object

complies with a rule, Cloud Storage performs a specified action on an object automatically.

When multiple rules with the same action are specified, the action is taken when the object in any of the rule(s) matches the requirement(s). Only one action should be included in each rule.

Requester Pays

When a user has access to a cloud storage resource like a bucket or object, the request is charged and executed. Usually, those access charges are charged to the project owner of the resource. You can request that requestors include a billing project in their applications with the Requester pays enabled on your bucket and therefore bill the project of your request.

Retention Policies using Bucket Lock

The Bucket Lock feature allows you to configure a Cloud Storage bucket's data retention policy in order to determine how long the bucket objects must be maintained. The feature also allows you to lock the retention policy to prevent a decrease or deletion of the policy permanently. This feature can provide immutable storage on Cloud Storage.

To specify a period of retention, you can add a retention policy to a bucket. In cases where a bucket has a retention policy, bucket objects can be deleted or overwritten only once the age exceeds the retention term. Retroactively, a retention policy applies for existing items in the bucket and new items in the bucket.

You can lock policy to keep it on the bucket permanently. You can not remove or minimize the retention period when you lock a retention policy. A bucket with a locked retention policy may not be removed unless the retention period has been met by every object in the bucket. The retention time of the locked retention policy can be increased. The locking of a retention policy can assist in the compliance of your data with records.

Note: Retention Policy Locking is an irreversible action. Once it is locked, you must delete the entire bucket to "remove" the bucket's retention policy.

Cloud Audit Logging with Cloud Storage

Cloud audit logging with Cloud storage is used for logging for cloud storage API operations. There are two types of logs within Cloud Audit Logging, i.e., admin activity logs and data access logs.

Admin Activity Logs are operating entries that modify the project, bucket or object settings or metadata. **Data Access Logs** are project, bucket or object entries for operations that modify or read objects.

Cross-Origin Resource Sharing (CORS)

Cloud Storage supports CORS so that your buckets can be configured for resource sharing among the different origin. For example, "the.storage.googleapis.com" bucket can be configured to allow a browser to share resources with scripts of "such.appspot.com". You can only set CORS at the bucket level. With the Gsutil command-line tool, the XML API, or the JSON API, you can set the CORS configuration to your bucket.

Access Control

With the Access Control option, you can control the access of your bucket and objects in Cloud Storage with the type of access you require. There are multiple options available for Access Control:

- **Cloud Identity and Access Management (Cloud IAM) Permissions**: Grant access to buckets as well as bulk access to a bucket's objects. You have wide control over your projects and buckets through cloud IAM permissions, but not fine grain control over individual objects
- **Access Control Lists (ACLs):** Give the individual buckets or objects read and write access to users. Using Cloud IAM permissions rather than ACLs, in most cases. Use ACLs when control of individual objects is fine grained
- **Signed URLs:** Specify read or write access for an object with a time-limited URL you create. Whoever sharing the URL can access the object, whether or not it has an account with Google, for the time you specify
- **Bucket Policy Feature:** Only allows you to control access to your storage cloud resources uniformly. Only the Cloud IAM bucket level allows access to the bucket and objects when enabled on the bucket, the access lists (ACLs) are disabled, and access granted to ACLs is revoked. Cloud IAM is used across GCP and enables you to give you fine-grained bucket and project levels permissions. Cloud Storage is the only way to use ACLs and has fewer permission options, but allows permissions to be granted per object. So that is why bucket policy's only feature is used.

Encryption

In Cloud Storage, the encryption of data is performed at server side before it is uploaded to disk with no additional cost. However, you can try other ways for encryption using Cloud Storage.

Google Managed Encryption Keys

When Cloud Storage get the data, it performs encryption before writting on disk. Cloud Storage manages on your behalf the server-side encryption keys via the key management

systems, which we use for our encrypted data, use AES-256 to encode user data at rest in Cloud Storage.

Customer-Supplied Encryption Keys

You can create your server-side encoding key, which acts as a further encoding layer over a standard Cloud Storage encoding and manages it. You can choose your AES-256 key that need to be provided by you. Cloud Storage does not permanently store your key on Google's servers or manage your key if you provide a customer-supplied encryption key. Therefore, you should instead use a Cloud Storage key because after the operation is complete, your key will be removed from Google's servers. Cloud Storage only stores a cryptographic key hash to validate future requests with the hash. It is not possible for your key to recover from this hash, and hash cannot be used to decrypt your information.

Customer Managed Encryption Keys

In customer managed key, you use the Cloud Key Management Service, you can generate and manage your encryption keys as an additional encryption layer above a standard Cloud Storage encryption layer. In this, you use the key generated by Cloud KMS. This encryption key is stored within Cloud KMS.

Client-Side Encryption

You have to create and manage, your encryption keys and use your tools to encrypt data before sending it into Cloud Storage in client-side encryption. Cloud Storage has encrypted data that you encrypt on the client's side, and Cloud Storage does not know which keys you used to encrypt the details. Cloud Storage is encrypted for a second time when your data is received. This second encryption is referred to as Cloud storage server-side encryption. Cloud storage removes the server layer of the encryption when retrieving your data, but the customer-side layer must be decrypted by you.

Consistency

Cloud Storage provides strong consistency for some operation and eventual consistency on some operations. The operations on which strong consistency globally provided are:

- Read-after-write
- Read-after-metadata-update
- Read-after-delete
- Bucket listing
- Object listing
- Granting access to resources

While the operation on which eventual consistency occurs is Revoking access from resources like; If the access of a user to a bucket is removed, these changes are immediately reflected in bucket metadata, but it may still take a short time for the user to have access to the bucket.

Cache Control and Consistency

Objects in the cache that can be read publicly may not be very consistent. The object cache is not updated or deleted until its cache life expires, if you allow an object to be cached in the cache. The object resides in the cache when it is updated or deleted.

Gcloud

Overview

Gcloud is a command line tool, which is used to interact with GCP, but you can use "gsutil" and "bq" as well. All of them share the same configuration, which is set via gcloud config. Gsutil in command line could have been the gcloud storage and bq in command line could have been the gcloud BigQuery.

All of these tools gcloud, gsutil and bq are available in Cloud SDK tool. Via this tool, you can access the Google Compute Engine, Google Cloud Storage, Google Big Query, and other services. In general command line tool are more powerful than console but less than the Rest API. Some of the things are not possible to do with the console so you can do that via Command line tool. Nonetheless, some operations are only possible via REST API.

There are three releases level named as general, alpha and beta. In general, there is an availability of commands that are fully stable and available for production use.

There are some additions that Google performs on gcloud, which you can access via gcloud alpha and gcloud beta. For example, gcloud beta billing account list command is used to list the billing account as its new addition but is not fully applied. In alpha releases, the commands are in the early stage of release and it can be changed without notice while the beta commands are completely functional but still have some issues.

Syntax

The basic syntax of gcloud is given below. In the syntax, the command runs from left to right.

"gcloud <global flags> <service/product> <group/area> <command> <flag> <parameters>"

e.g: gcloud –project myprojid compute instances list, gcloud compute instances create testvm (in this command, we did not define the project id as you specify it in the configuration).

There are many other commands you can use like "gsutil ls" is used to list the Google Cloud Storage.

- **Global Flags**- Users can set several global flags to modify the control behavior for all commands within the gcloud CLI
  --help (to display detailed help)
  --h (to display a summary of help)
  --project <projectID> (project name for invocation)
  --account <Account> (User account for the invocation of Google Cloud Platform)
  --format (Set the format to be used to print output command resources. The default is a human-friendly output format for commands)
  --quiet (disable the interactive prompts for gcloud commands)

Configuration Properties

These are the values that are entered once and can be used by any command that needs them; this is the way you specify the project. These values can be overwritten on specific command with a correspondence flag. The configuration properties are used for an account, project, region, and zone. For example, if you do not want to write account name every time to run gcloud, you can set the account property. Similarly, you can set project, region by defining every time –account, --project and --region. To set these properties, the syntax you have to use is " gcloud config set <property> <value>". After setting up the value, you can check the configuration by "gcloud get-value <property>". To clear the value, you use the command "gcloud config unset <property>".

Configurations

A set of SDK properties is a configuration. These features are key-value pairs that govern the gcloud command line tool's behavior and other SDK tools. It is used to maintain the group settings and switching the settings between them. It is useful when you have multiple projects. With the command "gcloud init", you can go into configuration to set an interactive flow of properties that are common. Some commands can be used to view some settings like:

- gcloud config list (to list all properties in the configuration you set)
- gcloud config configuration list (list all configurations)

"gcloud config configuration list" command will show you a table of configuration in which the configuration you are using will be shown in "IS_ACTIVE" column while other

column shows a list of account, project, zone, region and name of the configuration. In the beginning, you have only one configuration, but you can create a new configuration as well. The command to create new configuration is "gcloud config configurations create <name>". To switch on this new configuration type "gcloud config configurations activate <name>".

Configuration Analogy

Action	Directory	Configuration
Make new	mkdir newdir	gcloud config configurations create newconfig
Switch to	cd newdir	gcloud config configuration activates newconfig
List the content	ls	gcloud config list
List nonactive directory	ls ~/newdir (path of the directory whose content want to list)	gcloud --configuration=newconfig config list or gcloud config configurations describe newconfig

Table 3-03: Configuration Analogy

Lab 3-2: Creating VM

Scenario:

A company wants to create a virtual test server to check if they migrated their infra to the Cloud. Which service in GCP is best to use?

Solution:

GCE is the service that will be used to create a virtual VM.

1. Before creating a VM, you first need to enable Compute Engine API either via Console or via Command line tool. Here we will enable it via console. Login to "GCP" and from the list, select "API and Services".

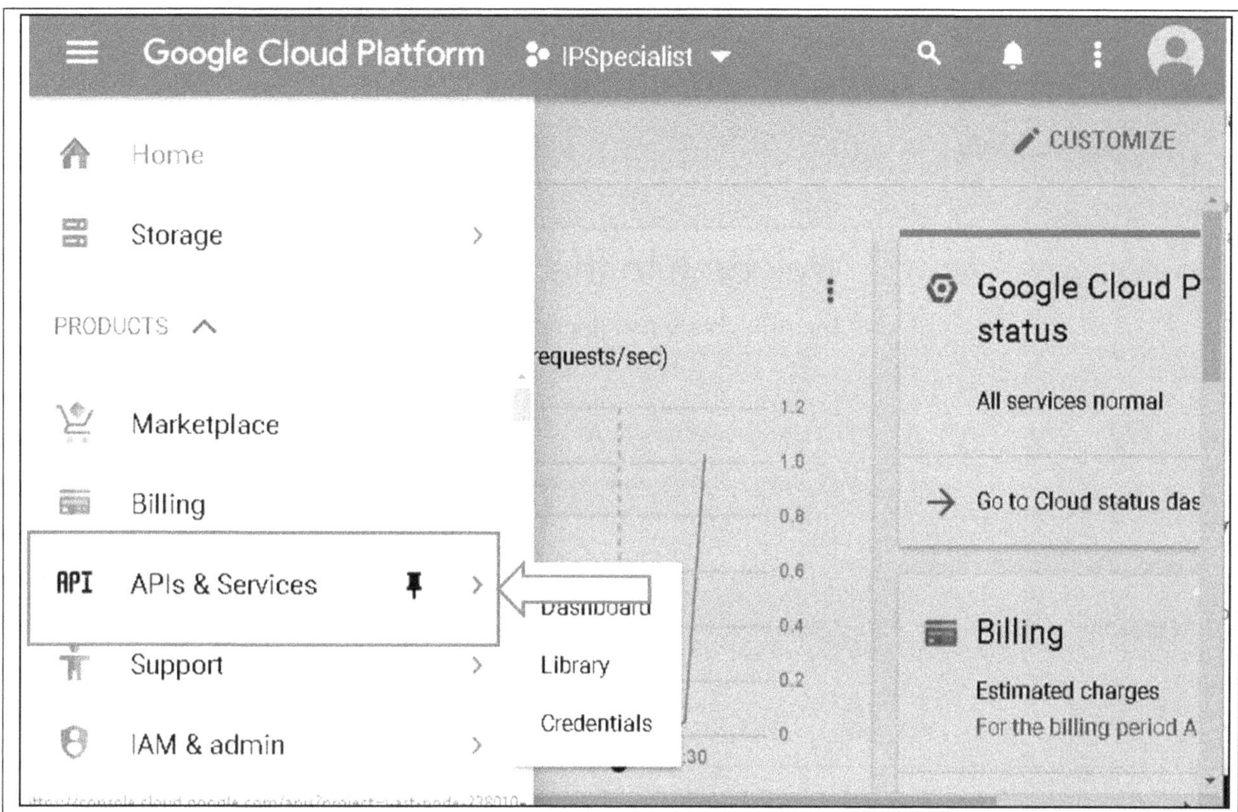

2. Click on "ENABLE APIS AND SERVICE". Search for "Compute Engine" and then click on "ENABLE".

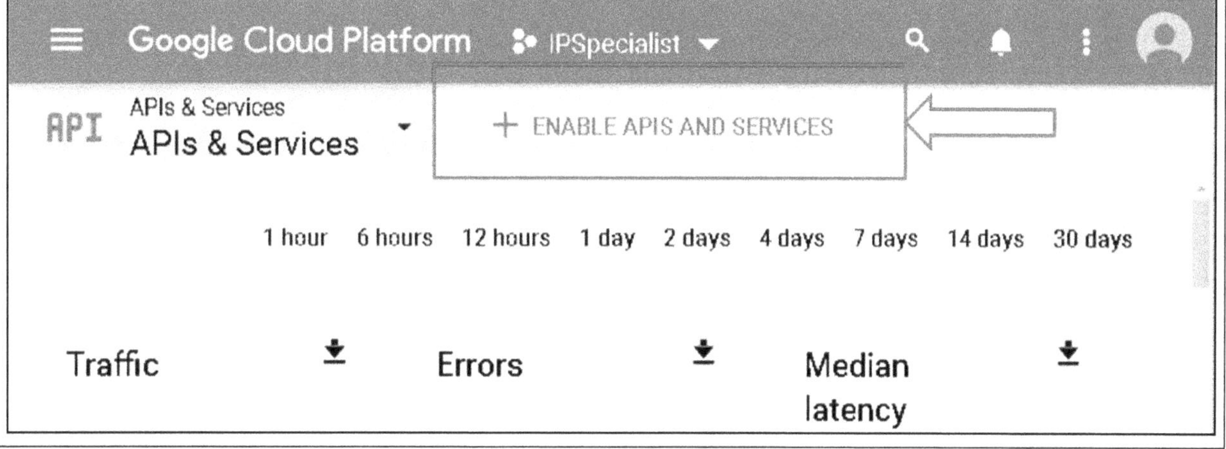

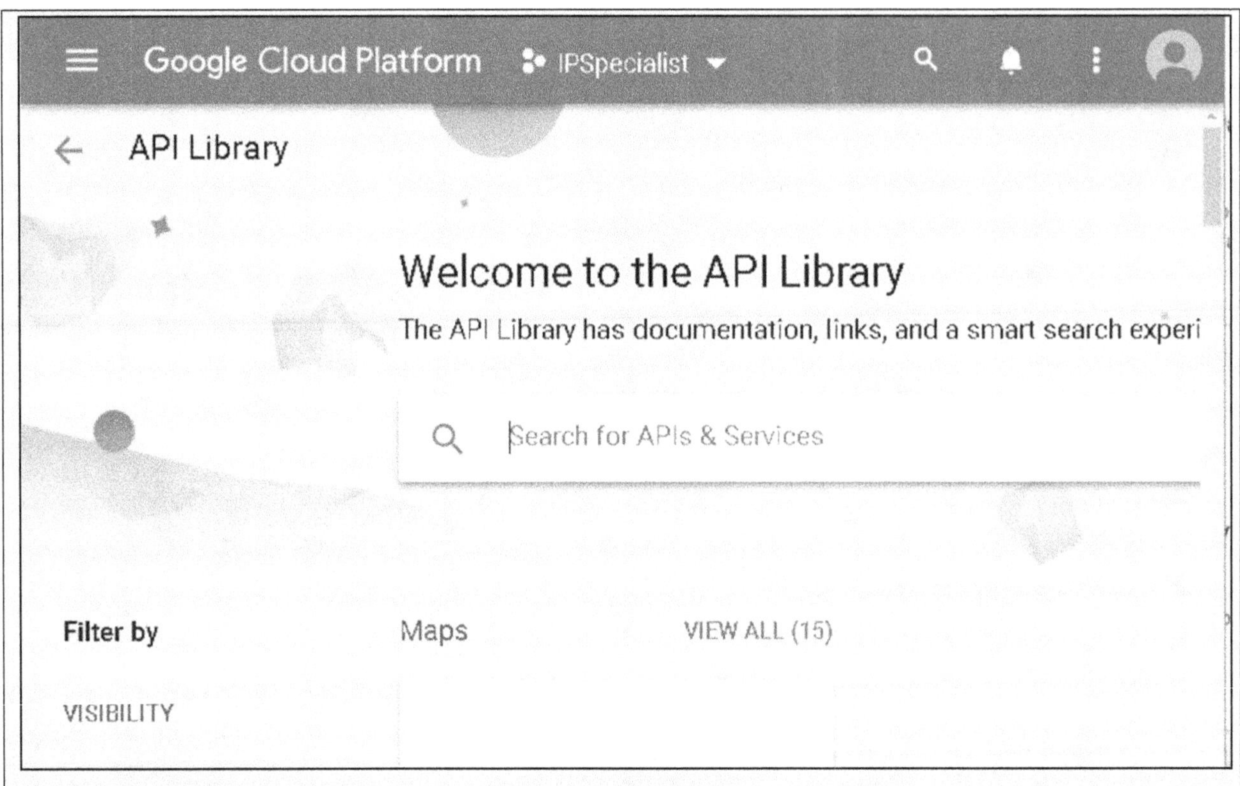
Google Cloud Platform
IPSpecialist
API Library
Welcome to the API Library
The API Library has documentation, links, and a smart search experi
Search for APIs & Services
Filter by
Maps
VIEW ALL (15)
VISIBILITY

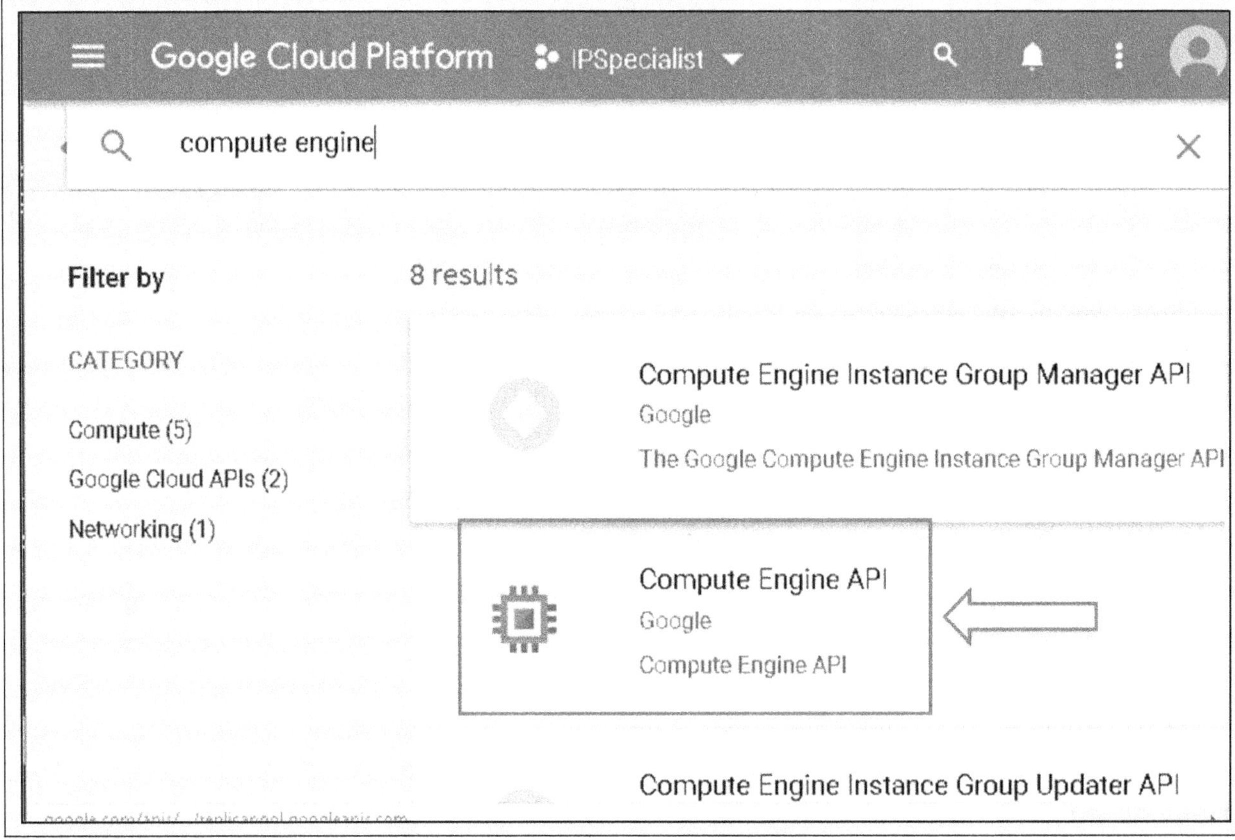
Google Cloud Platform
IPSpecialist
compute engine
Filter by
8 results
CATEGORY
Compute (5)
Google Cloud APIs (2)
Networking (1)
Compute Engine Instance Group Manager API
Google
The Google Compute Engine Instance Group Manager API
Compute Engine API
Google
Compute Engine API
Compute Engine Instance Group Updater API

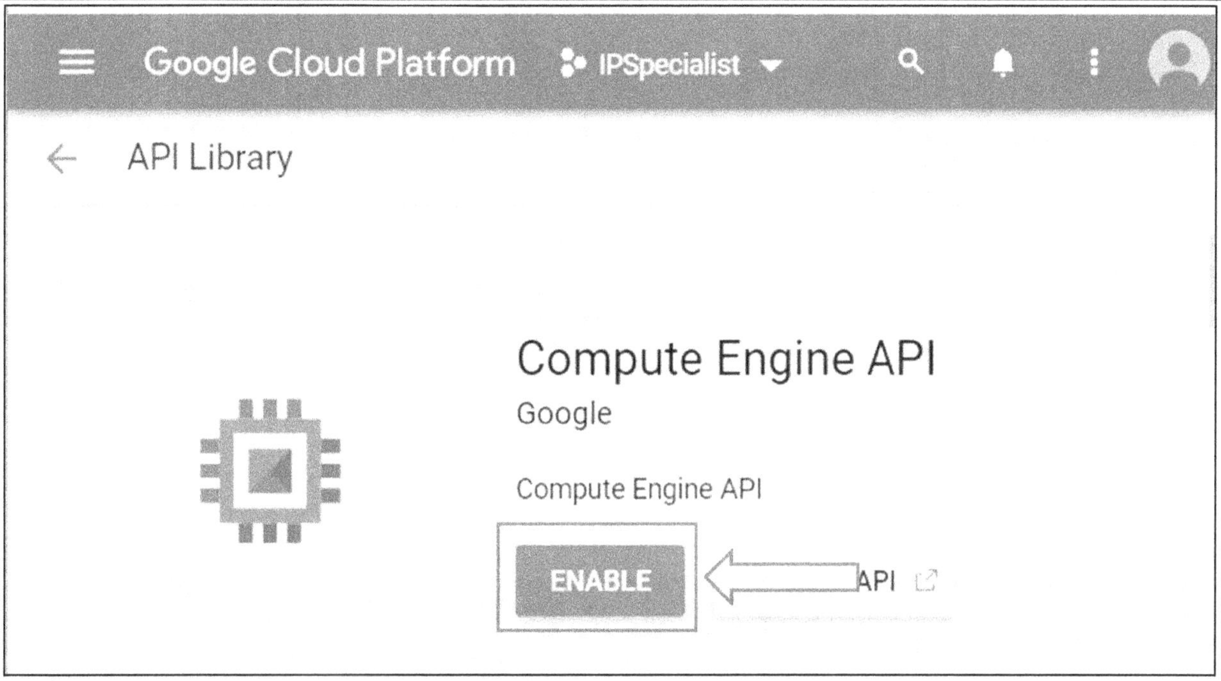

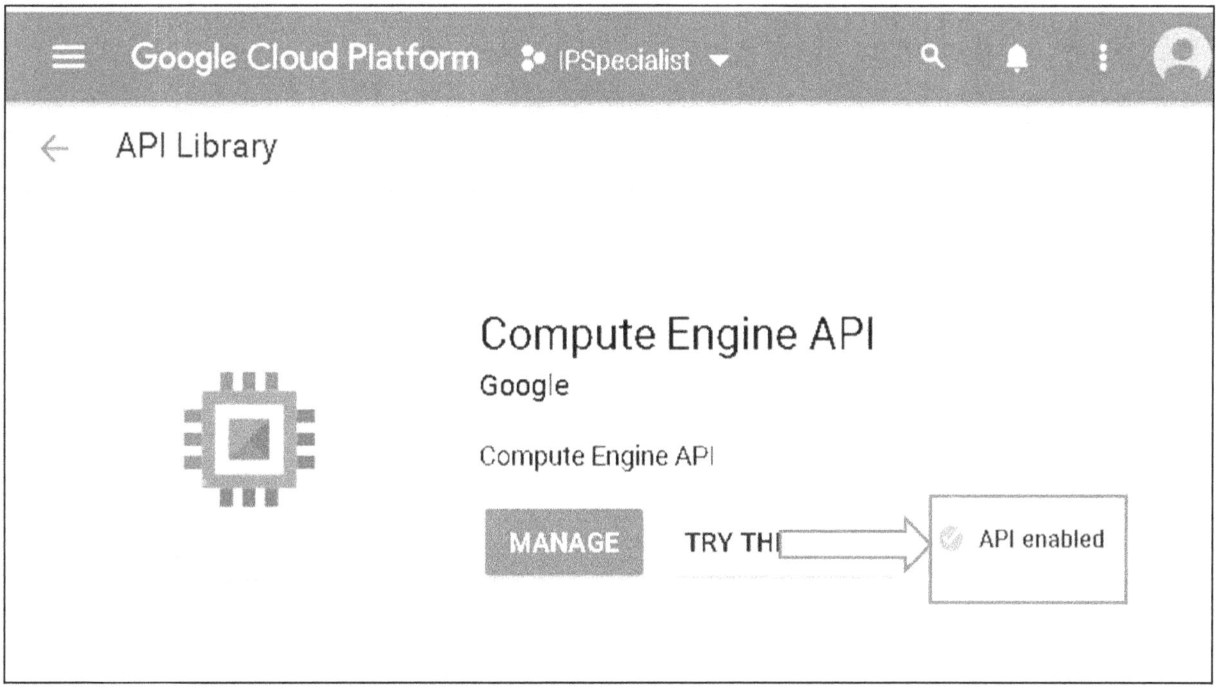

3. After enabling Compute Engine API, go to the Google Cloud SDK Shell and follow the same steps as we followed in Lab 3.1. Now. to identify in which project you are, type "gcloud config get-value project". This will show you your project name as an output.

```
Google Cloud SDK Shell
C:\Users\user\AppData\Local\Google\Cloud SDK>gcloud config get-value project
vast-node-238010

C:\Users\user\AppData\Local\Google\Cloud SDK>
```

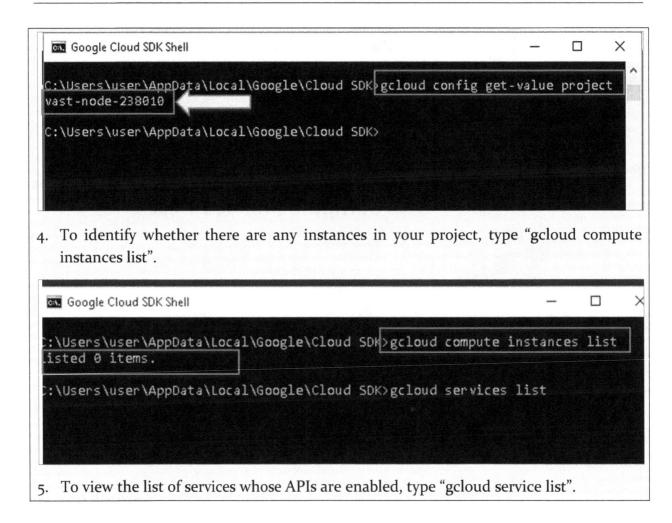

4. To identify whether there are any instances in your project, type "gcloud compute instances list".

```
Google Cloud SDK Shell
:\Users\user\AppData\Local\Google\Cloud SDK>gcloud compute instances list
isted 0 items.

:\Users\user\AppData\Local\Google\Cloud SDK>gcloud services list
```

5. To view the list of services whose APIs are enabled, type "gcloud service list".

```
Google Cloud SDK Shell
Listed 0 items.

C:\Users\user\AppData\Local\Google\Cloud SDK>gcloud services list
NAME                                  TITLE
bigquery-json.googleapis.com          BigQuery API
cloudapis.googleapis.com              Google Cloud APIs
cloudbuild.googleapis.com             Cloud Build API
clouddebugger.googleapis.com          Stackdriver Debugger API
cloudresourcemanager.googleapis.com   Cloud Resource Manager API
cloudtrace.googleapis.com             Stackdriver Trace API
composer.googleapis.com               Cloud Composer API
compute.googleapis.com                Compute Engine API
container.googleapis.com              Kubernetes Engine API
containerregistry.googleapis.com      Container Registry API
datastore.googleapis.com              Cloud Datastore API
deploymentmanager.googleapis.com      Cloud Deployment Manager V2 API
iam.googleapis.com                    Identity and Access Management (IAM) API

iamcredentials.googleapis.com         IAM Service Account Credentials API
logging.googleapis.com                Stackdriver Logging API
monitoring.googleapis.com             Stackdriver Monitoring API
oslogin.googleapis.com                Cloud OS Login API
pubsub.googleapis.com                 Cloud Pub/Sub API
replicapool.googleapis.com            Compute Engine Instance Group Manager AP
I
replicapoolupdater.googleapis.com     Compute Engine Instance Group Updater AP
I
```

6. As we enabled "Compute Engine API" in the beginning, it will automatically create its respective roles in IAM. You can check this by going into "IAM" under "IAM and admin".

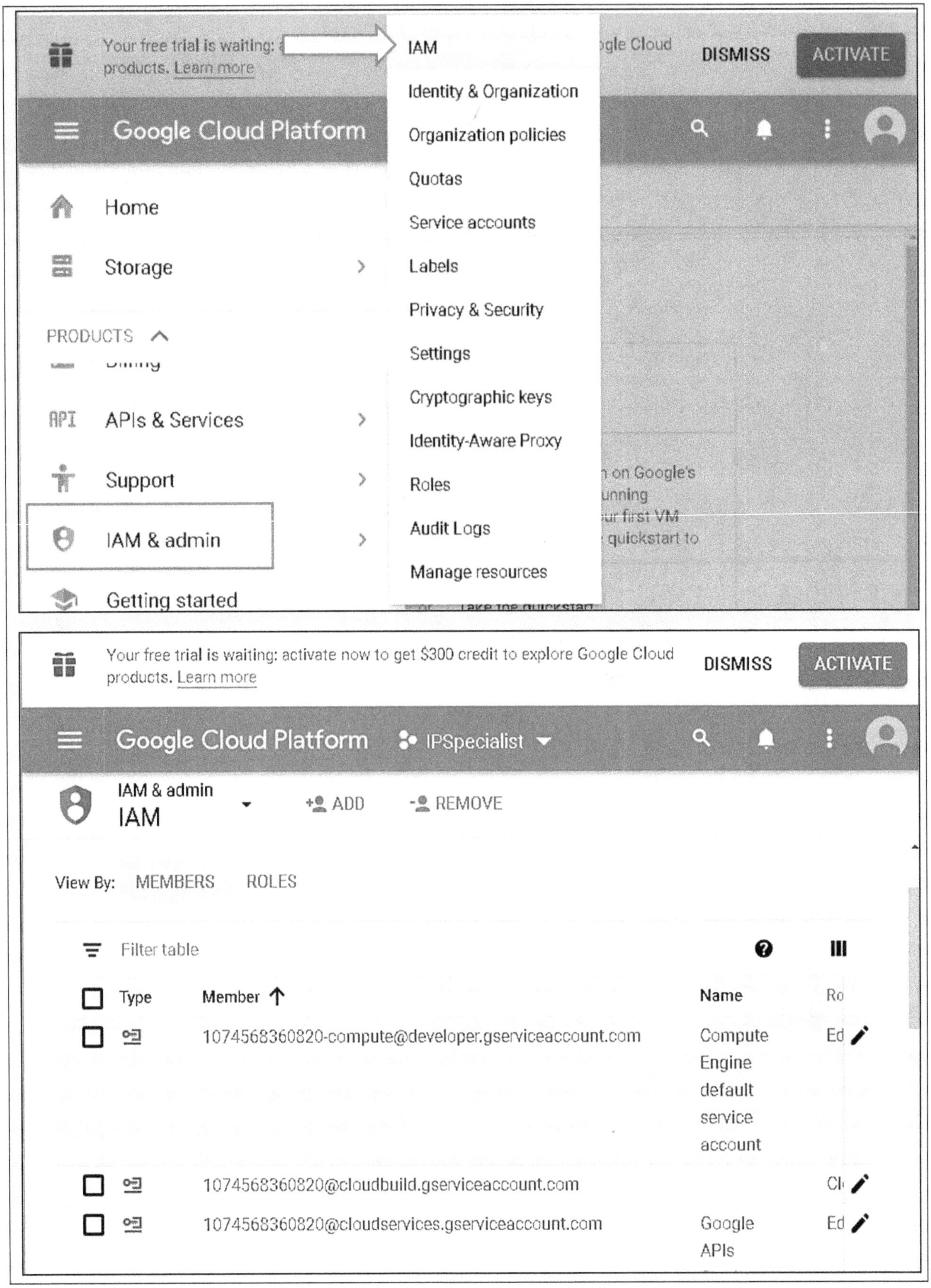

Your free trial is waiting: a... ...gle Cloud products. Learn more
DISMISS
ACTIVATE

Google Cloud Platform

Home
Storage
PRODUCTS
APIs & Services
Support
IAM & admin
Getting started

IAM
Identity & Organization
Organization policies
Quotas
Service accounts
Labels
Privacy & Security
Settings
Cryptographic keys
Identity-Aware Proxy
Roles
Audit Logs
Manage resources

Your free trial is waiting: activate now to get $300 credit to explore Google Cloud products. Learn more
DISMISS
ACTIVATE

Google Cloud Platform IPSpecialist

IAM & admin
IAM
ADD
REMOVE

View By: MEMBERS ROLES

Filter table

Type	Member	Name	Ro
	1074568360820-compute@developer.gserviceaccount.com	Compute Engine default service account	Ed
	1074568360820@cloudbuild.gserviceaccount.com		Cl
	1074568360820@cloudservices.gserviceaccount.com	Google APIs	Ed

7. A default service account is also created for the Compute Engine, which you can view in "Service accounts" under "APIs and Services".

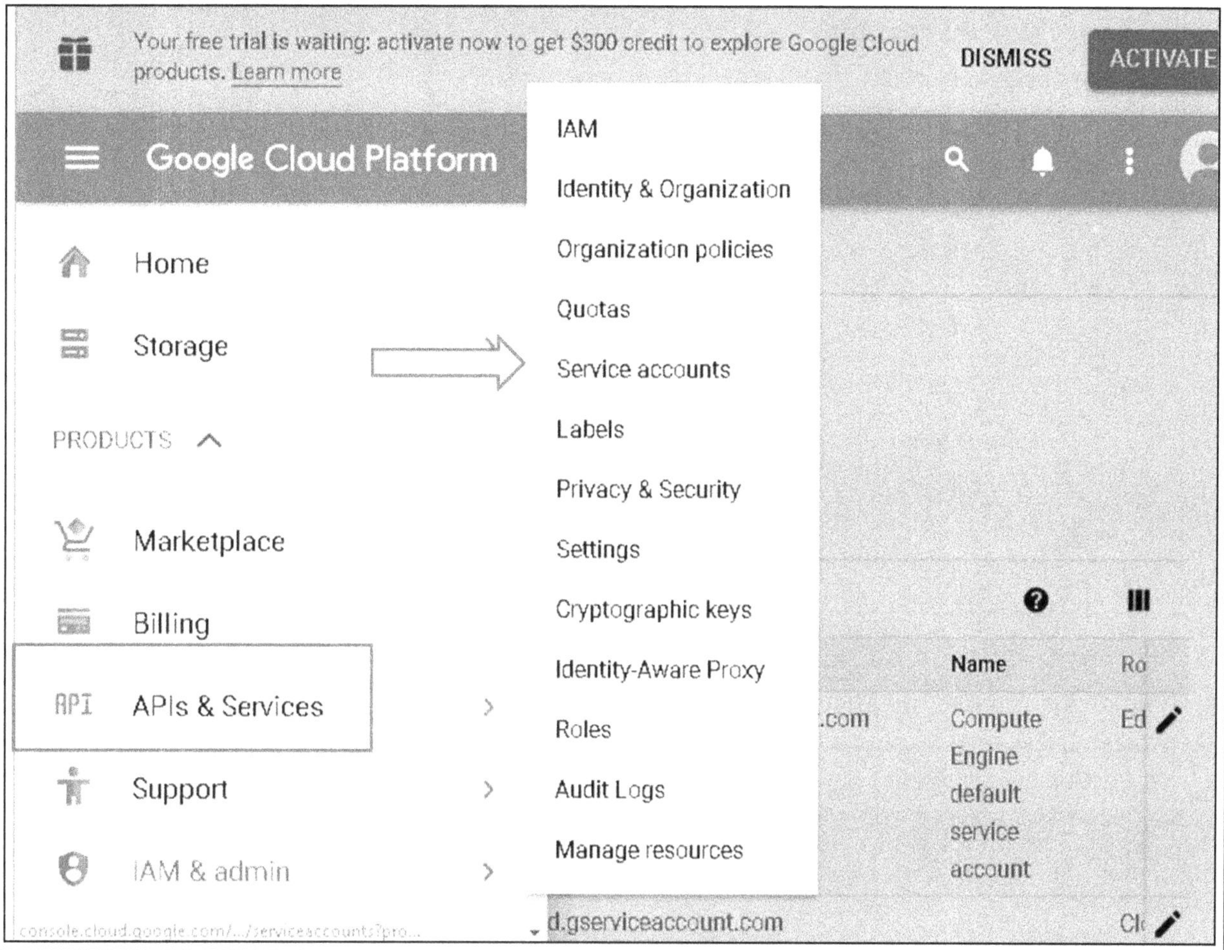

Your free trial is waiting: activate now to get $300 credit to explore Google Cloud products. Learn more
DISMISS
ACTIVATE
Google Cloud Platform
Home
Storage
PRODUCTS
Marketplace
Billing
APIs & Services
Support
IAM & admin
IAM
Identity & Organization
Organization policies
Quotas
Service accounts
Labels
Privacy & Security
Settings
Cryptographic keys
Identity-Aware Proxy
Roles
Audit Logs
Manage resources
Name
Compute Engine default service account
d.gserviceaccount.com

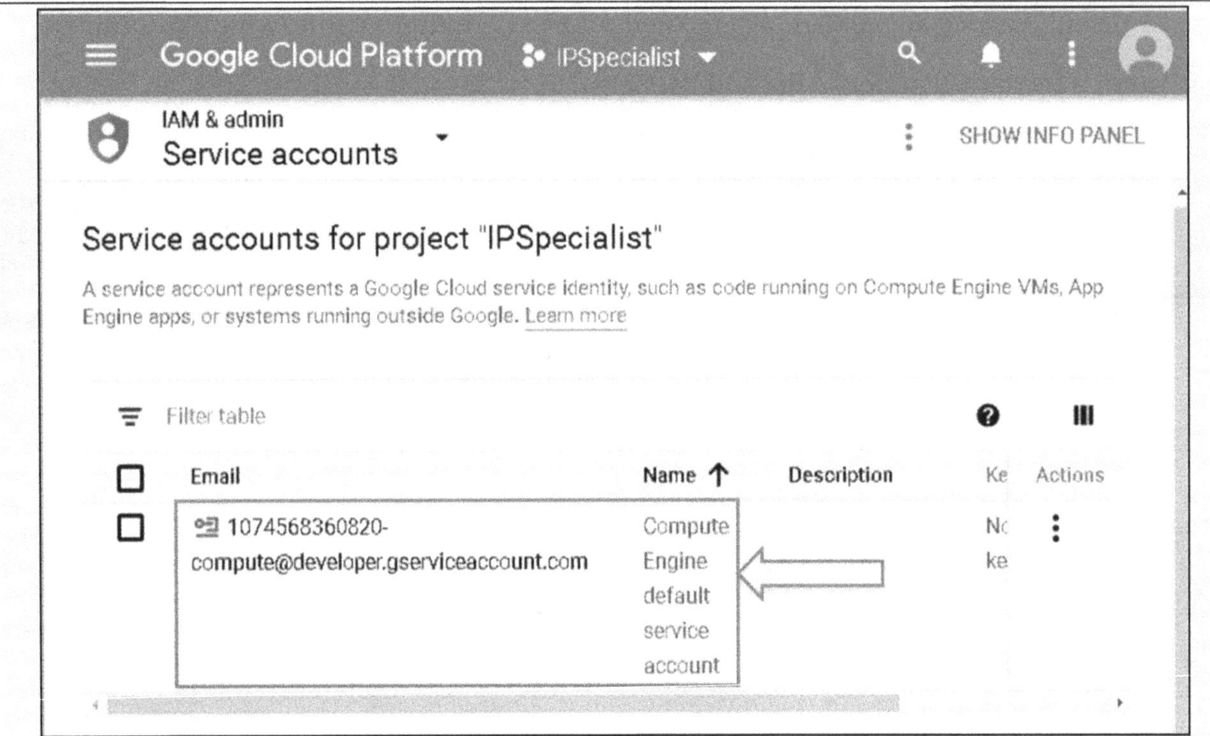

8. To create a VM via Command Line tool, go to Google Cloud SDK Shell and type “gcloud compute instances create <vmname>”.

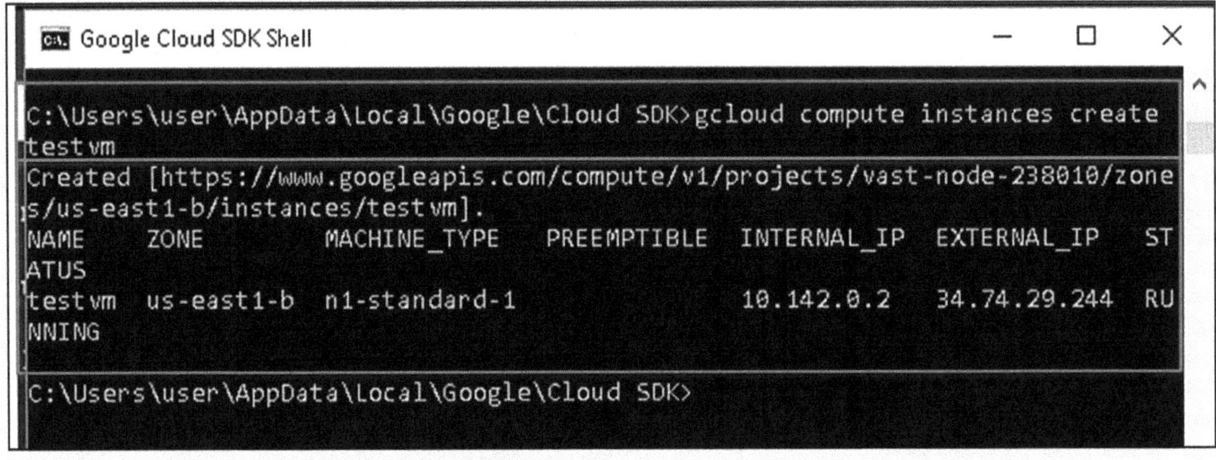

9. After the VM has been created, you can view it in the GCP console as well.

Google Cloud Platform   IPSpecialist

Compute Engine   VM instances   SHOW INFO PANEL

Filter VM instances   Columns

Name	Zone	Recommendation	In use by	Internal IP	External IP	Connect
testvm	us-east1-b			10.142.0.2 (nic0)	34.74.29.244	SSH

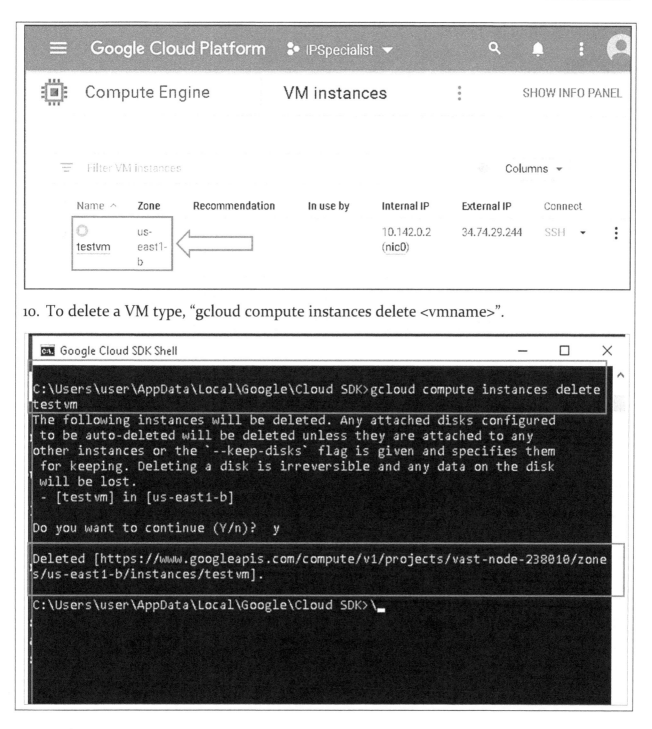

10. To delete a VM type, “gcloud compute instances delete <vmname>”.

Google Cloud SDK Shell

```
C:\Users\user\AppData\Local\Google\Cloud SDK>gcloud compute instances delete
testvm
The following instances will be deleted. Any attached disks configured
 to be auto-deleted will be deleted unless they are attached to any
other instances or the `--keep-disks` flag is given and specifies them
 for keeping. Deleting a disk is irreversible and any data on the disk
 will be lost.
 - [testvm] in [us-east1-b]

Do you want to continue (Y/n)?  y

Deleted [https://www.googleapis.com/compute/v1/projects/vast-node-238010/zone
s/us-east1-b/instances/testvm].

C:\Users\user\AppData\Local\Google\Cloud SDK>\_
```

Google Compute Engine

You can create and run virtual machines on Google infrastructure with Google Compute Engine. Compute Engine provides scale, performance, and value that let you start large computing clusters on Google's infrastructure easily. There are no upfront investments and a system designed for fast and consistent performance can be used by thousands of virtual CPUs.

Virtual Machine Instances

Overview

An instance is a Google-based Virtual Machine (VM). The Google Cloud Platform Console, gcloud Command-line Tool or Compute Engine API allows you to create an instance. The instances of Compute Engine can run Linux public images and Windows Server images provided by Google and private custom images, which can be produced or imported from existing systems. Docker containers can also be used, which are launched automatically in instances where the Optimized OS image runs. You can use a pre-determined machine type, set or create your custom machine types to select the machine characteristics of your instances, such as the number of virtual CPUs and the number of memory.

When you are a using console, you can view that the price changes depend on the machine type.

Instances and Projects

Each instance is part of the console project for a Google Cloud Platform, and one or more instances may exist. You specify the operating system, zone and machine type of the instance when you create an instance in a Project. These are removed from the project if you remove the instance.

Instances and Storage Options

Each Computes Engine, by default, has a small boot persistent disk, which contains the OS. You can also add additional storage based on the requirements of the application that is running on the instance.

Instances and Networks

Up to five VPC networks can be used in a project, and each Compute Engine instance is in one VPC network. Instances in the same network interact via a LAN protocol. Instances use the Internet to communicate outside their network with any machine that may be virtual or physical.

Instances and Containers

Instances from Compute Engine support a declarative way to launch container-based applications. You can provide a name for a Docker image and start configuration when creating a VM or instance template. Compute Engine will take care of the rest, including the installation of a Docker installed and starting your container when the VM starts.

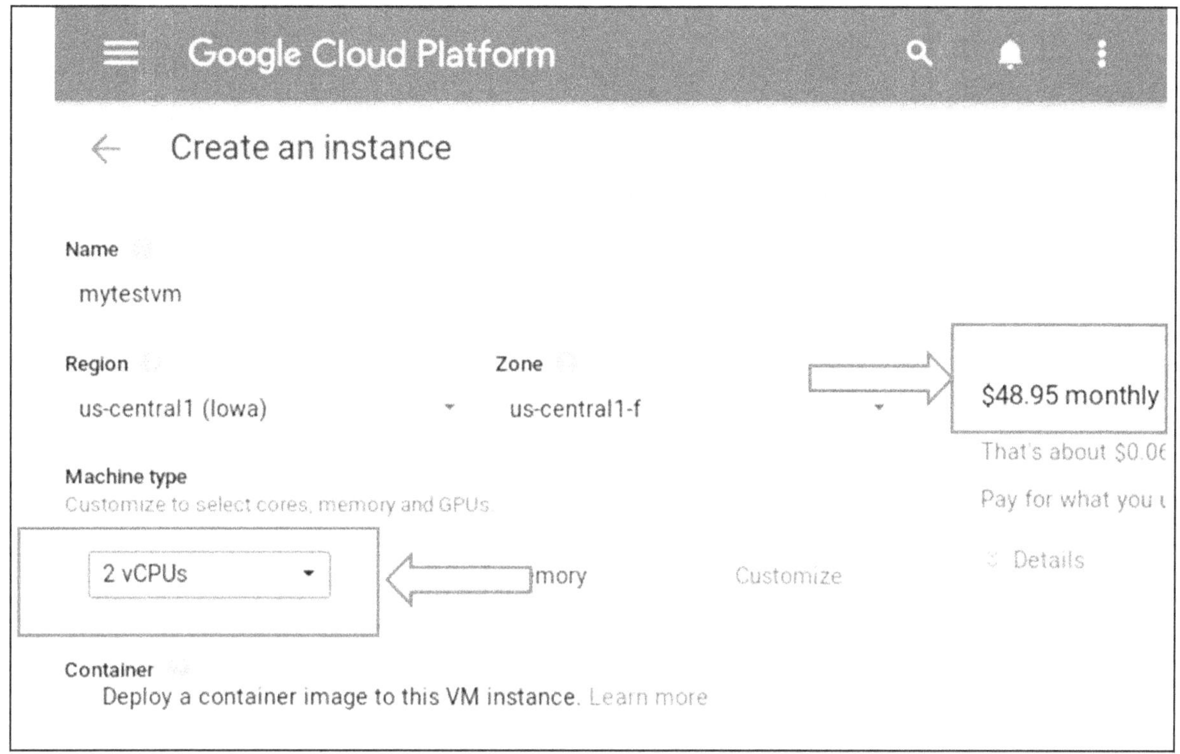

Figure 3-02: Instance Type with Price (a)

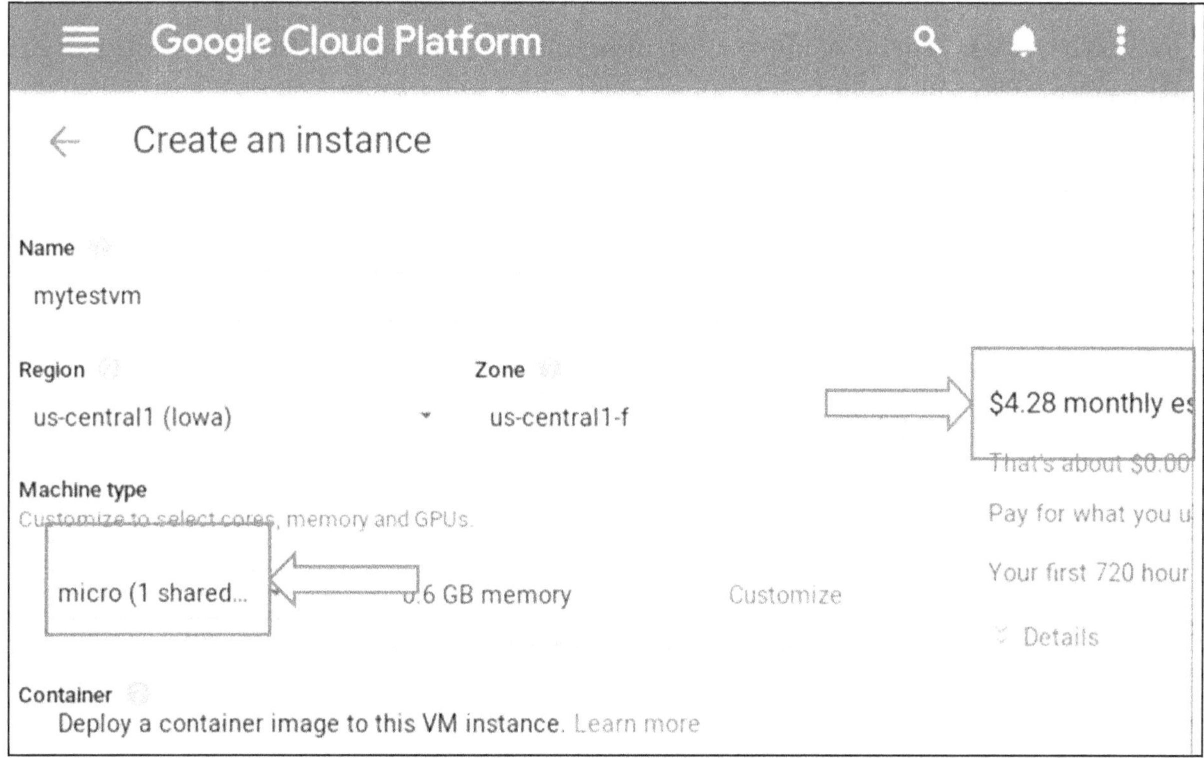

Figure 3-03: Instance Type with Price (b)

For Managing Instances

There are a variety of tools like GCP console, gcloud Command line tool or REST API for creating and managing the instances. For configuring the instance, you first need to connect the instance via SSH (Linux) and RDP (Windows) instances.

To manage the access of your Linux instances via OS login, you need to associate the SSH keys with your Google account or G suite account. If you do not want to use OS login to manage access, you can manage the SSH keys in the project or the instance metadata through which you get access to instances.

For windows instances, you only need to manage the password for the server.

Instance Lifecycle

In the entire life cycle of an instance, its transition can be through many states. The Compute Engine provides resources to start the instance when you first create an instance. Next, the instance moves to the stage in which it is ready to boot for the first time. When it is finally booted, it goes to running state. During its lifetime, a running instance can be stopped and restarted several times.

Instances of states are defining below:

- **PROVISION**–Resources are being allocated, and it is not yet in operation
- **STAGING**–Resources have been attained, and the first boot of instance is ready
- **RUNNING**-Boots execute the instance. Shortly after you enter this state, you can connect to the instance
- **STOP**-The instance is halted. This is because a user requested to stop the instance or a failure occurred. This is a temporary status, and once the instance has stopped, the instance will move to TERMINATED
- **TERMINATED**—The instance has been stopped by a user, or the instance has failed. Restart or delete the instance

If you no longer need an instance but want to keep it for future use, you can stop an instance. If you only need to wipe the content of your instance memory or application state, you may otherwise reset an instance. When you stop an instance, the instance moves into another TERMINATED instance where resetting an instance retains the instance during the entire procedure in a RUNNING state.

With some exceptions, removing an instance removes the instance and the attached resources from your project. However, if the drives have an auto-delete status to incorrect and any static external IPs are returned to your project, you can again use the IP for another resource, then the Compute Engine will maintain persistent disk for a deleted instance. The removal of a VM instance is permanent so that a deleted instance can not

restart. You can recreate the instance with the same name and properties, but Compute Engine will use it as a new instance with new properties for all purposes.

Machine Types

A machine type specifies a specific set of virtualized hardware resources, including the system memory size, virtual CPU (vCPU) counts and maximum disk performance, available to a Virtual Machine (VM) instance. Machine types of vCPUs and memory are calculated based on the resource-based billing model. You can select your instance machine type but you must pay individually for each vCPU and GB of storage.

Pre-defined Machine Types

Pre-defined machine types are managed by Google Compute Engine and are available in several classes. Pre-defined machinery types have a fixed collection of resources.

- **Standard machine types** are suitable for tasks that have a balance of CPU and memory needs. Standard machine types have 3.75 GB of memory per vCPU
- Types of **high-memory machines** are ideal for jobs with more memory than vCPUs. high-memory machines are with a system memory of 6.50 GB per vCPU.
- Types of **high-CPU machines** are perfect for tasks, which require more vCPUs than a memory. The types of high CPU machines are 0.90 GB per vCPU
- **Shared-core types** provide one vCPU, which can run on a single hardware hyper-thread on your instance host CPU for one portion of the time. Shared-core instances may be more cost efficient than standard, high-memory or high-CPU machine-types for running small, non-resource-intensive applications
- **Memory-optimized machine types** are ideal for tasks requiring intensive use of memory with higher vCPU memory ratios than high-memory machine types. These types of machines are perfect for in-memory and memory analysis databases like SAP, Hana's and the BW's, genomic analysis, analytical services, and more. These types of machines are considerably perfect. Memory-optimized types of machines have a memory of more than 14 GB per vCPU.

Custom Machine Types

If any of the pre-defined machine types did not match your requirement, then you can define your required vCPU and memory for the instance. Although, it is costly to use this machine type as compared to the pre-defined machine types.

CPU Platforms

Instances using one of the CPU platforms are available on a Compute Engine when it starts. The instance uses the default platform zone where the instance will operate if you do not actively specify the desired CPU platform. On Compute Engine, every virtual CPU

(vCPU) is implemented as a hyperthread on one of the platforms. If your VM-instance is needed to run on a particular platform, you may specify a minimum CPU platform so that the VM never runs on a platform older than the one you specify and if available, you can also specify a minimum CPU platform.

GPUs on Compute Engine

Google Compute Engine provides the GPUs you can add to your virtual machine instances. You can use these GPUs to speed up your installations' particular workloads such as machine learning and data processing. If you have graphical workloads like 3D visualizing, 3D rendering, or virtual applications, you can create virtual workstations. NVIDIA ® Tesla ® GPUs are for your pass through instances, so the GPUs and their associated memory are directly controlled by your virtual machine instances.

Instance Templates

When you want to build VM instances from a previous configuration quickly, you can use instance templates. You need to use an installation template to create a managed instance group if you want to create a group of identical instances. It is a resource in which you define the machine type, boot disk image or container image, labels, and other instance properties. It is a global resource hence you can use it anywhere. Instance templates are a practical way to save the configuration of a VM instance so that you can later create new VM instances or groups of VM instances. As in the existing instance template you can not modify it if you want to make any change, you must create a new instance template.

Instance Group

It is a collection of VM instances that can be managed via a single entity. There are two types of VM instance groups:

- Managed Instance Groups (MIGs) can be used for multiple identical VM-based applications. The automatic MIG services, including auto-scaling, auto-healing; regional multi-zone deployment and self-updating, give you the scalability and high accessibility of your workloads
- Unmanaged Instance Groups allow you to load the balance of your fleet of VMs

Sole-Tenant Nodes

A sole-tenant node is a physical Compute Engine Server, which is only used for your particular project to host VM instances. You can use sole-tenant nodes to physically separate your instances from instances in other projects, or group your instances on the same host hardware. Each node is related to a single physical server and is the only node running on that server. Without sharing the host hardware with other projects, you can run multiple different-size instances.

Storage Options

By default, the single booting persists disk containing the operating system for each Compute Engine instance. You can add one or more extra storage options to your instance when your applications require additional storage space. For your instances, Compute Engine offers various types of storage options.

Storage Options	Zonal Standard Persistent Disks	Regional Persistent Disks	Zonal SSD Persistent Disks	Regional SSD Persistent Disks
Storage Type	Efficient and reliable block storage	Efficient and reliable block storage with synchronous replication across two zones in a region	Fast and reliable block storage	Fast and reliable block storage with synchronous replication across two zones in a region
Maximum Space per Instance	64 TB	64 TB	64 TB	64 TB
Scope of Access	Zone	Zone	Zone	Zone
Data Redundancy	Zonal	Multi-zonal	Zonal	Multi-zonal
Encryption at Rest	Yes	Yes	Yes	Yes
Read IOPS per GB	0.75	0.75	30	30
Write IOPS per GB	1.5	1.5	30	30
Read Throughput per GB	0.12	0.12	0.48	0.48
Write Throughput per GB	0.12	0.12	0.48	0.48

Storage Options	Local SSDs	Cloud Storage Buckets
Storage Type	High-performance local block storage	Affordable object storage
Maximum Space per Instance	3 TB	Almost infinite
Scope of Access	Instance	Global
Data Redundancy	None	Regional or Multi-regional
Encryption at Rest	Yes	Yes
Read IOPS per GB	266.7	453.3

Write IOPS per GB	186.7	240
Read Throughput per GB	1.04	1.77
Write Throughput per GB	0.73	0.94

Table 3-04: Storage Option

Access Control

By default, the original project creator is a single user for all Google Cloud Platform projects. No other users will have access to the project, and thus to Compute ngine resources until the user is added or linked with a particular resource as a project member. Also, you can use service accounts to authenticate your applications instead of using User Identifiers when running applications on a Virtual Machine (VM). Instance and the application need to have access to a Compute Engine or other Google Cloud Platform APIs.

You can add users as team members to your project and specific resources and permit them with the Cloud Identity and Access Management roles. This allows users to create and handle the resources of your Compute Engine.

You can use OS Login without creating and managing individual SSH keys, to manage SSH access to your IAM. OS Login keeps a consistent user identity for VM instances and is recommended for the administration of a multitude of users through multiple instances or projects.

Lab 3-3 – Configuration on GCE

Scenario:

An enterprise wants to use Google Cloud Platform to host their virtual server and perform configuration via command line. How will they do this?

Solution:

Use GCE in GCP by using Google Cloud Shell Command line tool.

1. Similarly, as we did in the above labs, go to "Google Cloud Shell". Now, check the configuration.
2. Now, type the following command to check user and hostname. You can also check this Cloud Shell as a client program for any URL, through which you can connect to this URL.

root@kali: ~/google-cloud-sdk

File Edit View Search Terminal Help

```
Run `gcloud topic configurations` to learn more.

Some things to try next:

* Run `gcloud --help` to see the Cloud Platform serv
ices you can interact with. And run `gcloud help COM
MAND` to get help on any gcloud command.
* Run `gcloud topic --help` to learn about advanced
features of the SDK like arg files and output format
ting
root@kali:~/google-cloud-sdk# gcloud config list
[compute]
region = us-east1
zone = us-east1-b
[core]
account = ipsareeba46@gmail.com
disable_usage_reporting = False
project = vast-node-238010

Your active configuration is: [default]
root@kali:~/google-cloud-sdk# whoami
root
root@kali:~/google-cloud-sdk# hostname
kali
root@kali:~/google-cloud-sdk# curl api.ipify.org
202.47.32.113root@kali:~/google-cloud-sdk#
```

3. Check whether there are any instance running or not by typing the command below.

```
root@kali:~/google-cloud-sdk# gcloud compute instanc
es list
Listed 0 items.
root@kali:~/google-cloud-sdk#
```

4. Now, we will perform some filtering to check the machine type for instances available in a specific zone. After that, set the zone and region by the commands.

```
root@kali:~/google-cloud-sdk# gcloud compute machine
-types list --filter="NAME:f1-micro AND ZONE~us-west
"
NAME      ZONE        CPUS  MEMORY_GB  DEPRECATED
f1-micro  us-west1-b  1     0.60
f1-micro  us-west1-c  1     0.60
f1-micro  us-west1-a  1     0.60
f1-micro  us-west2-b  1     0.60
f1-micro  us-west2-a  1     0.60
f1-micro  us-west2-c  1     0.60
root@kali:~/google-cloud-sdk# gcloud config set comp
ute/zone us-west1-b
Updated property [compute/zone].
root@kali:~/google-cloud-sdk# gcloud config set comp
ute/region us-west1
```

5. Now, type the command to create the instance, but it will give you an error as you do not have a network, so first create a network by running the command "gcloud compute networks create default".

```
ute/region us-west1
Updated property [compute/region].
root@kali:~/google-cloud-sdk# gcloud compute instanc
es create --machine-type=f1-micro mytestvm
```

```
root@kali:~/google-cloud-sdk# gcloud compute instanc
es create --machine-type=f1-micro mytestvm
ERROR: (gcloud.compute.instances.create) Could not f
etch resource:
 - Invalid value for field 'resource.networkInterfac
es[0].network': 'https://www.googleapis.com/compute/
v1/projects/vast-node-238010/global/networks/default
'. The referenced network resource cannot be found.

root@kali:~/google-cloud-sdk# ^C
root@kali:~/google-cloud-sdk# gcloud compute network
s create default
```

6. After that, add firewall rules shown in the figure below, to allow ICMP and SSH access.

```
$ gcloud compute firewall-rules create <FIREWALL_NAM
E> --network default --allow tcp,udp,icmp --source-r
anges <IP_RANGE>
$ gcloud compute firewall-rules create <FIREWALL_NAM
E> --network default --allow tcp:22,tcp:3389,icmp

root@kali:~/google-cloud-sdk# gcloud compute firewal
l-rules create default-allow-icmp --network default
--allow icmp --source-ranges 0.0.0.0/0
```

```
root@kali: ~/google-cloud-sdk
File  Edit  View  Search  Terminal  Help
root@kali:~/google-cloud-sdk# gcloud compute firewal
l-rules create default-allow-icmp --network default
--allow icmp --source-ranges 0.0.0.0/0
Creating firewall...:Created [https://www.googleapis
.com/compute/v1/projects/vast-node-238010/global/fir
ewalls/default-allow-icmp].
Creating firewall...done.
NAME                NETWORK  DIRECTION  PRIORITY  AL
LOW  DENY  DISABLED
default-allow-icmp  default  INGRESS    1000      ic
mp         False
root@kali:~/google-cloud-sdk# gcloud compute firewal
l-rules create default-allow-ssh --network default -
-allow tcp:22 --source-ranges 0.0.0.0/0
Creating firewall...:Created [https://www.googleapis
.com/compute/v1/projects/vast-node-238010/global/fir
ewalls/default-allow-ssh].
Creating firewall...done.
NAME               NETWORK  DIRECTION  PRIORITY  ALL
OW   DENY  DISABLED
default-allow-ssh  default  INGRESS    1000      tcp
:22        False
root@kali:~/google-cloud-sdk#
```

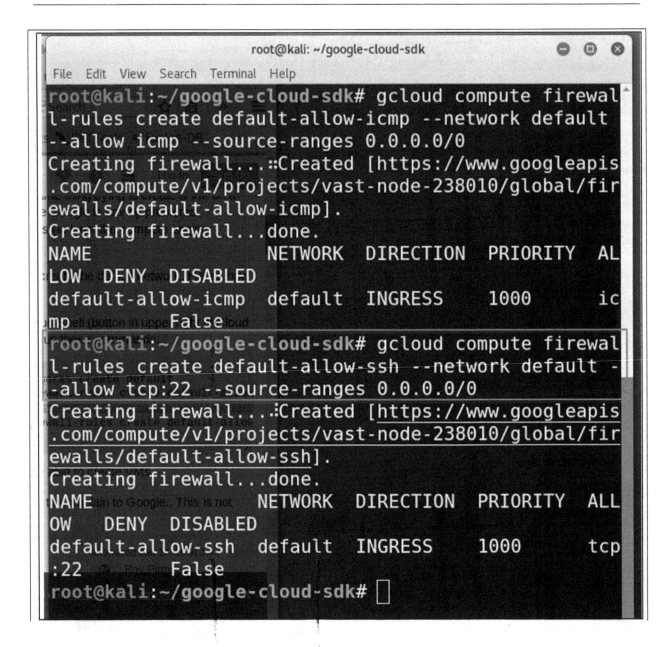

```
root@kali: ~/google-cloud-sdk
File Edit View Search Terminal Help
root@kali:~/google-cloud-sdk# gcloud compute firewall-rules create default-allow-internal --network default --allow tcp:0-65535,udp:0-65535,icmp --source-ranges 10.128.0.0/9
Creating firewall...:Created [https://www.googleapis.com/compute/v1/projects/vast-node-238010/global/firewalls/default-allow-internal].
Creating firewall...done.
NAME                    NETWORK  DIRECTION  PRIORITY  ALLOW                       DENY  DISABLED
default-allow-internal  default  INGRESS    1000      tcp:0-65535,udp:0-65535,icmp        False
root@kali:~/google-cloud-sdk# 
```

7. When all rules for firewall have been created, create an instance. Now, your instance has been created. Check connectivity by pinging the external IP as with VM name and internal IP; you cannot ping the VM.

```
  tcp:0-65535,udp:0-65535,icmp        False
root@kali:~/google-cloud-sdk# gcloud compute instances create --machine-type=f1-micro mytestvm
Created [https://www.googleapis.com/compute/v1/projects/vast-node-238010/zones/us-west1-b/instances/mytestvm].
NAME      ZONE        MACHINE_TYPE  PREEMPTIBLE  INTERNAL_IP  EXTERNAL_IP     STATUS
mytestvm  us-west1-b  f1-micro                   10.138.0.2   35.233.250.160  RUNNING
root@kali:~/google-cloud-sdk# 
```

```
root@kali:~/google-cloud-sdk# ping -c 3 mytestvm
ping: mytestvm: Name or service not known
root@kali:~/google-cloud-sdk# ping -c 3 10.138.0.2
PING 10.138.0.2 (10.138.0.2) 56(84) bytes of data.

--- 10.138.0.2 ping statistics ---
3 packets transmitted, 0 received, 100% packet loss, ti
me 2037ms

root@kali:~/google-cloud-sdk#
```

```
root@kali:~/google-cloud-sdk# ping -c 3 35.233.250.160
PING 35.233.250.160 (35.233.250.160) 56(84) bytes of da
ta.
64 bytes from 35.233.250.160: icmp_seq=1 ttl=52 time=77
7 ms
64 bytes from 35.233.250.160: icmp_seq=2 ttl=52 time=91
4 ms
64 bytes from 35.233.250.160: icmp_seq=3 ttl=52 time=11
13 ms

--- 35.233.250.160 ping statistics ---
3 packets transmitted, 3 received, 0% packet loss, time
 1999ms
rtt min/avg/max/mdev = 777.095/935.114/1113.849/138.257
 ms
root@kali:~/google-cloud-sdk#
```

8. Now, if you try to SSH the VM, you will still get permission issues. Try to SSH the VM with VM name. When you do this, it will ask for the password for generating the key, enter it.

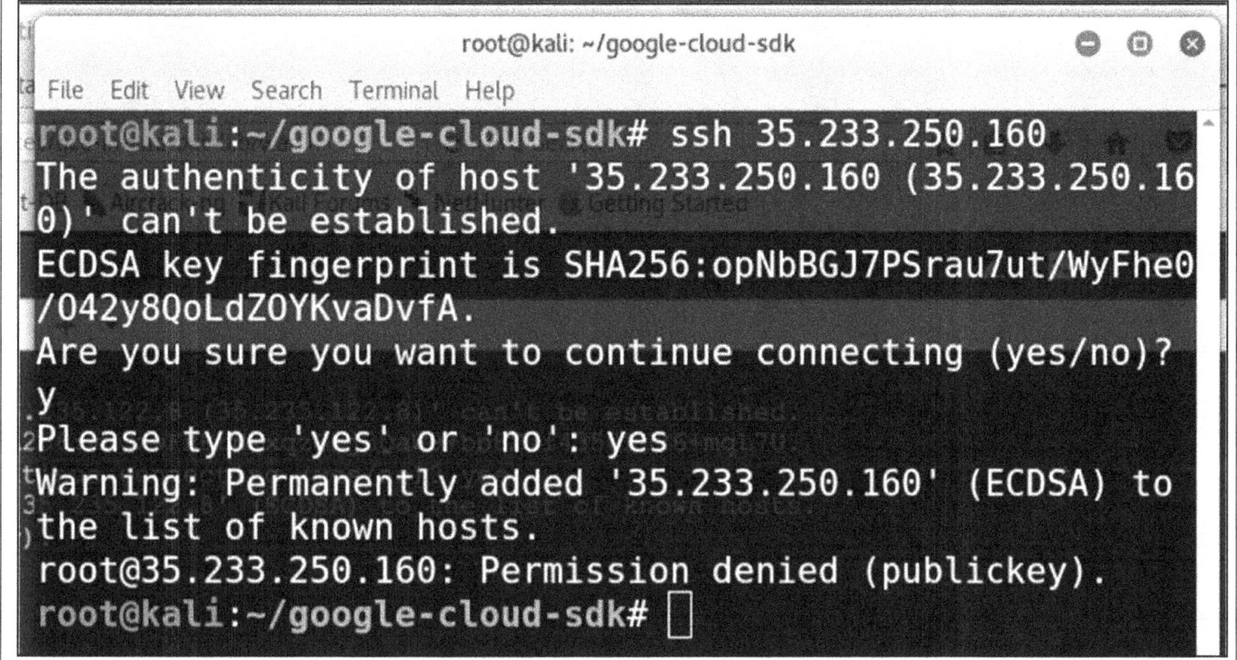
root@kali: ~/google-cloud-sdk
File Edit View Search Terminal Help
root@kali:~/google-cloud-sdk# ssh 35.233.250.160
The authenticity of host '35.233.250.160 (35.233.250.160)' can't be established.
ECDSA key fingerprint is SHA256:opNbBGJ7PSrau7ut/WyFhe0/042y8QoLdZOYKvaDvfA.
Are you sure you want to continue connecting (yes/no)? y
Please type 'yes' or 'no': yes
Warning: Permanently added '35.233.250.160' (ECDSA) to the list of known hosts.
root@35.233.250.160: Permission denied (publickey).
root@kali:~/google-cloud-sdk#

```
root@kali: ~/google-cloud-sdk
File  Edit  View  Search  Terminal  Help
root@kali:~/google-cloud-sdk# gcloud compute ssh mytest
vm
WARNING: The public SSH key file for gcloud does not ex
ist.
WARNING: The private SSH key file for gcloud does not e
xist.
WARNING: You do not have an SSH key for gcloud.
WARNING: SSH keygen will be executed to generate a key.
Generating public/private rsa key pair.
Enter passphrase (empty for no passphrase):
Enter same passphrase again:
Your identification has been saved in /root/.ssh/google
_compute_engine.
Your public key has been saved in /root/.ssh/google_com
pute_engine.pub.
The key fingerprint is:
SHA256:AYMdBoQ9GnqrWdzbdzVkXJJ1U/21zja23yM7ZMDPKiQ root
@kali
The key's randomart image is:
+---[RSA 2048]----+
|    +o+=.     o..=|
|   o +..o    o ..+|
| . o .   . .. o  +|
|. o       . o+  ..|
| o o     S  o+ o  |
|  + .   E .  o= * |
| +    o  o  .+.o o|
|o    . .  .... o o.|
|        . ..   .+ =|
+----[SHA256]-----+
```

```
|    . ..   .+ =|
+----[SHA256]-----+
Updating project ssh metadata...⠸Updated [https://www.g
oogleapis.com/compute/v1/projects/vast-node-238010].
Updating project ssh metadata...done.
Waiting for SSH key to propagate.
Warning: Permanently added 'compute.4100443191355525946
' (ECDSA) to the list of known hosts.
root@35.233.250.160: Permission denied (publickey).
ERROR: (gcloud.compute.ssh) Could not SSH into the inst
ance.  It is possible that your SSH key has not propaga
ted to the instance yet. Try running this command again
.  If you still cannot connect, verify that the firewal
l and instance are set to accept ssh traffic.
root@kali:~/google-cloud-sdk# 
```

9. Now, you can either try to do SSH with VM via Google Cloud SDK or via console. For SDK, type the below command and for the console, go the console and click on the VM that you created.

```
root@kali:~/google-cloud-sdk# ssh mytestvm.us-west1-b.v
ast-node-238010
```

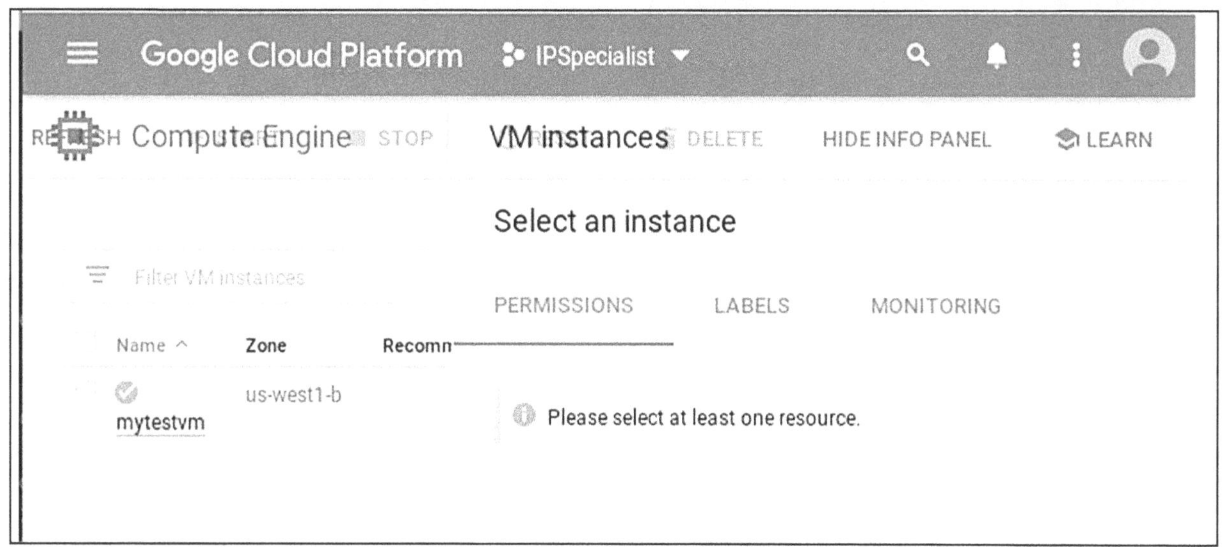

10. Click on "SSH" to connect to VM via SSH connectivity.

Your free trial is waiting: activate now to get $300 credit to explore Google Cloud products. Learn more
DISMISS
ACTIVATE
Google Cloud Platform
IPSpecialist
Compute Engine
VM instance details
Details
Monitoring
mytestvm
Remote access
SSH
Connect to serial console
Enable connecting to serial ports
Logs
Stackdriver Logging
Applications
Places
Firefox ESR
Tue 12:37
SSH: mytestvm @ vast-node-238010 - Mozilla Firefox
https://ssh.cloud.google.com/projects/vast-node-238010/zones/us-west1-b/instances/mytestvm?authuser=0&hl=en_US&project
Connecting...
Transferring SSH keys to the VM.

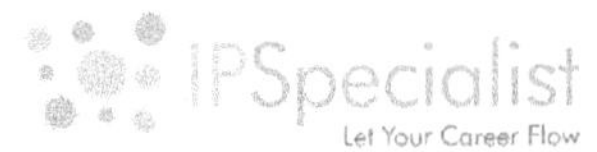

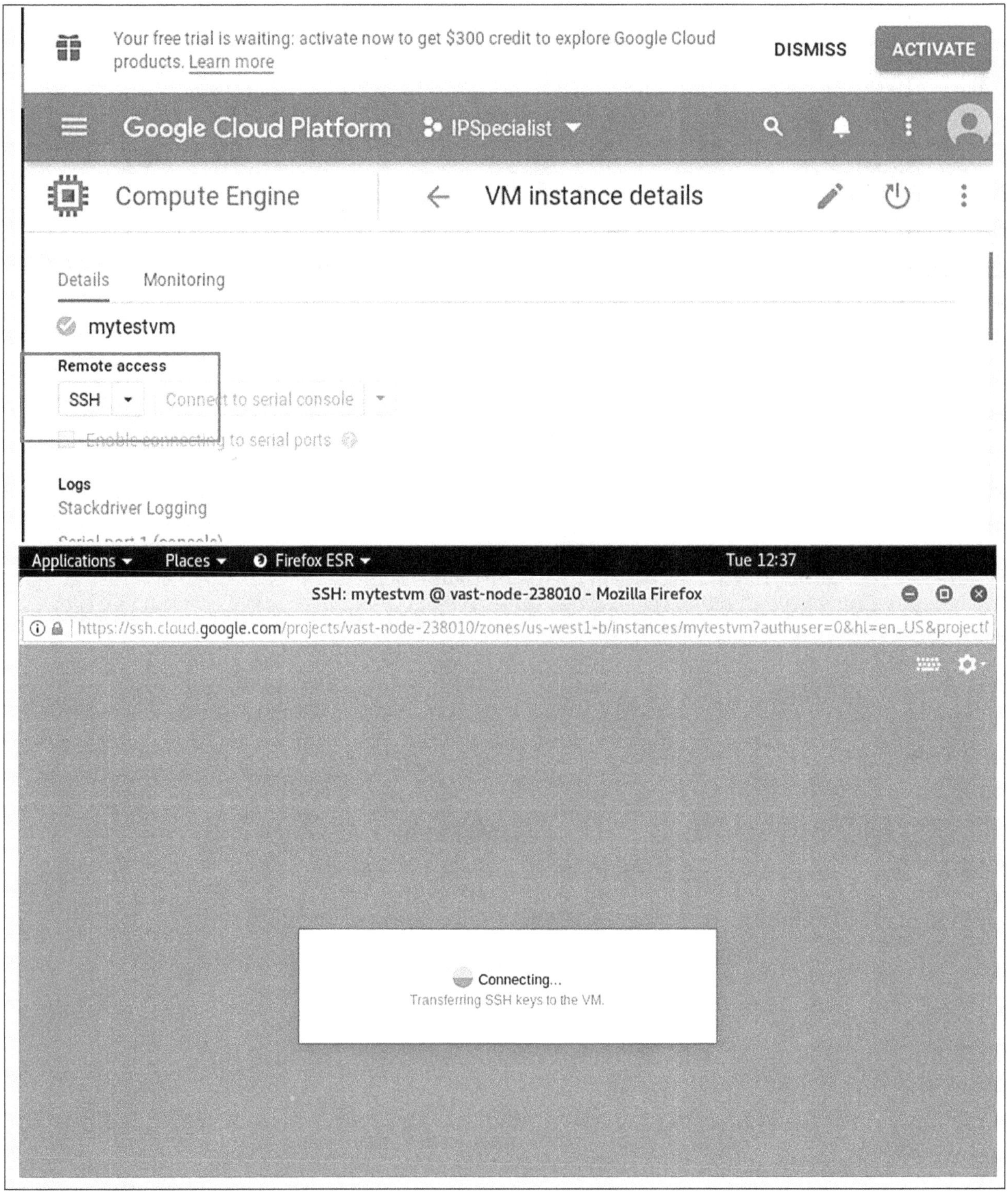

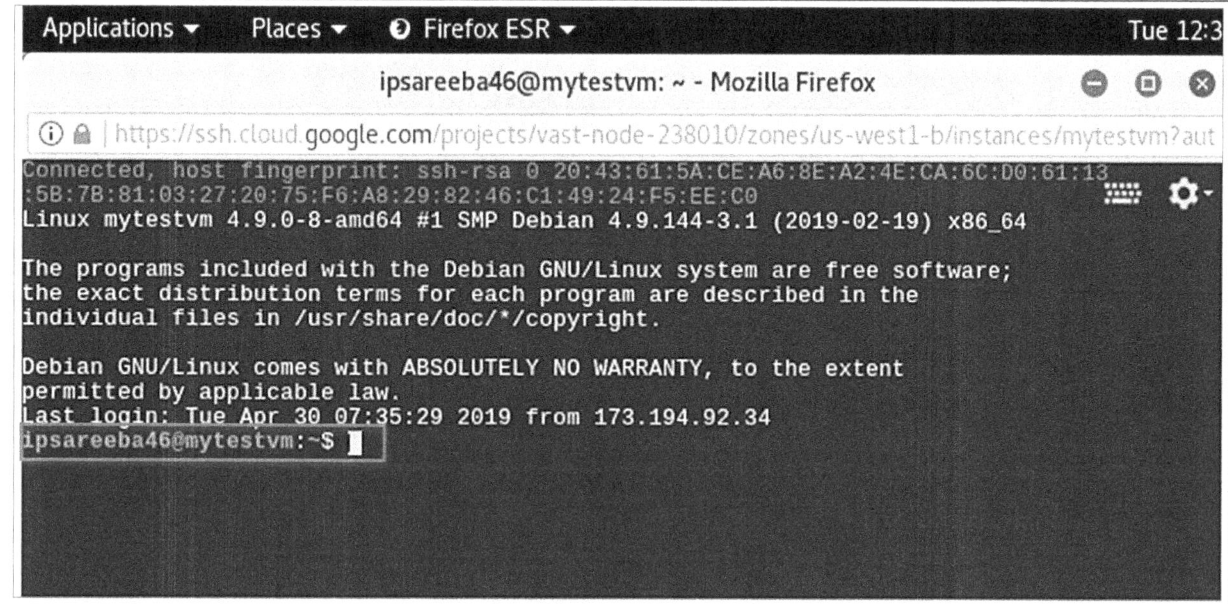

11. Here, when you type "whoami" and "hostname", you will get different information as you would in VM. It will give you VM hostname and user information. Similarly, if you check the URL connectivity, the IP address it will show will be different from the IP that was checked via Google Cloud SDK.

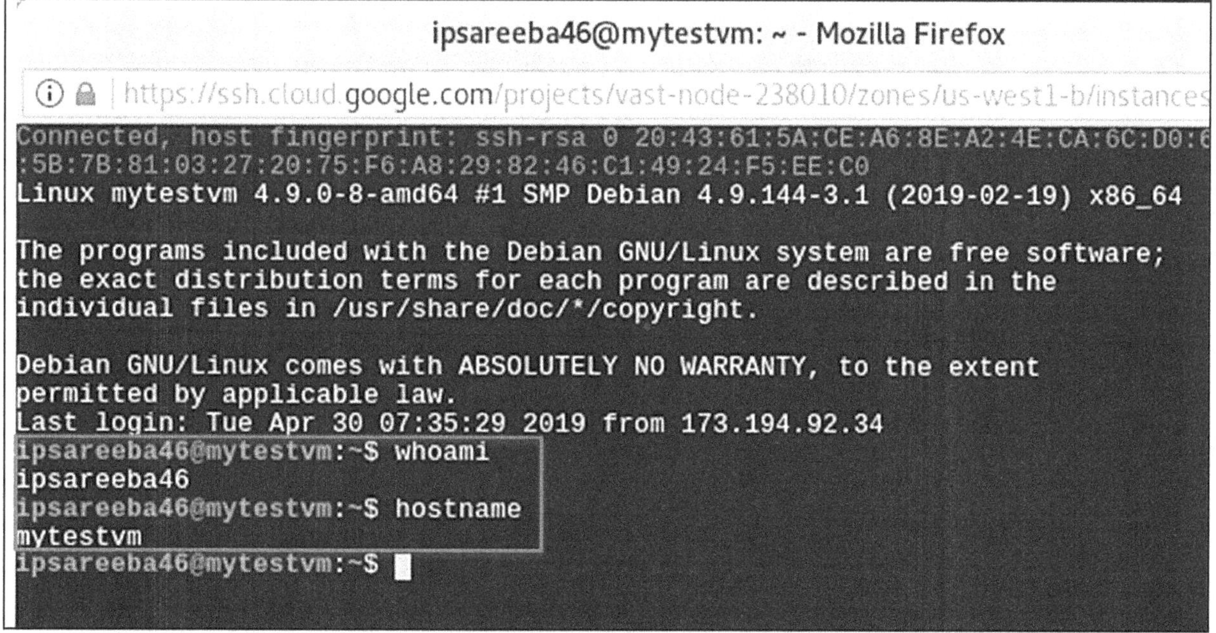

12. Go back to "Google Cloud SDK" and check the keys that are generated. One is the private key, and the other is the public key with ".pub" extension.

```
root@kali:~# cd google-cloud-sdk
root@kali:~/google-cloud-sdk# cd .ssh
root@kali:~/google-cloud-sdk/.ssh# ls
config                          google_compute_known_hosts
google_compute_engine           known_hosts
google_compute_engine.pub
root@kali:~/google-cloud-sdk/.ssh#
```

```
root@kali:~/google-cloud-sdk/.ssh# cat google_compute_e
ngine.pub
ssh-rsa AAAAB3NzaC1yc2EAAAADAQABAAABAQDorR9wE3uBXZuZAzc
4Cke8UhER1p1e0HfLTGqHq6vMYIqBVLmbU5BdH8A5m6TO+M2TKyBAC7
nFRnxjbmesL95crw/T4yst+hhcXhmodXPnxA0Voo/V4lzZQxjL0vLYY
J0ohh9suIa6jUDQg0YHJZhvzjjqNi7eBe03v4D+FncMK70EhwSWnflA
gNxOQ7EHF8pfjGs2SHcWZSLnC3E/ND5FiMi8/jLeVrtxM0VQS6OJLTf
jqhx8HzeS+nTGbpQiE3cN1EMpc3j/ObSMeLlI1S3arSnJ7pZDM14tIr
51fbDRT9s64F5ZSU2lr5RRjI40CJYzyHbvV1dmmQ16OytNEfoD root
@kali
```

```
root@kali:~/google-cloud-sdk/.ssh# cat google_compute_e
ngine
-----BEGIN RSA PRIVATE KEY-----
Proc-Type: 4,ENCRYPTED
DEK-Info: AES-128-CBC,D4287474CC3E8B2A6CBD573DD13C0312

6tMbfgPY8PRiZnoA147VubslTIbgHGRBYJbDNnnszTrRao9IxbOoMXy
8QDEEgcuA
pCyhBciBm/I0BKjL+7jLr895H+8sMNYy0W5t7GrZzB155B/SSMIqyVV
9Lf8r5b+a
```

13. Now, if you want to check the key in VM, then follow the command:

- "cd .ssh"
- "ls"
- "cat authorized_keys"

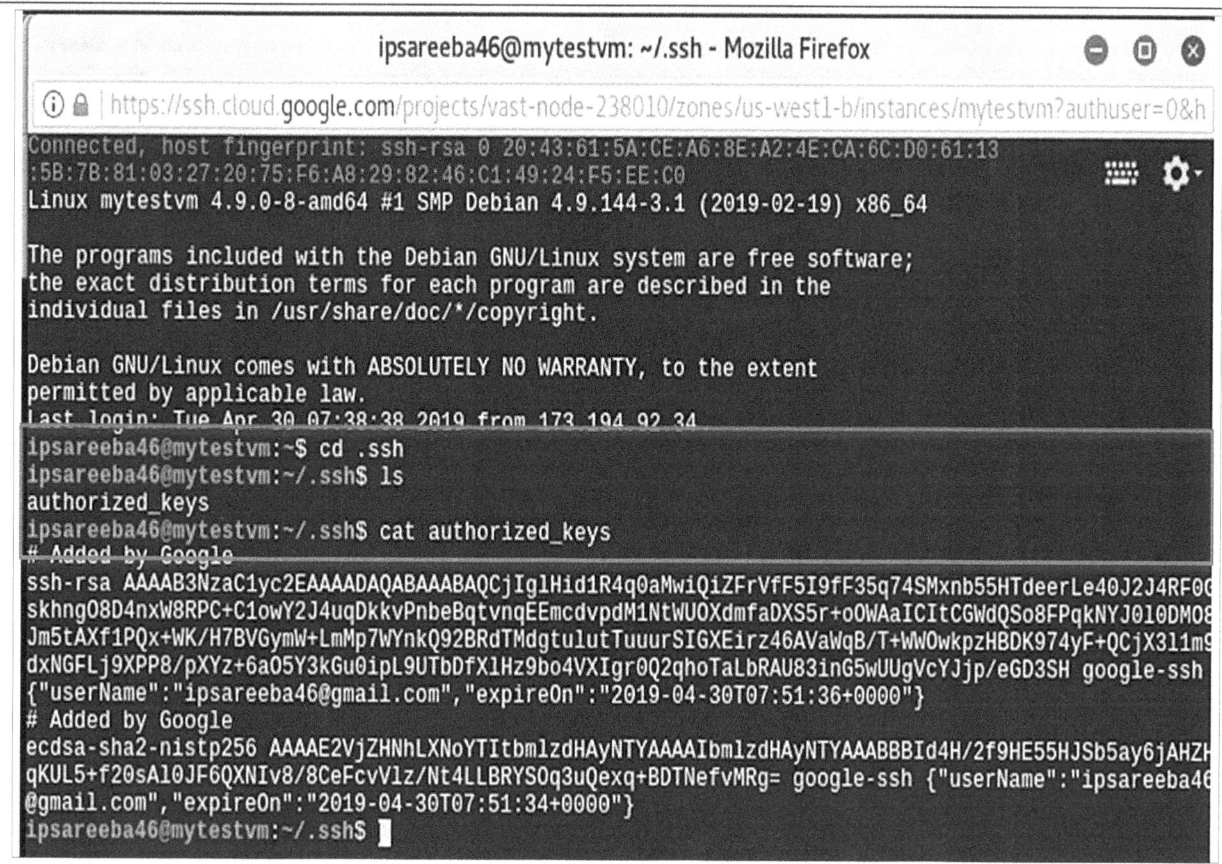

14. In SSH connectivity, you can also view metadata stored inside the VM by using different commands shown in the below figure.

```
ipsareeba46@mytestvm:~$ curl metadata.google.internal/computeMetadata/v1/
<!DOCTYPE html>
<html lang=en>
  <meta charset=utf-8>
  <meta name=viewport content="initial-scale=1, minimum-scale=1, width=device-w
  <title>Error 403 (Forbidden)!!1</title>
  <style>
    *{margin:0;padding:0}html,code{font:15px/22px arial,sans-serif}html{backgr
;padding:15px}body{margin:7% auto 0;max-width:390px;min-height:180px;padding:3
background:url(//www.google.com/images/errors/robot.png) 100% 5px no-repeat;pa
margin:11px 0 22px;overflow:hidden}ins{color:#777;text-decoration:none}a img{b
n and (max-width:772px){body{background:none;margin-top:0;max-width:none;paddi
ckground:url(//www.google.com/images/branding/googlelogo/1x/googlelogo_color_1
at;margin-left:-5px}@media only screen and (min-resolution:192dpi){#logo{backg
le.com/images/branding/googlelogo/2x/googlelogo_color_150x54dp.png) no-repeat
-border-image:url(//www.google.com/images/branding/googlelogo/2x/googlelogo_co
}@media only screen and (-webkit-min-device-pixel-ratio:2){#logo{background:ur
mages/branding/googlelogo/2x/googlelogo_color_150x54dp.png) no-repeat;-webkit-
 100%}}#logo{display:inline-block;height:54px;width:150px}
  </style>
  <a href=//www.google.com/><span id=logo aria-label=Google></span></a>
  <p><b>403.</b> <ins>That's an error.</ins>
  <p>Your client does not have permission to get URL <code>/computeMetadata/v1/
erver. Missing Metadata-Flavor:Google header. <ins>That's all we know.</ins>
```

```
Tue 12:57
ipsareeba46@mytestvm: ~ - Mozilla Firefox
https://ssh.cloud.google.com/projects/vast-node-238010/zones/us-west1-b/instances/mytestvm?authuser=0&h
ipsareeba46@mytestvm:~$ curl metadata.google.internak/computeMetadata/v1/
curl: (6) Could not resolve host: metadata.google.internak
ipsareeba46@mytestvm:~$ curl metadata.google.internal/computeMetadata/v1/
<!DOCTYPE html>
<html lang=en>
  <meta charset=utf-8>
  <meta name=viewport content="initial-scale=1, minimum-scale=1, width=device-w
  <title>Error 403 (Forbidden)!!1</title>
  <style>
    *{margin:0;padding:0}html,code{font:15px/22px arial,sans-serif}html{backgr
;padding:15px}body{margin:7% auto 0;max-width:390px;min-height:180px;padding:3
background:url(//www.google.com/images/errors/robot.png) 100% 5px no-repeat;pad
margin:11px 0 22px;overflow:hidden}ins{color:#777;text-decoration:none}a img{bo
n and (max-width:772px){body{background:none;margin-top:0;max-width:none;paddi
ckground:url(//www.google.com/images/branding/googlelogo/1x/googlelogo_color_15
at;margin-left:-5px}@media only screen and (min-resolution:192dpi){#logo{backgr
le.com/images/branding/googlelogo/2x/googlelogo_color_150x54dp.png) no-repeat 0
-border-image:url(//www.google.com/images/branding/googlelogo/2x/googlelogo_col
}@media only screen and (-webkit-min-device-pixel-ratio:2){#logo{background:url
mages/branding/googlelogo/2x/googlelogo_color_150x54dp.png) no-repeat;-webkit-b
 100%}}#logo{display:inline-block;height:54px;width:150px}
  </style>
  <a href=//www.google.com/><span id=logo aria-label=Google></span></a>
  <p><b>403.</b> <ins>That’s an error.</ins>
  <p>Your client does not have permission to get URL <code>/computeMetadata/v1/
erver. Missing Metadata-Flavor:Google header. <ins>That’s all we know.</ins>
ipsareeba46@mytestvm:~$ curl -H "Metadata-Flavor: Google" metadata.google.inte
rnal/computeMetadata/v1/
instance/
oslogin/
project/
ipsareeba46@mytestvm:~$ curl -H "Metadata-Flavor: Google" metadata.google.inte
rnal/computeMetadata/v1/project/
attributes/
numeric-project-id
project-id
```

15. To view the configuration list, type the command shown below.

```
https://ssh.cloud.google.com/projects/vast-node-238010/zones/us-west1-b/instances/my
ipsareeba46@mytestvm:~$ gcloud config list
[core]
account = 1074568360820-compute@developer.gserviceaccount.com
disable_usage_reporting = True
project = vast-node-238010

Your active configuration is: [default]
ipsareeba46@mytestvm:~$
```

16. If you try to delete the VM via SSH connectivity, then you will get an error as you are not authenticated to delete the VM. If you do this when creating a VM via console, then you will have rights to delete it because there you are the authenticated user who has created the VM.

```
https://ssh.cloud.google.com/projects/vast-node-238010/zones/us-west1-b/instances/mytestvm
ipsareeba46@mytestvm:~$ gcloud config list
[core]
account = 1074568360820-compute@developer.gserviceaccount.com
disable_usage_reporting = True
project = vast-node-238010

Your active configuration is: [default]
ipsareeba46@mytestvm:~$ gcloud compute instances delete mytestvm
ERROR: (gcloud.compute.instances.delete)        There was a problem
g your current auth tokens: Failed to retrieve http://metadata.google
/computeMetadata/v1/instance/service-accounts/1074568360820-compute@d
gserviceaccount.com/token from the Google Compute Enginemetadata serv
onse:
{'status': '404', 'content-length': '129', 'x-xss-protection': '0', '
flavor': 'Google', 'server': 'Metadata Server for VM', 'date': 'Tue,
19 08:01:31 GMT', 'x-frame-options': 'SAMEORIGIN', 'content-type': 'a
n/json'}
        Please run:

          $ gcloud auth login

        to obtain new credentials, or if you have already logged in w
        different account:

          $ gcloud config set account ACCOUNT

        to select an already authenticated account to use.
ipsareeba46@mytestvm:~$ exit
```

17. Go back to "Google Cloud SDK" and delete the VM with the command shown in the figure below.

```
File  Edit  View  Search  Terminal  Help
root@kali:~# cd google-cloud-sdk
root@kali:~/google-cloud-sdk# gcloud compute instances delete
 mytestvm
The following instances will be deleted. Any attached disks c
onfigured
 to be auto-deleted will be deleted unless they are attached
to any
other instances or the `--keep-disks` flag is given and speci
fies them
 for keeping. Deleting a disk is irreversible and any data on
 the disk
 will be lost.
 - [mytestvm] in [us-west1-b]

Do you want to continue (Y/n)?  y

Deleted [https://www.googleapis.com/compute/v1/projects/vast-
node-238010/zones/us-west1-b/instances/mytestvm].
root@kali:~/google-cloud-sdk#
```

GCE in Console

You have an easier way to work on console then command line. When you create a VM via GCP console, you have numerous options, on which you can perform hanging. However, the name and zone cannot be changed. You can change machine type, add labels, network interface changing, enable deletion protection or you can add additional storage options as well.

In Console, you have an option to make the instance pre-emptible, means you inform google that you are responsible for how long the instance is running, the pre-emptible instance will automatically be deleted after 24 hours, so be careful. When you enable pre-emptible instance, you cannot enable automatic restart option and on host maintenance.

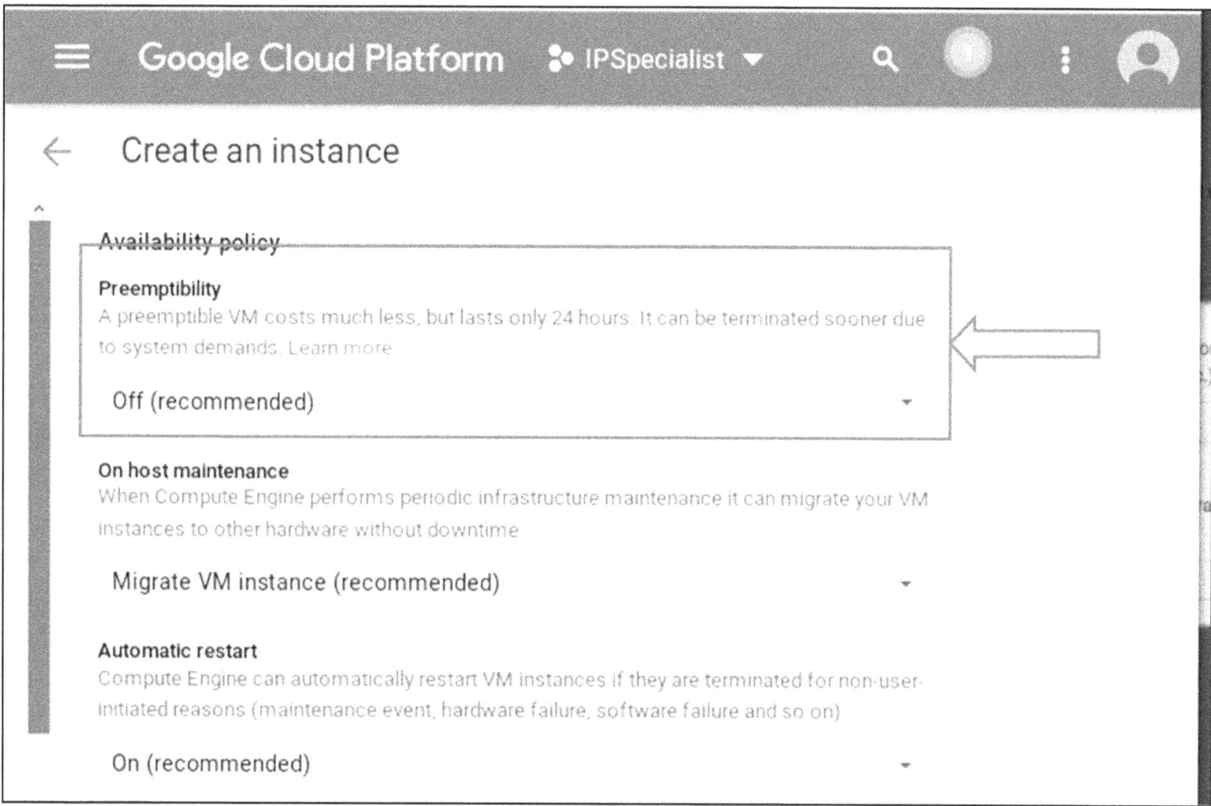

Figure 3-04: Pre-emptibility Off

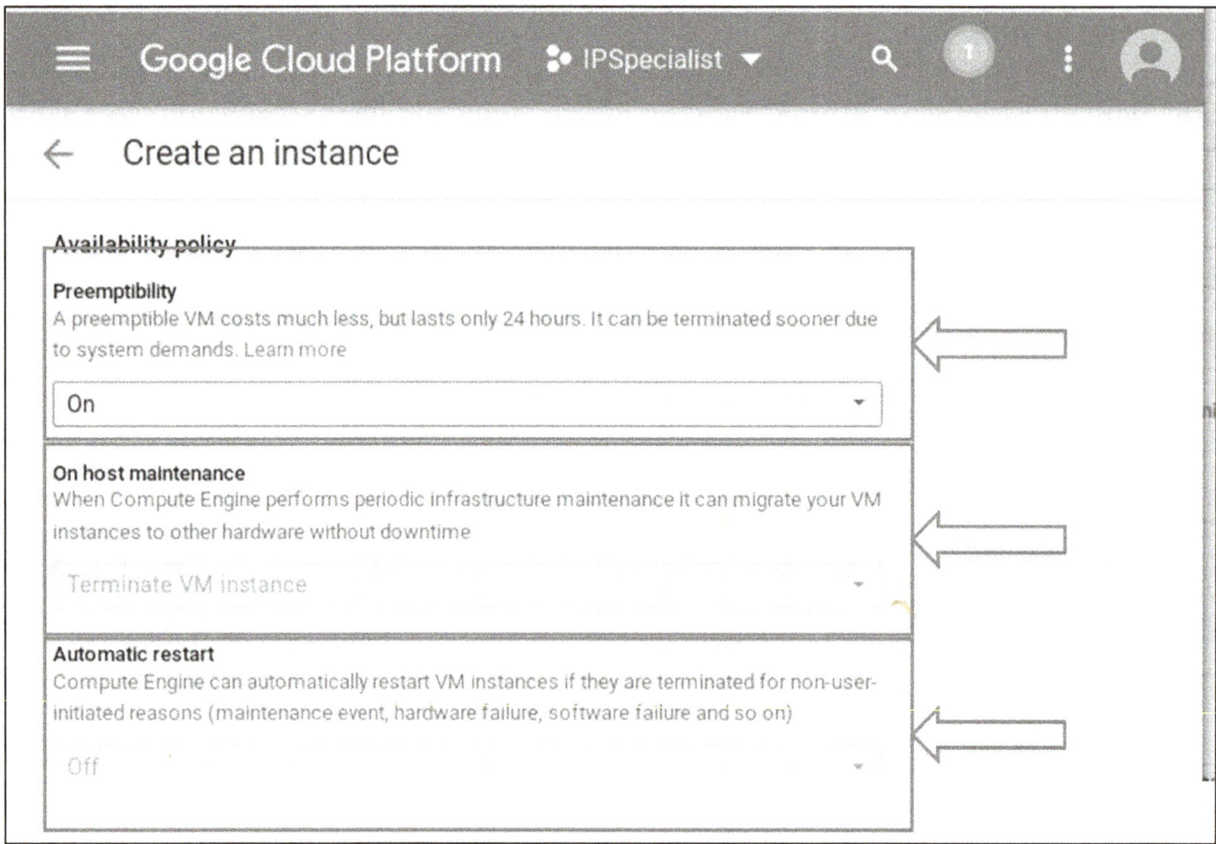

Figure 3-05: Pre-emtibility On

Here, you also have automation option, in which you define the startup script that will be used at the beginning of VM creation either to install the OS or to put metadata.

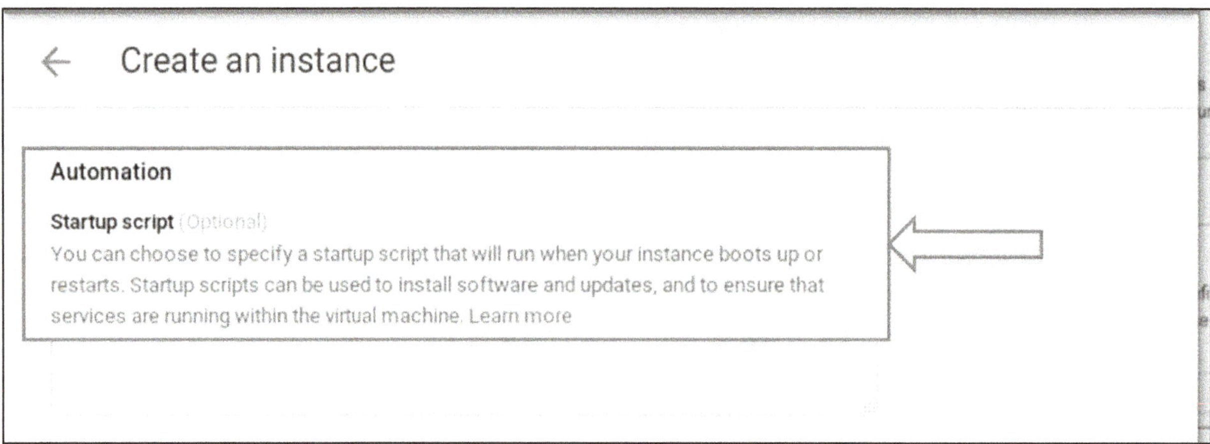

Figure 3-06: Automation Script

You can view that default deletion of boot disk with deletion of instance is enabled. You can also select the encryption method for the data in the console.

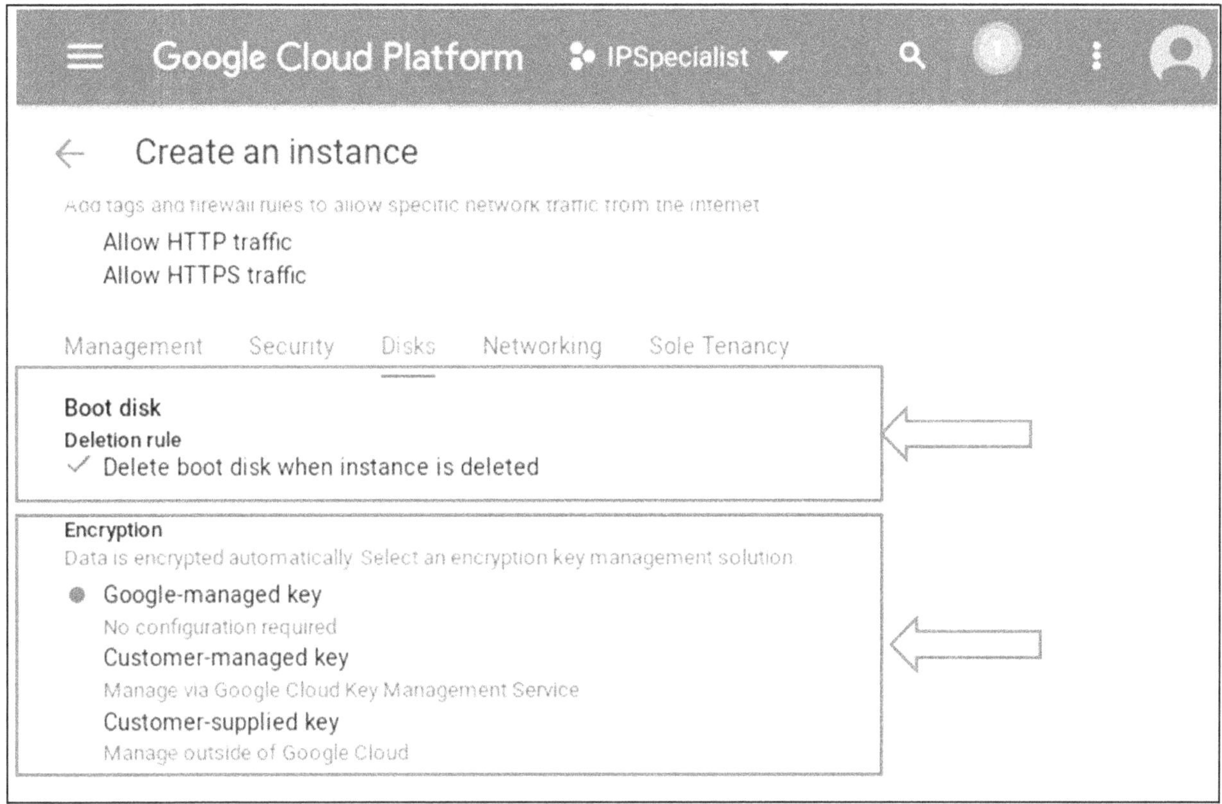

Figure 3-07: Boot Disk and Encryption Option

Lab 3.4- Creating a Virtual Machine and Attaching GCS to it

Scenario:

A company wants to use GCP to create a virtual machine with a custom script and save it as log files into a safe place after the script runs successfully. The most important thing is that they do not want to use SSH to perform any action on VM. How will they do this?

Solution:

They can achieve this by using GCE and GCS service and in the script, the command to store the resultant log file in the bucket must be defined.

1. Log in to "GCP Console" and go to "Compute Engine". Create a new instance. Also, simultaneously, create a bucket as the same as we created in the previous lab.

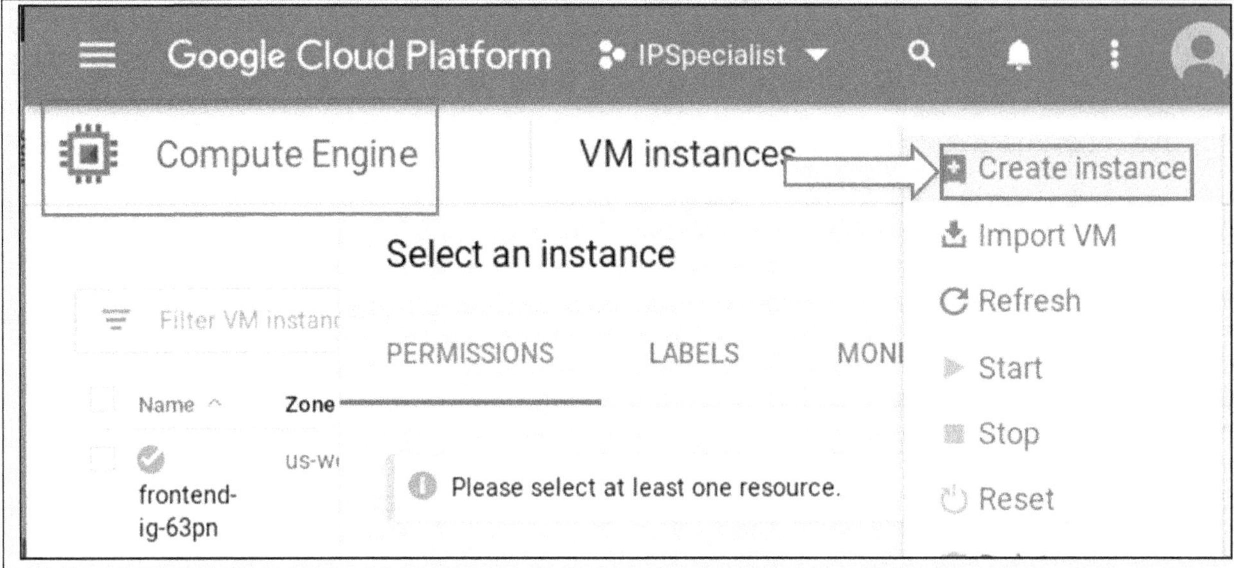

2. Enter the name, region, zone and machine type. Go to "default Compute engine service account" and select it.

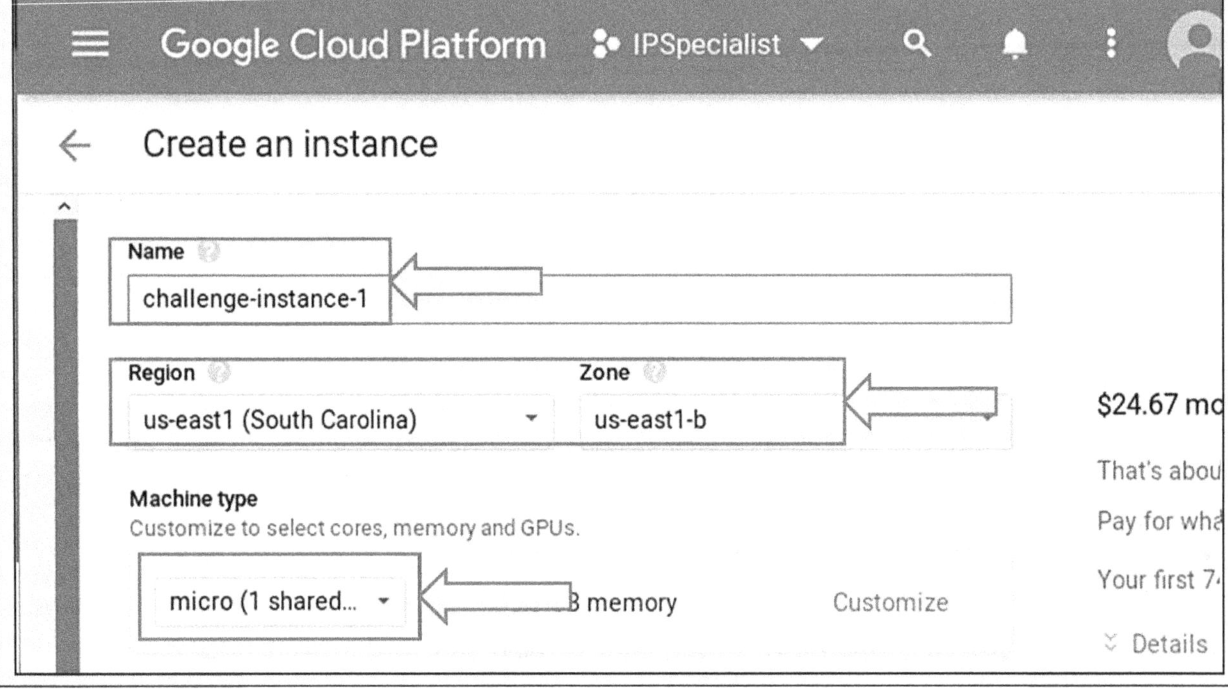

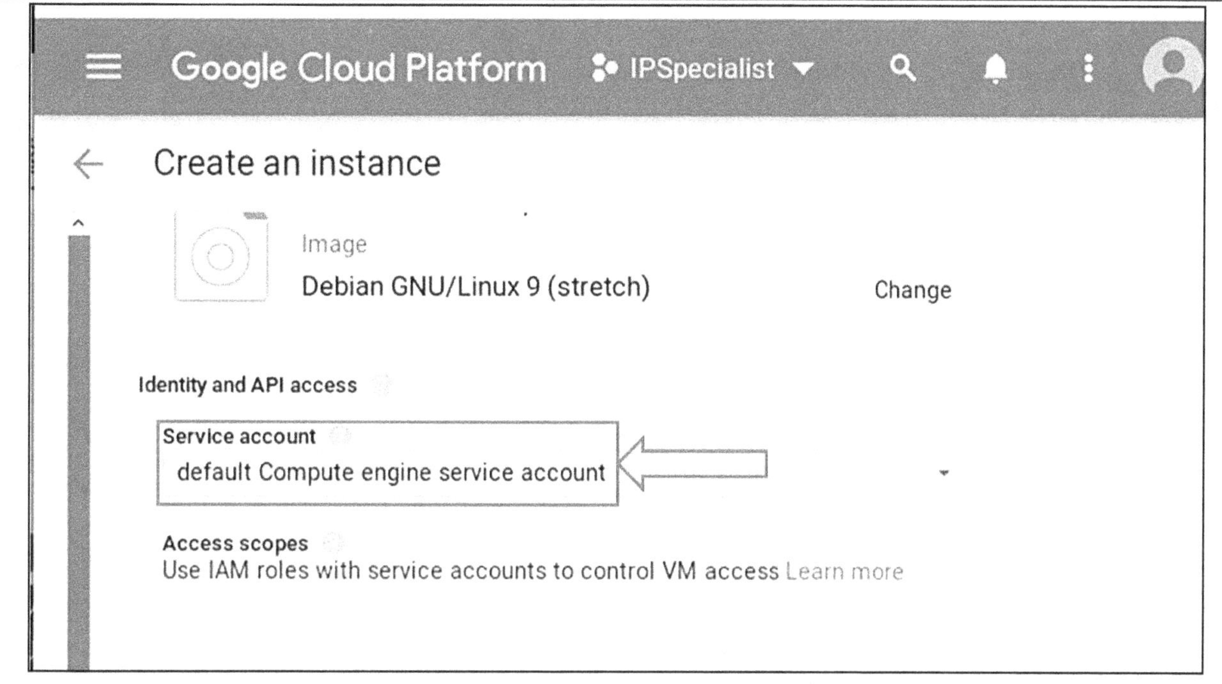

3. Set an appropriate rule for the service account in order to allow GCE to write the log file in GCS. Follow the steps shown below.

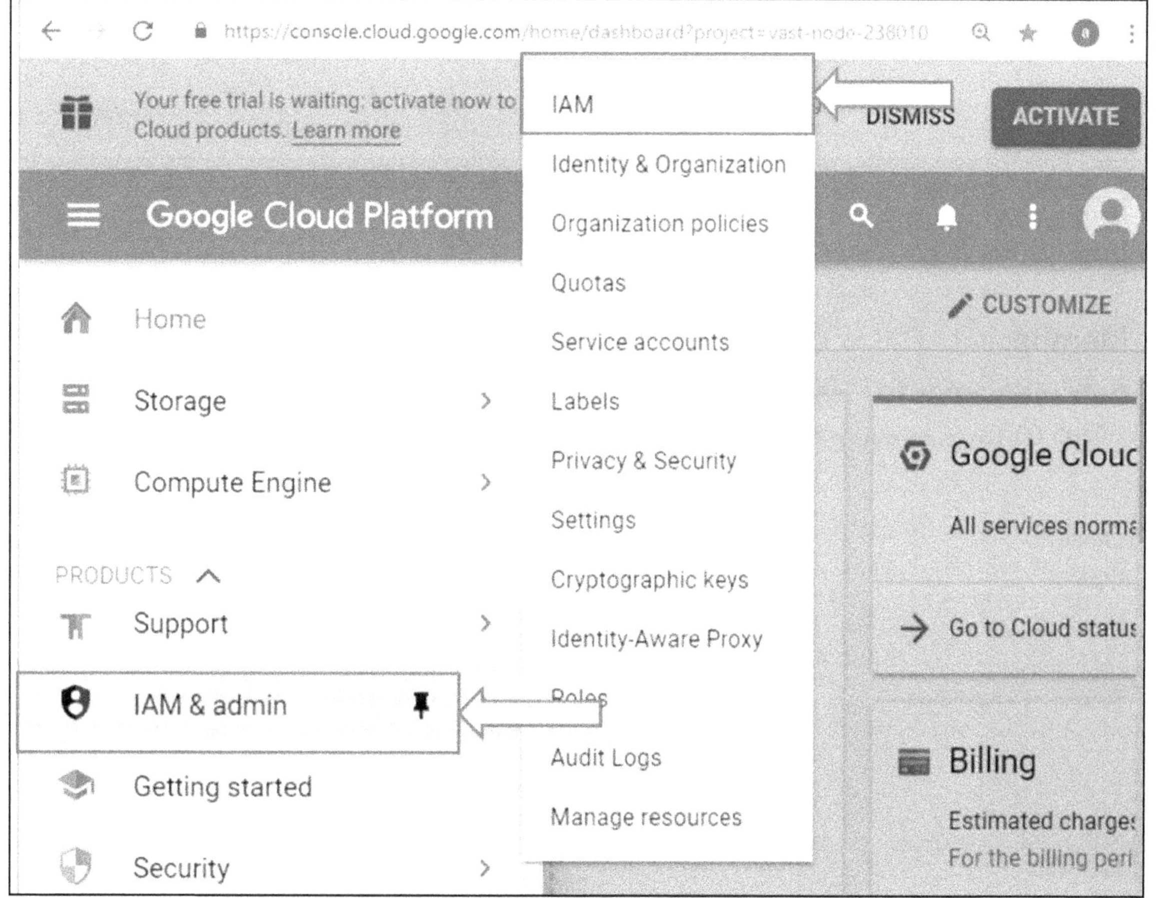

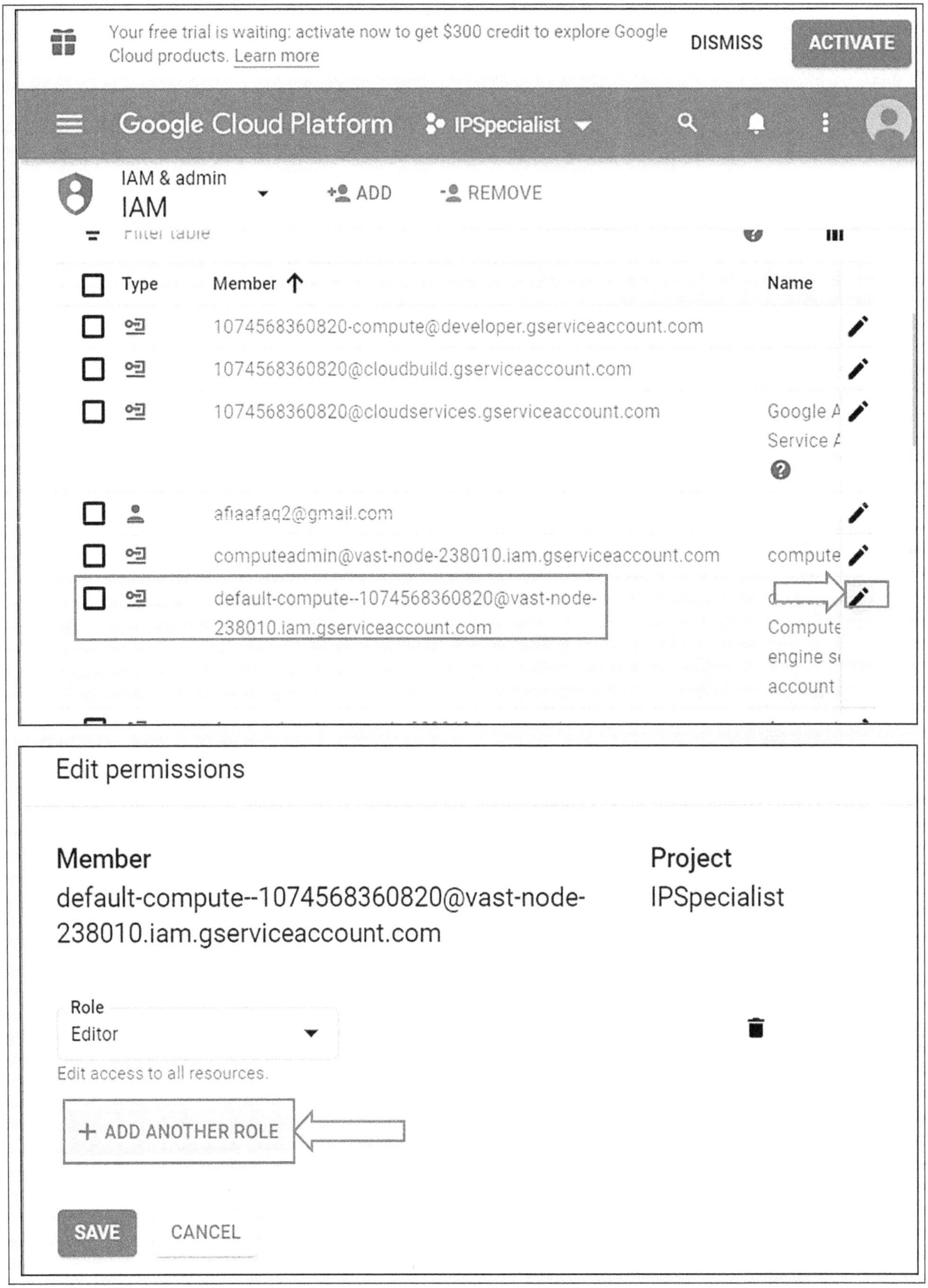

Your free trial is waiting: activate now to get $300 credit to explore Google Cloud products. Learn more DISMISS ACTIVATE

Google Cloud Platform IPSpecialist

IAM & admin
IAM ADD REMOVE

Filter table

Type	Member ↑	Name
	1074568360820-compute@developer.gserviceaccount.com	
	1074568360820@cloudbuild.gserviceaccount.com	
	1074568360820@cloudservices.gserviceaccount.com	Google A Service A
	afiaafaq2@gmail.com	
	computeadmin@vast-node-238010.iam.gserviceaccount.com	compute
	default-compute--1074568360820@vast-node-238010.iam.gserviceaccount.com	Compute engine s account

Edit permissions

Member
default-compute--1074568360820@vast-node-238010.iam.gserviceaccount.com

Project
IPSpecialist

Role
Editor

Edit access to all resources.

+ ADD ANOTHER ROLE

SAVE CANCEL

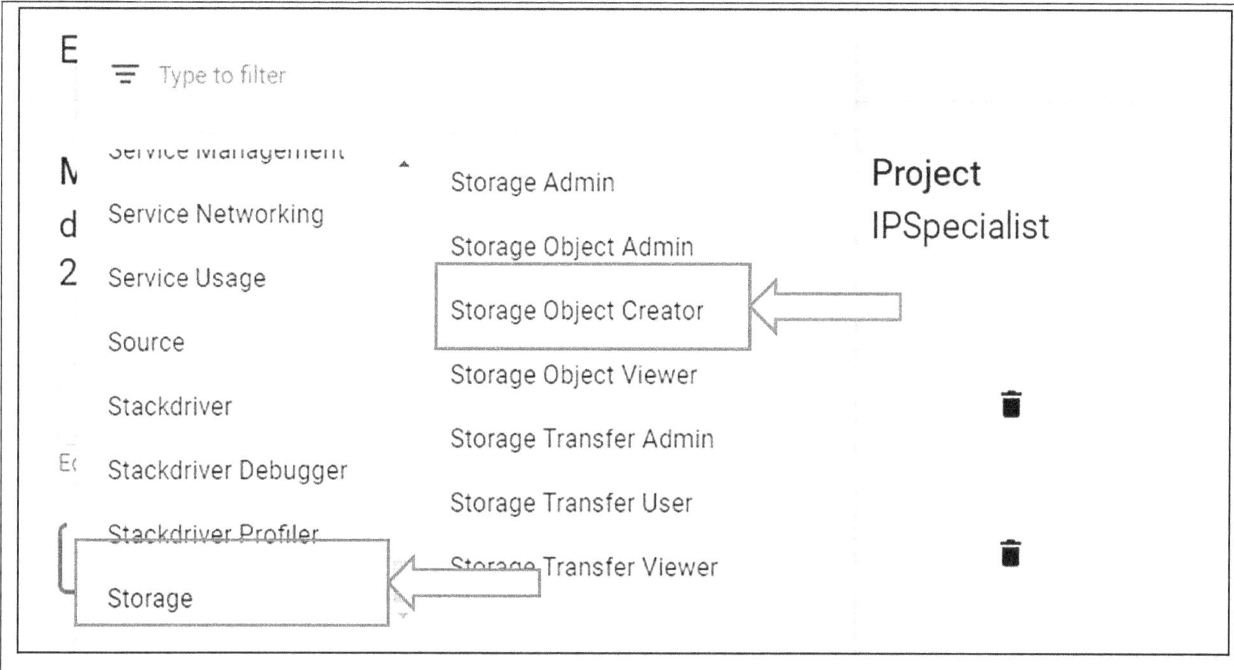

Edit permissions

Member
default-compute--1074568360820@vast-node-238010.iam.gserviceaccount.com

Project
IPSpecialist

Role
Editor
Edit access to all resources.

Role
Storage Object Creator
Access to create objects in GCS.

+ ADD ANOTHER ROLE

SAVE

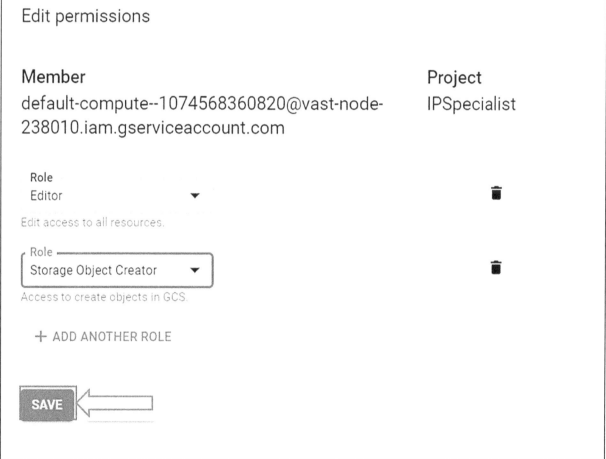

4. Now, go back to the instance creation window and go to management settings.

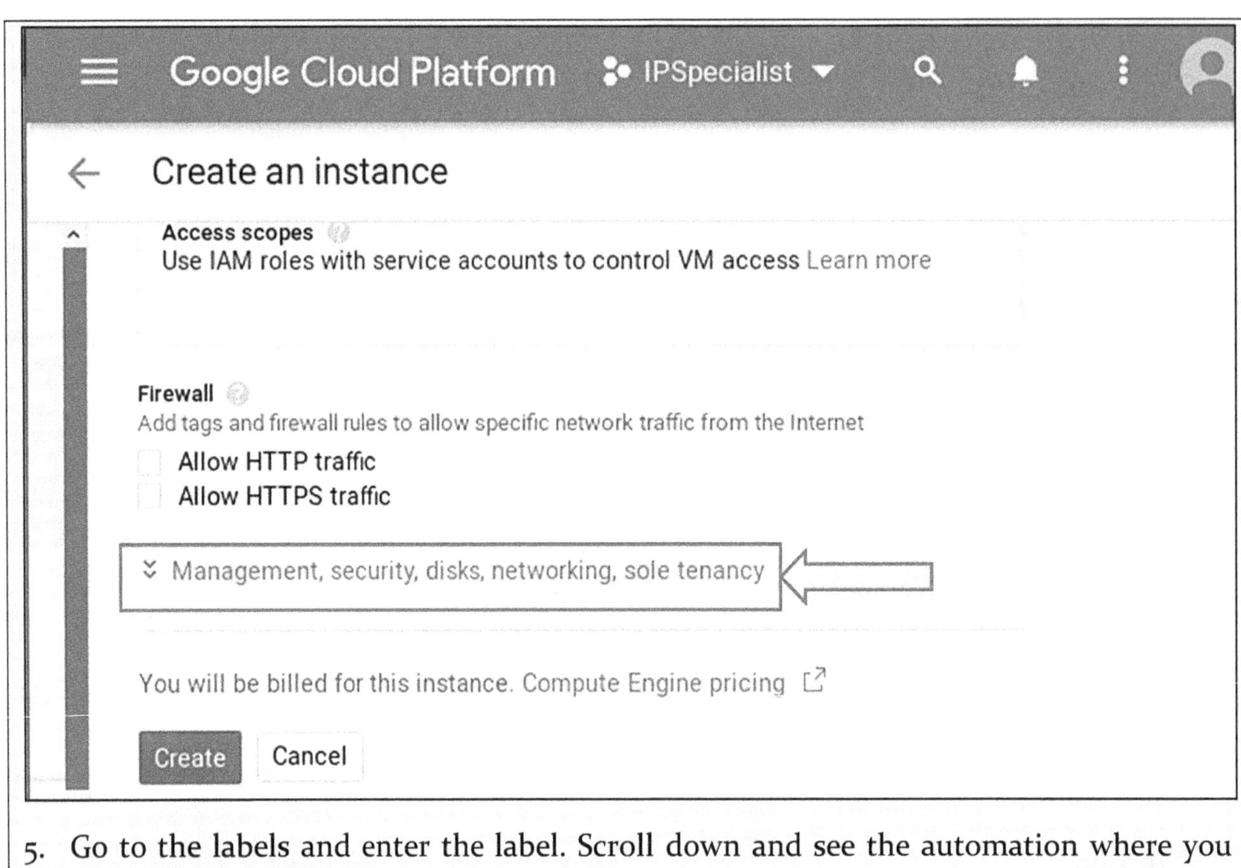

5. Go to the labels and enter the label. Scroll down and see the automation where you can enter the script, which is given below to the start-up script and in metadata, enter the bucket name and the name of bucket metadata.

"#! /bin/bash

#

 # Echo commands as they are run, to make debugging easier.

 # GCE startup script output shows up in "/var/log/syslog".

#

set -x

#

 # Make sure installed packages are up to date with all security patches.

#

```
apt-get update



#
# Install Google's Stackdriver logging agent, as per
# https://cloud.google.com/logging/docs/agent/installation
#
curl -sSO https://dl.google.com/cloudagents/install-logging-agent.sh
bash install-logging-agent.sh



#
# Install and run the "stress" tool to max the CPU load for a while.
#
apt-get install stress
stress -c 8 -t 120



#
# Report that we're done.
#

# Metadata should be set in the "lab-logs-bucket" attribute using the "gs://mybucketname/" format.
log_bucket_metadata_name=lab-logs-bucket
log_bucket_metadata_url="http://metadata.google.internal/computeMetadata/v1/instance/attributes/${log_bucket_metadata_name}"
worker_log_bucket=$(curl -H "Metadata-Flavor: Google" "${log_bucket_metadata_url}")
```

```
# We write a file named after this machine.
worker_log_file="machine-$(hostname)-finished.txt"
echo "Phew!  Work completed at $(date)" >"${worker_log_file}"

# And we copy that file to the bucket specified in the metadata.
echo "Copying the log file to the bucket..."
gsutil cp "${worker_log_file}" "${worker_log_bucket}"
```

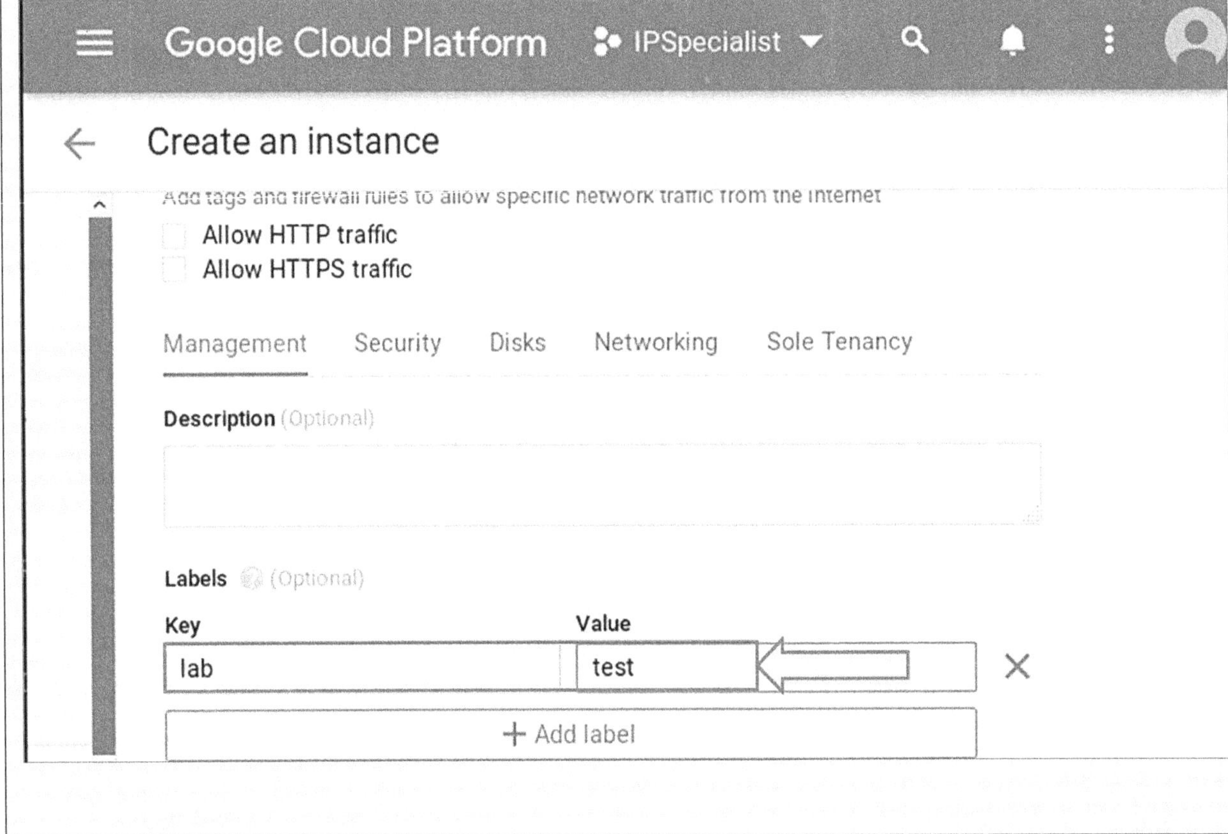

Google Cloud Platform IPSpecialist

Create an instance

Deletion protection

Enable deletion protection

When deletion protection is enabled, instance cannot be deleted. Learn more

Automation

Startup script (Optional)

You can choose to specify a startup script that will run when your instance boots up or restarts. Startup scripts can be used to install software and updates, and to ensure that services are running within the virtual machine. Learn more

Kali Tools Exploit-DB Aircrack-ng Kali Forums NetHunter Getting Started

to explore Google Cloud products. Learn more

restarts. Startup scripts can be used to install software and updates, and to ensure that services are running within the virtual machine. Learn more

```
echo "Copying the log file to the bucket..."
gsutil cp "${worker_log_file}" "${worker_log_bucket}"
```

Metadata (Optional)

You can set custom metadata for an instance or project outside of the server-defined metadata. This is useful for passing in arbitrary values to your project or instance that can be queried by your code on the instance. Learn more

lab-logs-bucket gs://challenge-gce-bucket/

+ Add item

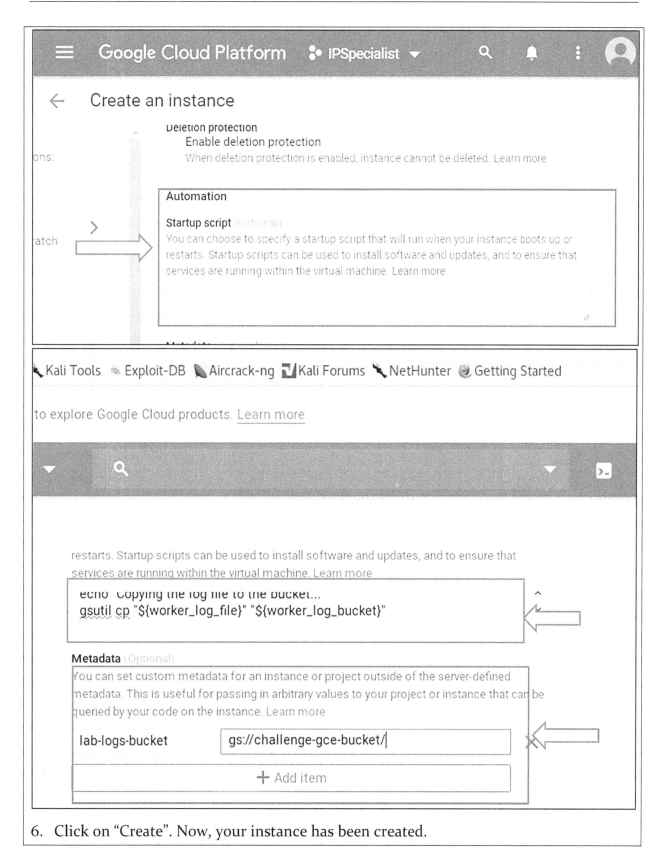

6. Click on “Create”. Now, your instance has been created.

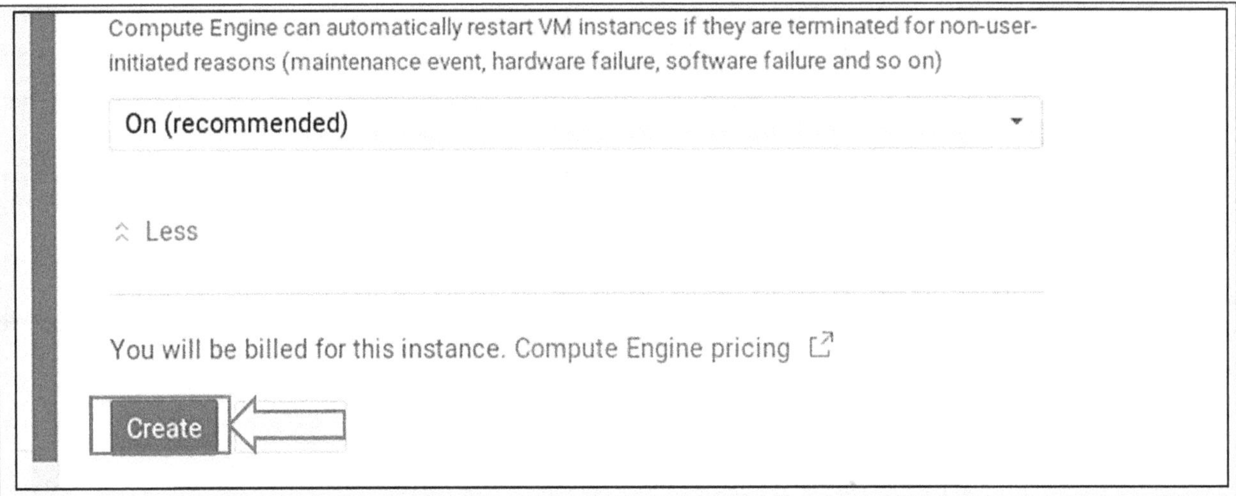

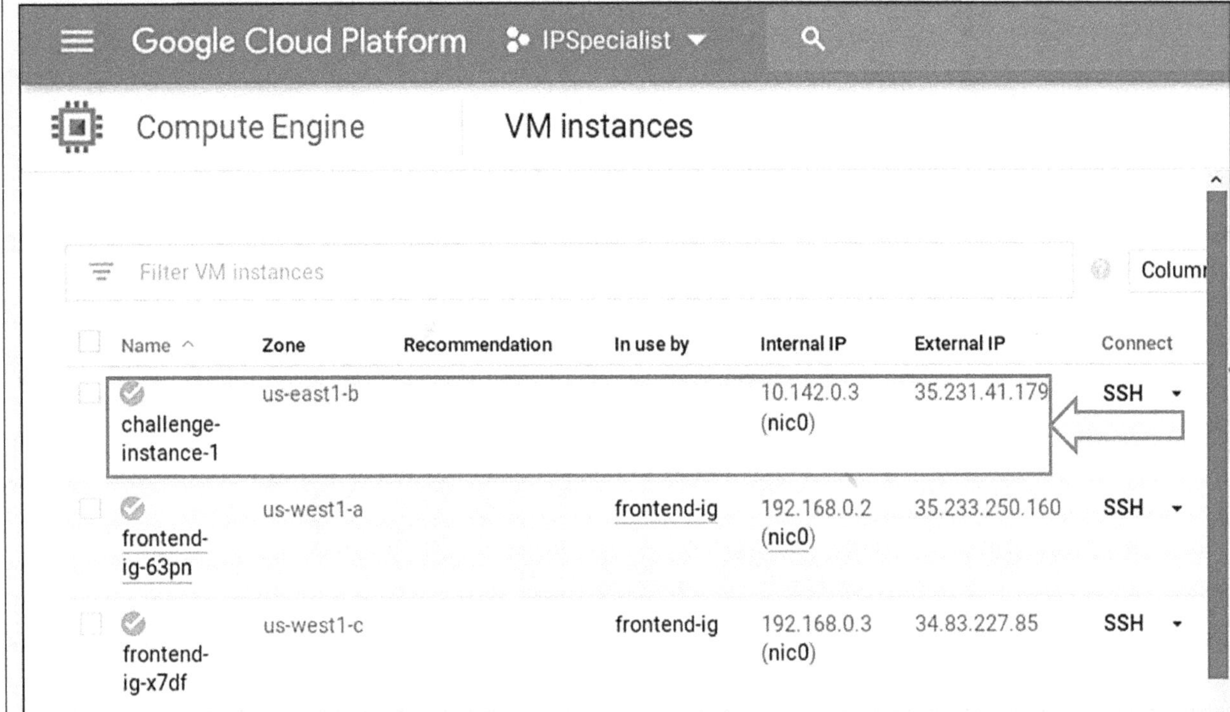

7. Click on the instance you created. Then go to "Stackdriver Logging" and open it. Also, open the "Monitoring" tab.

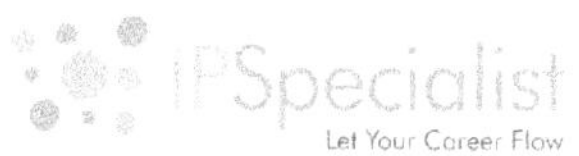

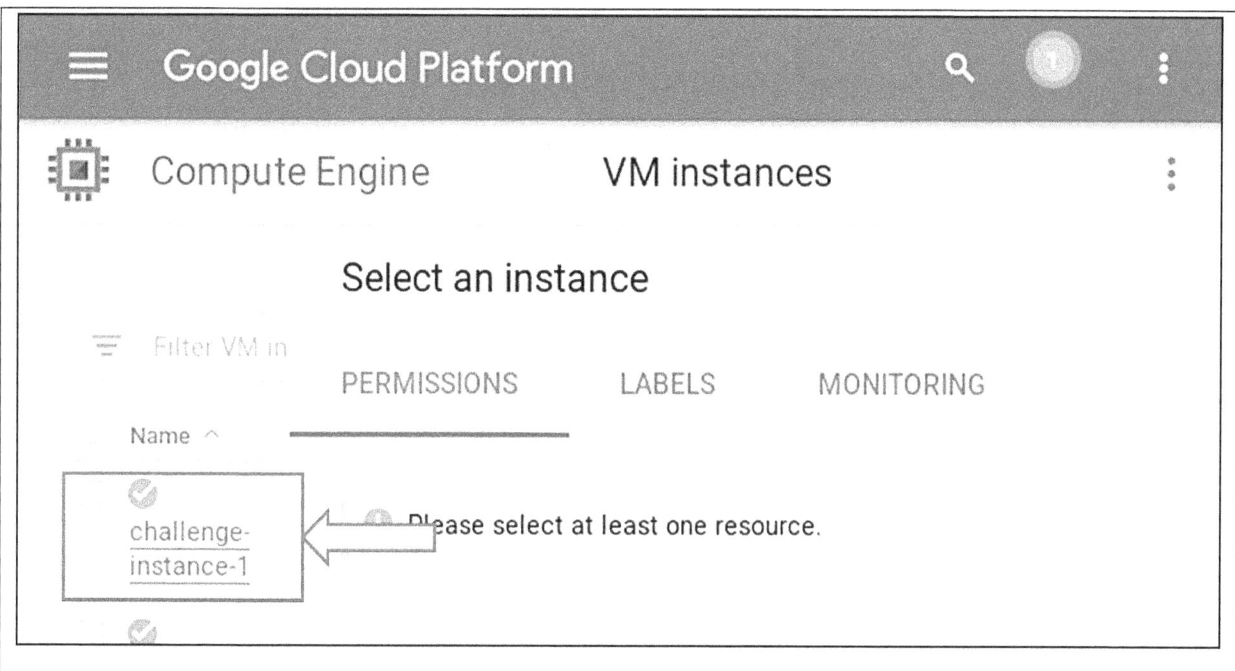

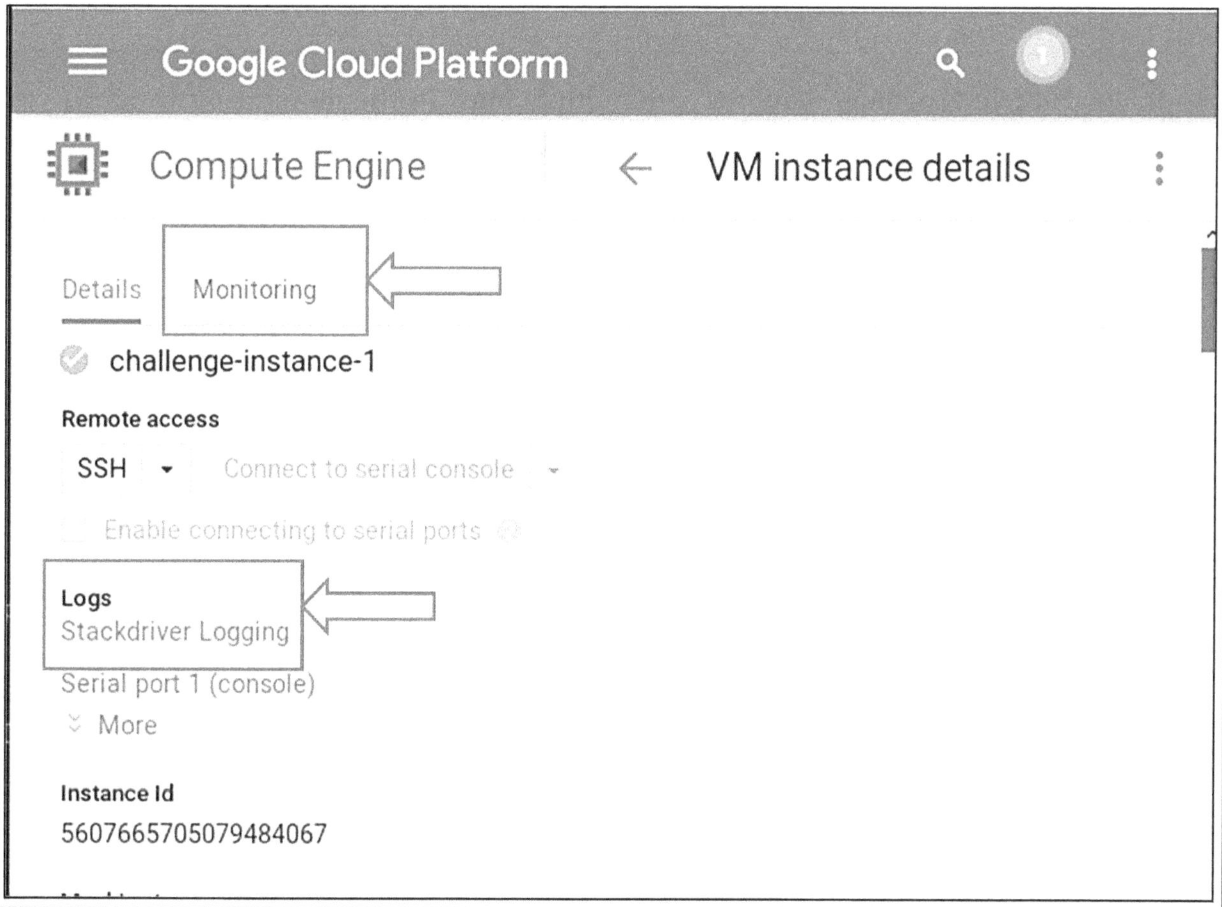

Google Cloud Platform
Compute Engine
VM instances
Select an instance
Filter VM in
PERMISSIONS
LABELS
MONITORING
Name
challenge-instance-1
Please select at least one resource.

Google Cloud Platform
Compute Engine
VM instance details
Details
Monitoring
challenge-instance-1
Remote access
SSH
Connect to serial console
Enable connecting to serial ports
Logs
Stackdriver Logging
Serial port 1 (console)
More
Instance Id
5607665705079484067

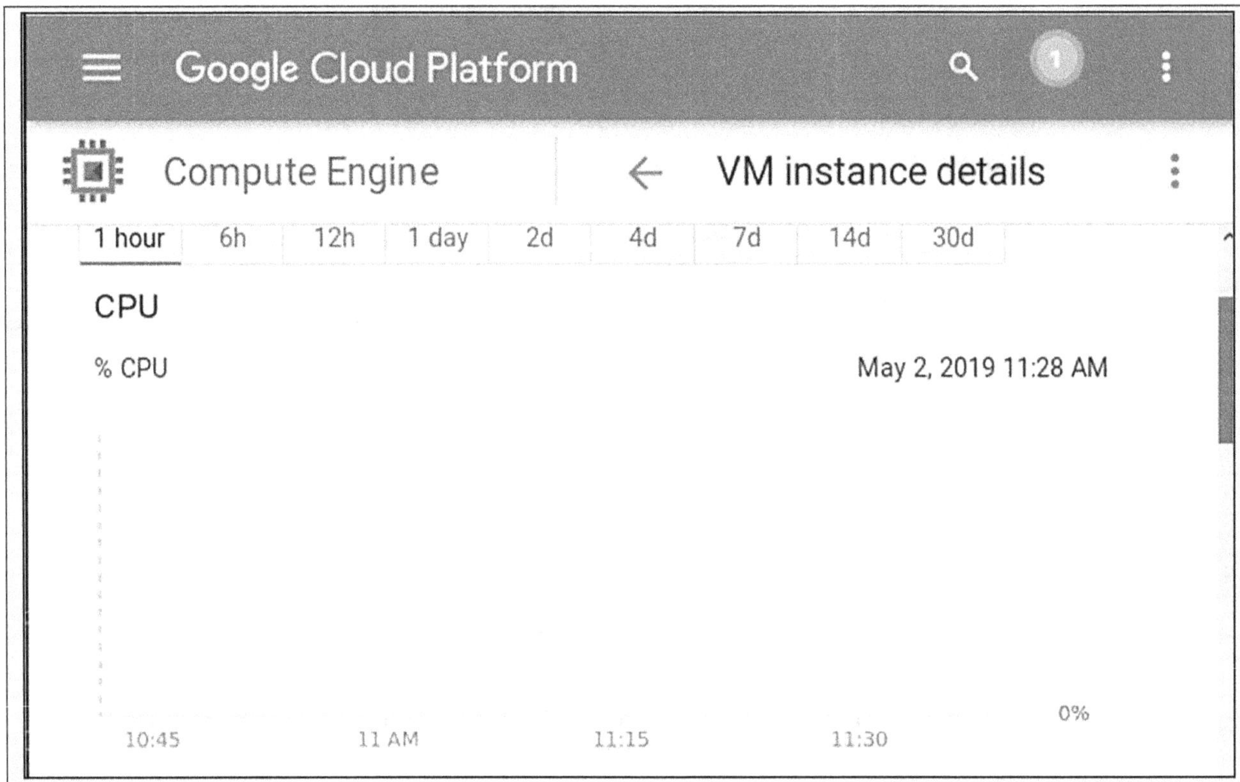

8. In "Stackdriver Logging", you will see multiple logs. In the monitoring window, you can see the CPU monitoring usage. If you go to the bucket, there you see the log file. When you open it, you will see the window that shows your work is completed as in stack driver log shows that startup is finished.

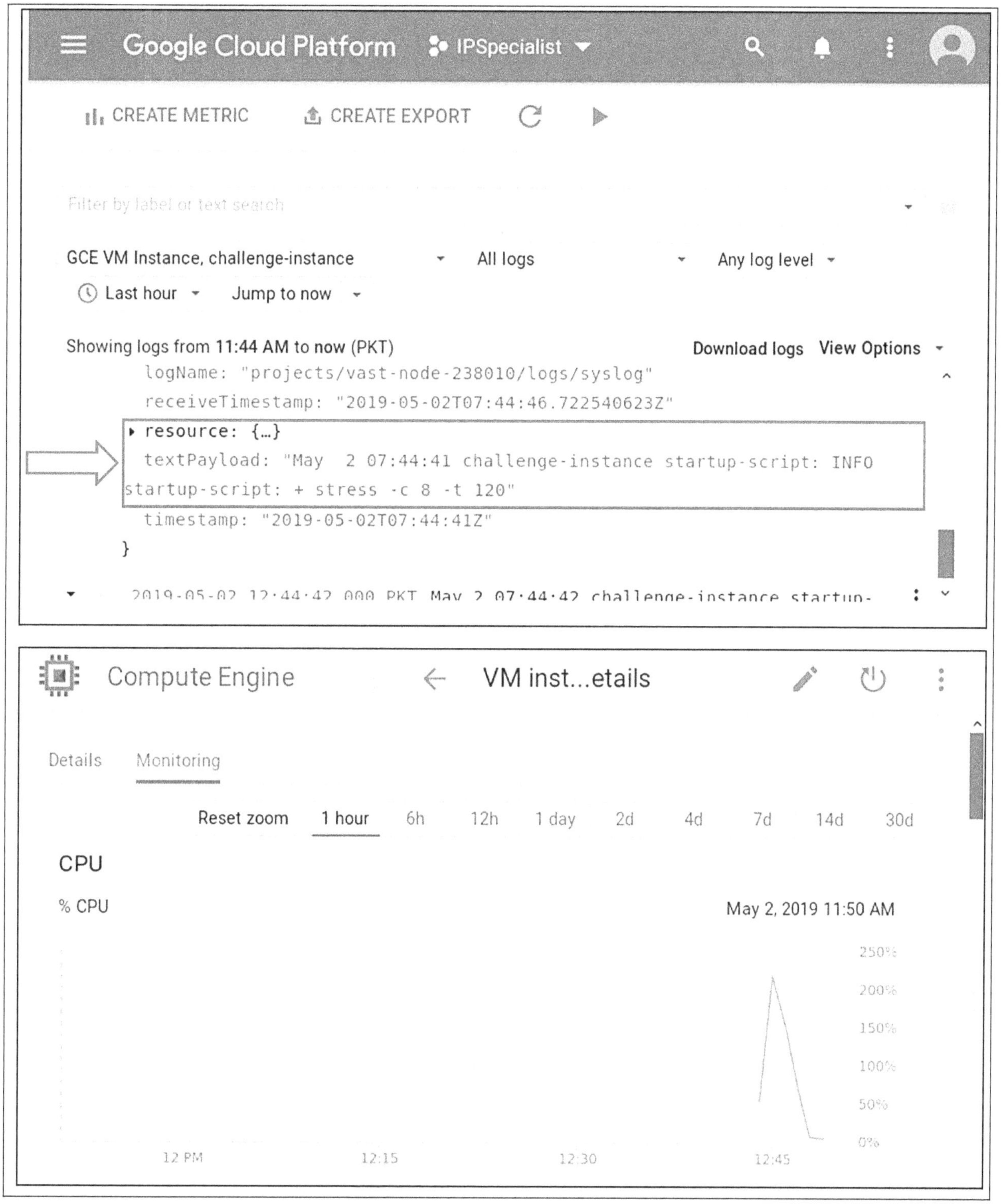

Google Cloud Platform IPSpecialist

CREATE METRIC CREATE EXPORT

Filter by label or text search

GCE VM Instance, challenge-instance All logs Any log level

Last hour Jump to now

Showing logs from 11:44 AM to now (PKT) Download logs View Options

```
logName: "projects/vast-node-238010/logs/syslog"
receiveTimestamp: "2019-05-02T07:44:46.722540623Z"
▸ resource: {…}
textPayload: "May  2 07:44:41 challenge-instance startup-script: INFO startup-script: + stress -c 8 -t 120"
timestamp: "2019-05-02T07:44:41Z"
}
▾ 2019-05-02 12:44:42.000 PKT May 2 07:44:42 challenge-instance startup-
```

Compute Engine VM inst...etails

Details Monitoring

Reset zoom 1 hour 6h 12h 1 day 2d 4d 7d 14d 30d

CPU

% CPU May 2, 2019 11:50 AM

250% 200% 150% 100% 50% 0%

12 PM 12:15 12:30 12:45

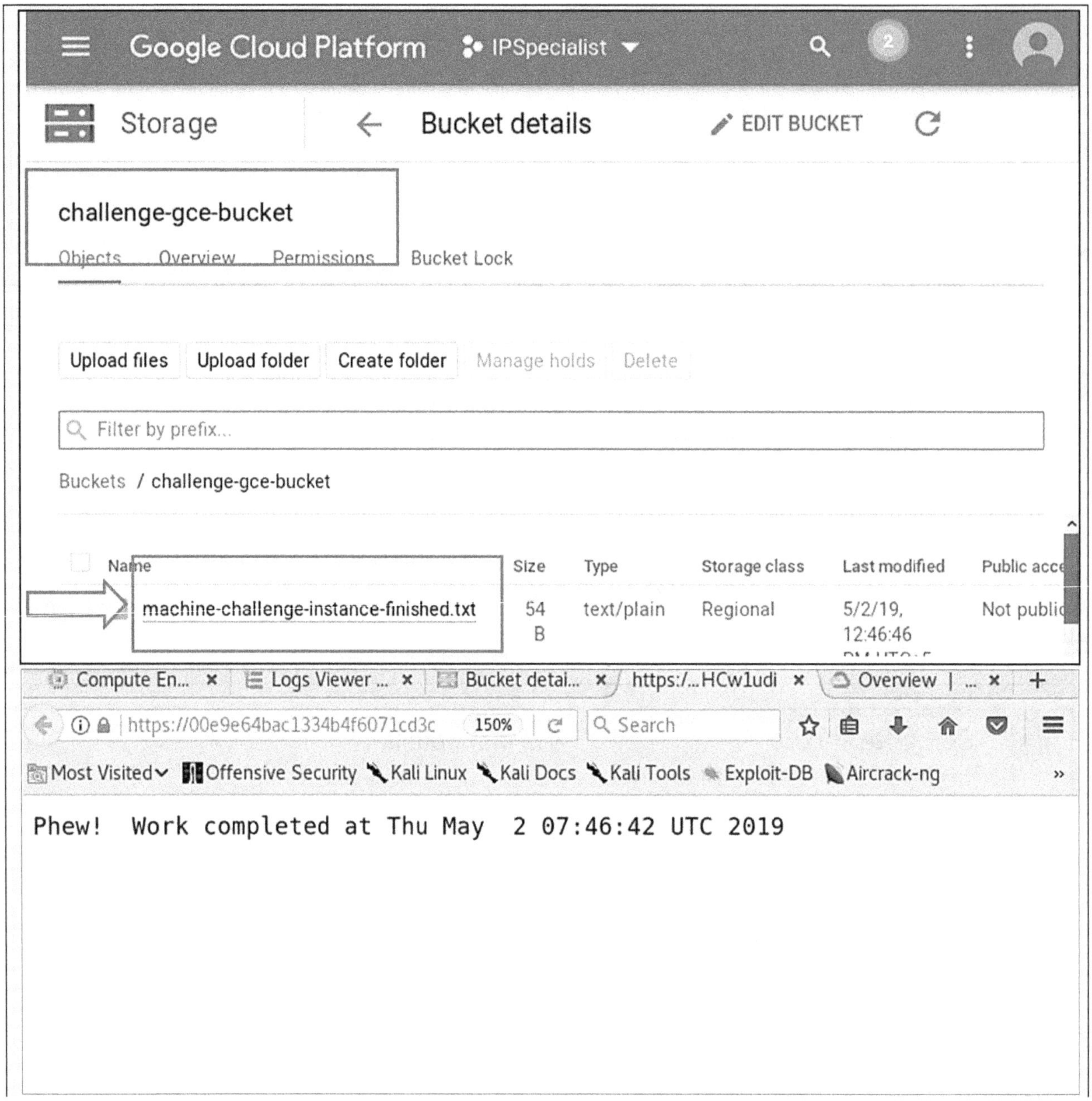

Google Cloud Platform IPSpecialist

Storage ← Bucket details EDIT BUCKET

challenge-gce-bucket

Objects Overview Permissions Bucket Lock

Upload files Upload folder Create folder Manage holds Delete

Filter by prefix...

Buckets / challenge-gce-bucket

Name	Size	Type	Storage class	Last modified	Public acce
machine-challenge-instance-finished.txt	54 B	text/plain	Regional	5/2/19, 12:46:46	Not public

Compute En... Logs Viewer ... Bucket detai... https:/...HCw1udi Overview | ...

https://00e9e64bac1334b4f6071cd3c 150% Search

Most Visited Offensive Security Kali Linux Kali Docs Kali Tools Exploit-DB Aircrack-ng

```
Phew!  Work completed at Thu May  2 07:46:42 UTC 2019
```

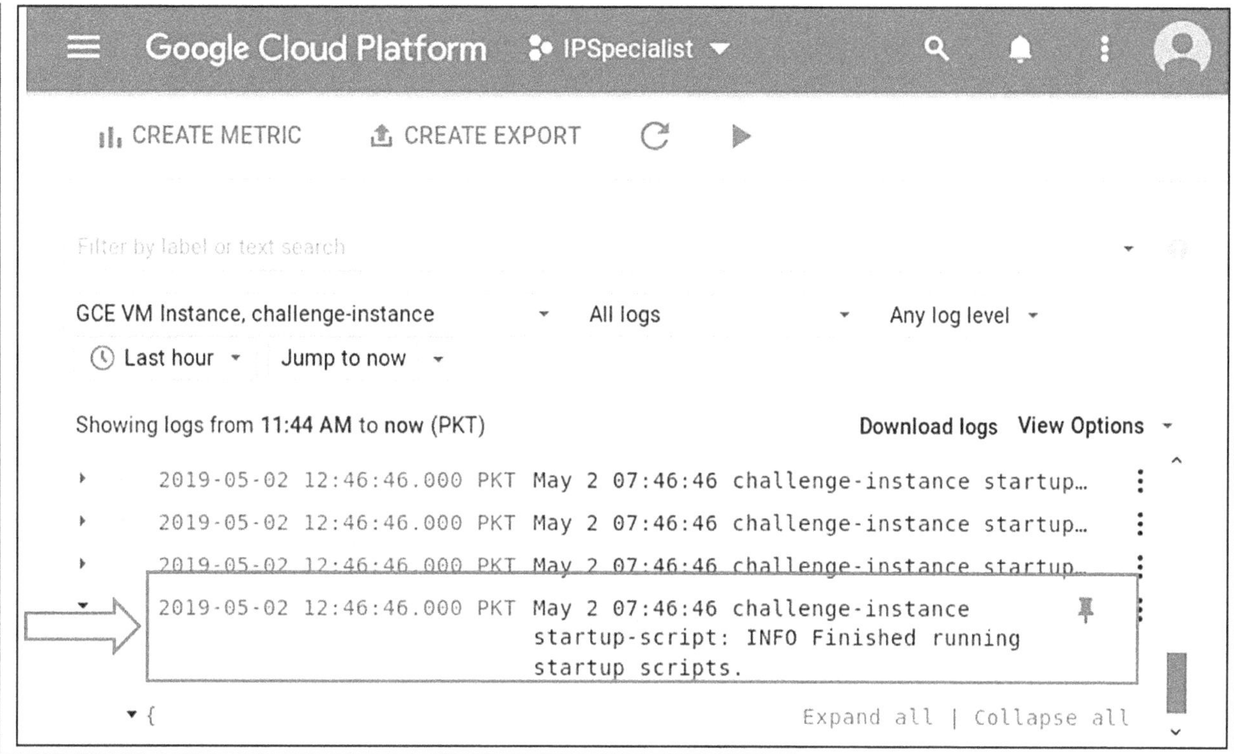
Google Cloud Platform
IPSpecialist
CREATE METRIC
CREATE EXPORT
Filter by label or text search
GCE VM Instance, challenge-instance
All logs
Any log level
Last hour
Jump to now
Showing logs from 11:44 AM to now (PKT)
Download logs
View Options
2019-05-02 12:46:46.000 PKT May 2 07:46:46 challenge-instance startup...
2019-05-02 12:46:46.000 PKT May 2 07:46:46 challenge-instance startup...
2019-05-02 12:46:46.000 PKT May 2 07:46:46 challenge-instance startup...
2019-05-02 12:46:46.000 PKT May 2 07:46:46 challenge-instance startup-script: INFO Finished running startup scripts.
Expand all | Collapse all

Mind Map

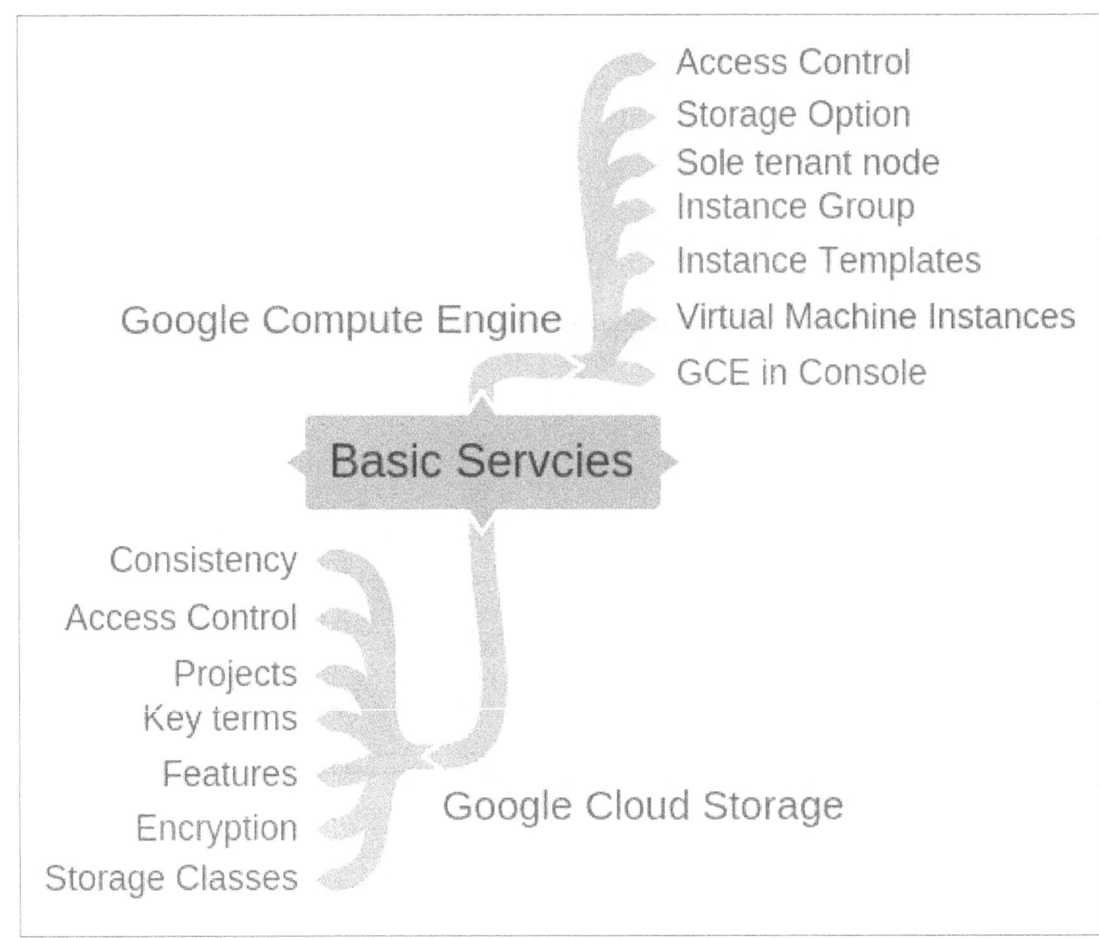

Figure 3-08: Chapter's Mind Map

Practice Questions:

1. ______________ consists of a set of users, a set of APIs, and settings for those APIs.
   A. Bucket
   B. Project
   C. Object
   D. None of the above

2. There is a limit of ____ labels per bucket.
   A. 10
   B. 30
   C. 64
   D. 20

3. In Google Cloud Storage, the object size is ____________.

A. 2046 bytes
B. 64 bytes
C. 16 bytes
D. 1024 bytes

4. If you want to keep the older version of any object, then what should you do?
   A. Bucket Policy
   B. Object Immutability
   C. Versioning
   D. None of the above

5. Objects are immutable and cannot be modified throughout their storage life after uploading. True or false?
   A. True
   B. False

6. From the following options, which role is only able to list a bucket?
   A. Editor
   B. Owner
   C. Viewer
   D. None of the above

7. Which storage option stores data in data centers worldwide with 99.95% availability?
   A. Multi-Regional Storage
   B. Regional Storage
   C. Nearline Storage
   D. Coldline Storage

8. Which storage option is best suited for computing, analytical and machine learning work?
   A. Multi-Regional Storage
   B. Regional Storage
   C. Nearline Storage
   D. Coldline Storage

9. From the following storage options, which one is for storing data that are

infrequently accessed?

A. Multi-Regional Storage
B. Regional Storage
C. Nearline Storage
D. Coldline Storage

10. From the following option, which storage is best to use at low cost for backup, DR and archiving?

A. Multi-Regional Storage
B. Regional Storage
C. Nearline Storage
D. Coldline Storage

11. Fixed key metadata are those in which you set both key and key value. True or false?

A. True
B. False

12. Which service is used to notify about any changes in an object, which is stored in GCS?

A. Error Reporting
B. Pub/Sub
C. Logging
D. Trace

13. Which feature allows you to configure a Cloud Storage bucket data retention policy to determine how long the bucket objects must be maintained?

A. Logging
B. Bucket Lock
C. Bucket Label
D. None of the above

14. How many types of logs are there in Cloud Audit Logging?

A. 4
B. 3
C. 2
D. 5

15. For fine-grained access control to the individual object, you can use ____________.
    A. Signed URL
    B. Bucket Policy
    C. ACL
    D. Cloud IAM

16. Within a project, you can use up to _______ number of VPC.
    A. 1
    B. 2
    C. 4
    D. 5

17. From the following states, name the state in which resources have been attained and the first boot of instance is ready.
    A. Provision
    B. Staging
    C. Running
    D. None of the above

18. From the following states, name the state in which resources are being allocated, and they are not yet in operation.
    A. Provision
    B. Staging
    C. Running
    D. None of the above

19. Which machine type is perfect for tasks, which require more vCPUs than memory?
    A. High Memory Machine
    B. Shared Core Type
    C. High CPU Machines
    D. Memory-Optimized Machine

20. From the following options, which one is a Google account that represents an application, as opposed to representing an end user?
    A. IAM User
    B. Service Account
    C. Quotas
    D. None of the above

Chapter 04: Scaling and Security

Introduction

This chapter is about scaling of instances and Security features provided by Google. Security of different resources are controlled by using IAM policy.

Scaling

Instance templates are global and once you create a particular template, user can use it to create multiple instances in different zones.

Instance Groups are of two types, either Managed or Unmanaged. Unmanaged instance groups are created by selecting instances whereas Managed instance groups based on a single selected instance template and the user is allowed to enable Auto-scaling.

Lab 4.1: Managed Instance Groups

Scenario:

In your organization, you are assigned with a task to monitor an instance in GCP. If the CPU usage of the instance exceeds 30% then launch more instances to balance the capacity load. You are allowed to launch up to 5 instances based on the CPU usage.

Solution:

You decided to Auto-scale the instance by creating an instance template and then, create a managed instance group and an unmanaged instance group.

1. Go to "Compute Engine" and select "Instance templates".

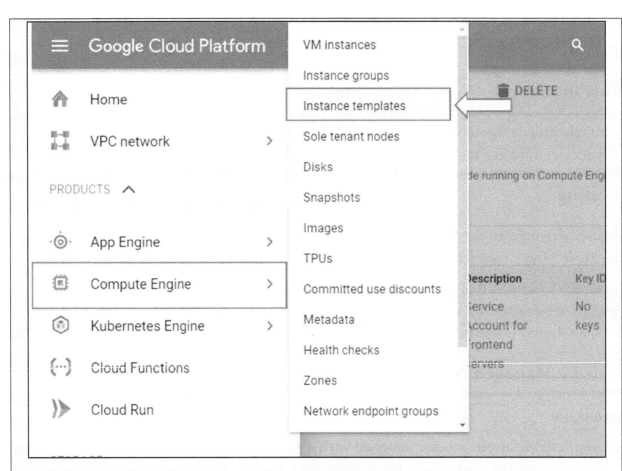

2. Click on 'Create instance template'

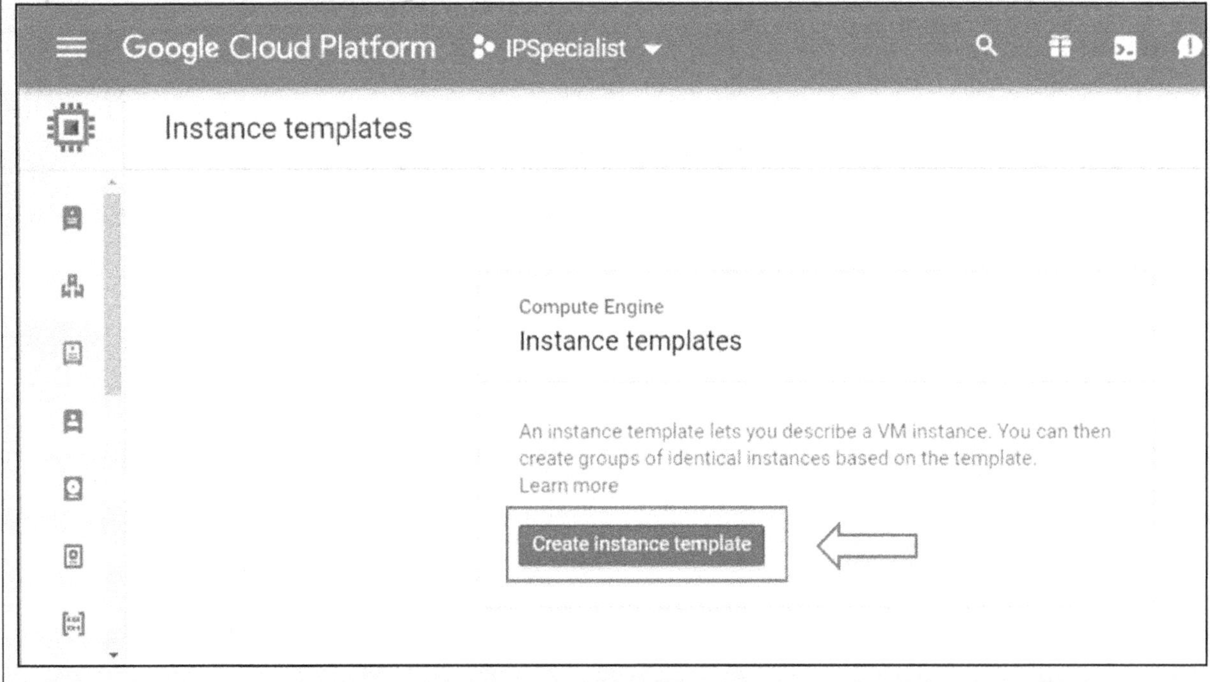

3. Enter a name and select the Machine type 'micro'

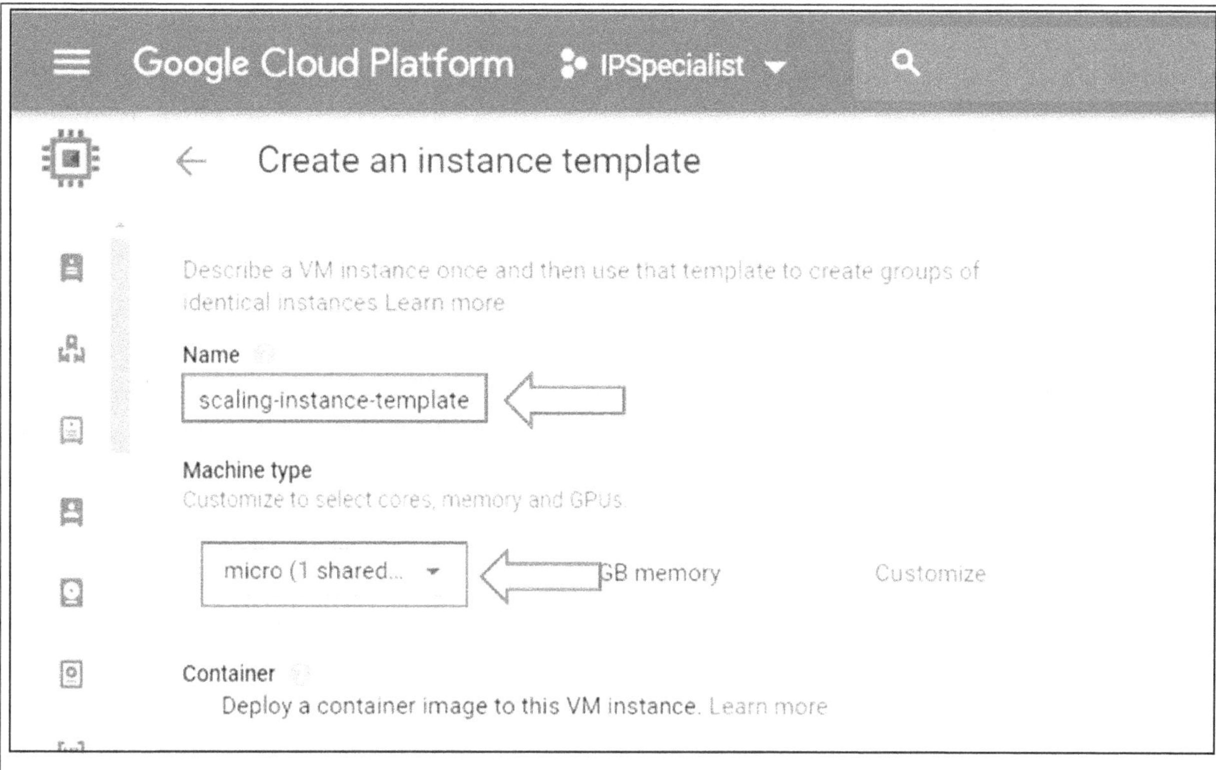

4. Extend Advanced setting to Add Labels

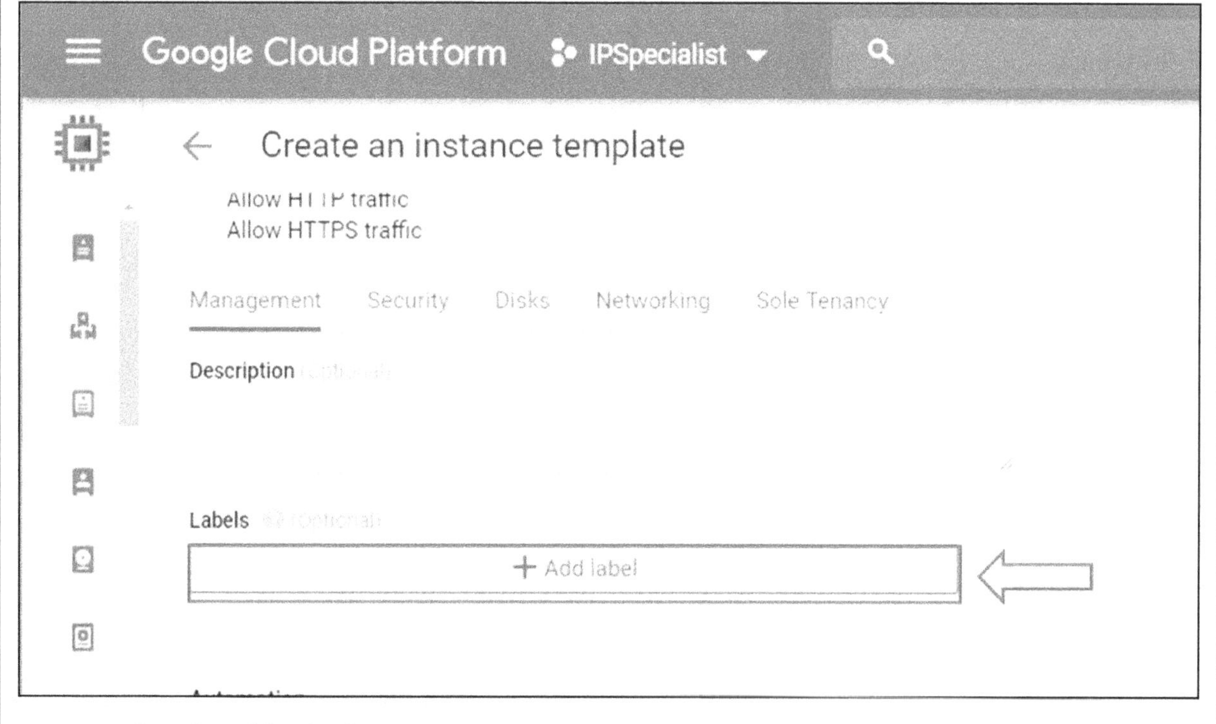

5. Enter 'Key' and 'Value'

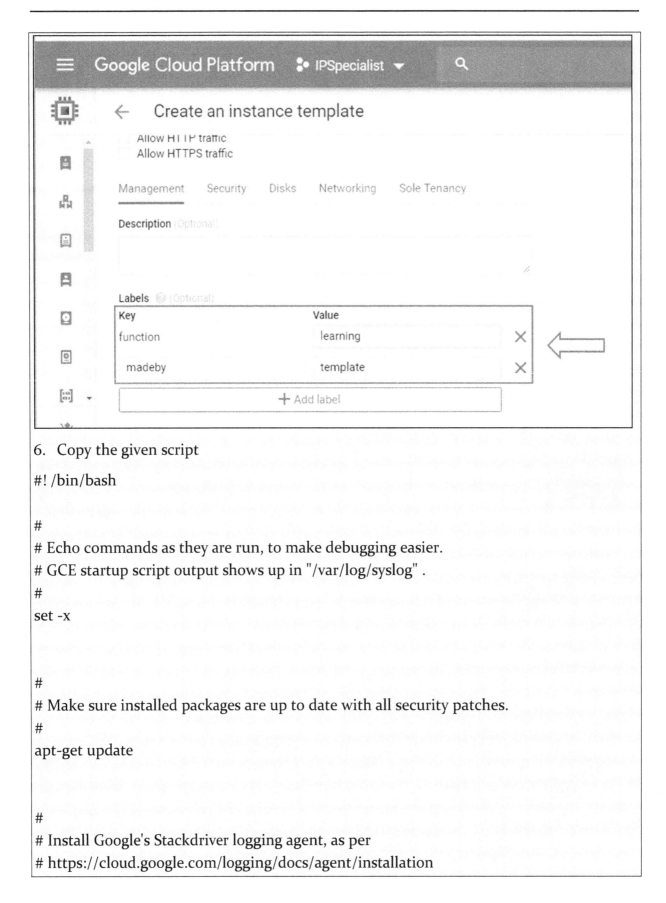

6. Copy the given script

```
#! /bin/bash

#
# Echo commands as they are run, to make debugging easier.
# GCE startup script output shows up in "/var/log/syslog" .
#
set -x


#
# Make sure installed packages are up to date with all security patches.
#
apt-get update


#
# Install Google's Stackdriver logging agent, as per
# https://cloud.google.com/logging/docs/agent/installation
```

```
#
curl -sso https://dl.google.com/cloudagents/install-logging-agent.sh
bash install-logging-agent.sh


#
# Install and run the "stress" tool to max the CPU load for a while.
#
apt-get install stress
stress -c 8 -t 120


#
# Report that we're done.
#

# Metadata should be set in the "lab-logs-bucket" attribute using the "gs://mybucketname/" format.
log_bucket_metadata_name=lab-logs-bucket
log_bucket_metadata_url="http://metadata.google.internal/computeMetadata/v1/instance/attributes/${log_bucket_metadata_name}"
worker_log_bucket=$(curl -H "Metadata-Flavor: Google" "${log_bucket_metadata_url}")

# We write a file named after this machine.
worker_log_file="machine-$(hostname)-finished.txt"
echo "Phew!  Work completed at $(date)" >"${worker_log_file}"

# And we copy that file to the bucket specified in the metadata.
echo "Copying the log file to the bucket..."
gsutil cp "${worker_log_file}" "${worker_log_bucket}"
```

7. Paste the script in 'Startup script' and copy the metadata name

Google Cloud Platform IPSpecialist

Create an instance template

madeby template

+ Add label

Automation

Startup script (Optional)

You can choose to specify a startup script that will run when your instance boots up or restarts. Startup scripts can be used to install software and updates, and to ensure that services are running within the virtual machine. Learn more

"gs://mybucketname/" format.
log_bucket_metadata_name=lab-logs-bucket
log_bucket_metadata_url="http://metadata.google.internal/computeMetadat

Metadata (Optional)

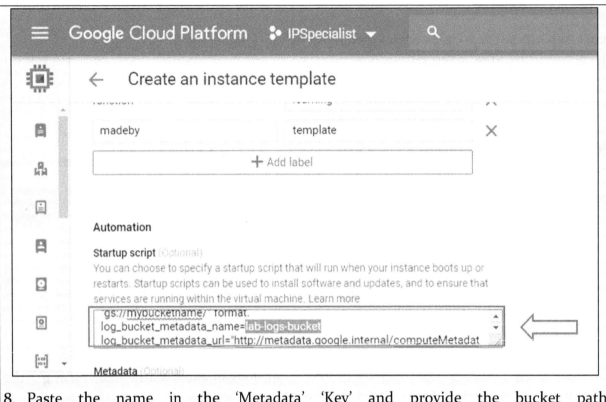

8. Paste the name in the 'Metadata' 'Key' and provide the bucket path <gs://bucketname/> in 'Value'

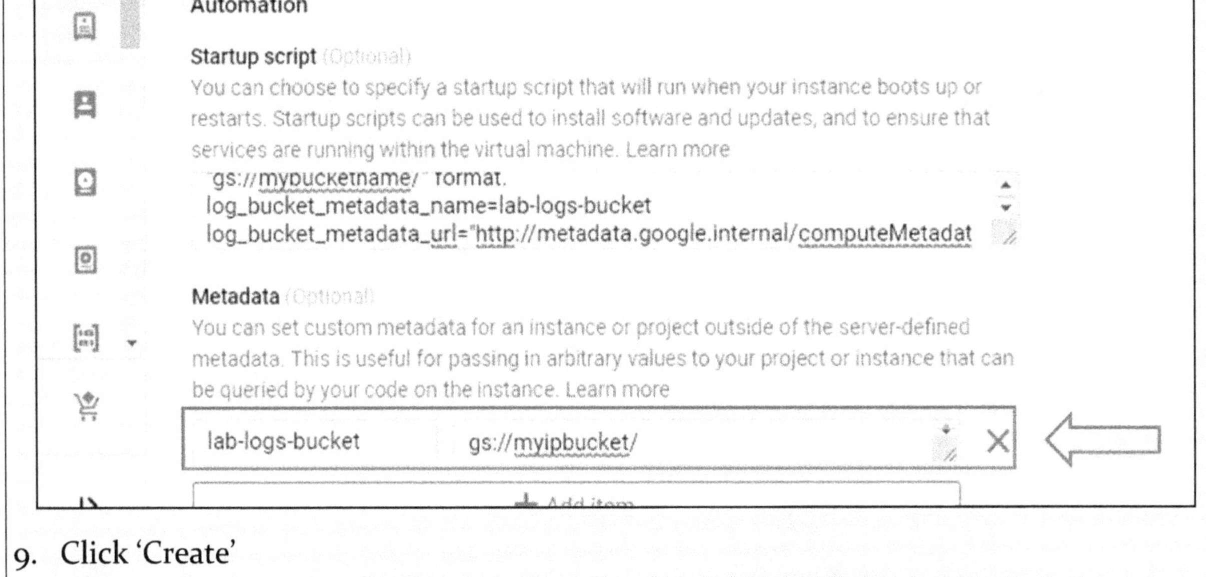

9. Click 'Create'

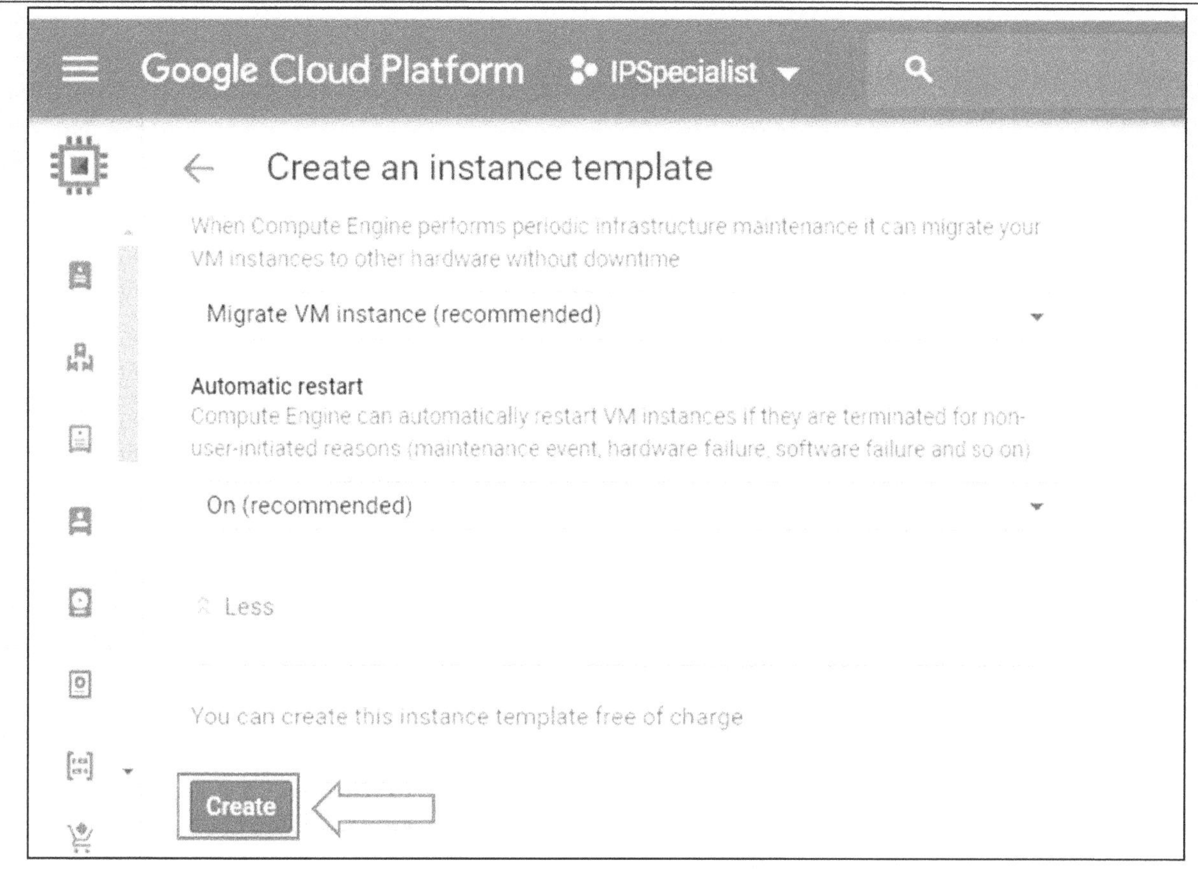

10. Click the created instance template

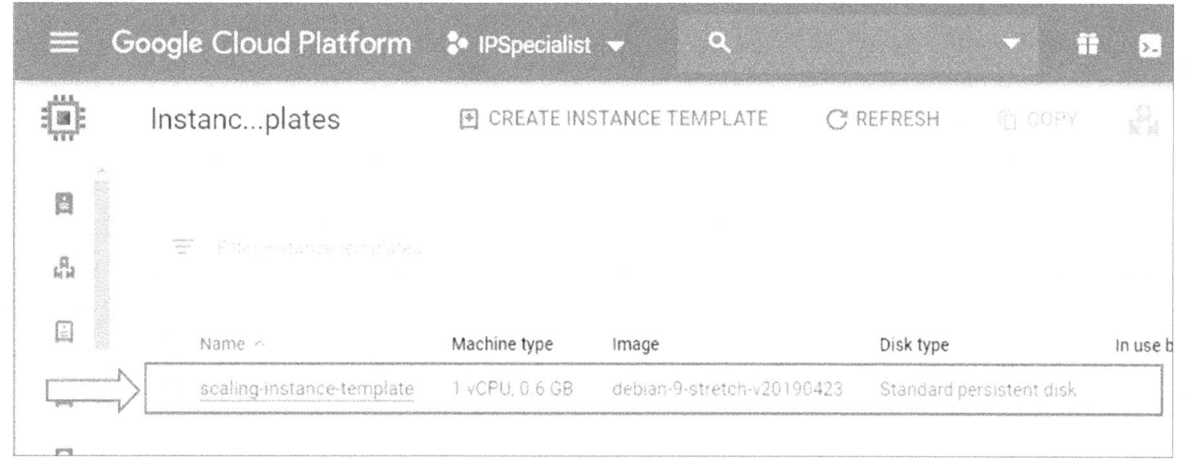

Instance template cannot be edited. You can create a template same as the previous one

11. Click 'CREATE VM'

Google Cloud Platform IPSpecialist

Instance templates CREATE VM ATE SIMILAR

scaling-instance-template

Machine type

f1-micro (1 vCPU, 0.6 GB memory)

Display device

Turn on a display device if you want to use screen capturing and recording tools.

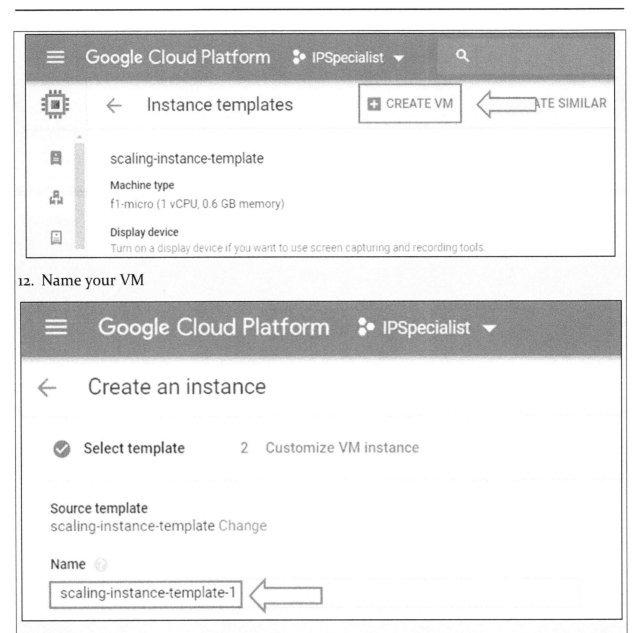

12. Name your VM

Google Cloud Platform IPSpecialist

Create an instance

Select template 2 Customize VM instance

Source template

scaling-instance-template Change

Name

scaling-instance-template-1

13. Click 'Create'

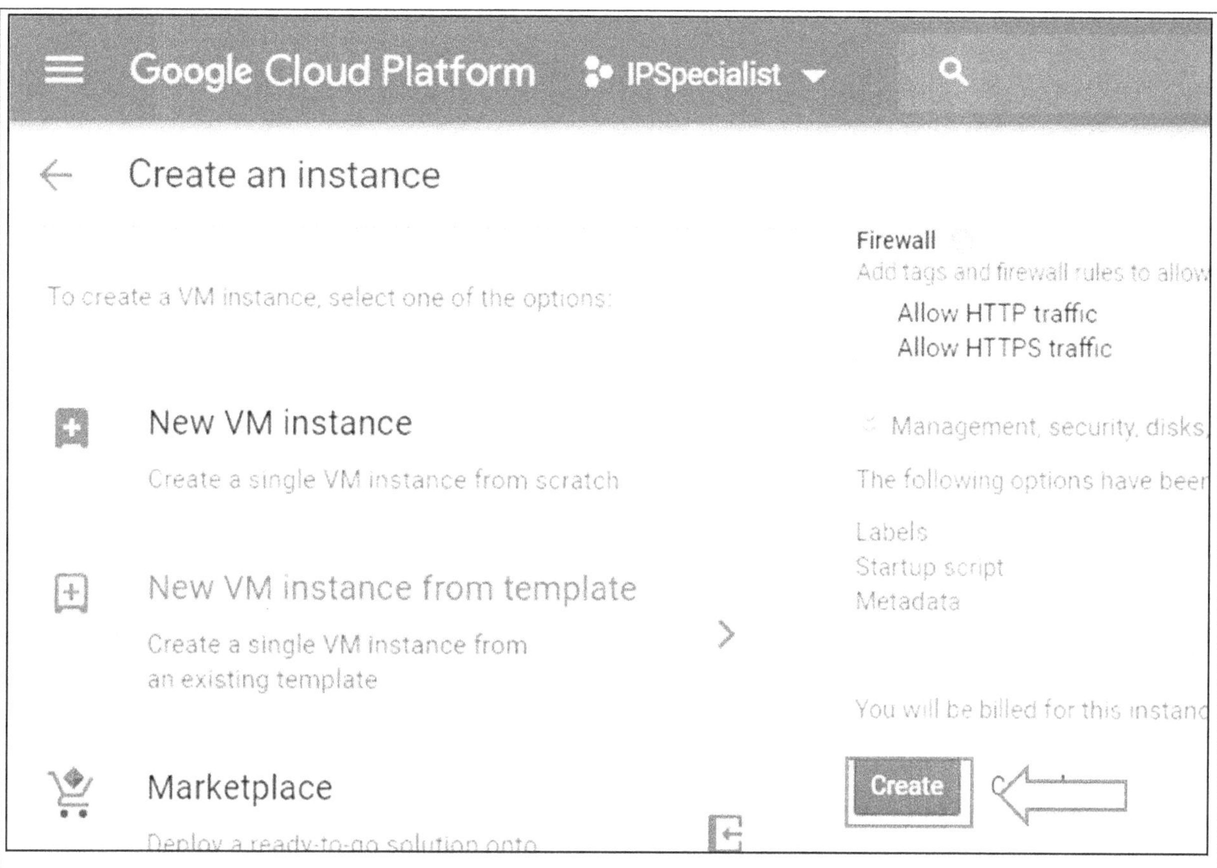

14. Click 'CREATE INSTANCE'

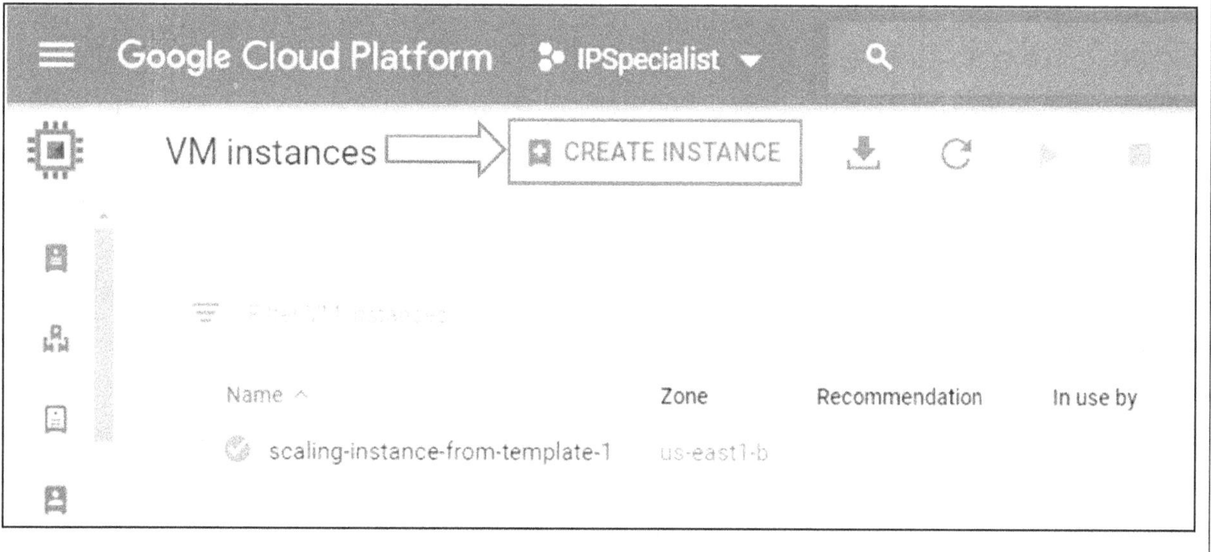

15. Click 'New VM instance from template'

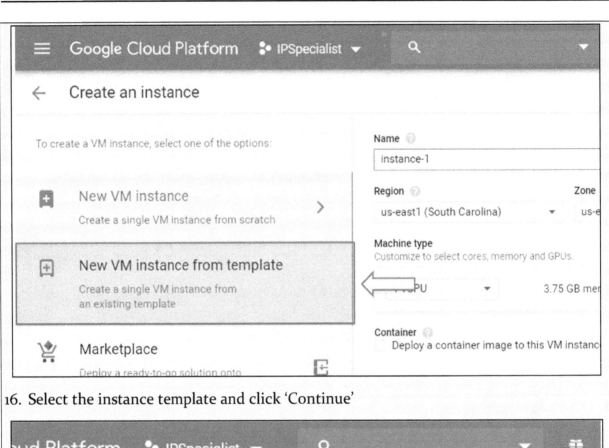

16. Select the instance template and click 'Continue'

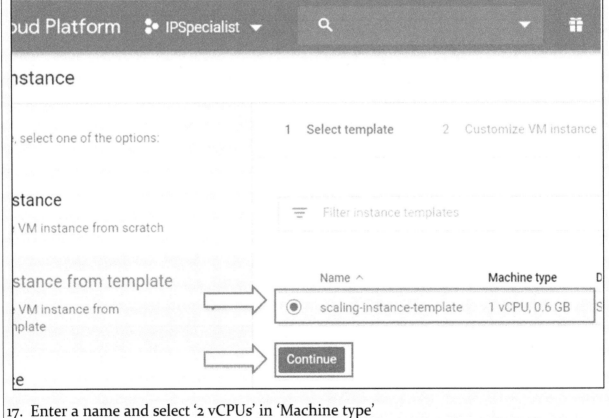

17. Enter a name and select '2 vCPUs' in 'Machine type'

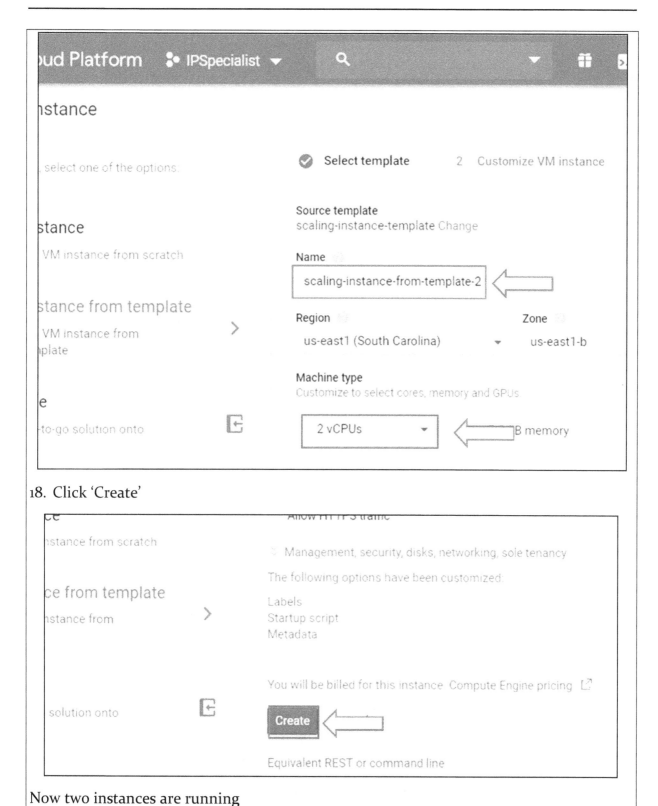

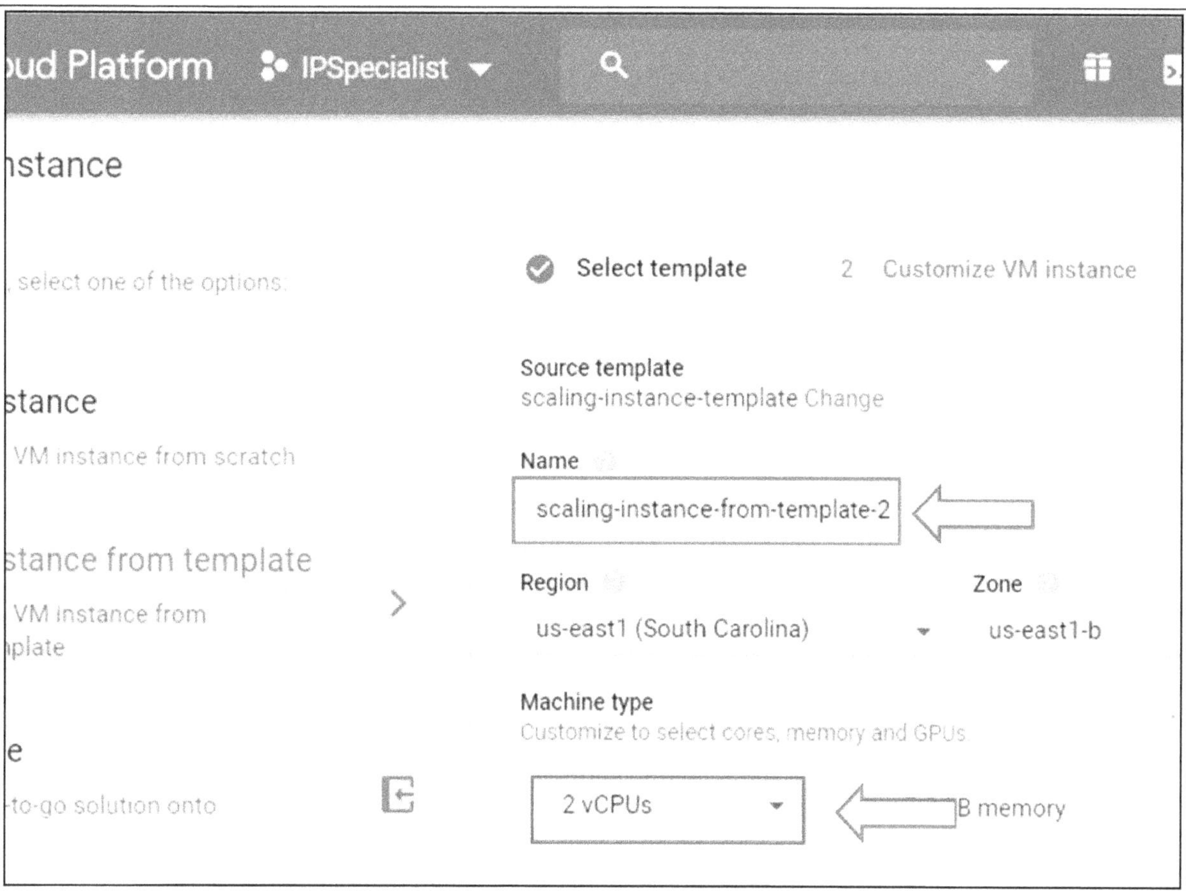

18. Click 'Create'

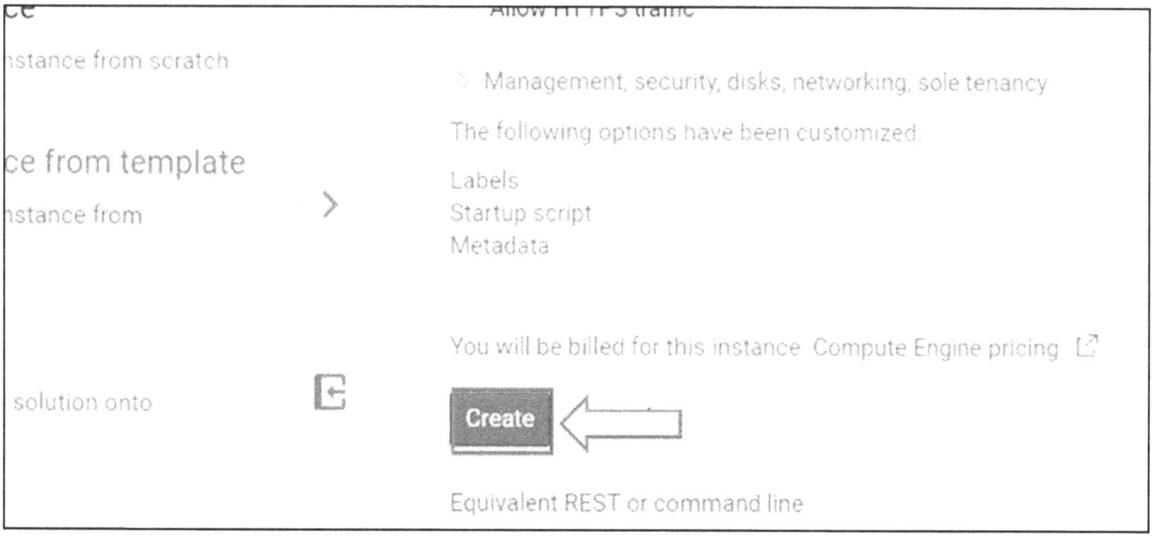

Now two instances are running

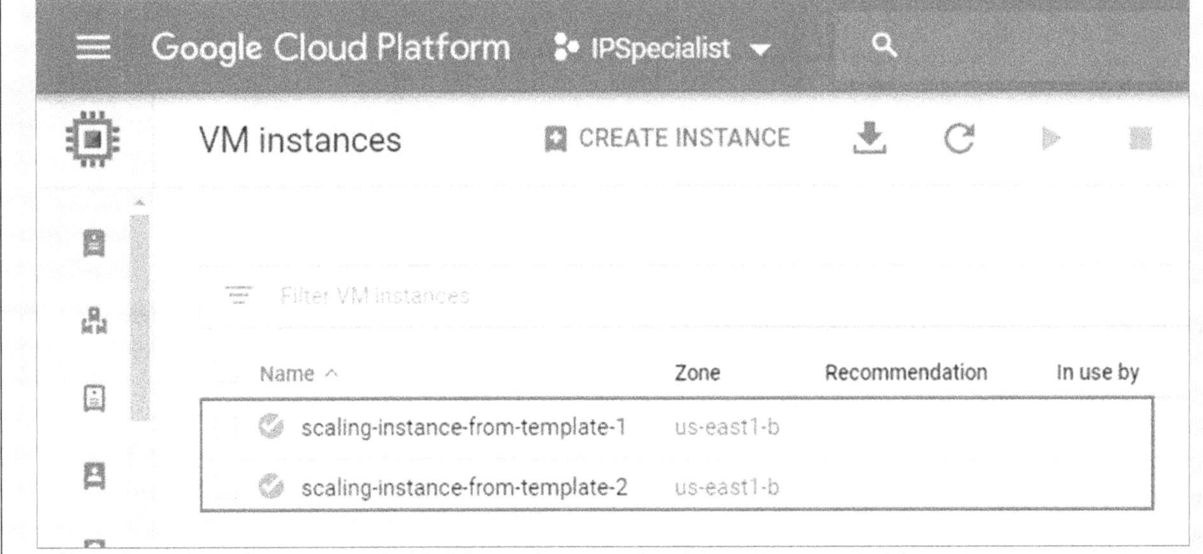

19. Click the first instance and select 'Monitoring'

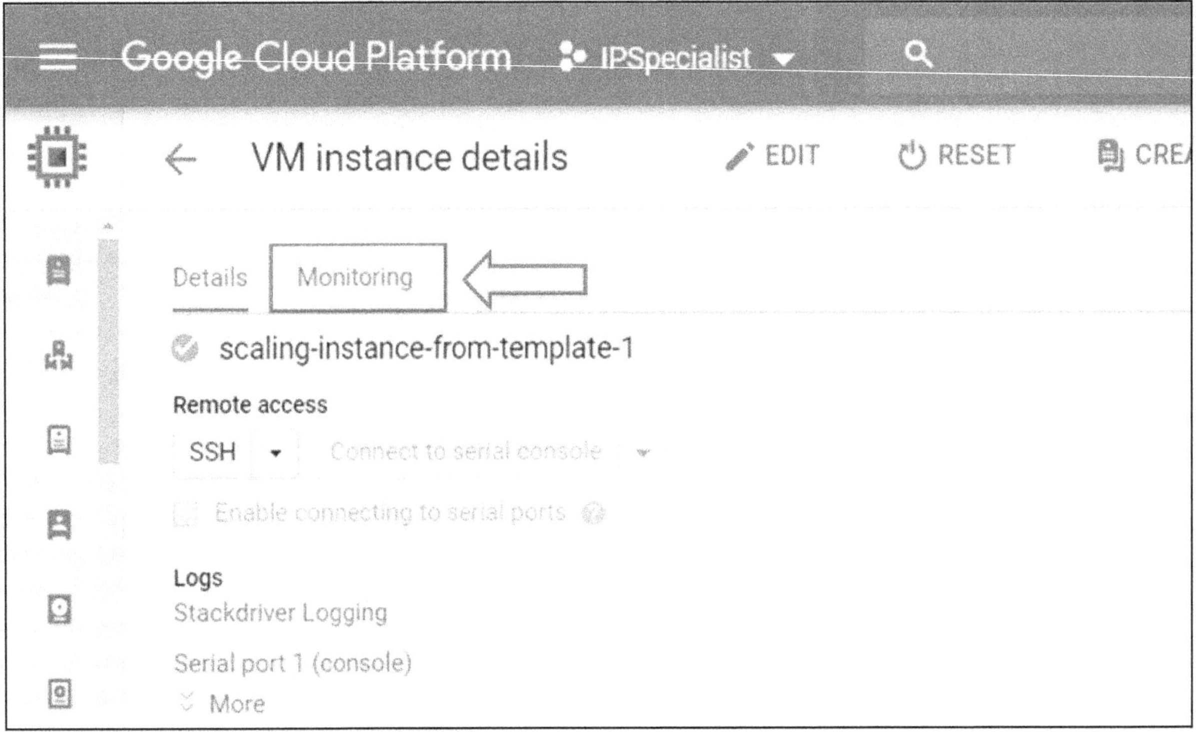

This instance has started working due to the script added in it. It is doing the PubSub and this machine does not have enough capacity, therefore, another instance will be used. Second instance has more CPUs

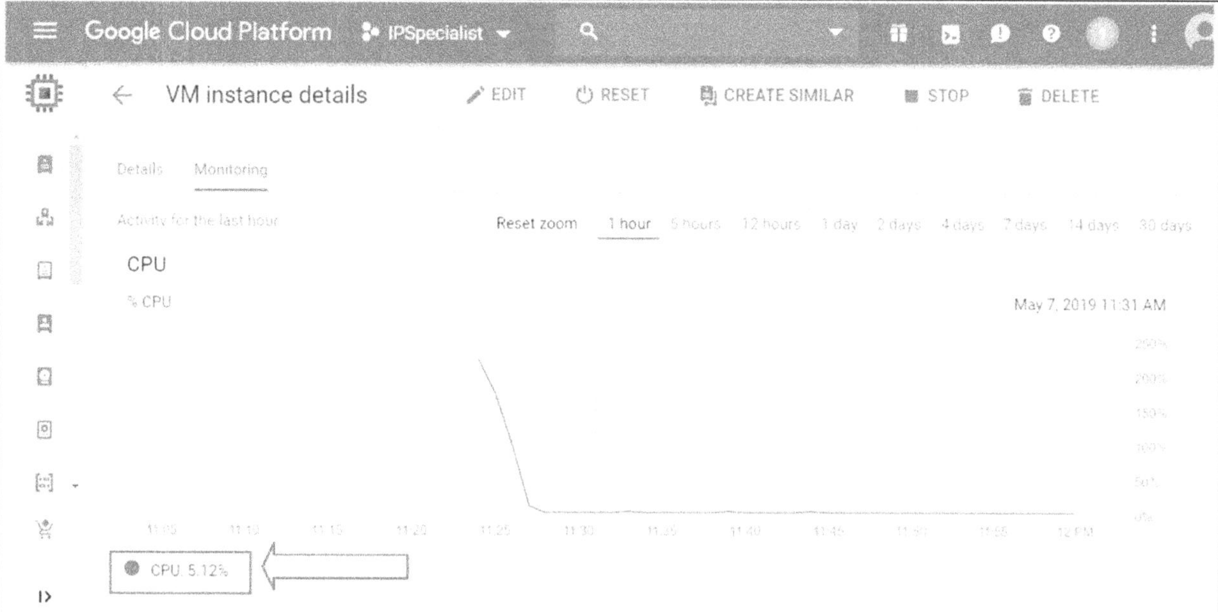

These instances are working separately

20. Go to 'Instance groups' to group these instances

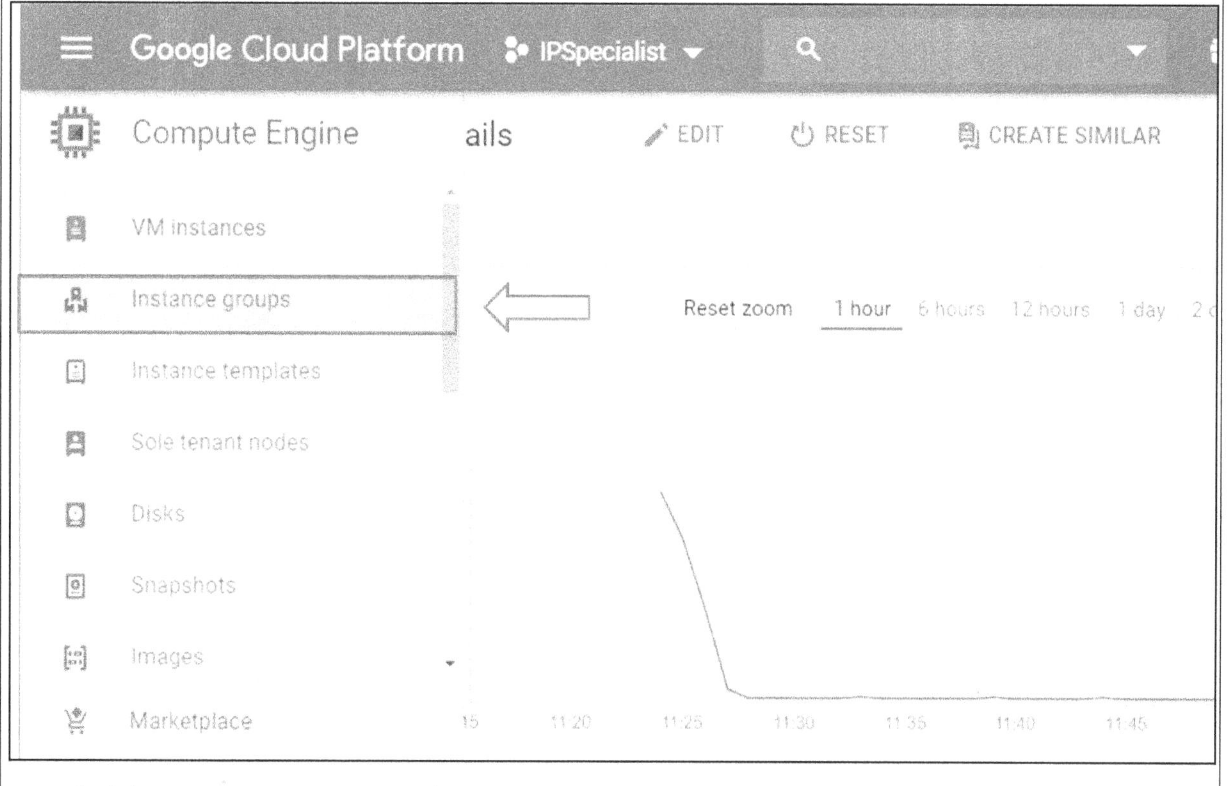

21. Click 'Create Instance group'

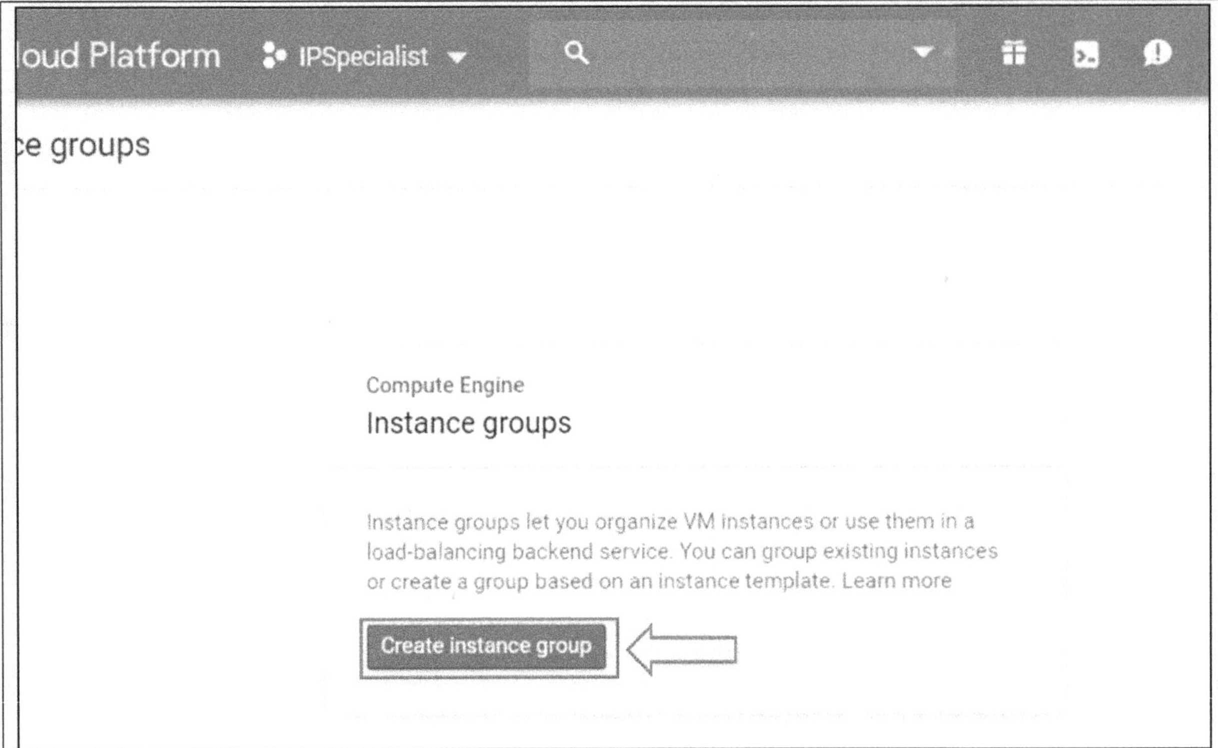

22. Give it a name

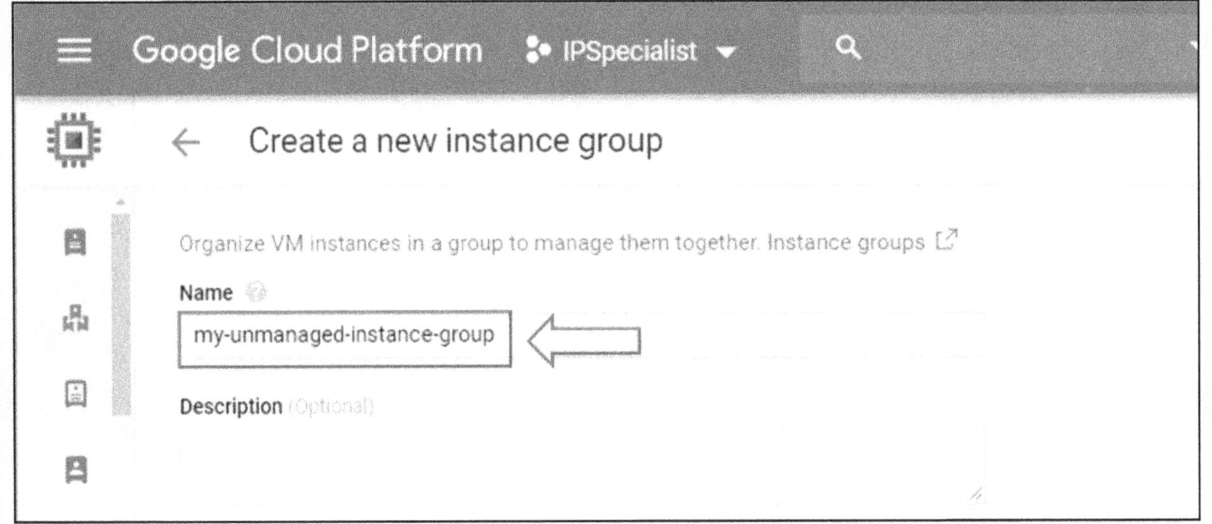

23. Select 'Unmanaged instance group'. Unmanaged instance group cannot be Multiple zone

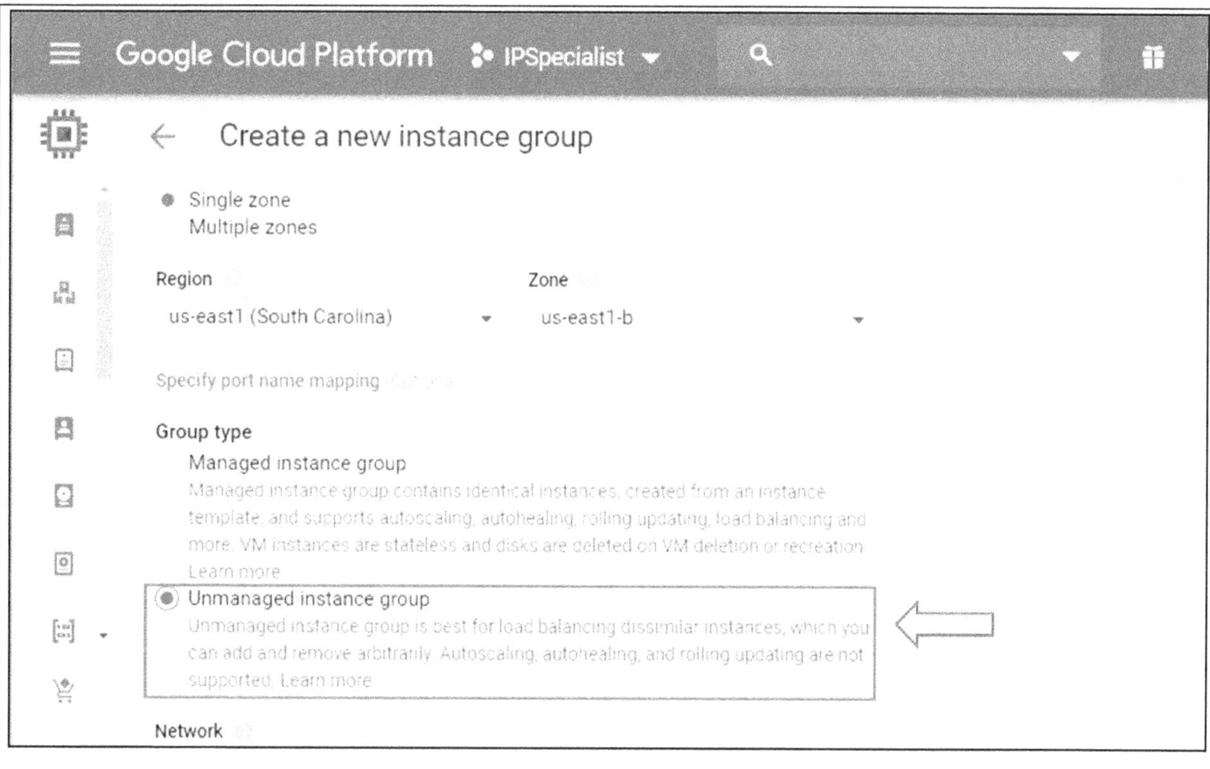

24. Add both the instances

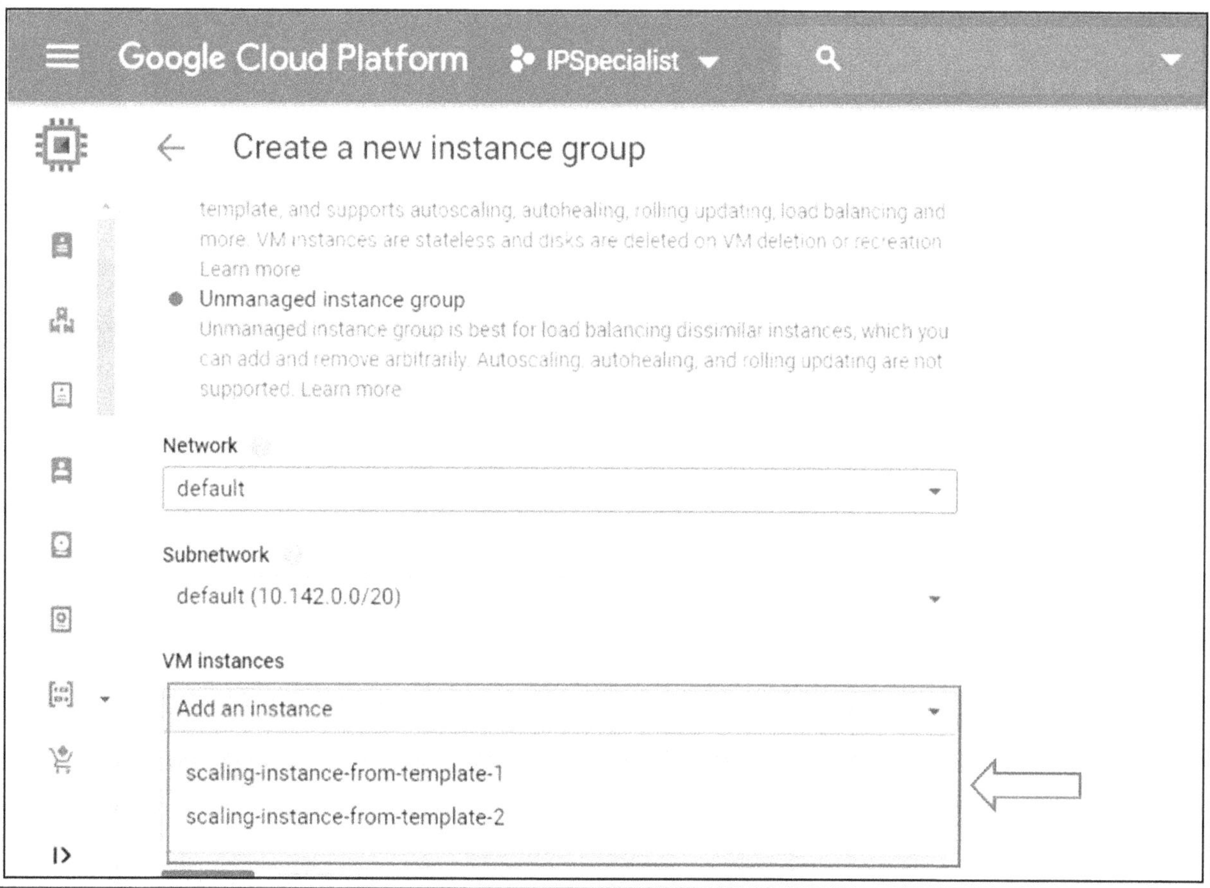

25. Click 'Create'

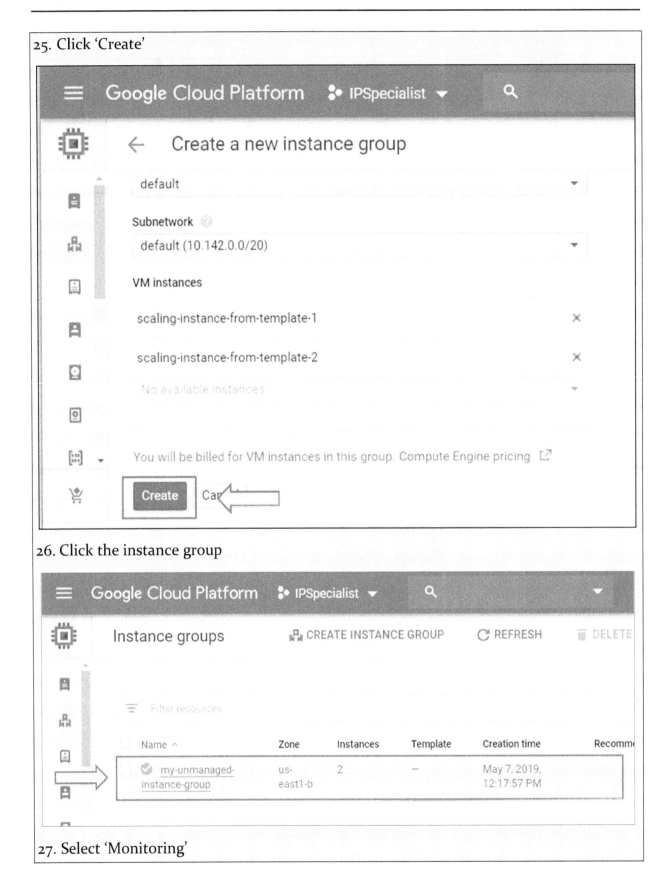

26. Click the instance group

27. Select 'Monitoring'

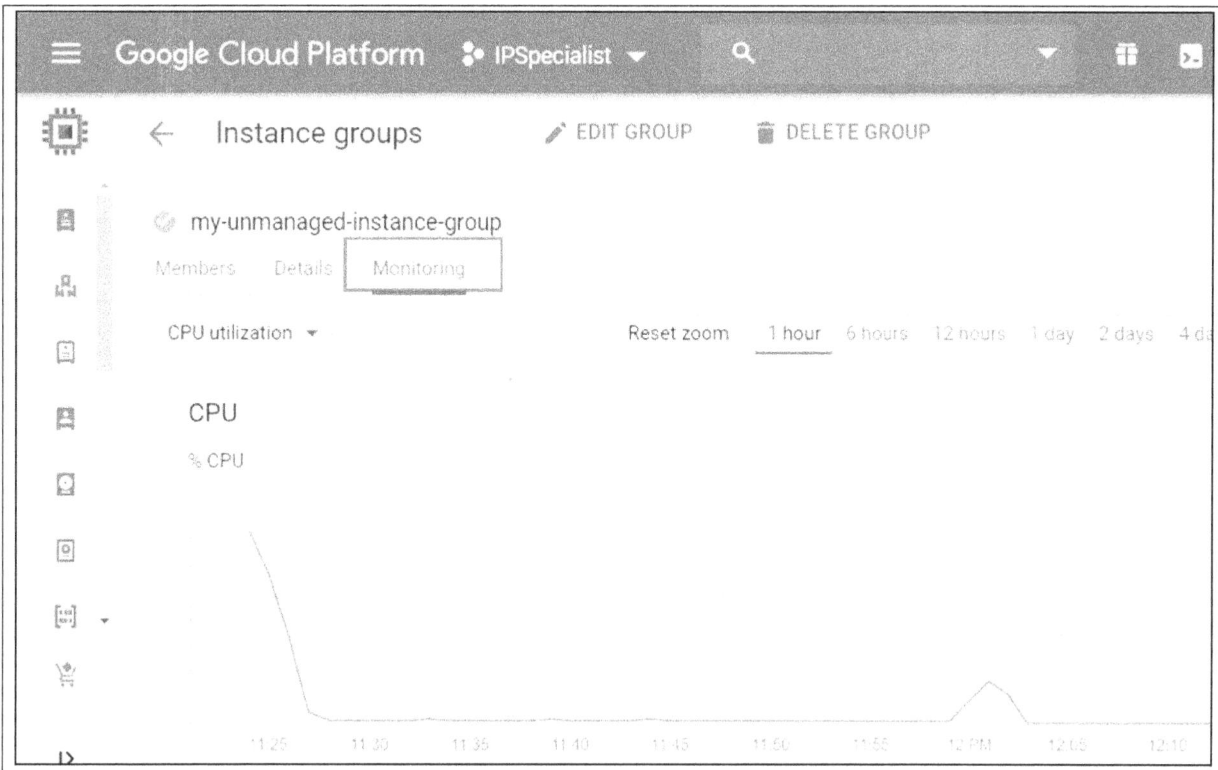

The instance does not have much load, therefore, the second instance can be stopped and turned on when needed. But this is not a good practice. This process should be automatic.

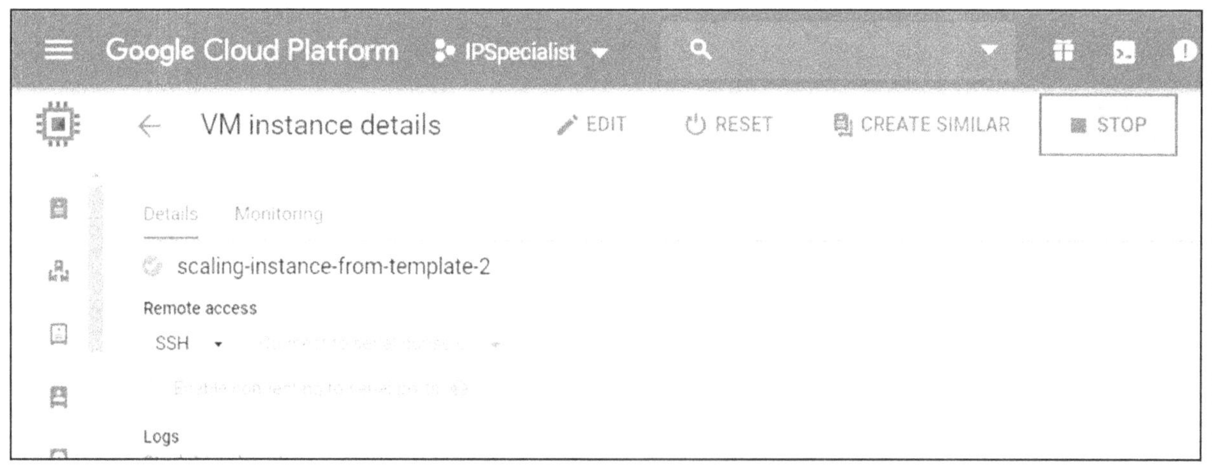

28. Go to the instance groups and click 'CREATE INSTANCE GROUP'

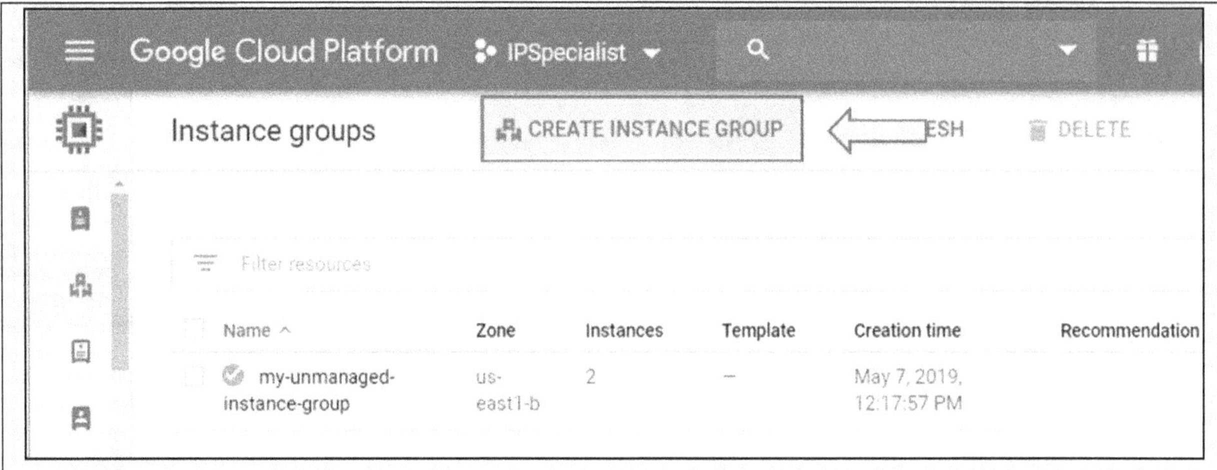

29. Enter any name and select 'Multiple zones'

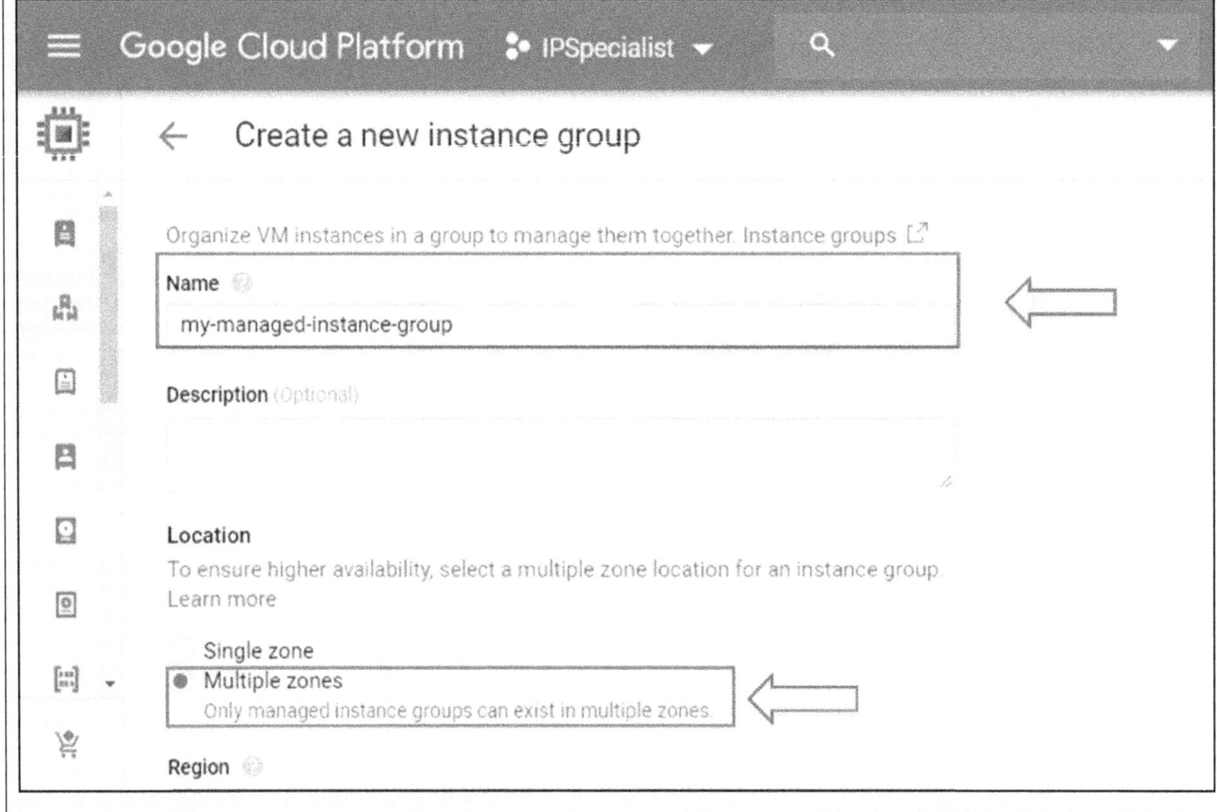

30. Select the region 'us-central1' and select all zones

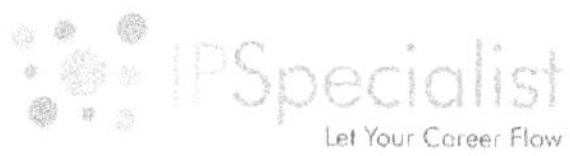

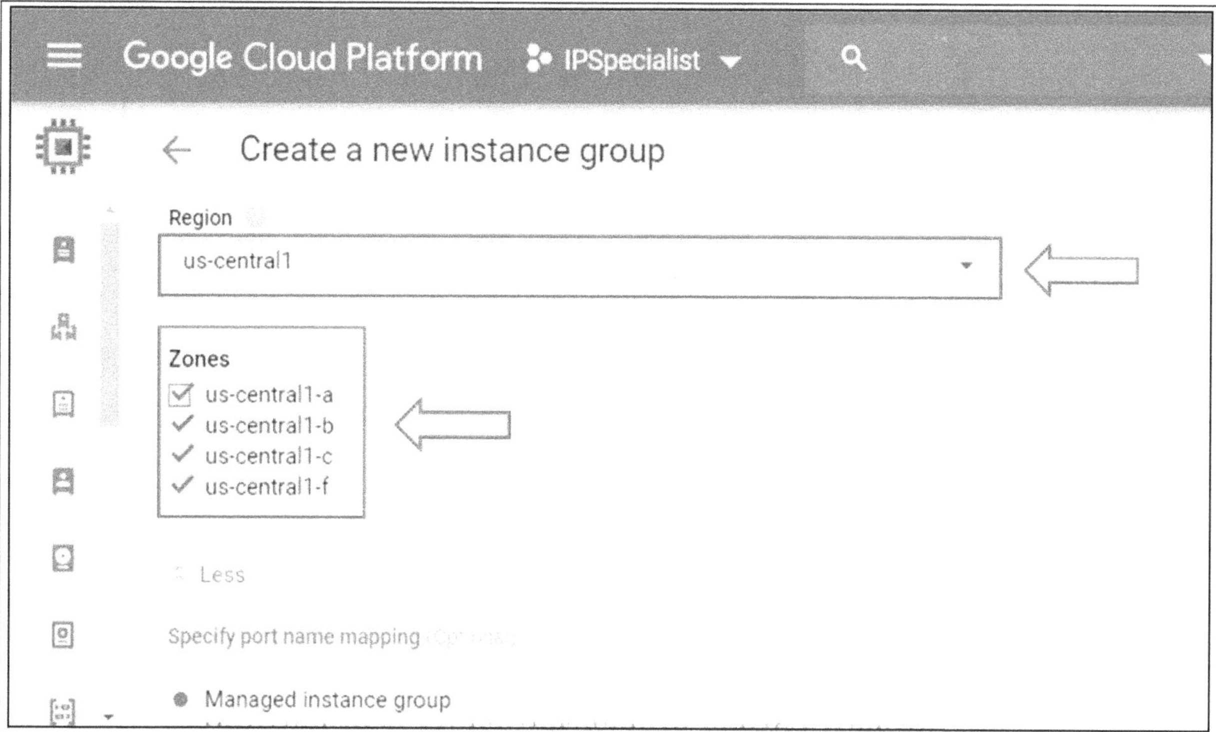

31. Select 'Managed instance group' and here select the instance template (no option to select instances)

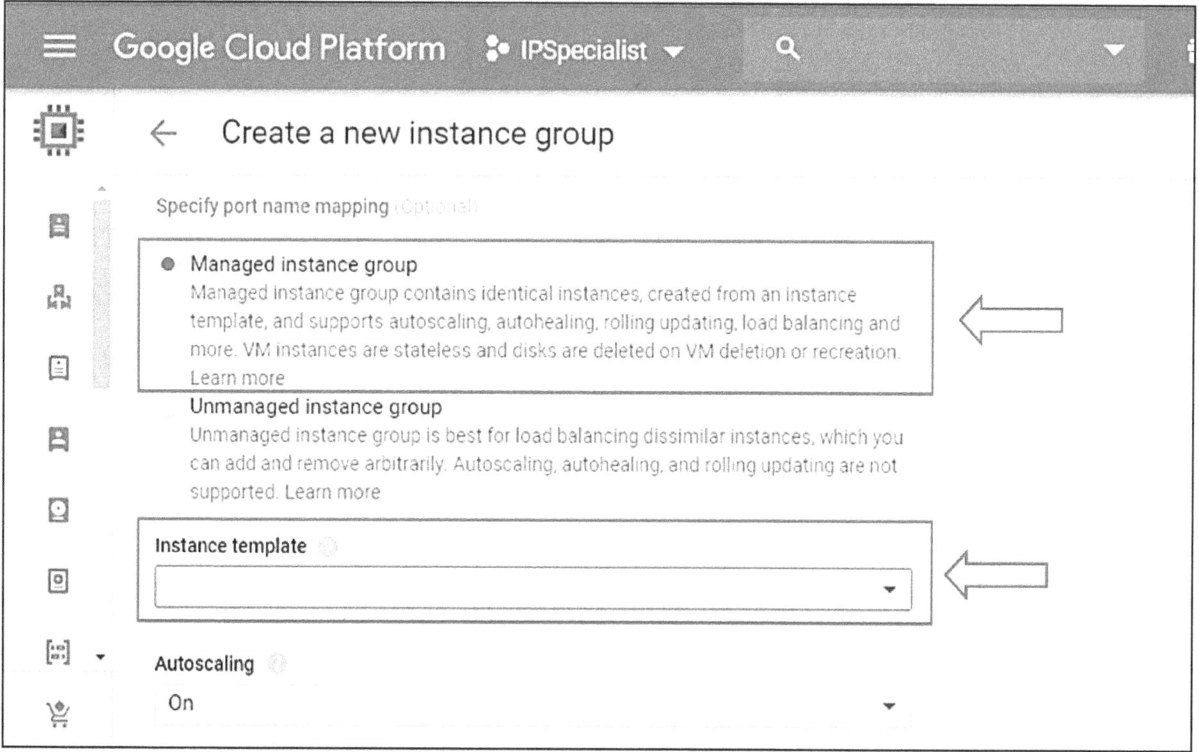

Autoscaling 'On' based on 'CPU usage' means that Google will automatically add or remove instances according to the CPU utilization

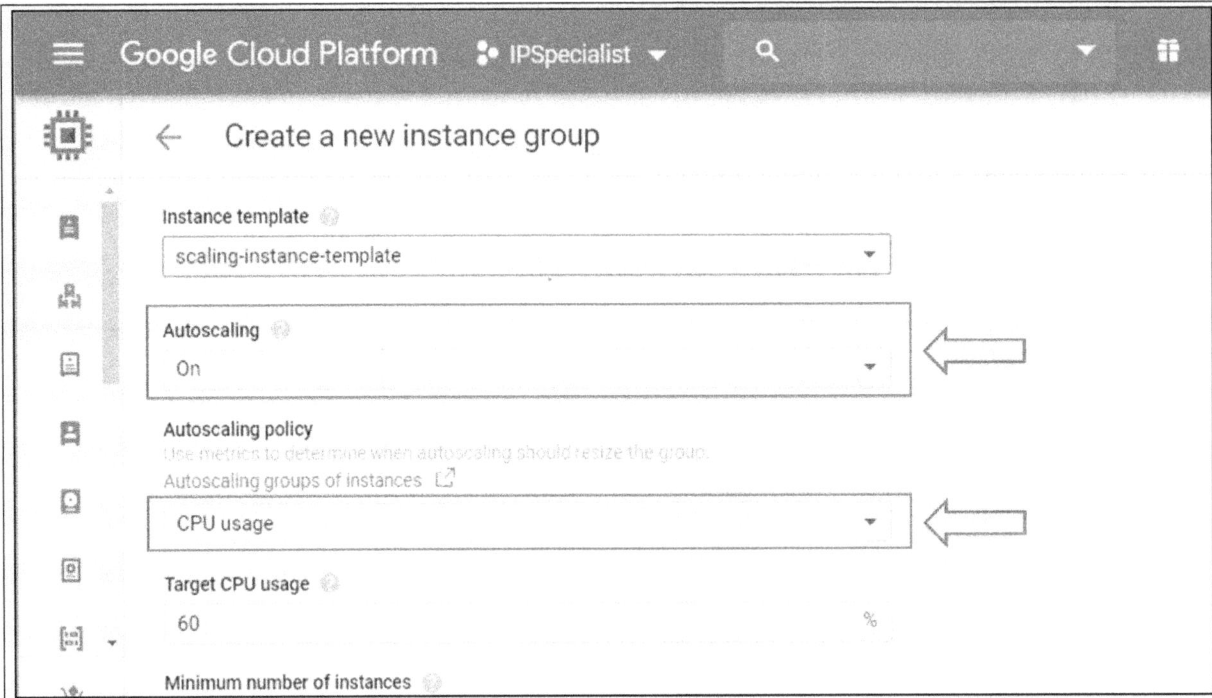

32. Change the 'Target CPU usage' to '30', 'Minimum number of instances' to '1' and 'Maximum number of instances' to '5' and 'Cool-down period' to '30'

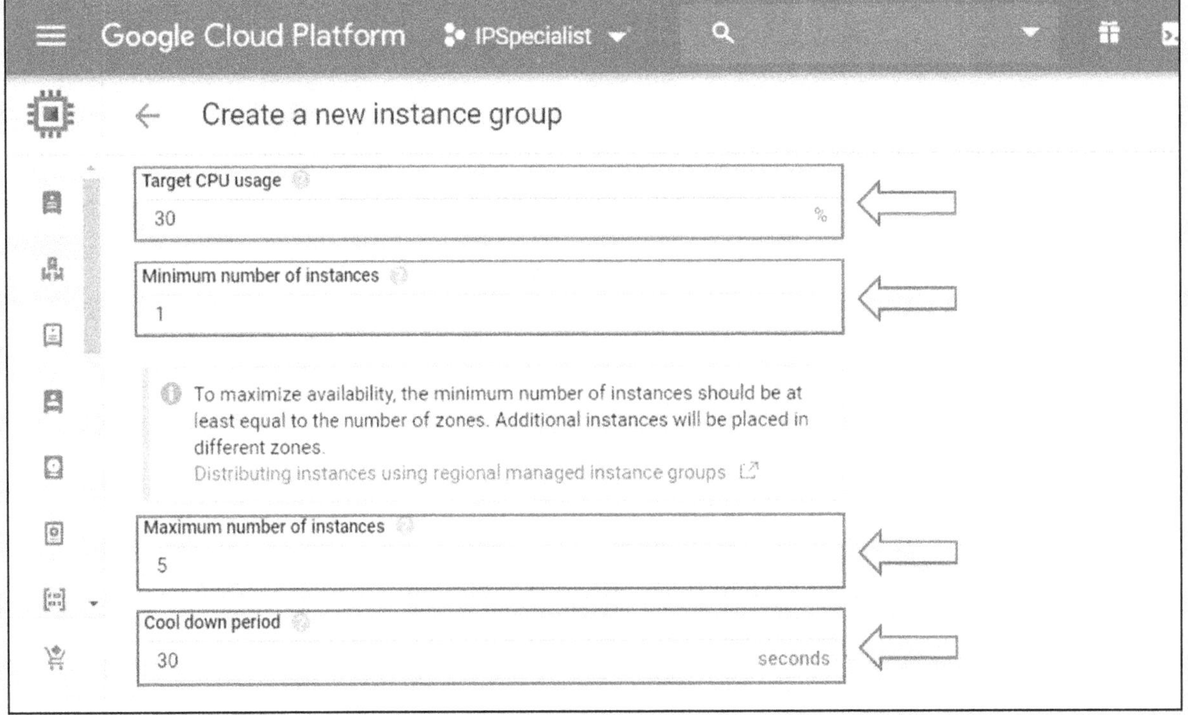

33. Click 'Create'. 'Autohealing' will enable to reload the instances if they failed to work and Health check means that the instances are continuously monitored and if they do not responds then the group will shut down that instance and launch a new one.

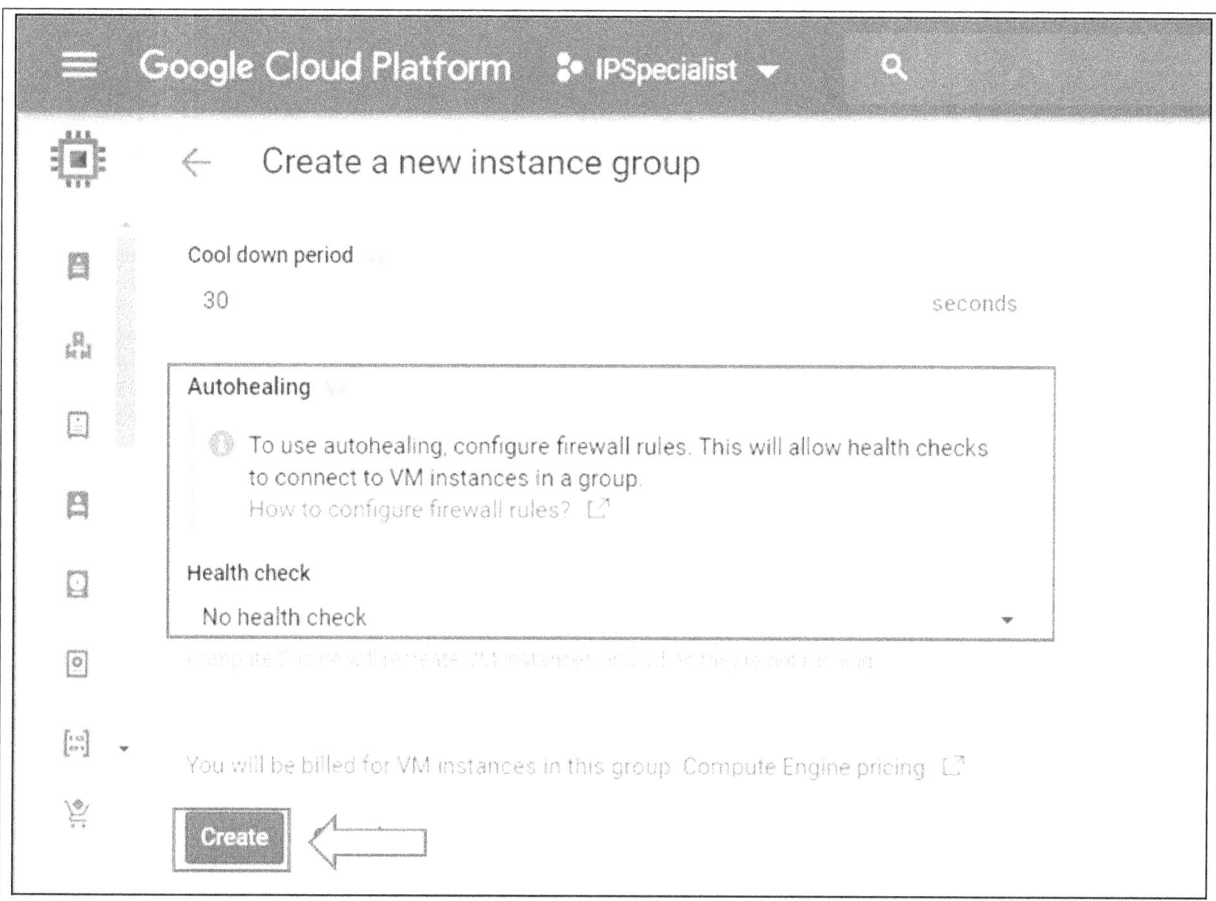

34. Go to the bucket. The two instances logged their files in the bucket

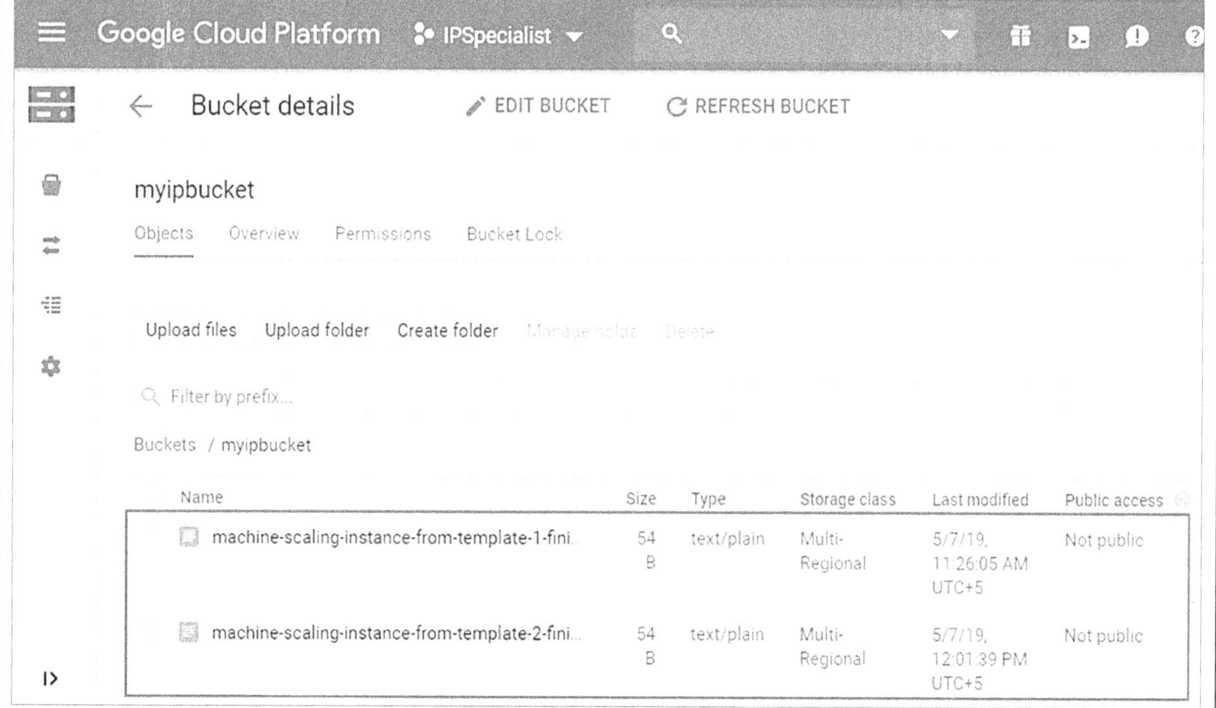

35. Go to the 'my-managed-instance-group'

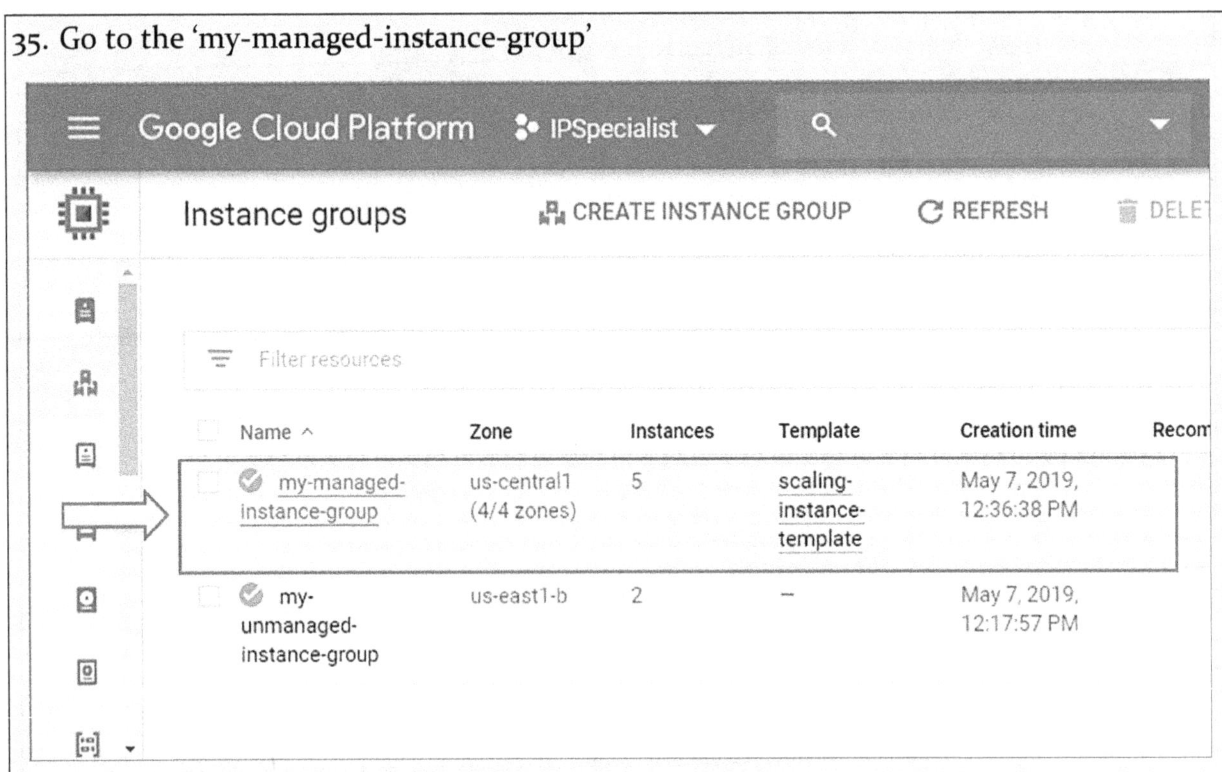

Five instances are created spread along different zones

36. Go to the 'Monitoring' tab.

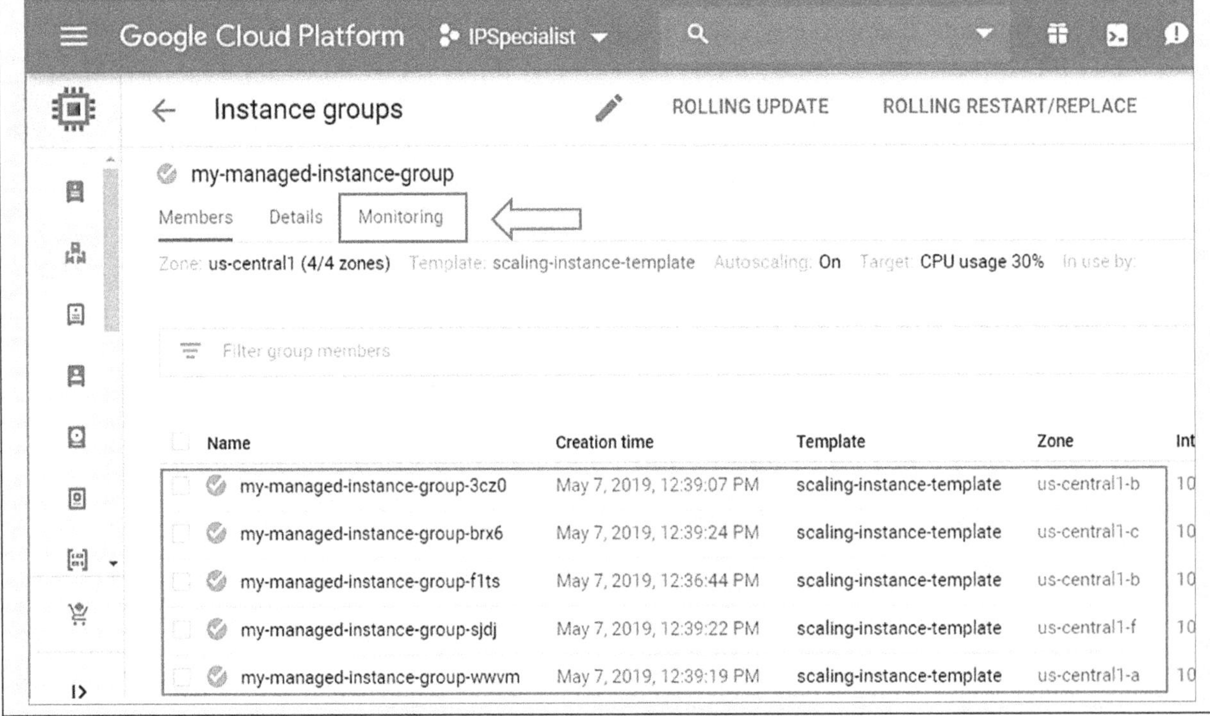

When there was one instance, the load on the CPU was high and it was distributed among multiple instances in the managed instance group reaches to the maximum number of instances from 1-5.

When total CPU usage falls below the threshold (green line) then the instance group will start removing the instances.

37. Delete both instance groups

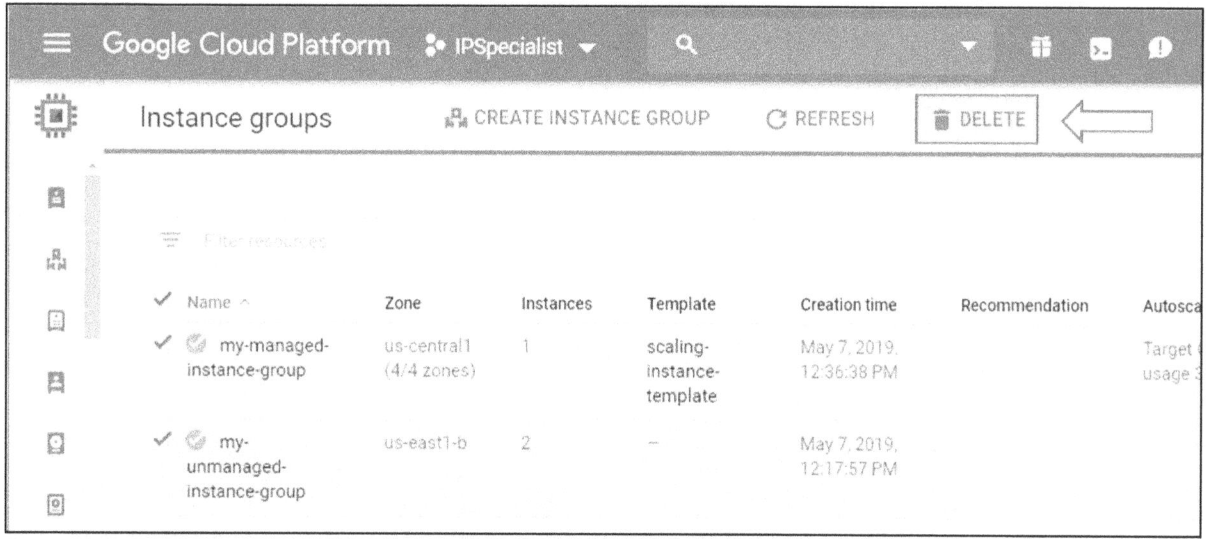

The bucket has more than two log files due to more launched instances

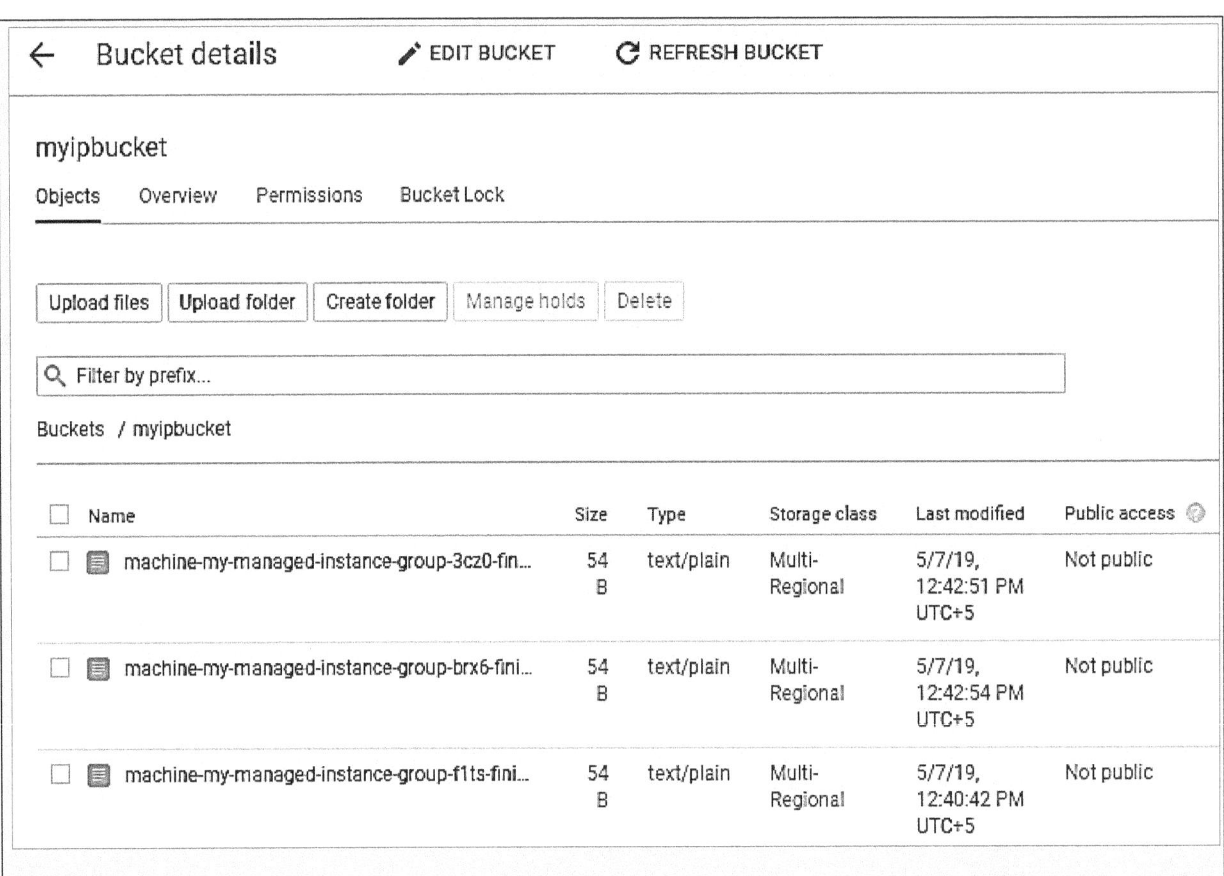

38. Copy any one instance name of the managed instance group (Here rest of the instances are shut down and disappear)

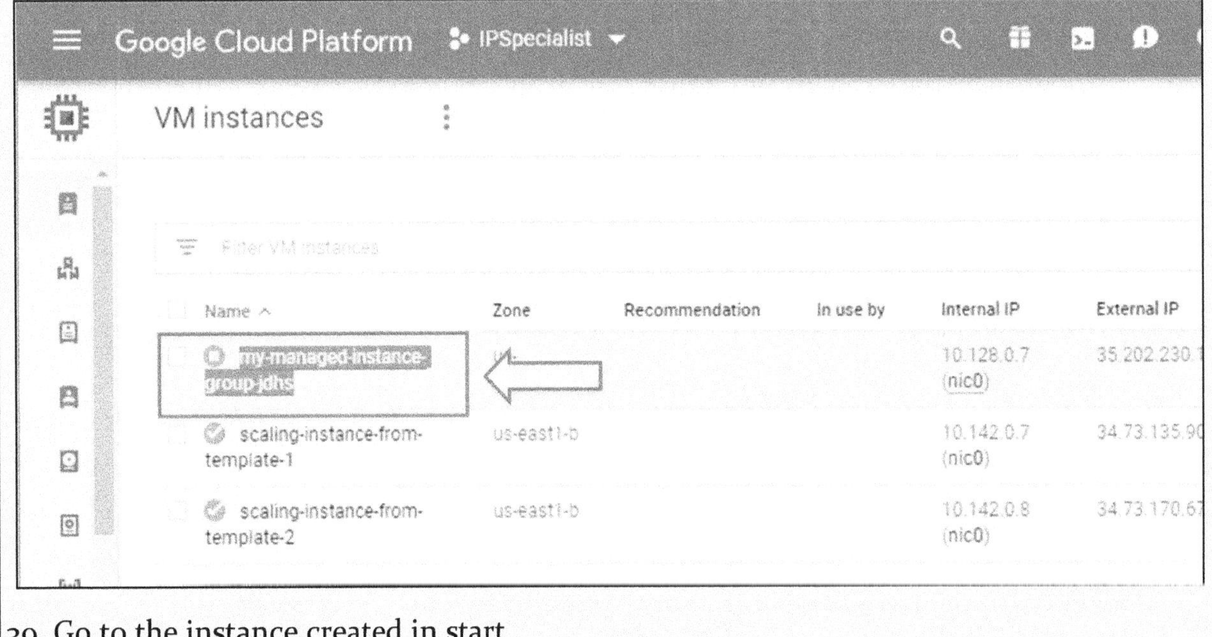

39. Go to the instance created in start

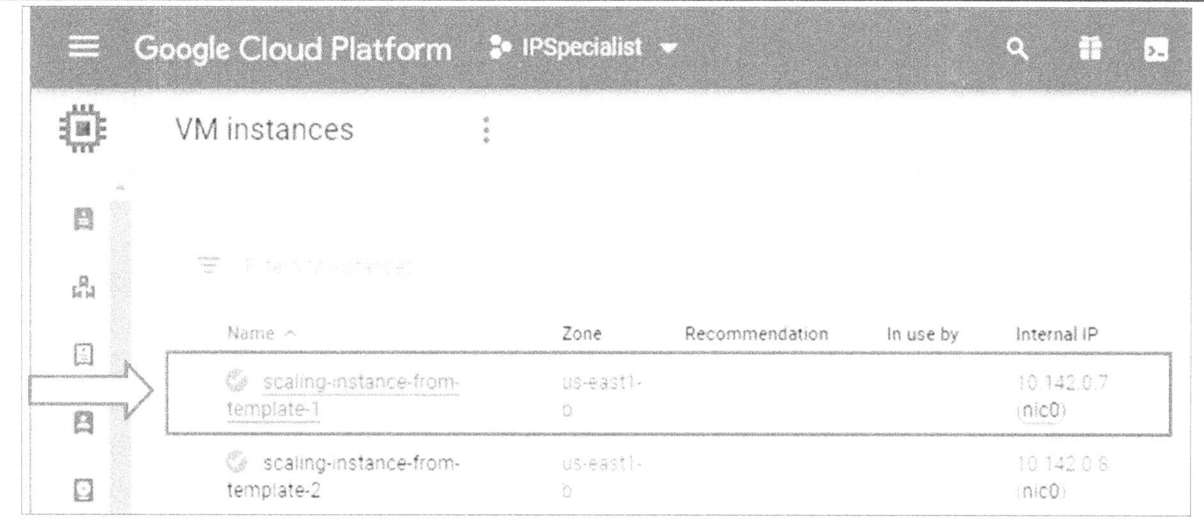

40. Select 'Stackdriver logging'

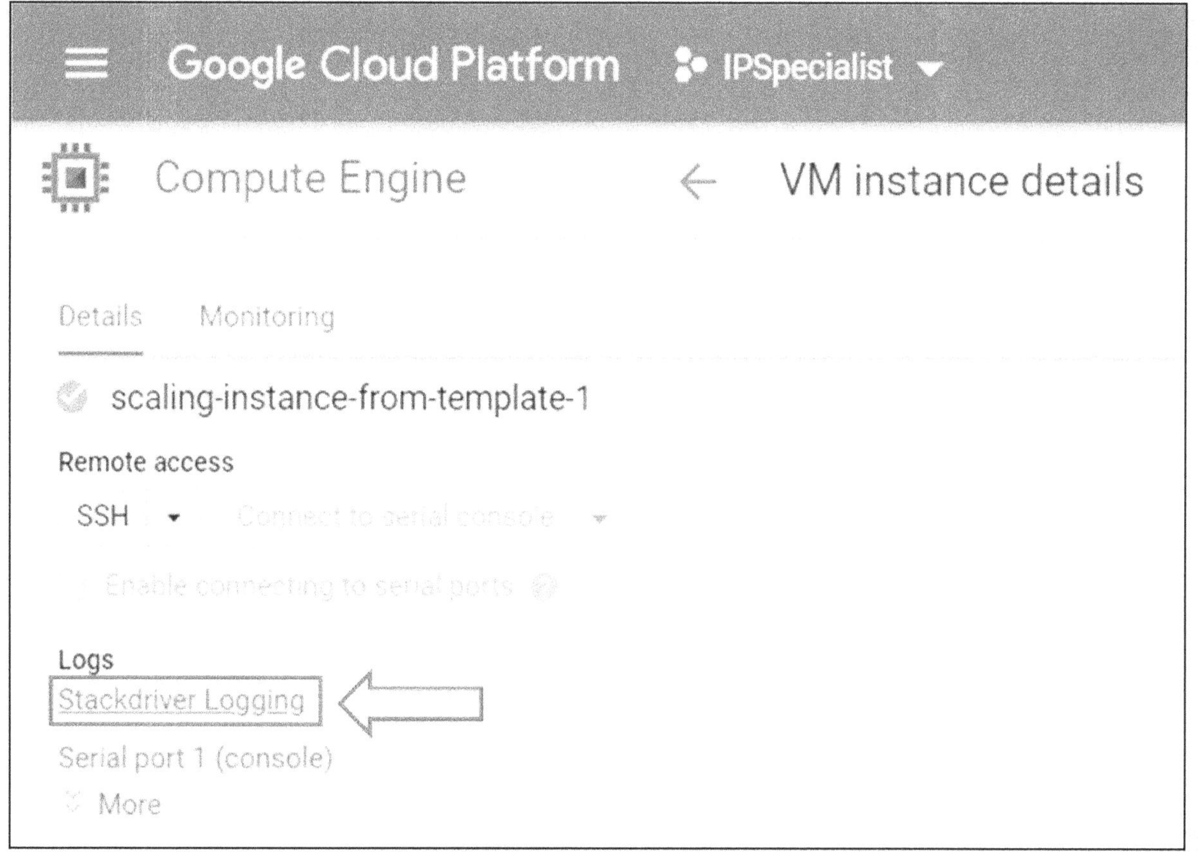

41. Select 'All instance_id'

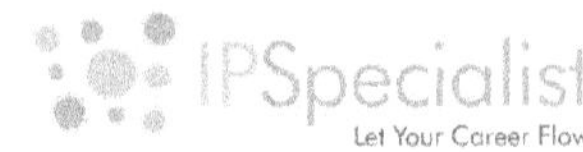

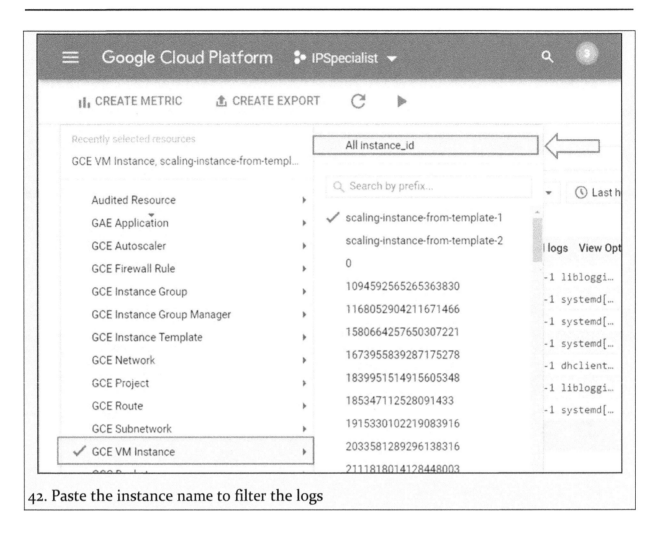

42. Paste the instance name to filter the logs

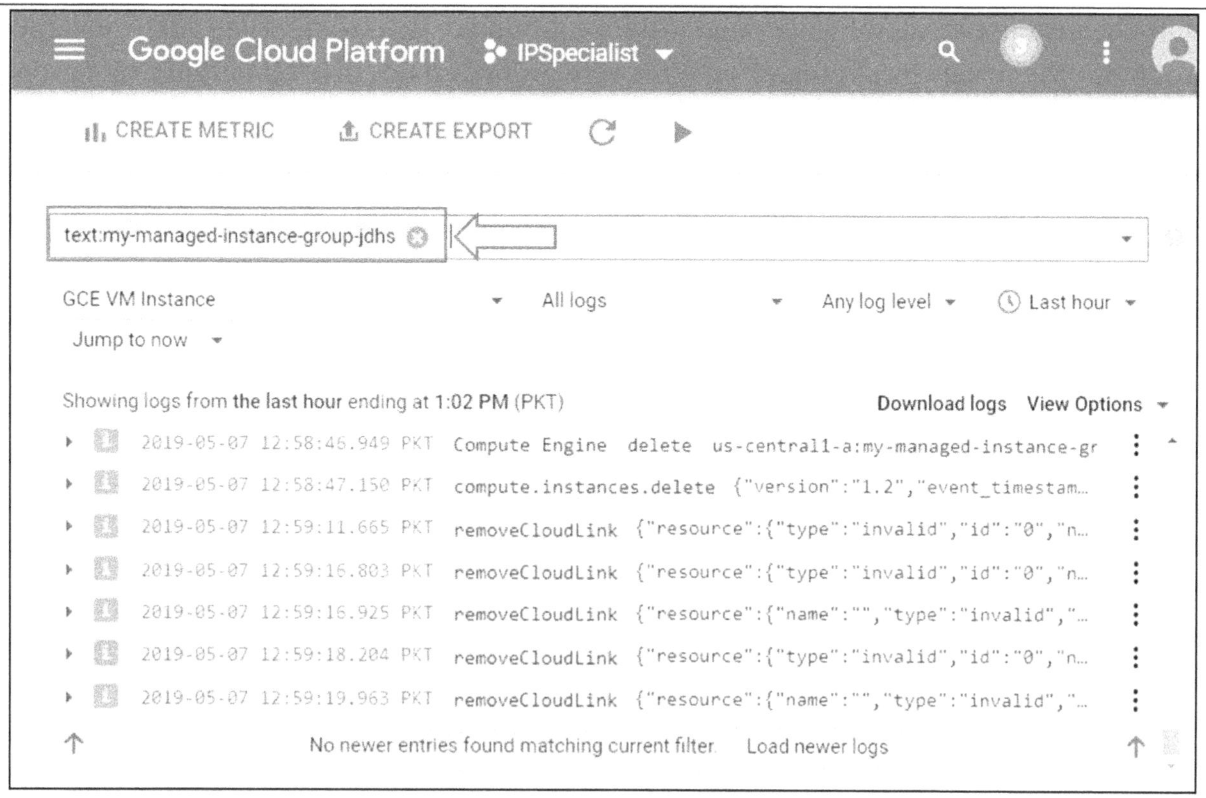

This will show the logs of this instance

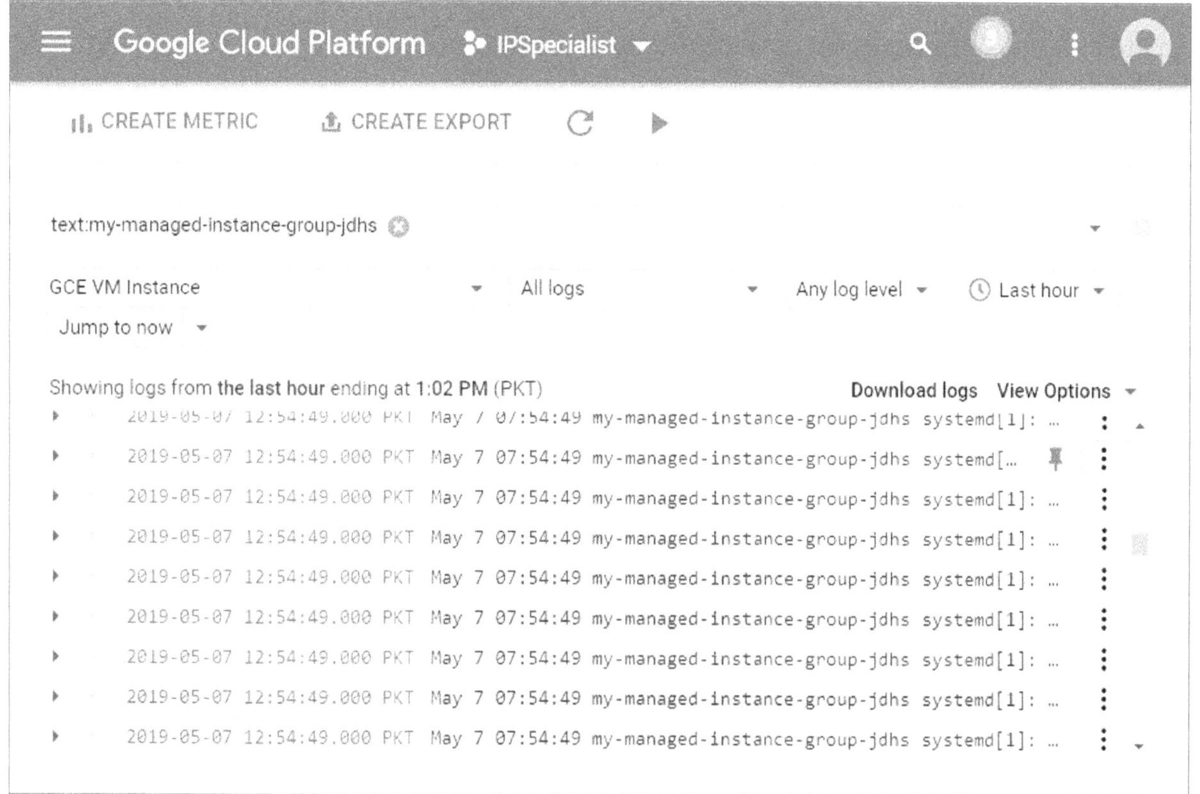

Only the instance created by managed instance group are deleted by deleting the instance group but the instances of unmanaged instance group are not deleted because this group does not owns them.

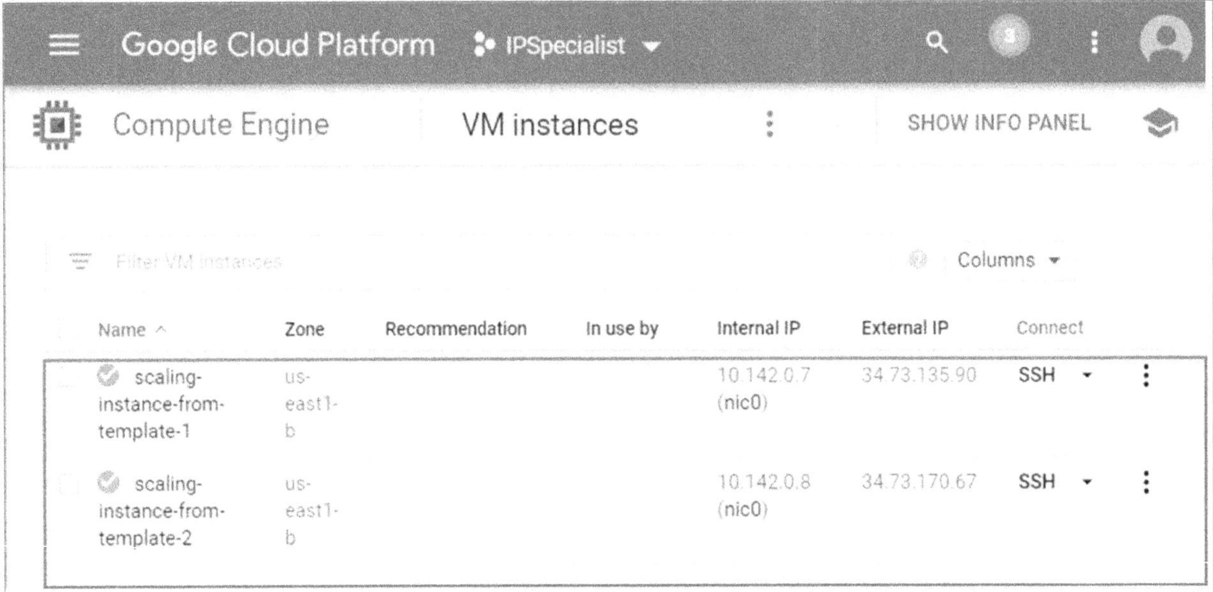

43. Click 'SEE ALL ACTIVITIES', this will show the things you have done

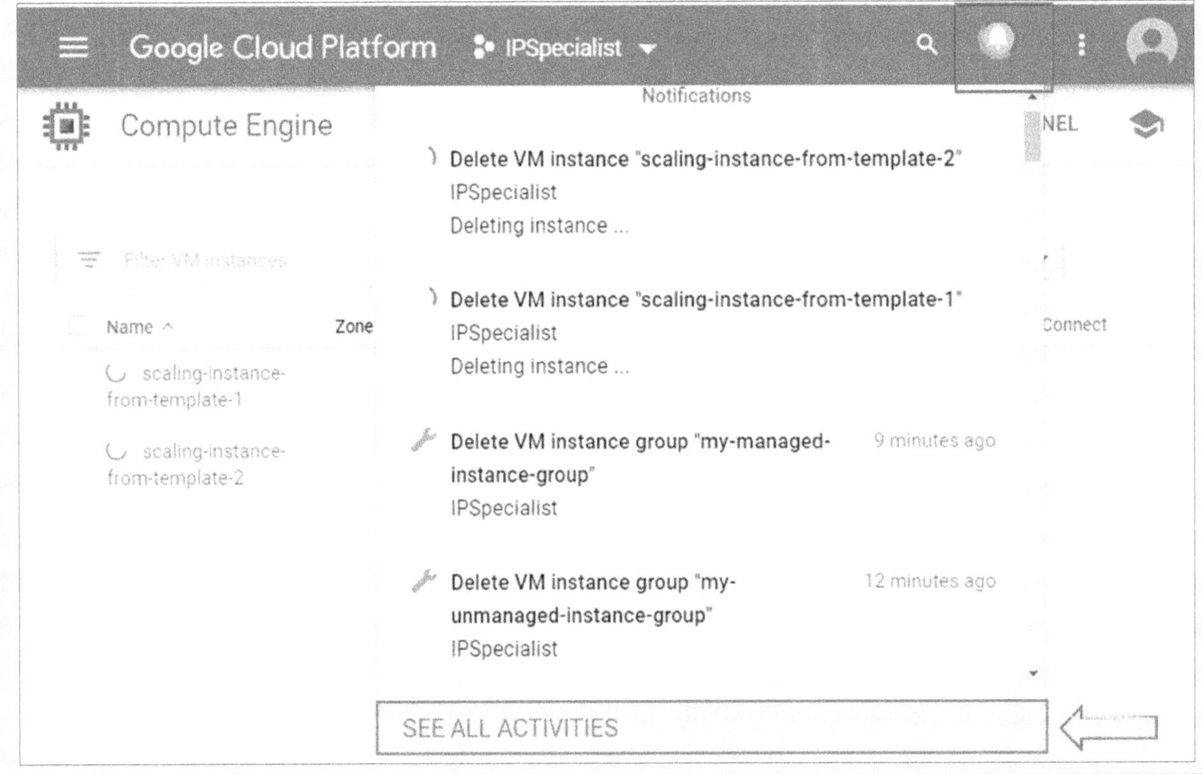

Security

The practice of preventing unauthorized access, use, disclosure, disruption, modification, inspection, recording, or destruction of information is information security, which is also known as InfoSec. The data or information can be of any type like electronic or physical. The focus of the information security system is balanced confidentiality, integrity and data accessibility (also known as CIA triad), while keeping a focus on effective implementation of policies, all without compromising the productivity of the organization.

Security is for maintaining proper Data flow.

Proper Data flow

Three main goals for information security are known as CIA Triad

Confidentiality (C)

It is that the data should be viewed only by the concerned person.

Integrity (I)

Integrity is to prevent data or information modifications by unauthorized users. It also prevents authorized users to make inappropriate changes.

Availability (A)

Availability is that the data should only be accessible when required.

Controlling Data flow

Control of Data flow refers to the AAA model of security. AAA stands for Authentication, Authorization, and Accounting.

Authentication

Authentication is based on the question "Who are you?". Authentication provides a way to identify a user, typically by requiring the user to enter a valid user name and password prior to access. The authentication process is based on the fact that each user has a unique set of access criteria.

Authorization

Authorization is based on the question "What are you allowed to do?"

The process of authorization determines if the user has the authority to issue such commands. Authorization is the policy enforcement process: To determine what types or qualities of activities, resources, or services a user is allowed to perform. Authorization usually takes place within the authentication context. Upon authentication of a user,

different types of access or activity may be permitted. Authorization is related to the permission of both reading and writing information.

Accounting

Accounting is based on the question “What did you do?”.

Accounting that measures the user's resources during access. The amount of time or data sent and/or received by the user during a session can be included. Accounting is performed by logging session statistics and usage information and is used for the activities of authorization control, billing, trend analysis, use of resources, and capacity planning.

Resiliency

Resiliency should be maintained in order to keep things running.

AAA Data flow

If a user wants to access some data then:

- It will first pass through the authentication process and then get the certified credentials from the authentication system.
- Authentication system also records this user in the acounting system that it gets certified credentials.
- User proceeds to the desired data
- The system verifies the certified credentials and then approaches the authorization system to check that this user have the required access or not.
- Whatever the result from the authorization system, it also logs in the accounting system
- If the user is authorized then the data is accessible for that user.

What enables security in GCP?

To enable security in GCP, following are available:

- Security products/services
- Security features are some aspects that can be used to help with security like serial number on any product so serial number is a security feature.
- Security Mindset is necessary for example keeping record of the products with their serial numbers that will help in identifying any stolen or lost product. Security Mindset includes Availability mindset is that the security system should be available every time whether the system is over loaded or facing any other problem.

Key Security Mindset Principles

Least privilege

Everyone can access the information, which will avoid the confidentiality aspect that is problematic. Least privilege is an important concept for computer security, is to limit users ' access rights to the minimum permissions they need to carry out their work. Only files or resources needed to do their work can be read, written or performed by users. This means that they have the least privileges.

Defence in Depth

Security layers are added i.e., not relying on single security procedure.

Fail Securely

For many reasons, applications often fail to process transactions. How they fail can determine whether or not application is secure.

Don't Trust services

Any third party services have their own security policies. Therefore, while using them ensure that information is according to your security policies.

Separation of duties

Administrators and users should be separated means administrators have the access to change anything but cannot login as a user.

Key Security Products/Features

For Authentication (AuthN)

Identity

In identity space, use G Suite or Cloud Identity for the Humans. Use Service Accounts for applications and services

Identity Hierarchy

You can also manage the identities for different roles and purposes by creating Google Groups. For managing identities, use Google Cloud Directory Sync (GCDS) to pull from LDAP (no push)

For Authorization (AuthZ)

- Identity Hierarchy (Google Groups)
- Resource Hierarchy (Organization, Folders, Projects)
- Identity and Access Management (Permissions, Roles, Bindings)

- Google Cloud Storage Access Control list (GCS ACLs)
- Billing Management
- Networking Structures and restrictions

For Accounting

- Audit or Activity logs that are provided by Stackdriver
- Billing Export to BigQuery or to a file in GCS (json or csv file)
- GCS object lifecycle management

IAM Resources Hierarchy

Resources are the things which are setup or created by the user. Projects are the container which for a set of related resources. Folder is for combining multiple projects. Folders can contain subfolders. Organization is tied to G Suite or Cloud Identity domain.

Different projects can contain different resources. User is able to access GCS from Compute Engine if both are in same project but if GCS bucket is in different project then it can not be accessable.

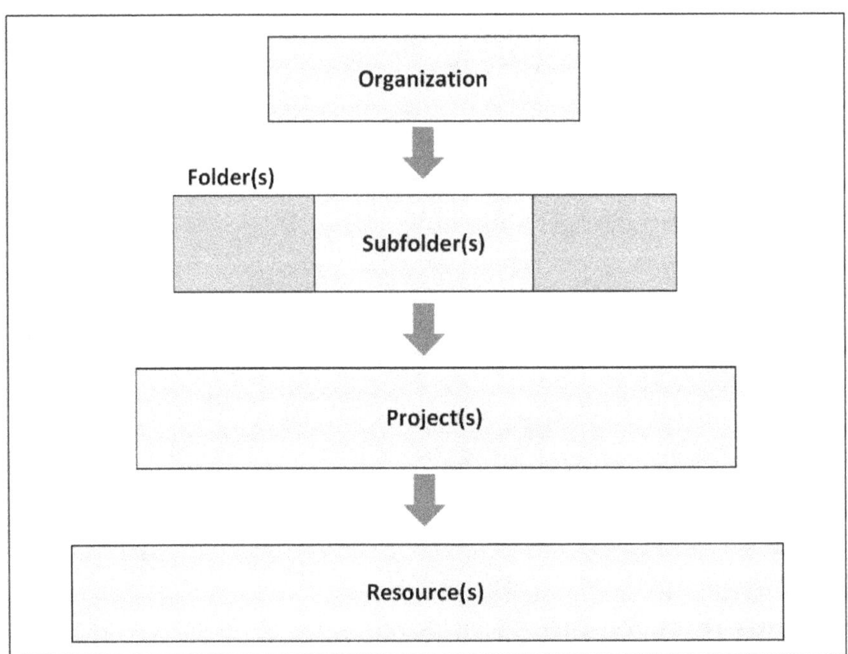

Figure 4-01: IAM Resources Hierarchy

IAM Permissions & Roles

Permissions allow user to perform certain actions. They follow the form Service.Resource.Verb .

Examples

- pubsub.subscriptions.consume
- pubsub.topics.publish

These permissions will allow a user to get data or put data to pubsub but restricts the user to add new topics or subscriptions.

Roles contain a set of permissions for using or managing GCP resources. If a role provides every permission for any service then the user having that role will act as an administrator for that service.

Primitive Roles

Primitive Roles are Project level roles. They are of three types:

- Viewer (Read-only)
- Editor (Read/Write)
- Owner (Read/Write and control access and billing)

Predefined Roles

Provide granular access to specific GCP resources.

Examples

roles/bigquery.dataEditor

roles/pubsub.subscriber (This will also allow to setup a subscription not only consuming the existing subscription)

Role Name	Role Title	Description
roles/appengine.appAdmin	App Engine Admin	Read/Write/Modify access to all application configuration and settings
roles/appengine.serviceAdmin	App Engine Service Admin	Read-only access to all application configuration and settings. Write access to module-level and version-level settings. Cannot deploy a new version.
roles/appengine.deployer	App Engine Deployer	Read-only access to all application configuration and settings. Write access only to create a new version; cannot modify existing versions other

		than deleting versions that are not receiving traffic.
roles/appengine.appViewer	App Engine Viewer	Read-only access to all application configuration settings.
roles/appengine.codeViewer	Code Engine Viewer	Read-only access to all application configuration ,settings and deployed source code.

Table 4-01: Examples of Predefined Roles

Custom Role

This type is project level or organization level Role in which any type of permissions can be defined.

IAM Members & Groups

A Member is a person with Google-known Identity i.e., each member have a unique email address.

Types of Members

- *User* is a specific google account. This account can be of G Suite, Cloud Identity, Gmail or any validated email
- *ServiceAccount* is not used by humans. It used by applications or services
- *Group* Members are used by Google groups in order to combine Users and service accounts
- *Domain* is for allowing access for any specific resource to all accounts. Domain should be managed by G Suite or Cloud Identity
- *All Authenticated Users* give access for any resource publicly i.e, the resource is available for any google account or service account
- *All Users* members do not require any authentication i.e., completely public access (Anyone on internet)

Group should be the default choice for member .

Groups

Google accounts and service accounts combine to form a Google Group. A Group contains multiple users with a unique email address of that group. The email address of the group can not be used to login (user cannot act as a group). Nest groups can also be

used for an organization such as different groups for different departments can be combined to form a single group.

IAM Policies

Policies are the method to bind Members with roles for Resources. A policy is attached within a Resource Hierarchy. Policy can be attached anywhere in an organization,folder, project or Resources. Policies contains the members and roles while the resources are identified by the attachment of policies. Policies is for giving permission to something i.e., allow only.

Limitations

- Single policy per resource and by default each resource have an empty policy
- Maximum 1500 member bindings per policy. Use groups instead of binding too many members in a single policy
- Maximum 250 groups per policy

It takes less than 60 seconds to apply changes when any policy is attached. It may take up to 7 minutes for full modification.

Example

```
{
   "bindings": [
        {
              "role": "roles/owner",
                  "members": ["user:bob@example.com"]        Binding 1
        },
        {
               "role": "roles/compute.networkViewer",
               "members" : [
                  "user : alice@example.com",
    Binding 2     "group: admins@example.com",
                  "domain : example2.com",
                "serviceAccount : my-other-app@appspot.gserviceaccount.com"
               ]
        }
]
}
```

This policy has two bindings, the first binding states that Bob is the owner for which this policy is defined. If this policy is attached to any folder or project then Bob would be the owner of that folder or project. Second binding is related to members for the role "compute.networkViewer"

Managing Policy Bindings

Method 1

User can use get-iam-policy function, edit the JSON or YAML file, and finally use set-iam-policy function to push the changed document. However, method 1 is not recommended to use.

Method 2

User can use add-iam-policy-binding and remove-iam-policy-binding

```
gcloud [GROUP] add-iam-policy-binding [RESOURCE-NAME] - -role [ROLE-ID-TO-GRANT] - -member user : [USER-EMAIL]
gcloud [GROUP] remove-iam-policy-binding [RESOURCE-NAME] - -role [ROLE-ID-TO-GRANT] - -member user : [USER-EMAIL]
```

These two functions are better because they are simple and less error prone than editing the JSON or YAML file. These operations will avoid race condition means multiple users can make changes simultaneously but if user will use method 1, then only one user can win in updating the changed document at same time. By using Method 1, the data called and pushed is more than the changed data, therefore, the machine will be required to process entire data everytime. Whereas in method 2, only two operations are needed to be processed.

Billing Access Control

Billing account is the type of resource, which stays outside any project and represents the amount to pay for GCP services usage. Any organization can be the owner of billing account. Billing account can be linked to any project. Multiple billing accounts can also be created. Single project can only be linked to single billing account.

Role: Billing Account User

This role is used to link projects to billing accounts. If this role is attached to a user on the billing account level, then that user can link any project to this billing account. If this role is attached on organization level, then the user can link any project to any billing account.

Role	Purpose	Scope
Billing Account Creator	Create new self-serve billing accounts	Organization
Billing Account Administrator	Manage Billing Accounts (but not create them)	Billing Account

Billing Account User	Link projects to billing accounts	Billing Account
Billing Account Viewer	View billing account cost information and transactions	Billing Account
Project Billing Manager	Link/unlink the project to/from a billing account	Project

Table 4-02: Billing Account Roles Example

Monthly Invoiced Billing

Instead of charged automatically by credit card, user is able to opt option for charges on monthly basis on the invoice due date. Monthly invoice billing provides you three payment options i.e., Cheque, Wire transfer or Credit card. By using invoiced billing, projects, and quota limit can be increased. Billing administrator can contact to Cloud billing support in order to check the eligibility for invoice billing and transferring the billing method to Monthly invoice billing.

Eligibility for invoice billing depends on:

- Account age
- Monthly expenditure
- Country

Scenario 1

You are working in a small-to-medium enterprise with preference for centralized control. There are three different users i.e., CEO, CTO and Development teams.

The task and IAM roles for billing Access control are given below:

User	Task	IAM Roles attached
CEO	• Manage payment instruments • View and approve invoice	Billing Account Administrator
CTO	• Set budget alerts • View spend • Create new billable projects	Billing Account Administrator project creator
Developers	None	None

Table 4-03: Scenario 1 Billing Account Roles

Scenario 2

You are working in a small-to-medium enterprise with preference for delegated authority.

User	Task	IAM Roles attached
CEO	Manage payment instruments but can delegate the authority to any other staff member	Billing Account Administrator
CFO	• Set budget alerts • View spend	Billing Account Administrator
Accounts payable	View and approve invoices	Billing Account Viewer
Developers	Developers are trusted because of delegated authority therefore they are responsible to create new billable projects	Billing Account User Project Creator

Table 4-04: Scenario 2 Billing Account Roles

Mind Map

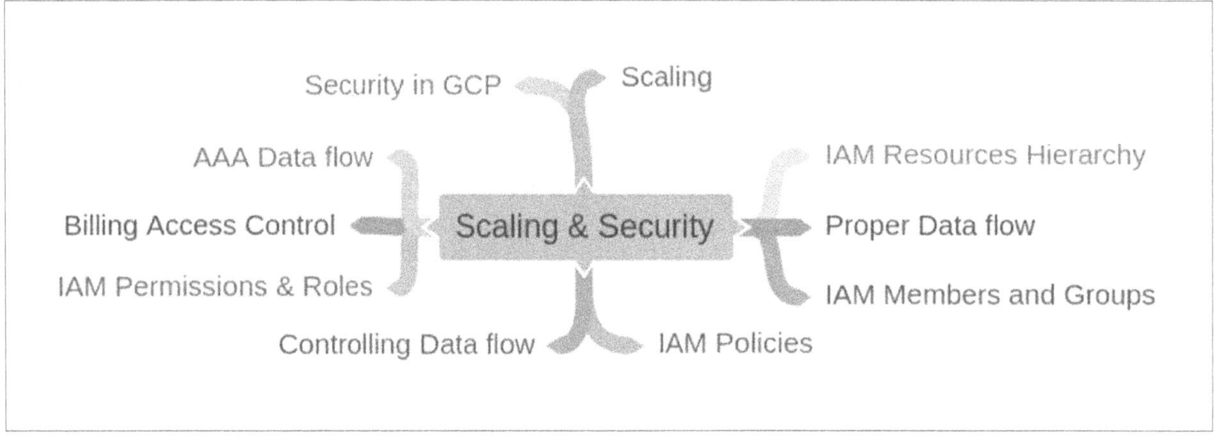

Figure 4-02: Chapter Mind Map

Practice Questions

1. Which of the following combinations is known as CIA triad?
   A. Creativity, Information, Availability
   B. Confidentiality, Information, Accessibility
   C. Confidentiality, Integrity, Availability
   D. None of the above

2. Which of the following options refers to the AA model of security?
   A. Information security system
   B. Control of Dataflow
   C. Data security
   D. Security control

3. Which of the question relates Authorization?
   A. What are you allowed to do?
   B. Who are you?
   C. What did you do?
   D. How to do it?

4. When a user wants to access any data, the first process is authorization. True or False?
   A. True
   B. False
5. Which of the following options are not the type of IAM roles?
   A. Custom role
   B. Predefined role
   C. User role
   D. Primitive role

6. Which type of access is allowed in Primitive role of Viewer type?
   A. Read and Write
   B. Read-only
   C. Administrative
   D. Custom Read-only

7. Select the type of role "roles/bigquery.dataEditor" belongs to
   A. Custom Role

B. Primitive Role
C. Predefined Role
D. User defined Role

8. Which of the following Roles provide Read/Write/Modify access to all application configuration and settings?
A. roles/appengine.appAdmin
B. roles/appengine.serviceAdmin
C. roles/appengine.deployer
D. roles/appengine.appViewer

9. serviceAccount is used by
A. Humans
B. Applications
C. Functions
D. All of the above

10. A Google Group consists of Google Accounts. True or False?
A. True
B. False

11. Multiple grouping within the group is called
A. Sub groups
B. Combine groups
C. Mix groups
D. Nest groups

12. User should attach the policy within the Resource Hierarchy. True or False?
A. True
B. False

13. Which of the following is defined by policy?
A. Deny only
B. Allow/Deny
C. Allow only
D. Allow only/Deny only

14. Binding too many members in a single policy is preferable. True or False?

A. True
B. False

15. What is the limitation of number of groups per policy?
   A. 150
   B. 200
   C. 250
   D. 300

16. Indicate the option which does not represent add-iam-policy-binding and remove-iam-policy-binding
   A. Error prone
   B. Simple to apply
   C. Avoid Race condition
   D. Full data is called and pushed

17. Which of the following resource is used to check the amount to pay for GCP services usage?
   A. Billing Account
   B. GCS
   C. IAM
   D. Cloud Shell

18. Which of the following role is used to link projects to billing account?
   A. Billing Account Viewer
   B. Billing Account Creator
   C. Billing Account Administrator
   D. Billing Account User

19. Google Cloud provides an option for monthly based payment. True or False?
   A. True
   B. False

20. Which of the following option does not belongs to eligibility criteria for invoice payment?
   A. Account age
   B. Monthly spend
   C. No. of Resources in use

D. Country

21. Choose the two types of instance groups provided by GCP:
    A. Managed instance group
    B. Unmanaged instance group
    C. Autoscaling instance group
    D. Autohealing instance group
22. What is the nature of instance templates?
    A. Regional
    B. Cross-Regional
    C. Global
    D. User defined

23. Unmanaged instance group provide both single and Multiple zones option. True or False?
    A. True
    B. False

24. Information Security is also referred as:
    A. InformationSec
    B. InfoSecurity
    C. InfoSec
    D. All of the above

25. Single billing account can be linked to multiple projects. True or False?
    A. True
    B. False

Chapter 05: Networking

Introduction

This chapter contains information about Networking in Google Cloud Platform. VPC modes i.e., Auto-mode VPC and Custom-mode VPC are discussed in detail with their practical application. Firewall rules for different scenarios are also discussed in this chapter.

OSI Model

The OSI model defines a networking framework for implementing protocols in seven layers. The data is transferred between two points by moving in 7 layers, from Application layer of the first connection to the bottom layer of the second connection and then moving back by following the same hierarchy.

OSI Layers

1. Application Layer (Layer 7)
2. Presentation Layer (Layer 6)
3. Session Layer (Layer 5)
4. Transport Layer (Layer 4)
5. Network Layer (Layer 3)
6. Data Link Layer (Layer 2)
7. Physical Layer (Layer 1)

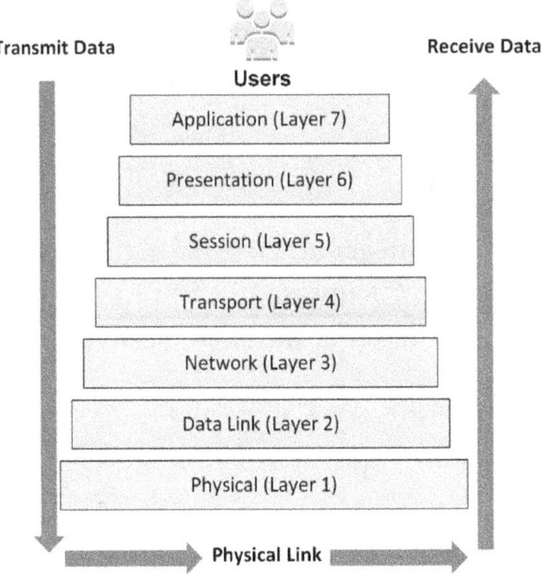

Figure 5-01: OSI Layers

Routing

Routing is a path defined for data to travel. Routing means to take decisions for moving the data from one point to another. When data is transmitted, it should be decided that from where and how the data must be passed to the destination. When the data is at the client's system, its routing decisions have to be made on the way to Google's network. When the data reaches to Google's network then the routing decisions have to be made on the way to the right resource, and then from one resource to another.

There are three steps of routing:

- Routing to Google's Network
- Routing to Resources
- Routing from one resource to another

Routing to Google's Network

VPC Routing Tier is used to transfer data between Clients and GCP. Google provides Standard Routing Tier and Premium Routing Tier for this purpose. Standard Routing is hot potato and it is performed over public internet. Premium Routing is cold potato and it is performed mostly on Google Network. Premium routing involves least distance and hops resulting in faster and securer communication. Hot potato routing assumes the problem as someone else's but cold potato routing does the routing by its own. For example, a website is running where users are connected from all over the world. If the website is hosted in California, then the data is sent across the world to California, that is if standard routing is used. If Premium routing is used, then the Google Network will

decide whether California is the best option to send data or any other place. For this you can use multiple copies of your server in different places.

Routing to the Right Resources

Following are the reasons for distributing data to different resources:

- **Latency Reduction:** If the servers are physically close to the clients, this will reduce Latency period. User can use Cross-Region Load balancing with Global Anycast IPs in order to obtain Latency Reduction. If Premium Tier routing is used and Global Anycast IP address is used to point the Google Network, then Google would decide where to send the data inside Google's network.
- **Load Balancing:** For dividing the load among different machines. Cloud Load Balancer is used for Load balancing.
- **System Design:** When the system is designed in such a way that different servers handle different parts of the system especially when using micro-services. For this purpose, HTTP(S) Load Balancers with URL map are used.

Unicast vs Anycast

When Unicast is used then the data can be handled by a single device, whereas Anycast will allow data to be handled by multiple devices.

Layer 4 vs Layer 7

TCP is a primary protocol used to send data over the internet. It is associated with the Layer 4 of OSI model. This layer works solely with IP addresses. Layer 7 deals with protocols such as HTTP and HTTPS therefore this layer is known to the URLs and paths. For URL based routes, routing should be able to understand Layer 7, and not only Layer 4.

DNS

Other Cloud and System uses DNS for Global Load Balancing. Name resolution by DNS is the first step for routing but the problem is that, DNS only returns the layer 4 IP address and does not know the full path. DNS queries are often cached and reused for huge set of clients. DNS lookup has a TTL, which defines the lookup time and if TTL is high, then the user is stuck and cannot lookup for another machine until TTL is expired but if TTL is very low, it will increase the refreshing cost.

Premium Tier 'cold potato' routing with Global Anycast IP addresses would avoid above mentioned problems.

Routing Among Resources

VPC is used to carry data from one resource to the other resource. VPC is a Global resource. VPC is a private Software Defined Networking (SDN) space in GCP. VPC also manages doors to outside and peers i.e., connection to internet, VPN or any other VPC.

The VPC space is then divided into subnets, which are region-based. Subnets are the logical space and they can contain multiple resources. All subnets are able to connect with each other without any additional configuration.

Routes define the 'next hop' for the traffic based on IP address of destination. Routes are global and network tags can be defined for GCE instances for restricting any route. Data flow also depends on the Firewall rules on VPC.

Firewall rules are Global and they can be defined by using IP addresses, Network tags and, Service accounts. By default, Firewall rule is restrictive inbound and permissive outbound. Priority number decides which rule overrides the other. For example, by default inbound restrictive and outbound permissive rule is set with the priority number 65535. Therefore, in order to allow incoming traffic, the rule should have high priority number (low priority number) than 65535.

IPs and CIDRs

IP addresses (IPv4) format is abc. def. ghi. jkl (dotted quad) in which each piece ranges from 0 to 255. E.g. 192.168.10.0

A group of IP addresses is known as CIDR block (<IP>/xy notation). E.g. 192.168.10.0/24

0.0.0.0/0 means any IP address i.e., include all IP addresses.

RFC1918 defines private address ranges i.e., 10.0.0.0/8, 172.16.0.0/12 and 192.168.0.0/16

Lab 5.1: Creating Auto-Mode VPCs

Scenario:

An organization ask you to create a VPC which have all regions provided by Google Cloud and will updates its region whenever new region is introduced.

Solution:

You decided to create an Auto-mode VPC

1. Go to the GCP console

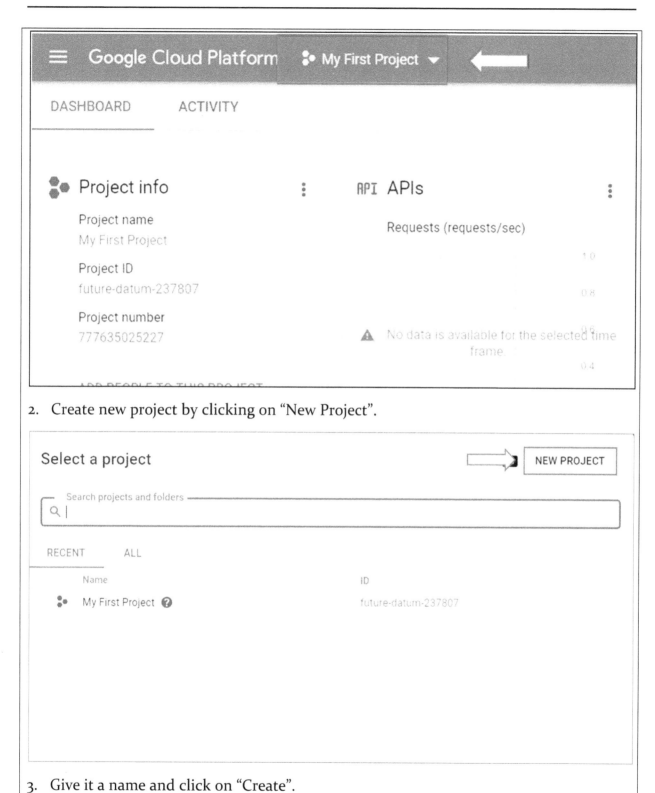

2. Create new project by clicking on "New Project".

3. Give it a name and click on "Create".

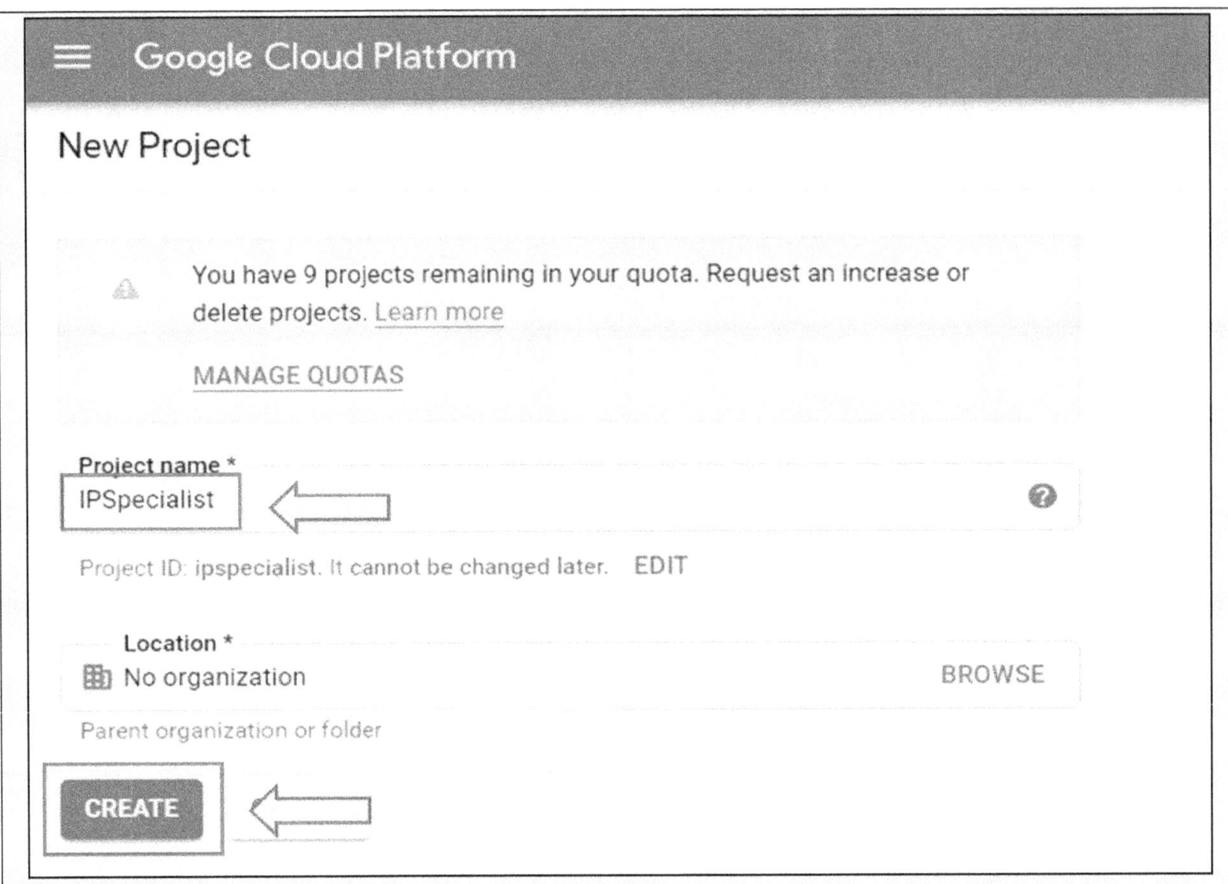

4. Enter into the new project.

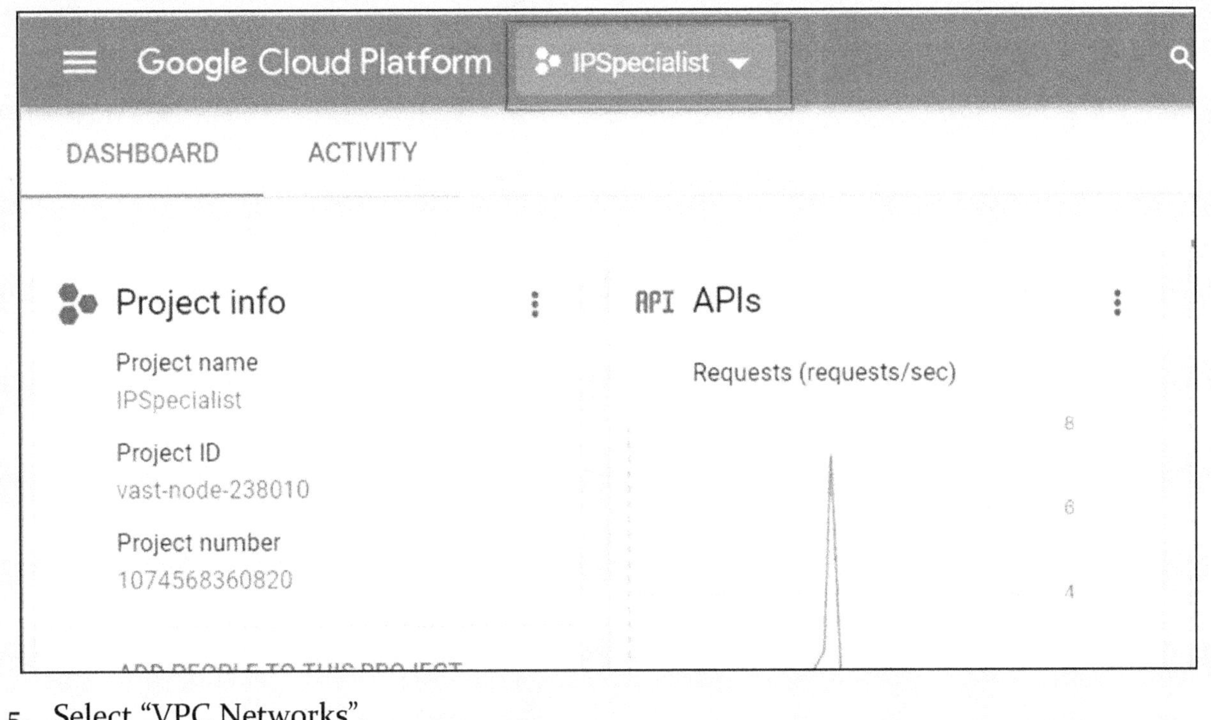

5. Select "VPC Networks".

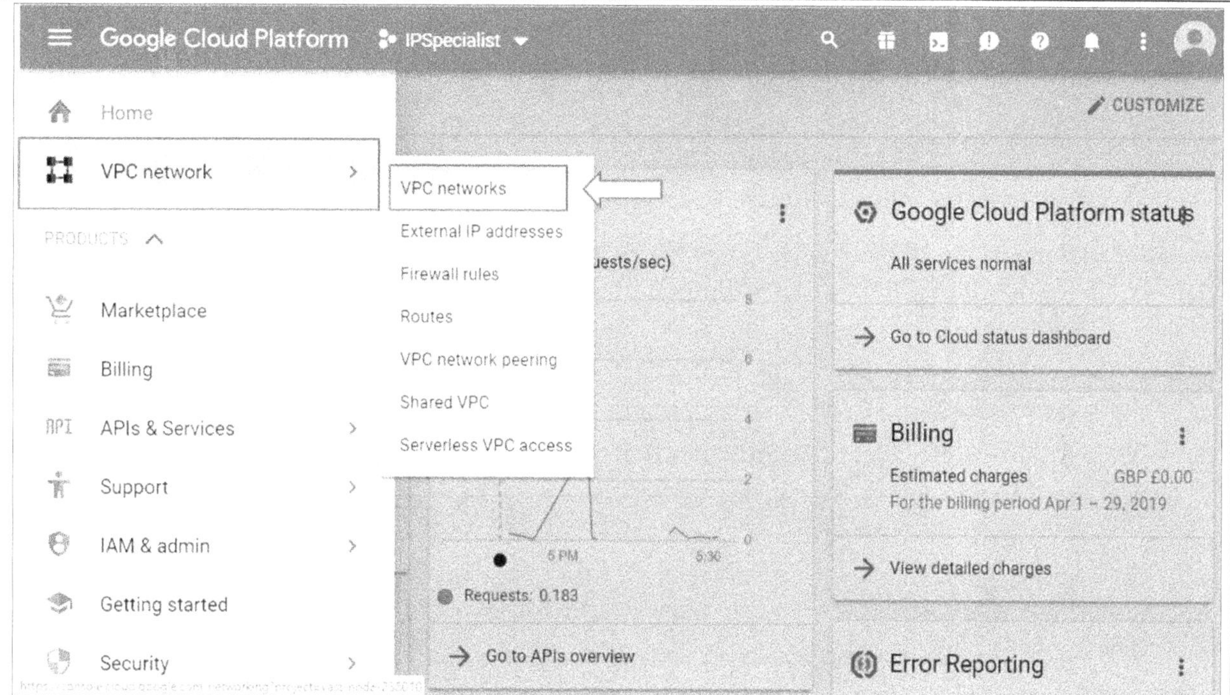

It has a default VPC with "Auto" mode. There is one subnet in each region due to auto mode network. IP Address ranges are the same. There are 4 Firewall Rules by default.

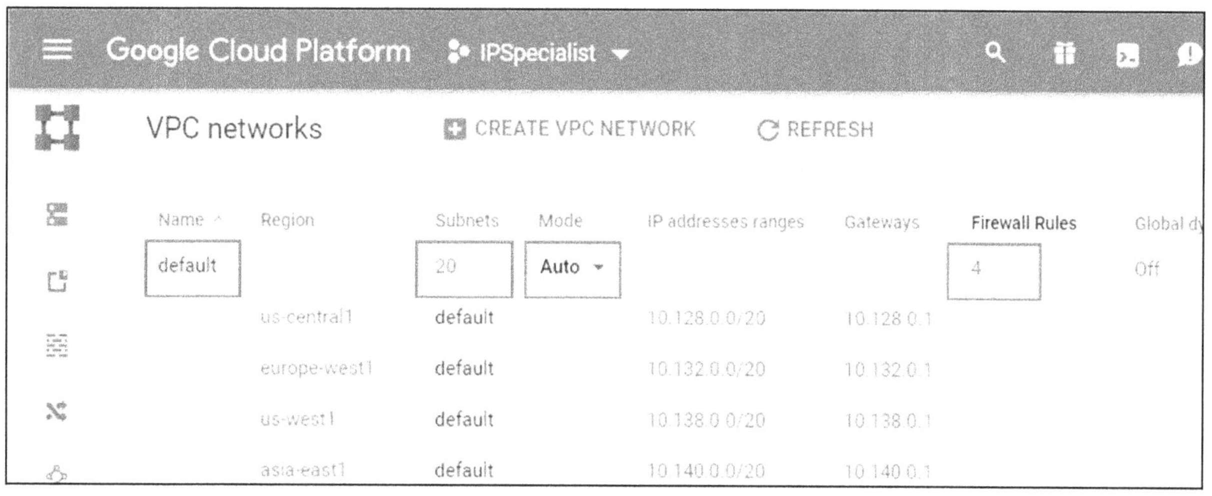

6. Click "CREATE VPC NETWORK".

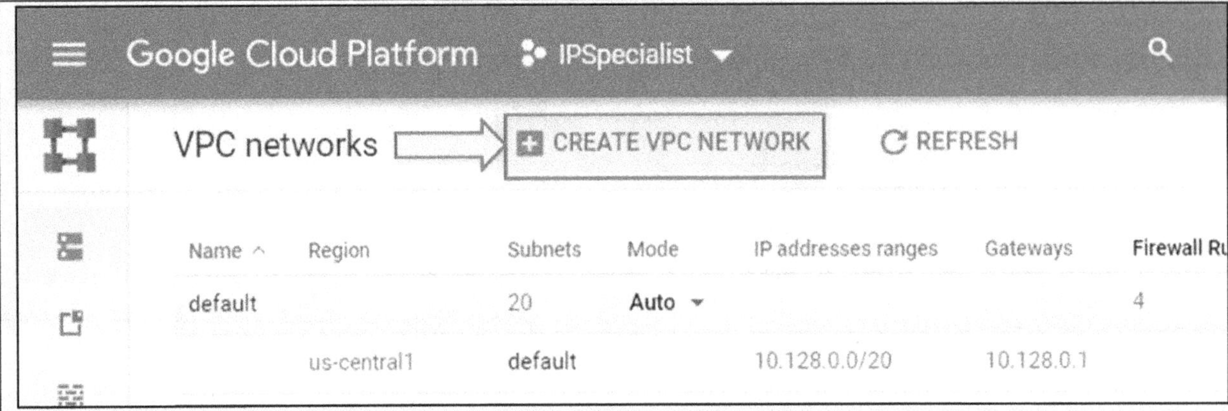

7. Give it a name and select the subnet creation mode as "Automatic".

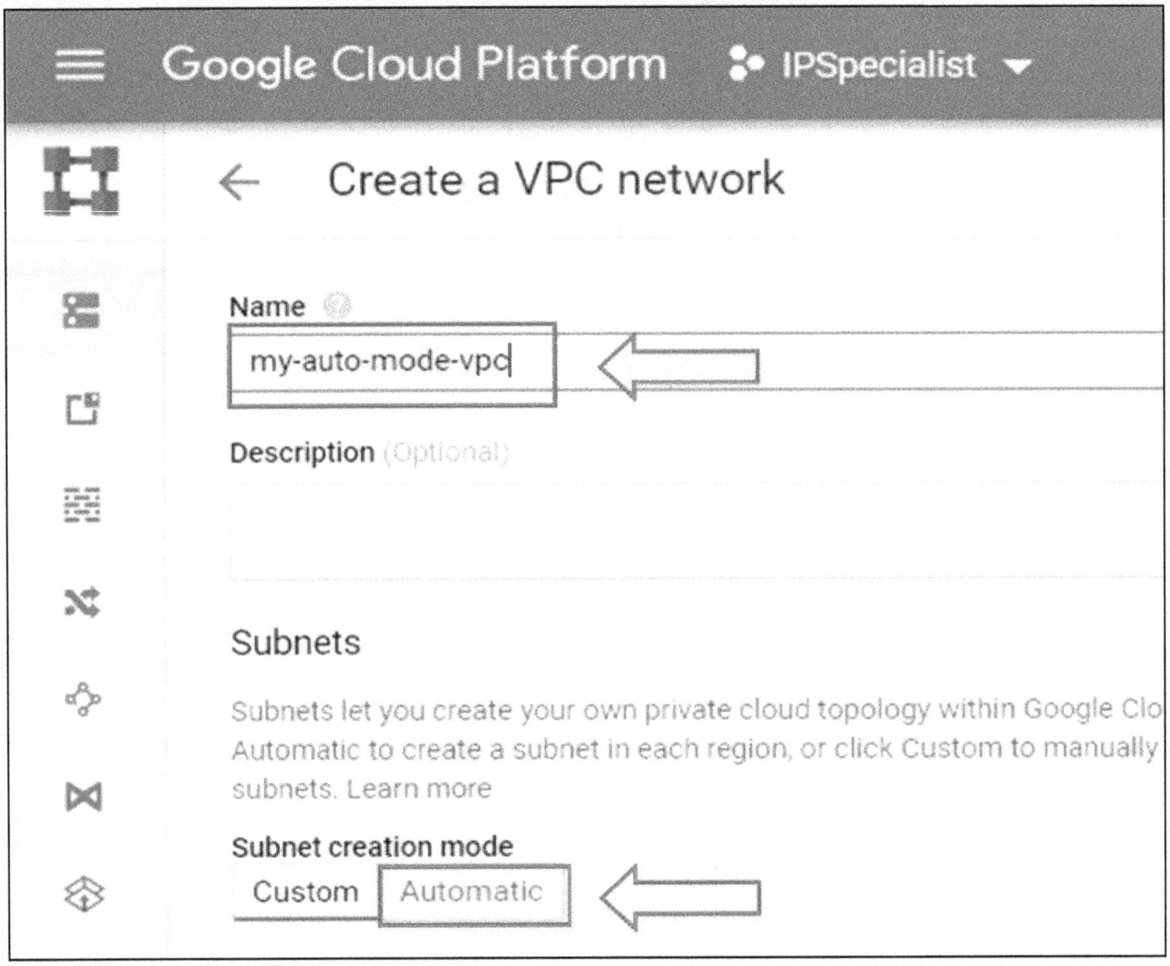

Automatic mode provides creation of subnet in each region, whereas if user selects the custom mode, subnets region has to be defined. If Google adds a new region in a Cloud, Automatic mode adds a new subnet in that region.

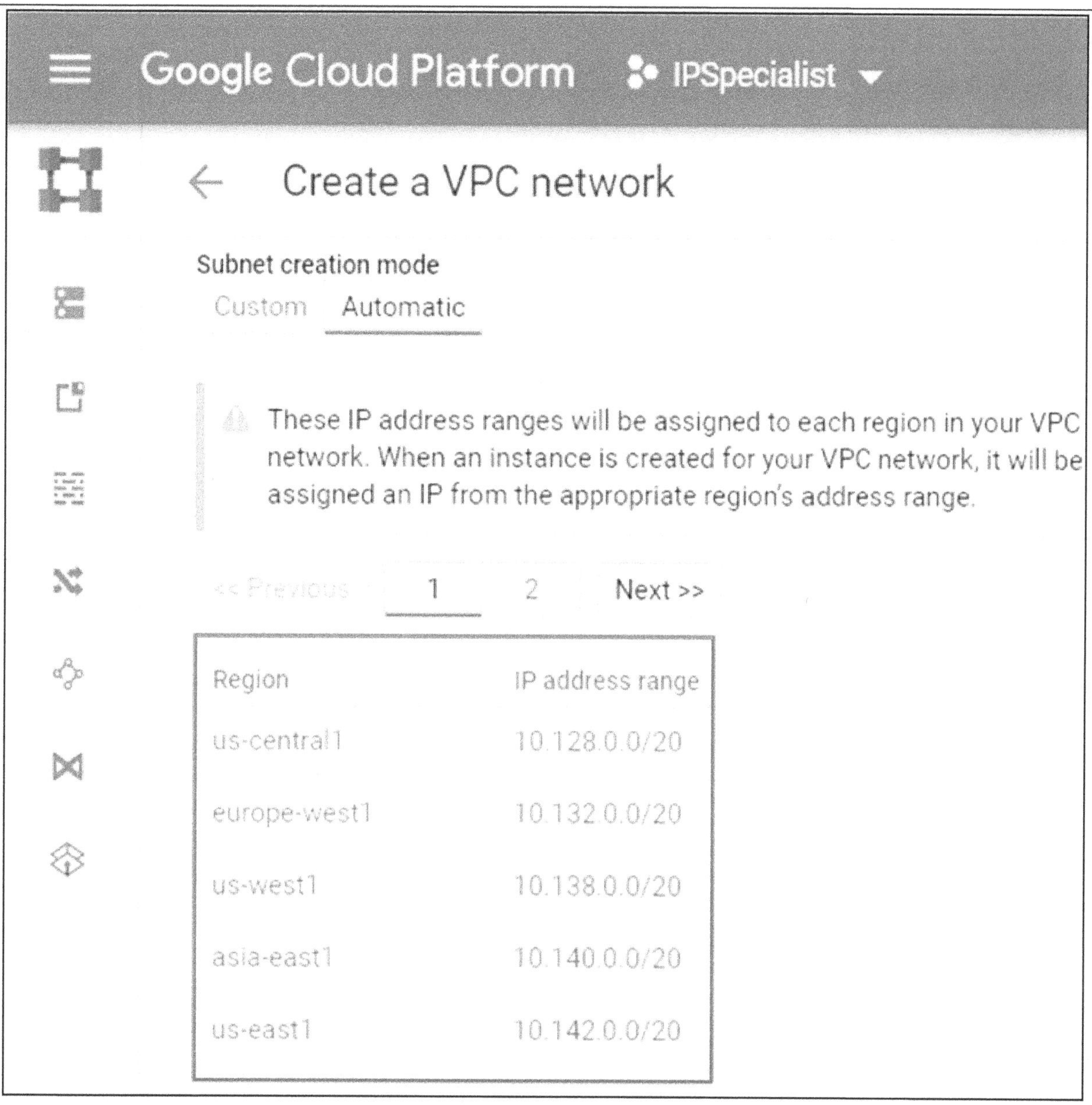

Google Cloud Platform IPSpecialist

Create a VPC network

Subnet creation mode

Custom Automatic

These IP address ranges will be assigned to each region in your VPC network. When an instance is created for your VPC network, it will be assigned an IP from the appropriate region's address range.

<< Previous 1 2 Next >>

Region	IP address range
us-central1	10.128.0.0/20
europe-west1	10.132.0.0/20
us-west1	10.138.0.0/20
asia-east1	10.140.0.0/20
us-east1	10.142.0.0/20

Here are the four Firewall rules and the two other rules are included by default.

Google Cloud Platform IPSpecialist

Create a VPC network

Firewall rules

Select any of the firewall rules below that you would like to apply to this VPC network. Once the VPC network is created, you can manage all firewall rules on the Firewall rules page.

Name	Type	Targets	Filters
my-auto-mode-vpc-allow-icmp	Ingress	Apply to all	IP ranges: 0.0.0.0/0
my-auto-mode-vpc-allow-internal	Ingress	Apply to all	IP ranges: 10.128.0.0/9
my-auto-mode-vpc-allow-rdp	Ingress	Apply to all	IP ranges: 0.0.0.0/0
my-auto-mode-vpc-allow-ssh	Ingress	Apply to all	IP ranges: 0.0.0.0/0
my-auto-mode-vpc-deny-all-ingress	Ingress	Apply to all	IP ranges: 0.0.0.0/0
my-auto-mode-vpc-allow-all-egress	Egress	Apply to all	IP ranges: 0.0.0.0/0

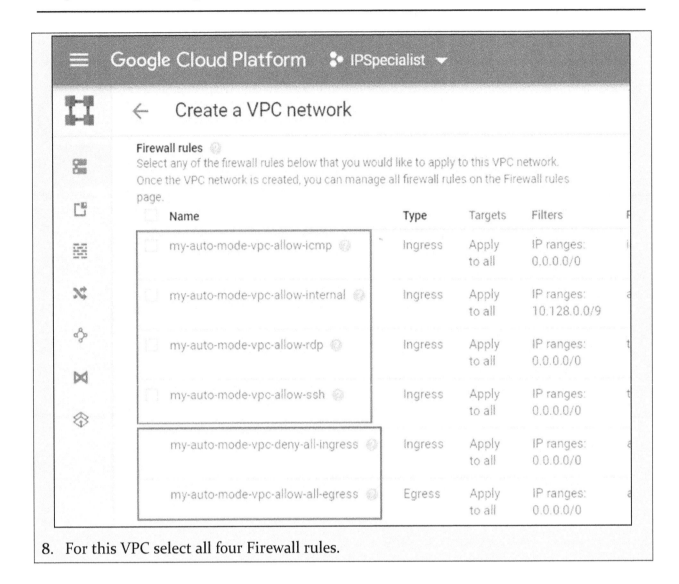

8. For this VPC select all four Firewall rules.

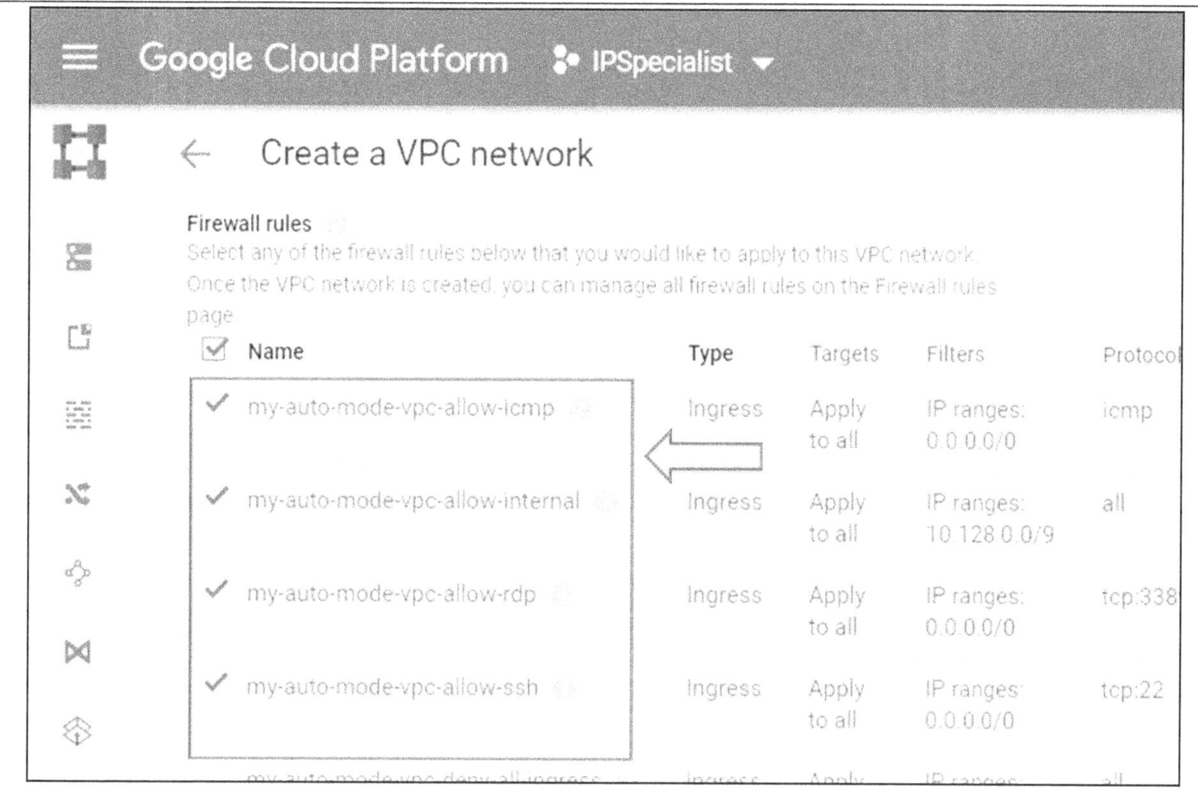

First rule is to allow icmp, it is the protocol for managing ping, trace routes etc. Rule for allowing SSH is to allow TCH traffic at port 22. SSH connections are secure if the SSH keys are managed properly. A rule is present for allowing internal traffic in VPC for a particular sider range.

Dynamic Routing Mode only impacts when the routes are learned through BGP, therefore leave it to default.

9. Click "Create".

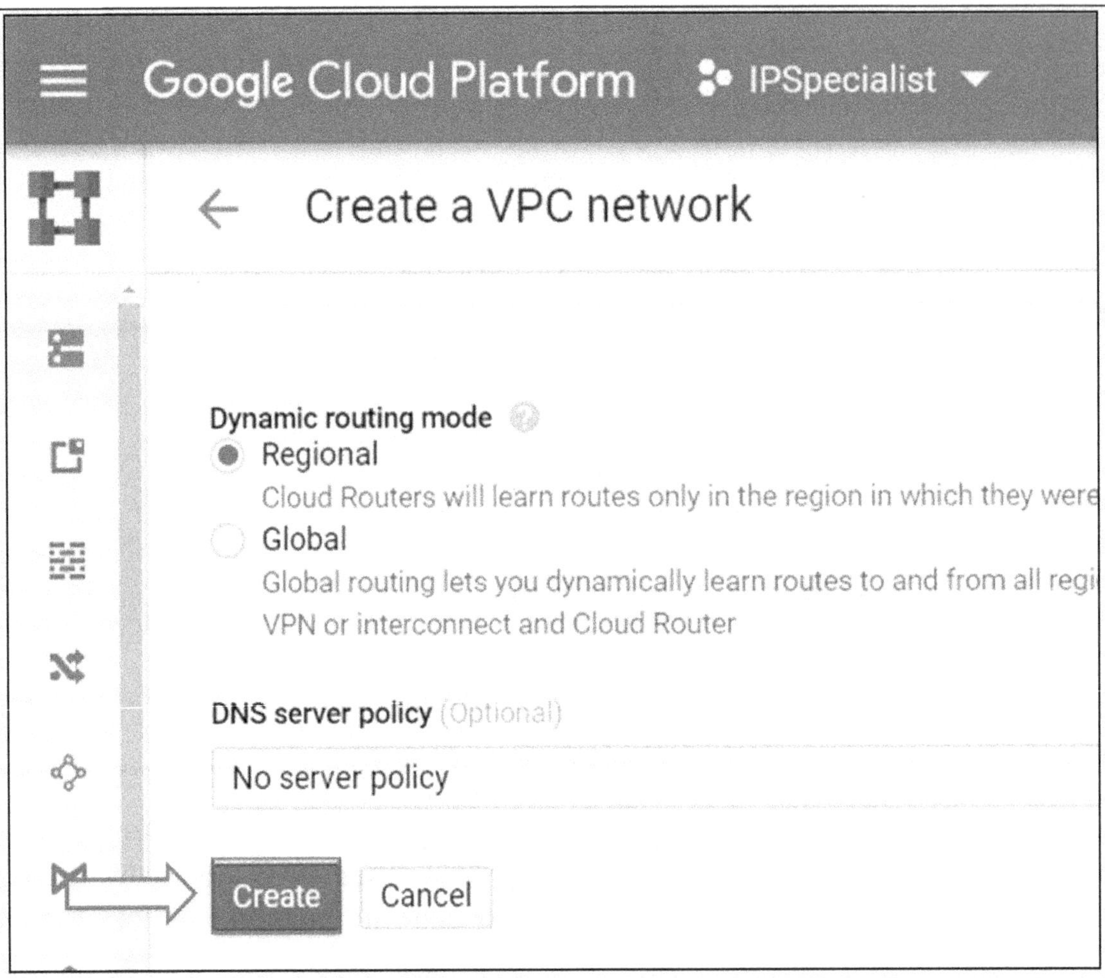

Auto mode VPC is created.

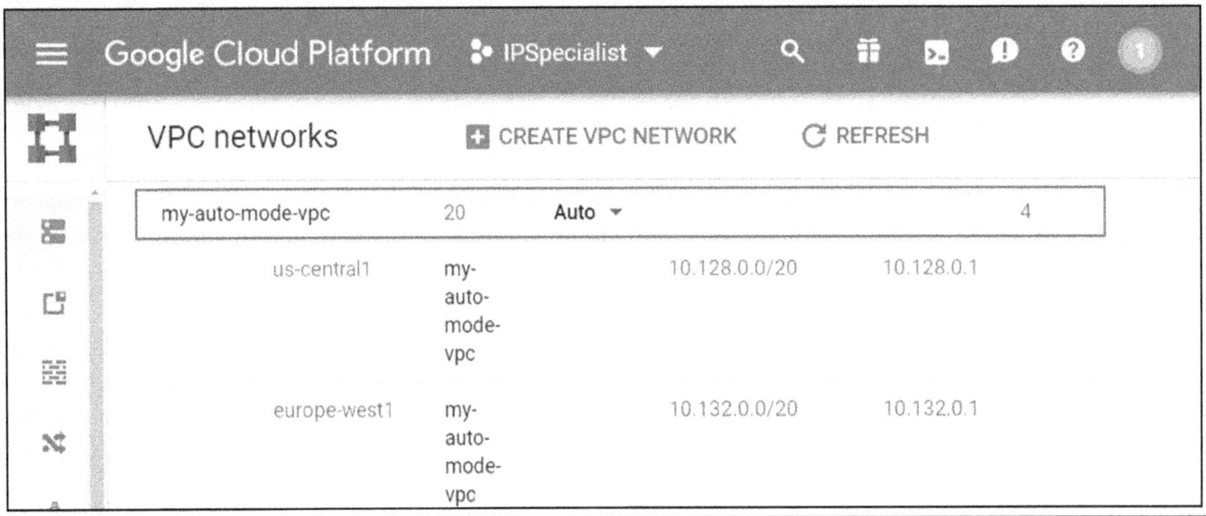

Lab 5.2: Custom-Mode VPCs

Scenario:

Your Company has assigned you a task to launch multiple instances in specific subnet and control the access of traffic to these instances

Solution:

You will launch instances by using instance group in a Custom-mode VPC. The traffic is controlled by introducing firewalls. These Firewall rules are defined by using service accounts and Network tags.

1. Log in to the GCP console.
2. Go to the Project.

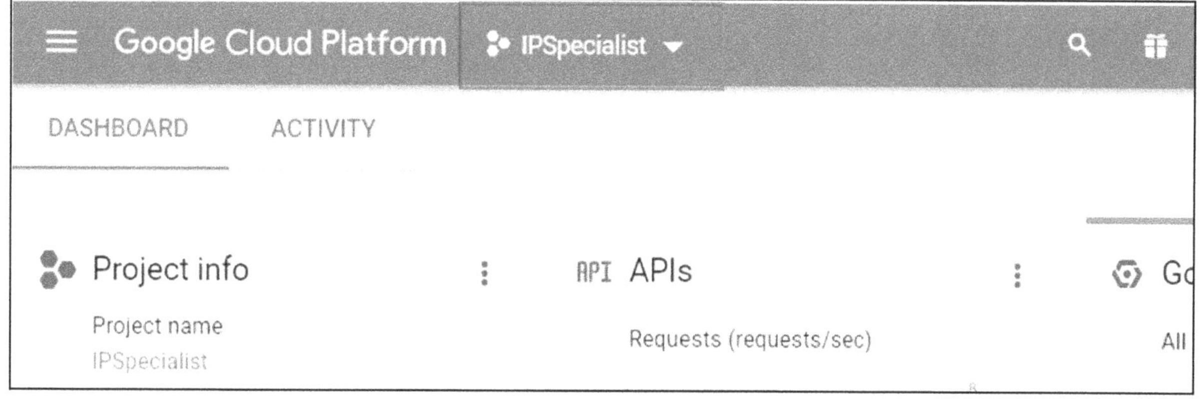

3. Go to the VPC Network and select "default".

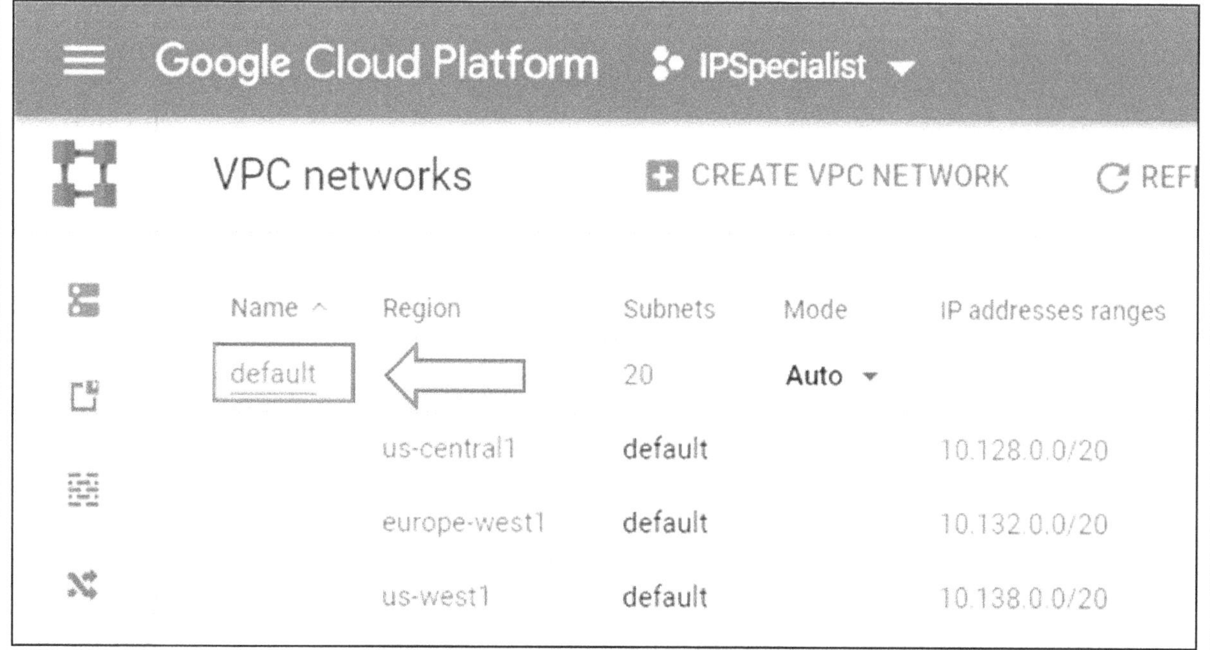

4. Click "DELETE VPC NETWORK".

Google Cloud Platform IPSpecialist
VPC network details EDIT DELETE VPC NETWORK
default
Description
Default network for the project
Subnet creation mode
Auto subnets
Select a subnet
PERMISSIONS

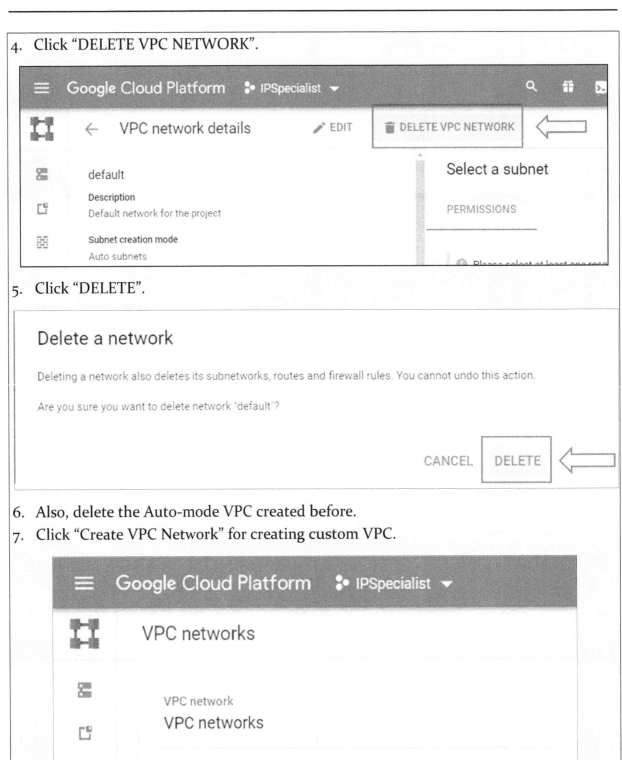

5. Click "DELETE".

Delete a network

Deleting a network also deletes its subnetworks, routes and firewall rules. You cannot undo this action.

Are you sure you want to delete network "default"?

CANCEL DELETE

6. Also, delete the Auto-mode VPC created before.
7. Click "Create VPC Network" for creating custom VPC.

Google Cloud Platform IPSpecialist
VPC networks
VPC network
VPC networks
There are no local VPC networks in the current project
Create VPC network

8. Give it a name and select the Subnet creation mode as "Custom".

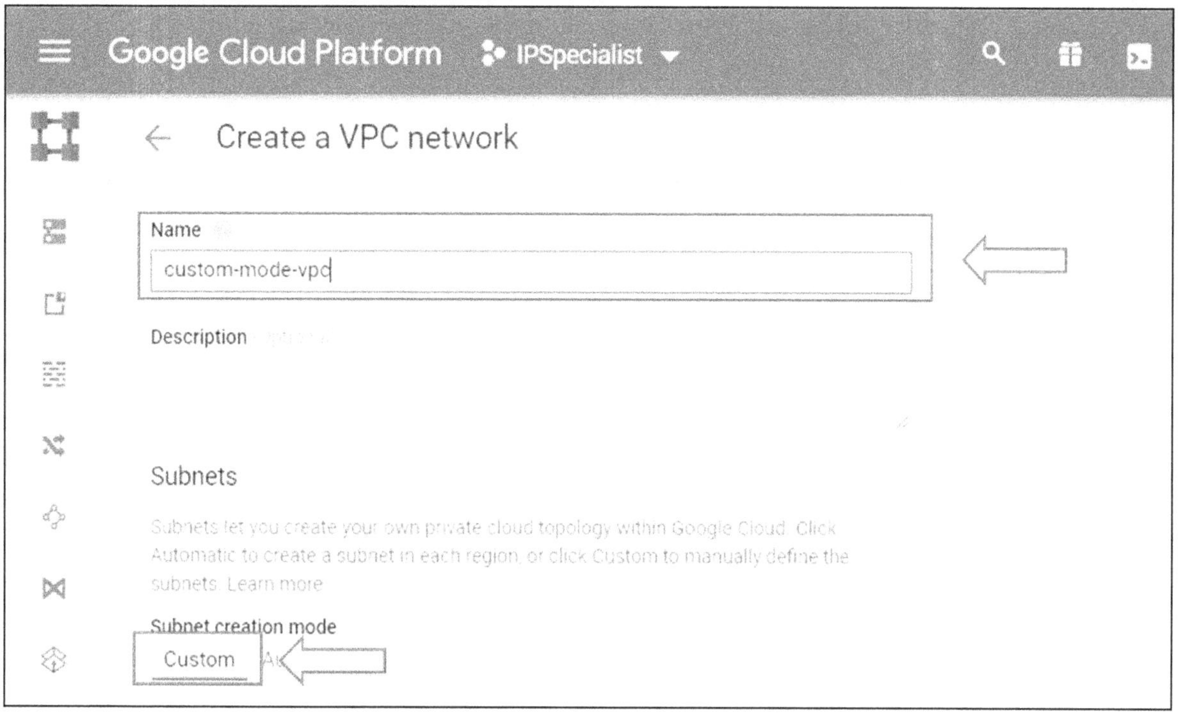

9. Create a subnet in us-west1 region.

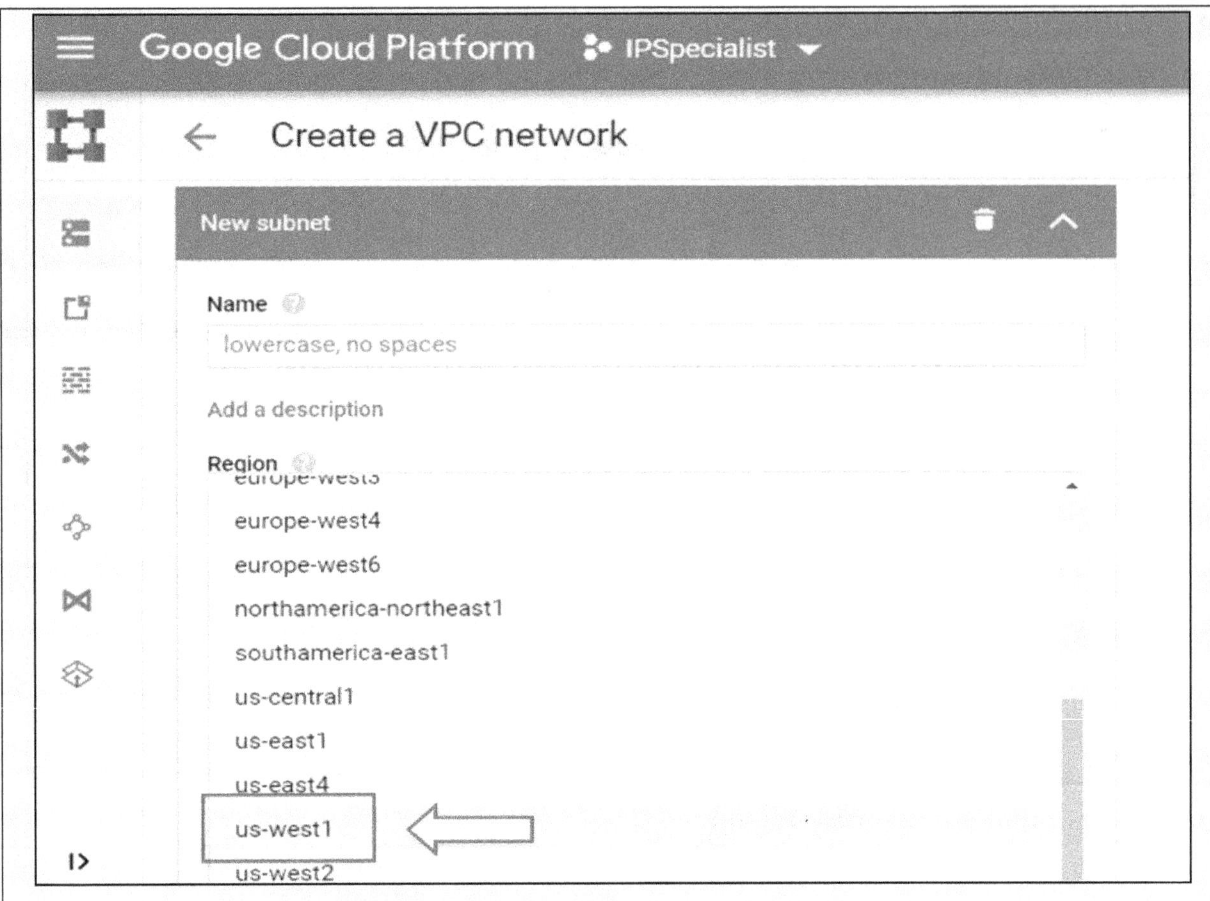

10. Enter any name for this subnet.

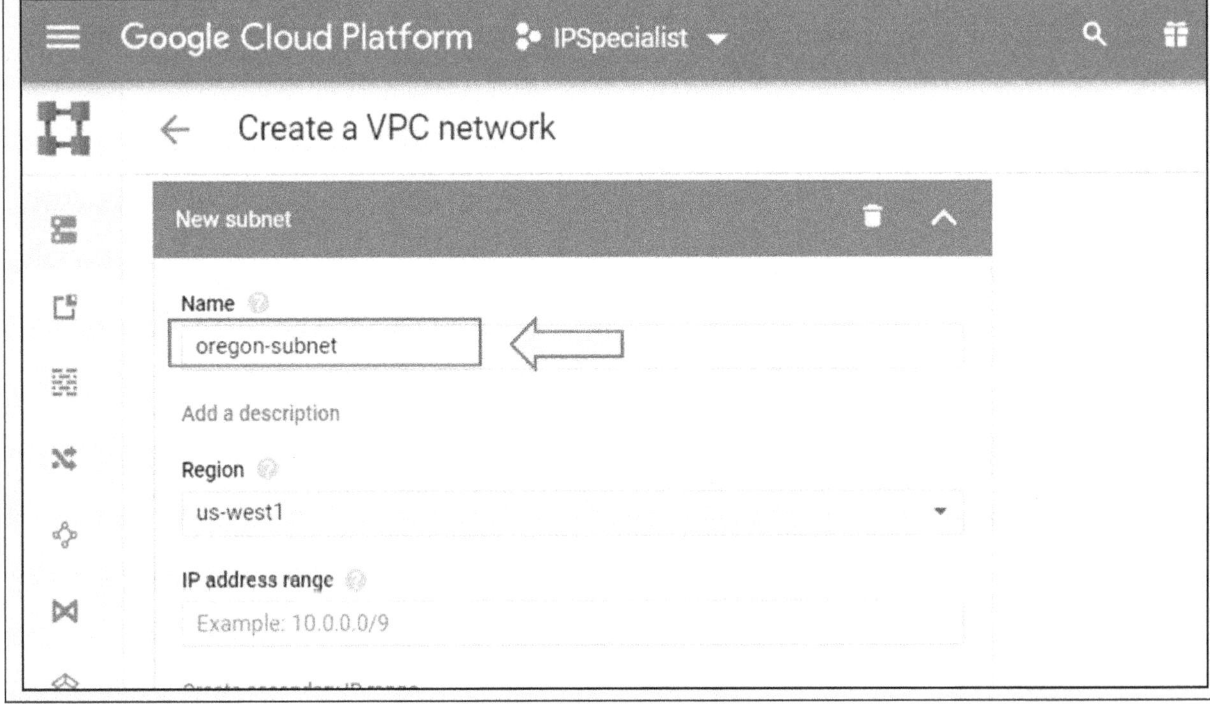

11. Provide the private IP address CIDR range and leave Private Google access and flow logs “Off”.

Private Google access allow you to connect to Google services even when you are not connected to the internet.

Flow logs enable you the access of t=detailed information of traffic of subnet.

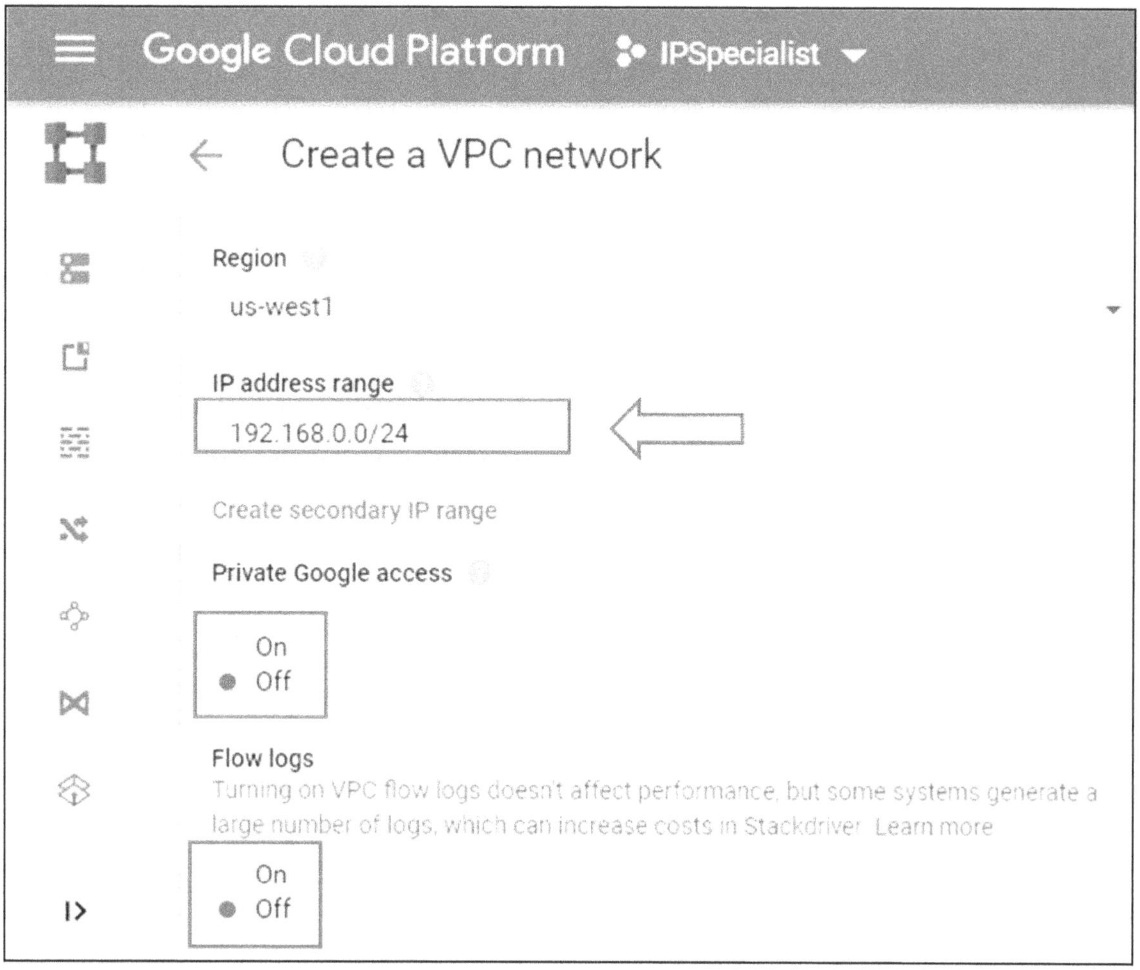

Google Cloud Platform IPSpecialist

Create a VPC network

Region

us-west1

IP address range

192.168.0.0/24

Create secondary IP range

Private Google access

On

Off

Flow logs

Turning on VPC flow logs doesn't affect performance, but some systems generate a large number of logs, which can increase costs in Stackdriver. Learn more

On

Off

12. Click “Done”.
13. Select “Global” in Dynamic Routing Mode in case you have to connect to any VPN for accessing the subnets globally.

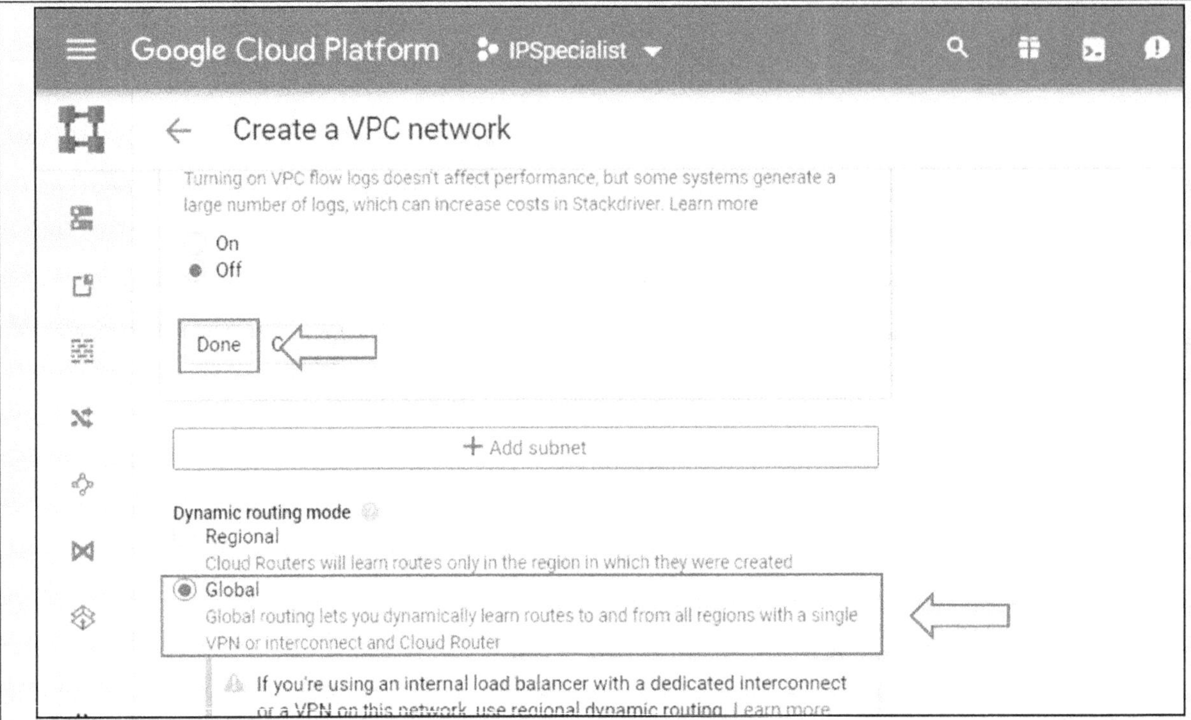

14. Click “Create”.

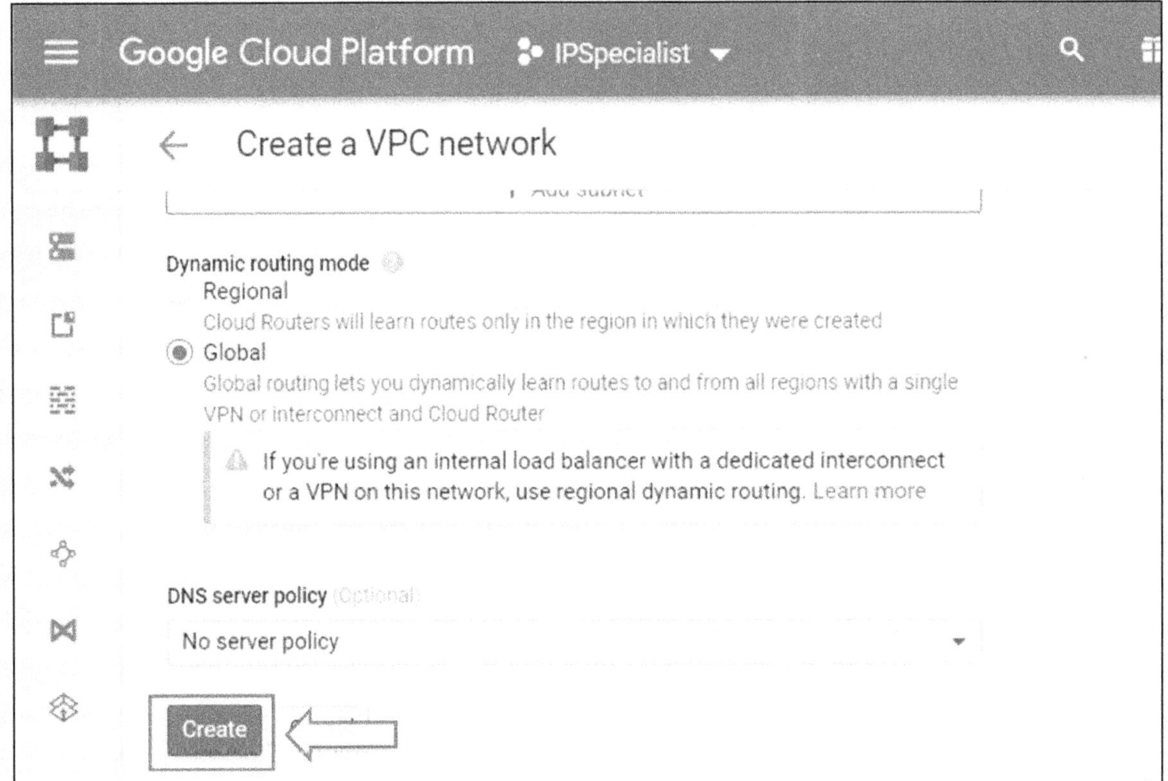

The Custom mode VPC is created. There are no Firewalls and nothing is using this subnet (custom-mode-vpc) so this VPC is static and devoid of purpose.

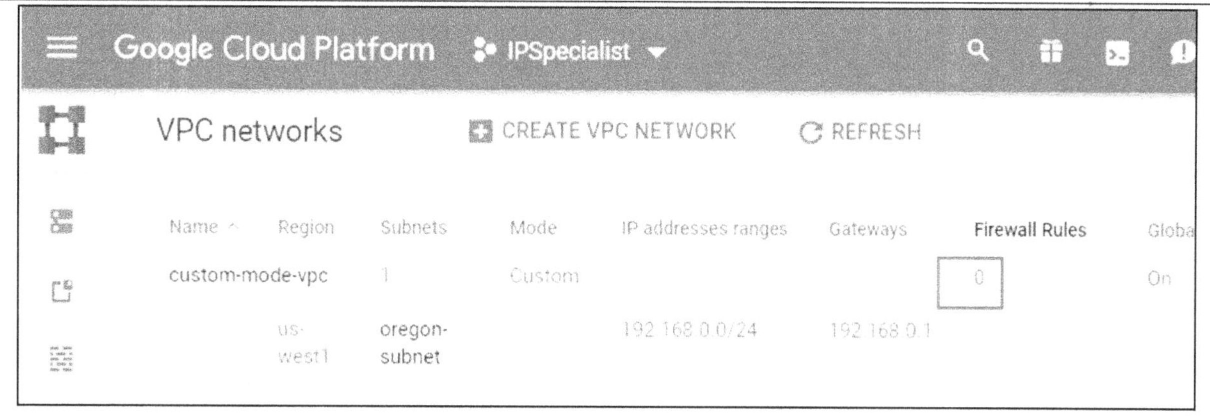

13. Go to "IAM & admin" and select "Roles".

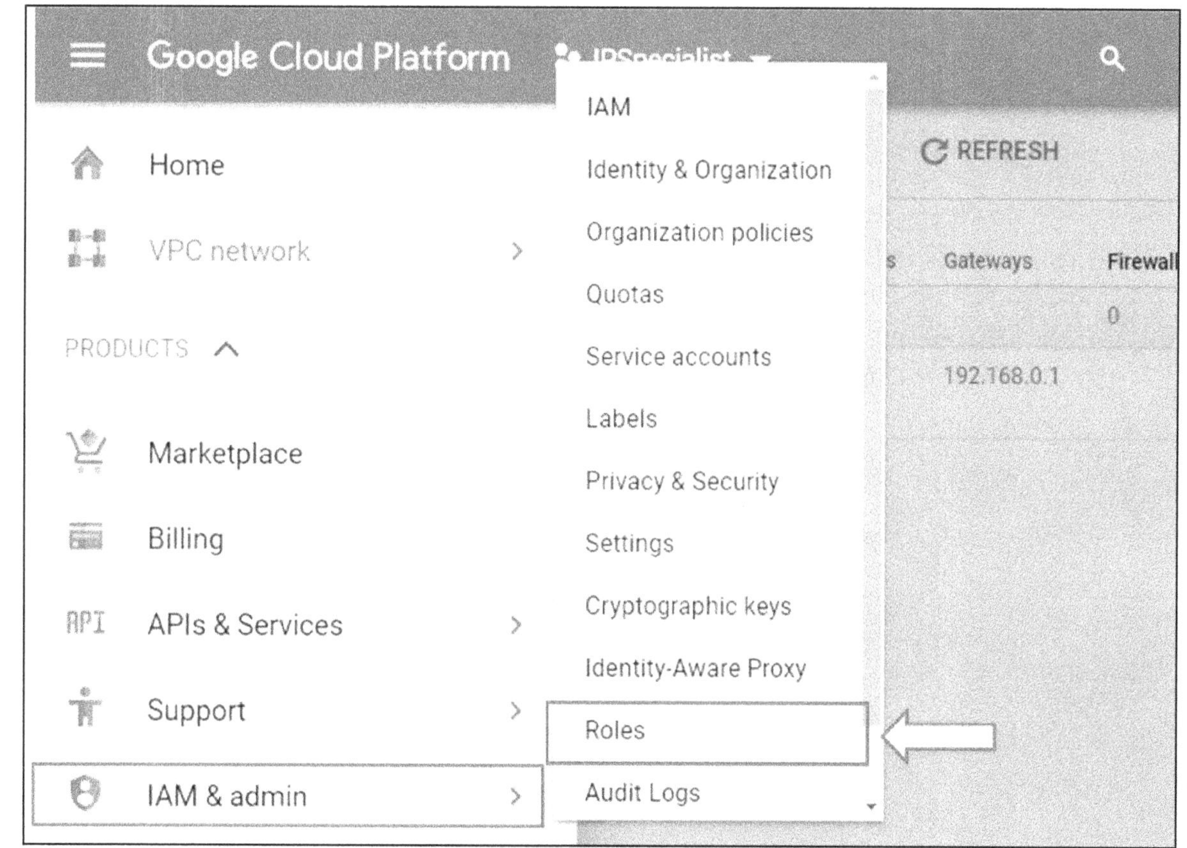

You can select any Role to view the permissions associated with it.

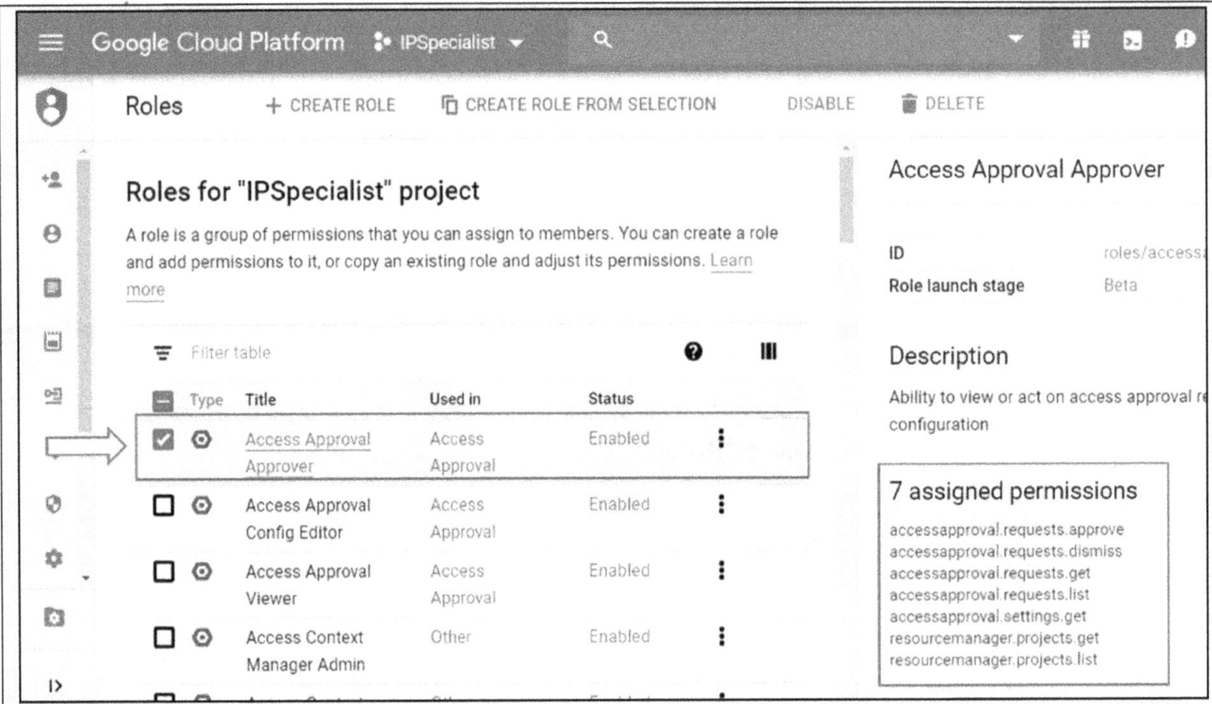

15. Filter this table with "Title: *writer*", this table only display the roles including writer.

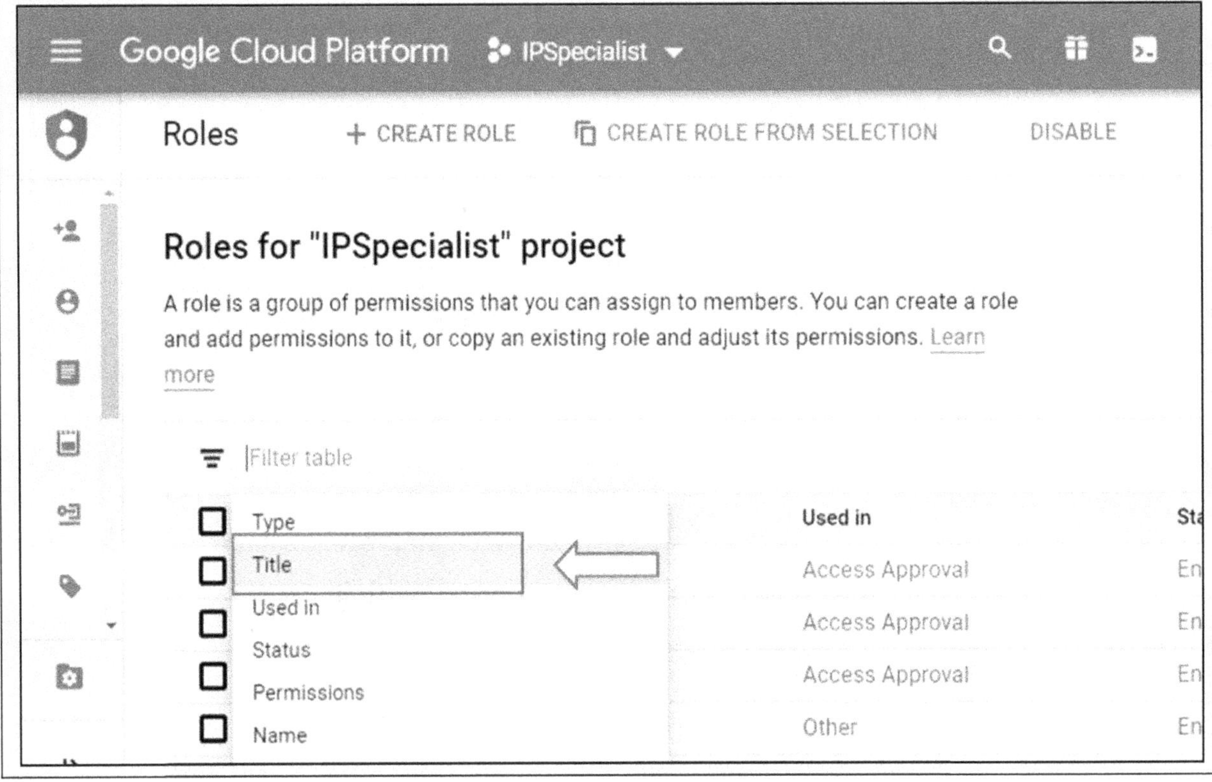

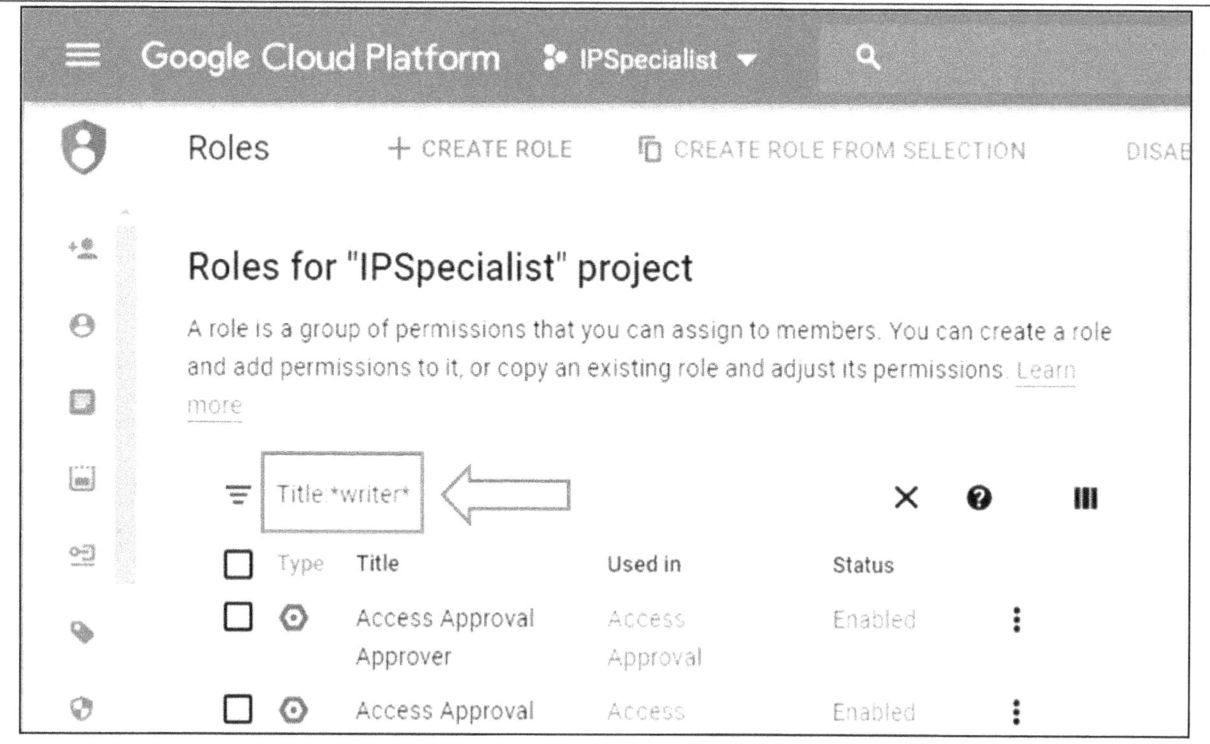

16. Select "Log Writer" and "Monitoring Metric Writer". These roles allow instances to write logs and metrics to stackdriver.

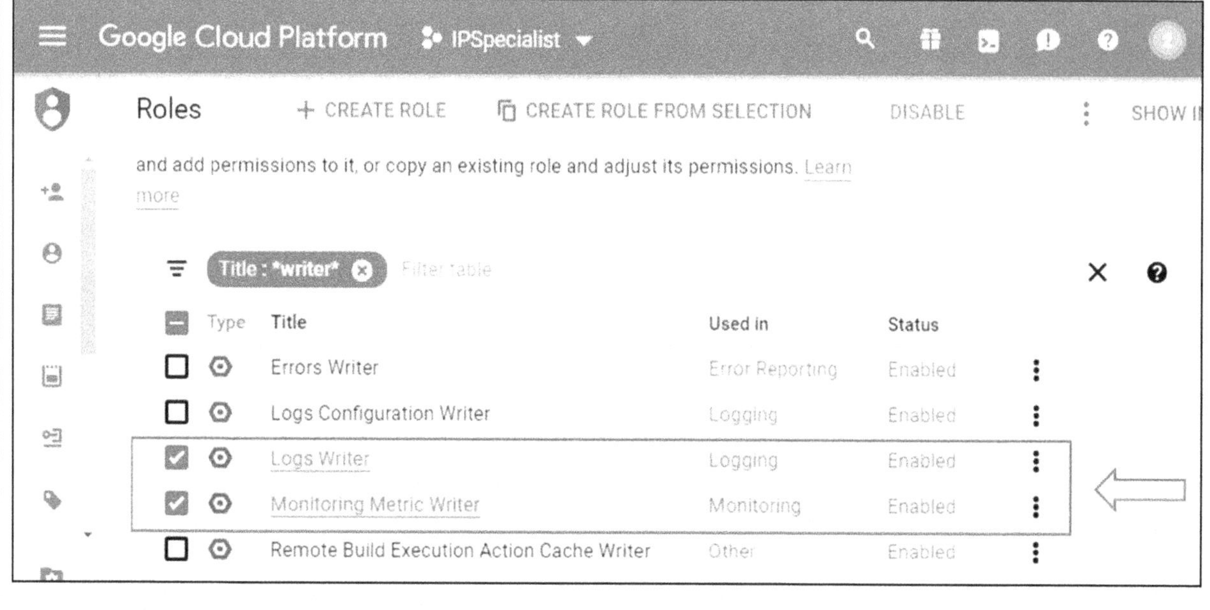

17. Click "CREATE ROLE FROM SELECTION".

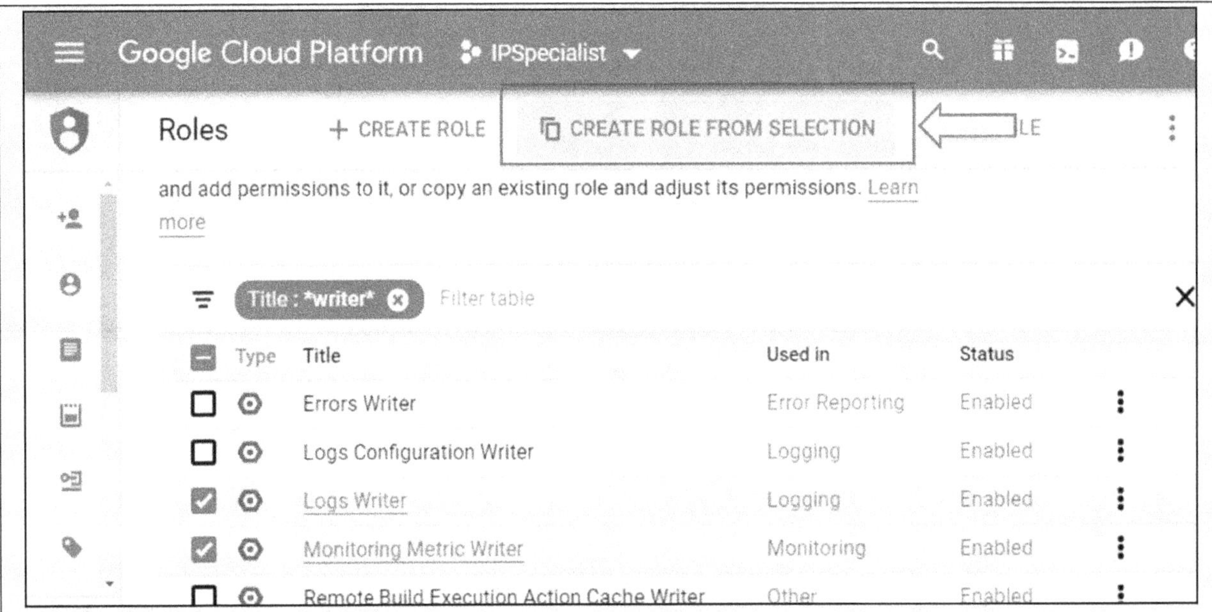

18. Provide this role a general name so that this role can be attached in multiple services where these permissions are required

This is a combine role, if Google adds new permission in any of the one i.e., "Logs Writer" or "Metric Monitoring Writer" then user has to update it manually.

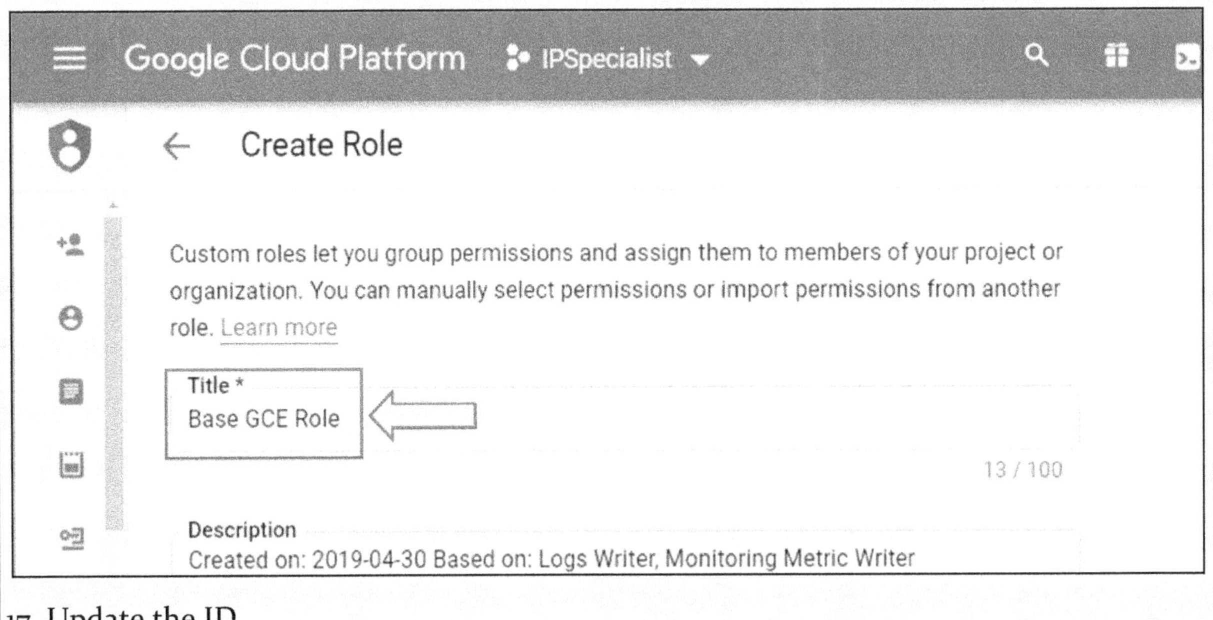

17. Update the ID.

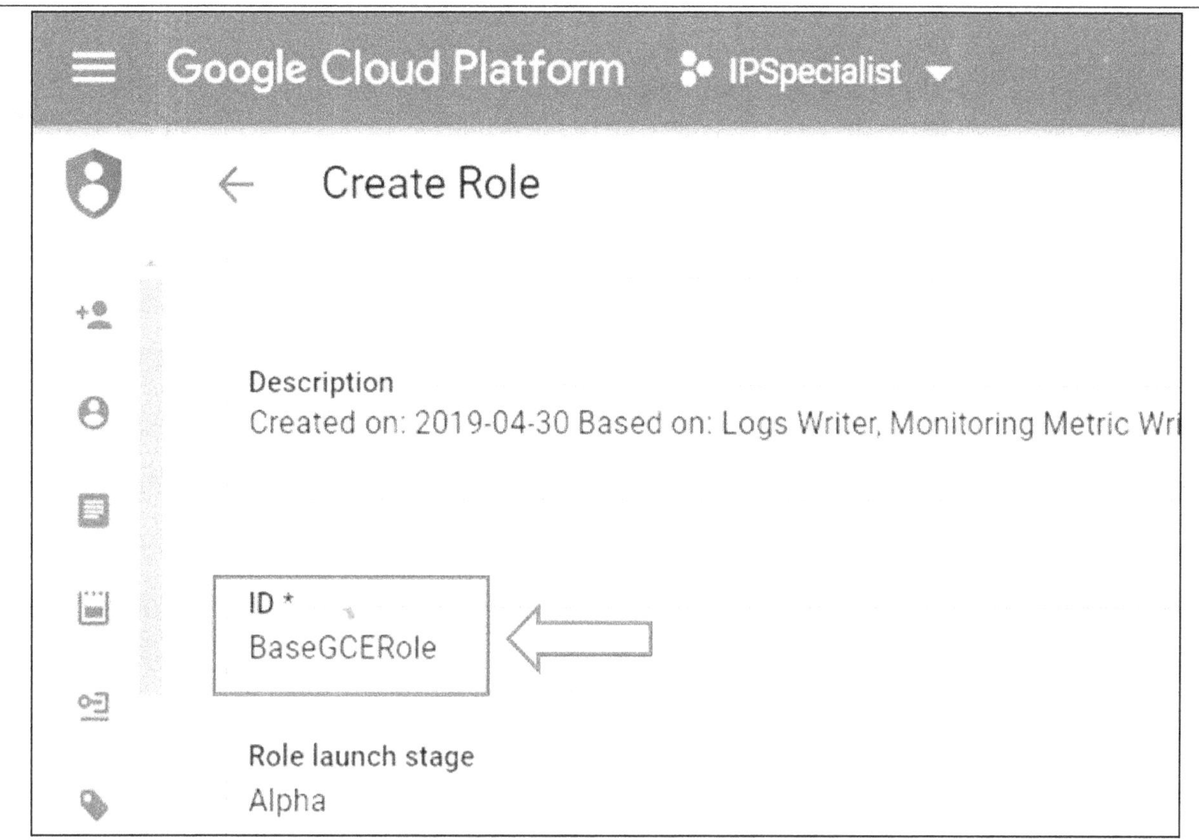

19. You can set a role to lifecycle but here select "General Availability".

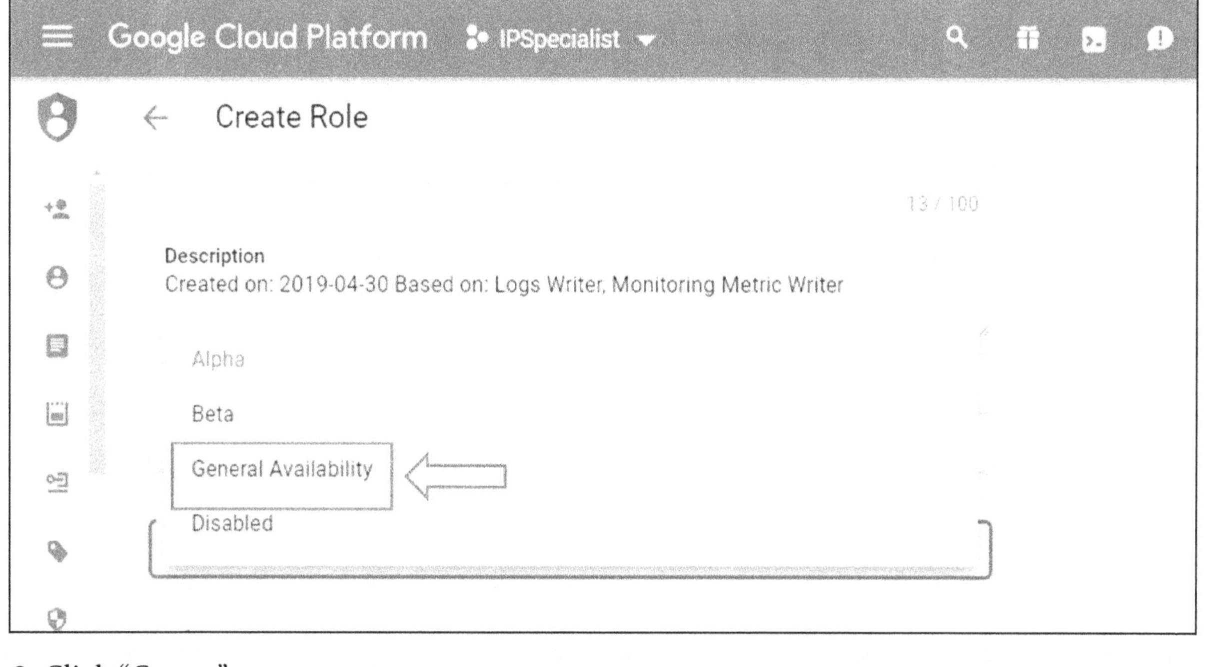

18. Click "Create".

Google Cloud Platform IPSpecialist

Create Role

7 assigned permissions

Filter table

Permission	Status
logging.logEntries.create	Supported
monitoring.metricDescriptors.create	Supported
monitoring.metricDescriptors.get	Supported
monitoring.metricDescriptors.list	Supported
monitoring.monitoredResourceDescriptors.get	Supported
monitoring.monitoredResourceDescriptors.list	Supported
monitoring.timeSeries.create	Supported

CREATE

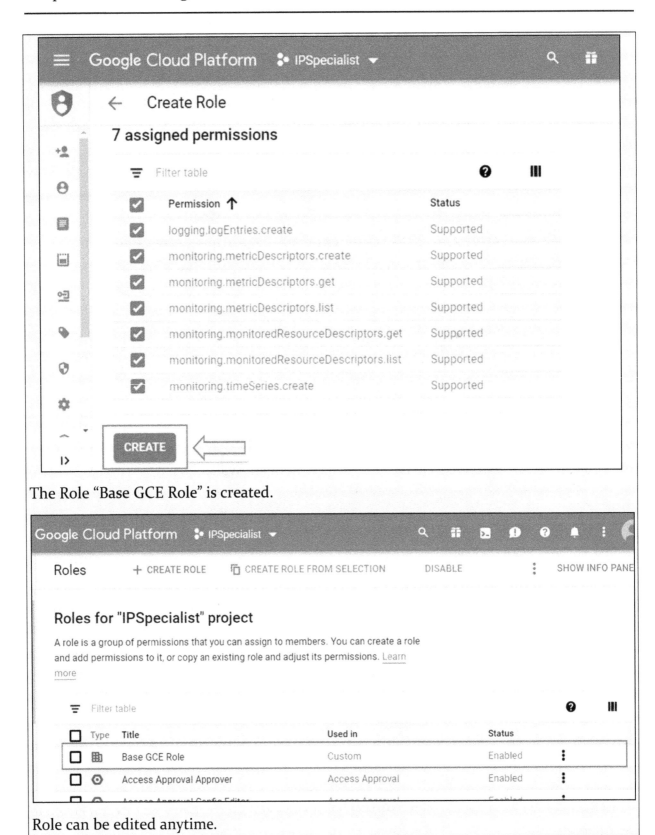

The Role “Base GCE Role” is created.

Google Cloud Platform IPSpecialist

Roles + CREATE ROLE CREATE ROLE FROM SELECTION DISABLE SHOW INFO PANE

Roles for "IPSpecialist" project

A role is a group of permissions that you can assign to members. You can create a role and add permissions to it, or copy an existing role and adjust its permissions. Learn more

Filter table

Type	Title	Used in	Status
	Base GCE Role	Custom	Enabled
	Access Approval Approver	Access Approval	Enabled

Role can be edited anytime.

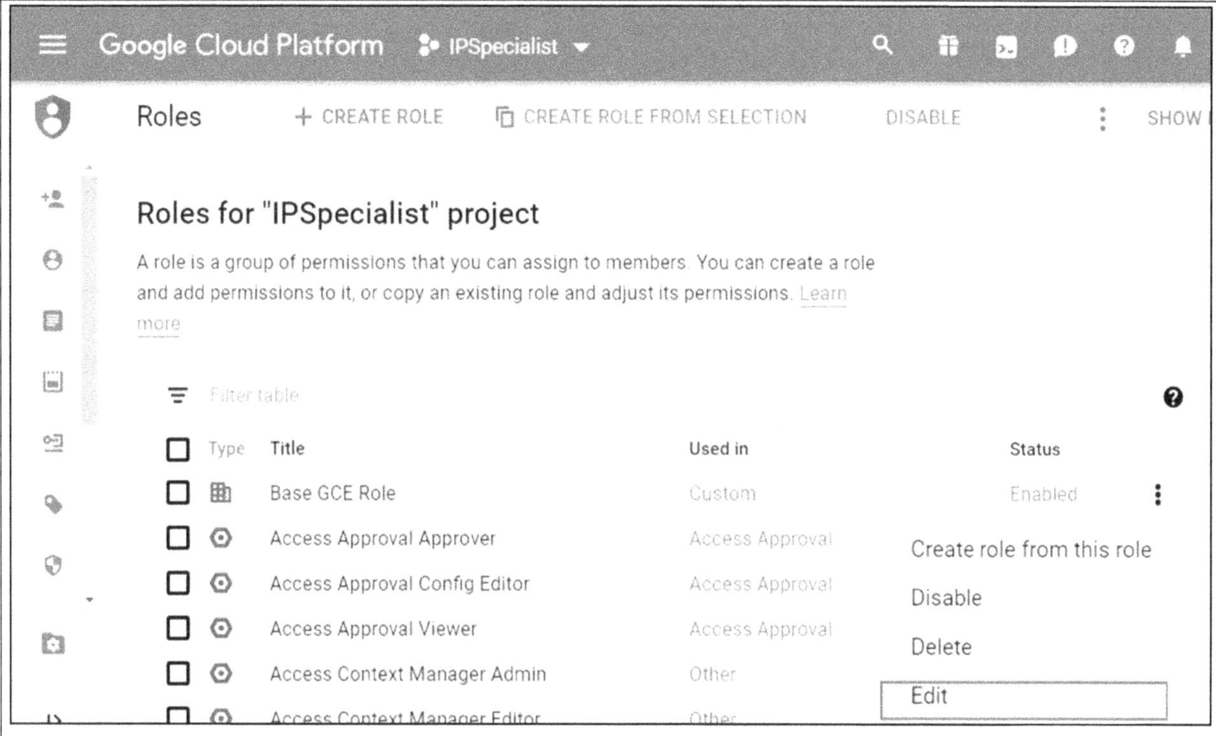

20. Go to the "Service accounts".

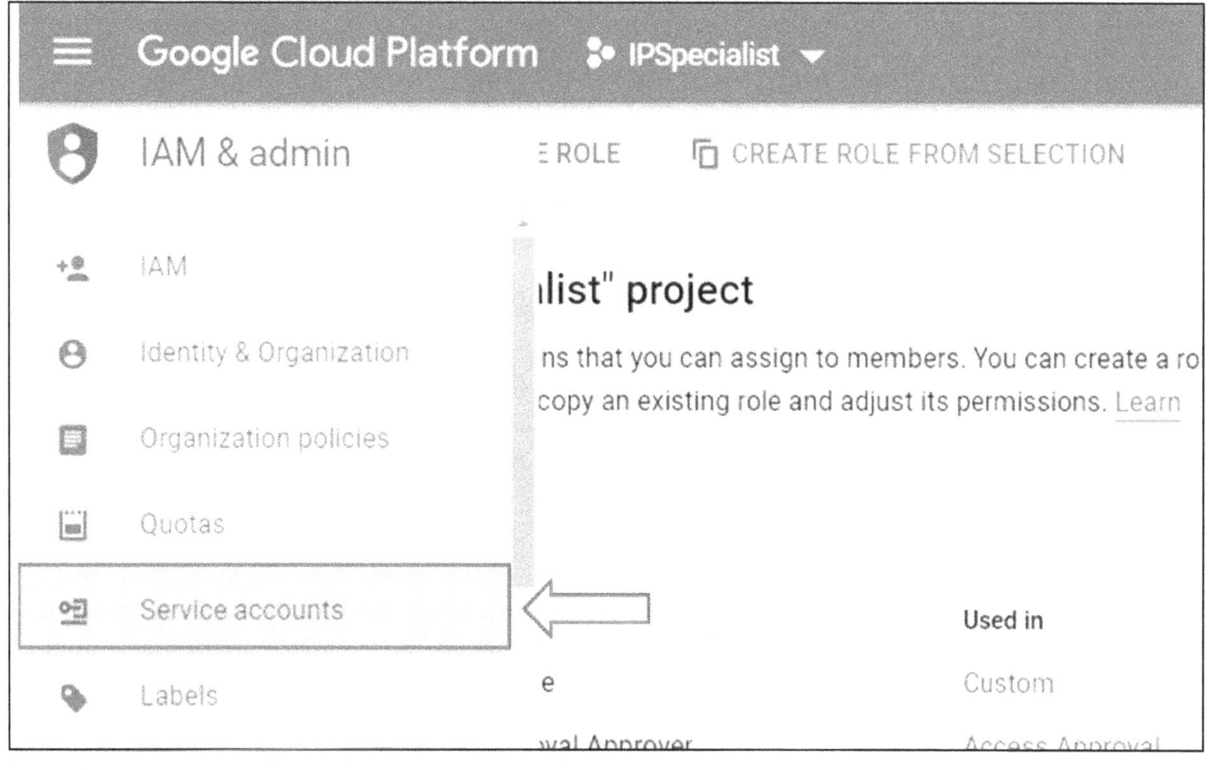

21. This default service account can be used or edited. But for this lab, delete it by clicking on "Delete".

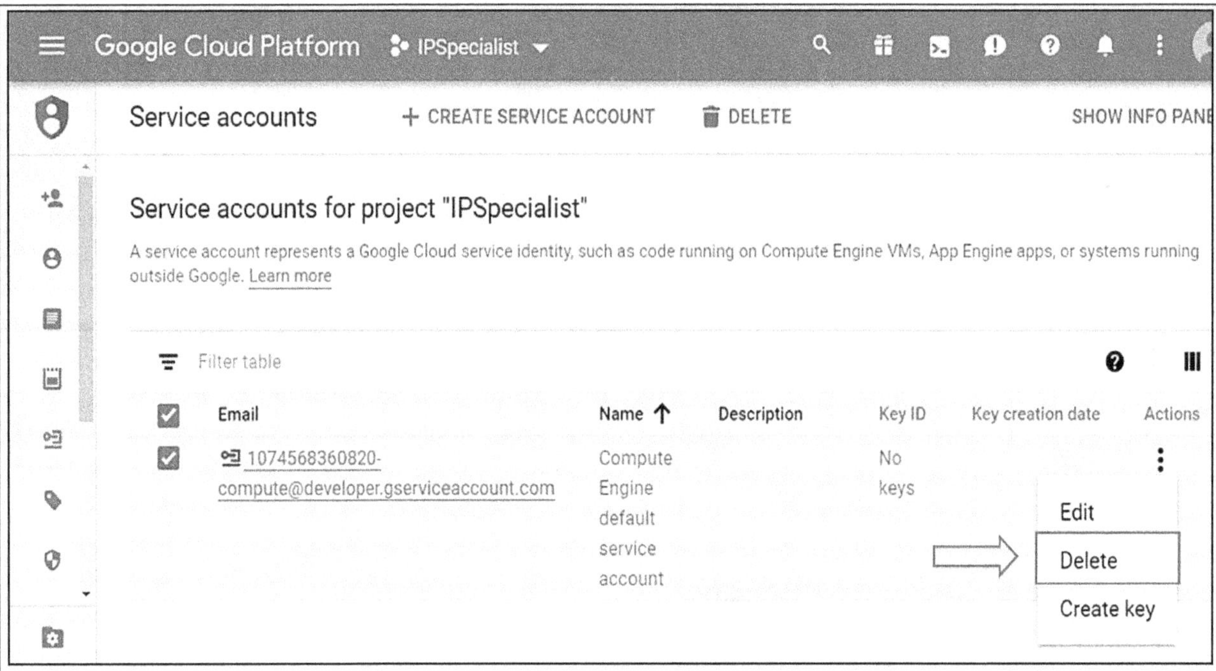

22. Paste the service account email and click "Delete".

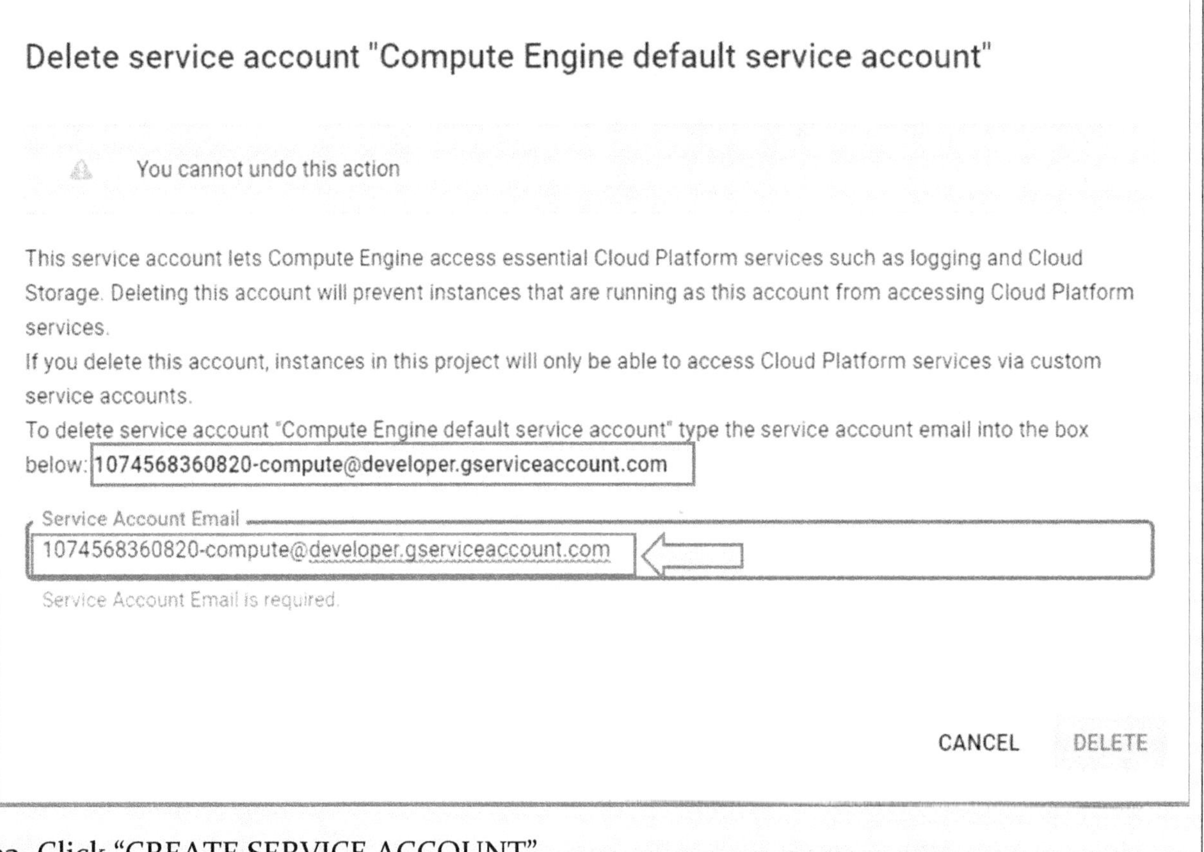

23. Click "CREATE SERVICE ACCOUNT".

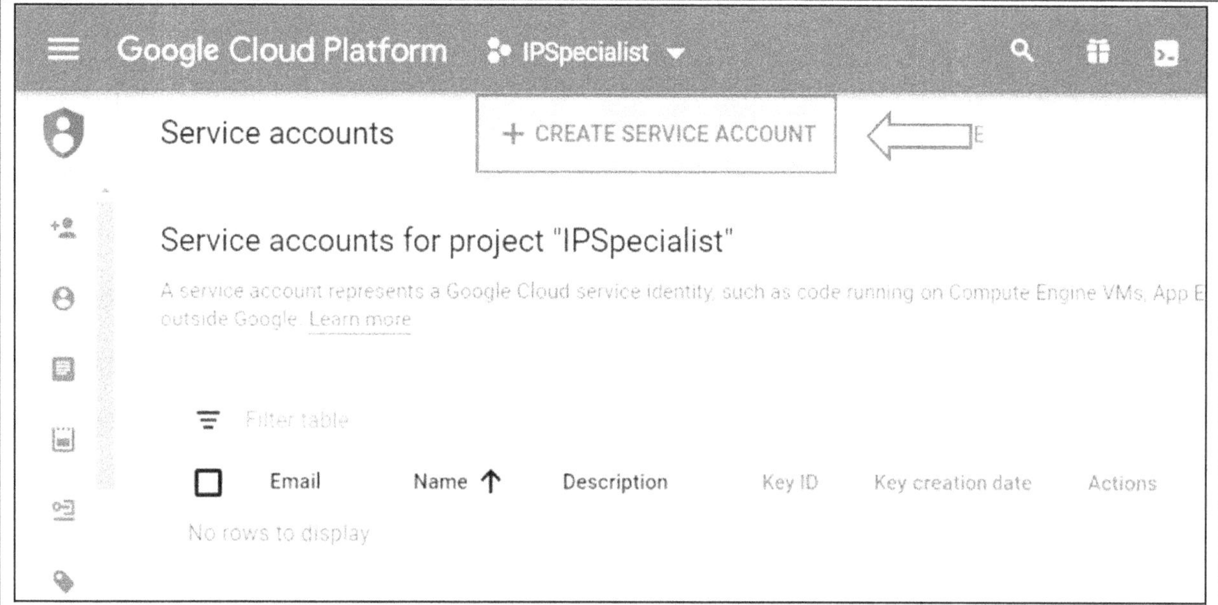

24. Provide the name and description and click "CREATE".

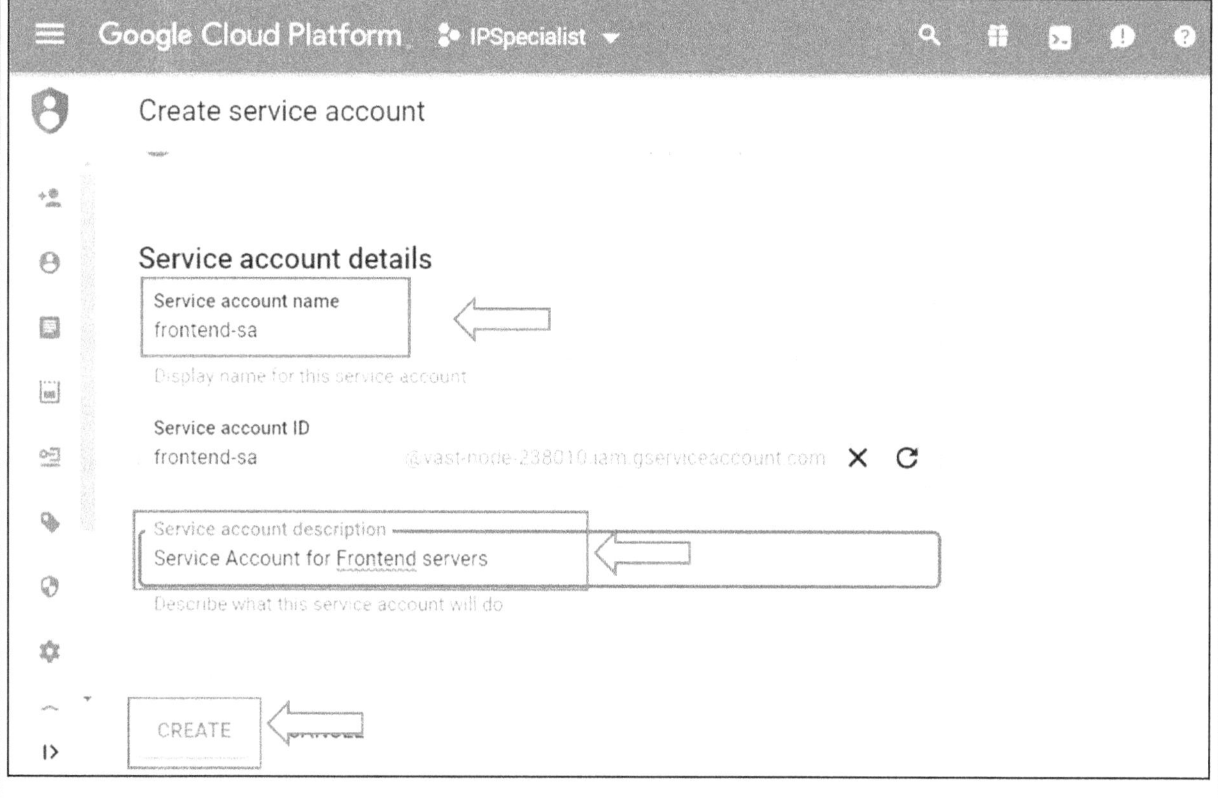

25. Select the created custom role.

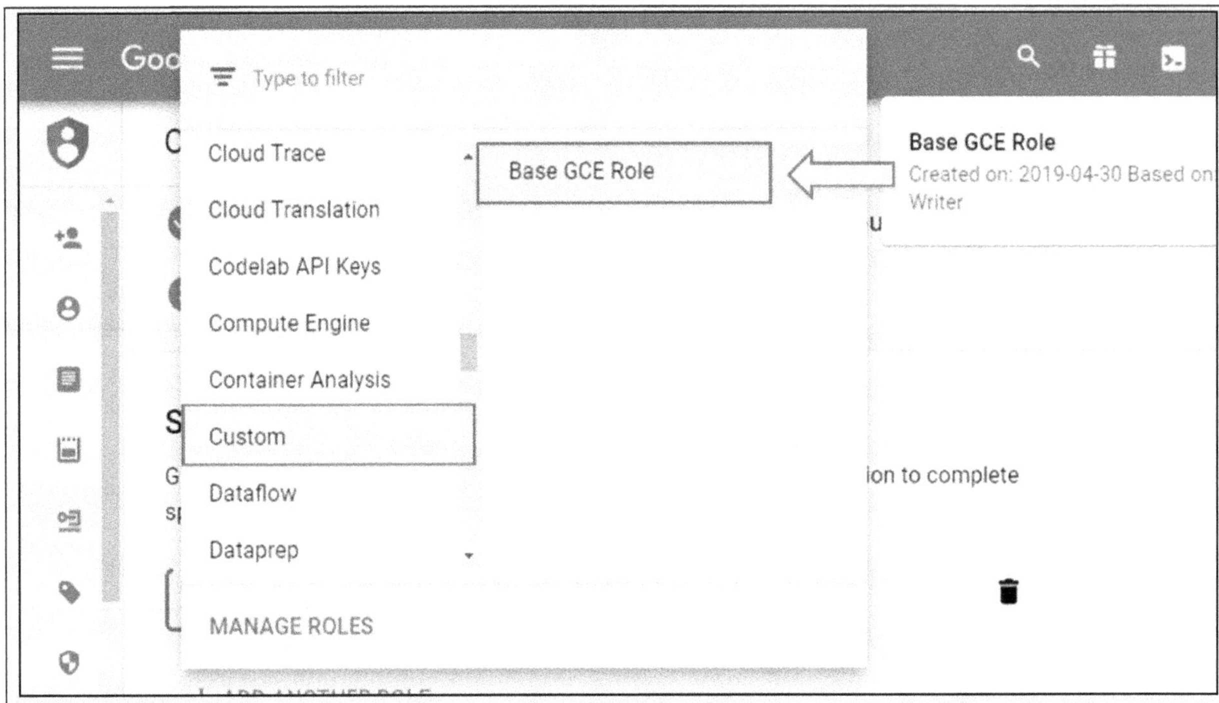

26. Click "CONTINUE".

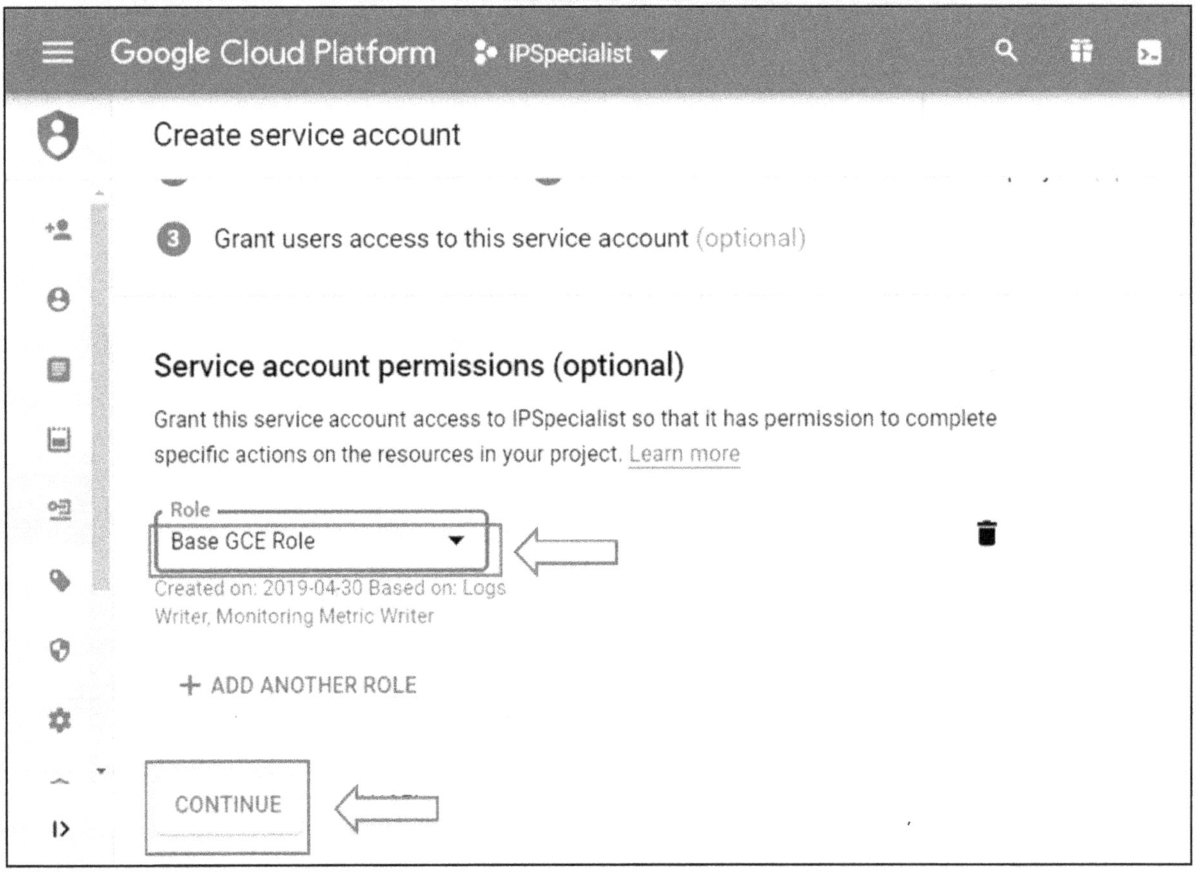

27. Click "DONE".

Google Cloud Platform IPSpecialist

Create service account

Grant users the permissions to deploy jobs and VMs with this service account

Service account admins role

Grant users the permission to administer this service account

Create key (optional)

Download a file that contains the private key. Store the file securely because this key can't be recovered if lost. However, if you are unsure why you need a key, skip this step for now.

+ CREATE KEY

DONE

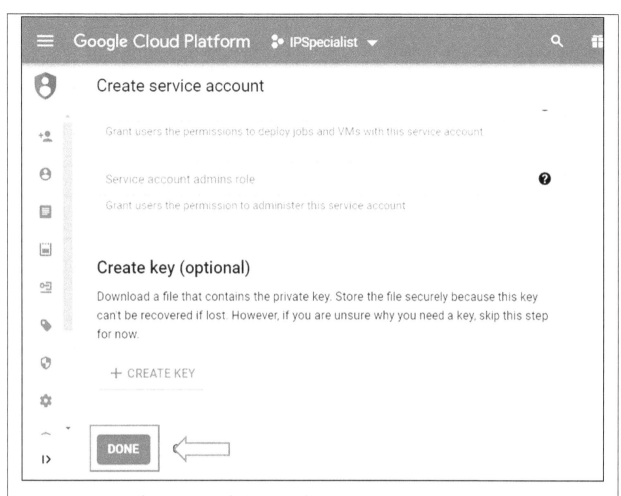

Service account with Custom Role is created.

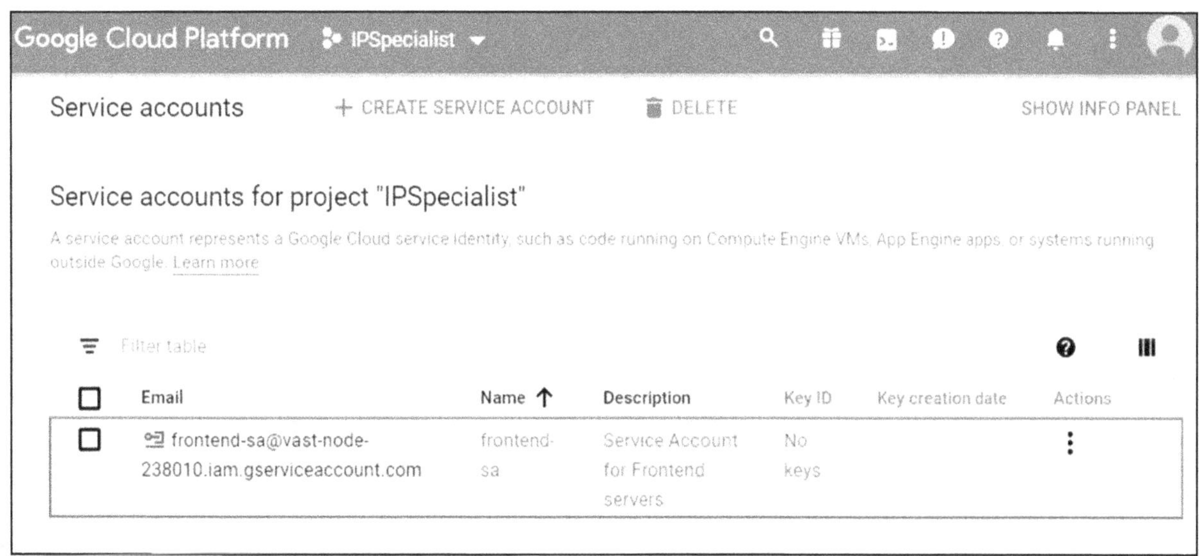

28. Go to “Compute Engine” and select “Instance templates”.

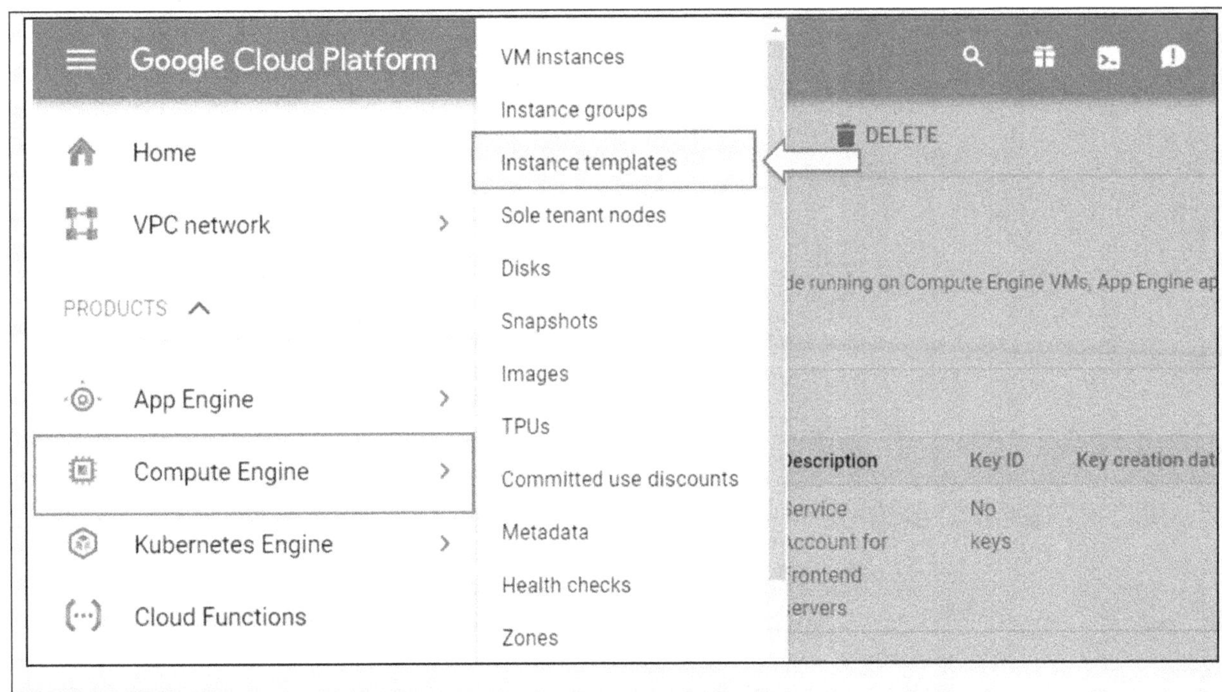

29. Click "Create Instance template".

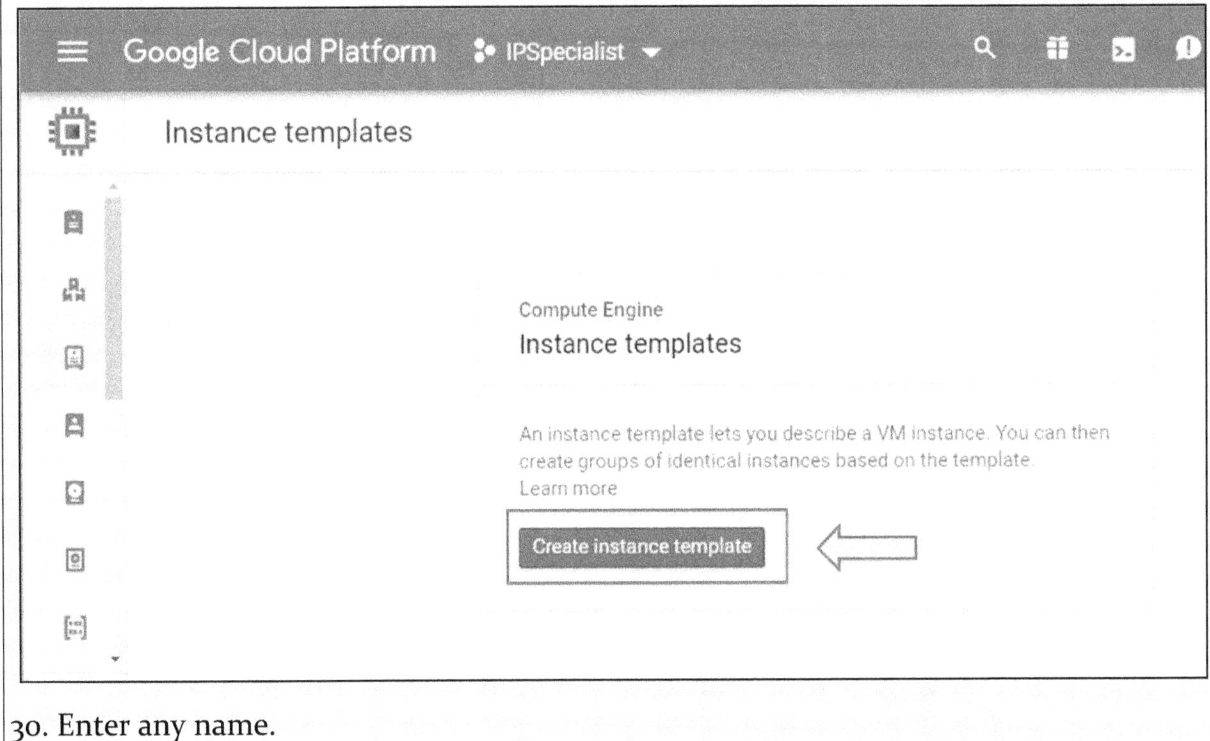

30. Enter any name.

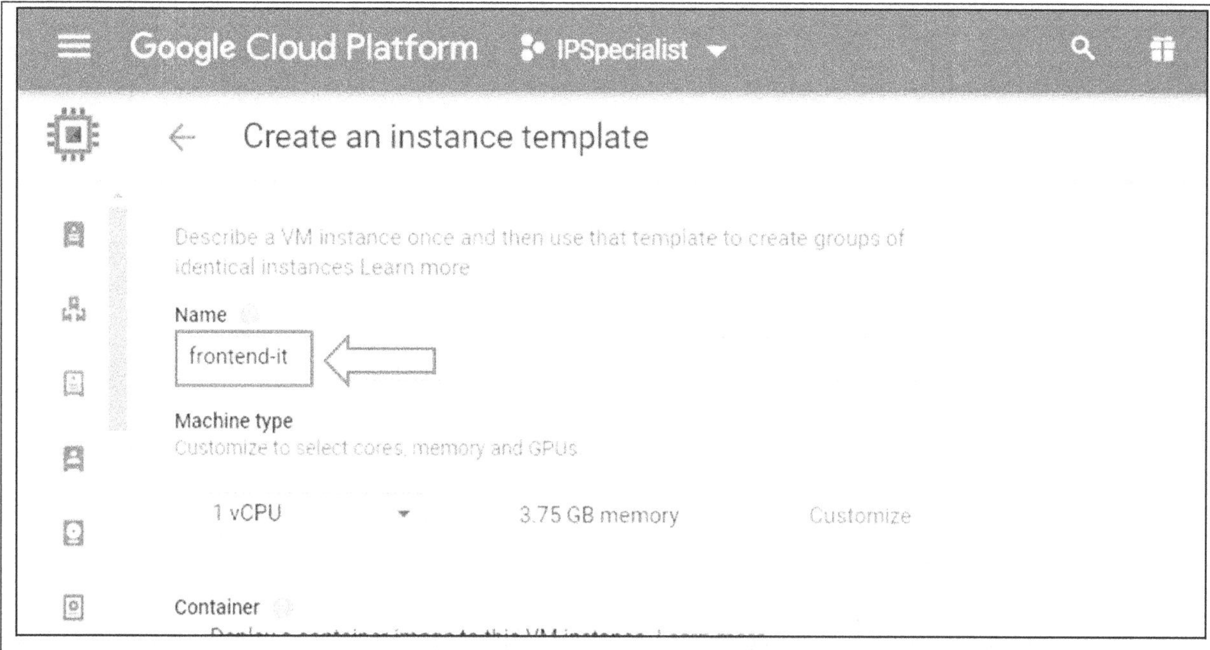

31. Select Machine type "micro (1 shared vCPU)"

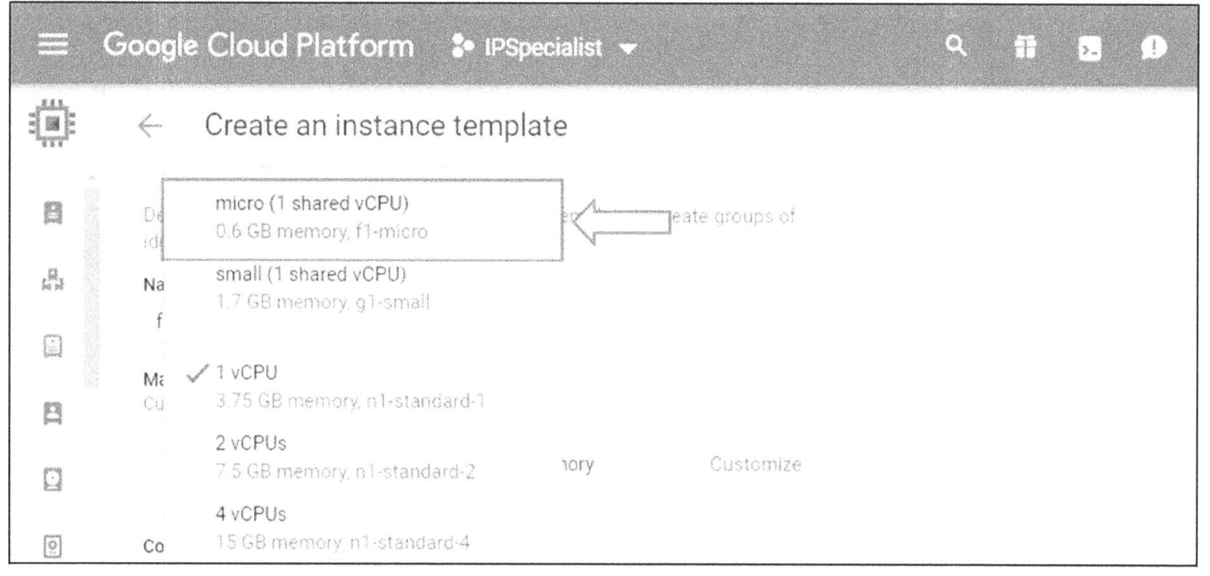

32. Select the created service account.

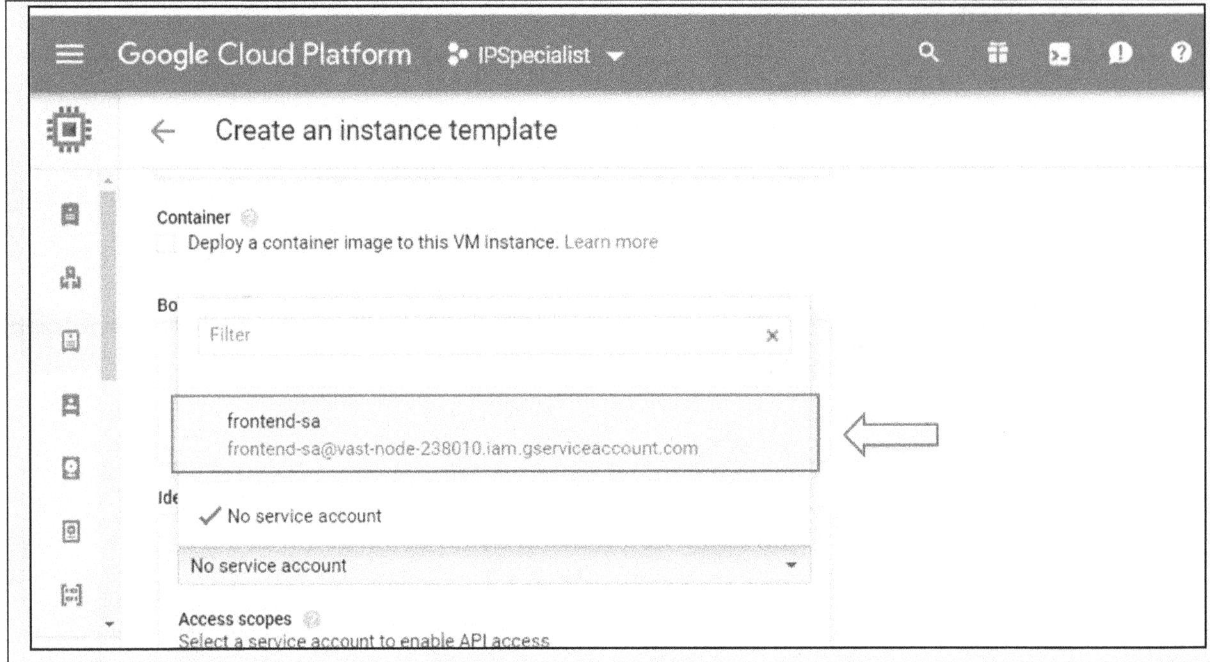

Access scopes are applied on default service account.

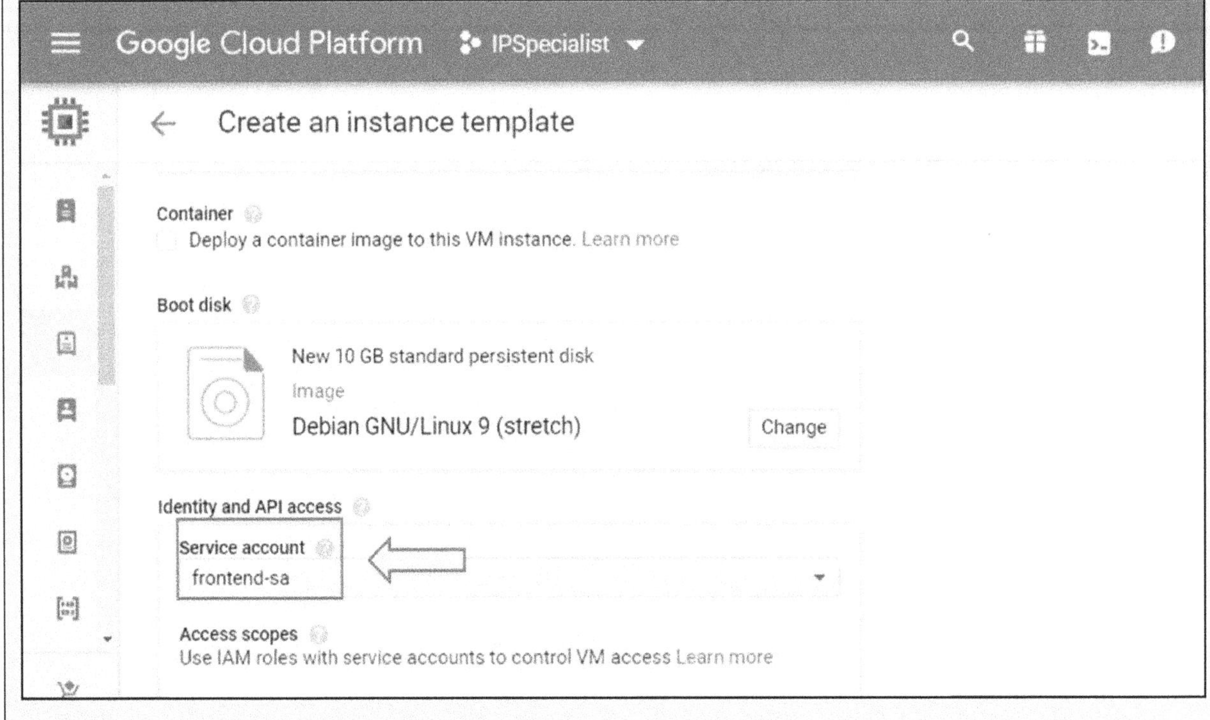

33. Dropdown this advance setting.

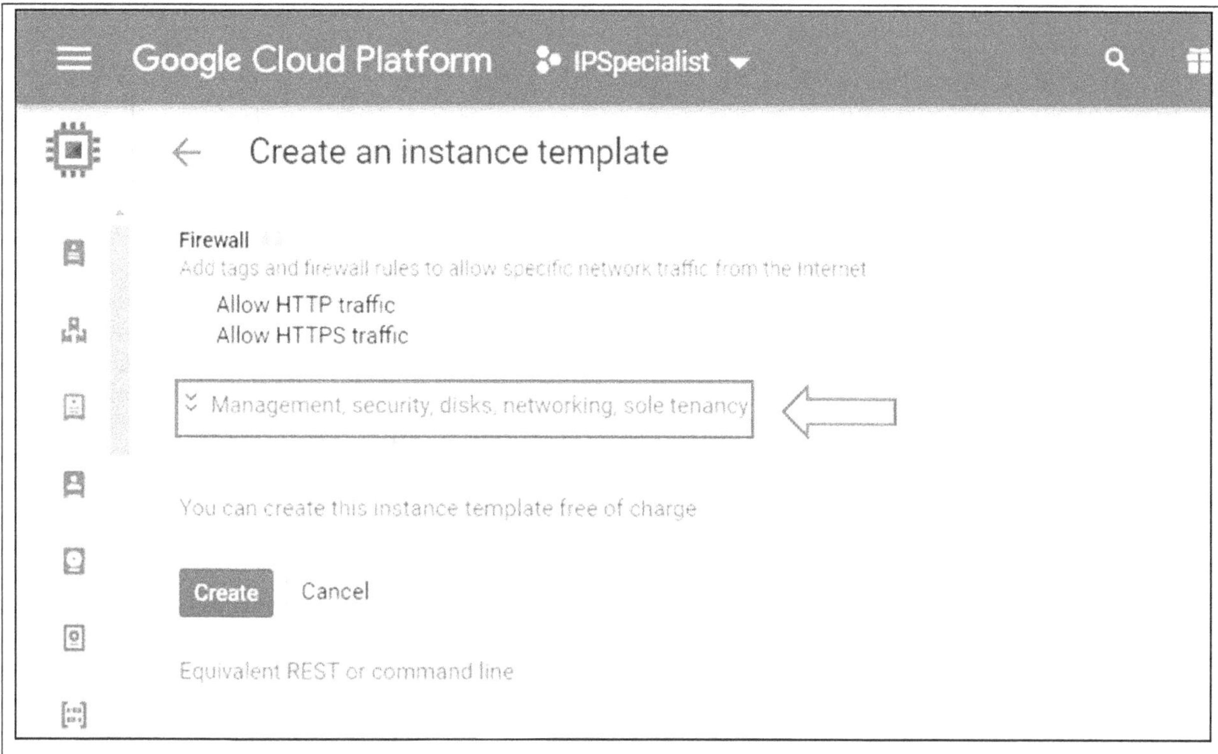

34. Select "Networking" tab.

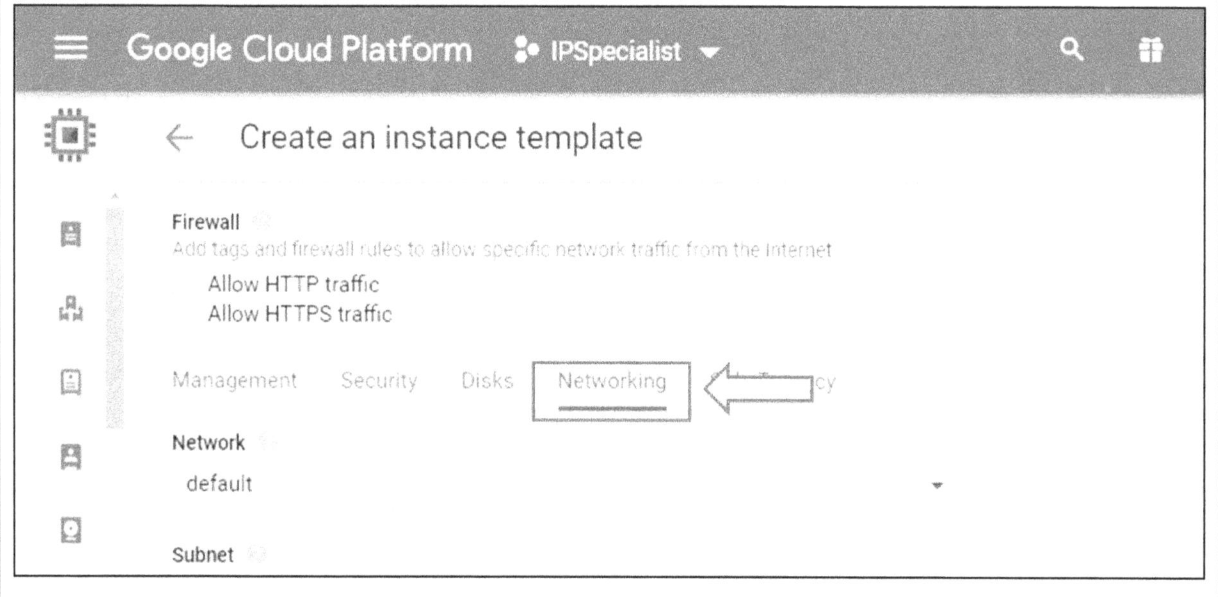

35. Select the VPC that was created and select the Subnet.

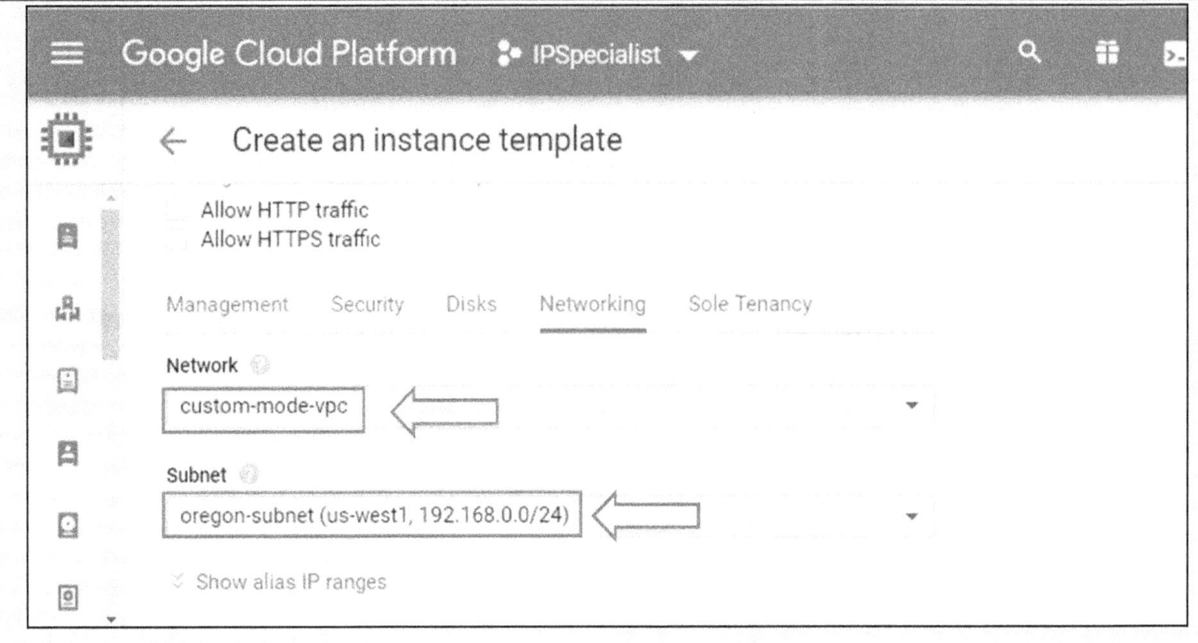

36. Click “Create”.

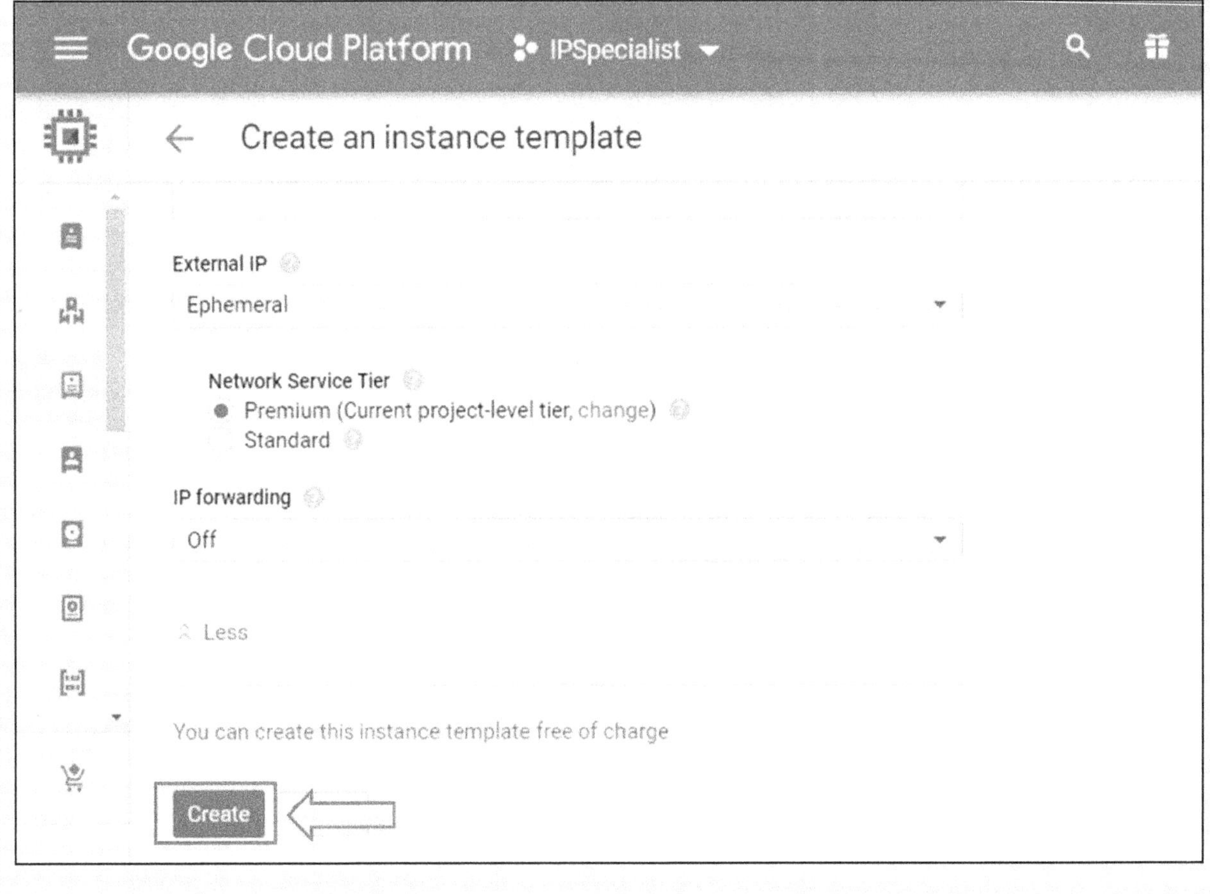

Instance template is created.

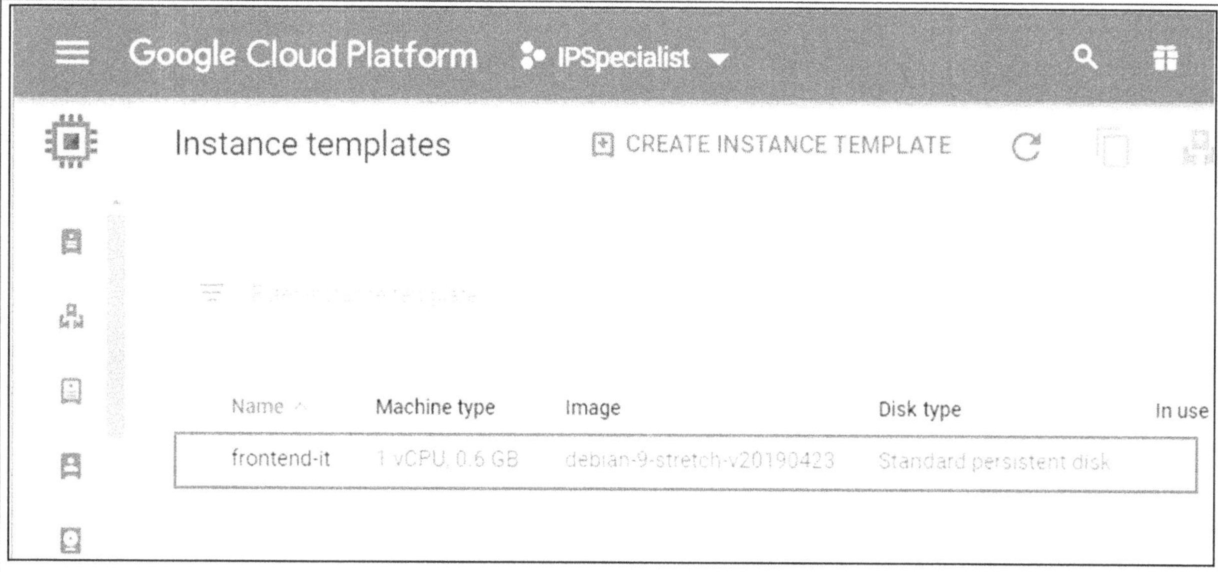

37. Go to "Instance groups".

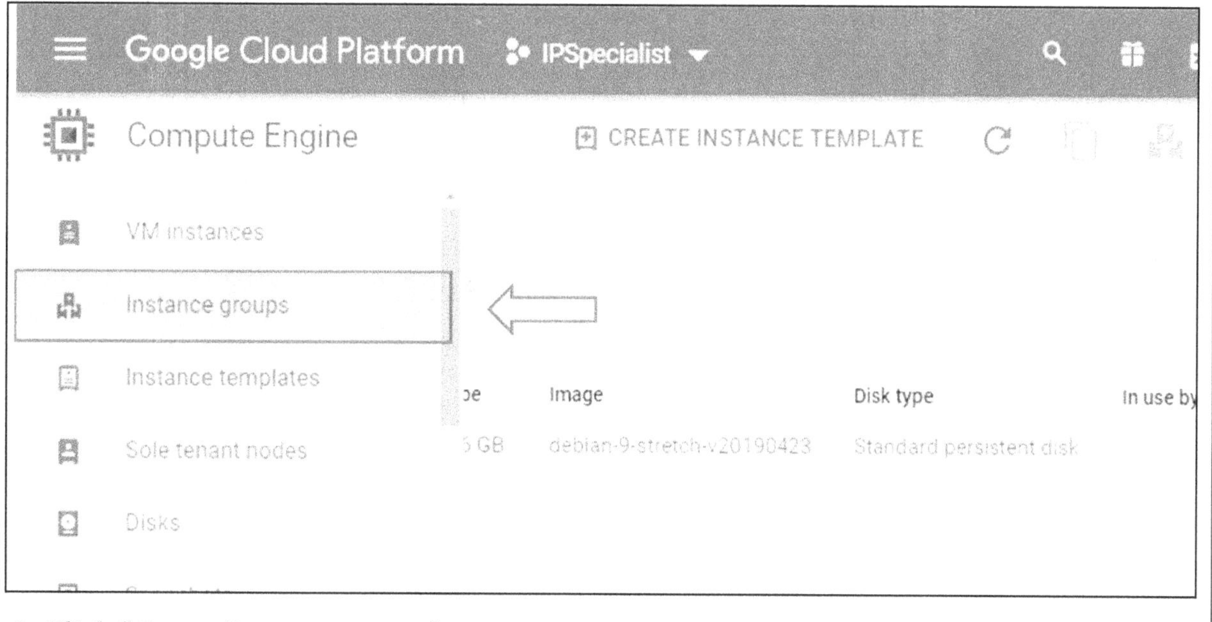

38. Click "Create Instance group".

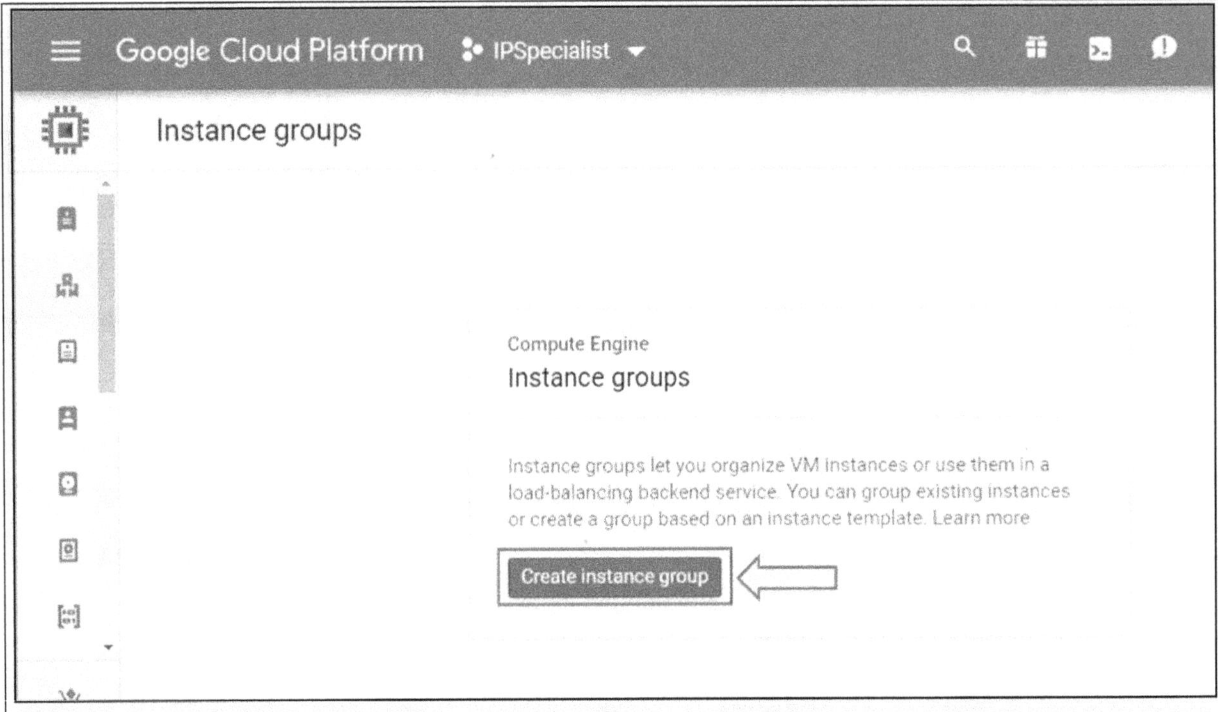

39. Enter any name and select "Multiple zones".

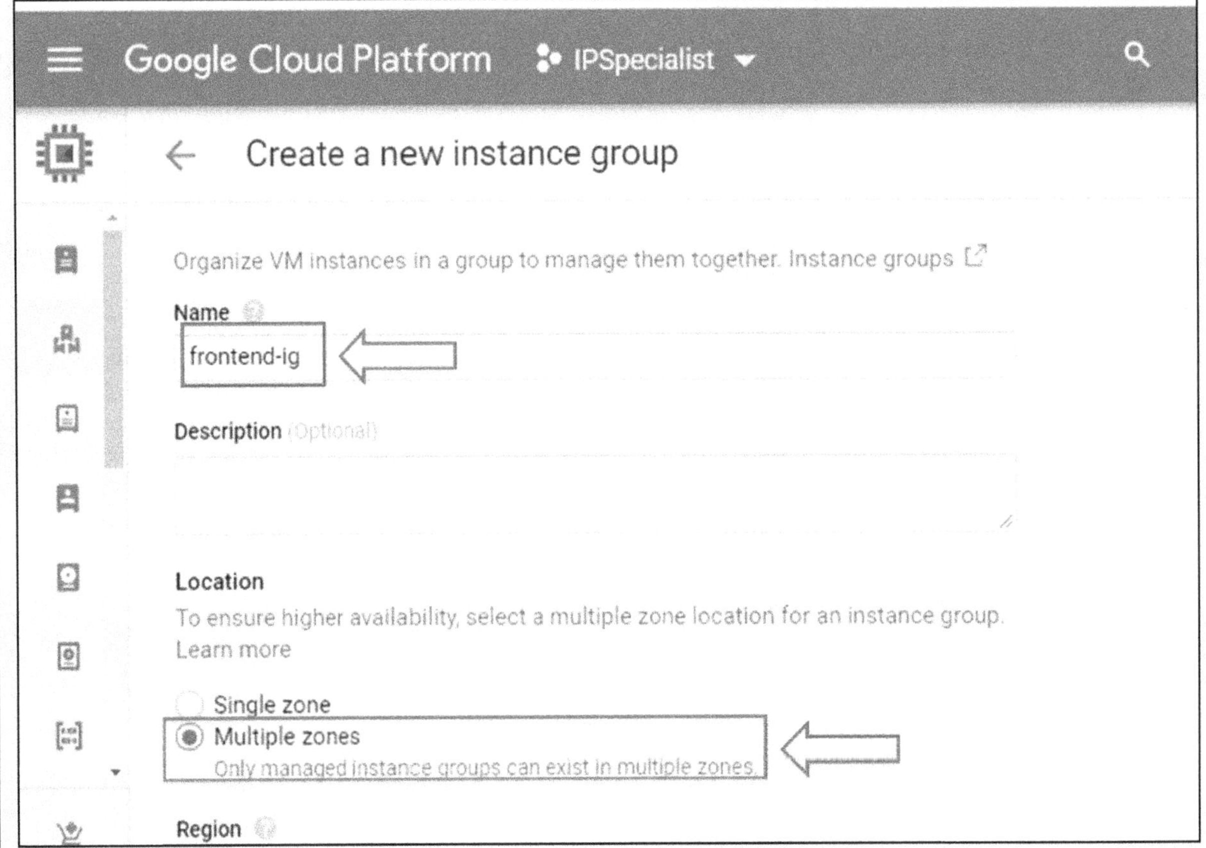

40. Select Region "us-west1" same as the VPC region and ensure that all zones are included.

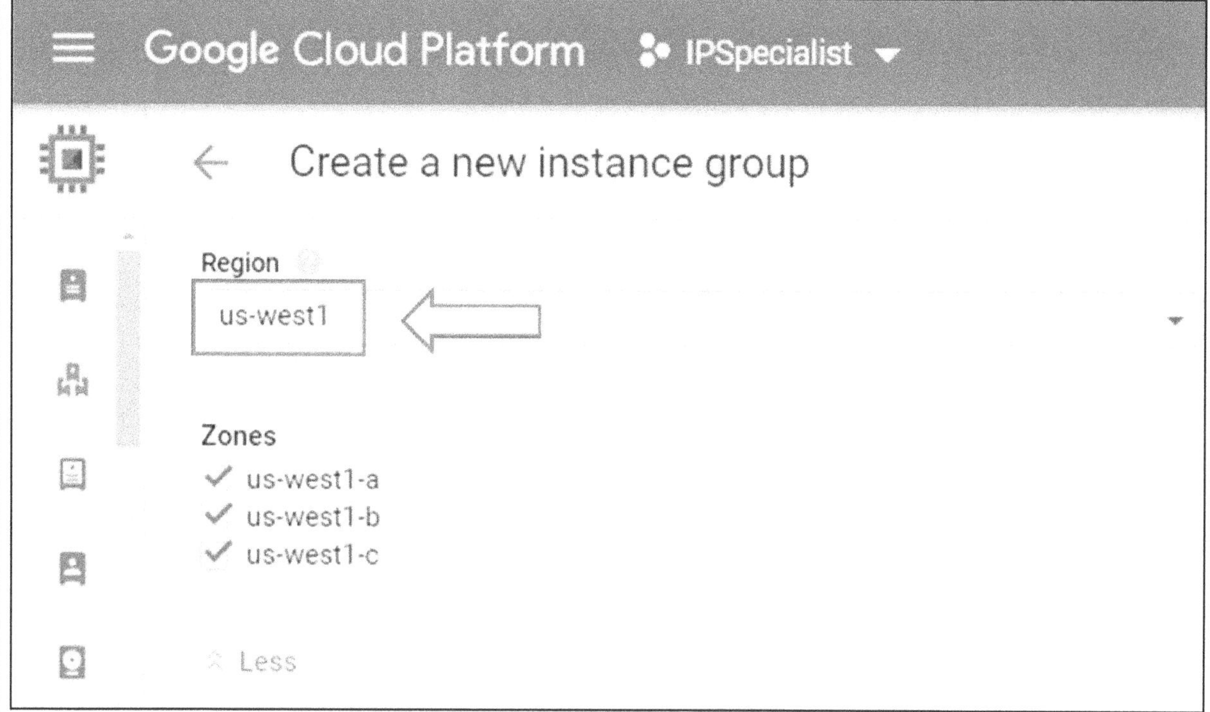

41. Select the Instance template created before.

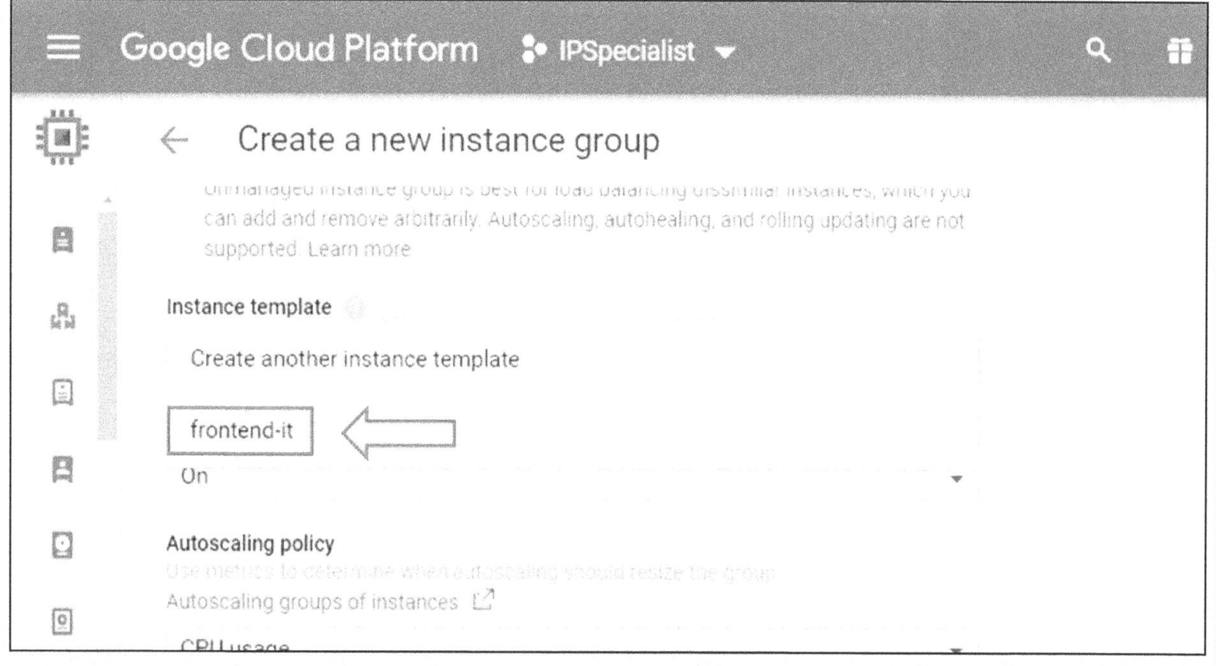

42. Change the Minimum number of instances "2" and Maximum number of instances "3".

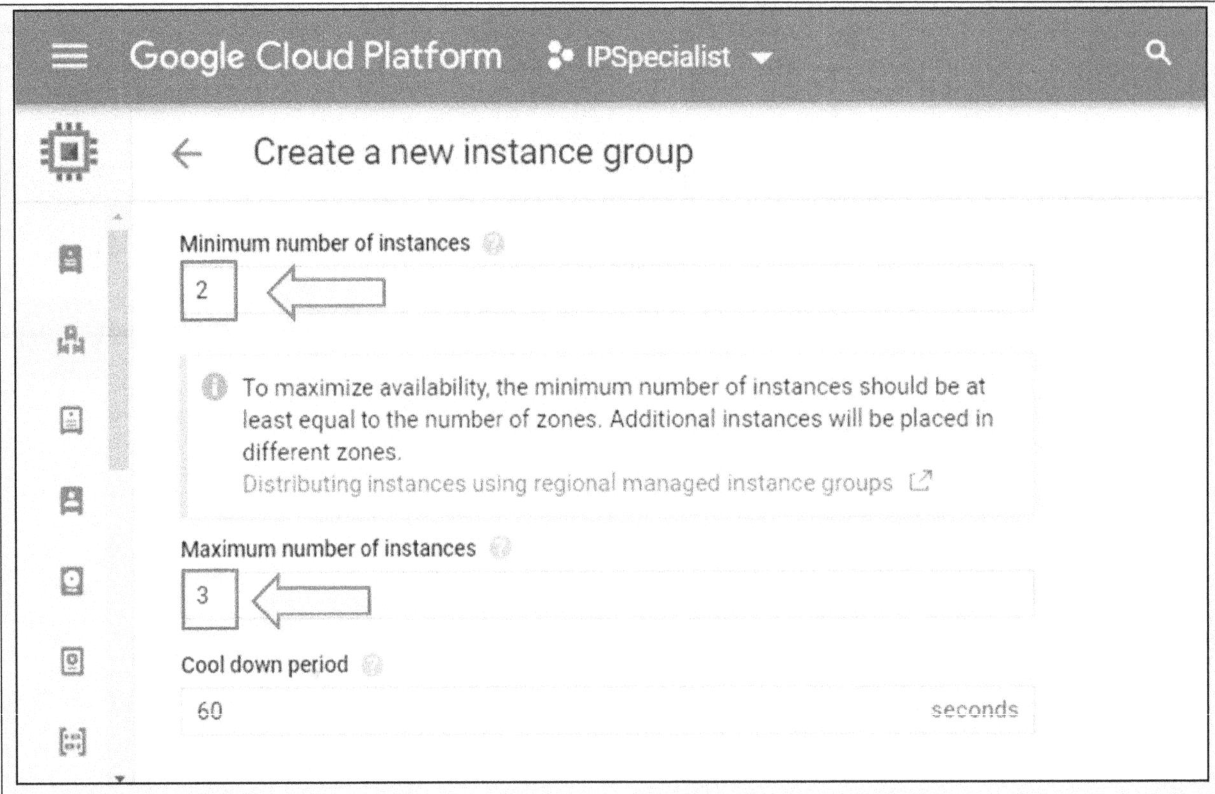

43. Click “Create”.

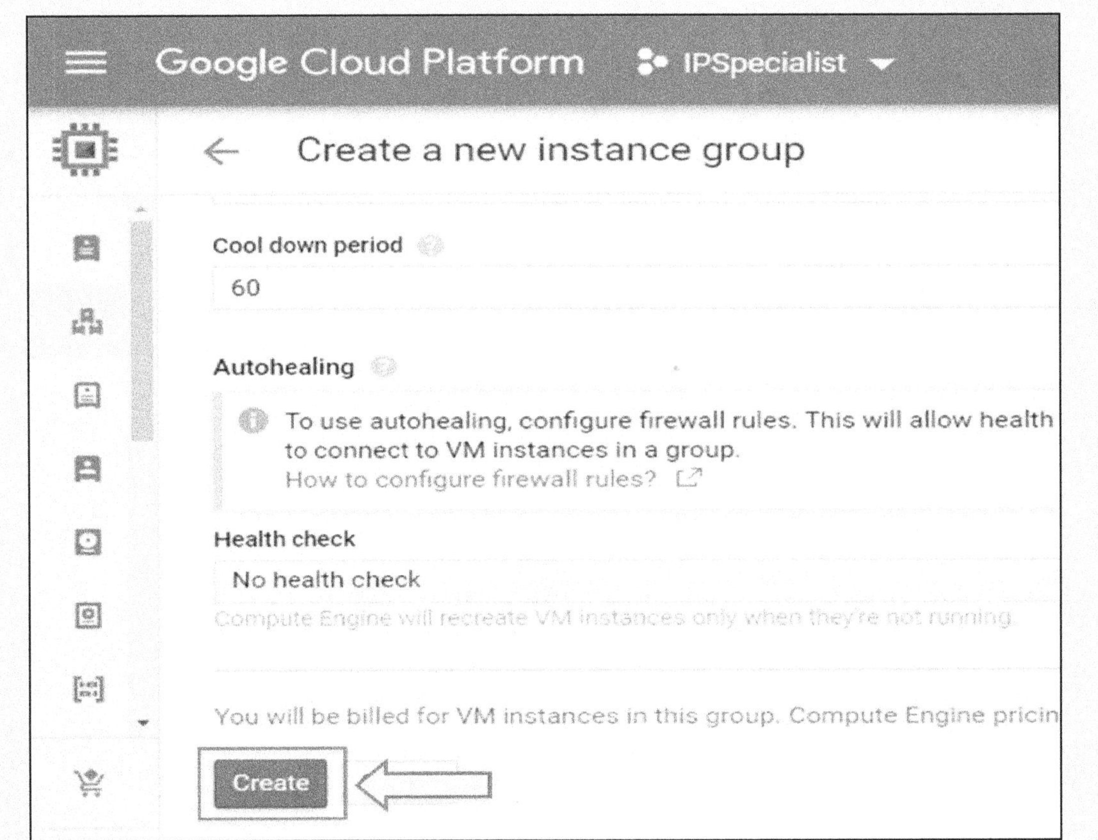

44. Click the instance.

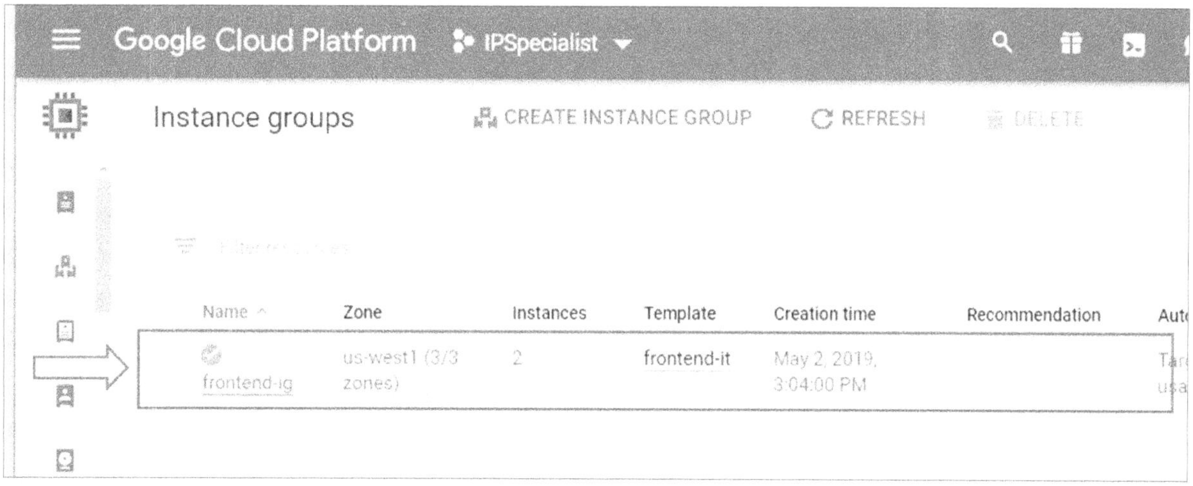

45. Copy one External IP address.

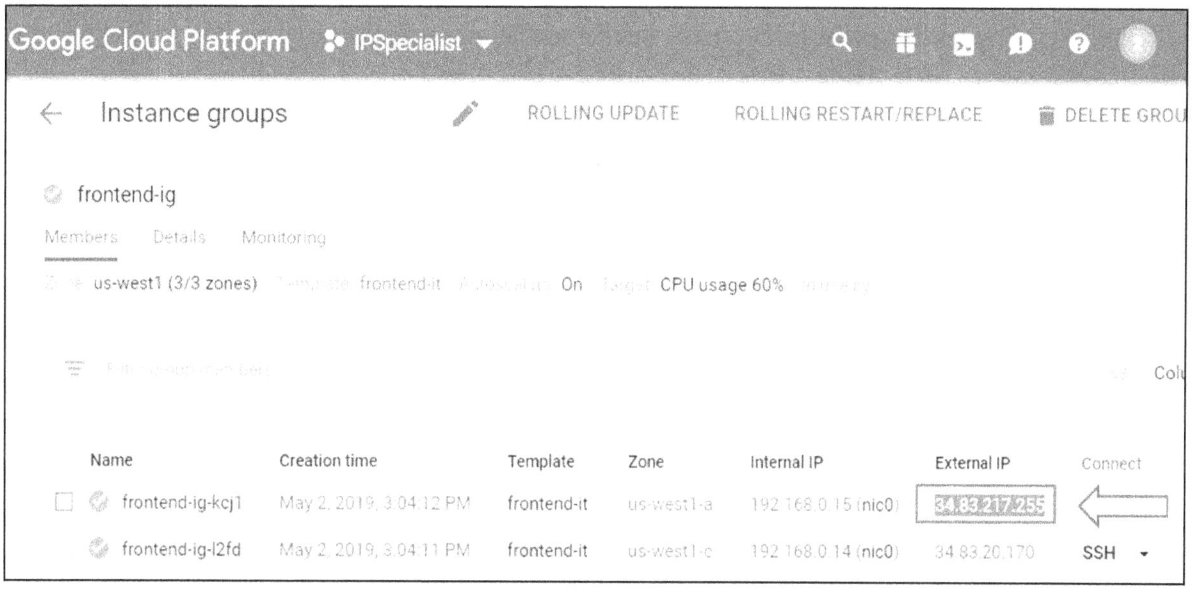

46. Activate Cloud Shell.

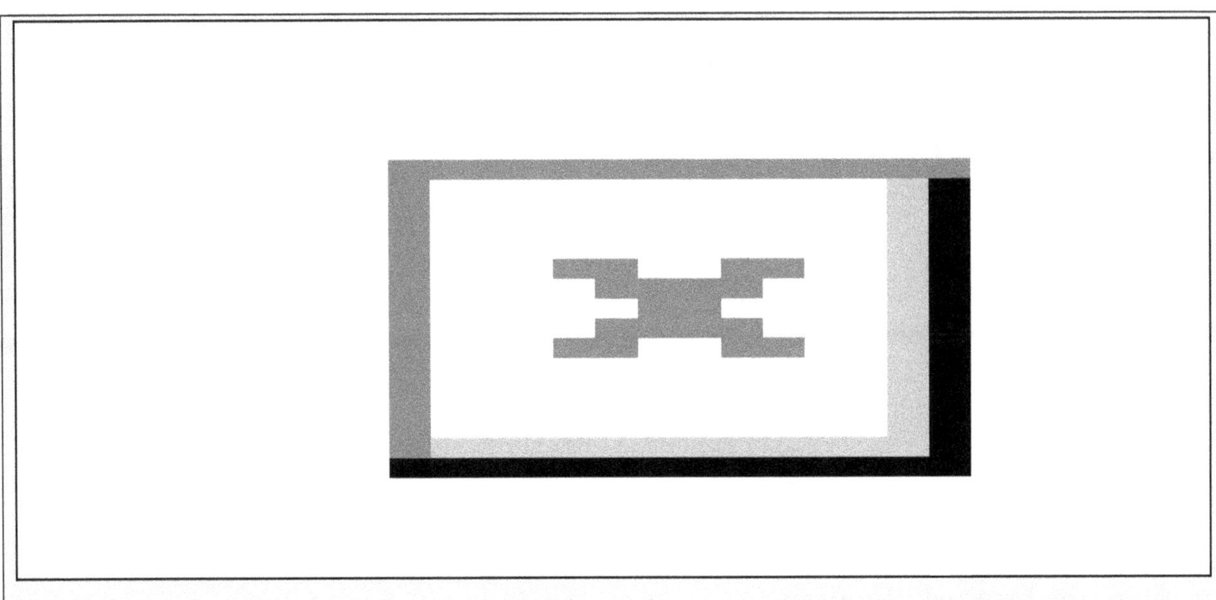

47. Ping that external IP address by using command "ping –c 3 <IPaddress>".

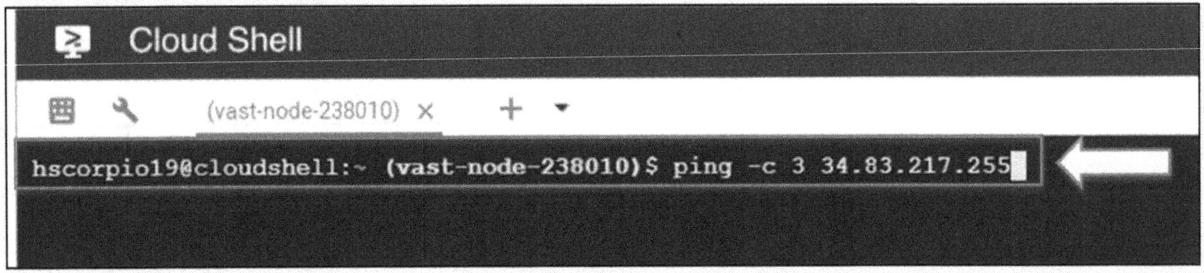

Ping is unsuccessful.

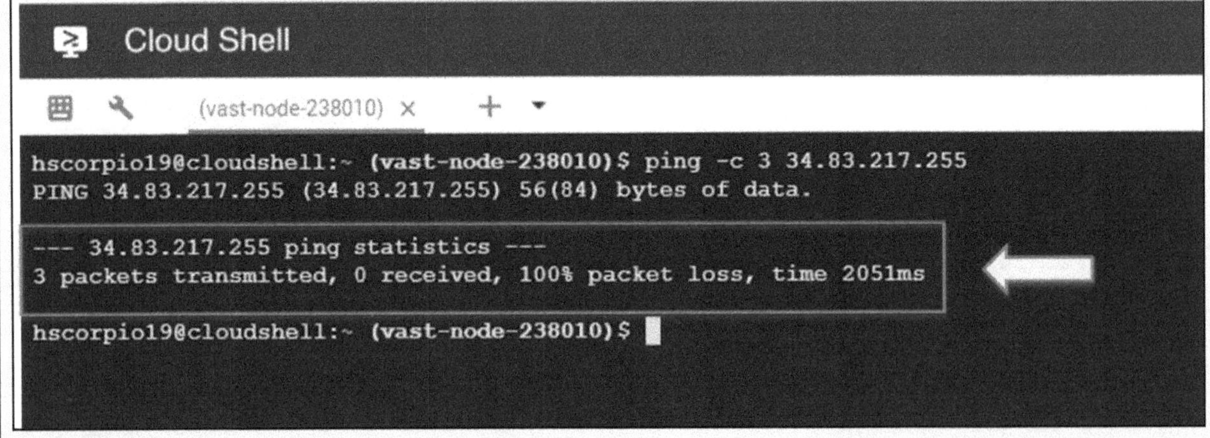

For checking the reason of failed ping.

48. Go to the VPC Networks in the console.

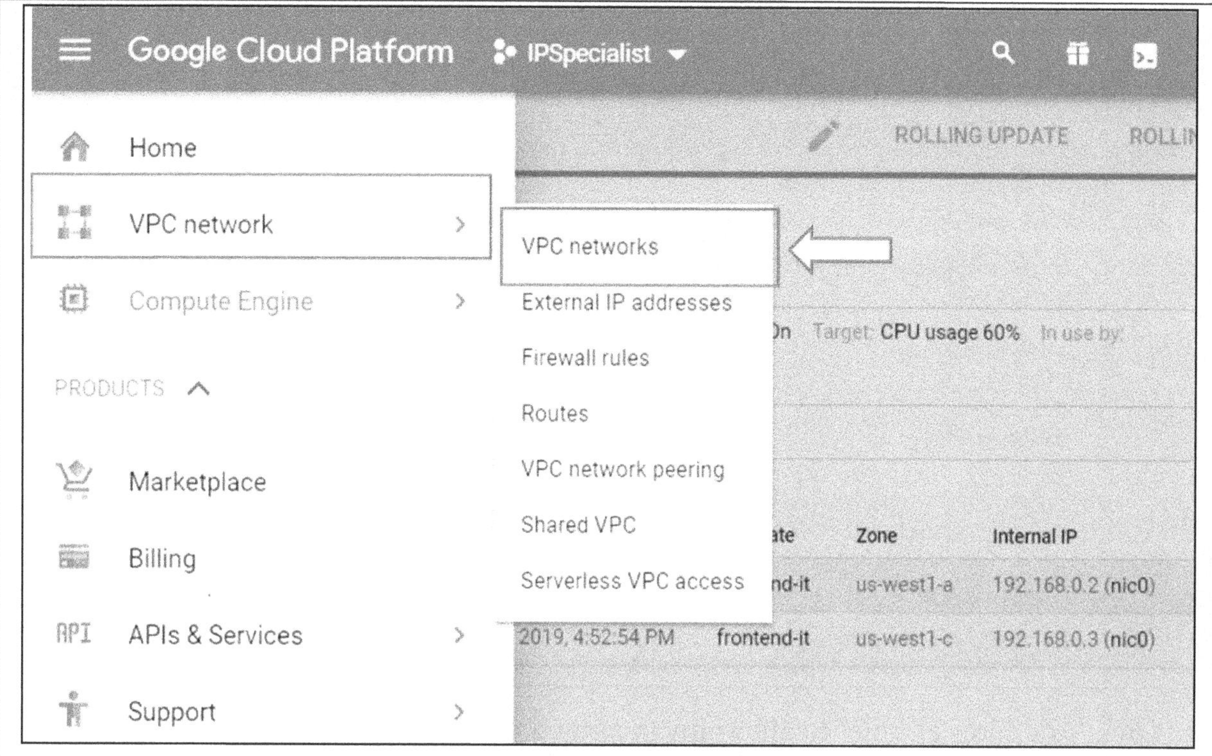

49. Select your VPC.

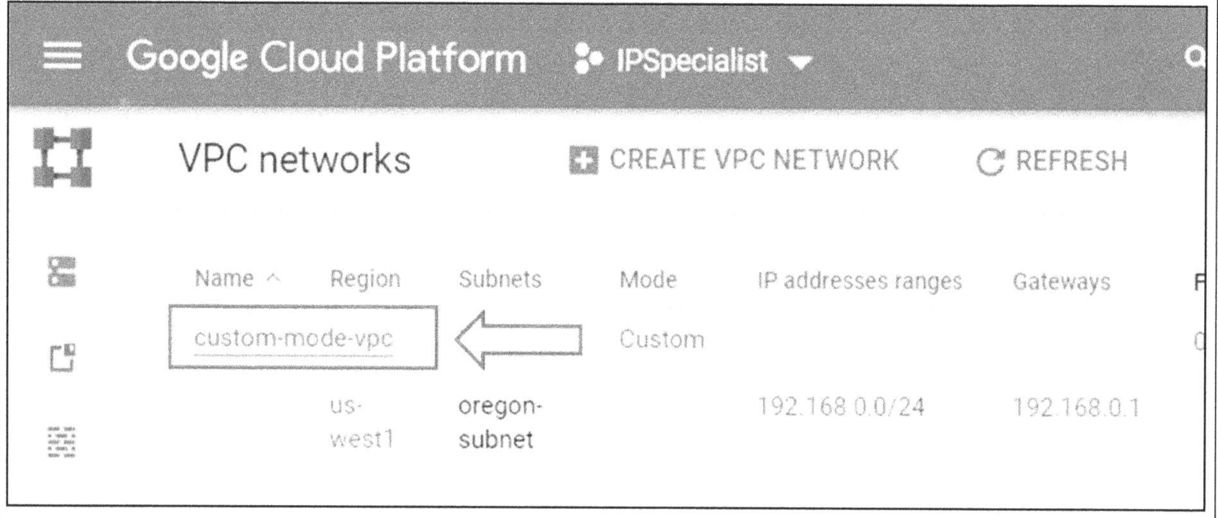

50. Select "Firewalls rule". There are no Firewall rules.

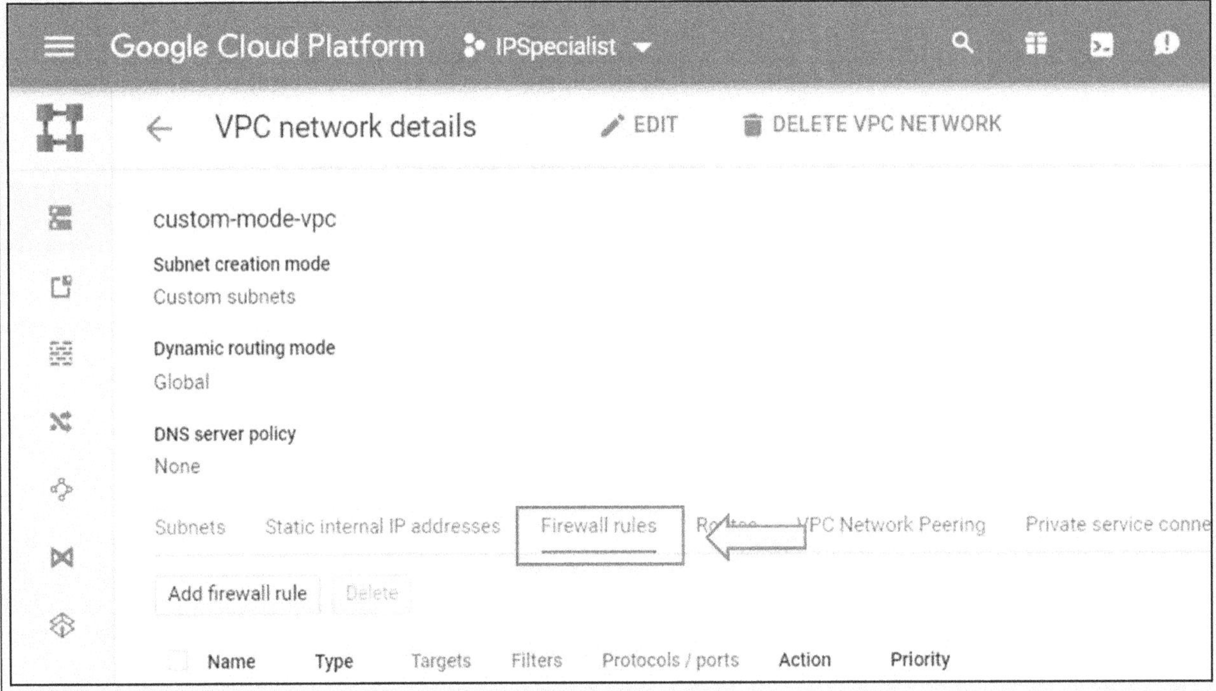

51. Click "Add Firewall rule" to allow any incoming traffic to the instance.

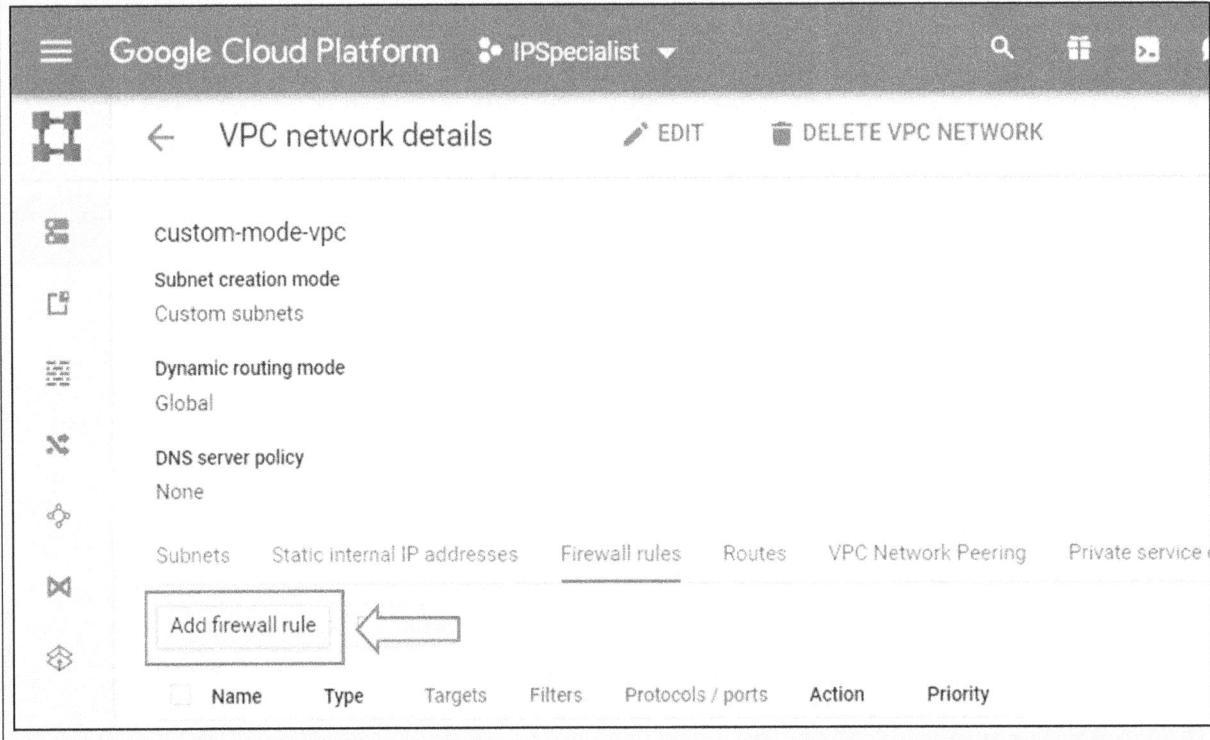

52. Enter any name that you can remember that it is a Firewall rule.

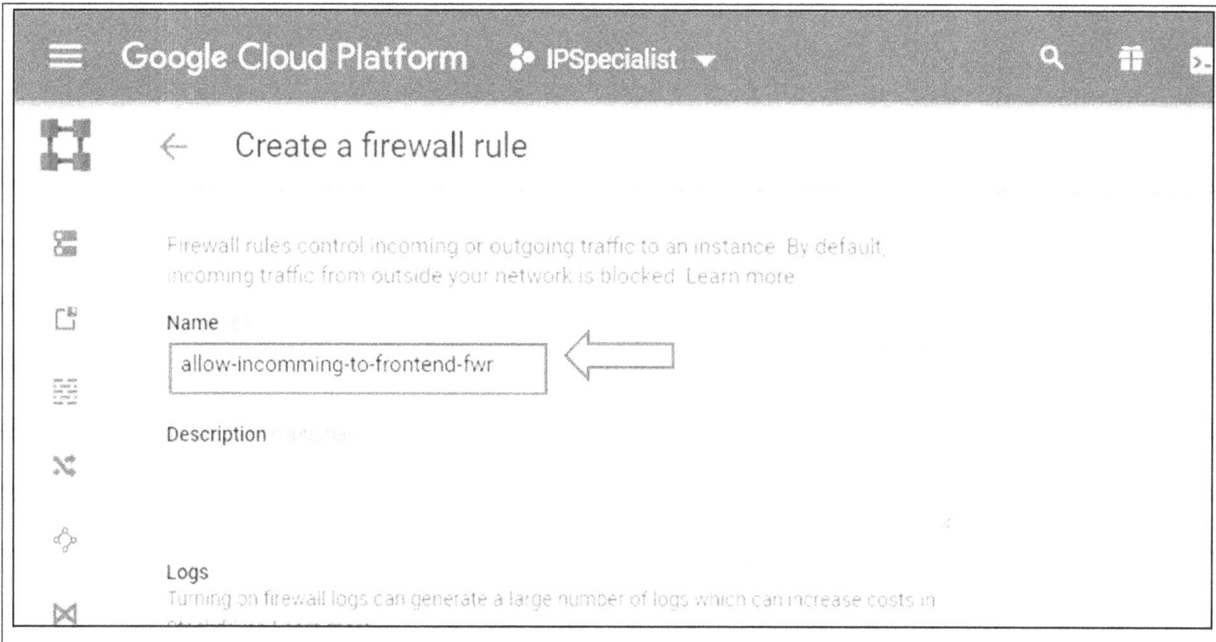

53. Select the Direction of traffic "ingress" and Action as match "Allow".

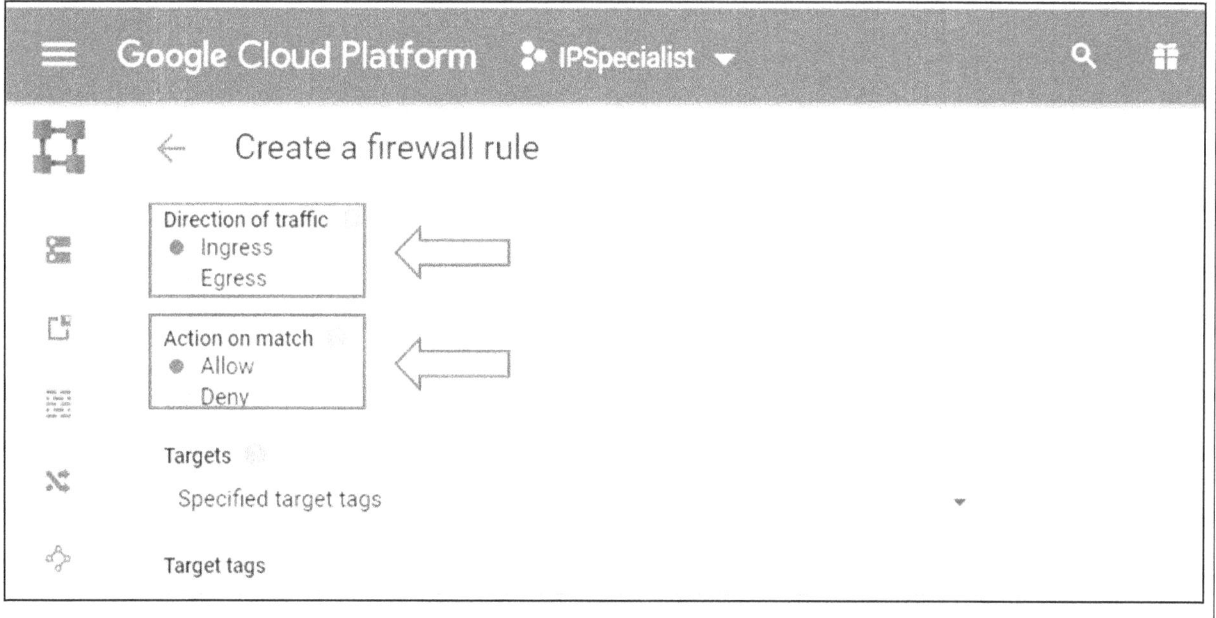

54. Select the Target "Specified service account".

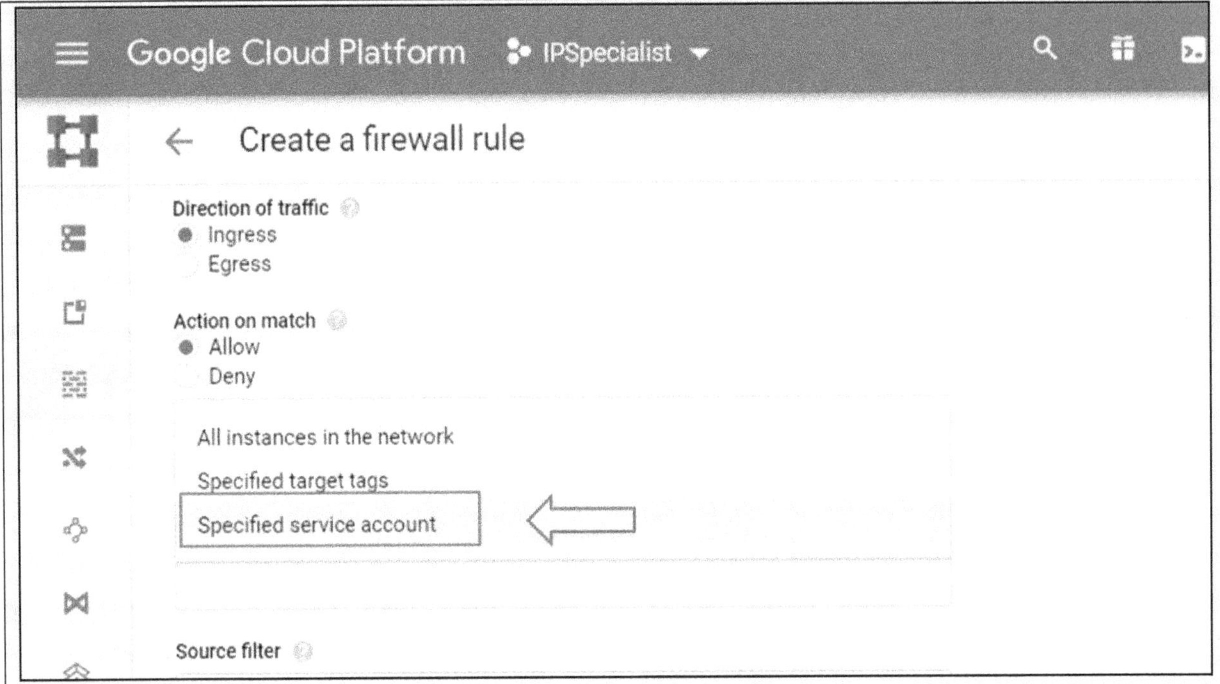

55. Select Service account scope "In this project" and select your Target service account.

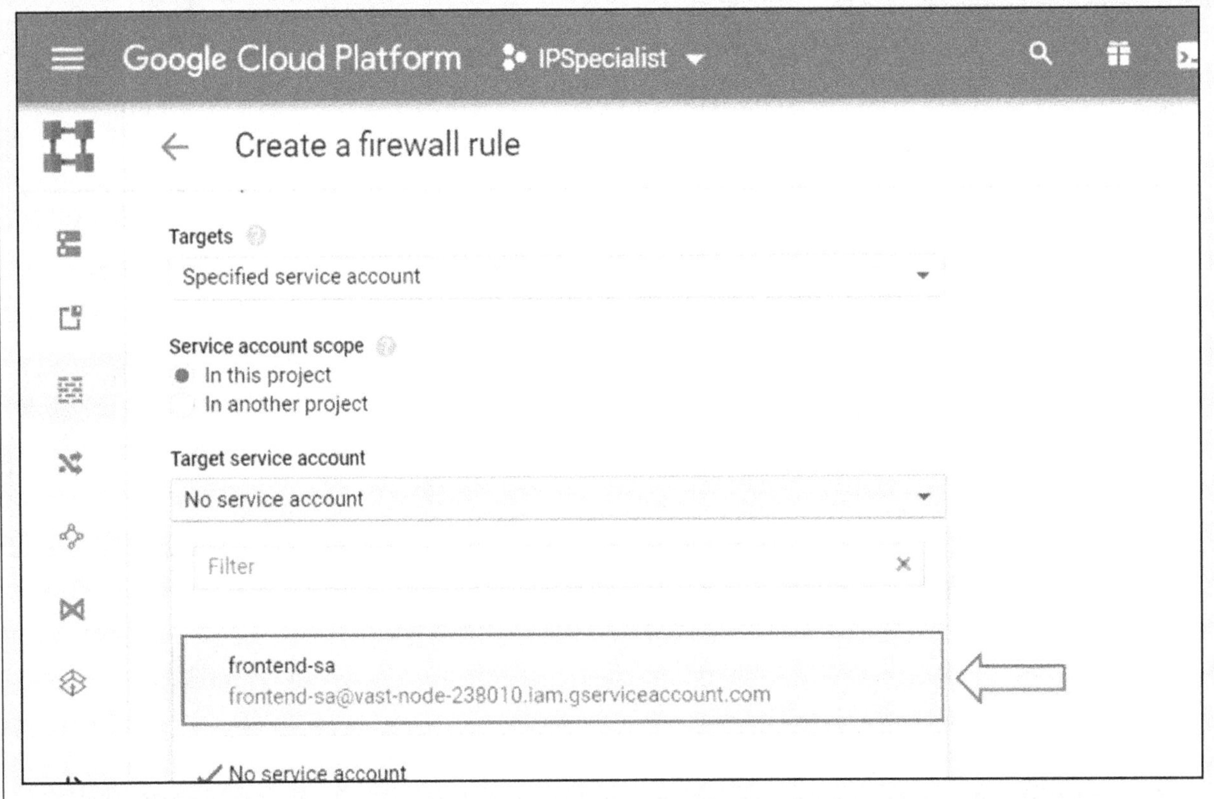

56. Enter Source IP ranges "0.0.0.0/0" for allowing traffic from anywhere and Enter Other protocols "icmp" for ping.

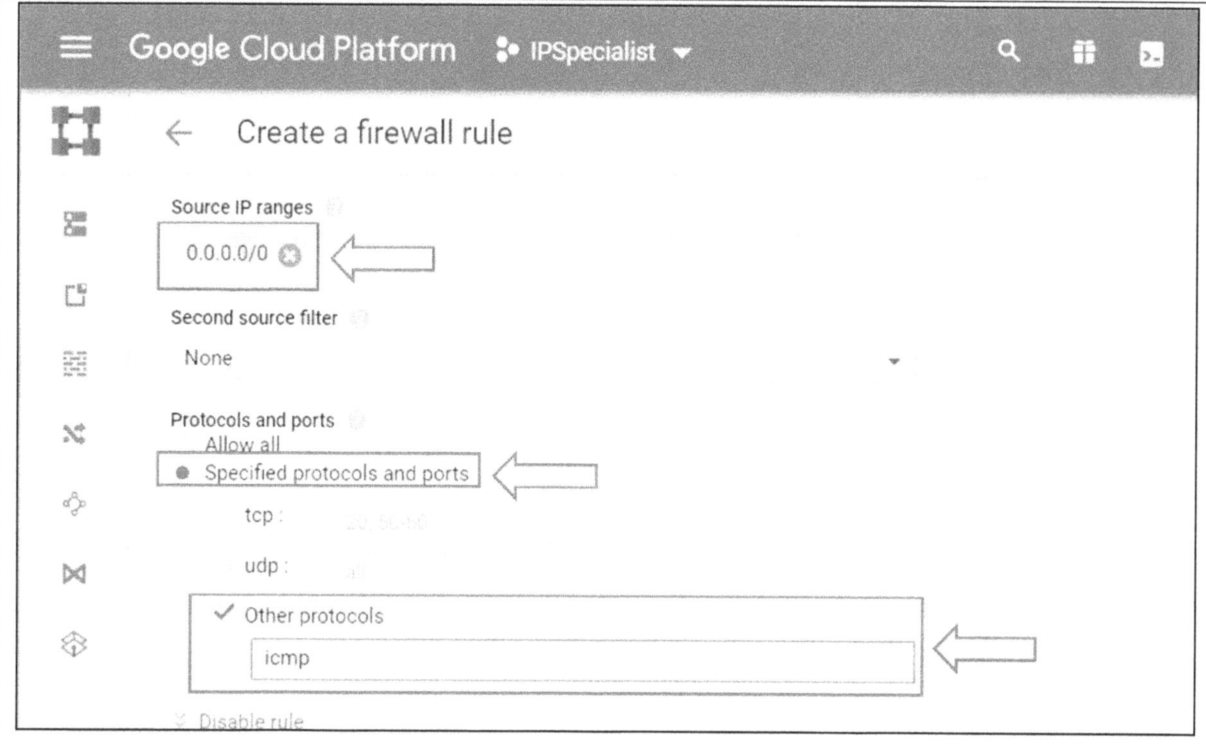

57. Click "Create".

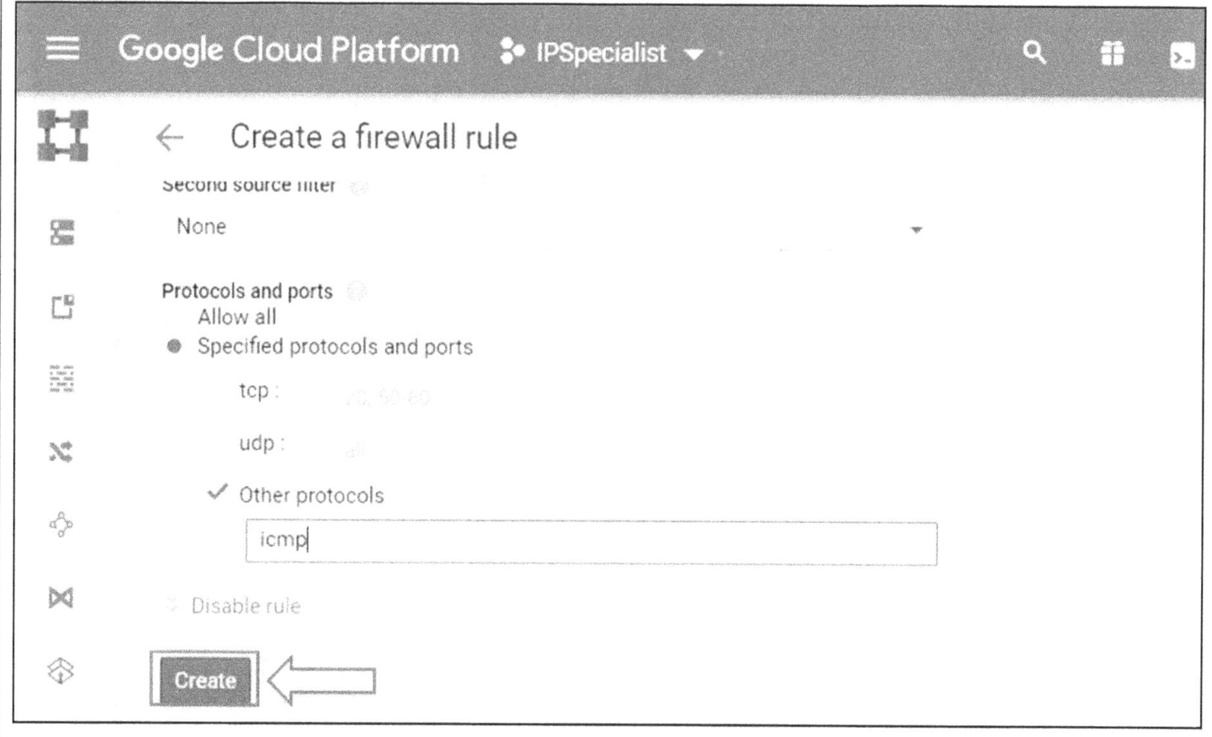

58. Switch back to Cloud Shell when Firewall rule is created and ping the instance again.

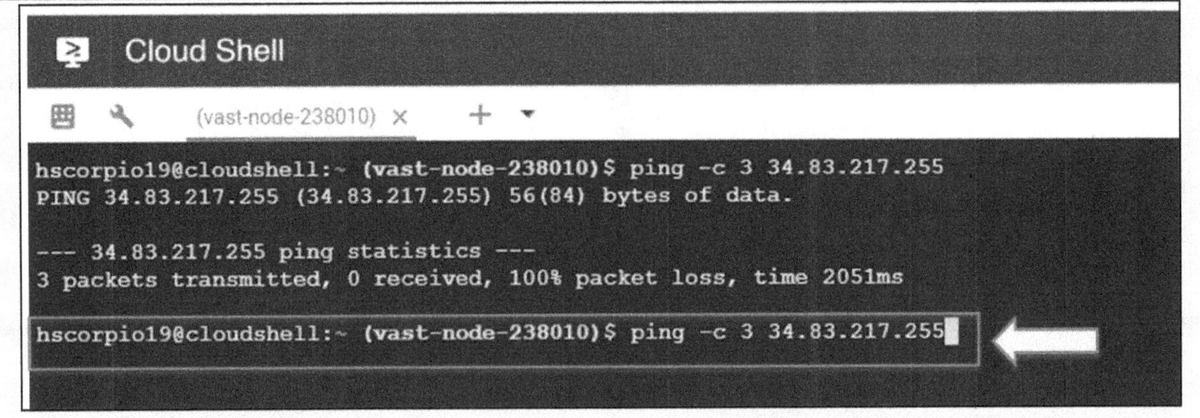

Ping is successful.

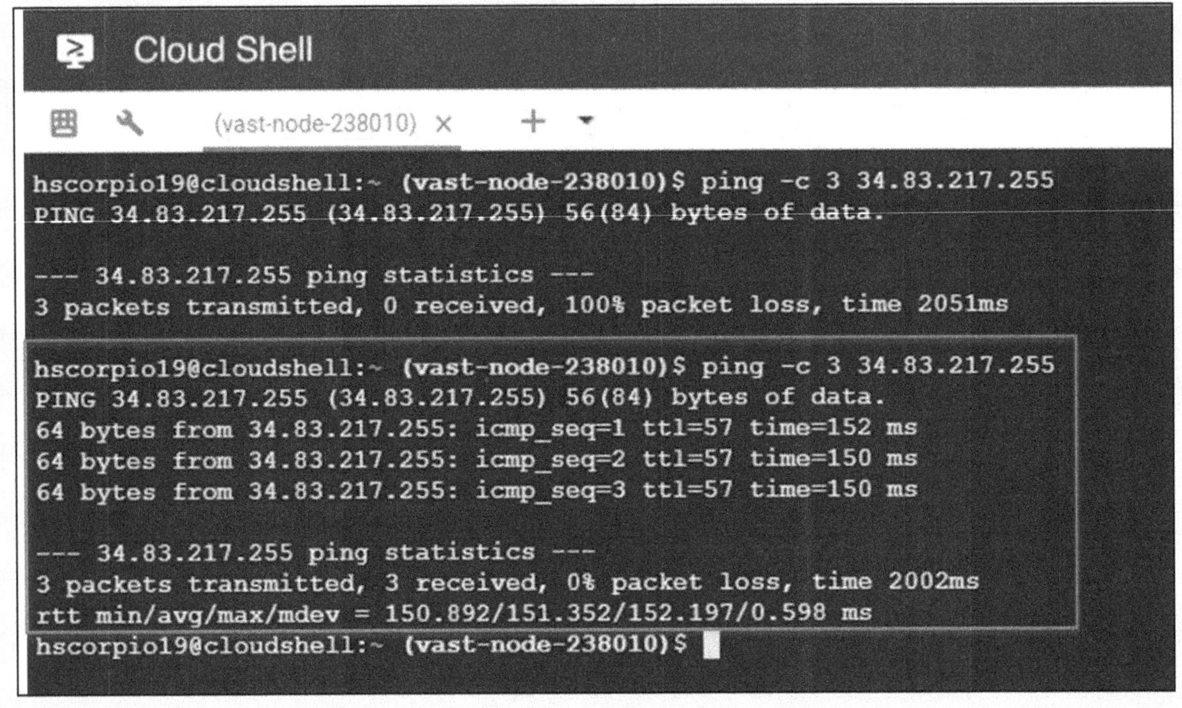

59. Go to instance groups and try to connect to an instance through SSH.

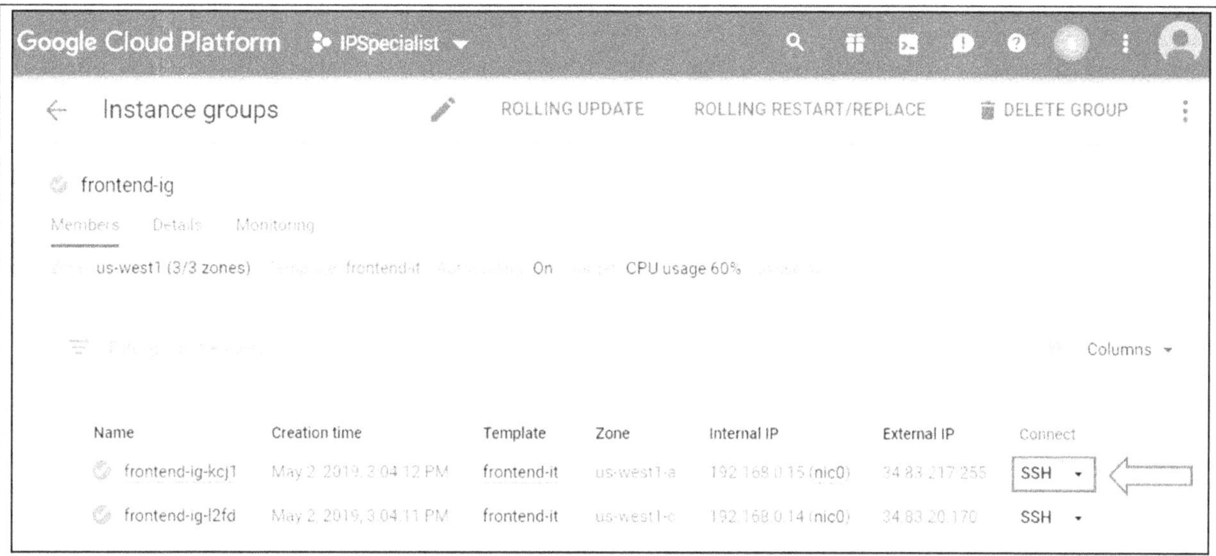

You are unable to connect to this instance through SSH as we have not allowed SSH in the Firewall rule.

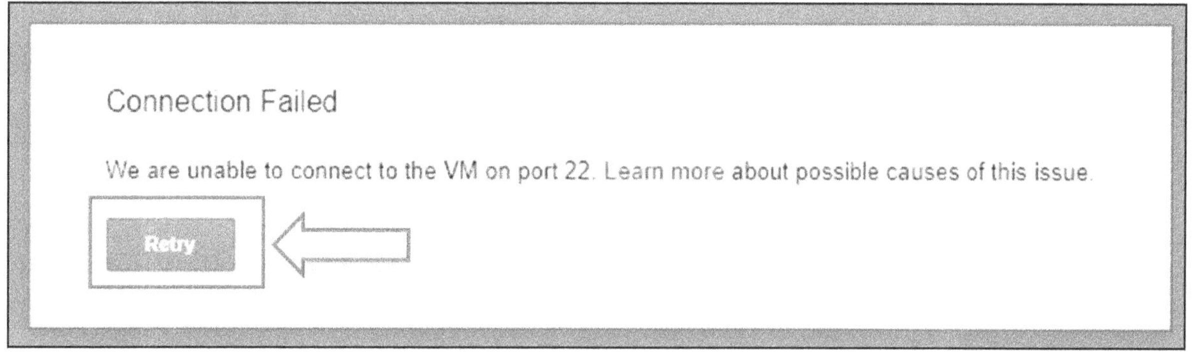

60. Go to that instance if you want to allow SSH to only one instance in the group.

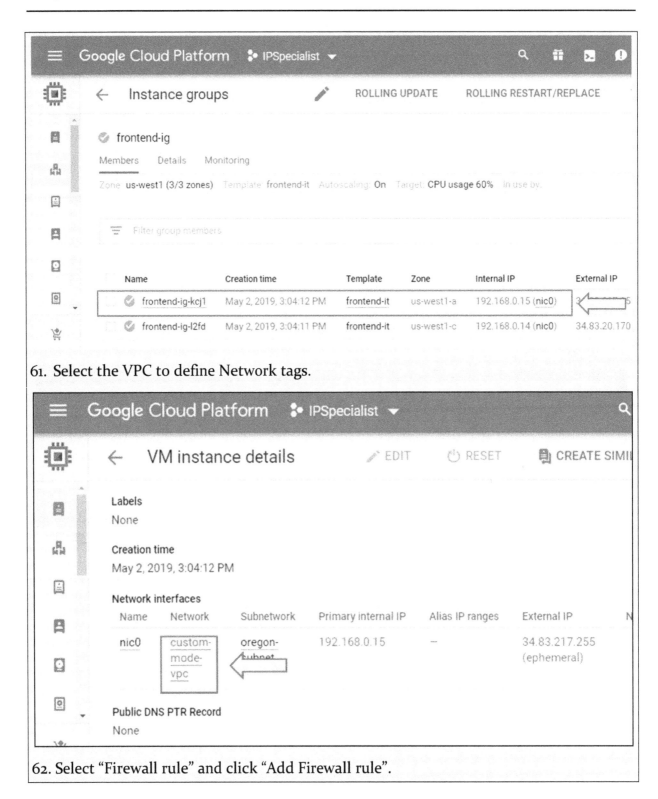

61. Select the VPC to define Network tags.

62. Select "Firewall rule" and click "Add Firewall rule".

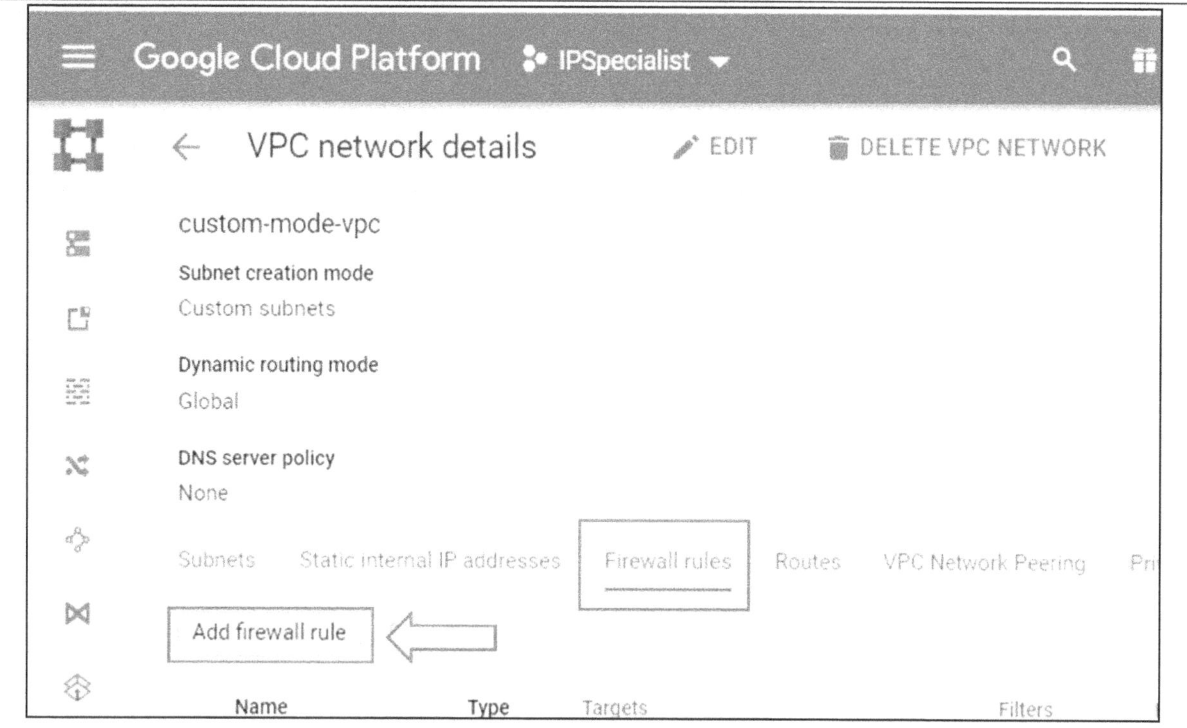

63. Enter any name.

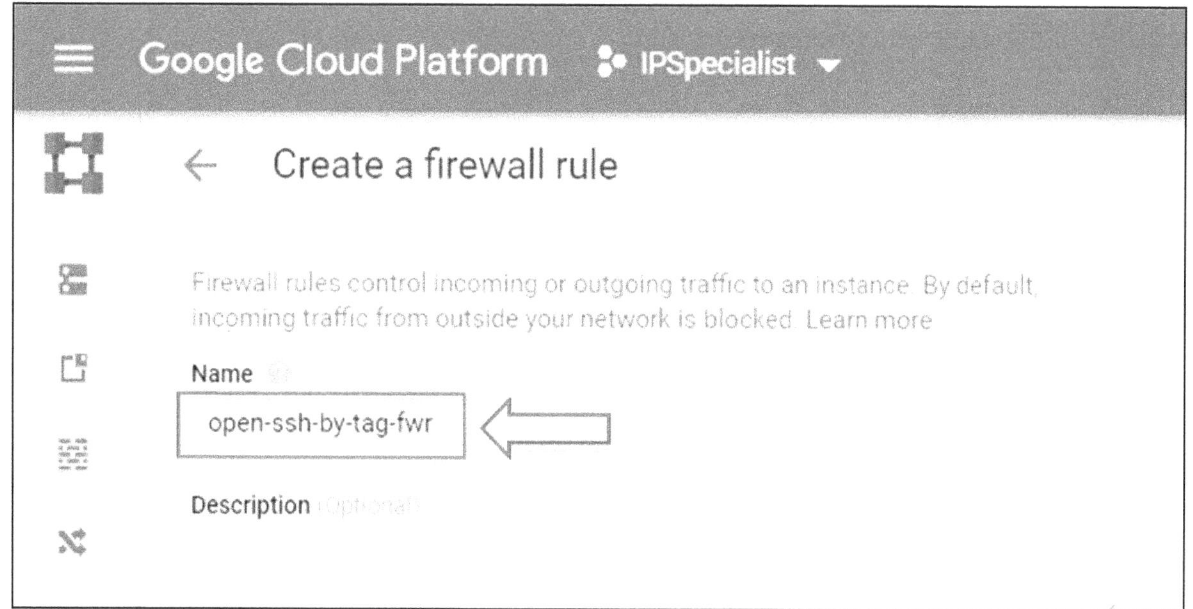

64. Set traffic ingress to allow and Targets as "Specified target tags".
65. Provide a target tag.

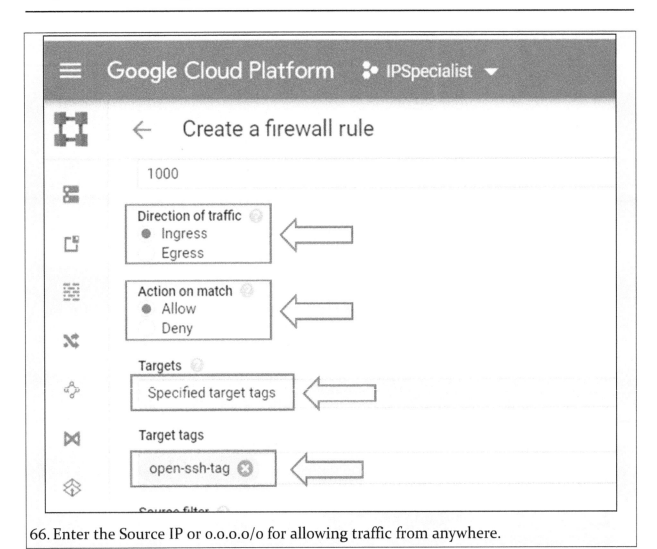

66. Enter the Source IP or 0.0.0.0/0 for allowing traffic from anywhere.

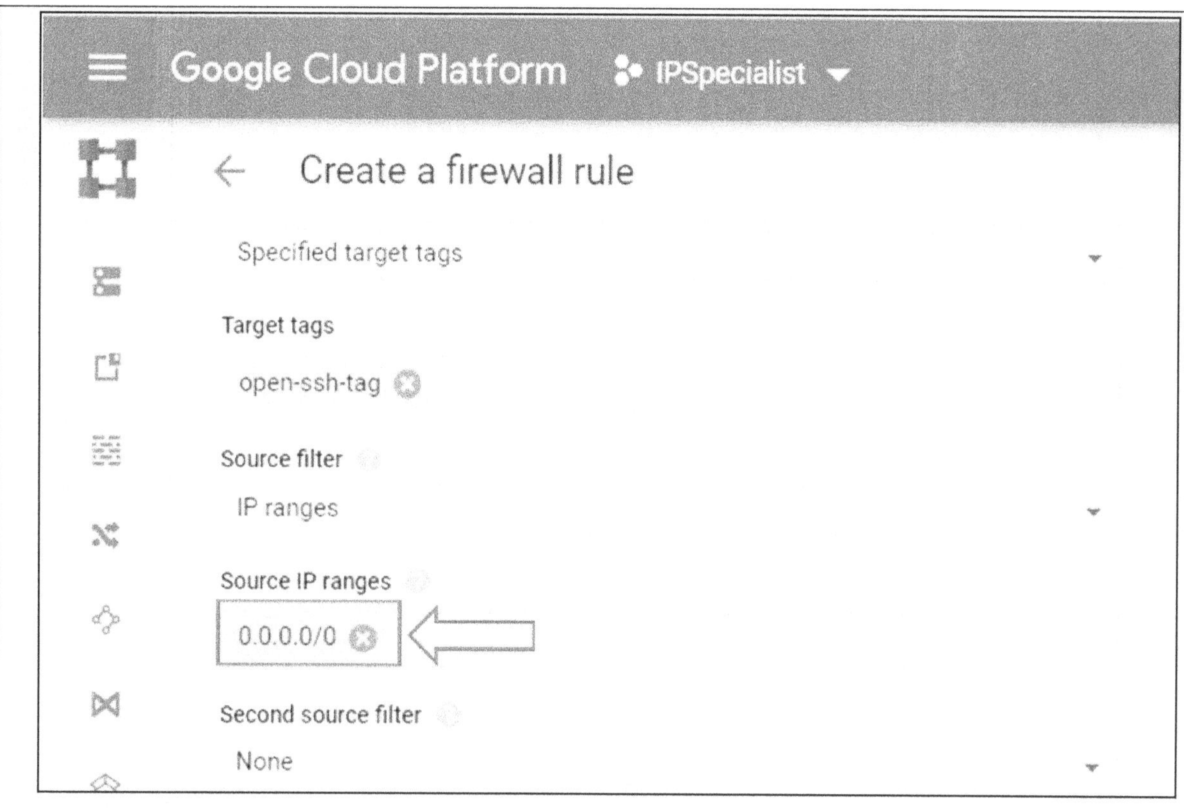

67. Select protocol tcp to 22 for SSH.

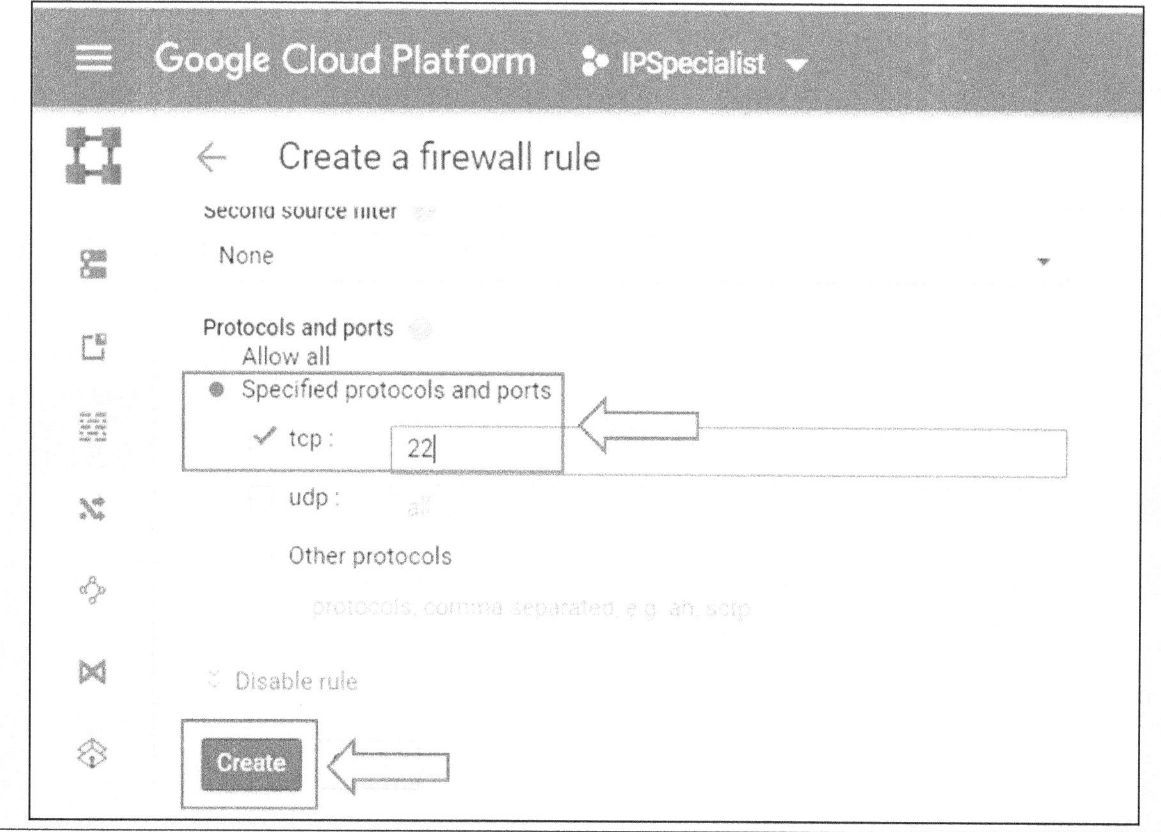

Firewall specified tag is created.

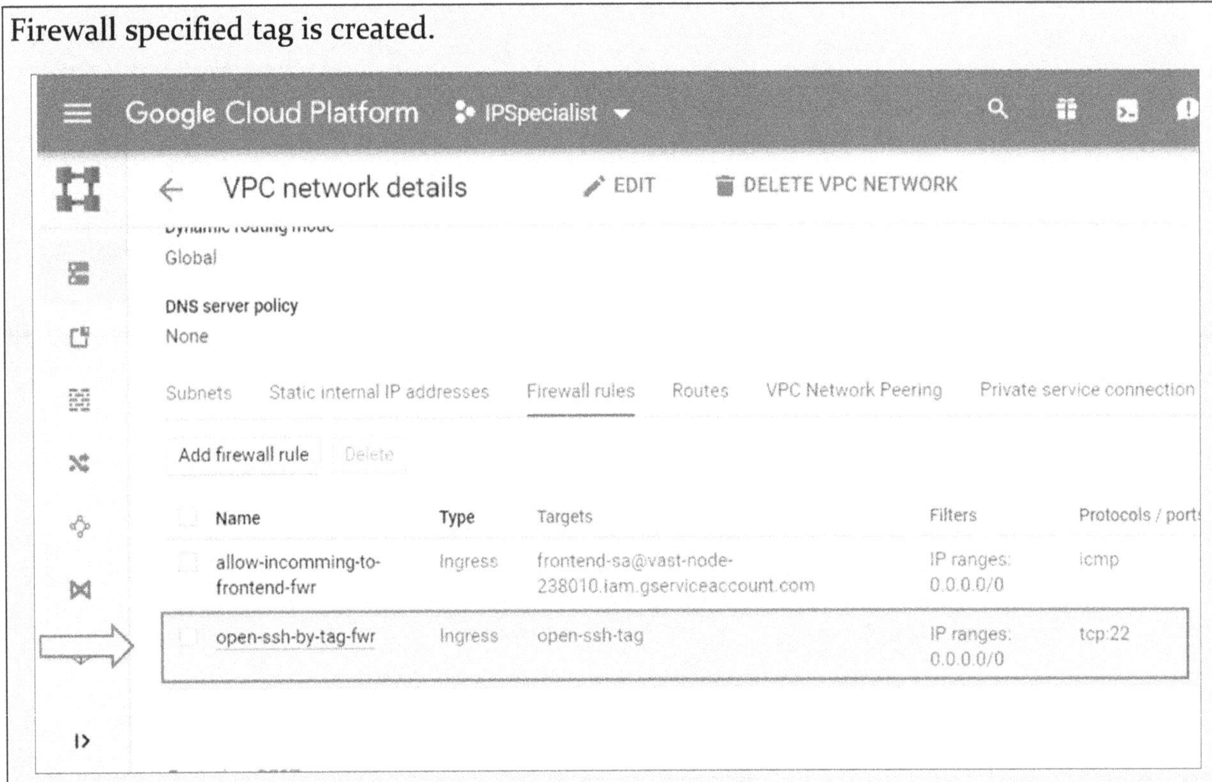

68. Now, go to the Cloud Shell and enter the command "gcloud compute instances add-tags instancename --tags=open-ssh-tag" to edit network tag in the particular instance.

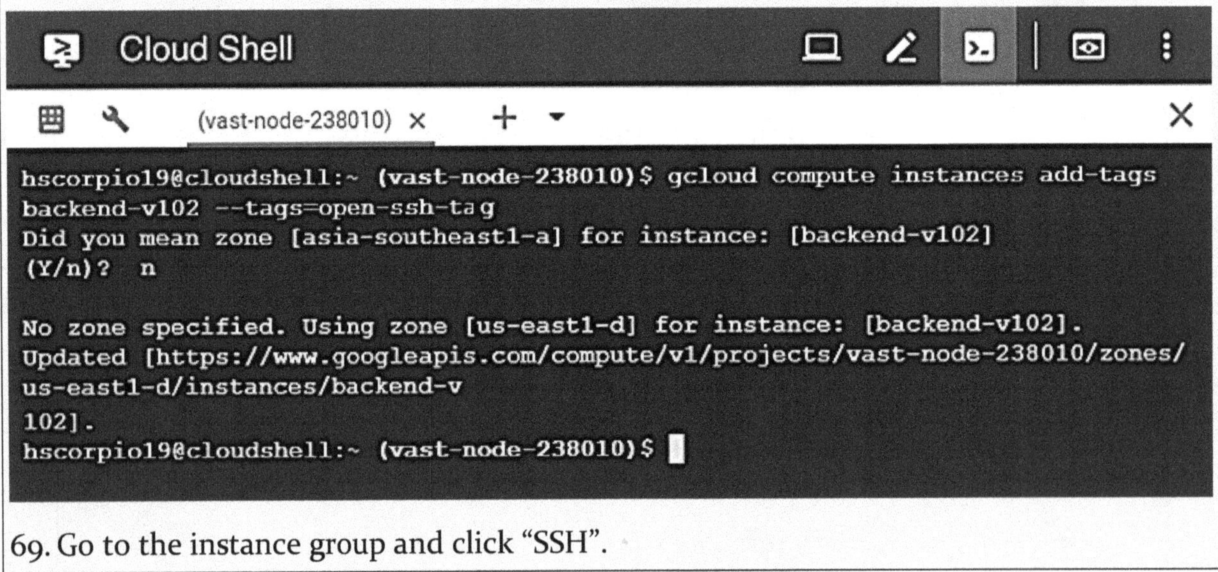

69. Go to the instance group and click "SSH".

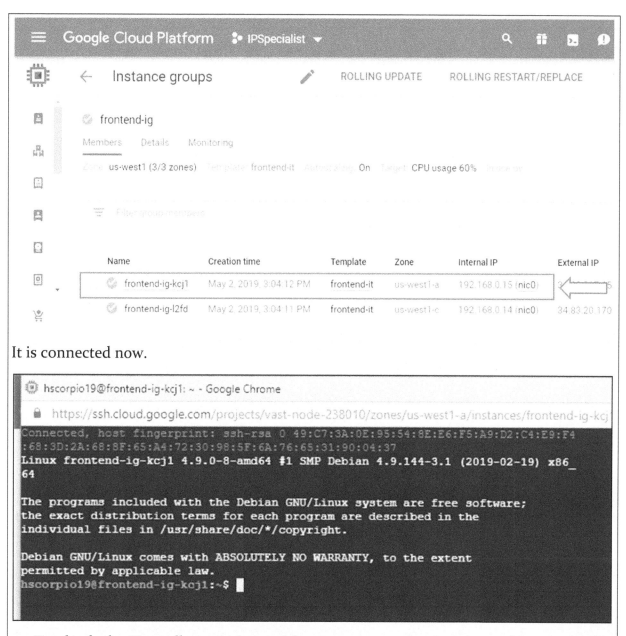

It is connected now.

```
Connected, host fingerprint: ssh-rsa 0 49:C7:3A:0E:95:54:8E:E6:F5:A9:D2:C4:E9:F4
:68:3D:2A:68:8F:65:A4:72:30:98:5F:6A:76:65:31:90:04:37
Linux frontend-ig-kcj1 4.9.0-8-amd64 #1 SMP Debian 4.9.144-3.1 (2019-02-19) x86_
64

The programs included with the Debian GNU/Linux system are free software;
the exact distribution terms for each program are described in the
individual files in /usr/share/doc/*/copyright.

Debian GNU/Linux comes with ABSOLUTELY NO WARRANTY, to the extent
permitted by applicable law.
hscorpio19@frontend-ig-kcj1:~$
```

70. To check the Firewall restrictions with respect to service account and Network tags, Create a new instance template i.e., frontent-it2 with a different service account and Network tag "frontend-ig2".

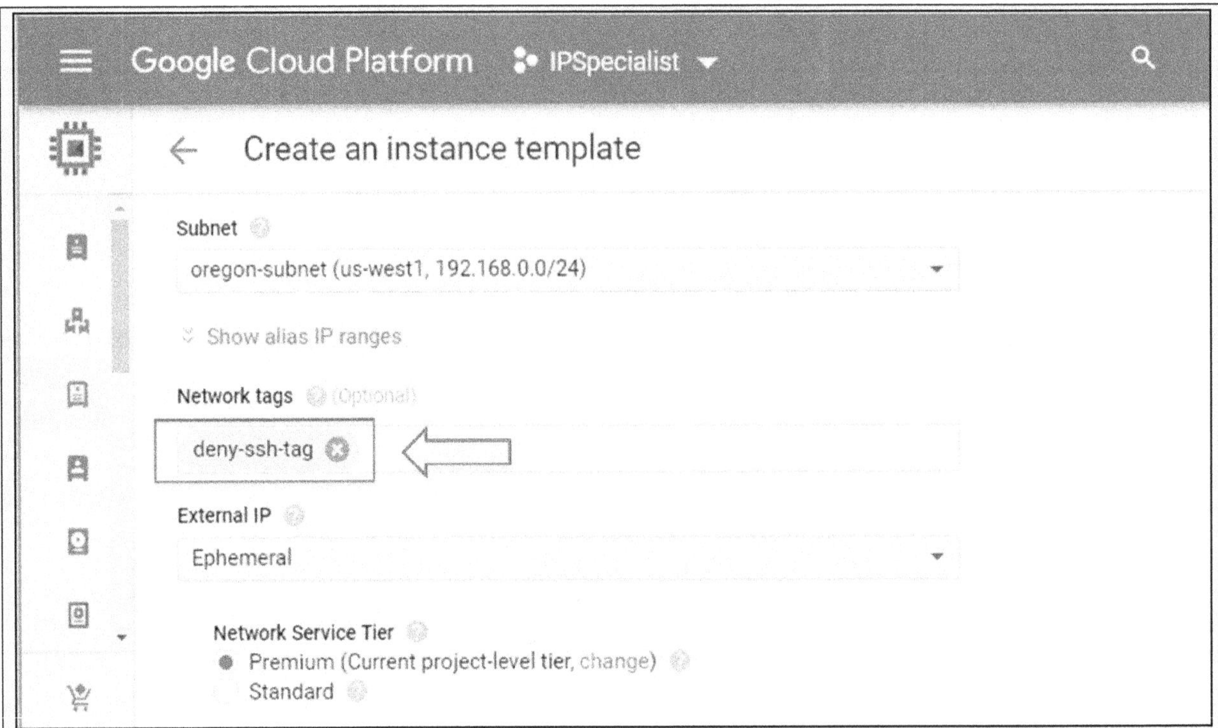

71. Create instance group "frontend-ig2" with this instance template and VPC.

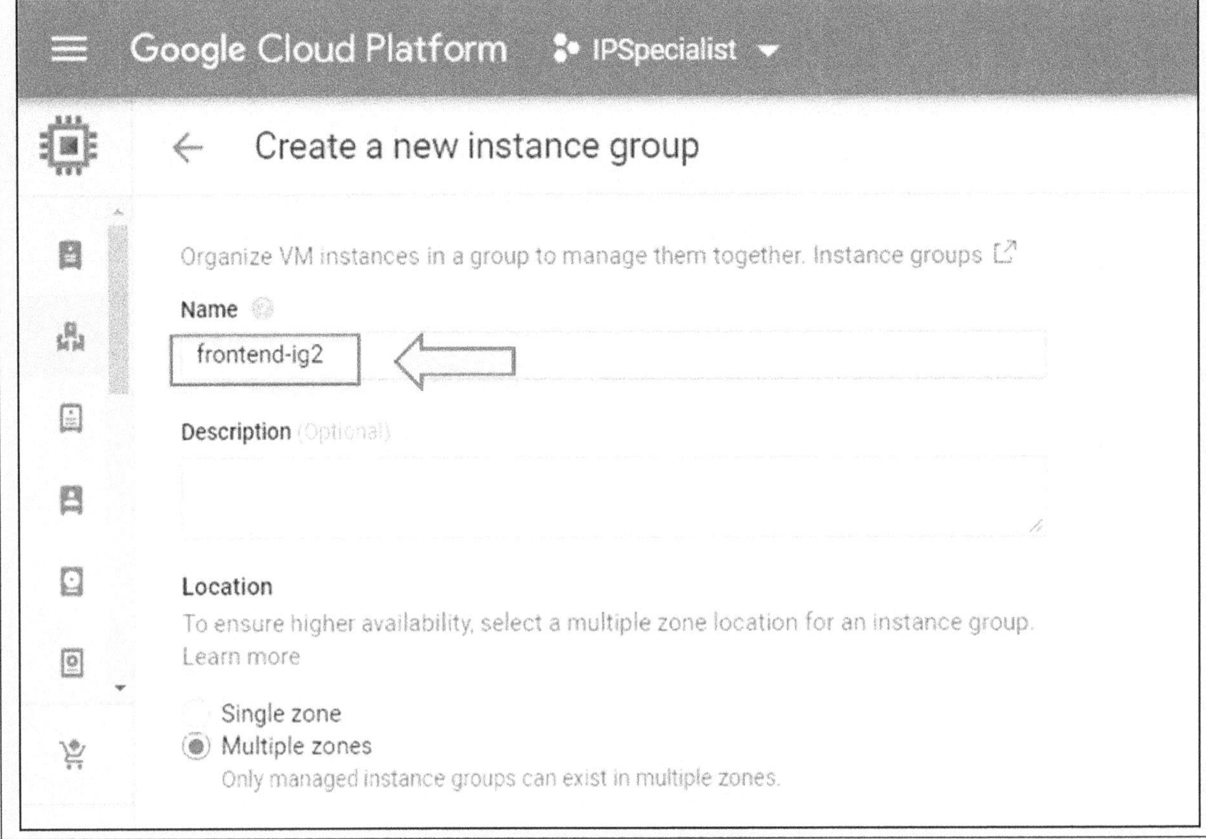

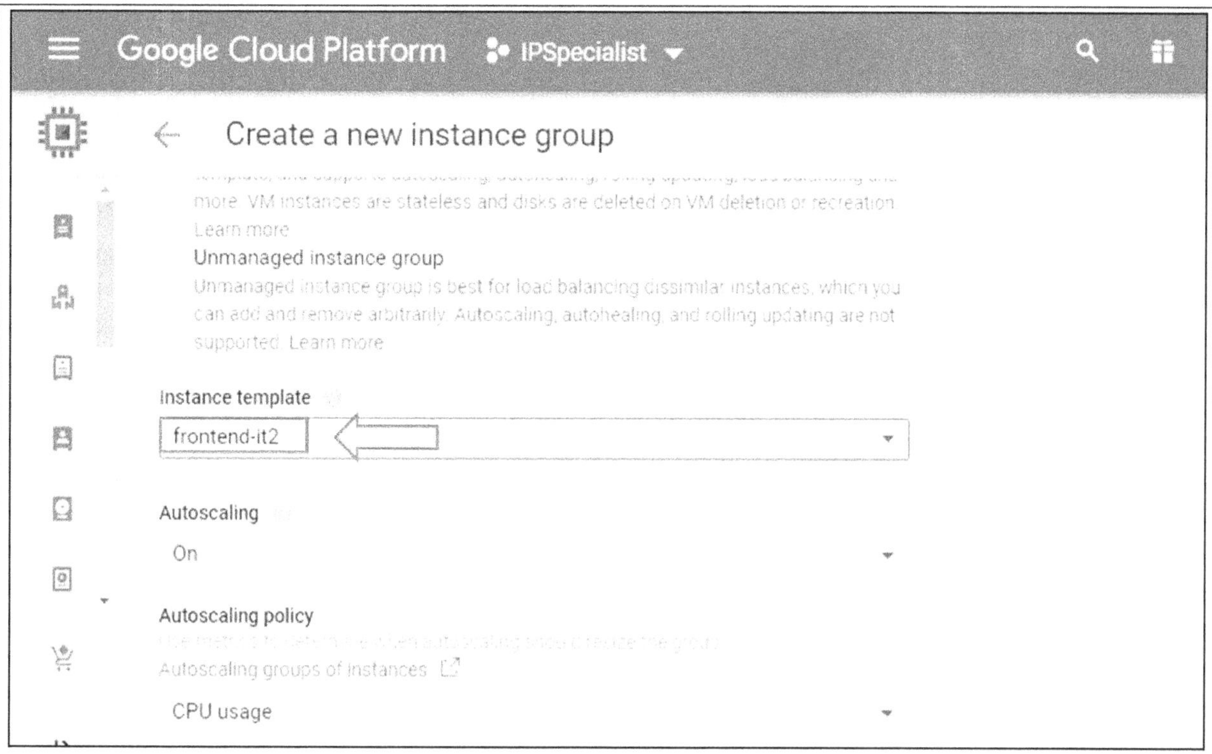

72. Copy External IP of any instance in the frontend-ig2 and ping it through Cloud Shell.

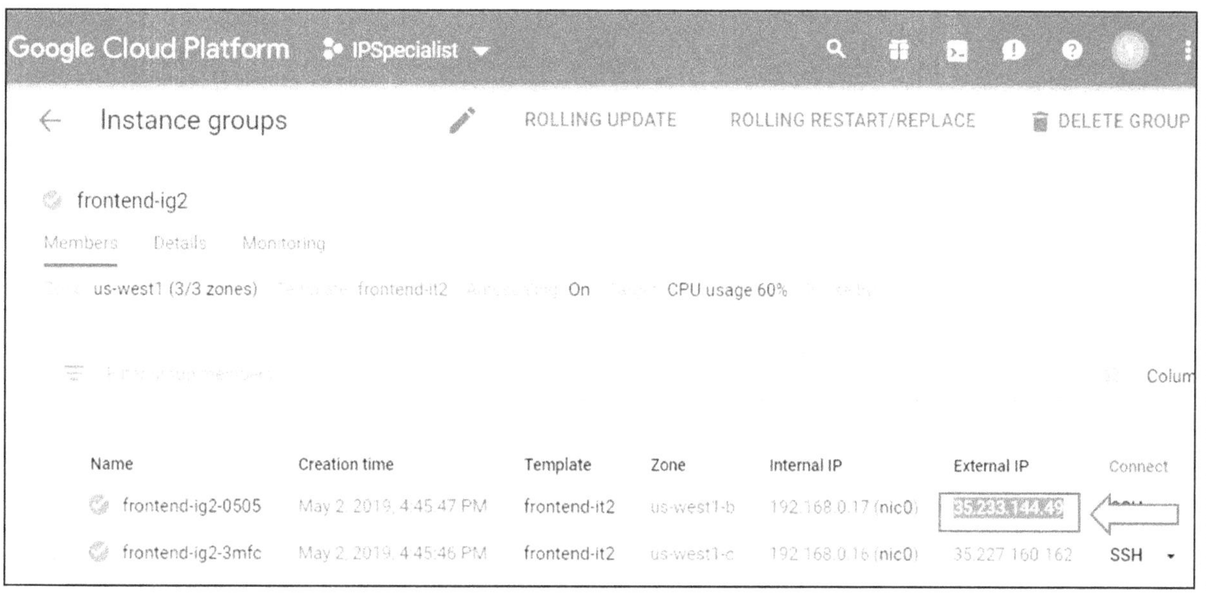

Ping unsuccessful as the Firewall rule for icmp is allowed only for the specified service account.

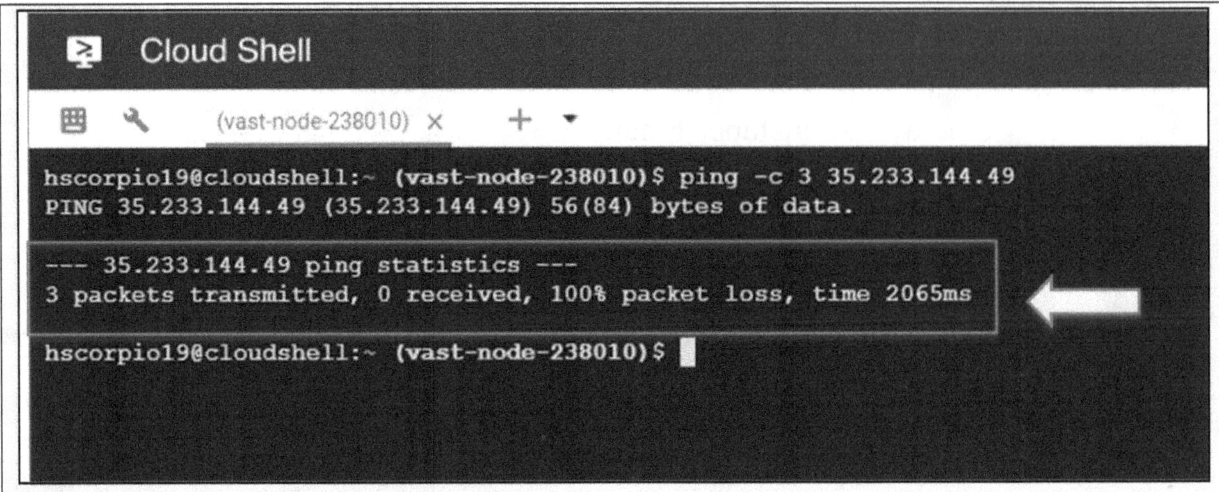

73. Now, try to connect through SSH.

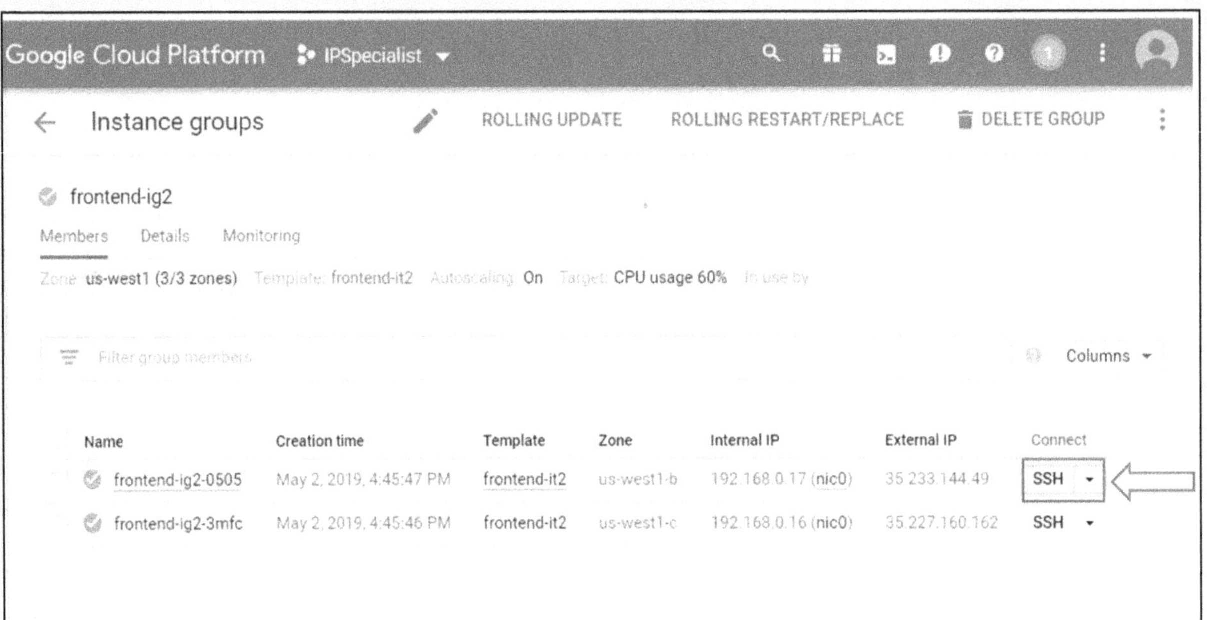

Connection denied because Network tag of this instance is different from the specified network tag in the Firewall Rule.

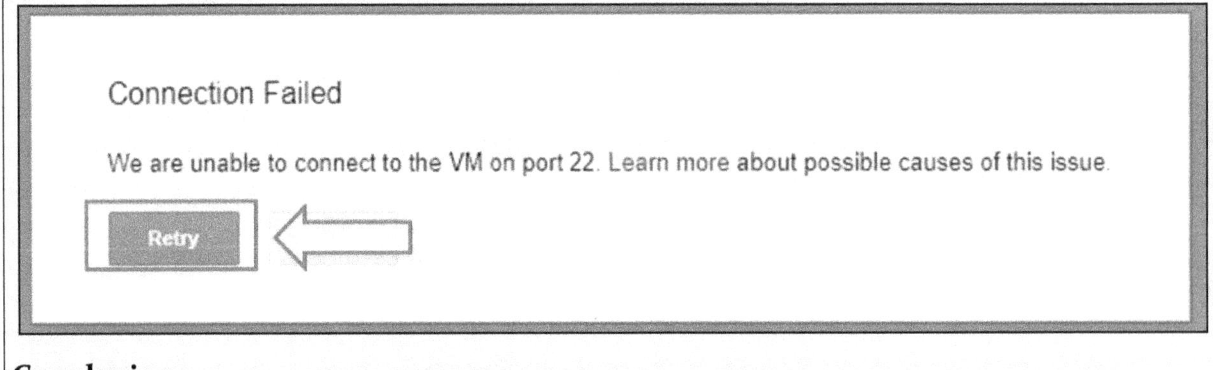

Conclusion:

For any traffic control, user should set the Firewall rules according to the defined Network tags, service accounts or specific Network instances.

Lab 5.3: Two-Tier Custom Mode VPC

Scenario:

You are currently working on a project, which demands the following things:

- Two Tier setup (Frontend instances and backend instances)
- Frontend instances should allow traffic from anywhere and can send traffic to backend instances and internet
- Backend instances allow traffic from frontend and backend instances only and they are unable to send traffic anywhere

Solution:

You have completed this project by defining Firewall rules in Custom-mode VPC. For Firewall rules you have used IP ranges and Network tags.

For frontend instances, you can use the same instance group as in Lab 02 or you can create a new one.

1. Delete the Firewall rules in the custom-mode-vpc in order to define new set of rules

Backend Instances

2. Create a service account for backend instances (Repeat Steps 23-27 of lab 02)
3. Create a new instance template "backend-it"

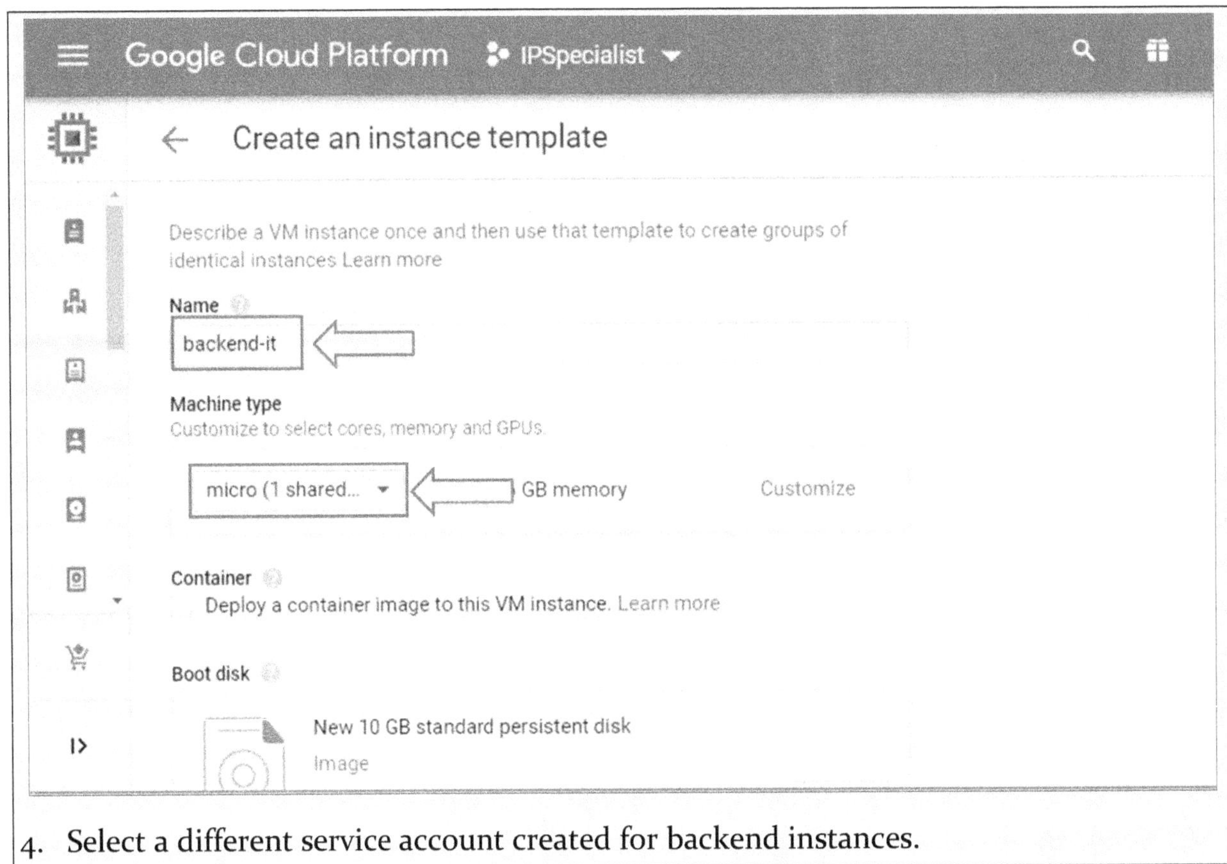

4. Select a different service account created for backend instances.

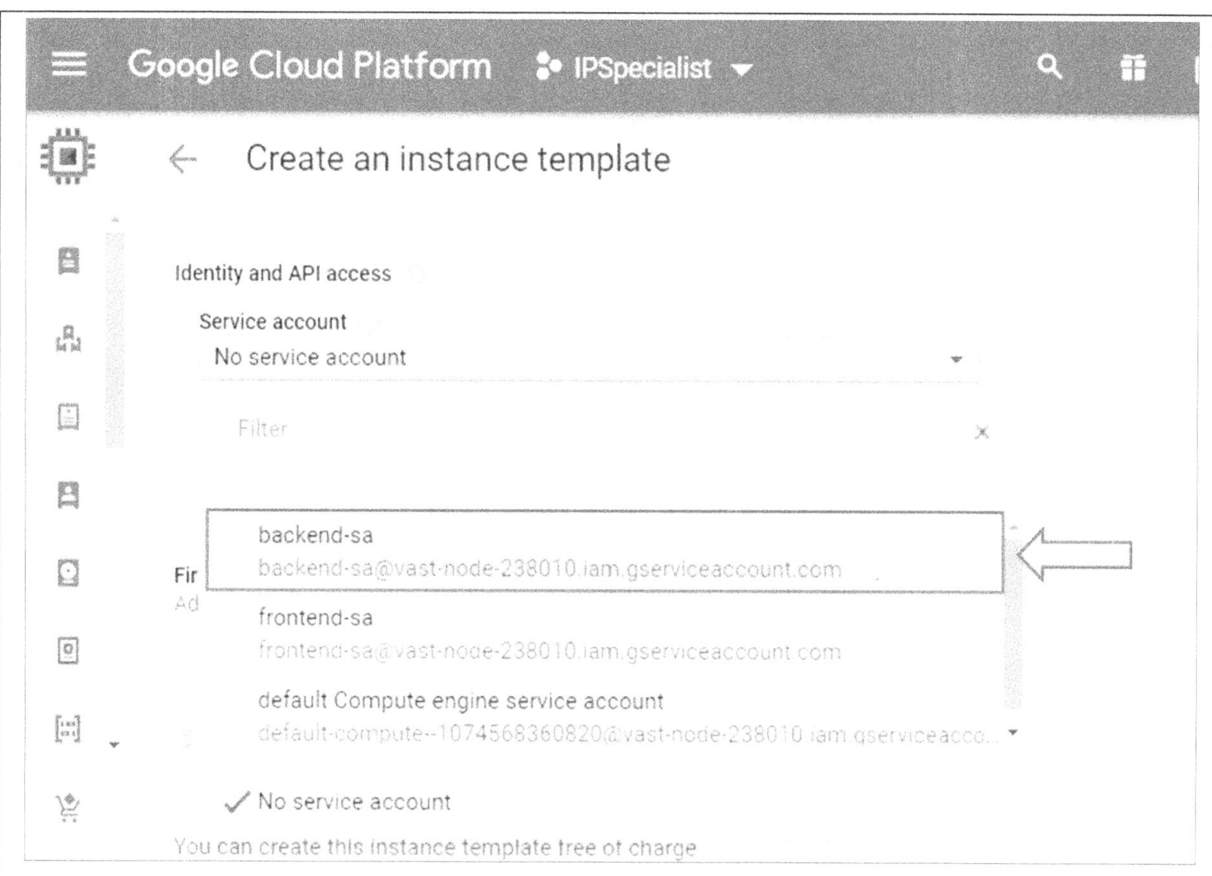

5. Select the same VPC in Networking tab.

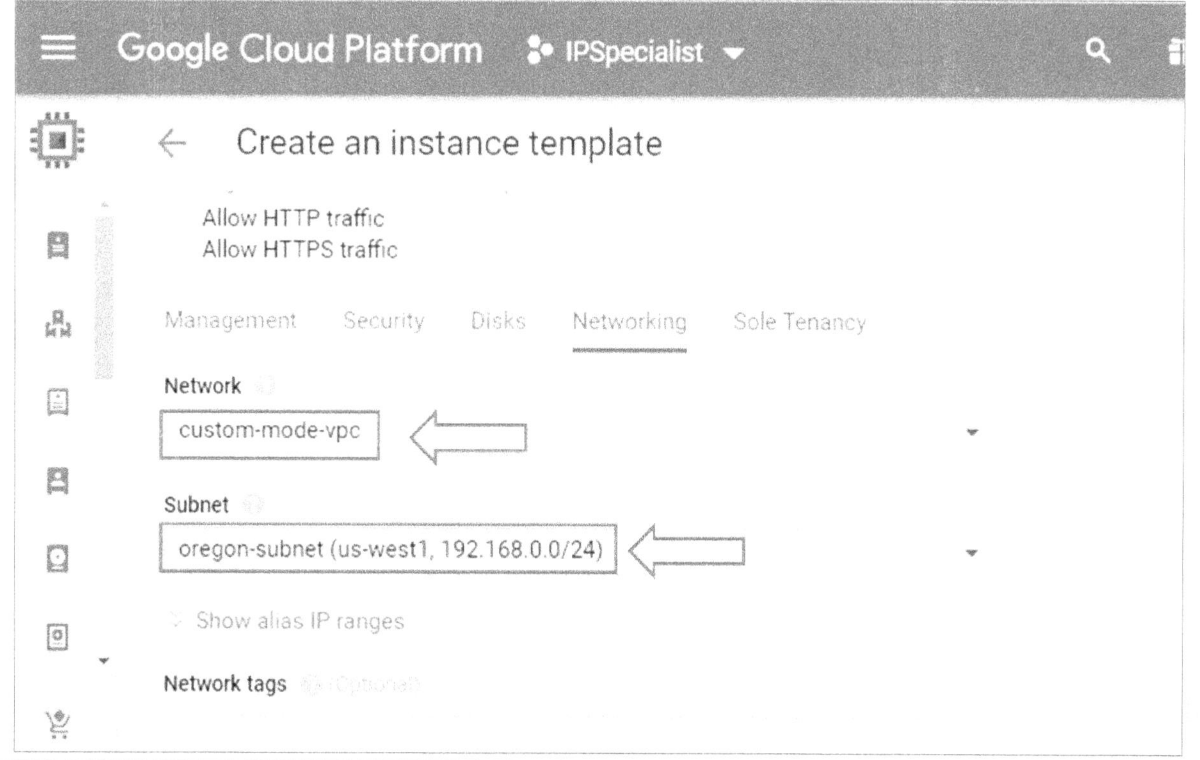

6. Create an instance group for backend instance in Multiple zones of "us-west1" region.

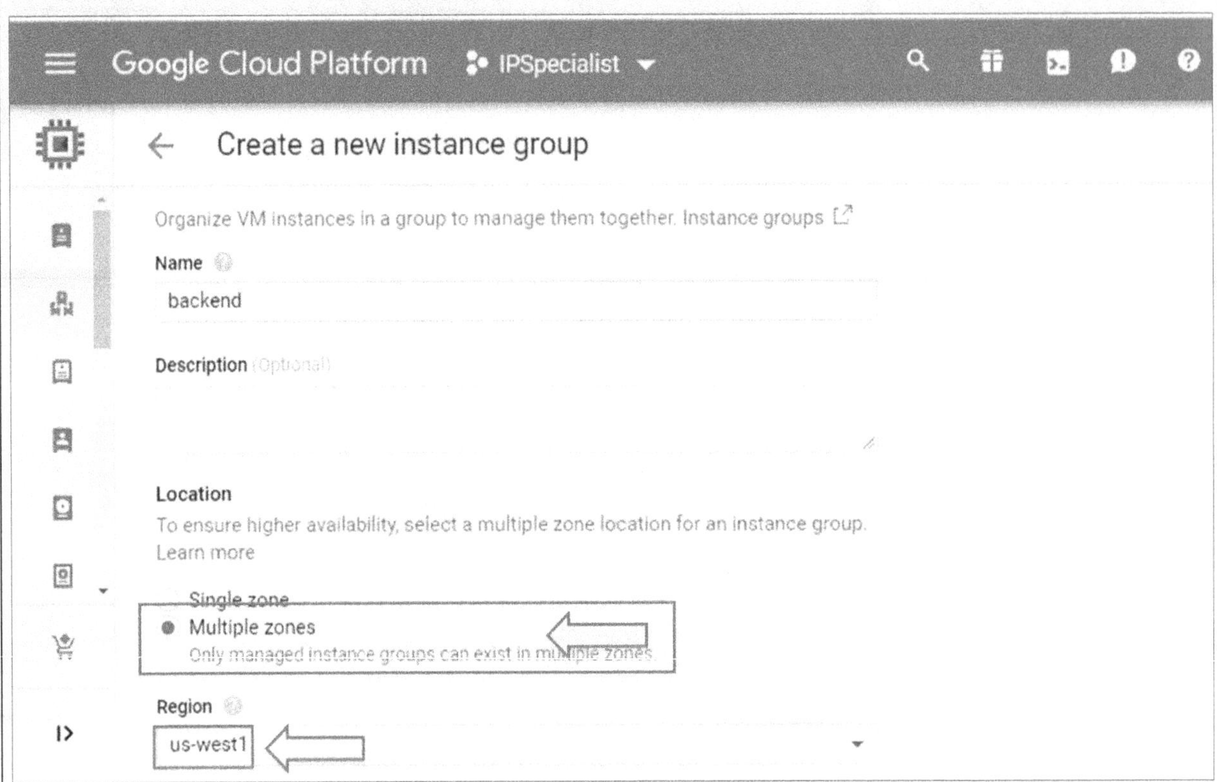

7. Attach the backend instance template and set the "Minimum number of instances" to 2.

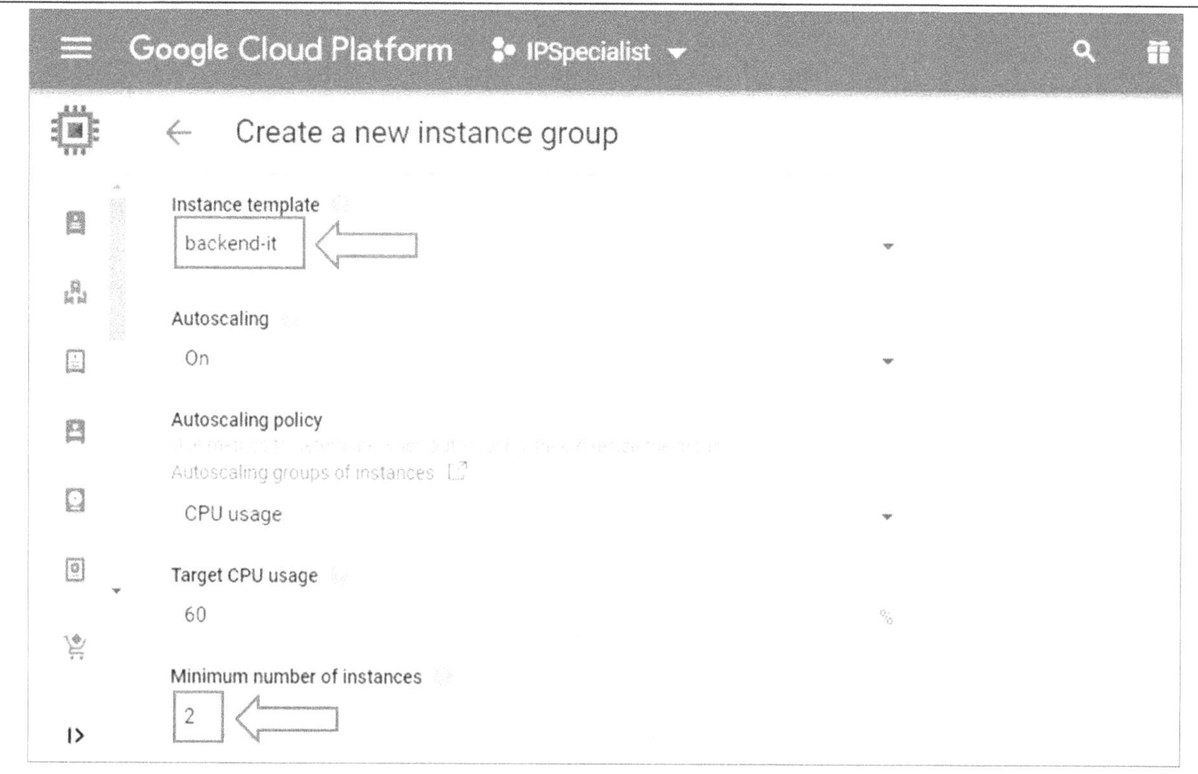

8. "Maximum number of instances" to "3" and click "Create".

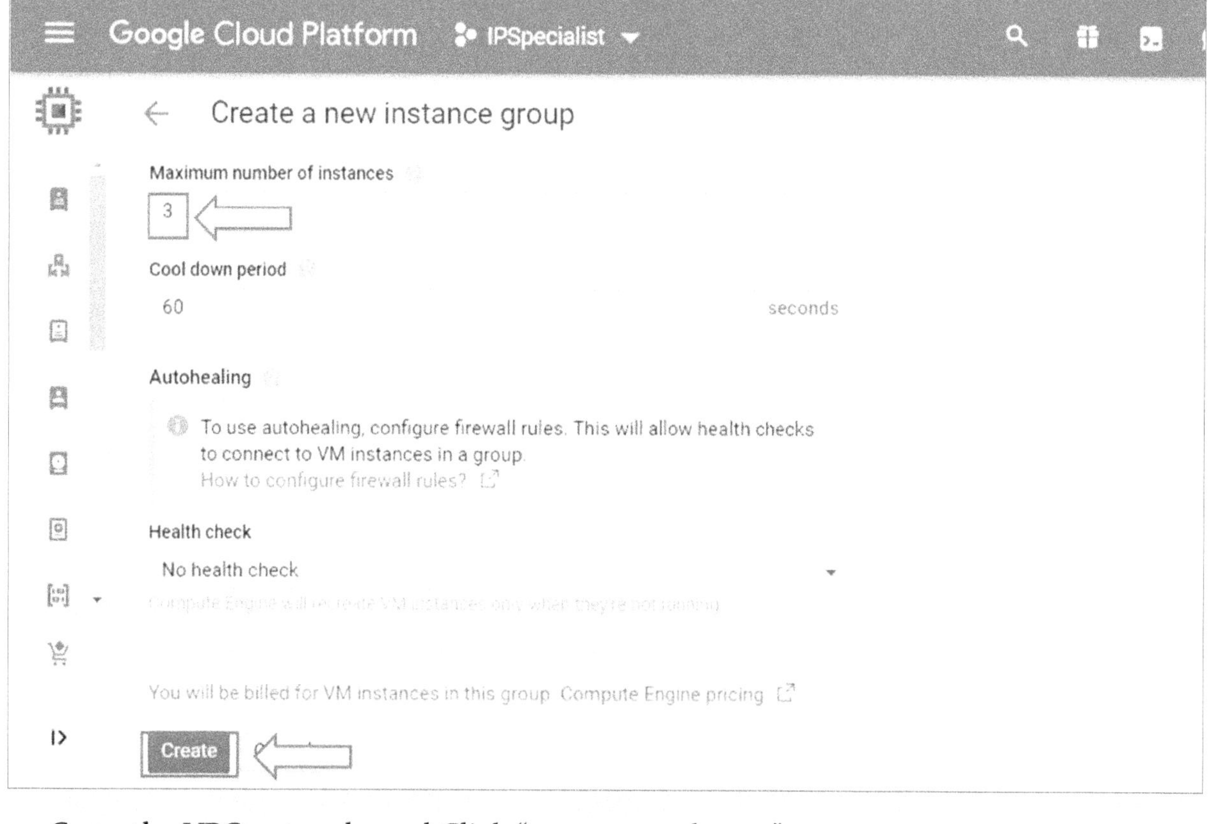

9. Go to the VPC networks and Click "custom-mode-vpc".

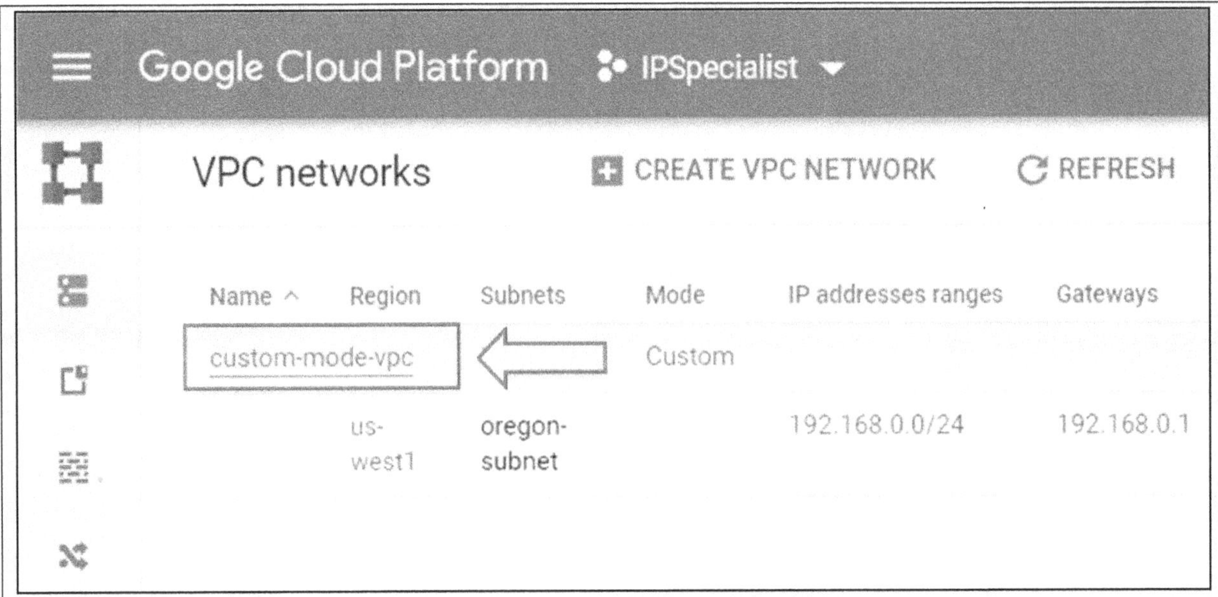

10. Click "Add firewall rule" in Firewall rules tab.

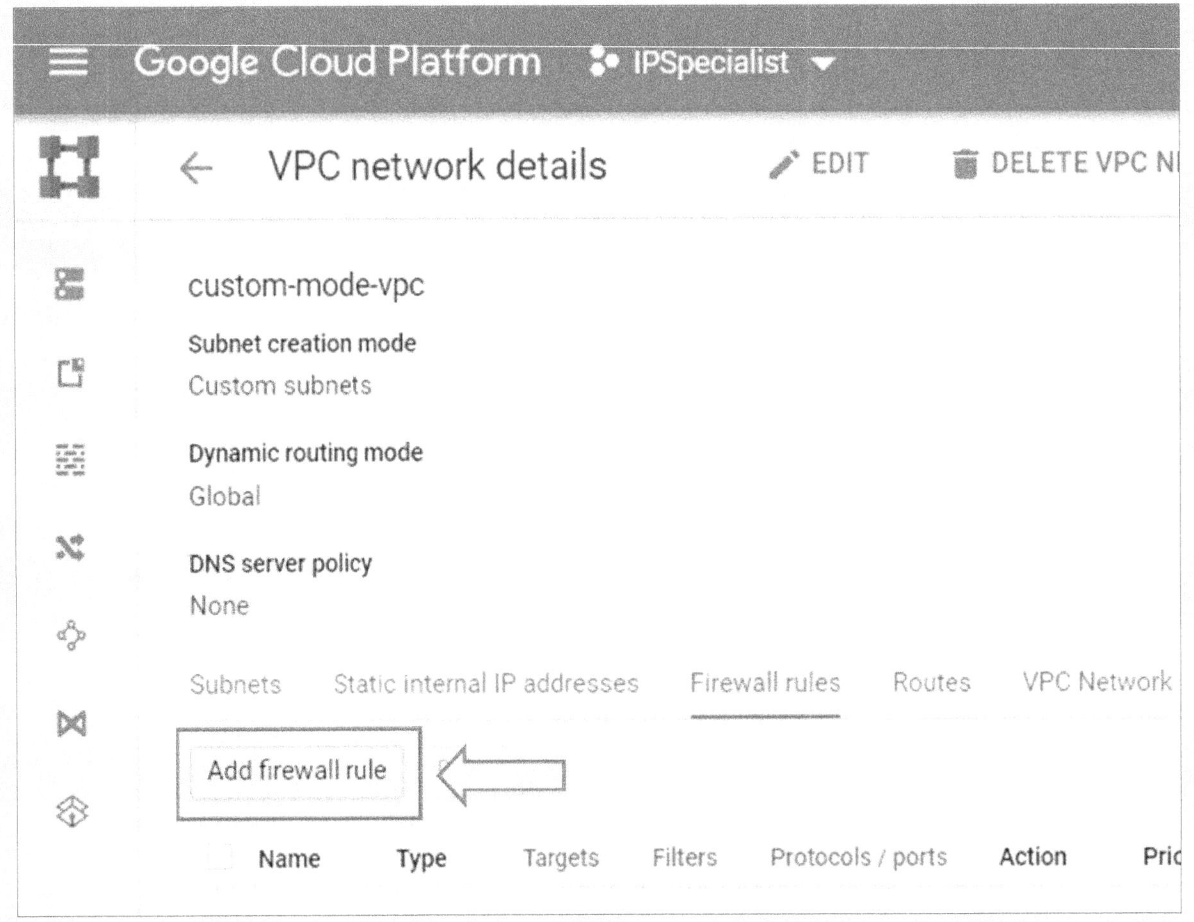

Rule 1 (Allow SSH to the instances having "open-ssh-tag" from anywhere)

Repeat steps 63-67 of Lab 02.

Firewall rules for Frontend instances

Rule 2 (Allow incoming to frontend instances from everywhere)

11. Repeat steps of lab 02 from 53 - 57 to create a rule for allowing traffic from internet to frontend instances and select "Allow all" in "Protocols and ports" option.

Firewall rules for Backend instances

Rule 3 (Allow incoming from frontend and other backend instances)

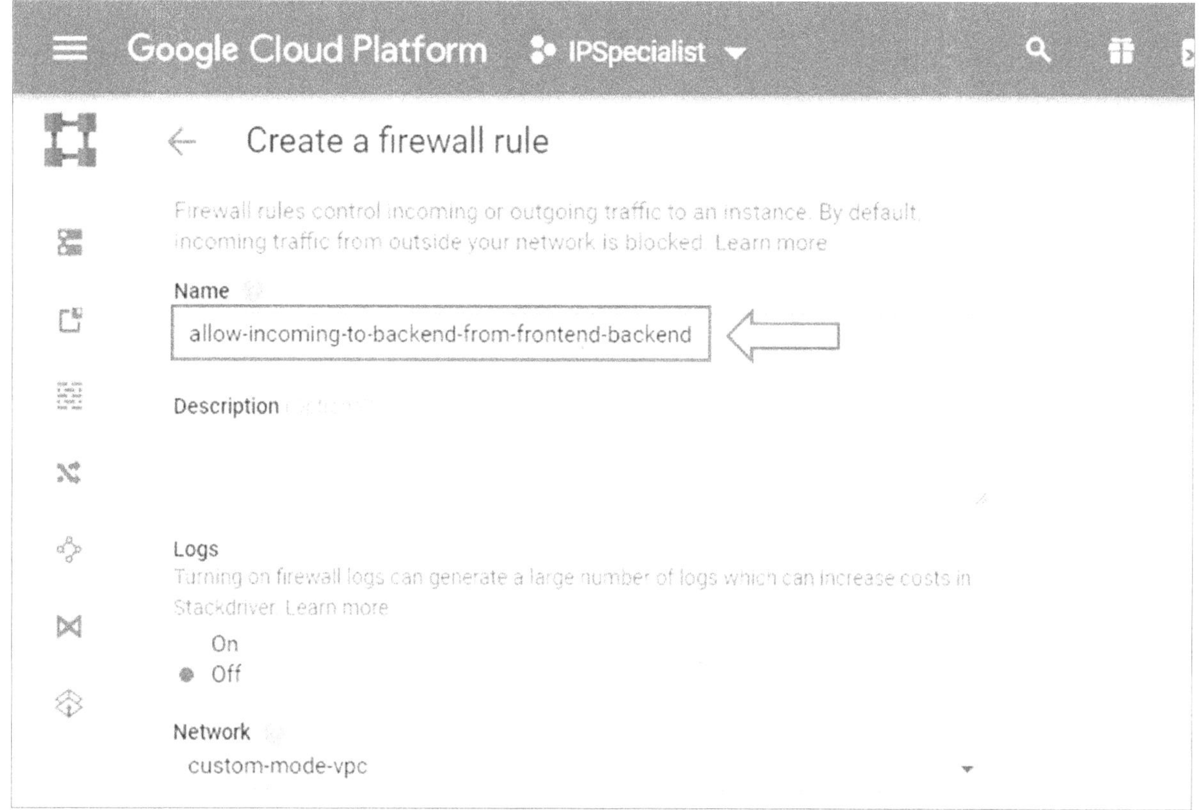

12. Add firewall rule in which select "Ingress" in direction, "Allow" in actions and target should be set to the backend service account.

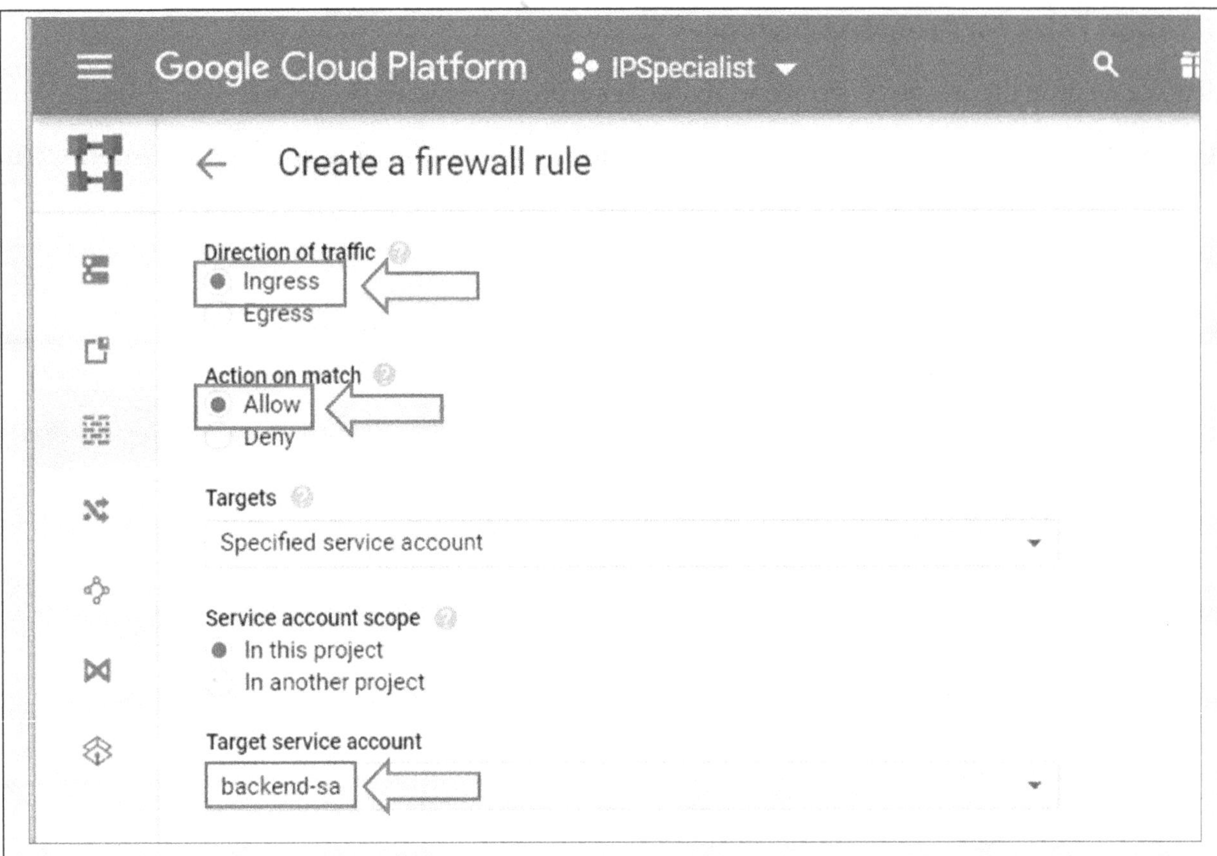

13. Enter the External IP addresses of the frontend and backend instances in source. Select "Allow all" in Protocols.

Google Cloud Platform IPSpecialist

Create a firewall rule

Target service account

backend-sa

Source filter

IP ranges

Source IP ranges

34.74.127.244 34.73.226.102 34.73.251.149
34.73.135.90

Second source filter

None

Protocols and ports

Allow all

Specified protocols and ports

Disable rule

Create Cancel

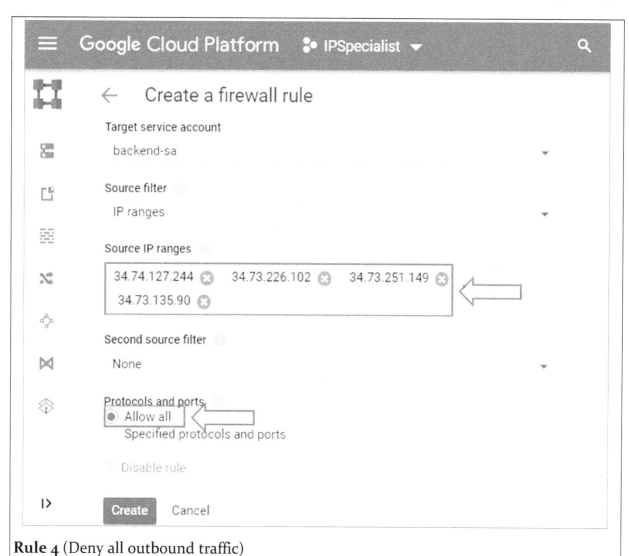

Rule 4 (Deny all outbound traffic)

14. Add firewall rule in which select "Egress" and "Deny" to restrict outbound.

Google Cloud Platform IPSpecialist

Create a firewall rule

Network
custom-mode-vpc

Priority
Priority can be 0 - 65535 Check priority of other firewall rules
1000

Direction of traffic
Ingress
Egress

Action on match
Allow
Deny

Targets
Specified target tags

Target tags

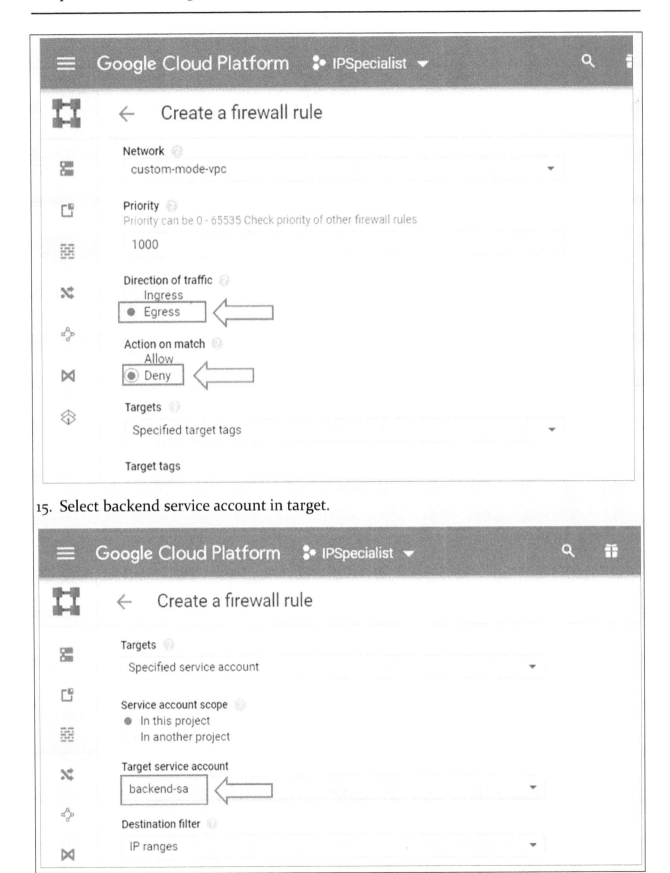

15. Select backend service account in target.

Google Cloud Platform IPSpecialist

Create a firewall rule

Targets
Specified service account

Service account scope
In this project
In another project

Target service account
backend-sa

Destination filter
IP ranges

16. Enter “0.0.0.0/0” in “Destination IP ranges”.
17. Select “Deny all” and click “Create”.

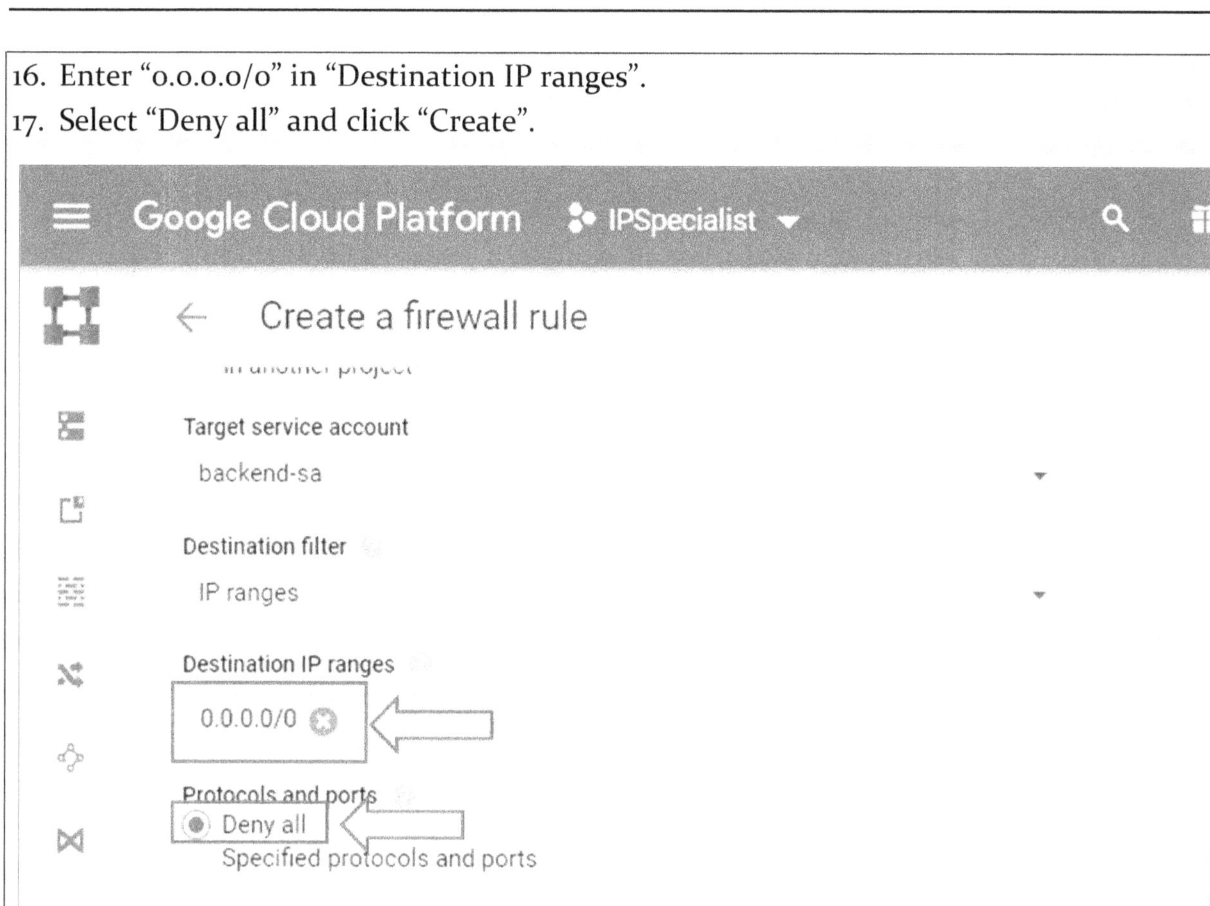

Rule 5 (Allow outbound to backend instances only)

18. Add Firewall rule in which set priority number lower than the priority number of Rule three.

Google Cloud Platform IPSpecialist

Create a firewall rule

Name
allow-outbound-from-backend-to-backend

Description (Optional)

Logs
Turning on firewall logs can generate a large number of logs which can increase costs in Stackdriver. Learn more
On
Off

Network
custom-mode-vpc

Priority
Priority can be 0 - 65535 Check priority of other firewall rules
100

Direction of traffic

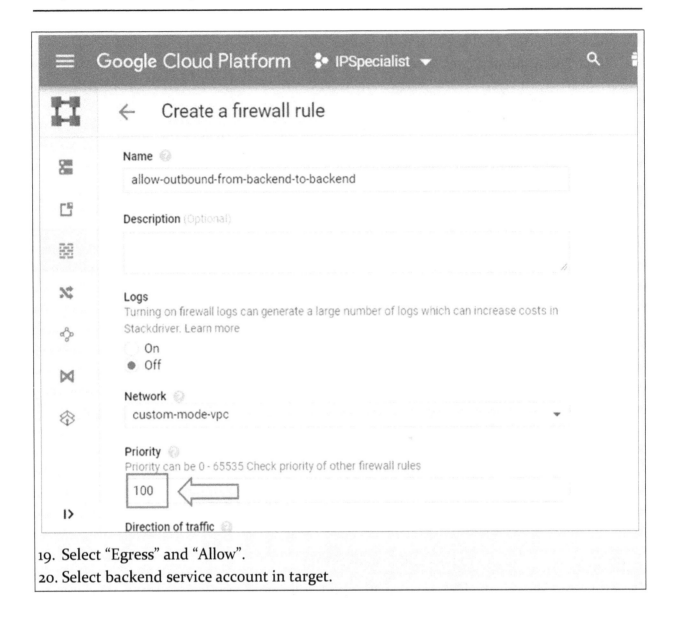

19. Select "Egress" and "Allow".
20. Select backend service account in target.

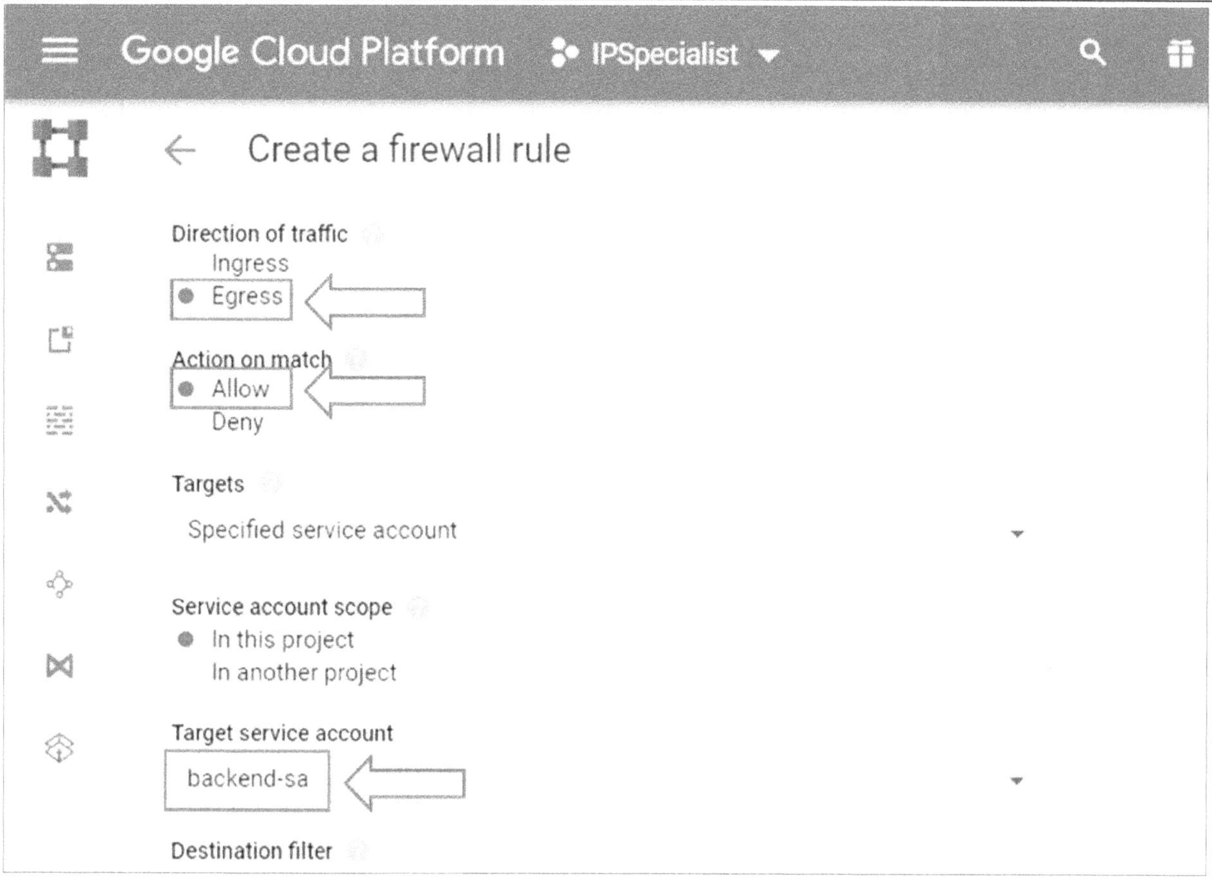

Google Cloud Platform IPSpecialist

Create a firewall rule

Direction of traffic
Ingress
Egress

Action on match
Allow
Deny

Targets
Specified service account

Service account scope
In this project
In another project

Target service account
backend-sa

Destination filter

21. Enter IP addresses of backend instances.
22. Select "Allow all" and Click "Create".

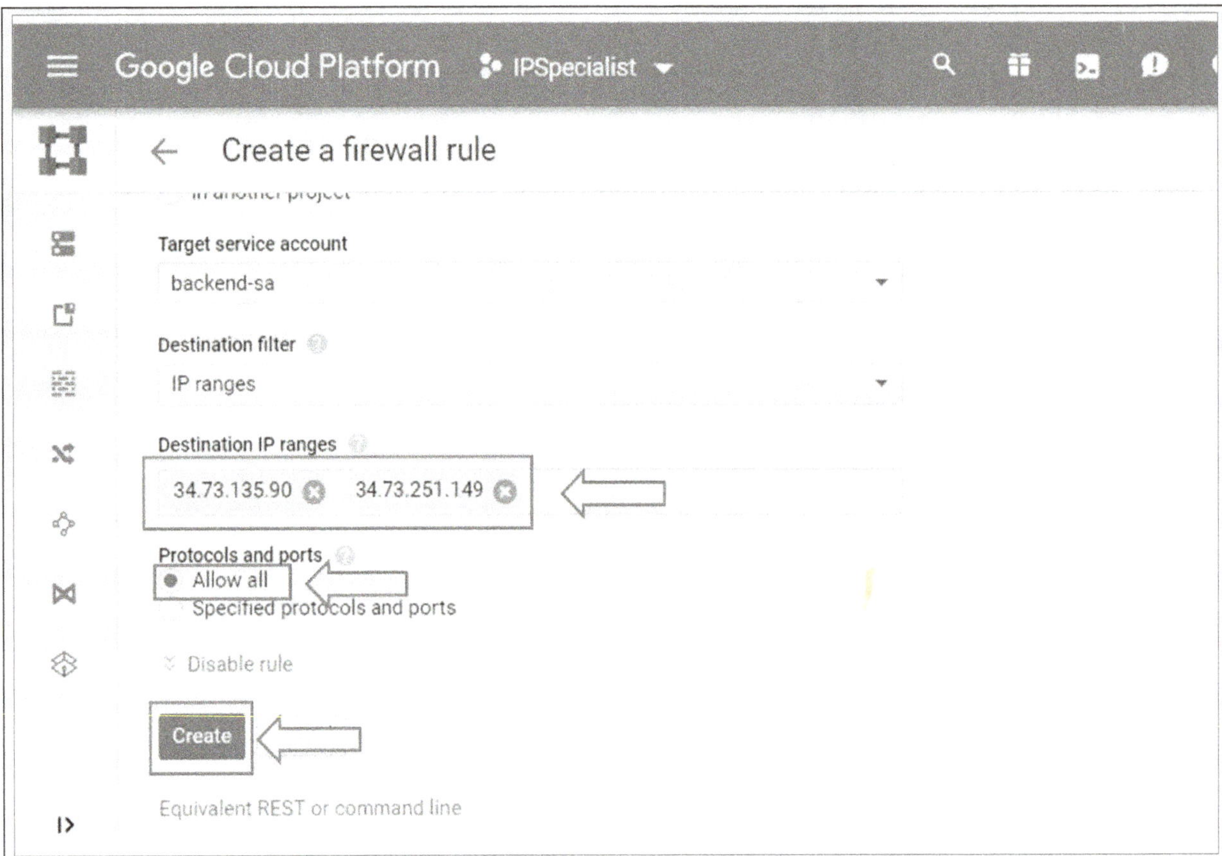

Checking the connections by using ping

Traffic from Internet

23. Open Cloud Shell and ping both frontend instances one by one by using External IP address and Enter command "ping –c 3 <External IP address>".

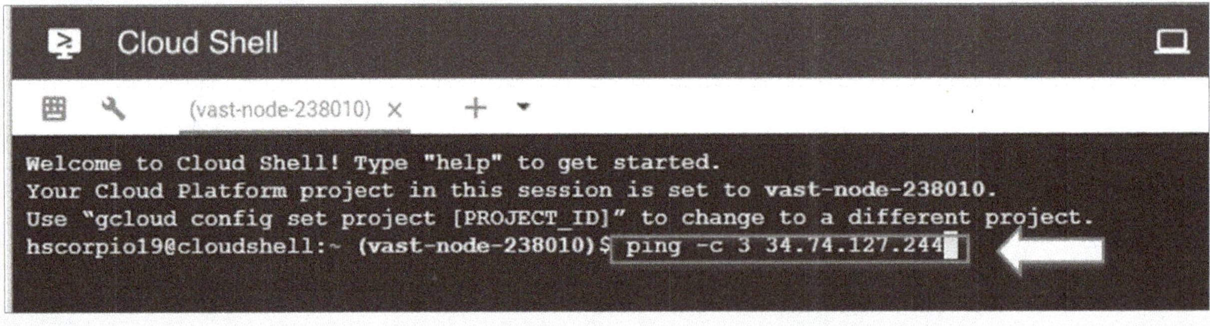

Ping is successful, which means frontend instances allowed traffic from anywhere.

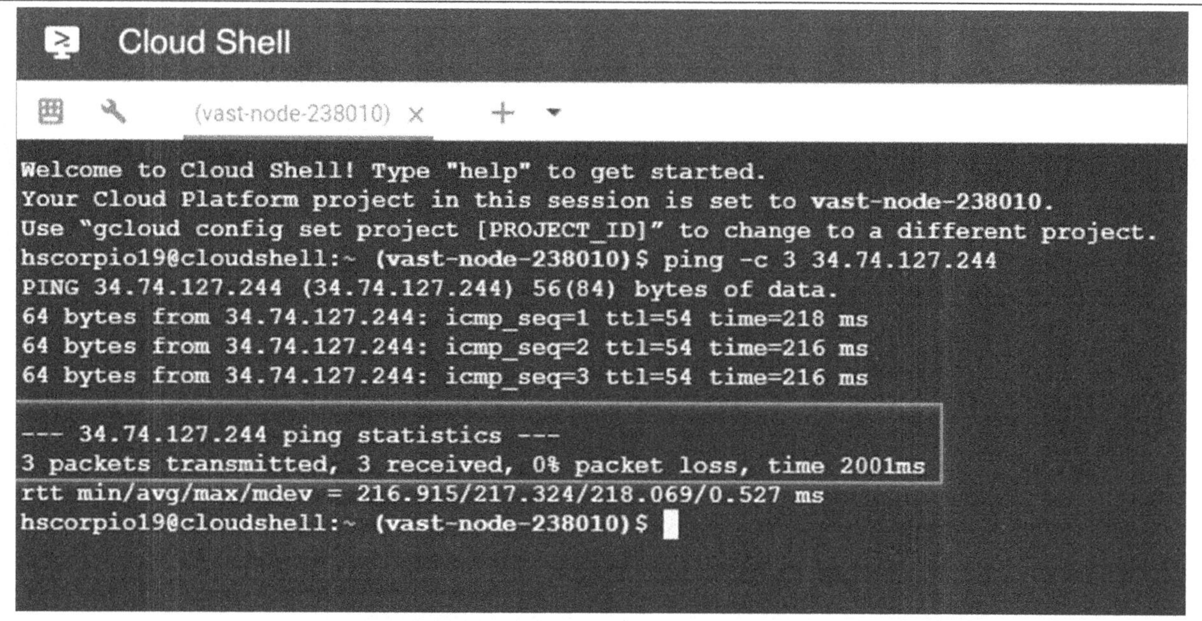

24. Ping backend instances. Packets loss means backend instances are not allowing traffic from the internet.

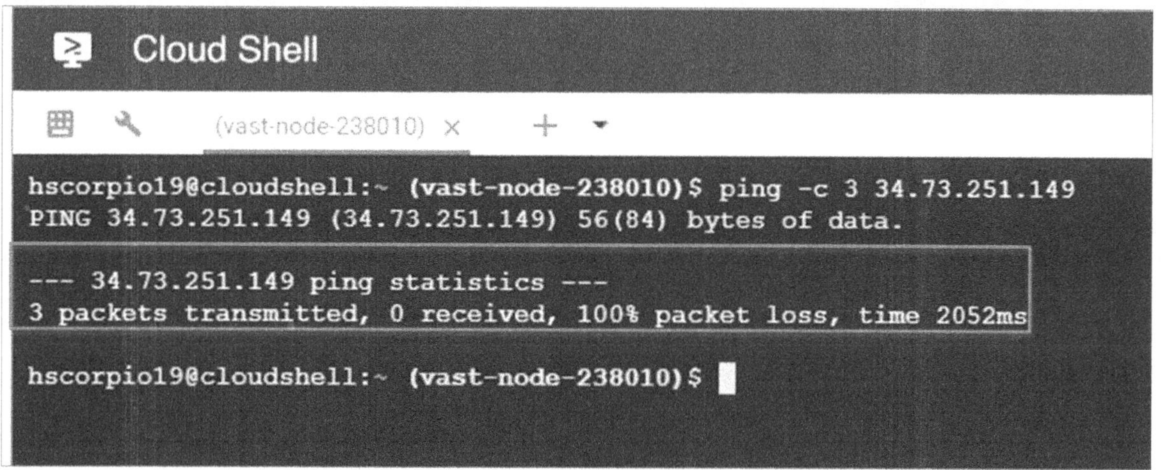

Traffic from Frontend instances

25. SSH to any one frontend instance.
26. Ping backend instances by using command "ping –c 3 <External IP address>".

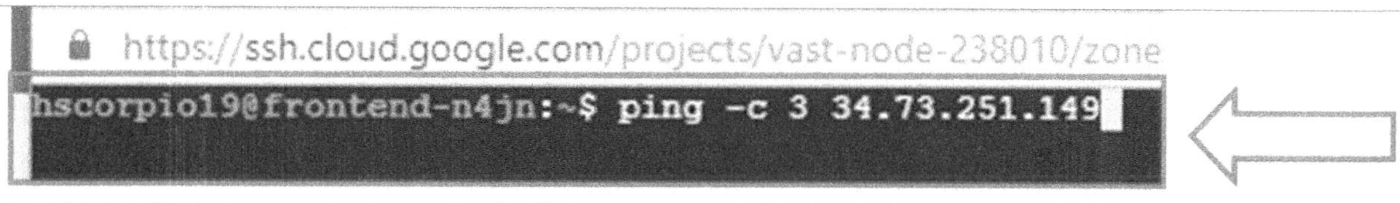

Ping successful means backend instances allows traffic from frontend instances.

```
https://ssh.cloud.google.com/projects/vast-node-238010/zones/us-east1-d/instances/frontend-n4jn
hscorpio19@frontend-n4jn:~$ ping -c 3 34.73.251.149
PING 34.73.251.149 (34.73.251.149) 56(84) bytes of data.
64 bytes from 34.73.251.149: icmp_seq=1 ttl=64 time=1.63 ms
64 bytes from 34.73.251.149: icmp_seq=2 ttl=64 time=0.563 ms
64 bytes from 34.73.251.149: icmp_seq=3 ttl=64 time=0.472 ms

--- 34.73.251.149 ping statistics ---
3 packets transmitted, 3 received, 0% packet loss, time 2015ms
rtt min/avg/max/mdev = 0.472/0.889/1.632/0.526 ms
hscorpio19@frontend-n4jn:~$
```

27. Ping google.com by using IP address 8.8.8.8. Ping is successful, which means frontend instances can send and receive traffic from the internet.

```
https://ssh.cloud.google.com/projects/vast-node-238010/zones/us-east1-d/instances/fronte
hscorpio19@frontend-n4jn:~$ ping -c 3 8.8.8.8
PING 8.8.8.8 (8.8.8.8) 56(84) bytes of data.
64 bytes from 8.8.8.8: icmp_seq=1 ttl=52 time=0.874 ms
64 bytes from 8.8.8.8: icmp_seq=2 ttl=52 time=0.299 ms
64 bytes from 8.8.8.8: icmp_seq=3 ttl=52 time=0.361 ms

--- 8.8.8.8 ping statistics ---
3 packets transmitted, 3 received, 0% packet loss, time 2020ms
rtt min/avg/max/mdev = 0.299/0.511/0.874/0.258 ms
hscorpio19@frontend-n4jn:~$
```

Backend instances traffic

28. For SSH to any backend instance first add "open-ssh-tag" to that instance as internet traffic is not allowed by backend instances. (Follow step 68 of lab 02)
29. Ping the frontend instances. Ping failed shows that backend instances cannot send traffic to frontend instances.

```
https://ssh.cloud.google.com/projects/vast-node-238010/zones/us-east1-c/instances
hscorpio19@backend-5t6g:~$ ping -c 3 34.74.127.244
PING 34.74.127.244 (34.74.127.244) 56(84) bytes of data.

--- 34.74.127.244 ping statistics ---
3 packets transmitted, 0 received, 100% packet loss, time 2043ms

hscorpio19@backend-5t6g:~$
```

30. Ping google.com. Ping failed shows that backend instances cannot send traffic to internet.

```
https://ssh.cloud.google.com/projects/vast-node-238010/zones/us-east1-c/instances/backe
hscorpio19@backend-5t6g:~$ ping -c 3 8.8.8.8
PING 8.8.8.8 (8.8.8.8) 56(84) bytes of data.

--- 8.8.8.8 ping statistics ---
3 packets transmitted, 0 received, 100% packet loss, time 2034ms

hscorpio19@backend-5t6g:~$
```

31. Ping the backend instances. Ping successful shows that backend instances can send traffic to backend instances.

```
https://ssh.cloud.google.com/projects/vast-node-238010/zones/us-east1-c/instances/back
hscorpio19@backend-5t6g:~$ ping -c 3 34.73.251.149
PING 34.73.251.149 (34.73.251.149) 56(84) bytes of data.
64 bytes from 34.73.251.149: icmp_seq=1 ttl=76 time=0.891 ms
64 bytes from 34.73.251.149: icmp_seq=2 ttl=76 time=0.317 ms
64 bytes from 34.73.251.149: icmp_seq=3 ttl=76 time=0.257 ms

--- 34.73.251.149 ping statistics ---
3 packets transmitted, 3 received, 0% packet loss, time 2004ms
rtt min/avg/max/mdev = 0.257/0.488/0.891/0.286 ms
hscorpio19@backend-5t6g:~$
```

Challenge

Perform the task of lab 6.3 by using only service accounts in firewall rules not IP ranges (except open-ssh-tag rule).

Mind Map

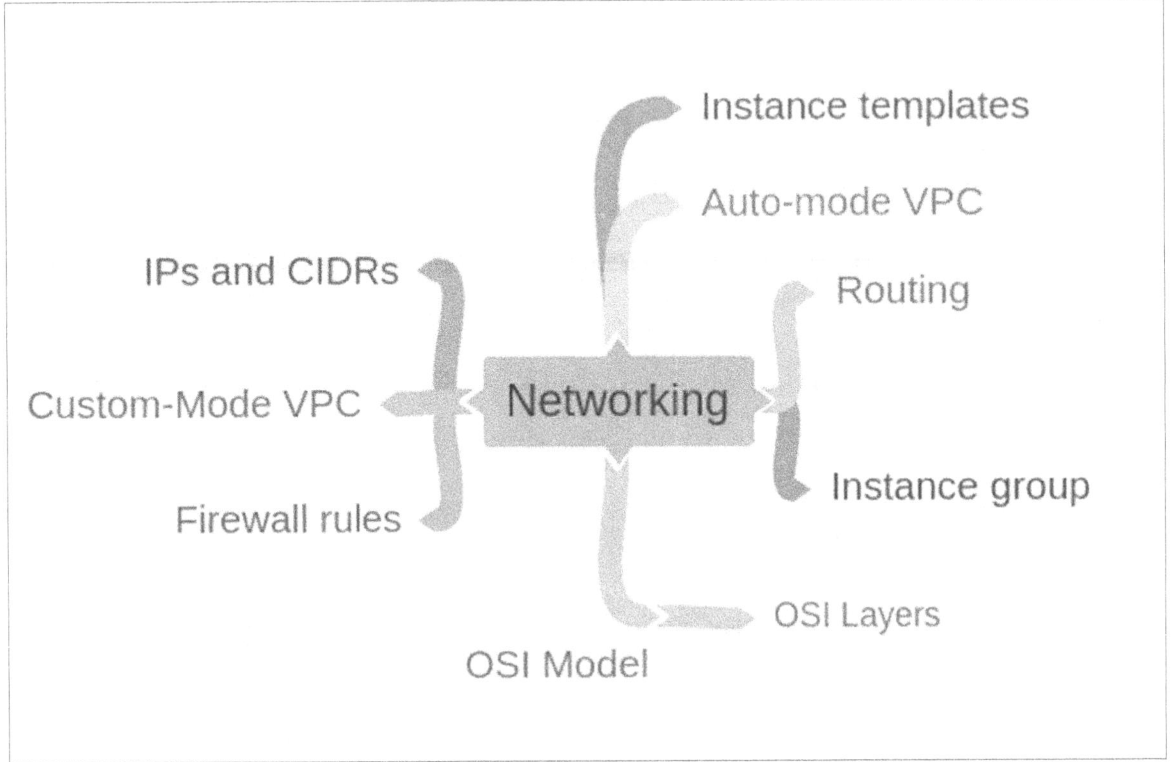

Figure 5-02: Chapter's Mind Map

Practice Questions

1. By default, in firewall rules which traffic is permissive?
   A. Ingress
   B. Egress
   C. All of the above
   D. None of the above

2. How many layers do the OSI model provides?
   A. 3
   B. 5
   C. 7
   D. 9

3. Choose the option representing layer 4 in OSI model
   A. Transport
   B. Network
   C. Application
   D. Physical

4. Data travelling path is known as?
   A. Mapping
   B. Routing
   C. Communication
   D. None of the above

5. Choose the two types of routing provided by GCP:
   A. Premium
   B. Custom
   C. Standard
   D. Simple

6. Which of the routing tier is fast?
   A. Simple
   B. Standard
   C. Custom
   D. Premium

7. Cross-Region Load Balancing with Global Anycast IPs can be used to obtain Latency

Reduction. True or False?

A. True

B. False

8. Which of the IP type allows data handling via multiple devices?

A. Unicast

B. Broadcast

C. Anycast

D. Multicast

9. Which is the primary protocol of internet?

A. HTTP

B. HTTPS

C. UDP

D. TCP

10. Which of the following option is used for Global load balancing?

A. Load balancer

B. Balancing Instance

C. Domain name system

D. None of the above

11. Firewall rules can only be defined by Network tags. True or False?

A. True

B. False

12. Select the priority number that default restrictive and permissive firewall rules have.

A. 1000

B. 65535

C. 0

D. 100

13. Which of the following CIDR represents all IP address range?

A. 0.0.0.0/24

B. 1.1.1.1/0

C. 0.0.0.0/0

D. 1.1.1.1/24

14. Choose the default VPC mode from the following options

A. Auto
B. Custom
C. Auto and Custom both
D. No default VPC exists

15. If you want to create VPC in a particular region, then which of the mode will you select?
    A. Auto
    B. Custom
    C. Impossible
    D. Contact google support

Chapter 06: Google Engines

Introduction

In this chapter, we will briefly discuss the Google Engines. The Google Kubernetes Engine (GKE) is becoming the most important cloud-native technology, and you should have a deep understanding of how it works. In this chapter, you will learn what a Kubernetes cluster is, and how to deploy and manage it on-premises and in the cloud. You will learn how Kubernetes fits into the cloud-native ecosystem and how its major components let us deploy and manage applications through it. You will also learn how declarative manifest files can control your configurations version. In this chapter we will learn about how the Google App Engine makes it easy to get started with your desired languages, frameworks, and libraries.

Google Kubernetes Engine (GKE)

Google Kubernetes Engine (GKE) helps you in providing a managed environment used for deploying, managing and scaling your containerized applications working on Google Infrastructure. The GKE consists of multiple machines which are grouped to form a cluster for example, GCE instances.

Cluster Orchestration with GKE

GKE clusters are powered via the Kubernetes open source cluster management system. Kubernetes offers the mechanisms through which you interact with your cluster. You operate Kubernetes commands and resources to set up and control your packages, to set policies, perform management tasks and monitor the performance of your workloads which are deployed.

Kubernetes draws on the same design standards that run popular Google services and offer equal advantages: Automated management, monitoring for application containers, rolling updates, automatic scaling and more. When you run an application on a cluster, you are using technology, totally based on Google's 10+ years' experience of running workloads in containers.

GKE on GCP

When you run a GKE cluster, you can also take some advantages of the advanced management features that GCP provides, which are:

- GCP load balancing for the instances of Compute Engine
- Node Pools are used to designate subsets of nodes inside the cluster to provide additional flexibility
- Automatic Scaling for instance count of cluster nodes
- Automatic Upgrade for node software of cluster
- Node Auto Repair used to maintain the availability and health of the node
- Logging and Monitoring with Stack driver to look after the cluster

GKE Workloads

GKE works with containerized applications or applications that are packed into hardware as an independent, isolated user-space instances, for example by using Docker. In GKE and Kubernetes, those containers, whether used for applications or batch jobs are collectively known as Workloads. Before you set up a workload on a GKE cluster, you first need to package the workload into a container.

Google Cloud Platform provides non-stop integration and continuous delivery tools that will help you build and serve application containers. Google Cloud Build is used to build the container images (such as Docker) using multiple source code repositories, and Google Container Registry to serve your container images and store the images.

Cluster Architecture

In GKE, a cluster consists of at least one cluster master and more than one worker machines referred to as nodes. Kubernetes cluster orchestration system runs on master and node machines.

A cluster is the most important aspect of GKE. The Kubernetes objects which represent your containerized applications will run on the top of a cluster.

Cluster Master

Cluster master runs Kubernetes Control Plane processes, such as the Kubernetes API server, scheduler, and core resource controllers. The master's lifecycle is managed using GKE, when you create or delete a cluster. Which includes the upgradation to the Kubernetes version running on the cluster master, which GKE performs either automatically or manually at your request in case you prefer to upgrade earlier than the automatic schedule.

Nodes

A cluster typically consists of one or more nodes called the worker machines, which runs your containerized applications and different workloads. The machines are Compute Engine VM instances that GKE creates on your behalf when you create a cluster.

Every node is managed from the master, which gets updates on each node's self-reported status. You can exercise a few manual controls over node lifecycle, or you could have GKE perform automatic repairs and automatic improvements for your cluster's nodes.

A node runs all the services which might be important to support the Docker containers that put your cluster's workloads up. Those consist of the Kubernetes Node Agent (kubelet) and the Docker runtime which communicates with the master and is responsible for initializing and running Docker containers which are scheduled on that node.

In GKE, there are several special containers that run as per-node agents to offer functionality which includes log collection and intra-cluster network connectivity.

What is POD?

Pods are the smallest and the most basic deployable objects in Kubernetes. Pod represents a single instance of the running process on your cluster.

Pods contain one or more containers, including Docker containers. A Pod runs multiple containers; the containers are managed as a single entity and share the Pod's resources. Commonly, running a couple of containers in a single Pod is an advanced use case.

Pods also include shared networking and storage resources for their containers:

- Network: Pods are automatically assigned specific IP addresses. Pod containers share the identical network namespace, along with IP address and the network ports. Containers in a Pod communicate inside the Pod on localhost with each other.
- Storage: Pods specify a set of shared storage volumes that can be shared between the containers.

A Pod can be considered to be a self-contained, isolated "logical host" that consists of the systemic needs of the application it serves.

A Pod is supposed to run a single instance of your application on your cluster. However, it is not recommended to create individual Pods directly. As a substitute, you generally create a set of identical Pods, referred as replicas, to run your application. A set of replicated Pods are created and managed using a controller, such as a Deployment.

Controllers manage the lifecycle of their Pods and can also perform horizontal scaling, and changing the number of Pods as necessary.

Although, you may occasionally interact with Pods directly to troubleshoot, debug or inspect them. As it is recommended that a controller is used to manage your Pods.

Pods run on nodes in your cluster. Once created, a Pod stays on its node until its process is complete, then the Pod is deleted. The Pod is evicted from the node due to lack of resources, or the node fails. If a node fails, Pods on the node are automatically scheduled for deletion.

What is Deployment?

Deployments are a set of multiple, identical Pods without any unique identities. A Deployment is capable of running multiple replicas of your application and can automatically replace any instances that stop working or turn out to be unresponsive. In this way, Deployments ensure that more than one instances of your application are available to serve the user requests. Deployments are managed through the Kubernetes Deployment controller.

Deployment uses a Pod Template. When changes occur in the Deployment Pod template, new Pods are automatically created at a time.

What are Stateful Sets?

Stateful Sets represent a set of Pods with unique, persistent identities and stable hostnames that GKE maintains irrespective of where they are scheduled. The Pod is maintained in persistent disk storage associated with the Stateful Set, the state information and other resilient data for any given Stateful Set is stored.

Stateful Sets use an ordinal index for the identity and order in their Pods. By default, Stateful Set Pods are deployed in sequential order and are terminated in reverse ordinal order. For example, a Stateful Set named web has its Pod named as web-zero, web-1, and web-2. While the web Pod specification is modified, its Pods are stopped and recreated in an ordered way; in this example, web-2 is terminated first, then web-1, and so on. As an alternative, you can specify the podManagementPolicy: Parallel field to have a Stateful Set launch or terminate all of its Pods in parallel, instead of waiting for Pods to run and get prepared or to be terminated before launching or terminating another Pod.

Figure 6-01: Stateful Sets.

Stateful Sets use a Pod template, which consists of specifications for its Pods. The Pod specification describes how each Pod should look, what applications have to run inside its containers, which volumes it needs to mount, its labels and selectors, and much more.

What is a Daemon Set?

Like other workload objects, Daemon Sets manage the groups of replicated Pods. But, Daemon Sets attempt to adhere to a One-Pod-per-node model, either across the whole cluster or a subset of nodes. As you upload nodes to a node pool, Daemon Sets automatically add Pods to the new nodes as needed.

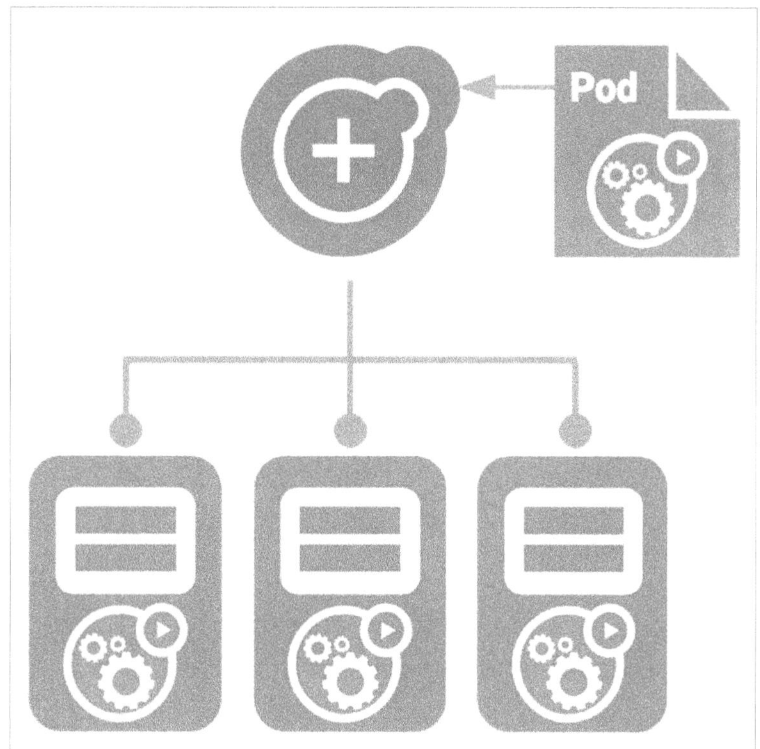

Figure 6-02: Daemon Sets.

Daemon Sets also uses a Pod template, which includes a specification for its Pods. The Pod specification describes how each Pod should look like, what programs should run inside its containers, which volumes it needs to mount, its labels and selectors, and more.

What is a Service?

The concept of a service is to gather a set of Pod endpoints into a single resource. You can configure multiple methods to access the grouping. By default, you receive a stable cluster IP address that clients within the cluster can use to contact Pods inside the service. A client generates a request to the stable IP address, and the request is routed to one of the Pods in the service.

A service identifies its member Pods by using a selector. For a Pod to become a member of the service, the Pod needs to have all the labels specified inside the selector. A label is an arbitrary key/value pair. This is attached to an object.

In a Kubernetes cluster, each Pod consists of an internal IP address. Pods in the Deployment come and go, and their IP addresses change. That is why Pod's IP address is not used directly. With a service, you get a stable IP address that lasts for the existence of the service, while the IP addresses of the member Pods change.

Service also provides Load Balancing. Clients can call a single and stable IP address, and their requests get balanced across the Pods, which are the members of the service.

Types of Services

There are five types of Services:

- ClusterIP (default): Internal clients generate a request to a stable internal IP address
- NodePort: Clients send requests to the node's IP address on node port which are specified by service
- LoadBalancer: Clients send the request to the IP address of Network Load Balancer
- ExternalName: Internal clients use the DNS name of a Service as an alias for an External DNS name
- Headless: Headless service is used in the situations where you want a Pod grouping, but do not need a stable IP address

HTTP(S) Load Balancing with Ingress

In GKE, an Ingress object defines rules for routing external HTTP(S) traffic to the programs running inside a cluster. An Ingress object is associated with service objects, each of which is concerned with a set of Pods.

When an Ingress Object is created, the GKE ingress controller creates a GCP HTTP(S) Load Balancer and configures it according to the data in the Ingress and its related services.

Features of HTTP(S) Load Balancing

The HTTP(S) Load Balancing which is configured by Ingress includes some of the following features:

- An Ingress defines how the traffic reaches to your services and how the traffic is routed to your application
- Ingress provides a single IP address for multiple services within the cluster
- Ingress can configure GCP features such as Google Managed SSL Certificates (Beta), Cloud CDN, Cloud Armor, and Cloud Identity Aware Proxy
- Ingress is capable of specifying the use of multiple TLS certificates for request terminations

Storage Overview

There are numerous storage options for the applications running on GKE. The choices vary in terms of simplicity of use and flexibility. Google Cloud Platform (GCP) gives several storage solutions, which are defined for different desires. Kubernetes also provides storage abstractions, which are used to provide storage in your cluster.

The simplest storage options are GCP's Managed Storage Products.

If you require a database, consider Google Cloud SQL, Cloud DataStore, or Cloud Spanner. While Google Cloud storage is used for object storage and for Private Docker container images use container Registry for storing.

Use Cloud FileStore if your application needs a managed Network Attached Storage (NAS). For POSIX-compatible file storage, a file server can be used on Compute Engine. If your application requires block storage, use Persistent Disks. You may provision persistent Disks manually, or allow Kubernetes to dynamically provision disks for you.

Kubernetes Storage Abstractions

Kubernetes Storage Abstractions provide block-based storage and file system to your Pods. They cannot be used with Cloud Storage and Managed Databases.

Volumes: Volumes are storage accessible to containers within a Pod. Some volume types are backed by ephemeral storage and are useful for storing configuration data and scratch space for programs. Different volume types are backed via durable storage.

Persistent Volumes: Persistent Volumes are cluster resources that Pods can use for long lasting storage. Persistent Volumes Claims can be used to dynamically provision persistent Volumes backed through Compute Engine persistent disks for the use in your cluster. You may additionally use Persistent Volume Claims to provide other kinds of backing storage like NFS.

Google App Engine (GAE)

App Engine is the original Google Cloud service and fairly easy to learn. Google App Engine (referred to as GAE or certainly App Engine) is a framework and a cloud computing platform used for developing and hosting web applications in Google-managed data centers. Applications are sandboxed and run throughout multiple servers. App Engine offers automatic scaling for web applications—because the variety of requests will increase for an application. App Engine automatically allocates more resources to the web application to handle the additional demand.

Google App Engine is free of cost up to a certain level of consumed resources and only in the standard environment but not in the inflexible surroundings. Charges are charged for extra storage, bandwidth, or instance hours required through the application. It was first released in April 2008 as a preview version and came out of preview in September 2011.

Codelabs

Google developers Codelabs offer a guided, tutorial, hands-on coding experience. Most codelabs will step you via the method of building a small application or adding a new function to a present application. They cover an extensive range of topics such as Android wear, Google Compute Engine, Project Tango, and Google APIs on iOS.

Lab 6.1 – For Analyzing Data

Scenario:

To improve the performance of an application, web developers need a Profiling tool to analyze the data in the Google Cloud Platform.

Solution:

Client app and Web developers commonly use profiling tools to improve their code's performance. Equivalent techniques are not as accessible or well adopted by backend services. Stack driver Profiler brings the same capabilities to service developers, regardless of whether their code is running, either on the GCP or elsewhere.

1. To target some learning objective, we have designed a bunch of labs to cover about how the Google Cloud works and how it can be used for a system.
2. To get familiarity with the lab environment, we will perform a lab in your trial account.
3. This is the link of Google Cloud Code Labs.

https://codelabs.developers.google.com/?cat=Cloud.

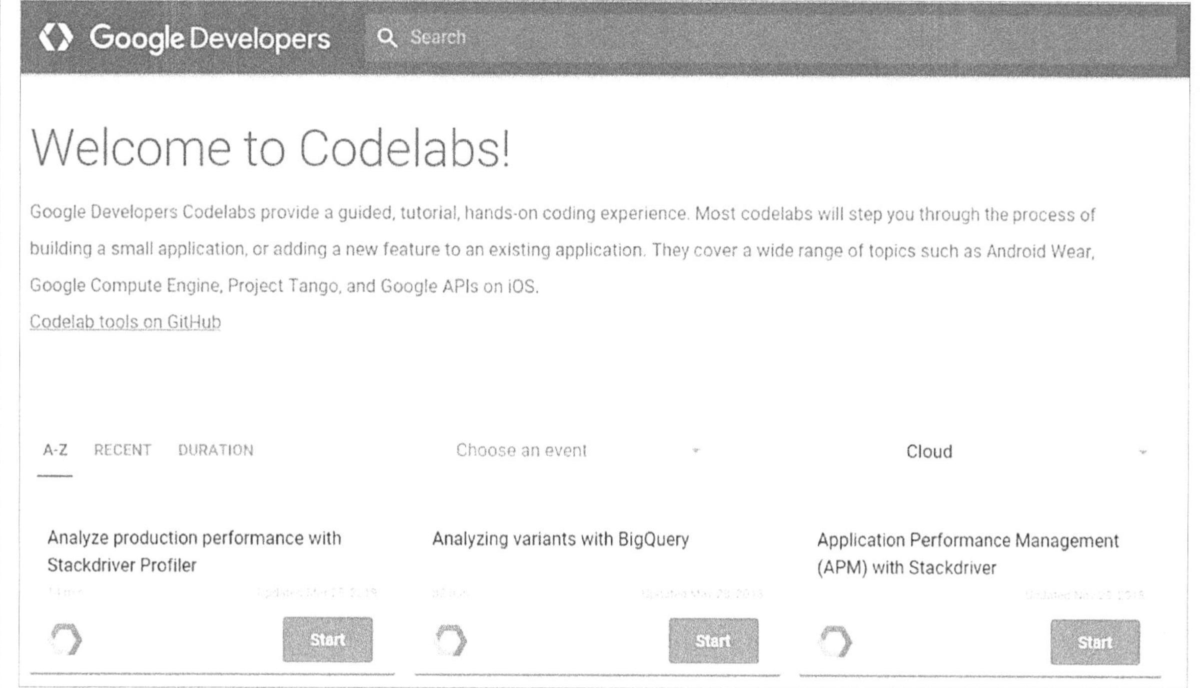

4. Open up the code lab using the given link. And perform any of the labs that you want to perform as it will provide you a complete guide of what you can do and how you can do.
5. Right here we are performing the very first lab to analyze production performance with "Stackdriver Profiler".

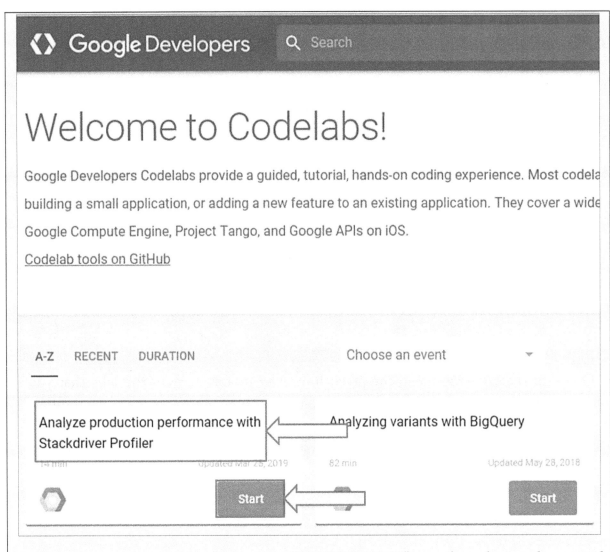

6. Create a new project by clicking on “NEW PROJECT” or select the newly created project.

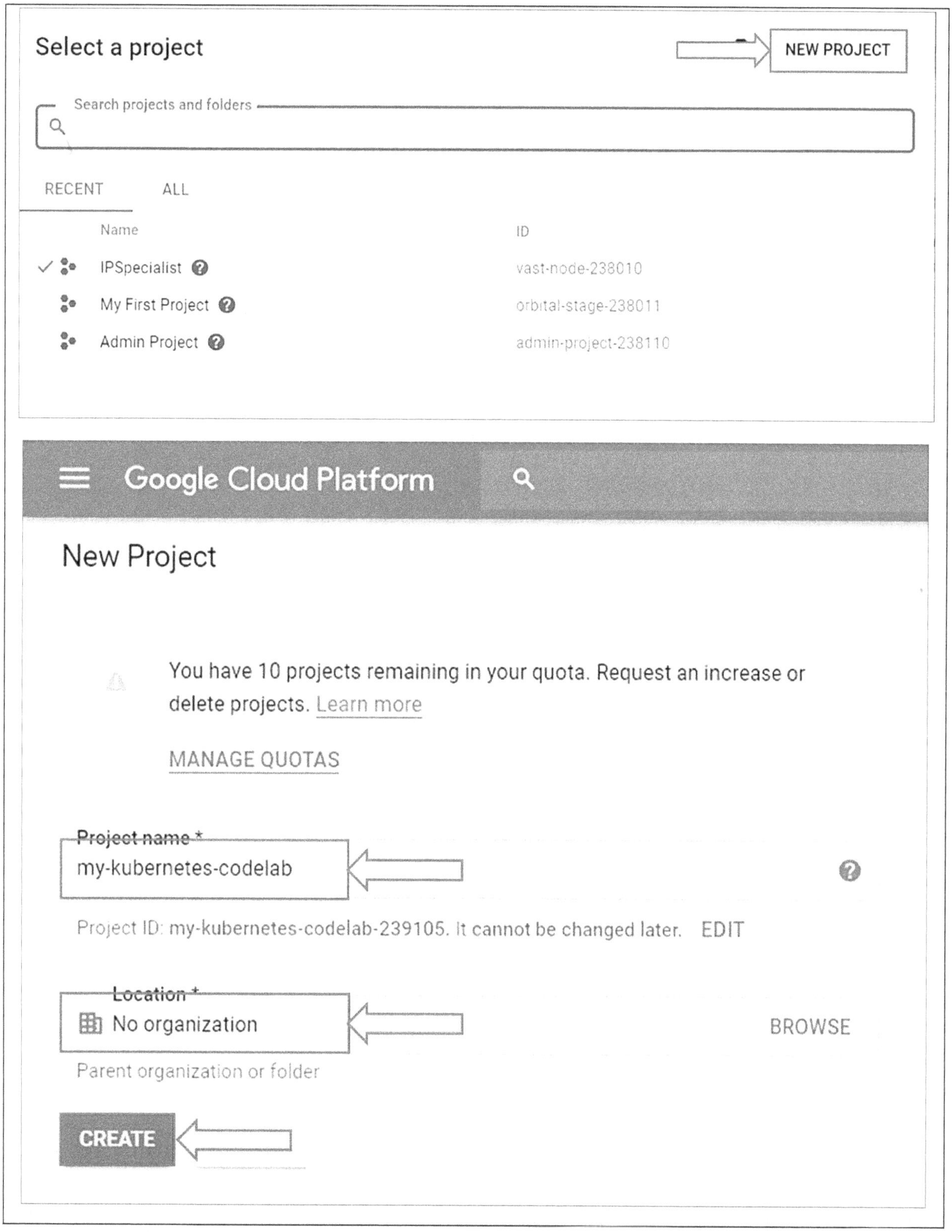

Select a project

NEW PROJECT

Search projects and folders

RECENT ALL

Name	ID
✓ IPSpecialist	vast-node-238010
My First Project	orbital-stage-238011
Admin Project	admin-project-238110

Google Cloud Platform

New Project

You have 10 projects remaining in your quota. Request an increase or delete projects. Learn more

MANAGE QUOTAS

Project name *

my-kubernetes-codelab

Project ID: my-kubernetes-codelab-239105. It cannot be changed later. EDIT

Location *

No organization

BROWSE

Parent organization or folder

CREATE

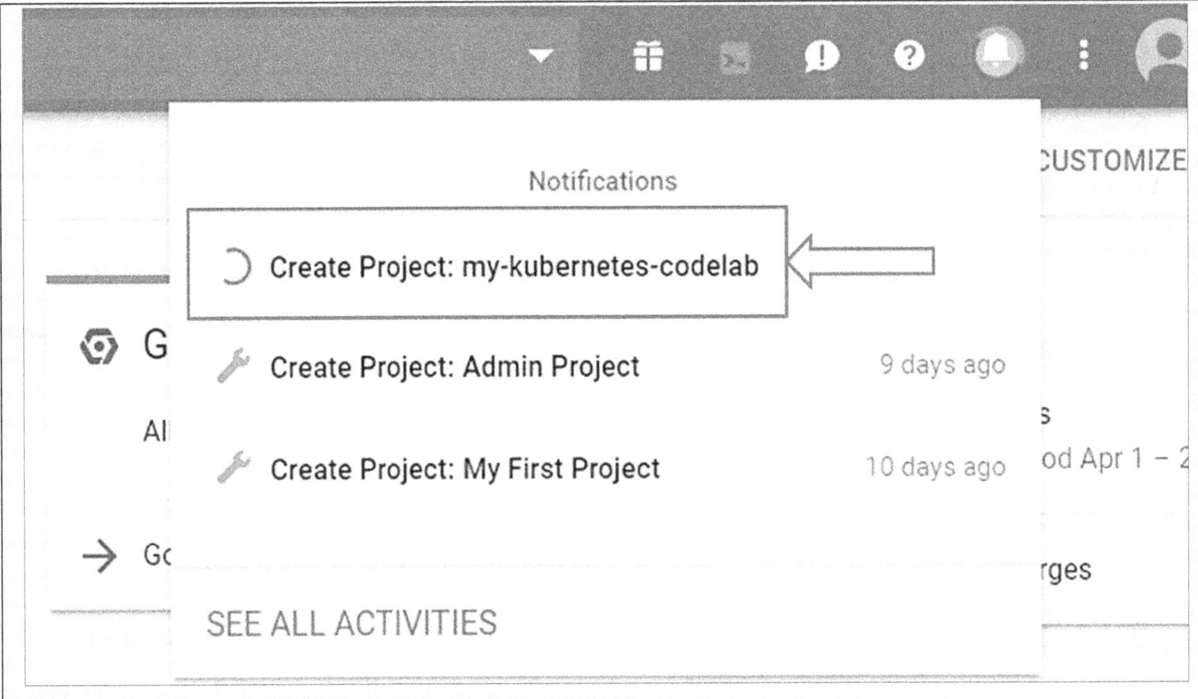

7. Next, you need to enable the billing to use Google Cloud resources.
8. Click on "Activate Cloud Shell".

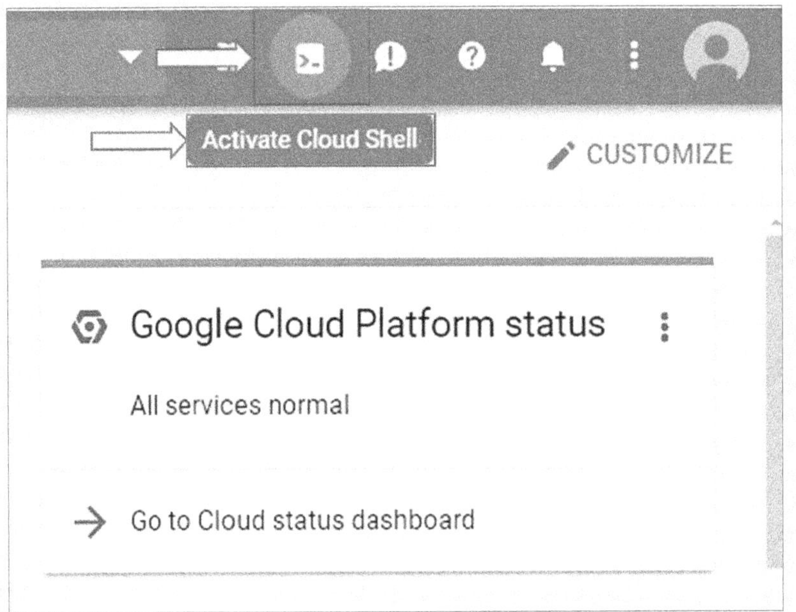

9. Run the described command in the Cloud Shell to check if you are authenticated or not.

```
afiaafaq2@cloudshell:~ (my-kubernetes-codelab-239105)$ gcloud auth list
   Credentialed Accounts
ACTIVE  ACCOUNT
*       afiaafaq2@gmail.com

To set the active account, run:
    $ gcloud config set account `ACCOUNT`

afiaafaq2@cloudshell:~ (my-kubernetes-codelal gcloud config list project
[core]
project = my-kubernetes-codelab-239105

Your active configuration is: [cloudshell-10363]
afiaafaq2@cloudshell:~ (my-kubernetes-codelab-239105)$
```

10. Go to "Profiler" from Navigation Panel in GCP console.

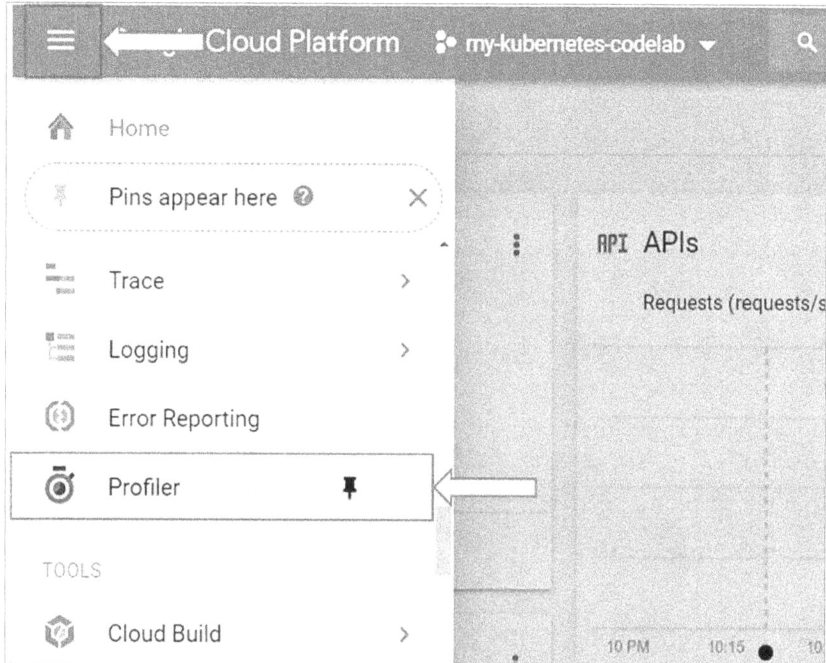

11. Here you can see that there is no such data to display.

Stackdriver Profiler

No data to display

No profiling data is found for project "my-kubernetes-codelab", likely because no profiling agent has been configured or the selected time period is too short.

To configure the data collection, follow the setup instructions, or take a 5-minute quickstart.

12. Write this command to upload the data.

```
started.
 is set to my-kubernetes-codelab-239105.
" to change to a different project.
ab-239105)$ gcloud auth list

ab-239105)$ go get -u github.com/GoogleCloudPlatform/golang-samples/profiler/...

ab-239105)$ cd ~/gopath/src/github.com/GoogleCloudPlatform/golang-samples/profiler/hotapp
```

13. Add the directory.
14. Run this file named as "main.go" by using the command "go run main.go".

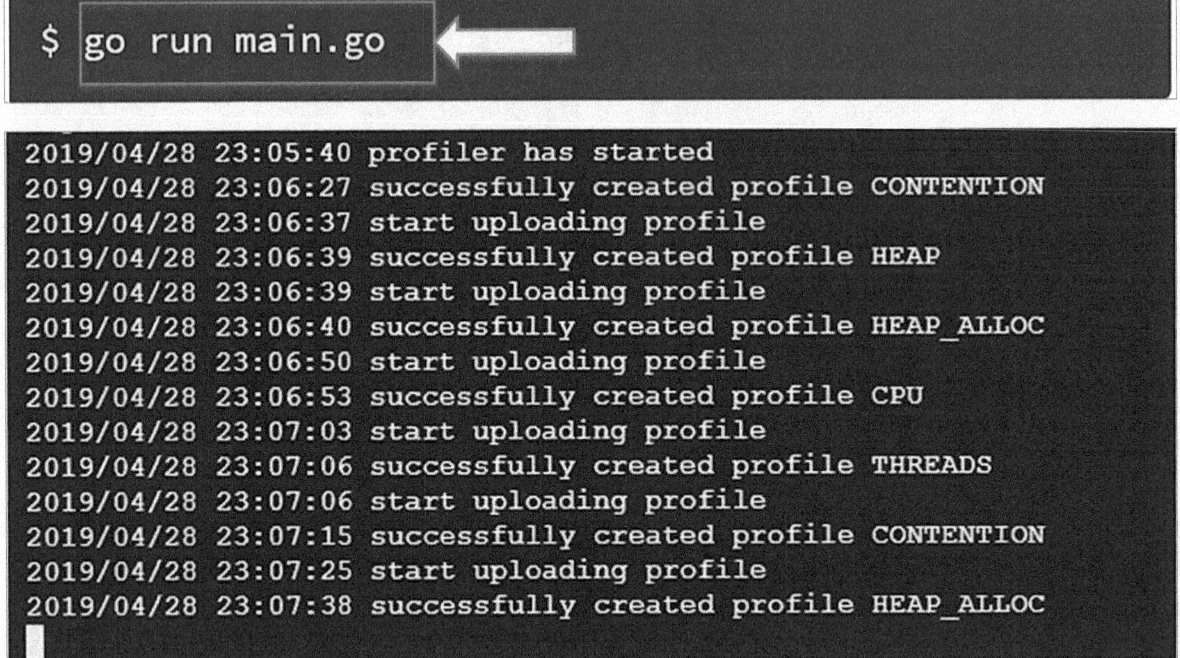

```
$ go run main.go
```

```
2019/04/28 23:05:40 profiler has started
2019/04/28 23:06:27 successfully created profile CONTENTION
2019/04/28 23:06:37 start uploading profile
2019/04/28 23:06:39 successfully created profile HEAP
2019/04/28 23:06:39 start uploading profile
2019/04/28 23:06:40 successfully created profile HEAP_ALLOC
2019/04/28 23:06:50 start uploading profile
2019/04/28 23:06:53 successfully created profile CPU
2019/04/28 23:07:03 start uploading profile
2019/04/28 23:07:06 successfully created profile THREADS
2019/04/28 23:07:06 start uploading profile
2019/04/28 23:07:15 successfully created profile CONTENTION
2019/04/28 23:07:25 start uploading profile
2019/04/28 23:07:38 successfully created profile HEAP_ALLOC
```

15. Now, go back to Profiler, and click on the button "Now".

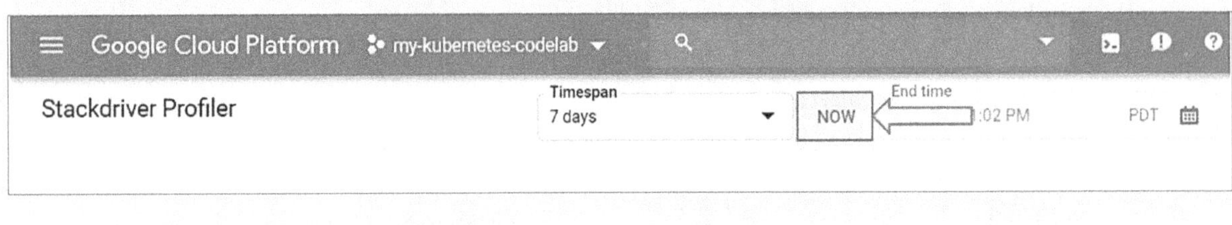

16. Now, you can analyze all the data.
17. You can also analyze the stack.

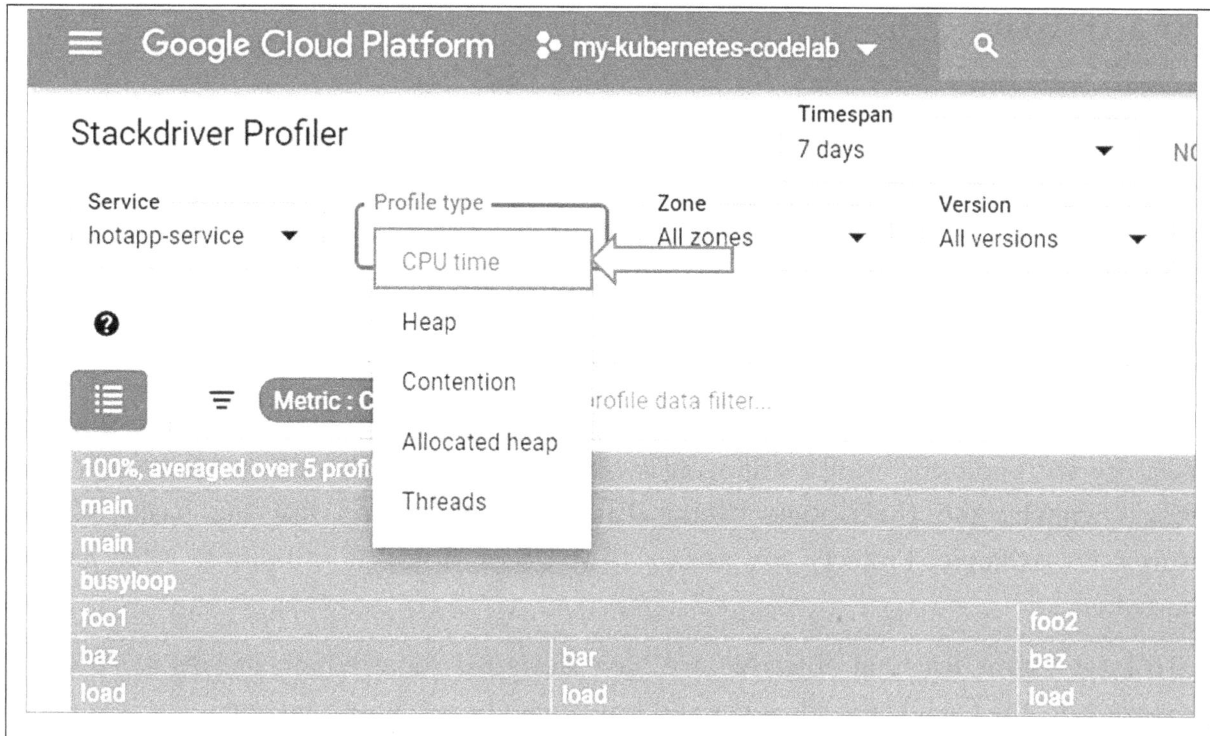

18. In this lab, you get to know about how a Go program could be configured with Stackdriver Profiler. You also learn about how to collect, view and analyze the performance data by using Stackdriver. You can apply your new skill to the services you run on GCP.

Qwiklabs

Qwiklabs provide you with temporary credentials to Google Cloud Platform and enable you to learn the Cloud using the real thing. From 30-minute individual labs to multi-day courses, from introductory level to expert, instructor-led or self-paced, with topics like machine learning, security, infrastructure, app dev, and more.

Lab 6.2- Qwiklabs

Scenario:

Qwiklab provides a temporary credential to GCP and AWS, so you can learn the Cloud using real environment. To get familiar with the Qwiklab environment or, how a Qwiklab works and how many different services they provide, this lab is designed.

Solution:

It is expected that students have some IT, or computing background, and have some familiarity with administering computing systems. In this first hands-on lab, you will access Qwiklabs and the Google Cloud Platform Console and use the basic GCP features, for example, Projects, Resources, IAM Users, Roles, Permissions, APIs, and Cloud Shell.

1. To target some learning objective, we have designed some bunch of labs to cover about how the Google Cloud works and how it can be used for a system.
2. To get familiarity with the lab environment, we will perform the lab using Qwiklab.
3. Click on "Join to Start This Lab".

A Tour of Qwiklabs and the Google Cloud Platform

4. Click on "Start Lab".

Start Lab 00:45:00

A Tour of Qwiklabs and the Google Cloud Platform

5. Click on "Open Google Console".

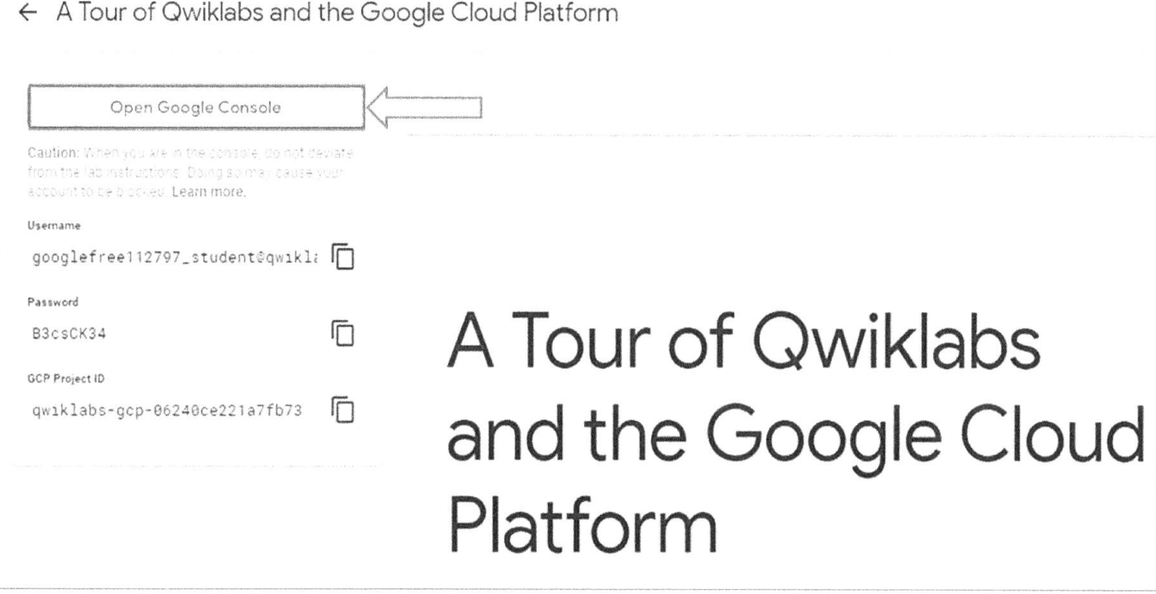

6. Copy the email address.

← A Tour of Qwiklabs and the Google Cloud Platform

Open Google Console

Caution: When you are in the console, do not deviate from the lab instructions. Doing so may cause your account to be blocked. Learn more.

Username

googlefree112797_student Copied!

Password

B3csCK34

GCP Project ID

qwiklabs-gcp-06240ce221a7fb73

A Tour of Qwiklabs and the Google Cloud Platform

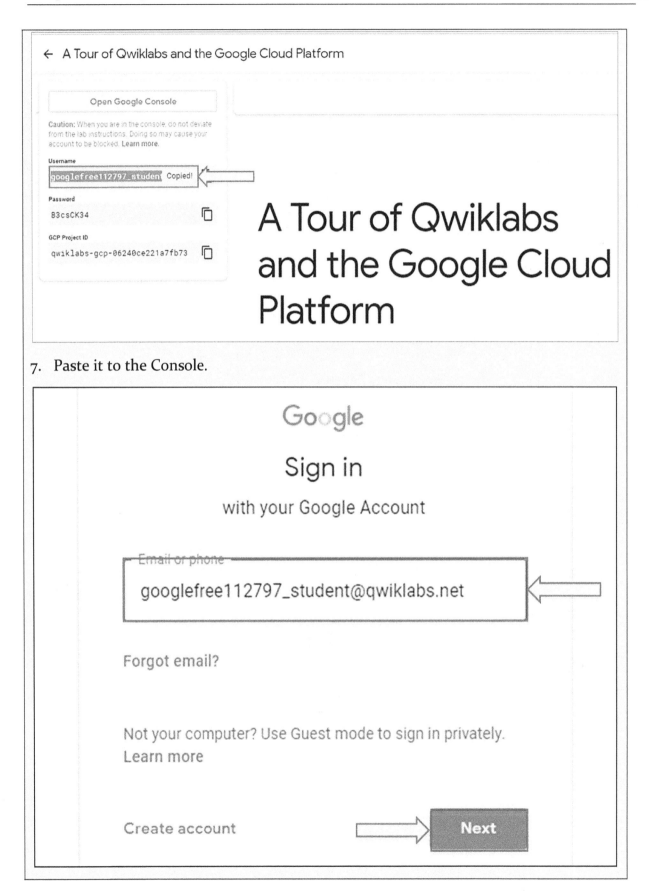

7. Paste it to the Console.

Google

Sign in

with your Google Account

Email or phone

googlefree112797_student@qwiklabs.net

Forgot email?

Not your computer? Use Guest mode to sign in privately.
Learn more

Create account

Next

8. Copy the Password.

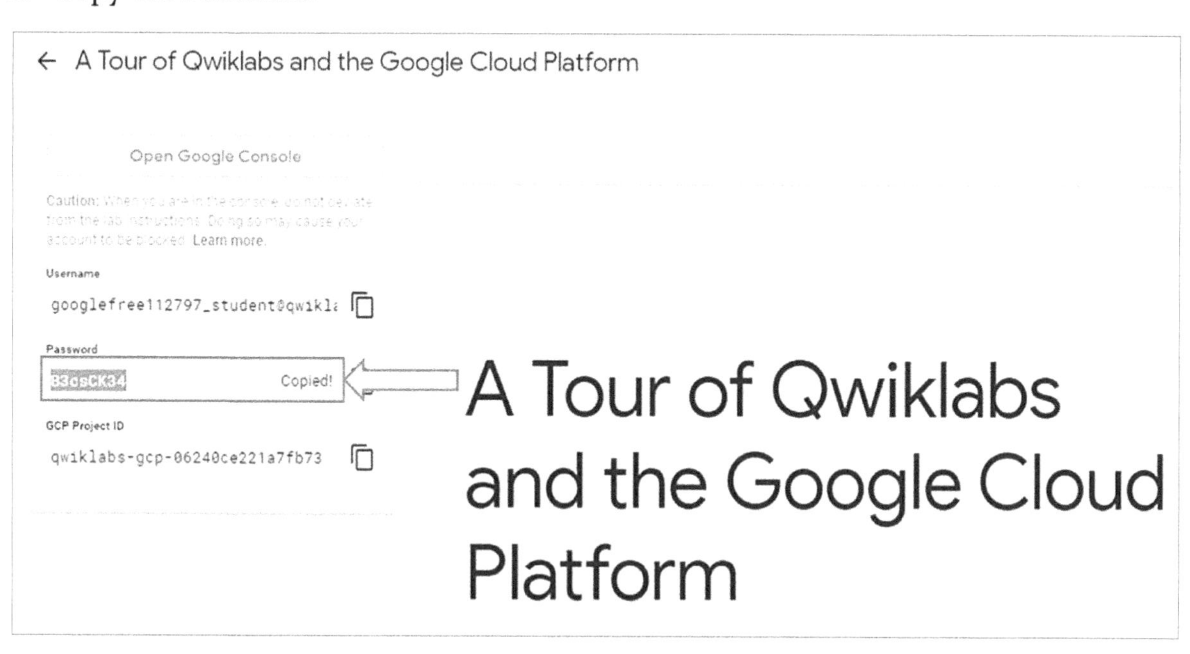

9. Paste it to the Console.

10. After reading the privacy and policy, click on "Accept".

Google

Welcome to your new account

Welcome to your new account: googlefree112797_student@qwiklabs.net. Your account is compatible with many Google services, but your qwiklabs.net administrator decides which services you may access using your account. For tips about using your new account, visit the Google Help Center.

When you use Google services, your domain administrator will have access to your googlefree112797_student@qwiklabs.net account information, including any data you store with this account in Google services. You can learn more here, or by consulting your organization's privacy policy, if one exists. You can choose to maintain a separate account for your personal use of any Google services, including email. If you have multiple Google accounts, you can manage which account you use with Google services and switch between them whenever you choose. Your username and profile picture can help you ensure that you're using the intended account.

If your organization provides you access to the G Suite core services, your use of those services is governed by your organization's G Suite agreement. Any other Google services your administrator enables ("Additional Services") are available to you under the Google Terms of Service and the Google Privacy Policy. Certain Additional Services may also have service-specific terms. Your use of any services your administrator allows you to access constitutes acceptance of applicable service-specific terms.

Click "Accept" below to indicate that you understand this description of how your googlefree112797_student@qwiklabs.net account works and agree to the Google Terms of Service and the Google Privacy Policy.

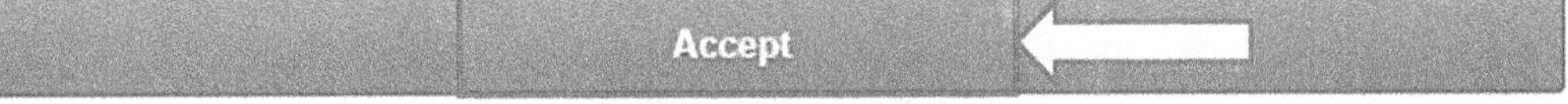

11. Your screen will appear like this.
12. This is your project selector.

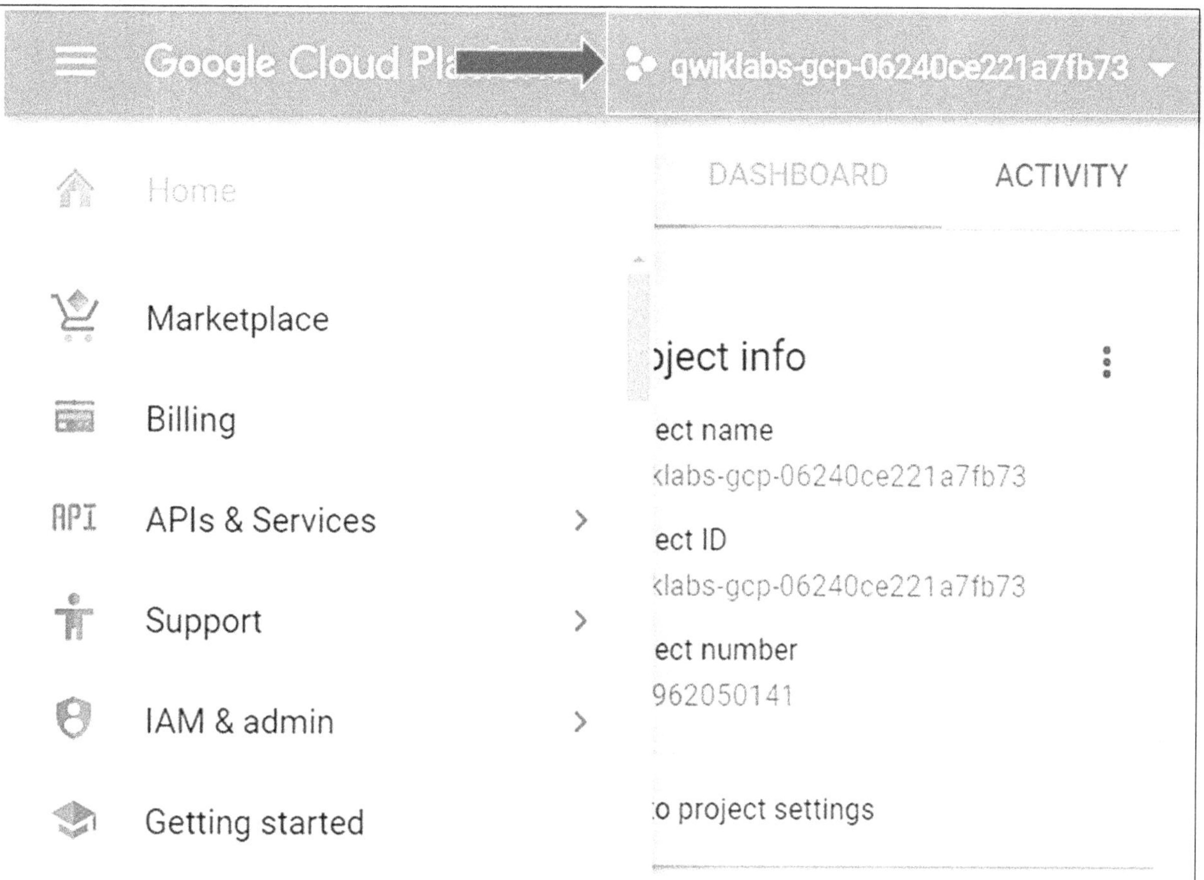

13. You can access the products and service from the Navigation Panel.

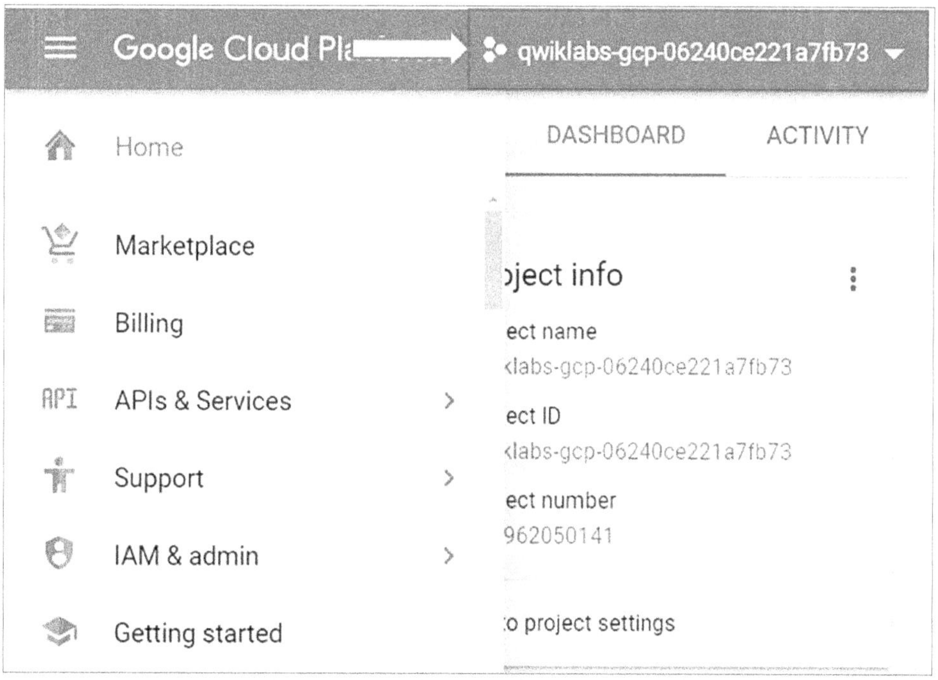

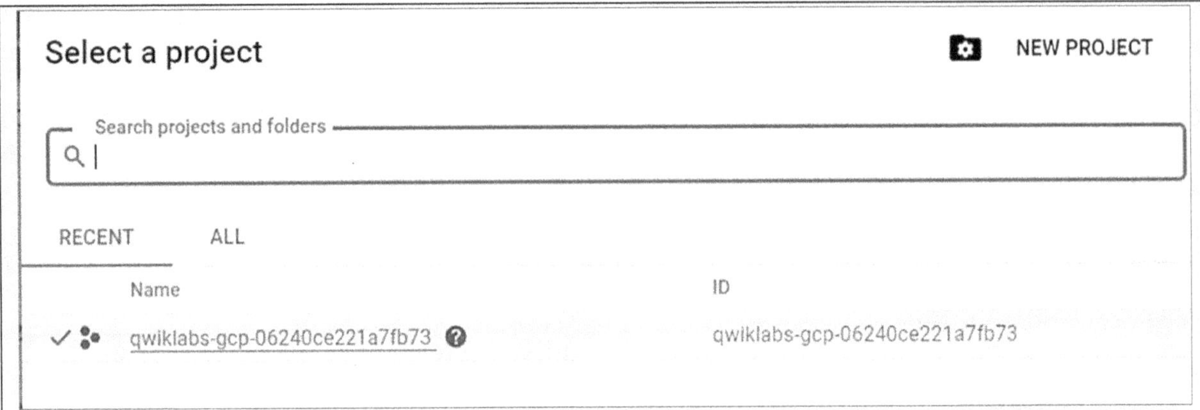

14. You can activate Google Cloud Shell by clicking on "Activate Cloud Shell".

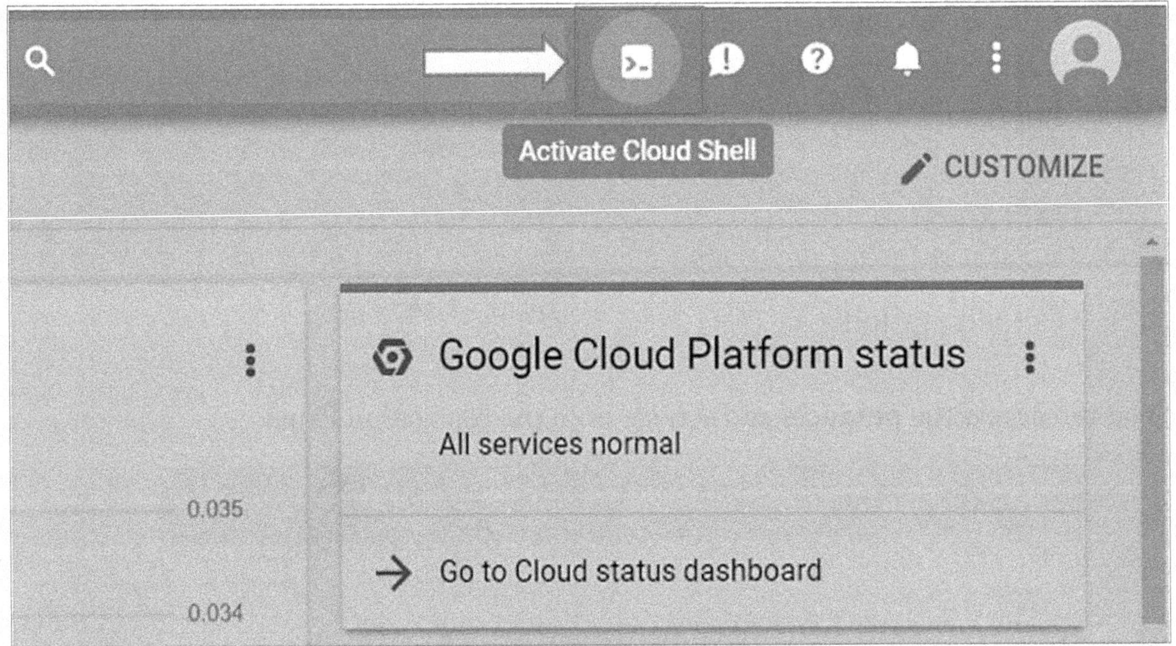

15. Back here you can see time is automatically running.
16. When you complete the entire lab, make sure to click on "End Lab".

IPSpecialist
Let Your Career Flow

End Lab 00:38:46

A Tour of Qwiklabs and the Google Cloud Platform

17. When you click on End Lab, you will be prompted with the screen.

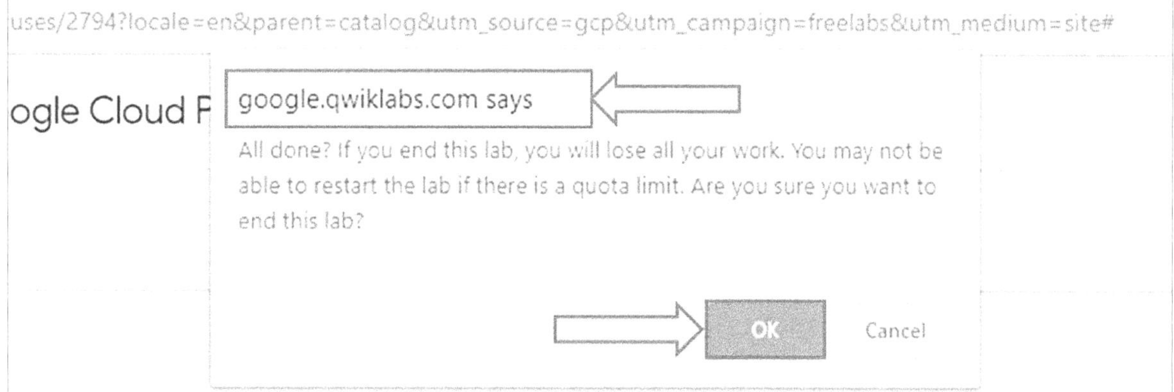
uses/2794?locale=en&parent=catalog&utm_source=gcp&utm_campaign=freelabs&utm_medium=site#
ogle Cloud F
google.qwiklabs.com says
All done? If you end this lab, you will lose all your work. You may not be able to restart the lab if there is a quota limit. Are you sure you want to end this lab?
OK
Cancel

A Tour of Qwiklabs and the Google Cloud Platform

18. Provide your feedback or either cancel it.

How satisfied are you with this lab?

Comment

Cancel Submit

19. Firstly, make sure to start or end the lab before the time runs out. Secondly, there is no way to pause the lab and lastly use the same credential by just copying to access the Qwiklab.

Mind Map

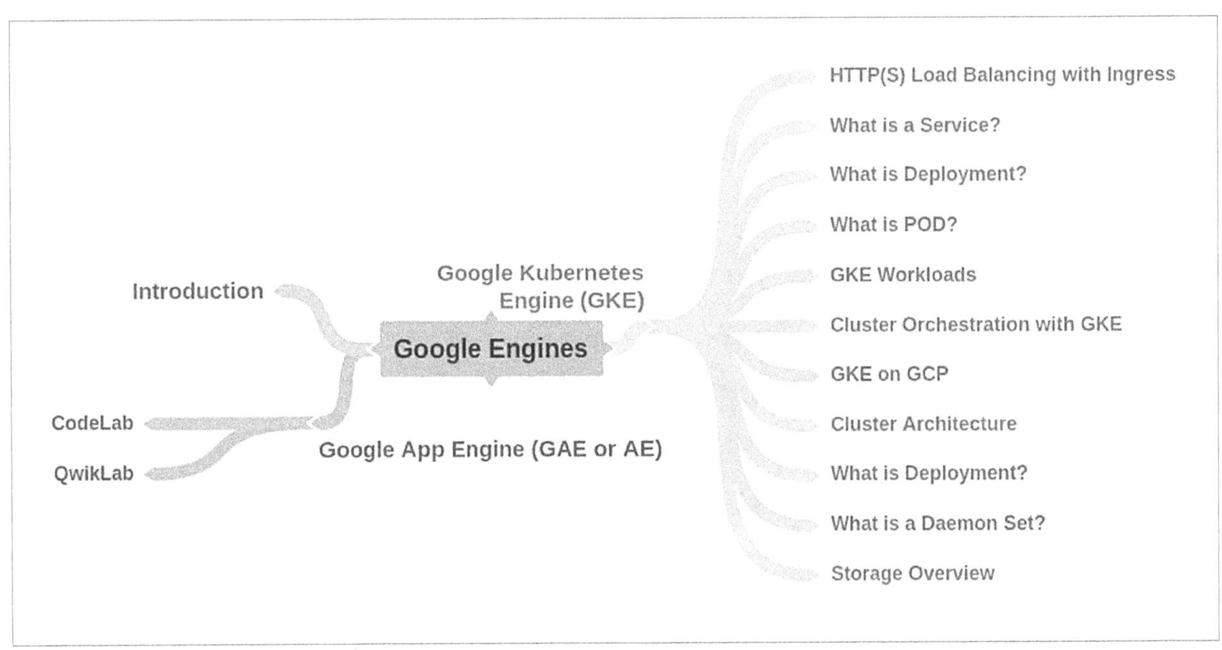

Figure 6-03: Chapter's Mind Map.

Practice Questions

1. GKE helps you in providing a managed environment used for ______________ your containerized applications working on Google Infrastructure.
   A. Deploying.
   B. Managing.
   C. Scaling.
   D. All of the Above.

2. The GKE consists of multiple machines which are grouped to form a __________.
   A. Cluster.
   B. Master Cluster.
   C. Node.
   D. None of the Above.

3. GKE clusters are powered via the _________________________system.
   A. Kubernetes Open Source Cluster Management.
   B. Kubernetes Storage Abstraction.
   C. Cluster Orchestration with GKE.
   D. All of the Above.

4. You operate Kubernetes commands and resources to:
   A. Set up and control your packages.
   B. Perform Management Tasks.
   C. Monitor the Workload Performance.
   D. All of the Above.

5. When you run a GKE cluster, you can also take some advantages of advanced management features that GCP provides, which are:
   A. GCP load balancing for the instances of Compute Engine.
   B. Node Pools are used to designate subsets of nodes inside the cluster to provide additional flexibility.
   C. Automatic Scaling for instance count of cluster nodes.
   D. Automatic Upgrade for node software of cluster.
   E. Node Auto Repair used to maintain the availability and health of the node.
   F. Logging and Monitoring with Stackdriver to look after the cluster.
   G. All of the Above.

6. GKE works with: (choose any 2)
   A. Containerized Application.
   B. Non-Containerized Application.
   C. Applications that are packed into hardware as an independent, isolated user-space instances.
   D. GKE Cluster.

7. In GKE and Kubernetes, those containers are known as:
   A. POD.
   B. Deployment.
   C. Workloads.
   D. Service.

8. In GKE, a cluster consists of worker machines referred as:
   A. Cluster.
   B. Nodes.
   C. Workloads.
   D. None of the Above.

9. Kubernetes cluster orchestration system runs on: (choose any 2)
   A. Master Cluster.
   B. Node Machines.
   C. Workloads.
   D. Cluster.

10. The Kubernetes objects which represent your containerized applications, they all run on the:
    A. On the top of Node.
    B. On the top of Cluster.
    C. On the top of Workload.
    D. None of the Above.

11. A cluster typically consists of one or more ______________, which are the worker machines that run your containerized applications and different workloads.
    A. Nodes.
    B. Cluster.
    C. Workloads.
    D. None of the Above.

12. A ________ runs all the services which might be important to support the Docker containers that make up your cluster's workloads.
    A. Nodes.
    B. Cluster.
    C. Workloads.
    D. None of the Above.

13. __________________ are the smallest and the most basic deployable objects in Kubernetes.
    A. Deployment.
    B. Pod.
    C. Stateful Set.
    D. Daemon Set.

14. A Pod runs:
    A. Single Container.
    B. Multiple Container.

15. For their containers, Pod includes:
    A. Shared Networking.
    B. Storage Resources.
    C. Both A and B.
    D. None of the Above.

16. __________ is a set of multiple, identical Pods without any unique identities.
    A. Pod.
    B. Deployment.
    C. Stateful Set.
    D. Daemon Set.

17. __________________ensures that more than one instances of your application are available to serve the user requests.
    A. Pod.
    B. Deployment.
    C. Stateful Set.
    D. Daemon Set.

18. ________________ represent a set of Pods with unique, persistent identities and

stable hostnames that GKE maintains irrespective of where they are scheduled.

A. Pod.
B. Deployment.
C. Stateful Set.
D. Daemon Set.

19. ______________ manages groups of replicated Pods.

A. Pod.
B. Deployment.
C. Stateful Set.
D. Daemon Set.

20. ________________ is used to gather a set of Pod endpoints into a single resource.

A. Cluster Architecture.
B. Service.
C. Storage Overview.
D. HTTP Load Balancing with Ingress.

21. In Service, you receive a stable cluster IP address that clients within the cluster can use to contact ___________ inside the service.

A. Pod.
B. Deployment.
C. Stateful Set.
D. Daemon Set.

22. In GKE, __________________ object defines rules for routing external HTTP(S) traffic to program the running inside a cluster.

A. Pod.
B. Deployment.
C. Ingress.
D. Cluster Master.

23. An Ingress object is associated with _____________, each of which is concerned with a set of Pods.

A. Service Objects.
B. Pod Objects.
C. Deployment Objects.
D. None of the Above.

24. _______________ provides block-based storage and file system to your Pods.
    A. Kubernetes Storage Abstraction.
    B. HTTP(S) Load Balancing with Ingress.
    C. Cluster Orchestration with GKE.
    D. None of the Above.

25. _______________ is a framework and cloud computing platform used for developing and hosting web applications in Google-managed data centers.
    A. Google App Engine.
    B. Google Kubernetes Engine.
    C. Both A and B.
    D. None of the Above.

Answers:

Chapter 01: Cloud Concepts
1. **A** (IaaS) **Explanation:** Infrastructure as a Software provides basic building blocks for Cloud. 2. **B** (Hybrid) **Explanation:** The hybrid deployment model is a mixture of on-premises Private Cloud and third part Public Cloud, and it is in between on-premises and Cloud. 3. **A** (Zone) **Explanation:** The zone is a concept where two or more data centers are logically grouped together. There are multiple zones around the globe, but each zone is independent of another zone. 4. **B** (Region) **Explanation:** Zones are grouped together in a region. Zones within the region can communicate with each other very quickly but not as quick as compared to the communication between the data centers in the zone. 5. **A** (Source) **Explanation:** In normal network, the data goes to the edge location, which is closest to the destination via the internet, but in Google network, the traffic enters from the internet to the edge location closest to the source. 6. **B** (Egress) **Explanation:** Network traffic is also charged but only for traffic going out of the network, not for incoming traffic. 7. **C** (PaaS)

Explanation:

Google App Engine is Platform as a Service (PaaS). Many of the resources are managed by Google for the user by using App Engine.

8. **A** (Google App Engine)

Explanation:

You can obtain the following by using the Google App Engine:

- Management of app hosting, scaling, monitoring, and infrastructure are done for user by Google

9. **B** (CaaS)

Explanation:

Google Kubernetes Engine is GCP's Container as a Service (CaaS). In Container-based service, the user does not have to consume time on deployment and integration into the hosting environment.

10. **B** (Cluster)

Explanation:

Creating and managing Compute Engine groups of instances running Kubernetes is called clusters. Kubernetes Engine uses compute engine instances as cluster nodes. Each node runs the Docker runtime, a Kubernetes node agent monitors the node's health, and is a simple network proxy.

11. **C** (IaaS)

Explanation:

Google Compute Engine is an unmanaged service of GCP works as Infrastructure as a Service (IaaS). Users should select and configure the platform components.

12. **B** (NoSQL)

Explanation:

Cloud Datastore and Cloud Bigtable for NoSQL data storage.

13. **A** (BigQuery)

Explanation:

GCP offers BigQuery for data analysis services.

14. **B** (Cloud Dataflow)

Explanation:

GCP provides managed services and sets of SDKs used for Batch and Streaming data processing tasks. This service is named as Cloud Dataflow. Dataflow is ideal for the processing task, which can be easily divided into parallel workloads.

15. **C** (Service Accounts)

Explanation:

A Service Account (SAC), instead of an individual end user, is a particular kind of Google Account that belongs to your application or VM.

16. **B** (12 months.)

Explanation:

When you create a free tier account for GCP, you also get USD 300 credit that you can use for up to 12 months, and this feature defines your free-tier account.

17. **C** (more than 8 Virtual CPUs at once.)

Explanation:

Business Accounts are not eligible for the free trial account. Free –tier account has some restrictions. When you are on the free trial, you are not allowed to have more than 9 Virtual CPUs together at once.

18. **A** (24 hours.)

Explanation:

From the Compute Side of things, each day you can run 24 hours' worth of f1-micro instance in most of the US regions, and you would not get charged for it.

19. **D** (28 hours.)

Explanation:

Also, in the Always Free Compute Category, we have App Engine, where an application can run 28 hours each day in North America without getting charged. You can also run two million Cloud Functions within certain size and time limit.

20. **A** (10 GB/ month of data.)

Explanation:

Cloud Pub/Sub has 10GB/ month of data because Cloud Pub/Sub is the global

messaging service in which you can write data from one region in the world and read from the other region.

21. **A** (120 minutes of build and 60 minutes of Voice Recognition.)

Explanation:

Every day you can perform 120 minutes of build, in Google Cloud Container Builders and can perform 60 minutes of Voice recognition each month in Google Cloud Speech API.

22. **C** (Both A and B.)

Explanation:

You can perform 1000 unit/ month of Cloud Vision API calls and 5000 unit/ month Google Cloud Natural Language API.

23. **A** (5 GB.)

Explanation:

Google also has a Cloud Shell existing in the console with 5GB of persistent disk storage quota. You can also perform 1GB f Google Cloud Source Repository Private Hosting.

24. **A** (The name of the project can be changed, but project number and ID cannot be changed.)

Explanation:

Google assigns a Project number and automatically generates an ID for the project as well. The name of the project can be changed, but the project number and ID cannot be changed.

25. **D** (All of the Above.)

Explanation:

According to GCP Documentation, tools for monitoring, analyzing and optimizing cost now become an important part of the managing development.

Chapter 02: Getting Started

1. **A** (Greg Wilson.)

Explanation:

It all comes back to a document made by Greg Wilson, who is the director of Developer relations at Google.

2. **E** (All of the Above.)

Explanation:

The cheat sheet is divided into multiple categories. We have Compute Products, Storage Products, Networking Products, Management Tools, Developer Tools and many more.

3. **B** (Google Commerce Search.)

Explanation:

Google has released a special version of its product for enterprise use. Google Commerce Search shows several navigations.

4. **B** (Analytics.)

Explanation:

This service is adopted by many websites as it is a free service.

5. **A** (Gears.)

Explanation:

Google Gear includes a database engine which is installed on the client that caches the data and synchronize it.

6. **A** (GCP.)

Explanation:

Google Cloud Platform, is a platform used for cloud computing which provides infrastructure tools and services for users which helps in building applications and services.

7. **B** (Google Cloud Platform.)

Explanation:

Google Cloud Platform is considered as the third biggest cloud provider in terms of revenue.

8. **D** (2008.)

Explanation:

Google announced its first cloud platform, Google App Engine, in 2008, and they continuously added more tools and services until it became known as the Google Cloud Platform later on.

9. **D** (All of the Above.)

Explanation:

Compute Engine in Compute products which are described as Virtual Machines, disks, and networks. This is the most relatable Google Cloud Product, just like computers you might buy from stores, and you can run whatever you want to run, and perform virtually anything you want to perform.

10. **A** (Event-driven server less function.)

Explanation:

Cloud Function which is a little way down in the list describes as Event-driven server less function. Cloud Function even perform faster than the Compute Engine within the 10th of the second and manages all the scaling for you automatically.

11. **B** (Cloud Storage.)

Explanation:

Cloud Storage is like the purest service at its core. It says give me some data, and I can give it back to you. That's why it is described as object storage and serving.

12. **B** (Cloud Storage.)

Explanation:

Nearline and Coldline are just versions of the Cloud Storage that are priced and optimized for less frequent data access, so they are perfect for backups.

13. **A** (Object-Based Storage.)

Explanation:

The Cloud Storage Product is object storage, but the persistent disk is block storage, so it works much like a hard drive works, and it only connects to Compute Engine instances.

14. **B** (Block Based Storage.)

Explanation:

The Cloud Storage Product is object storage, but the persistent disk is block storage, so it works much like a hard drive works, and it only connects to Compute Engine instances.

15. **A** (Cloud Storage and Persistent Disk.)

Explanation:

Cloud File Store sits between Cloud Storage and Persistent Disk and it is neither object based nor block based.

16. **D** (Neither Object-Based nor Block Based.)

Explanation:

Cloud File Store sits between Cloud Storage and Persistent Disk and it is neither object based nor block based.

17. **A** (Transfer Flow Processing Unit.)

Explanation:

The Cloud TPU is enlisted in AI and Machine Learning sections, but it is specialized hardware for Machine Learning (ML), so it's kind of like a Compute Engine Instances, but this one is built for Transfer Flow Processing instead of General Purpose Processing. TPU stands for Transfer Flow Processing Unit.

18. **C** (AI and Machine Learning Section.)

Explanation:

The Cloud TPU is enlisted in AI and Machine Learning sections, but it is specialized hardware for Machine Learning (ML), so it's kind of like a Compute Engine Instances, but this one is built for Transfer Flow Processing instead of General Purpose Processing. TPU stands for Transfer Flow Processing Unit.

19. **A** (Audio to Text.)

Explanation:

The Cloud Speech-to-Text will convert Audio to Text and Cloud Text-to-Speech will convert Text to Audio.

20. **B** (Text to Audio.)

Explanation:

The Cloud Speech-to-Text will convert Audio to Text and Cloud Text-to-Speech will convert Text to Audio.

21. **B** (Cloud Dataproc.)

Explanation:

In the Data and Analytics section, two of the core services that stand out are Cloud Dataflow and Cloud Dataproc. Spark and Hadoop manage cloud Dataproc. So, if you are already running Hadoop somewhere else, Cloud Dataproc is an efficient way to move that data to Google Cloud.

22. **A** (Cloud Dataflow.)

Explanation:'

The Cloud Dataflow also process a large amount of data but it is newer and better than Cloud Dataproc, and it handles both stream and batch data processing

23. **D** (BigQuery.)

Explanation:

Google BigQuery which is used as the Data Warehouse and Analytics. BigQuery is serverless; when you are not using it means you are not paying for it. It scales up automatically and handles it without a problem. You can store tons of data in BigQuery and still get incredibly fast responses for your queries.

24. **D** (All of the Above.)

Explanation:

Each GCP project contains:

- A project name

- A project ID
- A project number

25. **A** (USD 300.)

Explanation:

When you create a free tier account for GCP, you also get USD 300 credit that you can use for up to 12 months, and this feature defines your free-tier account.

Chapter 03: Basic Services

1. **B** (Project)

Explanation:

A project consists of a set of users, a set of APIs. Settings for those APIs to be billed, authenticated and monitored. You can have one or more projects.

2. **C** (64)

Explanation:

You have a limit of 64 labels per bucket.

3. **D** (1024 bytes)

Explanation:

The object size in GCS is 1024 bytes.

4. **C** (Versioning)

Explanation:

If versioning of object is enabled on the bucket, then all older versions are kept stored with generation number to identify it. In this way, you can restore the older version or either delete it depending on your requirement.

5. **A** (True)

Explanation:

Yes, objects are immutable and cannot be modified throughout their storage life after uploading.

6. **C** (Viewer)

Explanation:

Roles/Viewer: Members with this role can list buckets in the project.

7. **A** (Multi-Regional)

Explanation:

Multi-regional Google Cloud storage stores data in data centers worldwide with 99.95%

availability.

8. **B** (Regional)

Explanation:

Instead of spreading over a large geographic location, Regional Storage stores data in one geographic location at a low cost. It is best suited for computing, analytical and machine learning work.

9. **C** (Nearline Storage)

Explanation:

Nearline Storage is for storing data that are infrequently accessed. It is low-cost storage with low availability and a minimum of 30 days storage duration.

10. **D** (Coldline)

Explanation:

Coldline Storage is durable storage with low cost for DR, backup, and data archiving. In this, your data will be available within milliseconds.

11. **B** (False)

Explanation:

Metadata, for which you can define value, but the key that is set is known as fixed key metadata.

12. **B** (Pub/Sub)

Explanation:

If there are any changes in an object stored in the bucket, the Cloud Pub/Sub Notifications will send that information to Cloud Pub/Sub. Then this information will be added to the Cloud Pub/Sub topic.

13. **B** (Bucket Lock)

Explanation:

The Bucket Lock feature allows you to configure a Cloud Storage bucket data retention policy to determine how long the bucket objects must be maintained.

14. **C** (2)

Explanation:

There are two types of logs within Cloud Audit Logging, i.e., Admin Activity Logs and

Data Access Logs.

Admin Activity Logs are operating entries that modify the project, bucket or object settings or metadata. Data Access Logs are projects, buckets or object entries for operations that modify or read objects.

15. **C** (ACLs)

Explanation:

Access Control Lists (ACLs): Give the individual buckets or objects read and write access to users. Use Cloud IAM permissions rather than ACLs, in most cases. Use ACLs when control of individual objects is fine grained.

16. D (5)

Explanation:

Up to five VPC networks can be used in a project, and each Compute Engine instance is in one VPC network.

17. **B** (Staging)

Explanation:

STAGING–Resources have been attained, and the first boot of instance is ready.

18. **A** (Provision)

Explanation:

PROVISION–Resources are being allocated, and it is not yet in operation.

19. **C** (High CPU Machines)

Explanation:

Types of high-CPU machines are perfect for tasks, which require more vCPUs than memory. These types of high CPU machines are 0.90 GB per vCPU.

20. **B** (Service Account)

Explanation:

A service account is an application Google account, rather than the end user. These accounts may be used to allow Google Compute Engine to access non-sensitive information on behalf of the user.

Chapter 04: Scaling and Security

1. **C** (Confidentiality, Integrity, Availability)

Explanation

Three main goals for information security is known as CIA Triad

Confidentiality (C)

It is that the data should be viewed only by the concerned person.
Integrity (I)

Integrity is to prevent data or information modifications by unauthorized users. It also prevents authorized users to make changes, which are not appropriate.
Availability (A)

Availability is that data should be accessible when required.

2. **B** (Control of Dataflow)

Explanation

Control of Data flow refers to the AAA model of security. AAA stands for Authentication, Authorization and Accounting.

3. **A** (What are you allowed to do?)

Explanation

Authorization is based on the question "What are you allowed to do?" The process of authorization determines if the user has the authority to issue such commands.

4. **B** (False)

Explanation

If a user want to access some data then It will first pass through the authentication process and then get the certified credential from the authentication system.

5. **C** (User role)

Explanation

The IAM role is of three types i.e., Primitive, Predefined and Custom.

6. **B** (Read-only)

Explanation

Primitive Roles are Project level roles. They are of three types

- Viewer (Read-only)

- Editor (Read/Write)
- Owner (Read/Write and control access and billing)

7. **C** (Predefined Role)

Explanation

Predefined Roles provide granular access to specific GCP resources.

Examples

roles/bigquery.dataEditor

roles/pubsub.subscriber (This will also allow to setup a subscription not only consuming the existing subscription)

8. **A** (roles/appengine.appAdmin)

Explanation

roles/appengine.appAdmin provide Read/Write/Modify access to all application configuration and settings whereas roles/appengine.serviceAdmin, roles/appengine.deployer, roles/appengine.appViewer and roles/appengine.codeViewer roles provide Read-only access.

9. **B** (Applications)

Explanation

Service Account is not used by humans. It used by applications or services

10. **B** (False)

Explanation

Google accounts and service accounts combines to form a Google Group. A Group contain multiple users with a unique email address of that group.

11. **D** (Nest groups)

Explanation

Nest groups can also be used for an organization such as different groups for different departments can be combined to form a single group.

12. **A** (True)

Explanation

A policy is attached within a Resource Hierarchy. Policy can be attached somewhere in an organization,folder, project or Resources.

13. **C** (Allow only)

Explanation

Policies is for giving permission to something i.e., allow only.

14. **B** (False)

Explanation

Maximum 1500 member bindings per policy. Use groups instead of binding too many members in a single policy.

15. **C** (250)

Explanation

Maximum 250 groups per policy is the limitation of IAM policies.

16. **D** (full data is called and pushed)

Explanation

add-iam-policy-binding and remove-iam-policy-binding are simple and less error prone that editing the JSON or YAML file. These operations will avoid race condition means multiple users can make changes simultaneously

17. **A** (Billing Account)

Explanation

Billing account is the type of resource, which stays outside any project and represents the amount to pay for GCP services usage.

18. **D** (Billing Account User)

Explanation

"Billing Account User" role is used to link projects to billing accounts. If this role is attached to a user on the billing account level then that user can link any project to this billing account. If this role is attached on organization level then the user can link any project to any billing account.

19. **A** (True)

Explanation

Instead of charged automatically by credit card, user is able to opt option for charges on monthly basis on the invoice due date.

20. **C** (No. of Resources in use)

Explanation

Billing administrator can contact to Cloud billing support in order to check the eligibility for invoice billing and transferring the billing method to Monthly invoice billing.

Eligibility for invoice billing depends on:

- Account age
- Monthly spend
- Country

21. **A** (Managed instance group)
    B (Unmanaged instance group)

Explanation

Instance Groups are of two types, either Managed or Unmanaged. Unmanaged instance groups are created by selecting instances whereas Managed instance groups based on a single selected instance template and they allow the user to enable Autoscaling.

22. **C** (Global)

Explanation

Instance templates are global and once you create a particular template, user can use it to create multiple instance in different zones.

23. **B** (False)

Explanation

Unmanaged instance group cannot be Multiple zone. Only single zone option is available in GCP.

24. **C** (InfoSec)

Explanation

The practice of preventing unauthorized access, use, disclosure, disruption, modification, inspection, recording or destruction of information is information security, which is also known as InfoSec.

25. **B** (False)

Explanation

Billing account can be linked to any project. Multiple billing accounts can also be

created. Single project can only be linked to single billing account.

Chapter 5: Networking

1. **B** (Egress)

Explanation:

By default, Firewall rule is restrictive inbound and permissive outbound. Where inbound refers to Ingress and outbound refers to Egress.

2. **C** (7)

Explanation:

The OSI model defines a networking framework for implementing protocols in seven layers. The data is transferred between two points by moving in 7 layers from Application layer of the first connection to the bottom layer of the second connection and then moving back by following the same hierarchy.

3. **A** (Transport)

Explanation:

OSI layers are: Application Layer (Layer 7), Presentation Layer (Layer 6), Session Layer (Layer 5), Transport Layer (Layer 4), Network Layer (Layer 3), Data Link Layer (Layer 2), and Physical Layer (Layer 1)

4. **B** (Routing)

Explanation:

Routing is a path defined for data to travel. Routing means to take many local decisions for moving data from one point to another.

5. **A** (Premium)

C (Standard)

Explanation:

Google provides Standard Routing Tier and Premium Routing Tier for this purpose. Standard Routing is hot potato and the routing is performed over public internet, whereas Premium Routing is cold potato and routing is mostly performed on Google Network.

6. **D** (Premium)

Explanation:

Premium routing involves least distances and hops resulting in faster and secure communication.

7. **A** (True)

Explanation:

User can use Cross-Region Load Balancing with Global Anycast IPs in order to obtain Latency Reduction. If Premium Tier routing is used and Global Anycast IP address is used to point the Google Network, then Google would decide where to send the data inside Google's network.

8. **C** (Anycast)

Explanation:

When Unicast is used then the data can be handled by a single device whereas Anycast will allow data to be handle by multiple devices.

9. **D** (TCP)

Explanation:

TCP is a primary protocol used to send data over the internet. It is associated with the Layer 4 of OSI model. This layer works solely with IP addresses.

10. **C** (Domain name system)

Explanation:

Other Cloud and System uses DNS for Global load balancing. Name resolution by DNS is the first step for routing.

11. **B** (False)

Explanation:

Firewall rules are Global and it can be defined by using IP addresses, Network tags and, Service account.

12. **B** (65535)

Explanation:

By default, inbound restrictive and outbound permissive rule is set with the priority number 65535 so in order to allow incoming traffic the rule should have high priority (low priority number) than 65535.

13. **C** (0.0.0.0/0)

Explanation:

0.0.0.0/0 means any IP address i.e., include all IP addresses.

14. **A** (Auto)

Explanation:

VPC Network in GCP has a default VPC with "Auto" mode. There is one subnet in each region due to auto mode network. IP Address ranges are same. There are 4 Firewalls by default.

15. **B** (Custom)

Explanation:

Automatic mode provides creation of subnet in each region whereas if user select the custom mode, subnets region should be defined. If Google added new region in a cloud, Automatic mode adds the new subnet in that region.

Chapter 6: Google Engines

1. **D** (All of the Above.)

Explanation:

Google Kubernetes Engines (GKE) helps you in providing a managed environment used for deploying, managing and scaling your containerized applications, working on Google Infrastructure.

2. **A** (Cluster.)

Explanation:

The GKE consists of multiple machines which are grouped to form a cluster.

3. **A** (Kubernetes Open Source Cluster Management.)

Explanation:

GKE clusters are powered via the Kubernetes open source cluster management system. Kubernetes offers the mechanisms through which you interact with your cluster.

4. **D** (All of the Above.)

Explanation:

You operate Kubernetes commands and resources to set up and control your packages, perform management tasks and monitor the performance of your workloads which are deployed and set the policies.

5. **G** (All of the Above.)

Explanation:

When you run a GKE cluster, you can also take some advantages of advanced management features that GCP provides, which are:

- GCP Load Balancing for the instances of Compute Engine
- Node Pools are used to designate subsets of nodes inside the cluster to provide additional flexibility
- Automatic Scaling for instance count of cluster nodes
- Automatic Upgrade for node software of cluster
- Node Auto Repair used to maintain the availability and health of the node
- Logging and Monitoring with Stackdriver to look after the cluster

6. **A** (Containerized Application.)

C (Applications that are packed into hardware as an independent, isolated user-space instances.)

Explanation:

GKE works with containerized applications or applications that are packed into hardware independent, isolated user-space instances.

7. **C** (Workloads.)

Explanation:

In GKE and Kubernetes, those containers, whether used for applications or batch jobs are collectively known as Workloads.

8. **B** (Nodes.)

Explanation:

In GKE, a cluster consists of at least one cluster master and more than one worker machines referred to as nodes.

9. **A** (Master Cluster.)

   B (Node Machines.)

Explanation:

Kubernetes cluster orchestration system runs on master and node machines.

10. **B** (On the top of Cluster.)

Explanation:

The Kubernetes objects which represent your containerized applications, they all run on the top of a cluster.

11. **A** (Nodes.)

Explanation:

A cluster typically consists of one or more nodes called the worker machines which runs your containerized applications and different workloads.

12. **A** (Nodes.)

Explanation:

A node runs all the services which might be important to support the Docker containers that make up your cluster's workloads.

13. **B** (Pod.)

Explanation:

Pods are the smallest and the most basic deployable objects in Kubernetes. Pod represents a single instance of the running process on your cluster.

14. **B** (Multiple Container.)

Explanation:

A Pod runs multiple containers; the containers are managed as a single entity and share the Pod's resources.

15. **C** (Both A and B.)

Explanation:

Pods also include shared networking and storage resources for their containers.

16. **B** (Deployment.)

Explanation:

Deployments are a set of multiple, identical Pods without any unique identities.

17. **B** (Deployment.)

Explanation:

Deployments ensure that more than one instances of your application are available to serve the user requests. Deployments are managed through the Kubernetes Deployment controller.

18. **C** (Stateful Set.)

Explanation:

Stateful Sets represent a set of Pods with unique, persistent identities and stable hostnames that GKE maintains irrespective of where they are scheduled.

19. **D** (Daemon Set.)

Explanation:

Daemon Sets manage groups of replicated Pods. But, Daemon Sets attempt to adhere to a One-Pod-per-node model, either across the whole cluster or a subset of nodes.

20. **B** (Service.)

Explanation:

The concept of a service is to gather a set of Pod endpoints into a single resource. You can configure multiple methods to access the grouping.

21. **A** (Pod.)

Explanation:

You receive a stable cluster IP address that clients within the cluster can use to contact Pods inside the service.

22. **C** (Ingress.)

Explanation:

In GKE, an Ingress object defines rules for routing external HTTP(S) traffic to program running inside a cluster.

23. **A** (Service Objects.)

Explanation:

An Ingress object is associated with service objects, each of which is concerned with a set of Pods.

24. **A** (Kubernetes Storage Abstraction.)

Explanation:

Kubernetes Storage Abstractions provide block-based storage and file system to your Pods. They cannot be used with Cloud Storage and Managed Databases.

25. **A** (Google App Engine.)

Explanation:

Google App Engine (referred to as GAE or certainly App Engine) is a framework and Cloud computing platform used for developing and hosting web applications in Google-managed data centers.

Acronyms:

2-FA	2-Factor Authentication
AAA	Authentication, Authorization, and Accounting
ACL	Access Control List
AD	Active Directory
AE	Application Engine
AES	Advanced Encryption Standard
AI	Artificial Intelligence
API	Application Program Interface
AWS	Amazon Web Service
CDN	Content Delivery Network
CEO	Chief Executive Officer
CLI	Command Line Interface
Cloud TPU	Cloud Tensor Flow Processing Unit
CPU	Central Processing Unit
CTO	Chief Technical Officer
DDoS	Distributed Denial of Service
DLP	Data Loss Prevention
DNS	Domain Name System
FaaS	Function as a Service
GAE	Google App Engine
GCE	Google Compute Engine
GCP	Google Cloud Platform
GCS	Google Cloud Storage
GKE	Google Kubernetes Engine
GPU	Graphical Processing Unit
GUI	Graphical User Interface

HDD	Hard Disk Drive
HSM	Hardware Security Module
HTTP	Hyper Text Transfer Protocol.
HTTPS	Hyper Text Transfer Protocol Secure
IAM	Identity Access and Management
IP	Internet Protocol
IT	Information Technology
KMS	Key Management Service
LAN	Local Area Network
ML	Machine Learning
NAS	Network Attached Storage
NFS	Network File System
OS	Operating System
OSI	Open System Interconnection
SCIA	Confidentiality, Integrity, and Availability
SDK	Software Development Kit
SDN	Software Defined Networking
SLA	Service Level Agreement
SMBs	Small and Medium Business Solutions
SQL	Structured Query Language
SSH	Secure Shell
TLS	Transport Layer Security
TPU	Tensor Processing Unit
TTL	To Live
UI	User Interface
URL	Uniform Resource Locator
UTF	UniCode Transformation Format
VM	Virtual Machine

VPC	Virtual Private Cloud
VPN	Virtual Private Network
WAF	Web Application Firewall
WAN	Wide Area Network

References:

Cloud Concepts

https://en.wikipedia.org/wiki/Google_Cloud_Platform#Identity_&_Security

https://www.edureka.co/blog/what-is-google-cloud-platform/

https://cloud.google.com/compute/docs/faq

https://cloudplatform.googleblog.com/2014/10/simpler-billing-on-google-cloud-platform.html

https://cloud.google.com/docs/overview/

https://cloud.google.com/docs/overview/cloud-platform-services

Getting Started

https://www.techrepublic.com/article/google-cloud-platform-the-smart-persons-guide/

https://cloud.google.com/docs/overview/

https://acloud.guru/course/gcp-certified-associate-cloud-engineer/learn/getting-started/milestone-how-far-along/watch

https://cloud.google.com/docs/overview/cloud-platform-services

https://cloud.google.com/docs/overview/developer-and-admin-tools

https://cloud.google.com/free/

https://cloud.google.com/free/docs/gcp-free-tier#limitations

https://cloud.google.com/free/docs/gcp-free-tier

https://console.cloud.google.com/freetrial

https://cloud.google.com/docs/overview/#projects

https://cloud.google.com/billing/docs/how-to/budgets

https://cloud.google.com/billing/docs/how-to/billing-access

https://cloud.google.com/billing/docs/how-to/budgets

https://cloud.google.com/shell/

Basic Services

https://cloud.google.com/storage/docs/key-terms

https://en.wikipedia.org/wiki/Google_Storage

https://searchstorage.techtarget.com/definition/Google-Cloud-Storage

https://www.techrepublic.com/article/google-cloud-platform-the-smart-persons-guide/

https://cloud.google.com/storage/docs/storage-classes

https://cloud.google.com/storage/docs/metadata

https://cloud.google.com/storage/docs/cross-origin

https://cloud.google.com/storage/docs/access-control/

https://cloud.google.com/storage/docs/encryption/

https://cloud.google.com/sdk/docs/properties

https://cloud.google.com/sdk/docs/configurations

https://cloud.google.com/sdk/gcloud/reference/

https://cloud.google.com/compute/docs/containers/

https://cloud.google.com/compute/docs/nodes/

https://cloud.google.com/compute/docs/instances/

https://en.wikipedia.org/wiki/Google_Compute_Engine

Scaling and Security

http://www.pearsonitcertification.com/articles/article.aspx?p=2218577&seqNum=3

https://searchsecurity.techtarget.com/definition/authentication-authorization-and-accounting

https://searchsecurity.techtarget.com/definition/principle-of-least-privilege-POLP

https://www.owasp.org/index.php/Security_by_Design_Principles

Networking

https://www.webopedia.com/quick_ref/OSI_Layers.asp

https://cloud.google.com/compute/docs/access/

https://cloud.google.com/vpc/docs/using-firewalls

https://cloud.google.com/vpc/docs/using-firewalls#serviceaccounts

https://www.webopedia.com/quick_ref/OSI_Layers.asp

Google Engines

https://acloud.guru/learn/kubernetes-deep-dive

https://cloud.google.com/kubernetes-engine/docs/concepts/kubernetes-engine-overview

https://cloud.google.com/kubernetes-engine/docs/concepts/

https://cloud.google.com/kubernetes-engine/docs/concepts/cluster-architecture

https://cloud.google.com/kubernetes-engine/docs/concepts/pod

https://cloud.google.com/kubernetes-engine/docs/concepts/deployment

https://cloud.google.com/kubernetes-engine/docs/concepts/statefulset

https://cloud.google.com/kubernetes-engine/docs/concepts/daemonset

https://cloud.google.com/kubernetes-engine/docs/concepts/service

https://cloud.google.com/kubernetes-engine/docs/concepts/ingress

https://cloud.google.com/kubernetes-engine/docs/concepts/storage-overview

Summary and Exam Preparation

https://cloud.google.com/certification/cloud-engineer

https://cloud.google.com/certification/practice-exam/cloud-engineer

https://www.webassessor.com/wa.do?page=publicHome&branding=GOOGLECLOUD

https://cloud.google.com/certification/faqs/#0

https://cloud.google.com/docs/enterprise/best-practices-for-enterprise-organizations

https://cloud.google.com/solutions/best-practices-for-operating-containers

https://www.owasp.org/index.php/Security_by_Design_Principles

https://cloud.google.com/iam/docs/understanding-roles

https://cloud.google.com/products/calculator/

https://cloud.google.com/logging/docs/audit/

https://cloud.google.com/certification/guides/cloud-engineer/

https://codelabs.developers.google.com/?cat=Cloud

https://acloud.guru/exam-simulator/start?courseId=gcp-certified-associate-cloud-engineer

https://www.youtube.com/playlist?list=PLIivdWyY5sqIij_cgINUHZDMnGjVx3rxi

https://acloud.guru/learn/gcp-101

About Our Products

Other products from IPSpecialist LTD regarding Cloud technology are:

 AWS Certified Cloud Practitioner Technology Workbook

 AWS Certified SysOps Admin - Associate Workbook

 AWS Certified Solution Architect - Associate Technology Workbook

 AWS Certified Developer Associate Technology Workbook

 AWS Certified Solution Architect - Professional Technology Workbook

 AWS Certified DevOps Engineer – Professional Technology Workbook

 AWS Certified Advanced Networking – Specialty Technology Workbook

 AWS Certified Big Data – Specialty Technology Workbook

 AWS Certified Security – Specialty Technology Workbook

Upcoming products from IPSpecialist LTD regarding GCP technology are:

 Google Cloud Certified Professional Cloud Architect Technology Workbook

 Google Cloud Professional Data Engineer Technology Workbook

Note from the Author:

Reviews are gold to authors! If you have enjoyed this book and helped you along certification, would you consider rating it and reviewing it?

Link to Product Page:

www.ingramcontent.com/pod-product-compliance
Lightning Source LLC
Chambersburg PA
CBHW080144060326
40689CB00018B/3849

9781076568991